D1710796

BABYLONIAN WISDOM LITERATURE

BABYLONIAN WISDOM LITERATURE

BY

W. G. LAMBERT

OXFORD
AT THE CLARENDON PRESS

Oxford University Press, Ely House, London W. 1
GLASGOW NEW YORK TORONTO MELBOURNE WELLINGTON
CAPE TOWN SALISBURY IBADAN NAIROBI LUSAKA ADDIS ABABA
BOMBAY CALCUTTA MADRAS KARACHI LAHORE DACCA
KUALA LUMPUR HONG KONG TOKYO

FIRST PUBLISHED 1960
REPRINTED LITHOGRAPHICALLY IN GREAT BRITAIN
FROM CORRECTED SHEETS OF THE FIRST EDITION
AT THE UNIVERSITY PRESS, OXFORD
BY VIVIAN RIDLER
PRINTER TO THE UNIVERSITY
1967

PREFACE

THE science of Assyriology has been flourishing now for more than a century, and the pace of discovery shows no sign of abating. Old finds have scarcely begun to yield their secrets before new finds turn up. Owing to the paucity of labourers in the field, materials for study are very scattered, and of no branch of Assyriology is this more true than of Wisdom literature. This is an outstanding genre of Akkadian literature, second only to the epics in literary merit and content value. Yet the scholar can only use it from the piecemeal publication in dozens of books and scores of articles, many long since out of print, and some very unusual even in specialist libraries. In this scattered form the material is often very unreliable. Important texts are known only from copies of Craig or Langdon. Translations such as may be sought by those not initiated in the mysteries of cuneiform are often in German or French, and some contain inaccuracies in large numbers which any good student of today could correct. The aim of the present volume is to provide reliable copies of tablets, both published and hitherto unpublished, and careful editions with notes for the scholar, and translations and introductions explaining the background and content for the non-technical reader.

The copies of tablets are an attempt at compromise between the 'freehand' and 'accurate' schools. I do not believe that the scientific value of a copy is enhanced by its being almost illegible. I have therefore normally put space between the lines of script. It has been my principle, however, not to standardize the sign-forms, and to observe lateral spacing exactly. Every effort has been made to see all the tablets, but in a few cases the original cannot now be found, so that an old copy has had to be reproduced. Also I have been unable to reach the museums of Ankara and Baghdad, and for the few tablets preserved there I have relied upon and reproduced the copies of others. In the transliterations I have generally avoided the practice of some scholars who write ideograms in capitals rather than transcribe them into Akkadian. The justification urged, that this method communicates just what is on the tablet rather than an interpretation which might in fact be wrong, has some validity. But it does a great deal of harm to present the reader of a work of literature with a text partly written in a scribal code. To the ancient reader the ideograms were visual signs which, because of his profound acquaintance with the language of the work, he automatically read as Akkadian. To the modern scholar ideograms are Sumerian words no less and no more vocal than the parts of the text written in Akkadian, and it may be doubted if many modern scholars are so at home in Akkadian that the sight of, for example, GIŠ.ŠINIG brings *bīnu* to mind without the cumbrous process of equating a written and oral Sumerian word with its Akkadian equivalent. An ideogram written out in capitals ceases to be a sign representing a word. Those who regard Akkadian literature as a *corpus vile* for scholarly dissection will naturally find no objection, but those who care for literature as literature will hesitate to interpose a barrier of Sumerian between the reader and his understanding of the text. The objection is raised that the rendering of ideograms can often be a matter of doubt. This may be true of omens or mathematical texts, but it hardly ever applies to literature. The uncertainties about the endings need cause no hesitation, as the scribes from whom most of our copies of Akkadian literature come were quite indifferent about endings when they wrote words syllabically.

In the transliterated texts in this volume ideograms of very frequent occurrence are transferred into Akkadian without more ado, e.g. LUGAL becomes *šarru*, DINGIR *ilu*, and so on. With less-frequent examples, and where equally commonly attested alternatives exist (e.g. SILA and E.SÍR = *sūqu*), the Sumerian word is added in brackets. If, however, there is something to be gained by giving the Sumerian alone, as in critical and philological notes, I have not hesitated to do so.

In the composition of the transliterated texts the best-preserved manuscript has normally been followed, and the variant readings of other copies have been put in the apparatus. On the few occasions where the best-preserved text is obviously in error, or is plainly objectionable, the reading of another manuscript has been inserted in the text. In general, however, no attempt has been made to select the best readings eclectically from all the evidence, as it is doubtful whether our knowledge is adequate to do this scientifically. For those interested in scholarly minutiae the readings in the apparatus are no less important than those in the text. The symbols for the manuscripts are arranged so as to provide a general indication of the nature of the tablets without recourse to the lists. Roman capitals (A, &c.) refer to tablets in Assyrian script from Ashurbanipal's library. (No Ashurbanipal tablets in Babylonian script occur in this book.) Bold-face lower-case letters (**a**, &c.) refer to tablets from Assur or Sultantepe. Lower-case roman (a, &c.) refers to Neo-Late-Babylonian tablets.

In the Akkadian text no thoroughgoing differentiation between *i* and *e* has been attempted. Scribes of late literary tablets are often careless in this matter (cf. Commentary on *Theodicy* 215: *re-e-šú* and 218: *ri-i-ši*), and it is pointless to introduce an artificial consistency in part by using rare syllabic values. To be absolutely consistent it would be necessary to employ the value $i_{15} = e$, and to invent a further value $e_x = i$.

Many Wisdom texts are written in metre. It consists of a certain schematic balance of words such as can be observed even in the English renderings of the Psalms. It is nothing like the rigorous metres of Greek and Roman poets, except that a trochee must end the line. Lines normally fall into either three or four words or groups of words, and in the latter case there is a caesura after the second word or group. In the transliterated Akkadian texts this structure has been indicated by arranging the words in columns. Grouping of lines is also a part of Akkadian metre. The couplet is exceedingly common. In this book it is also accepted that poets at times intended single lines or groups of three as units. Extra spacing in the text and translation has been used to indicate this arrangement.

The translations do not strive after extreme literality, which is unnecessary for the reader of the original, and misleading for the layman. Some particularly hypothetical renderings have been italicized.

The undertaking of this work was suggested to me in 1950 by Professor Sidney Smith, from whose experienced counsel I benefited during the early stages of my work. Mr. D. J. Wiseman, of the British Museum, gave me valuable help in my first attempts at copying tablets, and has helped with collations when I have been out of London. This book owes much to the encouragement and advice so freely given by Professor A. Sachs during his periods at the British Museum, and his final assistance has been with the reading of the proofs. Dr. O. R. Gurney, with whose collaboration the first two tablets of *Ludlul* were published in 1954, has been my counsellor on many points. In all matters pertaining to the Berlin tablet collections Dr. Franz Köcher has been my learned consultant. In Istanbul I came to appreciate the helpfulness of Frau Kizilyay. Dr. E. I. Gordon, of the University Museum, Philadelphia, has helped me from his unique knowledge of Sumerian proverbs. During the latter stages of my work I was fortunate to be invited, through the good offices of Professor A. L. Oppenheim, to spend a summer at the Oriental Institute of the University of Chicago. There I was able to make use of the vast collections of Assyriological materials. Most of the newly found Assyrian fragments in the British Museum were identified in Chicago among the copies of the late Dr. F. W. Geers. I was also able to draw on the vast learning of Professors T. Jacobsen and B. Landsberger, from whom I received many valuable suggestions.

The following authorities have generously consented to the copying and publication of tablets under their charge:

The Trustees of the British Museum,
Dr. G. R. Meyer, Director-General of the Staatliche Museen, Berlin,
The Minister of Education of the Turkish Republic,
Professor S. N. Kramer, Curator of the Tablet Collections, University Museum, Philadelphia,
His Excellency Dr. Naji al-Asil, formerly Director-General of Antiquities in Iraq.

Professor Dr. E. Weidner supplied Pinches's copy of a now-lost fable fragment. The Deutsche Orient-Gesellschaft has consented to the reprinting of three copies by E. Ebeling in *KAR* of pieces which are not to hand. Dr. O. R. Gurney has allowed me to use his copies of Sultantepe tablets. Dr. J. J. A. Van Dijk similarly provided me with his copies of two Tell Harmal tablets now in Baghdad, and gave me the benefit of his experience with these tablets.

To all these persons and institutions I wish to acknowledge my indebtedness and express my thanks.

Scholars everywhere are under a debt of gratitude to the Delegates of the Clarendon Press for undertaking the publication of such a work, and to their staff for the craftsmanship bestowed on it.

W. G. L.

Baltimore, 1959

CONTENTS

GENERAL BIBLIOGRAPHY

HISTORICAL BACKGROUND

OWING to the rapid increase in knowledge in this field books soon become antiquated, and there is in 1959 no adequate work in English. The promised new edition of the *Cambridge Ancient History* should supply this want. Of older works, the relevant chapters in Volume III of the old *Cambridge Ancient History* (Cambridge, 1925, 1929) are worth mentioning. Among recent publications, the chapters on Mesopotamia in J. Finegan's *Light from the Ancient Past* (Princeton, 1946) give an up-to-date, if very brief, account. In German there are three recent works:

A. Scharff and A. Moortgat, *Ägypten und Vorderasien im Altertum* (Munich, 1950), pp. 193 ff.

A. Moortgat and G. Furlani in *Historia Mundi* II: *Grundlagen und Entfaltung der ältesten Hochkulturen* (Bern, 1953), pp. 224–330.

H. Schmökel, *Geschichte des alten Vorderasien: Handbuch der Orientalistik*, ed. B. Spuler, II/3 (Leiden, 1957).

In French there is:

G. Goossens in *Histoire universelle*, ed. R. Grousset and É. G. Léonard (Paris, 1956), I, pp. 287–495.

All four give a generally reliable account.

CULTURAL BACKGROUND

H. Schmökel, *Das Land Sumer* (Stuttgart, 1955).

B. Meissner, *Babylonien und Assyrien* (Heidelberg, 1920–5).

RELIGIOUS BACKGROUND

M. Jastrow, *The Religion of Babylonia and Assyria* (Boston, 1898).

M. Jastrow, *Die Religion Babyloniens und Assyriens* (Giessen, 1905–12).

É. Dhorme, *La Religion assyro-babylonienne* (Paris, 1910).

G. Furlani, *La Religione babylonese e assira* (Bologna, 1928–9).

C-F. Jean, *La Religion sumérienne* (Paris, 1931).

C-F. Jean, *Le Milieu biblique avant Jésus-Christ* III: *Les Idées religieuses et morales* (Paris, 1936).

É. Dhorme, *Les Religions de Babylonie et d'Assyrie* (Paris, 1945, 2nd ed. 1949).

F. M. Th. Böhl, *De Babylonisch-Assyrische Godsdienst*, in G. Van der Leeuw, *De Godsdiensten der Wereld*[2] I. 110–67 (Amsterdam, 1948).

S. N. Kramer, *Sumerian Religion*, in V. Ferm, *Forgotten Religions* (New York, 1950), pp. 45–62.

A. L. Oppenheim, *Assyro-Babylonian Religion*, in V. Ferm, op. cit., pp. 63–79.

N. Schneider, *Die Religion der Sumerer und Akkader*, in F. König, *Christus und die Religionen der Erde* II (Vienna, 1951), pp. 383–439.

F. M. Th. Böhl, *Die Religion der Babylonier und Assyrer*, in F. König, op. cit., pp. 441–98.

J. Bottéro, *La Religion babylonienne* (Paris, 1952).

S. H. Hooke, *Babylonian and Assyrian Religion* (London, 1953).

M. Rutten, *Les Religions asianiques* [including Sumerian], in M. Brillant and R. Aigrain, *Histoire des religions* IV (Paris, 1956), pp. 1–117.

R. Largement, *La Religion suméro-akkadienne*, in M. Brillant and R. Aigrain, op. cit., pp. 119–76.

LITERATURE

(i) *Descriptive Accounts*

O. Weber, *Die Literatur der Babylonier und Assyrer* (Leipzig, 1907).

C-F. Jean, *La Littérature des Babyloniens et Assyriens* (Paris, 1924).

B. Meissner, *Die babylonisch-assyrische Literatur* (Potsdam, 1928).

É. Dhorme, *La Littérature babylonienne et assyrienne* (Paris, 1937).

S. N. Kramer, *Sumerian Mythology* (Philadelphia, 1944).

H. A. Brongers, *De Literatuur der Babyloniërs en Assyriërs* (Den Haag, 1951).

A. Falkenstein, "Zur Chronologie der sumerischen Literatur", *CRR* II (1951), 12–27.

A. Falkenstein, "Zur Chronologie der sumerischen Literatur (nachaltbabylonische Stufe)", *MDOG* 85 (1953), 1–13.

W. von Soden, "Das Problem der zeitlichen Einordnung akkadischer Literaturwerke", *MDOG* 85 (1953), 14–26.

S. N. Kramer, *From the Tablets of Sumer* (Indian Hills, Colorado, 1956).

(ii) *Collections of Texts in Translation*

H. Zimmern, *Babylonische Hymnen und Gebete in Auswahl* (= *AO* 7/3, Leipzig, 1905).

A. Ungnad in H. Gressmann, *Altorientalische Texte zum alten Testamente*[1] (Tübingen, 1909), pp. 1–171.

H. Zimmern, *Babylonische Hymnen und Gebete, Zweite Auswahl* (= *AO* 13/1, Leipzig, 1911).

R. W. Rogers, *Cuneiform Parallels to the Old Testament* (New York, 1912; 2nd ed. 1926).

A. Ungnad, *Die Religion der Babylonier und Assyrer* (Jena, 1921).

E. Ebeling in H. Gressmann, *Altorientalische Texte zum alten Testament*[2] (Berlin/Leipzig, 1926), pp. 108–439.

J. B. Pritchard, ed., *ANET* (Princeton, 1950; 2nd ed. 1955).

A. Falkenstein and W. von Soden, *Sumerische und akkadische Hymnen und Gebete* (Zürich/Stuttgart, 1953).

ABBREVIATIONS AND REFERENCES

(i) TABLET SIGNATURES

British Museum, London
- BM British Museum
- DT Daily Telegraph
- K Kouyunjik
- Rm Rassam
- Sm Smith

(Tablets given a registration date only, e.g. 80–7–19, 289, are also British Museum tablets.)

Museum of the Ancient Orient, Istanbul
- A Assur
- Bo Boghazköy
- Si Sippar

University Museum, Philadelphia
- CBS Catalogue of the Babylonian Section
- N– Nippur
- UM University Museum

Vorderasiatisches Museum, Berlin
- BE Babylon Expedition
- VAT Vorderasiatische Abteilung Tontafel

Iraq Museum, Baghdad
- IM Iraq Museum

Archaeological Museum, Ankara
- SU Sultantepe-Urfa

(ii) PUBLICATIONS CITED BY INITIALS AND SHORT TITLES OF WORKS FORMING PART OF A SERIES

AASOR	*Annual of the American Schools of Oriental Research*
AB	*Assyriologische Bibliothek*
ABL	R. F. Harper, *Assyrian and Babylonian Letters*
ABRT	J. A. Craig, *Assyrian and Babylonian Religious Texts* (= *AB* XIII)
AfO	*Archiv für Orientforschung*
AGM	*Archiv für Geschichte der Medizin*
AJA	*American Journal of Archaeology*
AJSL	*American Journal of Semitic Languages*
AKA	E. A. Wallis Budge and L. W. King, *Annals of the Kings of Assyria*
AKF	*Archiv für Keilschriftforschung*
AMT	R. Campbell Thompson, *Assyrian Medical Texts*

ANET J. B. Pritchard, ed., *Ancient Near Eastern Texts*[1,2]
AnOr *Analecta Orientalia*
AO *Der Alte Orient*
AOTU *Altorientalische Texte und Untersuchungen*
ARM *Archives royales de Mari* (texts in transliteration)
ArOr *Archiv Orientální*
AS *Assyriological Studies*
Asarhaddon R. Borger, *Die Inschriften Asarhaddons Königs von Assyrien* (= *Archiv für Orientforschung*, Beiheft 9)
ASKT P. Haupt, *Akkadische und sumerische Keilschrifttexte* (= *AB* I)
BA *Beiträge zur Assyriologie*
Bab *Babyloniaca*
BASOR *Bulletin of the American Schools of Oriental Research* (S(upplementary) S(tudies))
BBK *Berliner Beiträge zur Keilschriftforschung*
BBR H. Zimmern, *Beiträge zur Kenntnis der babylonischen Religion* (= *AB* XII)
BBSt L. W. King, *Babylonian Boundary Stones*
BE *The Babylonian Expedition of the University of Pennsylvania* (*Series A* unless otherwise indicated)
Beer L. F. Hartman and A. L. Oppenheim, *On Beer and Brewing in Ancient Mesopotamia* (*JAOS* Supplement No. 10)
Belleten *Türk Tarih Kurumu, Belleten*
BIN *Babylonian Inscriptions in the Collection of James B. Nies*
BiOr *Bibliotheca Orientalis*
BMS L. W. King, *Babylonian Magic and Sorcery*
BRM *Babylonian Records in the Library of J. Pierpont Morgan*
CAD I. J. Gelb, T. Jacobsen, B. Landsberger, and A. L. Oppenheim, *The Assyrian Dictionary . . . of the University of Chicago*
CRR I, &c. *Compte rendu de la première* (&c.) *rencontre assyriologique internationale*
CT *Cuneiform Texts from Babylonian Tablets in the British Museum*
DP *Délégation en Perse, Mémoires*
Dreams A. L. Oppenheim, *The Interpretation of Dreams in the Ancient Near East* (= *Transactions of the American Philosophical Society*, N.S., Volume 46, Part 3)
Fauna B. Landsberger, *Die Fauna des alten Mesopotamien* (= *Abhandlungen der philologisch-historischen Klasse der Sächsischen Akademie der Wissenschaften*, Band 42, No. 6)
GAG W. von Soden, *Grundriss der akkadischen Grammatik* (= *AnOr* 33)
GCCI *Goucher College Cuneiform Inscriptions*
Gerichtsurkunden A. Falkenstein, *Die neusumerischen Gerichtsurkunden* (*Bayerische Akademie der Wissenschaften, Philosophisch-historische Klasse, Abhandlungen*, N.F., Heft 39–40, 44)
Glossar zu den neubabylonischen Briefen E. Ebeling, *Sitzungsberichte der Bayerischen Akademie der Wissenschaften, Philosophisch-historische Klasse*, Jahrgang 1953, Heft 1
GSG A. Poebel, *Grundzüge der sumerischen Grammatik*
Hippologica A. Salonen, *Hippologica Accadica* (= *Annales Academiae Scientiarum Fennicae*, Ser. B, Tom. 100)
HUCA *Hebrew Union College Annual*

IF — *Zeitschrift für indogermanische Forschungen*
JAOS — *Journal of the American Oriental Society*
JBL — *Journal of Biblical Literature*
JCS — *Journal of Cuneiform Studies*
JEOL — *Jaarbericht van het Vooraziatisch-Egyptisch Genootschap, Ex Oriente Lux*
JNES — *Journal of Near Eastern Studies*
JRAS — *Journal of the Royal Asiatic Society*
JSS — *Journal of Semitic Studies*
JTVI — *Journal of the Transactions of the Victoria Institute*
KAH — L. Messerschmidt and O. Schroeder, *Keilschrifttexte aus Assur historischen Inhalts* I, II (= *WVDOG* 16, 27)
KAJ — E. Ebeling, *Keilschrifttexte aus Assur juristischen Inhalts* (= *WVDOG* 50)
KAR — E. Ebeling, *Keilschrifttexte aus Assur religiösen Inhalts* I, II (= *WVDOG* 28, 34)
KAV — O. Schroeder, *Keilschrifttexte aus Assur verschiedenen Inhalts* (= *WVDOG* 35)
KB — *Keilinschriftliche Bibliothek*
KBo — H. H. Figulla *et al.*, *Keilschrifttexte aus Boghazköi* I–VI (= *WVDOG* 30, 36)
KUB — *Keilschrifturkunden aus Boghazköi*
Landfahrzeuge — A. Salonen, *Die Landfahrzeuge des alten Mesopotamien* (= *Annales Academiae Scientiarum Fennicae*, Ser. B, Tom. 72/3)
LKA — E. Ebeling, *Literarische Keilschrifttexte aus Assur*
LKU — A. Falkenstein, *Literarische Keilschrifttexte aus Uruk*
LSS — *Leipziger semitistische Studien*
LTBA — *Die lexikalischen Tafelserien der Babylonier und Assyrer in den Berliner Museen*
MAD — *Materials for the Assyrian Dictionary*
MAOG — *Mitteilungen der altorientalischen Gesellschaft*
MCS — *Manchester Cuneiform Studies*
MCT — O. Neugebauer and A. Sachs, *Mathematical Cuneiform Texts*
MDOG — *Mitteilungen der deutschen Orient-Gesellschaft*
MSL — B. Landsberger *et al.*, *Materialen zum sumerischen Lexikon*
MVAG — *Mitteilungen der vorderasiatisch-aegyptischen Gesellschaft*
MVEOL — *Mededeelingen en Verhandelingen van het Vooraziatisch-Egyptisch Genootschap, Ex Oriente Lux*
OECT — *Oxford Editions of Cuneiform Texts*
OIP — *Oriental Institute Publications* (Chicago)
OLZ — *Orientalistische Literaturzeitung*
Or — *Orientalia*
PB — A. Deimel, *Pantheon Babylonicum*
PBS — *Publications of the Babylonian Section, University Museum, University of Pennsylvania*
Physiognomatik — F. R. Kraus, *Texte zur babylonischen Physiognomatik* (= *Archiv für Orientforschung*, Beiheft 3)
PRT — E. G. Klauber, *Politisch-religiöse Texte aus der Sargonidenzeit*
PSBA — *Proceedings of the Society of Biblical Archaeology*
R — H. C. Rawlinson *et al.*, *The Cuneiform Inscriptions of Western Asia*
RA — *Revue d'Assyriologie*

RB *Revue biblique*
RLA *Reallexikon der Assyriologie*
RSO *Rivista degli studi orientali*
SBH G. Reisner, *Sumerisch-babylonische Hymnen*
SEM E. Chiera, *Sumerian Epics and Myths* (= *OIP* xv)
ŠL A. Deimel, *Šumerisches Lexikon*
SLT E. Chiera, *Sumerian Lexical Texts* (= *OIP* xi)
SO *Studia Orientalia*
SSS *Semitic Study Series*
STC L. W. King, *The Seven Tablets of Creation*
STT O. R. Gurney and J. J. Finkelstein, *The Sultantepe Tablets*
STVC E. Chiera, *Sumerian Texts of Varied Contents* (= *OIP* xvi)
Tammuz-Liturgien M. Witzel, *AnOr* 10
TCL *Musée du Louvre, Département des antiquités orientales, Textes cunéiformes*
TDP R. Labat, *Traité akkadien de Diagnostics et Pronostics médicaux*
VAB *Vorderasiatische Bibliothek*
VS *Vorderasiatische Schriftdenkmäler*
WO *Die Welt des Orients*
WVDOG *Wissenschaftliche Veröffentlichungen der deutschen Orient-Gesellschaft*
YOS *Yale Oriental Series, Babylonian Texts*
ZA *Zeitschrift für Assyriologie*
ZDMG *Zeitschrift der deutschen morgenländischen Gesellschaft*

CITATIONS FROM AKKADIAN TEXTS

EXCEPT where otherwise stated, quotations from the following works follow the line numbering of the following editions:

Code of Hammurabi (*CH*) A. Deimel, E. Bergmann, A. Pohl, and R. Follet, *Codex Ḫammurabi*[3]
Enūma Eliš/Epic of Creation R. Labat, *Le Poème babylonien de la Création*
Epic of Gilgameš R. Campbell Thompson, *The Epic of Gilgamish*
Era Epic F. Gössmann, *Das Era-Epos*
Maqlû G. Meier, *Die assyrische Beschwörungssammlung Maqlû* (= *AfO*, Beiheft 2)
Šurpu E. Reiner, *Šurpu* (= *AfO*, Beiheft 11)
Tukulti-Ninurta Epic E. Ebeling, *MAOG* XII/2 (see, however, *AfO* 18. 38–51 for a revision of the column numbers)

The following lexical texts are cited, with kind permission, from the editions of B. Landsberger, which are being published in the series *MSL*. Where the editions are as yet (1958) unpublished there can be no absolute guarantee that the line numbering will remain unchanged if new fragments should turn up. Where it has been possible to refer conveniently to a published copy, this has been given in addition to the tablet and line numbers. In some cases, however, such as where an unpublished text has been used, this has not been possible.

á.A	*Ea*	*Malku-šarru*
Alam-lānu	*Erim.ḫuš*	*Nabnītu*
AN	*Ḫargud* (*MSL* v ff.)	*OB. Lú*
Antagal	*Ḫarra* (*MSL* v ff.)	*Šumma izbu*, Commentary
Á-Tablet	*Izi-išātu*	
Diri	*Lú = amēlu*	

(For the full titles of these and the other lexical series see I. J. Gelb, *Standard Operating Procedure for the Assyrian Dictionary*, pp. 114–15. Note, however, that *OB. Lú* now replaces *LHC*.)

TIME CHART

B.C.	POLITICAL EVENTS		DEVELOPMENT OF LITERATURE	
3000	Arrival of Sumerians(?)			
2900			Invention of writing on clay tablets for business purposes	
2800				
2700				
2600				
2500–2400	Classical Sumerian period		The earliest traces of Sumerian literature	
2300–2200	Old Akkadian period		Semitic Old Akkadian written in Sumerian script	
2100	The Guti invaders			
2000–1900	Third Dynasty of Ur		Sumerian Renaissance: many new texts written	
1800	Isin-Larsa period The Amorites settle in S. Mesopotamia			
1700–1600	Old Babylonian period (First Dynasty of Babylon) Arrival of Cassites		Most Sumerian literature known from copies of this period. Development and spread of Babylonian literature	
1500–1200	Cassite period	Mitanni power in N. Mesopotamia and Syria Hittite empire in Asia Minor	Sifting and editing of old texts; Sumerian texts provided with Babylonian translations. Many new texts written, both Babylonian and bilingual	*c.* 1300. Copies of Babylonian texts from Hittite capital Boghazköy
1100	Second Dynasty of Isin	Rise of Assyria		*c.* 1100. Middle Assyrian copies of Babylonian texts
1000–700	Time of decline in the South Aramaeans settle in S. Mesopotamia	Assyrian empire	Rise of Marduk monolatry	
600	Late Babylonian empire			*c.* 650. Library of Ashurbanipal. A few new compositions
500–400	Persian period		Copies of traditional texts. Few original compositions	
300–200	Seleucid period		Copies of traditional texts from Uruk and Babylon. No new compositions	
100–A.D. 100	Parthian period		The last cuneiform tablets, from Babylon	

1

THE DEVELOPMENT OF THOUGHT AND LITERATURE IN ANCIENT MESOPOTAMIA[1]

'WISDOM' is strictly a misnomer as applied to Babylonian literature. As used for a literary genre the term belongs to Hebraic studies and is applied to Job, Proverbs, and Ecclesiastes. Here 'Wisdom' is a common topic and is extolled as the greatest virtue. While it embraces intellectual ability the emphasis is more on pious living: the wise man fears the Lord. This piety, however, is completely detached from law and ritual, which gives it a distinctive place in the Hebrew Bible. Babylonian has a term 'wisdom' (*nēmequ*), and several adjectives for 'wise' (*enqu*, *mūdû*, *ḫassu*, *etpēšu*), but only rarely are they used with a moral content (perhaps, e.g., *Counsels of Wisdom* 25). Generally 'wisdom' refers to skill in cult and magic lore, and the wise man is the initiate. One of the texts edited below begins, "I will praise the lord of wisdom", where Marduk is the lord, and his wisdom is skill in the rites of exorcism.

Though this term is thus foreign to ancient Mesopotamia,[2] it has been used for a group of texts which correspond in subject-matter with the Hebrew Wisdom books, and may be retained as a convenient short description. The sphere of these texts is what has been called philosophy since Greek times, though many scholars would demur to using this word for ancient Mesopotamian thought. Some of the works deal with ethics: practical advice on living (Chs. 4–5), others with intellectual problems inherent in the then current outlook on life (Chs. 2–3, and probably 6). Other types of literature not so intimately revealing thought patterns are included because they are conventionally classed as 'Wisdom': fables, popular sayings, and proverbs (Chs. 7–9). These are not discussed further in the present chapter, and the reader is referred to the introductions to the texts themselves. A case could be made for including many of the Babylonian epics in the Wisdom category, because they deal with cosmological problems. Their approach, however, is less direct, and they are clearly distinguished from the more openly rational attitude displayed in our texts. Since Wisdom as a category in Babylonian literature is nothing more than a

[1] This essay is not intended to replace the existing political and literary histories of ancient Mesopotamia, however inadequate they may be, but selects those matters which bear most directly on the Wisdom texts. A certain basic knowledge of Sumerian and Babylonian civilizations is presumed.

[2] Cf. T. Fish's criticism of J. J. A. Van Dijk's book-title, *La Sagesse suméro-accadienne*, in *JSS* I. 286–7.

group of texts which happen to cover roughly the same area, there is no precise canon by which to recognize them. In the present volume the writer has included all those works which obviously belong, but in the matter of border-line cases he has been compelled to use his own judgement.

The texts speak for themselves, but for a modern reader to gain anything approaching a full understanding it is necessary to know something of the intellectual world in which they were written. The attempt to supply this need is no light undertaking. The modern mind inevitably tries to fit ancient cogitations into the strait jacket of twentieth-century thinking, and any attempt to present the old *Weltanschauung* in modern terms can at the best be an inadequate introduction. Only by immersing oneself in the literature is it possible to feel the spirit which moves the writer. It must be made clear, too, that the only thought which can be recovered is that of a small group, presumably the intelligentzia of ancient society. Probably we shall never know how far the written forms of thought were understood and acknowledged by the mass of men and women. The handling of this written material—hymns, prayers, epics, &c.—has many pitfalls. Much Sumerian literature presents such difficulty to the translator that even the plain meaning of the words is often in question. Many texts are undated, and undatable. The ancients constantly rewrote old texts so that old and new stand side by side. We do not know how often in this process old words were reinterpreted to suit changed concepts. Even if a particular composition can be dated with certainty, can it be assumed that the outlook implied was characteristic of the age? Did individual authors hold views unorthodox in their age? One can only speculate whether further discoveries of contemporary documents would prove the existence of differing schools of thought. In addition to these problems the outlook and approach of the interpreter must inevitably result in a somewhat personal and subjective synthesis. The present attempt can make no claim to have escaped from these pitfalls, and the reader who is unable to make an independent evaluation of the conclusions offered is warned that other scholars might present a picture with quite substantial differences.

The first great civilization in Mesopotamia was that of the Sumerians. This people came from an uncertain region in the east or north-east and settled in the southernmost part of Mesopotamia. Their language has no known cognates, so that their origins are completely obscure. Territorially they did not expand beyond the southern end of the Tigris–Euphrates plain, and their system of government under city states prevented them from uniting to win an empire. Like the Greek city states, their chief contribution to mankind was cultural. In this sphere they established a pattern of civilization the influence of which lasted for many centuries after the Sumerians themselves had been absorbed into the infiltrating Semites. From the Sumerians the later Babylonians took over their system of writing, much of their religion, and some of their literature. It would, however, be a mistake to contrast Sumerian and Semite in the earliest historical periods, for so far back as our evidence reaches there is every indication of a peaceful symbiosis of the two stocks, though the Sumerians were culturally dominant. Nevertheless, the occurrence of Semitic words in Sumerian from early times[1] must caution us against forgetting that there was a second element in Sumerian civilization. Native tradition offers confirmation in that the third king after the flood, according to the *Sumerian King List*,[2] bore the Semitic name Palâ-kīnātim.

Very few literary texts have been recovered from the Classical Sumerian period.[3] Literature certainly existed, but probably much of it was oral, and no need was felt to write it down. There is no shortage of finds documenting the externals of religion—temples, names of deities, material of offerings, &c.—but they have little value for ascertaining the inner spirit, which is our concern. It is only from the period after the fall of the Semitic Agade Dynasty that literary documents are forthcoming. Under the Third Dynasty of Ur, Gudea, ruler of the town of Lagaš, made up for his lack of political independence by lavishing wealth on temples. Two large clay cylinders record in great detail his pious acts. From this Neo-Sumerian period, and from the following Isin-Larsa period, quite a number of works of literature have survived, though often in copies from the First Dynasty of Babylon: hymns, letters, parts of two codes of laws,[4] literary debates, all of which contain unambiguous evidence of their date of composition. It is also in copies of the First Dynasty of Babylon that most of the surviving traditional Sumerian literature has been recovered. It may not be an accident of discovery that the only big finds of traditional Sumerian literature are of tablets written when Sumerian was almost dead as a spoken language; a study of the period as attempted below suggests the explanation. It is, however, certainly an accident that the excavations at Nippur have yielded most of the material. Other contemporary libraries must have existed, though they have not been found.

Many scholars doubt whether it is possible with present knowledge to reconstruct the pattern of Sumerian thought. Certainly any detailed exposition would be premature, but for our purpose it is sufficient to note certain similarities and contrasts between a Sumerian view of the universe and that which the Babylonians had adopted by 1000 B.C., and retained little altered until their ultimate extinction. It would, however, be misleading to present this contrast in purely ethnic terms. It is the result of a change and a development in Mesopotamian culture, and to what extent fresh immigrants can be considered responsible is a very difficult question. Our plan then is to describe the two ends of this development in broad terms, to sketch the process of development, and finally to elaborate certain aspects of the Babylonian view of life as reflected in the texts edited later in this book.

According to the Sumerians and Babylonians two classes of persons inhabited the universe: the human race and the gods. Pre-eminence belonged to the gods, though they were not all equal. At the lower end of the divine scale came a host of minor deities and

[1] The earliest may be damgara (*mkr) 'dealer, merchant', which occurs in the Fara texts (A. Deimel, *Die Inschriften von Fara* I, p. 53, no. 523; ibid. III, p. 5*; cf. A. Salonen, *SO* XI/1. 23[1]), though its Semitic derivation has recently been doubted (A. Salonen, *Hippologica*, 247). For other certain Semitic loans see A. Salonen, *SO* XI/1. 23[1], and A. Falkenstein, *CRR* II. 13.

[2] *AS* 11.

[3] Cf. A. Falkenstein, *CRR* II. 18–19; G. A. Barton, *Miscellaneous Babylonian Inscriptions*, no. 1; S. N. Kramer, *From the Tablets of Sumer*, p. 106.

[4] The codes are of Urnammu (S. N. Kramer and A. Falkenstein, *Or* N.S. 23. 40–51) and Lipit-Ištar (F. R. Steele, *AJA* 52. 425–50).

demons, while a trinity of great gods, Anu, Enlil, and Ea, stood at their head. A modern scholar will observe that many of these gods are personifications of parts or aspects of nature. The sun and moon gods are obvious examples. The goddess Inánna (Sumerian), or Ištar (Babylonian), personifies love and procreation. The great gods are no exceptions: An (Anu) is the Sumerian word 'heaven', and that was his sphere. Enki (Sumerian) or Ea (Babylonian) was lord of a subterranean lake, strictly to be distinguished from the underworld. Enlil's name means 'Lord Wind', so that his cosmic location was between that of the other two. In the beginning, according to Sumerian and Babylonian speculations, only the gods had existed. Man was a later creation, and was intended as a servant of the gods. He had therefore duties to perform to his divine lords, and could offend them. This was 'sin', and the offence might be transgressing a ritual taboo or oppressing the widow and orphan. There was no distinction such as we tend to make between moral sin and ritual omission. The unwitting ritual neglect was an abomination to the gods. The Sumerian, and later Babylonian, pantheon was the elaboration of the theologians. In historical times their task consisted in reducing to an ordered whole all the gods which had their cognizance. Despite the large amount of duplication, since each locality had its own gods, conservative feeling did not allow the rejection of any one. Gods of wide popularity, or gods of politically important cities, were put at the top of the hierarchy, and lesser ones followed, or even became the attendants of the greater. In some cases, however, a syncretism of similar gods from different sources of origin took place, in which the more important took over the names and attributes of the lesser. Also in the course of time a more recent god might gradually take over the rank of an older one. Ningirsu, a local god of the Sumerian city Lagaš, and also a god of war, was later swallowed up in Ninurta, the popular war god of the Babylonians.

Some of the items in the preceding paragraph may not apply to the earliest periods of Sumerian history, but that is of no consequence here, where the aim is to lay the foundations on which the Babylonians rested. The most profound change which took place within these general conceptions between 2000 and 1000 B.C. was in the nature of the gods. When two Sumerian city states went to war the gods of each side were also participants. If the one state prevailed and sacked the other city, the local god shared in the disaster. This outlook is found in the Sumerian lamentations over cities[1] in which the god or goddess participates in the grief for his or her plundered home. The attitude of the conquered citizens to the victorious deity is vividly portrayed in the document written by a loyal citizen of Lagaš after the sack of his town by the men of the neighbouring Umma. After lamenting the sacking he adds: "As for Lugalzaggisi, ruler of Umma, may Nidaba his goddess bear this guilt on her neck."[2] In later times the Assyrians, close imitators of their southern neighbours in most matters of culture, plundered Babylon. First, about 1220 B.C. under Tukulti-Ninurta I, who has left an account in the form of an historical

[1] Cf. *AS* 12, lines 46–47 = 63–64:

"Thy lamentation which is bitter—how long
will it grieve thy weeping lord?
Thy lamentation which is bitter—how long
will it grieve thy weeping Nanna?"

[2] *VAB* I. 58, III. 11–IV. 3.

epic. At the beginning the writer portrays the gods of the Babylonian cities as angry with Kaštiliaš, the king, for his wickedness.[1] Consequently they forsake their cities, leaving them unprotected, so that an Assyrian victory follows. In the final battle of the campaign all the gods are on the side of Tukulti-Ninurta.[2] In this way was Babylon plundered. Also Sennacherib most savagely destroyed the city of Babylon. His successor Esarhaddon explains this disaster as follows:

> They (the citizens of Babylon) oppressed the weak, and gave him into the power of the strong. Inside the city there was tyranny, the receiving of bribes; every day without fail they plundered each other's goods; the son cursed his father in the street, the slave [abjured] his master, [the slave girl] did not listen to her mistress . . . . they put an end to offerings and entered into conspiracies . . . . they laid hands on the property of Esagil, the temple of the gods, and sold silver, gold and precious stones to the land of Elam . . . Marduk, the Enlil of the gods, was angry and devised evil to overwhelm the land and destroy the peoples.[3]

In the quotations given we have cited for the Sumerians, the complaints of the conquered, and for the Babylonians, the judgement of the victors. However, it is abundantly clear that the Babylonians themselves would have accepted the second part of the judgement, that the gods were angry with them, even if they did not confess to the crimes with which they are charged. In the Babylonian *Era Epic* when the destructive god Era was planning to destroy mankind he persuades Marduk to vacate his shrine, so that the destruction planned received the consent of Marduk.[4] A Late-Babylonian king, Nabonidus, freely mentions the gods' anger with Babylon, shown by their absenting themselves from their shrines.[5]

Thus between 2000 and 1000 B.C. the gods became more amicably disposed to each other, and learnt to act in unison. The same change is seen in the epic literature. The modern reader is immediately struck by the amoral character of the Sumerian gods in the epics. In one Inanna, goddess of Uruk, wishes to obtain certain things from Enki, so she visits him and together they enjoy a banquet, part of which was alcoholic. While he is under the influence of the food and drink Inanna easily obtains her wish, and at once makes off for Uruk with the spoils. On recovering Enki realizes his folly, and the remainder of the story is a contest between the cunning Enki, who tries to have the boat stopped, and Inanna, who evades all the attempts at stopping her and reaches her destination.[6] In another epic, the *Paradise Myth*, Enki mates with the goddess Ninḫursag, from which union a daughter is born. Enki then mates with the daughter, and a granddaughter is born. The previous performance is repeated, but Ninḫursag warns the fourth generation, so that Enki's advances are now met with a demand for certain plants and fruits. Enki is able to supply these bridal gifts, and mating takes place. This union, however, produces plants, which the uninhibited Enki proceeds to taste. For this deed Ninḫursag curses him,

1 *AfO* 18. 42. 33–46.
2 *MAOG* XII/2. 7. 23 ff.
3 R. Borger, *Asarhaddon*, pp. 12–13. The translation is a combination of pieces from different inscriptions.
4 End of Tablet I.
5 *VAB* IV. 284, col. x.
6 See S. N. Kramer, *Sumerian Mythology*, pp. 64–68.

so that he starts to wither away, and it is only by the intervention of all the gods in council that Ninḫursag is ultimately persuaded to restore Enki to health.[1]

When considering Babylonian epics it is necessary to bear in mind how much is directly owed to Sumerian forerunners. The *Descent of Ištar*, to take the obvious example, is nothing but a free rewriting of the Sumerian *Descent of Inanna*. Even where the actual story is not proved to be of Sumerian origin the motifs and phraseology can be strongly influenced by Sumerian. It will be understood that Babylonian epics are under a burden of tradition, for which their change in outlook is all the more remarkable. The nearest approach to Enki's libertinism in the whole range of Babylonian literature is in an incantation which describes how Sin, the moon god, fell in love with one of his cows called Geme-Suena ('Handmaid-of-Sin'), assumed the form of a bull, and secretly mated with her.[2] It is probably one of those old elements which have survived in incantations with their "fresh earthy pregnance", to quote a phrase of Landsberger,[3] and this metamorphosis of the god is better paralleled in Canaanite and classical Greek myths than in Mesopotamian sources.[4] In general the gods of Babylonian epics are more respectable, if more dull. Era, as already noted, does not let loose destruction without first persuading Marduk and the other gods of its desirability. In the *Gilgameš Epic* Ištar wishes to send a destructive divine bull to earth for revenge on Gilgameš, who had insulted her. By correct etiquette she begs permission from her father Anu, who only grants it after making careful inquiry if his daughter's intemperate revenge may not lead to the extinction of mankind by famine. Ištar satisfies her father, and use of the divine bull is sanctioned.[5] Another daughter of Anu, the demon Lamaštu, so provoked her father by her improper designs that he forthwith kicked her from heaven to earth.[6] In divine families naughty children have to be punished just as among humans. Two Babylonian epics do centre on fighting among the gods: the *Zû Myth*, in which the demon god Zû steals the Tablet of Destiny (a literal cuneiform tablet laying down the *status quo*), and the *Epic of Creation*, in which the old generation of gods, angry with the younger for its noise, try to destroy them, but are themselves destroyed by Marduk. In both of these epics the main body of gods are assumed to be in the right. Zû, the irresponsible demon, has robbed them of a thing the loss of which could bring chaos on the universe. In the *Epic of Creation* a primeval monster is threatening extinction on the gods and has to be faced. The responsible gods sit in committee like a group of civil servants, until a junior member is prevailed upon to take up the cause.

Despite the odd misdemeanour, the Mesopotamian gods learnt the art of being good citizens by 1000 B.C. The very fact that many of the old myths, such as the *Paradise Myth*, were not passed on is evidence of the change of outlook.

Finally, the change is also seen in the attitude to personal gods and demons. Demons

[1] Edited by S. N. Kramer, *BASOR* Supplementary Studies, I. Cf. also *ANET* 37–41 and H. Frankfort and others, *The Intellectual Adventure of Ancient Man*, pp. 157–60 = *Before Philosophy*, 170–4.

[2] *KAR* 196 rev. II and K 2413 rev. (*RSO* IV, Tav. II). Cf. E. Ebeling, *AGM* 14. 68; F. M. Th. Böhl, *JEOL* IV. 202–4; S. Langdon, *Semitic Mythology*, p. 97.

[3] *JNES* 14. 14.

[4] *ANET* 139. v; Roscher, *Lexikon* II/I. 263 ff.

[5] Tablet 6.

[6] *BIN* IV. 126 = *Or* N.S. 25. 141–8.

in all periods were bent on ill. The problem of how to escape their attacks became easier as time passed. In early times no one could be certain of immunity. In the second millennium the belief arose that the personal god could protect from demons, in return for services, that is offerings, rendered:

> One who has no god, as he walks along the street,
> Headache [a disease demon] envelops him like a garment.[1]

Though the personal god was necessarily a small god, he was able to take his client's case to the greater gods, and to see that it received attention.[2]

The three points listed—the nature of the gods' participation in the affairs of the world, the conduct of the gods to each other, and the restraining power of the personal gods—all reflect one fundamental change. The theology of the Sumerians as reflected in what seem to be the older myths presents an accurate reflection of the world from which they spring. The forces of nature can be brutal and indiscriminate; so were the gods. Nature knows no modesty; nor did the gods. This is not to deny that some Sumerian thinkers may have progressed beyond this stage, but many epics do reflect this outlook. It may seem primitive to a modern mind, but its abstinence from adding anything in interpretation gives it a permanent value. In contrast the Babylonians grappled with facts and tried to reduce the conflicting elements in the universe to parts of a harmonious whole. No longer using the analogy of natural forces, they imagined their gods in their own image, and tried to fit the universe into moral laws springing from the human conscience. Like all such attempts this raises intellectual and moral difficulties, and these are the background against which the texts here edited are to be set. First, however, the transitional period must be studied.

The years 1900–1700 were a period of political upheaval, ending in the establishment of the First Dynasty of Babylon over the whole of southern Mesopotamia. As a people the Sumerians had almost disappeared, though leaving a legacy of culture behind them. With our concern for the intellectual life we have to restrict consideration of these two centuries to the forces at work among the thinkers of the time. On the one hand there was a force favouring conservatism, on the other a force tending to change.

The conservative force was to be found in the scribal quarters of the old Sumerian centres. That of Nippur is best known,[3] though other cities must have had their counterparts. Here, with centuries of tradition behind them, lived and worked the most learned men of their day. They had a virtual monopoly of learning since they and their pupils, who were trained in the *Edubba* ('Tablet-House'), were the only educated persons. Although the scribal art was not an hereditary right, if we may believe a Sumerian satire on school life,[4] the length of the training could not but permeate the apprentices in this

[1] *CT* 17. 14, "O" 7–10; cf. *CT* 17. 19. 5–6 and *Šurpu* VII. 19–20.

[2] See von Soden, *ZDMG* 89. 143–69.

[3] University Museum, *Bulletin*, Philadelphia, vol. 16/2. 14–19.

[4] Published by S. N. Kramer, *Schooldays* (*Museum Monographs*, University Museum, Philadelphia), and in *JAOS* 69. 199–215.

art with the spirit of their teachers. One point of organization on which we are regrettably ill-informed is the relation of the scribes to the temple. General considerations would lead us to suppose that the scribal schools were attached to a temple, but we are in no position either to affirm or to deny if all scribes of the schools were *ipso facto* priests. The satire on the *Edubba* suggests a very secular spirit, but schoolboy activities do not constitute a valuable criterion. Because of their traditions these scholars were guardians of Sumerian literature, and so ideas. Though this was a rearguard action it was no mere rattling of dry bones. The Third Dynasty of Ur and the Isin-Larsa period had been prolific in new Sumerian compositions of many types, and many traditional works which were probably written down for the first time in these periods show signs of lateness, though the material is doubtless early.[1] It may be that a sense of pending loss prompted the writing down of works which had previously been oral, just as the fall of Jerusalem was a factor in the production of a written Mishnah. Thus in producing new and revising old texts there was little occasion to consider a literature in the vernacular. Though there is no reason to suppose that the old Sumerian scribal centres actively opposed the creation of a Babylonian literature, the overwhelming percentage of Sumerian texts recovered from Old Babylonian Nippur shows where their real interests lay.

Politically the Sumerians gave way to Semites. The forces of reform in literature were also Semitic, though both an old and a new Semitic element combined before much impact on Sumerian civilization was possible. Some variety of Semites had been living peacefully among the Sumerians from the beginning, and, as already observed, made at least a small contribution to Sumerian civilization. Outside the Sumerian centres in southern Mesopotamia a Semitic culture was more free to develop, though it owed many things to the brilliance of the southern cities. An impetus to Semitic creativity was given by the Agade Dynasty, which made common use of Semitic Akkadian instead of Sumerian for royal inscriptions. Historians of art consider this dynasty a profound influence on later Mesopotamian productions.[2] In the matter of thought and literature we are ill-informed. The earliest surviving works of Babylonian literature show a maturity which presumes a long development. The beginnings must certainly go back to the Agade Dynasty period, if not earlier, and from this period a school exercise tablet has been found inscribed with part of an historical writing.[3] The conquests of Sargon and Narām-Sin doubtless helped to spread Old Akkadian culture in the regions of the upper Euphrates and Tigris, but Mari on the middle Euphrates already had its own dialect of Old Akkadian,[4] and a fine school of local artists.

A new wave of Semitic migration started about 2000 B.C., and the invaders, called Amorites, moved down the Euphrates valley first into the Old Akkadian culture of places like Mari, and eventually into the Sumerian centres. Though Semitic-speaking, they belonged to a different branch of the stock from the Old Akkadians. Their original

[1] See A. Falkenstein, *RCC* II. 12–27.

[2] e.g. H. Frankfort, *The Art and Architecture of the Ancient Orient*, ch. 3.

[3] I. J. Gelb, *MAD* I, no. 172.

[4] *RA* 50. 1–10.

language can be recovered only from their personal names, since no documents written in Amorite have been found. The onomasticon reveals a Semitic dialect closely akin to Canaanite,[1] and their very name marks them as an offshoot of this group. It would be a mistake to regard their migration as a barbarian descent on Rome. These people had a culture of their own in the upper Euphrates area which owed something to the Sumerians, and their movement was gradual, so that when they reached the south they no longer spoke a kind of early Canaanite, but an Old Babylonian dialect. Unfortunately the details of this period in the crucial areas of the upper and middle Euphrates are unknown, which is particularly regrettable because it was a very significant phase for the Babylonian language, literature, and presumably thought. In script and language there is a great gulf between Old Akkadian and Old Babylonian. Old Akkadian script was a pioneer attempt at using Sumerian writing to express a totally different language. When the curtain of obscurity is lifted, the Old Babylonian culture appears fully developed, vast strides have been made towards perfecting cuneiform script as a means of writing Semitic Babylonian, and a brilliant classical literature is written in it.

As already commented, the Sumerian centres apparently remained aloof from this development. Several corroborative lines of evidence show that the rise of Babylonian literature took place outside the area where Sumerian traditions were strong. The tablets recovered from the library, if it was such, of Tell Harmal, in the Diyala region, can be contrasted with those of contemporary Nippur. In the literary texts from Tell Harmal there are about equal numbers of Babylonian and Sumerian tablets, and in addition there is a large group of bilingual tablets.[2] Another phenomenon is the obvious lack of any one cultural centre of Old Babylonian literature. The Diyala region writes literature in its own dialect.[3] The towns of Mari[4] and Babylon[5] do the same. In far Cappadocia the Assyrian merchants of a century or two earlier had literature written in the Old Assyrian dialect.[6] The impression is given of literary traditions springing up simultaneously in the regions where Sumerian literature was not strongly entrenched. The local traditions of writing seem strong, and show no sign of immaturity or experiment. There was certainly no opposition to Sumerian, for the odd Sumerian composition was written as far afield as Mari,[7] and in religion some Sumerian was probably used. At least the liturgy of a Mari ritual has Sumerian titles.[8] An incidental pointer to the origin and direction of reform comes from script. The history of Babylonian script, apart from a few archaizing tendencies, is the gradual introduction of signs to distinguish sounds which were not known, or not distinguished, in Sumerian script. Thus Babylonian writing at first did not

[1] The names have been studied by Th. Bauer, *Die Ostkanaanäer*, and by C-F. Jean in *Studia Mariana*, pp. 63–98.

[2] Reports on the excavations at Tell Harmal, and publications of texts, have appeared in the following volumes of *Sumer*: II. 19–30; III. 48–83; IV. 52–54, 63–102, 137–8; V. 34–86, 136–43; VI. 4–5, 39–54; VII. 28–45, 126–55; XI, pls. I–XVI, nos. 3, 4, 9, 10; XIII. 65–115.

[3] *JNES* 14. 14–21; 17. 56–58; cf. *JCS* 9. 31–35.

[4] *RA* 35. 1–13; 36. 12.

[5] The dialect of Babylon is well known from the Hammurabi correspondence.

[6] *JNES* 14. 17; *BIN* IV. 126 = *Or* N.S. 25. 141–8.

[7] There is an as yet unpublished bilingual letter addressed to the king of Mari, a literary composition of course (*Syria* 20. 100).

[8] *RA* 35. 1–13.

distinguish *g* and *q*. The introduction of separate signs for the *q* sound began first in Mari, Ešnunna, and Elam, and only later was this invention adopted in the more conservative Babylon. Being less bound by tradition, the peripheral areas were hot-beds of reform. As yet, however, this stream of ideas moving inwards had little impact on the Sumerian centres. The source of inspiration may well have been in the mingling of the Amorites with the long-established Old Akkadians. Cross-pollination in cultural matters is often the cause of increased fertility. Some of the dynamic achievements of the Amorites in politics are well known. An Amorite, Išbi-Era, "the man of Mari", took over when the Third Dynasty of Ur fell. Hammurabi united southern Mesopotamia under him, and ruled more territory and confirmed a longer dynasty than any known Sumerian dynasty. Wherever the Amorites settled they adopted the greater part of the conquered civilization, but since their introduction to southern Mesopotamia was through such places as Mari they arrived at their ultimate destinations with a good measure of Babylonian culture.

Old Babylonian literature is classical in every sense. It has vigour and freshness which was never matched later. Both the hymns and epics are outstanding, and even the omens, in which one does not look for beauty or style, promise a wider range of fates than the late-period texts. The two important questions in connexion with Old Babylonian literature are: (i) In what way does its outlook differ from Sumerian thought? (ii) To what are the changes to be attributed?

The chief differences are implicit in the change of conception about the gods which has already been described. So long as the gods were simple personifications of parts or aspects of nature a wonderful reality pervaded thought. But as soon as human reason tries to impose a man-made purpose on the universe, intellectual problems arise. The big problem in Babylonian thought was that of justice. If the great gods in council controlled the universe, and if they ruled it in justice, why . . .? All kinds of very real difficulties had to be faced, and the position must have been worsened by the growth of law codes, from the Third Dynasty of Ur onwards. If, in the microcosm, a matter could be taken to law and redress secured, why, in the macrocosm, should one not take up matters with the gods? The most common complaint is virtually about a broken contract. A man served his god faithfully, but did not secure health and prosperity in return. The problem of the righteous sufferer was certainly implicit from the time of the Third Dynasty of Ur. An Akkadian name of this period is *Mina-arni*, 'What-is-my-guilt?',[1] which implies the line of reasoning: I have suffered: I must have done wrong: What can it be? Suffering necessarily implies guilt. A Sumerian text is thought to deal with this problem more directly, though the difficulties of translation are considerable.[2] Two religious texts on tablets written during the First Dynasty of Babylon illustrate the problem. The first is a Babylonian dialogue between a man and his god, in which the man says, "The crime which I did I know not",[3] the same thought as, "What is my guilt?" The second takes the matter a

[1] E. Chiera, *Selected Temple Accounts from Telloh, Yokha and Drehem* 29. VI. 12.

[2] Edited by S. N. Kramer in *Supplements to Vetus Testamentum*, vol. III. 170–82.

[3] *RB* 59. 239–50, line 13. Since J. Nougayrol, the first editor, and others following him (e.g. Van Dijk, *La Sagesse*, pp. 120–1) have taken this text as "Une Version ancienne du 'Juste Souffrant' ", some account

step farther. This is a bilingual Sumero-Babylonian text in which the speaker says, "I have been treated as one who has committed a sin against his god".[1] Here the speaker evidently does not acknowledge any personal sin, though he finds himself beset with what should be the punishment for sin. Since two Sumerian texts, one being bilingual, know the problem of the righteous sufferer, it must have arisen in the Sumerian academies of at least the Isin-Larsa period, and perhaps under the Third Dynasty of Ur. It may then be a simple Mesopotamian development owing nothing to outside influences. No answers to this problem have yet been found in Old Babylonian texts, but so few texts have been recovered that this may well be an accident. The universal incidence of death seemed another injustice, since the ancient Mesopotamians looked for no rewards or bliss in the afterlife. The gods lived for ever, why not man? The Old Babylonian *Epic of Gilgameš* is written around this topic. Several Sumerian Gilgameš stories were taken, one of which, *Gilgameš and the Land of the Living*, describes how he was tormented by the thought of death and conceived a desire to achieve immortal fame by some outstanding deed. To this known Sumerian material the Semitic writer added much other legendary matter of uncertain origin and fused the whole together with the fear of death. In the end the inevitability of death has to be acknowledged, and Gilgameš is counselled on how to face life with this burden:

of it is demanded here. Nougayrol has certainly rendered a service in publishing this difficult text, and von Soden (*Or* N.S. 26. 315–19) has advanced the study of it with collations and his usual acumen. The present writer has also collated the tablet, but would hesitate to offer a complete edition for the reason of von Soden: only repeated collation of the original and prolonged study would yield even approximate results. In certain passages where Nougayrol and von Soden agree as to the reading, the present writer would hesitate to affirm its correctness. A number of von Soden's corrections were, however, seen independently by the writer, and he ventures to offer a further one for 26b: *ma-la al*!-*z*[*é*! ?-*nu* ?-*k*]*u* ? "(I have forgotten neither the extent of your kindness to me nor) the extent of my blasphemy against you" (cf. note on *Counsels of Wisdom* 29). As to the general scope and purpose of the work, the writer suggests the following modifications of Nougayrol's views:

(i) After an introduction in narrative form (1–11) the sufferer seems to speak, and apparently continues until line 38. The strophe 39–47 is badly preserved, but 45–47 are again narrative and introduce the reply of the god, which follows in 48–67. The intermediary, a friend, which Nougayrol assumes, seems not to exist. *ru-i-iš* in the first line, if derived from *ru'um* 'companion', would mean not "pour son ami", but *amice* 'in a friendly fashion'. Van Dijk, however, loc. cit., has questioned this etymology. The only other passage which could imply a mediator is 43b as read by von Soden: *šu-li-ia*$_8$-*šu qà-qá-ar-šu* "lasst ihn aufsteigen zur Erd(oberfläch)e". This could be a petition on behalf of the sufferer spoken by a friend or priest. Until the context of this line is recovered it would be unwise to build on it.

(ii) There is no evidence that this text deals with a righteous sufferer. Its being a dialogue between a man and his god proves nothing. Ashurbanipal in a famous text holds a discussion with Nābû, but not in the part of a righteous sufferer (*VAB* VII. 342–51). In 13 "the crime which I did I know not" can be an admission of sin, not a denial of it. The following line may also be a confession of sin. As seen by the writer 14 is to be read: ⌜*ú*⌝!-[*ka-ab-bi-i*]*s*! *an-zi-il-la-ka a-na-k*[*u i*]*k-ki-ba-am li-im-na-ma am-* × [×] × × × × "I have trespassed against you, I have . . . . . . a wicked abomination". These lines could, of course, be interpreted as questions, but even so they would not necessarily imply a negative answer. Most probably, however, the sufferer is here admitting his sin in the hope of forgiveness, and so prosperity. The answer of the god also does not make absolutely clear if the suffering is a consequence of sin or not. The general theme is summed up in the words *li-ib-bu-uk la i-li-im-mi-in* "Do not be downhearted" (48). However, after a promise of health (61) the sufferer is enjoined to perform charitable deeds (62–65), which could be interpreted as a penance.

(iii) The last two lines read more like a liturgical formula than a catch-line.

[1] Unpublished, but the relevant lines are cited in *CAD*, vol. Ḫ, 208b. Cf. in later texts E. Ebeling, *Handerhebung*, p. 134. 68; *VAB* VII. 252. 15.

Gilgameš, where are you rushing?
The life which you seek you will not find,
For when the gods created mankind
They assigned death to men,
But held life in their keeping.
As for yourself, Gilgameš, fill your belly,
Day and night be happy,
Every day have pleasure,
Day and night dance and rejoice,
Put on clean clothes,
Wash your head, bathe in water,
Gaze on the little one who holds your hand,
Let your spouse be happy in your bosom. (Tablet 10, Old Babylonian version, col. III)

This philosophy has not one word about religion, and is a moderate hedonism. Among the letters which Babylonians wrote to their personal gods there is also found in this period a very demanding tone. Unless satisfaction is secured, the gods can expect to be dropped, and will then get no offerings. It is not known how widespread this truculent attitude was, but it does suggest an overhasty exploitation of the newly grasped concept of cosmic justice.

While internal development is certainly a factor in the growth of Mesopotamian thought, outside influence also has to be recognized. The most striking case is seen in the development of the Sumerian text *Gilgameš and the Land of the Living*. The feat which Gilgameš set himself was the cutting down of cedar-trees on a remote mountain which was guarded by an ogre. The Sumerian writer clearly had no information about this mountain. The name is not given, and it is presented as a veritable fairyland. When this story was incorporated into the Babylonian *Gilgameš Epic* this skeleton became covered with flesh and sinews. The mountain is expressly named as Mount Hermon in the Lebanon range, and the mention of the Euphrates reveals an exact knowledge of the way cedar logs would be brought from Lebanon to Babylonia. The Amorites had come from this general area of Syria and could fill in details that a Sumerian writer would be ignorant of. What is more, this Mount Hermon is said to be the seat of the Sumerian pantheon![1] This is a completely Canaanite idea, for in the Canaanite myths from Ras Shamra, the ancient Ugarit, gods do in fact reside on Mount Hermon, just as Yahweh is associated with Sinai.

Another item of Old Babylonian civilization which is probably an Amorite importation is the *lex talionis* in the law code of Hammurabi.[2] Contrary to what might be expected from an oversimplified evolutionary approach, the *lex talionis* is a late-comer in Mesopotamian law. The Sumerian code of Urnammu (Third Dynasty of Ur) and the Babylonian

[1] *JNES* 16. 256 rev. 13 and 20; *Gilgameš* 5. I. 6. The fact of the gods' dwelling on the mountain explains the dreams received by Gilgameš and Enkidu, and the punishment which Enkidu suffered for his part in the exploit.

[2] §§ 196–201 (*ANET* 175).

laws of Ešnunna (*c.* 1850 B.C.) prescribe monetary payments for bodily injuries.[1] It is first in the *Code of Hammurabi* that the *lex talionis* appears, and its spirit pervades many laws not concerned with bodily injury, though it applies to free citizens only. The *Book of the Covenant* (Exodus 21–23) lays down "eye for eye, tooth for tooth", and as this collection of laws is from the point of view of legal draftsmanship and social development less advanced than the *Code of Hammurabi*, its later date does not compel the assumption of possible dependence on the *Code of Hammurabi*. More probably Hammurabi depends on an old Amorite legal principle.

The reign of Hammurabi was politically important, but equally significant for culture. He destroyed Mari and unified control which had previously rested with many cities. Whether for this reason only, or for other reasons also, the diversity of Mesopotamian culture ended. The details of this presumably gradual process are lost, but when the obscure end of the First Dynasty of Babylon and the equally obscure beginning of the Cassite period are over, we find many of the old Sumerian cities such as Nippur and Uruk back as leaders of culture, but with the significant addition of Babylon. Henceforth they set the tone, and all deviations were provincialisms. Their culture was now Babylonian, though tradition died hard; old Sumerian texts continued to be copied, though now often with an interlinear Babylonian translation, and new Sumerian texts were even composed.

The age of the Cassite kings was the second and last great constructive period in the history of Babylonian literature. It is, therefore, all the more regrettable that so little is known about it. A new small king list of the following dynasty was published in 1956, and this necessitated considerable emendations in all the hitherto reconstructed lists for that period.[2] Knowledge of the preceding Cassite period is much the same. Some account of conditions can, however, be given. Compared with the hey-day of the First Dynasty of Babylon, the country was immeasurably poorer, and the foreign rulers had none of the glory of a Hammurabi. Though they may have arrived as barbarians, they soon settled down and began to ape the culture of the conquered land. That their rule should have lasted for about four centuries is proof either of their ability as rulers, or of the dispiritedness of the subjects. Perhaps both reasons contributed. A feudal organization existed, in which nobles were granted pieces of land, and in many ways the Cassite period can be considered the Middle Ages of Babylonian history. Politically the whole land seemed in a stagnant phase, but certain social changes certainly began in this time. 'Guilds', or 'families', were springing up. Those in a particular trade or profession used the name of a particular person in their calling much as we use our surnames: "X son of Y" in the Cassite period often refers to profession rather than to parentage. One of these families can be traced back to the fourteenth century. Others are shown to be Cassite period by their names. The importance of this institution for literature is that scribal 'families', using the name of a scribal ancestor, existed. Moreover, in Uruk and Babylon at least, the same names continued in use by scribes into Seleucid and Parthian times, so that the continuity

[1] Urnammu laws 17 and 18 (*Or* N.S. 23. 48); *Laws of Ešnunna* 42–48 (*ANET* 163).
[2] A. Poebel, *AS* 15.

of tradition is established. The great span of time involved makes it improbable that these 'families' multiplied by physical descent only. No doubt apprentices were adopted. Although the ancestors belonged to particular professions and cities, in time their descendants included many who neither lived in the original town, nor belonged to the guild. The Uruk scribal families are best documented. From the ninth to the second century B.C. the scribes of these families were officers of the temple, and since nothing of an *Edubba* is heard of after the First Dynasty of Babylon, learning must have been the handmaid of religion, whether or not this was the case earlier. The continuity of tradition suggests that in the Cassite period the same organization prevailed. The Cassite-period scholars then were clerics. Their activity was twofold: preserving their heritage, and continuing the tradition. In their first part they were transcribers and editors. Part of a catalogue has been preserved in the libraries of Ashurbanipal which gives a series of literary works, each of which is said to be "according to" an editor of a particular town. Several of the editors, or their 'fathers', have been identified as scribal ancestors. For example, the *Gilgameš Epic* is "according to Sin-liqi-unninni", an ancestor from Uruk.[1] The task of editing is not to be underestimated. It often involved recasting and rewriting. In some cases, like *Enuma Anu Enlil*, several editions circulated in late times, presumably the product of the Cassite-period scholars of several towns. Often, however, only a single *textus receptus* survived, but the reasons for such textual uniformity are not known. The original compositions of the Cassite period are quite different in spirit from the Old Babylonian works, in that the writers were conscious of the fine tradition to which they were heirs. They tended to live in the past, and lacked the inspiration of the earlier works. Even in language this is apparent. Middle Babylonian, the contemporary vernacular, is a development on Old Babylonian, but it was not generally used for literature. A special literary dialect, Standard Babylonian, was created during the Cassite period, which, so far as our knowledge goes, was never a spoken dialect. It appears to be the result of taking Middle Babylonian as a basis and attempting to restore certain Old Babylonian forms. It is a curiosity that some phonetic features are morphologically older than Old Babylonian! There is no possible confusion between Standard and Old Babylonian. As in language, so in style. Self-consciousness results in a striving for stylistic effect, and some Cassite-period compositions are overloaded with rare words. The authors betray their very academic background and training.

In matters of thought it is possible to give a reasonably complete survey of the outlook and doubts of Cassite-period scholars. It must be stressed that some parts of the whole may in fact go back to Old Babylonian times, though lack of evidence prevents a decision. The main differences between surviving Old Babylonian texts and works either written or edited in the Cassite period are (i) a fuller understanding of the problems involved in the traditional approach to the universe, (ii) less confidence and self-assertion.

To deal with the first. The basic assumption of the gods ruling the universe in justice is maintained. Thus all misfortune and suffering should be punishment for neglect. Either

[1] For more details on the subject of ancestors, both scribal and otherwise, see *JCS* 11. 1–14 and 112.

the great gods themselves could invoke punishment, or the personal gods would withdraw their protection so that evil demons rushed in. The existence of such powers seems never to have been doubted, and no moral difficulty was felt since the just gods exercised a firm control over them. In this way the whole system of magic was retained, though to a modern western mind there is something incompatible with just gods ruling the universe, yet demons having supernatural powers for ill. The intellectuals of the Cassite period probably understood all the magic rites for exorcizing demons as divinely given means of protection with efficacy only for those in the gods' care. Under this system of thought an individual's fate was in his own hands. If he kept on the right side of the gods, no ill could assail him. This same idea provided an interpretation of history, of which no examples have yet been found from Old Babylonian times. The best example from the Cassite period is perhaps the *Weidner Chronicle.*[1] This text selects a number of important rulers from the earliest times onwards and explains their successes and failures as a reflection of their having provided, or having failed to provide, certain fish offerings for the Esagil temple in Babylon. The *Epic of Tukulti-Ninurta* and the records of Esarhaddon quoted above further document this philosophy. Many parts of the Old Testament presuppose the same interpretation of history, and as a doctrine it is not questioned in any known cuneiform text. The historical knowledge of the Cassite-period scholars was too inadequate for them to see the difficulties. The modern scholar finds an anachronism in the *Weidner Chronicle* before he can consider the premisses upon which it is based. The early kings did not take offerings to Esagil, because it did not then exist.

In the personal sphere the idea of piety as the guarantee of prosperity was more vulnerable. The suffering of an apparently righteous man was an irrefutable occurrence. Two long works of literature deal with this problem: *I will praise the lord of wisdom* (Bab. *ludlul bēl nēmeqi*; abbreviated *Ludlul*), and the Babylonian *Theodicy* (see Chs. 2–3). The first is certainly Cassite period, the *Theodicy* may be a little later. They approach the problem from different angles. The writer of the first was a devotee of Marduk, and in his monologue the only real question is why Marduk allows his servant to suffer. The agents responsible for the suffering—the personal gods, the devils, the human persecutors—receive little attention, as though no responsibility rested with them. The *Theodicy*, on the other hand, pays much attention to the human oppressors, and is a document of social history.

A whole range of answers to the problems are given in texts either written or circulating in the Cassite period. The traditional idea was apparently not without its supporters, whatever the difficulties. The orthodox friend in the *Theodicy* never seems to tire of telling the unfortunate sufferer that piety brings prosperity. Unlike Job's friends he abstains from directly accusing his interlocutor of some abominable hidden crime (the two speakers maintain mutual respect to the end), though this must surely have occurred to him. In the end the *Theodicy* leaves the question unanswered. Logical support for the traditional view was often sought in a subtle elaboration of the doctrine of sin. The basis of this lay in the complaint going back to the Third Dynasty of Ur that the sufferer did not know for what

[1] Published by H. Güterbock, *ZA* 42. 47–57.

crime he was being punished. Also hymns since Sumerian times had emphasized the remoteness of the gods. Putting these two things together the Cassite-period theologians, or their predecessors, evolved the doctrine that man has no intuitive sense of sin, and only the gods could reveal it to him. Thus sins of ignorance were common, if not universal, and explain why a man without any consciousness of sin can nevertheless be guilty before the gods, and so suffer. The following passages illustrate the idea:

> Mankind is deaf and knows nothing.
> What knowledge has anyone at all?
> He knows not whether he has done a good or a bad deed.[1]

> Where is the wise man who has not transgressed and [committed] an abomination?
> Where is he who has checked himself and not ba[ckslided?][2]

> Who is there who has [checked] himself and not done an abomination?
> People do not know their [. .] . which is not fit to be seen.
> A god reveals what is fair and what is foul.
> He who has his god—his sins are warded off.
> He who has no god—his iniquities are many.[3]

So far as the writer of *Ludlul* attempts to answer the problems he has raised, he has a variation on this answer. He goes beyond the view that man can only learn right and wrong by divine revelation, and asserts that man can never distinguish good and bad because of the gods' remoteness. To him the logical explanation was that moral standards must be inverted with the gods as compared with men (II. 34–38). A similar outlook occurs in a prayer:

> Mankind, as many as they be,
> Of themselves, who knows (anything)?
> Who has not transgressed? Which one has not offended?
> Who knows the way of a god?[4]

The writer of *Ludlul* advances his theory without enthusiasm, and turns away in despair. No solution seemed adequate. By the end of the work an answer was achieved, though not in the direction which the writer had explored. In time the sufferings were ended and bliss followed. Strictly this is narrative, but it implies an answer: the sufferings of the righteous are only temporary. The Psalmist said the same of the prosperity of the wicked (Psalm 73).

To the writer of the *Theodicy* the problem was why some men oppress others. The sufferer rejects the idea that the personal god can provide protection. An idea on which

1 IV R^2 10, rev. 29–34 = *OECT* VI. 43.

2 *BA* V. 640. 15–18 = *OECT* VI. 23.

3 *a-a-ú it-×[×]× gil-la-tú la ub-lam*
la i-da-nim-m[a ×]×-ši-na la na-aṭ-la
šá dam-qat ù [mas-]kàt ilu muš-kal-lim
šá i-šú-u ìl-šú [ku]š-šu-da ḫi-ṭa-tu-šú
šá ìl-šú la i-šú-u ma-'-du ar-nu-šú
(*BA* V. 394, K 3186+3419. 39–43. The writer has collated the tablet and constructed of it and other pieces a long hymn to Marduk, which he is planning to publish as "Hymns to Marduk in Paragraphs, No. 1", where these are lines 106–10.)

4 E. Ebeling, *Handerhebung*, p. 72. 8–11.

both the sufferer and his friend agree is that the gods made men prone to lies and oppression. This is certainly the boldest and most original thought which came out of the Mesopotamian thinkers. Unfortunately it demolishes the presupposition of a universe ruled in justice by its divine creators. The work ends as soon as this agreement is reached, and we do not know if the writer grasped any of the tremendous implications of his thesis.

This apparently greater profundity of reasoning in the Cassite period was not without its counterpart in a sobering of the Old Babylonian *joie de vivre*. Political conditions may also have contributed. A country under foreign rulers and in a somewhat backward state does not promote hedonism. Thus in place of the advice given to Gilgameš quoted above the emphasis now lay on accepting the wretched state imposed by the gods, and continuing the various religious and social duties. Acquiescence and submission naturally followed this emphasis, and a number of texts which we date in the Cassite period preach this philosophy. The most curious example is an old legend of Narām-Sin, king and great military leader of the Agade Dynasty. It is ironical that a story about him should be made the basis for teaching pacifism. The legend,[1] which may not be without historical basis, tells how Narām-Sin was confronted with a coalition of barbarian hordes. Twice he failed to secure a good oracle, but nevertheless rashly joined battle. The result on each occasion was a complete disaster. The third time a good oracle was secured and victory followed. The writer now draws the irrelevant moral: when confronted by an enemy do not risk battle. Instead submit, accept terms, and appease the aggressor. On a personal level a similar resignation is advised. One section of the *Counsels of Wisdom* (p. 100) warns the hearer not to get embroiled in other people's lawsuits, and, should a case of one's own have arisen, the other party should be placated with love and kindness. In short, do not take up a challenge. In the *Theodicy* the sufferer declares his intention of giving up all social responsibilities and living the life of a vagrant (133–43). The *Dialogue of Pessimism*, if it is to be taken seriously, takes the final step, declaring all life to be futile, and suicide to be the only good.

These excesses of despair may not have been universal. The orthodox friend in the *Theodicy* chides the sufferer with blasphemy for his despondency. These institutions he proposed to abandon were no mere human arrangements, but sacred things provided by the gods for man's benefit. Thus to reject them was sin. A number of Sumerian texts state plainly that rulership and other parts of communal life were divine appointments. History begins, according to the *Sumerian King List*, with the lowering of kingship from heaven, and after the flood another lowering was necessary. The gifts that Inanna stole from Enki during his feast were social institutions which she wanted for her people. The opening section of the *Fable of the Tamarisk and the Palm* (p. 155) shows that this idea lasted into later times, and it certainly formed the theoretical basis of morality.

Perhaps the plainest statement of the orthodox good life is found in the *Counsels of a Pessimist* (p. 108). After freely granting that all is vanity, the writer urges his hearers not to neglect farm, family, or gods. The preceptive hymns (Ch. 5) fall into the same general

[1] Published by O. R. Gurney in *Anatolian Studies* v. 93–113.

category. The adultery, slander, oppression, and fraud against which they inveigh are plainly stated to be abominations to the gods. The *Counsels of Wisdom* (Ch. 4) is less uniform in content. The advice not to marry a prostitute or give too much respect to a slave girl (66–80) reads like advice of a practical rather than a moral character. Also the warning to a vizier not to abuse his position of trust (81–94) is based on the dangers of being found out, rather than on the gods' displeasure. Another section, however (135–47), teaches orthodox religious duties. This diversity of outlook is certainly the result of the composite nature of the work. Two other of its topics deserve mention. The one, improper speech, occurs twice (26–30; 127–34) and the large vocabulary of approximate synonyms used both here and elsewhere in Babylonian literature (see note on line 28) shows the importance attached to this offence. It is difficult to define its exact nature in modern terms, since it included both slander and blasphemy. Even in private such speech was sinful, as line 132 explains. It belongs clearly to the realm of magic, as the utterance is *per se* effective. Since, once uttered, it could not be taken back, warning against the fatal word is particularly insistent. The second topic, found in lines 56–65, is in sharp contrast with the previous one, yet equally widespread. It teaches kindness to those in need, and does so with the authority of Šamaš, the god of justice. The number of approximate synonyms for 'poor man' is again considerable.[1] The antiquity of this theme is shown by the attention given to the widow and orphan in Sumerian texts. A hymn to the goddess Nanše mentions them, and traditions of rulership and justice regard them as persons needing protection.[2] The earliest reference is in the inscriptions of the first social reformer, Urukagina of Lagaš (*c.* 2400 B.C.), himself a testimony to the social conscience of the Sumerians. In Babylonian literature this Sumerian tradition is followed.[3] The *Theodicy* shows a keen awareness of social injustice, and the *Advice to a Prince* (p. 112) urges him to rule justly in order to secure his own safety from the gods.

[1] The ordinary Akkadian words for 'poor' are *lapnu* and *katû*, which occur together in both lists (*RA* 25. 125. 13–14) and hymns (K 3600+DT 75 (*ABRT* I. 54; H. Winckler, *Sammlung von Keilschrifttexten* II. 3; *BA* V. 628) IV. 12). The less ordinary words are given in *Malku-šarru* IV. 44–49:

la i-šá-nu-u	=	*muš-ke-nu*	
ma-ak-ka-nu-u	=	*a-ku-ú*	
lu-la-nu-u	=	*lil-lu*	
dun-na-mu-u	=	*en-šu*	
,,	=	*ú-la-lu*	
a-ši-šu-u	=	,,	(*LTBA* II. I. XII. 75–80.)

The series *Erim.ḫuš* also gives as a group *ú-la-lu*, *en-šú*, and *dun-na-mu-u* (IV. 167–9 = *CT* 18. 42 rev. 6–8), and the list *CT* 37. 25, III. 26–32, has a longer selection, with one addition: *lil-lu*, *še-e-ṭu*, *la-la-nu-u*, *muš-ke-nu*, and *dun-na-mu-*[*u*]. In literary texts combinations from this group are common, with occasional additions: *dunnamû*, *ekūtu*, *enšu*, and *lā išānû* (*LKA* 49 obv. 15–16 = E. Ebeling, *Handerhebung*, 50); *dunnamû*, *enšu*, *akû* (K 8663 obv. I. 14–15; *OECT* VI. 73 obv. 11); *enšu*, *dunnamû* (*PSBA* 17. 138. 2); *dunnamû*, *ulālu*, *enšu*, *ḫubbulu*, *muškênu* (*Šamaš Hymn* 132–3); *lillu*, *akû* (*Fable of Willow*, K 8413. 5); *lā šūšuru*, *ekû*, *enšu*, *lā le'û* (E. Ebeling, *Handerhebung*, p. 24. 20–21); *enšu*, *piznuqu*, *lā le'û*, *ulālu*, *maqtu*, *dunnamû* (*ZA* 4. 38. III. 13–16). It is certainly striking how many of these literary synonyms for 'poor' are in origin expressions for physical weakness: *enšu* (see note on *Theodicy* 19), *akû* 'cripple', *lillu* 'physically weak' and 'mentally defective'. Because of the attention given to this class of people by the gods they came to be considered as "the poor of this world, rich in faith", so that Nabopolassar considers himself one of them: *a-na-ku en-šu-um pí-iz-nu-qu* (*VAB* IV. 68. 19).

[2] A rendering of the hymn to Nanše is given by Kramer in University Museum, *Bulletin*, Philadelphia, vol. 16/2. 32–34. Urukagina (Cone B XII. 23–25), Gudea (Cylinder B XVIII. 6–7, Statue B VII. 42–43), and Urnammu (*Or* N.S. 23. 43, 162–3) all speak of care for widow and fatherless, cf. *RA* 48. 148–9.

[3] See the passages quoted on obv. 13–14 of the Ninurta hymn edited below, p. 317.

Šamaš was the god particularly concerned with justice and morality in Babylonian literature, and his worship must have been a salubrious element in an otherwise unprogressive religion. Apart from the *Šamaš Hymn* itself, it is noteworthy that the *Theodicy* concludes with his mention, and the *Counsels of Wisdom* connects him with humanitarianism. Throughout Babylonian history and literature his name keeps recurring, though he never achieved a place right at the top of the pantheon.[1] There is evidence that respect for him did reach to the masses. The popular sayings edited in Chapter 8 mention him several times, and the spread of similar material into the Ahiqar collections carried his name outside the area of strong Babylonian influence.

Thus the moral standards of the Babylonians were of very mixed origin. Some of the precepts continue primitive rites and taboos. Others are the outcome of cosmological thinking. Still others are a testimony to the force of the human conscience. The majority of scholars consider that the actual moral tone of Babylonian society, bedevilled by cult prostitution as it was, must have been very low indeed. Probably this was so in certain periods, though evidence is lacking and overall generalizations will certainly be wrong in part. Changes in ethical values must have taken place, and one example can be given. The pig was no offence to the Sumerians, but several of the popular sayings from the later period (p. 215) show a typical Semitic revulsion for it.

After the Cassite period the amount of new literature written was not very great, nor, with some exceptions, of much value. In thought the changes are so slight as to be almost unnoticeable. One tendency may be remarked which had already begun in the Old Babylonian period. Once the existence of a moral purpose in the universe had been established, a tendency to henotheism naturally followed. A single purpose could best be conceived as the responsibility of one god, rather than of the whole Mesopotamian pantheon. From time to time and in different places there were attempts to raise one god above the level of the rest: Marduk at more than one time in the history of Babylon, Ninurta in Middle Assyrian times, and Nābû a little later in Assyrian history. Some texts even go so far as to explain the other gods as aspects of the great god. A hymn says of Marduk:

> Sin is your divinity, Anu your counsel,
> Dagan is your lordship, Enlil your kingship,
> Adad is your strength, Ea your subtle wisdom.[2]

Ninurta is similarly praised,[3] and still farther in this direction Marduk is explained as being the other gods through having their qualities.[4] This certainly gives the impression of a striving for monotheism, but Babylon and its culture were extinguished before any such goal was reached.

The Assyrians have hitherto received no more than a passing mention. In matters of

[1] An attempt to elevate Šamaš is found in a hymn which speaks of his activities as essential to the operations of the other gods (*Or* N.S. 23. 209–16).

[2] E. Ebeling, *Handerhebung*, 14. 3–5.

[3] *KAR* 102; translated in A. Falkenstein and W. von Soden, *Sumerische und akkadische Hymnen und Gebete*, pp. 258–9.

[4] *JTVI* 28. 1–22; *CT* 24. 50 and p. 9.

culture they were completely under the influence of the Babylonians. As early as Ashur-uballiṭ I (*c.* 1350 B.C.) a Babylonian scribe was in the pay of an Assyrian king,[1] and Tukulti-Ninurta I (*c.* 1220 B.C.) used his sack of Babylon for seizing large numbers of cuneiform tablets as booty.[2] Kings before and after him doubtless shared his interest in Babylonian literature, and most of the native compositions were written in Standard Babylonian, not in the vernacular. At the end of the period of Assyrian supremacy Ashurbanipal was more successful in collecting tablets and amassing libraries than in arresting the break-up of the Assyrian power. We, at least, have cause to be glad, for it is from his tablet collections that the majority of the texts here edited have been recovered.

[1] *HUCA* 25. 127 = H. Fine, *Studies in Middle-Assyrian Chronology and Religion*, p. 109.
[2] *AfO* 18. 44. 3–8.

2

THE POEM OF THE RIGHTEOUS SUFFERER

LUDLUL BĒL NĒMEQI

INTRODUCTION

Ludlul bēl nēmeqi is a long monologue in which a certain noble relates how he met with every conceivable calamity, and was eventually restored to health and prosperity by Marduk. Originally the poem seems to have consisted of four tablets constituting together 400–500 lines. Of the first tablet the beginning and end are missing. The second tablet is preserved complete. Much of the third is preserved. There is a general opinion that part of the fourth is contained in some fragments from Assur, now joined by a piece from Sultantepe, but a careful consideration of the surviving material throws doubt on this conclusion, and there is no certainty even that this section is part of the work.

The plot of the first three tablets so far as preserved is clear:

[(*a*) Introduction (not preserved).]
(*b*) The narrator is forsaken by his gods.
(*c*) All his fellow men from the king to his slaves turn against him.
(*d*) Every kind of disease afflicts him.
(*e*) His deliverance is promised in three dreams.
(*f*) He is freed of all the diseases.

* * * * *

The first problem arises from the loss of the introduction. Who is the speaker? The opening words, "I will praise the lord of wisdom", i.e. Marduk, which are known from their use as the title, show the general atmosphere, and one presumes that, without in any way sparing praise, the speaker must eventually have introduced himself, and perhaps gave some biographical details. The only surviving section which provides information is (*e*), where, in the narration of the dreams, three names occur: Laluralimma, Urnindinlugga, and Šubši-mešrê-Šakkan. To anticipate our conclusion, it is Šubši-mešrê-Šakkan who speaks. It is clear that he was once a man of affluence and authority. He occupied several high offices (I. 60, 61, 103, 104), owned slaves and fields (I. 89, 101), had a family (I. 99), and even speaks of "my city" as though it belonged to him (I. 102). His whole personal bearing had been that of a man of authority (I. 70–78). At the same time he had been a model of piety both to the gods and to the king (II. 23–32). The three names quoted belong to the Cassite period (see the notes on III. 25, 39, 43), and we should probably conclude that the writer, who also belonged to this period, set the scene in the recent past. No doubt a modern author would have put such a story into the distant past, but that is no criterion for judging an ancient poem. The author had sufficient learning to find old Sumerian names, had he wished, instead of employing names in current use. One may conjecture that Šubši-mešrê-Šakkan was a feudal lord ruling a city for the Cassite monarch.

When the text first becomes coherent this noble describes how he was forsaken by his whole pantheon (I. 41–46). This calls to mind the *Tukulti-Ninurta Epic*, where all the gods of Babylonia forsake their cities in their anger at the wickedness of Kaštiliaš (BM 98730 obv. 33–46, in *AfO* 18/1. 42–43). Just as Kaštiliaš discovered his plight by failure to obtain a good omen, so our noble is beset by ominous signs (I. 49–54). The fulfilment of these ensues. The king becomes irreconcilably angry, and the seven courtiers seize the opportunity to plot every kind of mischief against him (55–69). The result is a total eclipse of his previous position (70–76), and he becomes a social outcast, hated by his friends, abused by his slaves, and disowned by his family (77–92). In this situation his persecutors are public heroes, while any kindness to him meets with a fell reward (93–98). Meanwhile all his property is confiscated and his duties are taken over by others (99–104). At this the sufferer gives himself up wholly to lamentation (105–10), which we cannot follow since the text breaks off at this point.

The first tablet then, so far as it is preserved, deals with the narrator's suffering at the hands of his fellow men. The second tablet is quite different. The first few lines intimate that suffering from those supernatural agencies which were thought responsible for disease is the theme of this part of the work. First, however, the speaker complains that his consultation of those clergy who were concerned with the exorcizing of evil demons has been of no avail (4–9). Then by a quick change the writer leaves the field of magic and incantations and addresses himself to the problem of the suffering of the righteous—another clear indication that these people had no dichotomy of ethical and cultic values. The sufferer, assuming that the gods repay good and evil, complains at some length that he has met the fate of a wrongdoer (12–22), a sentiment expressed more succinctly elsewhere,[1] and then reassures himself by stressing the pious tenor of his past life (23–32). What solution then can he find? He takes hold of the old theologoumena about the remoteness and inscrutability of the gods, and turns them round to mean that all values must be inverted with the gods, so that what is considered right among men must be wrong with the gods, and vice versa (33–38). This in itself, however, is more a complaint than an answer, and he follows it up by pointing out the very uncertain nature of human existence, and the preponderating influence which circumstances, such as famine and prosperity, have in human conduct (39–47). In the face of all this the sufferer expresses blank resignation (48). He has, however, no time to ponder, for Disease, a theme with which the writer deals thoroughly *con amore*, is upon him.

There now follows a long section reminiscent of incantations. It begins with a recital of the diseases, conceived as evil spirits, which arrive from their several other-world dwellings (49–58), and then lists the many disabilities which they inflict upon him (59–

[1] See pp. 10–11.

107). The listing of the parts of the body affected begins apparently in the conventional Babylonian manner, commencing with the head downwards,[1] but after a few lines the desire to include a good selection of the stock phrases of the incantation literature necessitated a breaking off of this plan and several changes of metre. When the recital is over, the narrator again stresses the helplessness of the priests who were consulted and the gods who were petitioned (108–13), mentions the outrageous behaviour of those who exploited his downfall (114–18), and concludes the tablet with what seems to be a confession of faith in his ultimate recovery (119–20). This confession, if it be such, brings to mind Job's outburst, "I know that my redeemer liveth", but it must be observed that there are textual difficulties in both passages.

With the third tablet we reach the very heart of the work. The opening phrase, "His hand was heavy upon me", is of great importance for the understanding of the whole poem. Whose hand? The following lines repeat the "his" but offer no explanation. The writer gives dark hints, but avoids openly using the name Marduk in this connexion. Marduk, with whose praise the poem began, is not mentioned during the 200 lines describing the suffering. Yet it was not the king, the courtiers, household, slaves, or demons that were really responsible. The almighty Marduk was at the root of the trouble, and although the pious hero dare not openly expostulate with him, he cannot leave the subject without a guarded allusion to the cause of his sufferings. Next come the dreams (9–44). The first begins very abruptly, and there is cause for asking if these were really dreams, and not psychic experiences in a semi-conscious state. In the first and third phenomena Šubši-mešrê-Šakkan speaks to the visitant (17, 34), which was not usual in dreams.[2] Yet the second and third are expressly called dreams. The first experience is the appearance of a young man of superlative physique; his message is not preserved. In the second another young man appears, but in the part of an exorcist priest, who duly performs rites on the sufferer after announcing that Laluralimma of Nippur has sent him. The last dream begins with the appearing of a divine-looking young woman, who answers the sufferer's pleas with a message of consolation. Then in the same dream a man Urnindinlugga, from Babylon if the traces have been read correctly, appears. He is described as bearded, though this was usual in the Cassite period, and he is specifically called an incantation priest. Appropriately he carries a tablet, no doubt written with incantations. He announces that he is the messenger of Marduk, and that he has brought prosperity to Šubši-mešrê-Šakkan, thus giving the name of the hero of the poem. The two named figures are very arresting. We know of nothing that lends support to the idea that these were dead worthies who in their disembodied state cared for this unfortunate man. The shades of the Babylonians troubled the living if not provided with burial and offerings, but never helped them. It is probable that all five who appeared were, in the story, religious dignitaries of the time. The young woman may have been intended as an *entu*-priestess. The man from Nippur

[1] This procedure is found in the series *ana marṣi ina ṭeḫêka* (Labat, *TDP*, pp. 18 ff.), *CT* 17. 9, and the hymn *KAR* 102. 10–33. Contrast Song of Songs vii. 1–5.

[2] For an exhaustive study of dreams in the ancient Near East see A. L. Oppenheim, *Dreams*.

who sent his representative may have been the author's ruse for calling in the help of the ancient sanctuary of Nippur without conceding any of Marduk's supremacy to Enlil, which would have happened if Enlil had sent the messenger. This also throws light on the nature of the dreams. A god may appear in a dream, but gods themselves did not perform ritual curing. This was the task of priests, and they did not normally practise their rites in other people's sleep. So the writer resorts to a succession of none too convincing dreams as a means of bringing the necessary priests to the sick man's bedside.

All these experiences are signs that Marduk's wrath is now appeased (50–53), another confirmation that he was held responsible. After a gap in the text the undoing of the evil begins, and each of the disease demons is sent away in the same florid style (Si 55 rev.). The text breaks off before this process is finished, but lines quoted in the cuneiform commentary allow us to follow it to the end, at least in excerpts (a–k). According to the next two lines (l, m) the healed man underwent the river ordeal, and then had his slave mark removed. However, we do not know if he had ever been sold into slavery, and it is probable that these lines are not to be interpreted more literally than q, which speaks of a lion which had been devouring him. Next he proceeds along the processional streets of Babylon to the temple of Marduk, declaring himself an example to all who have sinned against Marduk, a none too clear declaration. Marduk then begins to suppress his human enemies, and with this the Commentary breaks off.

Many scholars, following B. Landsberger (*apud* H. Zimmern, *Berichte über die Verhandlungen der Sächsischen Gesellschaft der Wissenschaften*, Phil.-hist. Klasse, 70/5. 45[2]), connect the three Assur and one Sultantepe fragments and regard them as part of Tablet IV (here cited as 'Tablet IV(?)'). The evidence offered is twofold: first it is claimed that two lines from this text are actually cited in the cuneiform commentary. If proved, this would be decisive. Then the suitability of the text as the ending of *Ludlul* is claimed. This may be granted in principle, but similarities of style and subject matter are so common in Babylonian literature that they are not usually compelling. Other compositions of the same kind as *Ludlul* may have existed. The lines claimed as identified are 13–14 of the text with q in the Commentary, and 15–[16] with r. A minute examination of the two passages shows that their identification is a mistake.[1]

There are several lines of reasoning which bring to light objections against the idea that the Assur and Sultantepe fragments are the ending of *Ludlul*. An approximate estimate of the length of the entire work can be made. A general premiss is that a literary tablet normally contains more writing on the obverse than on the reverse, rarely the same amount,

[1] The first group of signs in 13 is three at the most, and while the last might be *i*, the first cannot be *ina*(aš); thus *ina pi-i* is excluded. The *girru* is certainly the same in both passages, but the last word of 13 begins with *za*, not *a*, and there is room for one sign only between this and [*i*]*a*. The only possible reconciliation is to emend and restore: *a*!-[*kil-i*]*a*, which results in peculiar grammar. In 14 [d]*marduk* at the end is the same as in r, but the preceding -*š*]*am-ma* can only be made to conform to *nap-sa-ma* by assuming the rare value *sam*, or another form of *napsamu* with *š*. In the attempt to force 15–[16] into r, [d]*marduk* would have to stand under *ušaddi*, and then one is left wondering why *mu-ka-* is so far to the right, when only one sign (*ša*) would go between them; especially so when the following sign might be *á*[*š*, but not *š*[*i*, and then there is not enough room for the three signs -*ši-di-ia*. Landsberger's statement in *AfO* 18. 378[5] does not answer these objections.

and very rarely less. The only complete tablet of *Ludlul* is II, of 120 lines. Of the manuscripts of III, q was a full-length tablet, and **p**, which contains roughly half of this, has exactly 60 lines, with a catch-line added. The only assumption possible is that the tablets extended for about 120 lines. The Commentary, which is written on a single tablet, changes from obverse to reverse just before dealing with the end of Tablet II. This suggests that four tablets is the maximum possible. Commentaries can be very erratic in the number of lines they select for comment, and this one is no exception in that in one place three consecutive lines are cited, and in another almost 20 lines are passed over. The general picture, however, is more reliable. In the first tablet one out of every seven lines receives a comment. In Tablet II, one out of every six. The first half of Tablet III, the dreams, did not offer similar scope, and only one out of every twelve has attention, but the driving out of the demons marks a return to one in six. On the obverse of the Commentary the broken-off portion covered some 40 lines of text, according to the computed line numbering of Tablet I. On the reverse there is no sign of compressing the writing to get all the lines on the tablet, and if on the obverse about seven individual lines were commented upon in the missing top portion, it follows that the corresponding bottom portion on the reverse can have dealt with no more, and probably dealt with fewer.

More evidence comes from j and k, which appear to be parts of one big tablet containing the whole work, though with rulings separating the sections which elsewhere occupy complete tablets. If our estimate of 120 lines a tablet is about correct, these two pieces allow the deduction from the material they contain of Tablet I that each column of this large tablet had about 90 lines. Parts of three columns of the obverse are preserved, which gives a total of six columns and a maximum of about 540 lines. This agrees very well with the deduction that the poem is of four tablets of about 120 lines each, a total of 480. If four columns each side were to be postulated for j and k, this would result in a total of not more than 720 lines, or six tablets. The small amount of missing space at the end of the Commentary seems decisively against this.

Another factor, connected with the MS. q, which contained the whole of Tablet III, at once disproves the simple idea that the text under discussion is Tablet IV. q lacks the first 21 lines on the obverse. If allowance is made for even a short colophon and a little blank space on the reverse it follows that less than 20 lines are now wanting at the end of Tablet III. Thus not all the 21 lines a–u excerpted by the commentator can belong to Tablet III. Probably the majority belong to Tablet IV. If the ratio of one in six—the lowest attested—is assumed, the surviving portion of the Commentary must cover the first 100 lines of Tablet IV. With only a few lines missing at the end of the Commentary, and with Tablet IV almost finished, where can the 100 lines of the text of the Assur and Sultantepe fragments belong? Was Tablet IV twice as long as the other tablets? Was there perhaps a Tablet V which was not used by the commentator? Only the recovery of more evidence can answer these questions, and for the present a scholarly reserve must be maintained.

Whatever uncertainties may arise about its connexions, this text lacks nothing in interest. The narrator begins by declaring how Marduk has saved him (1–14). After a gap the citizens of Babylon, seeing his recovery, burst into acclamation of Marduk and his consort (29–48). After a further gap the sufferer passes through eleven gates of the Esagil temple complex in Babylon, and at each receives a blessing corresponding with the Sumerian names of the gates (77–90). Having arrived inside, the speaker supplicates his saviour, makes for him a veritable feast of fat things, at which the manuscripts end. The text, however, is not ended, for the last preserved line is a catch-line (on **u**; cf. **p** for a similar style of tablet). The suitability of this text for the end of *Ludlul* can readily be appreciated. It should, however, be pointed out that a plan does emerge from what is preserved of the first three tablets, and if this plan was carried through, further problems are raised. There is an orderly procedure through the departure of the gods to the persecutions, first by human, and secondly by demonic agencies. After the turning-point, the dreams, the writer starts to take up these topics in reverse order. First the diseases are driven out. Now surely he must pass on to the human tormentors: the estates and offices must be returned, the insulting slaves must bow again, the family must recognize the outcast, the courtiers must repent, and the king must receive him back. Next should come the return of the personal deities. If the author did follow out this scheme he must have written with a quite unusual brevity at the end.

The first attestation the poem receives is in the libraries of Ashurbanipal. Nine manuscripts come from this source, and the Commentary. The latter is listed on an Ashurbanipal tablet of literary titles (*mu-kal-lim-tú šá lud-lul bēl né-me-qí*, Rm 618. 19, *apud* Bezold, *Catalogue*). Late Assyrian copies from Assur and Sultantepe confirm that *Ludlul* was a classic of Babylonian literature in the seventh century B.C. The copies from Babylon and Sippar are probably later. The date of composition is almost certainly Cassite period. The three names do not permit an earlier date, and stylistic considerations are opposed to one later.

The whole work shows to an extreme degree the characteristics of Cassite-period scholarship (see p. 14). The range of vocabulary is far wider than in most religious texts, and *hapax legomena* or meanings not otherwise attested occur frequently. The author has certainly not coined these rare words himself. He was steeped in the magic literature and seems to have culled from it all the obscure phrases and recondite words. Even the extensive lexical work *Ḫarra* does not know so many terms for parts of the body. As literature the originality of the work lies in the overall design rather than in its parts. Much of the material, even complete couplets, and the themes are traditional. The Babylonians had long been accustomed to mention or expatiate on their troubles both in letters addressed to their gods and in literary prayers. The first tablet seems to have drawn much inspiration from these two genres. The many lines devoted to the arrival and departure of the demons, however, are clearly based on incantations. Among these there are many examples of a story of healing: a man is set upon by a demon; he does not know how to be rid of it; the aid of Marduk is sought, who goes to his father Ea for advice; the prescription, a ritual, is given by which the sufferer will be made whole. The chief formal difference is that the incantations are written in the third person. In individual cases there are very close parallels. The arrival of the demons reads just like *CT* 17. 12 or *Šurpu* VII. Their seizing parts of the body is told in the same style as, for example, *Maqlû* I. 97–102. At the point where, if *Ludlul* were an incantation, the prescriptions for the ritual would be found, the dreams occur in which the ritual is performed and an incantation priest presents himself. Though it is rare in incantations to find as much attention given to the clearing up of a malady as to its onset, there is a short piece directed against a sorceress which first gives the members affected, and then repeats the list as they are cured (*ZA* 45. 25–26).

One legitimate criticism of the style is that the abundance of verbiage blunts the edge of the argument. Some explanation comes from the general theme of the work. For a long time it has been customary to refer to *Ludlul* as "The Babylonian Job", and so long as knowledge was restricted to the second tablet such a description was justified. Seen now in a more complete form it will not bear the title so readily. Quantitatively the greater part of the text is taken up with showing how Marduk restores his ruined servant, and only a small part with trying to probe the reason for the suffering of the righteous. In places the writer deliberately sheers away from plainly facing this problem because of its blasphemous implications. Perhaps "The Babylonian *Pilgrim's Progress*" would be a better title. Under the surface, however, the writer is perplexed by the same problem as Job. The world is ruled by the lord Marduk, from whom justice is expected by his servants. Yet Marduk allows even the most devoted to suffer. The author of *Ludlul* finds no answer adequate to solve this mystery. All he can say is that though it be the lord who has smitten, yet it is the lord who will heal.

LITERATURE

TEXT WITH OR WITHOUT EDITION

1875 H. C. Rawlinson, IV R^1 67, no. 2 (text of B).

1888 B. T. A. Evetts, *PSBA* 10. 478 and pls. I–II (text of K 2518).

1891 [T. G. Pinches], IV R^2 60* (text of B, E, K 2518).

1902 V. Scheil, *Une Saison de Fouilles à Sippar*, no. 37, p. 105 (an extract from Si 37).

1906 M. Jastrow, *JBL* 25. 135–91 (an edition using *inter alia* an unpublished copy of Si 37 by Messerschmidt).

1910 R. C. Thompson, *PSBA* 32. 18–24 (text of q).

1919 E. Ebeling, *KAR* 108 (= **h**) and 175 (= **p**).

1923 E. Ebeling, *KAR* 326 (= **n**).

1923 S. H. Langdon, *Bab* 7. 131–94 and pls. XIII–XV = *Babylonian Wisdom*, 3–66 and pls. III–V (text of K 3323, DT 358, F, C).

1937 O. R. Gurney, *AfO* 11. 367 and pl. IV, no. 2 (text of j).

1952 R. J. Williams, *JCS* 6. 4–7 and pls. I–II (photograph of l).

1953 W. von Soden, *BiOr* 10. 8–12 (transliteration of O).

1954 W. G. Lambert and O. R. Gurney, *Anatolian Studies* IV. 65–99 (text of **i** and **m**).

1957 O. R. Gurney, *STT* I. 32–33 (revised copies of **i** and **m**).

EDITIONS, TRANSLATIONS, STUDIES

1882 J. Halévy, *Documents religieux de l'Assyrie et de la Babylonie*, pp. 195–7.

1887 A. H. Sayce, *Hibbert Lectures*, pp. 535–6.

1888 T. G. Pinches, *Academy* (London), 21 Jan., pp. 46–47.

1903 H. Zimmern, in E. Schrader, *Die Keilinschriften und das alte Testament*[3], pp. 385–7.
1904 A. Jeremias, *Monotheistische Strömungen*, pp. 40–42.
1905 H. Zimmern, *AO* 7/3. 27–31.
1907 P. Dhorme, *Choix de Textes religieux assyro-babyloniens*, pp. 372–9.
1909 A. Ungnad, in H. Gressmann, *Altorientalische Texte zum alten Testamente*[1], pp. 92–93.
1910 F. Martin, *Journal Asiatique*, 16, Xe Série, 75–143.
1911 P. Landersdorfer, *Eine babylonische Quelle für das Buch Job?* (*Biblische Studien*, XVI/2).
1912 M. Jastrow, *Die Religion Babyloniens und Assyriens* II. 120–2.
1912 R. W. Rogers, *Cuneiform Parallels to the Old Testament*[1], pp. 164–9.
1913 A. Jeremias, *Handbuch der altorientalischen Geisteskultur*[1], pp. 330–2.
1921 R. Reitzenstein, *Das iranische Erlösungsmysterium*, p. 253.
1922 C. J. Ball, *The Book of Job*, pp. 9–30.
1922 B. Landsberger, in E. Lehmann and H. Haas, *Textbuch zur Religionsgeschichte*[2], pp. 311–16.
1925 B. Meissner, *Babylonien und Assyrien* II. 140–1.
1926 E. Ebeling, in H. Gressmann, *Altorientalische Texte zum alten Testament*[2], pp. 273–81.
1926 R. W. Rogers, *Cuneiform Parallels to the Old Testament*[2], pp. 164–9.
1929 A. Jeremias, *Handbuch der altorientalischen Geisteskultur*[2], pp. 420–4.
1935 M. Witzel, *Or* N.S. 4. 107–23 (edition of Tablet II).
1943 J. J. Stamm, *JEOL* IX. 99–107.
1946 T. Jacobsen, in H. Frankfort and others, *The Intellectual Adventure of Ancient Man*, pp. 213–16 = *Before Philosophy*, pp. 228–31.
1946 J. J. Stamm, *Das Leiden des Unschuldigen in Babylon und Israel* (*Abhandlungen zur Theologie des Alten und Neuen Testaments*, 10).
1950 R. H. Pfeiffer, *ANET*[1], pp. 434–7.
1955 R. H. Pfeiffer, *ANET*[2], pp. 434–7.
1956 A. L. Oppenheim, *Dreams*, pp. 217, 250.
1959 W. G. Lambert, in H. Franke (ed.), *Akten des vierundzwanzigsten Internationalen Orientalisten-Kongresses*, pp. 145–8.

COMMENTARY ONLY: TEXT

1884 H. C. Rawlinson, V *R* 47.
1923 S. H. Langdon, *Bab* 7, pls. XI–XIII = *Babylonian Wisdom*, pls. I–III.

TABLET IV(?), TEXT

1915 E. Ebeling, *KAR* 10 (= **t**) and 11 (= **u**).
1953 E. Ebeling, *LKA* 67 (= **v**).
1957 O. R. Gurney, *STT* I. 27 (SU 1952, 302).

TABLET IV(?), EDITIONS (when not included in the editions of the whole work)

1918 H. Zimmern, *Zum babylonischen Neujahrfest, Zweiter Beitrag* (*Berichte über die Verhandlungen der Sächsischen Gesellschaft der Wissenschaften*, Philologisch-historische Klasse, 70/5). 45–48.

SUMMARY LIST OF MANUSCRIPTS

(*Details are given in the lists for the separate tablets*)

Symbol	*Museum or Excavation Number*	*Tablet*(*s*)
A	K 2518+DT 358	II
B	K 3972	II
C	K 8396	II
D	K 3323+Rm 941	II
E	DT 151	II
F	Sm 1745	II
G	K 3291 (Commentary)	I, II, III, IV
h	VAT 10657	II
i	SU 1951, 32	II
j	BM 32214 (S+ 76–11–17, 1941)	I, II
k	BM 32694 (S+ 76–11–17, 2463+2478)	I, II
l	Si 37+881	II
m	SU 1951, 10	I
n	VAT 11100	I
O	K 9237	I
p	VAT 9954	III
q	Si 55	III
r	VAT 10601	II
s	VAT 10071 and VAT 10756 (Exercise Tablets)	I
[**t**	VAT 9303	IV?
u	VAT 9442	IV?
v	VAT 10538	IV?
w	SU 1952, 212+291 with 302	IV?]
X	K 10503+Sm 2139	I
Y	K 6935	II
z	VAT 11565	I

ADDENDA TO *LUDLUL*, TABLET I

WHILE this book was in press **z** (VAT 11565 = *KAR* 279) was discovered to be the lost ending of *Ludlul* I. It overlaps lines 110–12 and duplicates and restores the last four lines of the tablet as preserved on j. Since the original, VAT 11565, is mislaid in Berlin, Ebeling's copy is reproduced on Pl. 74.

110 trace

111	. . . *a-di-ra*]*t lib-*[*bi-ia*]
112	. . .] *pi-rit-tu* [××]
113	. . . g]i? ri lu d[i? × (×)]
114	. . .] be ri i [××]
115	. . . ta]ḫ? be di a kur [××]
116	. . .]× bu ḫu u s[u ××]
117	. . .] *ki-ma* da ×[××]
118	. . .] *nap-ra-ku na-pa-lu-ú*
119	. . .] *iš-ši-ra* ^{mí}*damiqtim*(sig$_5$)^{tim}
120	. . . *ú*]*-nam-me-ra* ^{d}*šamši*^{ši}

(Illegible remains of a colophon appear on the bottom edge of **z**.)

Variants of j: 119 *-š*]*i-ir* 120 *-na*]*m-mir*

The new piece had rulings after every tenth line, like **p**, and ends on a tenth line, 120 according to our calculations. These calculations started from the assumption that the tablet was of 120 lines, and unless it is a coincidence that the new fragment ends at exactly 120, the evidence confirms the basis and accuracy of our calculations. It is then almost certain that Tablets I, II, and III all consisted of 120 lines. The author probably intended them to be construed as 60 couplets each, 60 being an important figure in Babylonian numerology, derived from their sexagesimal system. This result confirms our conclusions about the extent of *Ludlul*. There is every reason to assume that Tablet IV had 120 lines exactly, therefore the Commentary must have ended with this Tablet. The text here called Tablet IV(?) is either Tablet V or no part of *Ludlul* at all.

A further discovery too late to be incorporated in the text is the identification of K 10503 as a piece of *Ludlul* I, and its joining to Sm 2139. The obverse of the new piece has parts of lines 43–52, and its reverse follows Sm 2139 after a gap of four lines with parts of lines 86–91. The following new variants are offered:

44 ⸢*i*⸣*-bé-eš* ×[	50 *á*[*r-*
48 *-r*]*i-is ta-ra-ni*	87 *-a*]*r-ras kak-ki*
49]*-da-a-ti*	91 *-t*]*u*? *i-m*[*e*?-

The variant in line 48 *ipparis* "has been cut off" seems preferable to the reading of **m** *ippariš*.

TABLET I

MANUSCRIPTS

Symbol		*Lines on* *Obverse*		*Reverse*	*Plates*
Sultantepe					
m	= SU 1951, 10	38–72		73–104	1–2
Assur					
n	= VAT 11100	66–86		92–112	3
s	= VAT 10071 rev. 3–4, and VAT 10756 rev. 5–6 (The extracts on these exercise tablets can be taken together, since all the extracts run consecutively from the one on to the other.)		82–85		73
z	= VAT 11565 (see Addenda, p. 30)				
Ashurbanipal					
O	= K 9237	47–65		66–84	3
X	= Sm 2139*	..		75–81	3
G	= K 3291 (Commentary)	47, 48, 61, 69, 71, 78, 86, 87, 89, 93, 105, 106			15–17
Babylon					
k	= BM 32694 (S+ 76–11–17, 2463+2478)	Col. I? 48–54; 56–62		..	4
j	= BM 32214 (S+ 76–11–17, 1941) (k and j are probably parts of the same tablet)	Col. II? Last 4 lines		..	4

Since the beginning is lacking the numbering has been computed from the assumed total of 120 lines (see Introduction), and the places at which the scribes of **m**, **n**, and O changed from obverse to reverse. The approximate numbering thus gained has been adjusted to the wedges marking each tenth line on O.

* Now joined to K 10503; see p. 30.

1 *lud-lul bēl né-me-qí* [. . . (from the colophons)

38	[× × ×] × × × [. . . . .]	
39	[×] × × *nišī*^{meš} *kit-ru-b*[*a* . . . .]	
40	× *-m/l/nat-su da-me-eq-tú*	[. . . . .]
41	[*d*]*a-liḫ-tam-ma be-lum*	[. . . . .]
42	*ù qar-ra-du* ^{d}en.×	*pu-su* × [. . . . . . .]
43	*id-dan-ni ili-i*$_{14}$	*šá-da-šu i-*[*mid*]
44	*ip-par-ku* ^{d}*iš-tar-*⌜*i*⌝$_{14}$	*i-bé-*[*eš* . . .]
45	[*i*]*s-li-it še-*⟨*ed*⟩ *dum-qí*	*šá i-di-*[*ia*]
46	*ip-ru-ud la-mas-si-ma*	*šá-nam-ma i-še-'*[*e*]
47	[*i*]*n-ni-ṭir ba-al-ti*	*du-ú-ti ú-tam-mil*
48	*si-im-ti ip-pa-ri-iš*	*ta-ra-na iš-ḫi-iṭ*
49	*iš-šak-na-nim-ma*	*i-da-at pi-rit-ti*
50	*uš-te-ṣi* ⟨*ina*⟩ *bīti-ia*	*ka-ma-a-ti ar-pu-*⌜*ud*⌝
51	*dal-ḫa te-re-tu-ú-a*	*nu-up-pu-ḫu ud-da-kám*
52	*it-ti* ^{lú}*bārî*(ḫal) *u šá-'-i-li*	*a-lak-ti ul par-sat*
53	*ina pi-i su-qí*	*le-mun egirrû*(enem. gar-*ú*)*-a*
54	*at-til-ma ina šat mu-šu*	*šu-ut-ti pár-da-at*
55	*šarru šīr ilī*	^{d}*šamši šá nišī*^{meš}*-šú*
56	*lìb-bu-uš ik-ka-ṣir-ma*	*pa-ṭa-ru-uš lim-niš*
57	*na-an-za-zu tés-li-tu*	*uš-ta-na-ad-da-nu elī-ia*$_{5}$
58	*paḫ-ru-ma ra-man-šu-nu*	*ú-šaḫ-ḫa-zu nu-ul-la-a-ti*
59	*šum-ma iš-ten-ma*	*na-piš-ta-šu ú-šat-bak-šu*
60	*i-qab-bi šá-nu-ú*	*ú-šat-bi ter-tu-uš*
61	*šá ki-ma šal-ši*	*qip-ta-šú a-tam-ma-aḫ*
62	*er-ru-ub bīt-uš-šu*	*rebû*^{ú} *i-tam-mi*
63	*ḫa-áš-šu pi-i ḫa-še-e*	*šu-bal-kut*
64	*šeš-šu u si-bu-u*	*i-red-du-u še-du-uš-šú*
65	*ik-ṣu-ru-nim-ma*	*ri-kis sibit il-lat-su-un*
66	[*u*$_{4}$-]*mi-iš la pa-du-u*	*ú-ri-kiš maš-lu*
67	[*u*] *iš-ten še-er-šu-nu-ma*	*pa-a i-te-ed-di*

COMMENTARY (comments only)

[The first four preserved lines, of which little remains, seem to have dealt with lines of the text which have not been recovered.]

47 *du-ú-tu bu-un-n*]*a-nu-ú*   48 *ta-ra-nu ṣil-lu*   61 *ta-*]*ma-ḫu ṣa-ba-tum*

VARIANTS

49 k: *pi*]*-rit-tum*   50 k: *á*[*r-p*]*u-du*   53 O: e.sír   k: *-r*]*u ú-a*   54 O: *at-til*   k: *pár-*

1 I will praise the lord of wisdom [. . .

---

41 The lord [. . . . . the] confusion
42 And the warrior . . . . . . [. . . . . . .]
43 My god has forsaken me and disappeared,
44 My goddess has failed me and keeps at a distance.
45 The benevolent angel who (walked) beside [me] has departed,
46 My protecting spirit has taken to flight, and is seeking someone else.
47 My strength is gone; my appearance has become gloomy;
48 My dignity has flown away, my protection made off.
49 Fearful omens beset me.
50 I am got out of my house and wander outside.
51 The omen organs are confused and inflamed for me every day.
52 The omen of the diviner and dream priest does not explain my condition.
53 What is said in the street portends ill for me.
54 When I lie down at night, my dream is terrifying.
55 The king, the flesh of the gods, the sun of his peoples,
56 His heart is enraged (with me), and cannot be appeased.
57 The courtiers plot hostile action against me,
58 They assemble themselves and give utterance to impious words.
59 Thus the first, "I will make him pour out his life."
60 The second says, "I will make him vacate his post."
61 On this wise the third, "I will seize his position."
62 "I will take over his estate", says the fourth.
63 The fifth . . . .
64 The sixth and seventh will persecute . . . .
65 The clique of seven have assembled their forces,
66 Merciless like a demon, equal to . . .
67 One is their flesh, united in purpose.

---

da-t]um 55 **m**: dingir.dingir O: dingir.meš 56 k: *li-i]m-ni* 57 O: *na-an-za-zi tés-lit* k: *elī-iá* 58 O: *ra-man-šú-nu* k: *n]u-ul-la-a-tú* 59 O: *na-piš-ta-šú* k: ⌜*ú*⌝*-šat-bak* 60 k: *t]e-er-tu-šú* 61 **m**: *qip-ta-*⌜*šu*⌝ G: *a-tam-maḫ* k: *-ma]ḫ* 62 O: *i-t[a-* k: *i-tam-m]u?* 63 O: 5-*šu* 64 O: 6-*šu* 7-*ú i-rad-du-u* 65 O: *ik-ṣur-nim-ma, si-bit* 66 O: *pa-du-ú* 67 O: [*ù*]?, uzu.meš-*šú-nu-ma* mnO

68 *[li]bba na-ad-ru-nim-ma* *na-an-ḫu-uz-zu i-šá-tíš*
G 69 *tuš-šu u nap-ra-ku* *ú-šam-ga-ru elī-ia*$_5$
70 *mut-tál-lu pi-ia* *a-pa-tíš i-téš-ʾ-ú*
G 71 *šap-ta-a-a šá it-ta-aṣ-ba-ra* *ḫa-šik-kiš e-me*
72 *šá-pu-tum šá-gi-ma-ti* *šá-qum-meš* × *-še-[. .]*
73 *šá-qa-a-tum ri-šá-a-a* *ik-nu-uš qaq-qar-[šu]*
X 74 *lìb-bi kab-ba-ra-a* *pi-rit-ti ú-tan-[niš]*
75 *ra-pa-áš-tum i-ra-a-ti* *a-ga-áš-gu-u it-te-ʾ-[i]*
76 *ša-di-ḫa a-ḫa-a-a* *ki-la*!*-[a]t-ta i-taḫ-za*
77 *šá e-til-liš at-tal-la-ku* *ḫa-la-la al-mad*
G 78 *šar-ra-ḫa-ku-ma* *a-tur ana re-e-ši*
79 *a-na rap-ši ki-ma-ti* *e-te-me e-da-niš*
80 *su-qa a-ba-ʾa-ma* *tur-ru-ṣa ú-zu-na-a-ti*
81 *er-ru-ub ēkal-liš* *i-ṣa-pu-ra i-na-a-ti*
s 82 *āli-i*$_{14}$ *ki-i a-a-bi* *ni-kil-man-ni*
83 *tu-šá-ma nak-ra-ti* *na-an-du-ur-tú ma-a-ti*
84 *a-na a-ḫi-i* *a-ḫi i-tu-ra*
85 *a-na lem-ni u gal-le-e* *i-tu-ra ib-ri*
G 86 *na-al-bu-bu tap-pe-e* *ú-nam-gar-an-ni*
G 87 *ki-na-a-ti qaq-dà-a* *ú-mar-ras-s[u]* [giš]*kakkī*[meš]
88 *ru-ù'-a ṭa-a-bi* *ú-kar-r[i]* ? *na-piš-ti*
G 89 *šu-piš ina* ⸢*puḫri* *i*⸣*-ru-ra-ni ar-di*
90 *bi-ti* mu/ik × × an *um-ma-ni ṭa-pil-ti iq-bi*
n 91 *i-mu-ra-ni-ma m[u-d]u-u* *šá-ḫa-ti i-mid*
92 *a-na la šīrī*[meš]*-šú* *iš-ku-na-ni kim-ti*
G 93 *a-na qa-ab* [mí]*dameqti*(sig$_5$)*-ia* *pi-ta-as-su ḫaš-ti*
94 *mu-ta-mu-ú ṭa-pil-ti-ia* *šá-kin ana re-e-ši*
95 *da-bi-ib nu-ul-la-ti-ia* *ilu ri-ṣu-šú*
96 × *ša iq-bu-u a-ḫu-lap* *ḫa-muṭ-su mu-tú*
97 *šá la amāta*(inim) *rig-ma i-te-me* *uballiṭ*(ti.la) *še-du-uš*
98 *ul ar-ši a-lik i-di* *ga-me-lu ul a-mur*
99 *a-na ṣi-in-di u bir-ti* *zu-ʾ-ú*!*-zu mim-ma-a-a*

COMMENTARY

69 *nap-ra-ku pi-ir-ku* 71 *[ṣa-ba-ru da-b]a-bu*: *ḫa-šik-ku suk-ku-ku*: *e-mu-u ma-šá-lu* 78 *re-e-šu* [lú]*ardu* 86 *na-al-bu-bu ši-gu-ú* 87 *[ki]-na-*⸢*ti*⸣ ? *[d]a-mi ta-[li-mu]* 93 *ḫa-áš-tum šu-u[t-ta-tum]*

VARIANTS

68 m: *na-a[n-ḫu]-zu* 70 n: *a]-p[a]-a-tíš* 72 n: *-qu]m-m[iš* 73 O: *šá-qa-a-ti*

68 Their hearts rage against me, and they are ablaze like fire.
69 They combine against me in slander and lies.
70 My lordly mouth have they held as with reins,
71 So that I, whose lips used to prate, have become like a mute.
72 My sonorous shout is [reduced] to silence,
73 My lofty head is bowed down to the ground,
74 Dread has enfeebled my robust heart.
75 A novice has turned back my broad chest.
76 My arms, (though once) strong, are both paralysed.
77 I, who strode along as a noble, have learned to slip by unnoticed.
78 Though a dignitary, I have become a slave.
79 To my many relations I am like a recluse.
80 If I walk the street, ears are pricked;
81 If I enter the palace, eyes blink.
82 My city frowns on me as an enemy;
83 Indeed my land is savage and hostile.
84 My friend has become foe,
85 My companion has become a wretch and a devil.
86 In his savagery my comrade denounces me,
87 Constantly my associates furbish their weapons.
88 My intimate friend has brought my life into danger;
89 My slave has publicly cursed me in the assembly.
90 My house . . . ., the mob has defamed me.
91 When my acquaintance sees me, he passes by on the other side.
92 My family treat me as an alien.
93 The pit awaits anyone who speaks well of me,
94 While he who utters defamation of me is promoted.
95 My slanderer slanders with god's help;
96 For the . . . who says, "God bless you", death comes at the gallop.
97 While he who utters a libellous cry is sustained by his guardian spirit.
98 I have no one to go at my side, nor have I found a helper.
99 My household has been enslaved,

---

75 **n**: *ra-pa-áš-tú* **n**O: *i-ra-ti* 76 O: *šá-di-ḫa* **n**: *šad-de-e-ḫa* á.II.me-*a-a* *ki-la*!- is an emendation of X**m**: *ki*-TA-*at-ta* **n**: KU-*l*[*a*?- 77 O: *e-liš* 78 G(**n**)X: *a-na* 80 O: *su-qu* 81 O: *e-ru-ub e-k*[*al-* **n**: *e-kal-liš-ma* 82 **s**: uru 83 **n**: *tu-šá-a-ma* **s**: *nak-ra-tum na-an-dur-ti* 84 **ns**: *a-ḫe-e* 85 **n**: *lim-ni gal-l*[*e-* 86 **n**: *-bu-u*]*b* G: *ú-nam-ga-ra-an-ni* 87 G: *ki-n*]*a-a*[*t*?, ⌜*ú*⌝-[*mar*]-⌜*ra-áš* giš⌝.[tukul] 89 G: *pu-uḫ-ri e-ru-ra-an-ni* × ×[93 G: *ḫaš-tum* 94 **n**: *mu-*[*t*]*a-m*[*u-u*] 95 **n**: *nu-ul-la-te-*[96 **n**: *a-ḫu-l*[*a-p*]*í* 99 *zu-'-ú-zu* is an emendation of **m**: *ú-zu-'u-zu*

mn		
	100 *ina-at ak-mu-ú*	*man di lu s[a]-ki-ka*
	101 *ina qir-bé-ti-ia*	*ú-šes-su-u* [d]*a-la-la*
	102 *ki-i āl na-ki-ri*	*uš-qa-me-mu āli*
	103 *par-ṣi-ia*	*ú-šal-qu-u šá-nam-ma*
	104 *ina pil-lu-di-ia*	*a-ḫa-a uš-zi-zu*
G	105 u_4*-mu šu-ta-nu-ḫu*	*mu-šú gir-ra-a-ni*
G	106 *arḫu qí-ta-a-a-u-lu*	*i-dir-tú šat-t[ú]*
	107 [*ki-m*]*a su-um-me a-dam-mu-ma*	*gi-mir* u_4*-me-i*[*a*]
	108 [*ana za*]*-ma-a-ru*	*qu-ub-bi-ia ú-šá-aṣ-rap*
	109 [*ina bi*]*-tak-ke-e*	*šu-ub-ra-a īnā*[II]*-a-a*
	110 [× × × *di-m*]*a-ti*	*ṣur-ru-pu ú-suk-ka-a-a*
	111 [. . . . .]*-e*	*a-di-rat lìb-b*[*i-ia*]
	112 [. . . . .] ×	⌜*pi-rit*⌝*-t*[*i* . . . .]

[For ending of Tablet I see Addenda, p. 30]

100 And the oxen which I . . . .
101 They have excluded the harvest cry from my fields,
102 And silenced my city like an enemy city.
103 They have let another take my offices,
104 And appointed an outsider in my rites.
105 By day there is sighing, by night lamentation,
106 Monthly—wailing, each year—gloom.
107 I moan like a dove all my days;
108 [For a] song I emit groans.
109 My eyes . . . . [through] constant weeping,
110 My lower eyelids are distended [through abundance of] tears.
111 [. . . . .] . the fears of [my] heart
112 [. . . . .] . panic [. . . . . . .]

COMMENTARY

105 *gir-ra-a-ni bi-*[*ki-tum*] 106 *qí-ta-a-a-ú-lu qu-ú-*[*lu*]

VARIANTS

100 **n**: *i-na-*[, *šá-k*[*i-* 101 **n**: *a-l*[*a*]*-la* 102 **n**: [*uš*]*-qam-me-m*[*u*] uru.mu 105 G: *mu-šu* 106 G: *qí-ta-a-a-ú-lu*, *i-dir-tu* mu.an.[na 108 Landsberger (Lehmann-Haas, *Textbuch*[2], p. 312): [*kīma lal-l*]*a-a-ru* 109 Von Soden (*BiOr* 10. 10): [u_4*-um*? *bi*]*-tak-ke-e*

TABLET II

MANUSCRIPTS

Symbol		Lines on Obverse	Reverse	Plates
Ashurbanipal				
A	= K 2518+DT 358	1–47	96–120	4
B	= K 3972	21–48	98–120	5
C	= K 8396	44–65	66–90	5
D	= K 3323+Rm 941	18–23	105–20	6
	(C and D are almost certainly parts of the same tablet)			
E	= DT 151	1–11	(Colophon)	6
F	= Sm 1745	3–9	..	4
Y	= K 6935	..	90–99	7
G	= K 3291 (Commentary)	3, 7, 9, 11, 21, 24, 43, 44, 53, 57, 61, 69, 70, 88, 90, 96, 97, 98, 100	101, 107	15–17
Assur				
h	= VAT 10657	..	82–94	6
r	= VAT 10601	63–74	..	6
	(**h** and **r** are probably parts of the same tablet)			
Sultantepe				
i	= SU 1951, 32	1–56; 61–72	73–83; 85–120	8–11
Babylon				
j	= BM 32214 (S+ 76–11–17, 1941)	Col. II? 1–17	..	4
k	= BM 32694 (S+ 76–11–17, 2463+ 2478)	Col. II? 16–33	..	4
	(j and k are probably parts of the same tablet)			
Sippar				
l	= Si 37+881	8–29; 37–48	76–120	6–7

1	*akšud*(kur-*ud*)-*ma a-na ba-laṭ*	*a-dan-na i-te-eq*
2	*a-saḫ-ḫur-ma*	*le-mun le-mun-ma*
3	*za-pur-ti ú-ta-ṣa-pa*	*i-šar-ti ul ut-tu*
4	*ila al-si-ma*	*ul id-di-na pa-ni-šú*
5	*ú-sal-li* ^{d}*iš-tar-ri*	*ul* ⸢*ú*⸣-*šá-qa-a ri-ši-šá*
6	^{lú}*bārû*(ḫal) *ina bi-ir*	*ár-kàt ul ip-ru-us*
7	*ina ma-áš-šak-ka* ^{lú}*šā'ilu*(en.me.li)	*ul ú-šá-pi di-i-ni*
8	*za-qí-qu a-bal-ma*	*ul ú-pat-ti uz-ni*
9	^{lú}*mašmaššu ina ki-kiṭ-ṭe-e*	*ki-mil-ti ul ip-ṭur*
10	*a-a-i-te ep-še-e-ti*	*šá-na-a-ti ma-ti-tan*
11	*a-mur-ma ár-kàt*	*ri-da-ti ip-pi-ru*
12	*ki-i šá tam-qí-tum*	*a-na ili la uk-tin-nu*
13	*ù ina ma-ka-le-e*	^{d}*iš-tar-ri la zak-ru*
14	*ap-pi la e-nu-ú*	*šu-kin-ni la am-ru*
15	*ina pi-i-šú ip-par-ku-ú*	*su-up-pe-e tés-li-ti*
16	*ib-ṭi-lu* u_4-*mu ili*	*i-še-ṭú eš-še-ši*
17	*id-du-ú aḫ-šú-ma*	*mi-šu-nu i-mi-šu*
18	*pa-la-ḫu ù it-'u-du*	*la ú-šal-me-du nišī*^{meš}-*šú*
19	*ìl-šú la iz-kur*	*e-kul a-kal-šú*
20	*i-zib* ^{d}*iš-tar-ta-šú*	*mas-ḫa*-⸢*tu*⸣ *la ub-la*
21	*a-na šá im-ḫu-ú*	*bēl-šú im-šu-ú*
22	*niš ili-šú kab-ti*	*qal-liš iz-kur*
	a-na-ku am-šal	
23	*aḫ-su-us-ma ra-man*	*su-up-pu-ú tés-li-ti*
24	*tés-li-ti ta-ši-mat*	*ni-qu-u sak-ku-ú-a*
25	u_4-*mu pa-la-aḫ ilī*^{meš}	*ṭu-ub lìb-bi-ia*
26	u_4-*mu ri-du-ti* ^{d}*iš-tar*	*né-me-li ta-at-tur-ru*

COMMENTARY

3 *za-pur-tum ru-ub-*[*bu*] 7 *maš-šak-ku sur-qí-nu šá* ^{lú}*šā'ili*(en.⸢me.li⸣) 9 *kì-kìṭ-ṭu-ú né-pi-ši* 11 *ip-pi-ri*: [*m*]*a-na-aḫ-tum*: *murṣu* 21 *im-ḫu-ú ka-ba-tum* 24 *sak-ku-u par-ṣi*

VARIANTS

1 j: *a-da*]*n-nu i-ti-iq* i: -]*nu i-ti-*[2 i: *a*[*s-ḫur-m*]*a* 3 EG: *za-pur-tum* Gi: *ú-ta-aṣ-ṣa-pa* G: ⸢*i*⸣-*šar-tum* j: *ú-šar-tú, ú-ṣu* 4 j:]-*nu pa-nu-uš* i: *pa-ni-*[*š*]*u* 5 i: *ú-*[*sal-l*]*a* E: ^{d}*iš-t*[*a-ri* A: *i-šaq-qa-a* i: *ri-ši-šu* j: *ri-ši-šú* 6 E(i): *bi-ri* i: [*a*]*r-ka-at* 7 G: *i-na maš-šak-ki* AF insert *u* before *šā'ilu*. i:]×-⸢*ki*⸣ *šá-'-i-li* G: *i-šá-pi d*[*i-n*]*i* i: *di-nim* j: *di-in-šú-nu* 8 i: *za-*[*qí-q*]*ú a-*BA.BI-(ras.)-*ma* j: *ú-pat-ta uz-nu* 9 i: *ma*[*š-m*]*aš-šu* Gi: *kì-kìṭ-ṭè-e* l:]-*ṭe-*⸢*e*⸣ j: *ki-mil-tú* 10 Ei: *a-a-it* i: *ep-še-ti šá-na-at* l: -*š*]*e-t*[*u*]

1 I survived to the next year; the appointed time passed.
2 As I turn round, it is terrible, it is terrible;
3 My ill luck has increased, and I do not find the right.
4 I called to my god, but he did not show his face,
5 I prayed to my goddess, but she did not raise her head.
6 The diviner with his inspection has not got to the root of the matter,
7 Nor has the dream priest with his libation elucidated my case.
8 I sought the favour of the *zaqīqu*-spirit, but he did not enlighten me;
9 And the incantation priest with his ritual did not appease the divine wrath against me.
10 What strange conditions everywhere!
11 When I look behind, there is persecution, trouble.
12 Like one who has not made libations to his god,
13 Nor invoked his goddess at table,
14 Does not engage in prostration, nor takes cognizance of bowing down;
15 From whose mouth supplication and prayer is lacking,
16 Who has done nothing on holy days, and despised sabbaths,
17 Who in his negligence has despised the gods' rites,
18 Has not taught his people reverence and worship,
19 But has eaten his food without invoking his god,
20 And abandoned his goddess by not bringing a flour offering,
21 Like one who has grown *torpid* and forgotten his lord,
22 Has frivolously sworn a solemn oath by his god,
(like such an one) do I appear.
23 For myself, I gave attention to supplication and prayer:
24 To me prayer was discretion, sacrifice my rule.
25 The day for reverencing the god was a joy to my heart;
26 The day of the goddess's procession was profit and gain to me.

šá-na-ti j: *šá-na-tum* 11 **i**: *a-mur a[r-k]a-te ri-da-ta* l: *-ka-]t[u* G: *ar-ka-t[um] ri-da-a-tum ip-pe-e-ri* j: *-t]um ri-da-tú ip-pi-r[i* 12 **i**: *tam-q[í-s]u* j: dingir.meš 13 l: ^{d}15 **i**: ^{d}*iš-ta[r, iz-za-kar* j: *i-zak-ru* l: *iz-[* 14 **i**: *e-nu-u, šu-[ki]n-na* jl: *šu-kin-nu* j: *am-ri* 15 **i**: *i[p-p]ar-ku-u su-pu-u tés-li-tú* j: *su-pe-e u* l: *su-pu-ú tés-⌜li⌝-t[u* 16 k: *ib-ṭi-la* **i**: *u_4-u]m* j: dingi]r.meš *i-še-eṭ eš-še-e-šu* **i**: *eš-še-šu* l: ud.[è]š.è[š 17 A: *aḫ-šú-nu* l: *me-šú-nu* j:] × × × ⌜dingir.meš *i-me-e-šu*⌝ **i**: *me-e-šu-⌜nu⌝ i-me-šu* 18 **i**: *pa-la-ḫa i[t-]ú-du* k: *u* 19 **i**: *iz-ku-ru i-⌜ku-lu⌝* l: ⌜*i*⌝*-ku-lu* 20 l: *i[z-* **i**: *iz-bu, -ḫ]a-[s]u* A: *mas-ḫas* 21 **i**: *ša im-ḫu-u be-la-šu [im]-šu-u* G: *be-la-šú* 22 **i**: *ni-iš*, ⌜*kab*⌝*-tú, i]z-qur* l: *-k]u-ru* 23 **i**: *ra-ma-ni,]-pu-u tés-li-tú* B: *-u]p-pu-u tés-⌜li-tum⌝* l: *-]u tés-l[i-* 24 **i**: *tés-li-tú ta-ši-ma-tú* G: *tés-li-tum ta-ši-ma-tum* B: *ta-ši-ma-⌜ti⌝* GB: *ni-qu-ú* l: *-qu]-ú* 25 Bi: *ili* 26 **i**: *ri-du-ut* B: *né-me-la ta-at-tu-ru*

27	*ik-ri-bi šarri*	*ši-i ḫi-du-ti*
28	*ù ni-gu-ta-šú*	*a-na da-me-eq-ti šum-ma*
29	*ú-šar a-na māti-ia*	*mê*^{meš} *ili na-ṣa-ri*
30	*šu-mi* ^{d}*iš-tar šu-qur*	*nišī*^{meš}*-ia uš-ta-ḫi-iz*
31	*ta-na-da-a-ti šarri*	*i-liš ụ-maš-šil*
32	*ù pu-luḫ-ti ēkalli*	*um-man ú-šal-mid*
33	*lu-u i-di ki-i it-ti ili*	*i-ta-am-gur an-na-a-ti*
34	*ša dam-qat ra-ma-nu-uš*	*a-na ili gul-lul-tu*[*m*]
35	*ša ina lìb-bi-šú mu-us-su-kàt*	*eli ili-šú dam-qat*
36	*a-a-ú ṭè-em ilī*^{meš}	*qí-rib šamê*^{e} *i-lam-mad*
37	*mi-lik šá* ^{d}*za-nun-ze-e*	*i-ḫa-ak-kim man-nu*
38	*e-ka-a-ma il-ma-da*	*a-lak-ti ili a-pa-a-ti*
39	*šá ina am-šat ib-lu-ṭu*	*i-mut ud-de-eš*
40	*sur-riš uš-ta-dir*	*za-mar uḫ-ta-bar*
41	*ina ṣi-bit ap-pi*	*i-za-am-mur e-li-la*
42	*ina pi-it pu-ri-di*	*ú-ṣar-rap lal-la-re-eš*
43	*ki-i pi-te-e ù ka-ta-mi*	*ṭè-en-ši-na šit-ni*
44	*im-mu-ṣa-ma*	*im-ma-a šá-lam-tíš*
45	*i-šib-ba-a-ma*	*i-šá-an-na-na ìl-šin*
46	*ina ṭa-a-bi i-ta-ma-a*	*i-li šá-ma-'i*
47	*ú-taš-šá-šá-ma i-dab-bu-ba*	*a-rad ir-kal-la*
48	*ana an-na-a-tú uš-ta-*×	*qí-rib-ši-na la al-tan-d*[*a*]
49	[*u*] *ia-a-ti šu-nu-*[*ḫu*]	*i-*⟨*ri*⟩*-*⌜*id*⌝*-di mi-ḫu-u*
50	*murṣu mun-ni-šú*	*elī-ia in-neš-ra*
51	*im-ḫul-li* [*iš-tu i-šid*]	*šamê*^{e} *i-zi-qa*
52	[*u*]*l-te i-rat erṣetim*^{tim}	*i-ši-ḫa ṭi-'-i*
53	⌜*šu-ú*⌝*-lu lim-nu*	*it-ta-ṣa-a ap-su-uš-šú*
54	[*ú-tuk-ku l*]*a* [*ni*]*-'i*	*ú-ṣa-a ul-tu ēkur*
55	[*la-maš-tu ú-ri*]*-da*	*ul-tu qí-rib šadî*^{i}

COMMENTARY

43 *u*$_4$*-mu ù mu-ši* 44 [*u*]⌜*n-ṣu bu-bu-tum*⌝ 53 *šu-lum e-ṭím-mu*

VARIANTS

27 **i**: *ik-rib* 28 **l**:]⌜sig$_5$*-ti*⌝ 29 **Bik**: *ú-šá-ri* **i**: *ana* **B**: *me-e* **i**: *n*[*a-ṣ*]*a-ru* 30 **k**: *šu-ú* **i**: *šu-ma* ^{d}*iš-ta-*⌜*ri*⌝ **B**: *šu-qu-ru* 31 **i**: *ta-na-da-at* **Ai**: *e-liš* 32 **k**: *u* **k**(**i**): *pu-luḫ-tú* **A**: *pu-luḫ-tu* **i**: *um-ma-nu* 33 **A**: *lu* **k**: *lu*]*-ú* **i**: *ilī*^{meš} *i-tam-ku-ra*

27 The king's prayer—that was my joy,
28 And the accompanying music became a delight for me.

29 I instructed my land to keep the god's rites,
30 And provoked my people to value the goddess's name.

31 I made praise for the king like a god's,
32 And taught the populace reverence for the palace.

33 I wish I knew that these things were pleasing to one's god!

34 What is proper to oneself is an offence to one's god,
35 What in one's own heart seems despicable is proper to one's god.

36 Who knows the will of the gods in heaven?
37 Who understands the plans of the underworld gods?
38 Where have mortals learnt the way of a god?

39 He who was alive yesterday is dead today.
40 For a minute he was dejected, suddenly he is exuberant.

41 One moment people are singing in exaltation,
42 Another they groan like professional mourners.

43 Their condition changes like opening and shutting (the legs).

44 When starving they become like corpses,
45 When replete they vie with their gods.

46 In prosperity they speak of scaling heaven,
47 Under adversity they complain of going down to hell.

48 I am *appalled* at these things; I do not understand their significance.

49 As for me, the exhausted one, a tempest is driving me!
50 Debilitating Disease is let loose upon me:
51 An Evil Wind has blown [from the] horizon,
52 Headache has sprung up from the surface of the underworld,
53 An Evil Cough has left its *Apsû*,

54 The irresistible [Ghost] left *Ekur*,
55 [The *Lamaštu*-demon came] down from the Mountain,

---

34 A: *šá* **i**: om. *ana* 35 A: *šá* **i**: om.(?) *eli*, [*il*]*i-šu* 38 **i**: *a-lak-tú* 39 **i**: *i-*]*mu-ú-tu* l: ⌜*ú*⌝-[*de-eš* 40 **i**: *uš-ta-di-ru* l: *r*]*a*? *za-am-ra* **i**: *uḫ-tab-*[*bar* 41 **i**: *ap-pa i-za-mu-ra* l: *i-za-am-mu-ru* 42 l: *ú-*⌜*ṣar*⌝*-ra-pa* **i**: *lal-*⌜*la*⌝-[*ri*]*š* 43 A: *pi-te* **i**: *pi-ti-e* Ail: *u* G: *ka-ta-me* l: *ṭè-em-*[44 **i**: *im-mu-ṣa-a-ma*,]-IM-*tíš* 45 A: *i-šib-ba-ma* **i**: *ìl-ši-in* 46 **i**(A): *i-na* **i**: *e-la-a* 47 **i**: *ú-ta-šá-šá*[-, *i-dab-bu-ub a-*⌜*ri*⌝*-du* 48 B: ⌜*an-na-ti*⌝ l: ⌜*al-ta-an*⌝-[*da* 49 C: *me-ḫ*[*u-u* 50 C: *in-né-eš-ra* 52 C: *ṭi-'-ú* 53 G: *šu-lum* C(G): zu.ab-*uš-šú* 54 C: *ni*]-'-*i* **i**: *i*[*š-t*]*u* 55 **i**: *iš-tu*

56 [. . . . . .] e$_4$.la$_6$ — *šu-ru-up-pu-u i-nu-šu*
57 *it-ti ur-qí-tum erṣetim*^{tim} — *i-pi-ṣi lu-'-tú*
58 [. . . . . .] *pu-ḫur-šú-nu* — *ištēniš*^{niš} *iṭ-ḫu-ni*
59 [. . . . *qaq-qa-d*]*u* — *i-te-'-ú muḫ-ḫi*
60 [*bu-né-ia*] *i-ki-lu* — *i-na-i-lu īnā*^{II}*-ia*
61 *la-ba-ni* ⌜*e*⌝*-te-qu* — *ú-ram-mu-ú ki-šá-du*
62 [*ir-ti*] *im-ḫa-ṣu* — *tu-le-e iṭ-ṭe*$_4$-⌜*ru*⌝
63 [*ši-*]⌜*i*⌝*-ri il-pu-tú* — *ra-'i-ba id-*⌜*du-ú*⌝
64 [*ina r*]*e-eš lìb-bi-ia* — *ip-pu-ḫu i-šá-t*[*u*]
65 *qir-bi-ia id-lu-ḫu* — *ú-na-ti-iá ut-ti-*[×]
66 *šu-u*[*d*?*-d*]*u*?*-u uḫ-ḫu* — *ú-la-'i-bu* ⌜*ḫa*⌝-[*še-e-a*]
67 *meš-re-ti-ia ú-la-'-ib* — *ú-niš-šu pi-*⌜*it-ri*⌝

68 *la-na zaq-ru* — *i-bu-tú i-ga-ri-iš*
69 *gat-ti rap-šat* — *ú-ru-ba-iš uš-ni-i-la*
70 *ki-i ú-lil-te an-na-bi-ik* — *bu-pa-niš an-na-di*

71 *a-lu-ú zu-um-ri* — *i-te-di-iq ṣu-ba-ti*
72 *ki-ma šu-uš-kal-li* — *ú-kàt-ti-man-ni šit-tú*

73 *pal-ṣa-a-ma* — *ul i-na-aṭ-ṭal* — *i-na-a-a*
74 *pi-ta-a-ma* — *ul i-šim-ma-a* — *uz-na-a-a*

75 *kal pag-ri-ia* — *i-ta-ḫaz* — *ri-mu-tú*
76 *mi-šit-tu* — *im-ta-qut* — *eli šīrī*^{meš}*-ia*

77 *man-gu* — *iṣ-bat* — *i-di-ia*
78 *lu-'-tú* — *im-ta-qut* — *eli bir-ki-ia*
79 *ma-šá-ma* — *na-mu-ši-šá* — *ši-pa-a-a*

80 [*mi*?*-i*]*ḫ*?*-ṣu šuk-šu-du* — *ú-nap-paq ma-aq-t*[*i-i*]*š*
81 [×-]*du-ud mu-tu* — *i-te-rim pa-ni-ia*

82 [*i-ḫa*]-⌜*sa*⌝*-sa-ni-ma* — *šá-'i-li ul ap-pal*
83 [× ×]A *i-bak-ku-u* — *ra-man ul i-ši*

84 *ina pi-ia* — *na-aḫ-bal* — *na-di-ma*
85 ⌜*ù*⌝ *nap-ra-ku* — *si-ki-ir* — *šap-ti-ia*

86 [*b*]*a-bi e-di-il* — *pi-ḫi maš-qu-u-a*

COMMENTARY

57 *lu-'-tum mur-ṣu tum su-un-gir-tum* 61 *i-ti-qú*: *ra-mu-u*: *še-bé-ru* 69 *ur-ba-tu*: ^{giš}*ur-ba-nu* 70 *ú-lil-*

VARIANTS

57 G: *ur-qit* ki-*tum i-pi-iṣ-ṣu lu-'-tum* 61 G: *i-ti-qú* 66 **r**: *ú-la-i-*[67 **i**: *meš-re-te-ia ú-la-'i-bu ú-niš-šú* **r**: *ú-la-i-bu* 68 **i**: *la-a-ni* **r**: *zaq-*]*ra* 69 **ir**: *rap-šá-ta* **i**: *ur-ba-ti*

56 Cramp set out [from . . . .] the flood,
57 Impotence cleaves the ground along with the grass.
58 [. . . . . .] their host, together they came on me.
59 [. . . .] head, they enveloped my skull;
60 [My face] is gloomy, my eyes are in flood.
61 They have wrenched my neck muscles and taken the strength from my neck.
62 They struck [my chest,] drubbing my breast.
63 They affected my flesh and caused convulsions,
64 [In] my epigastrium they kindled a fire.
65 They upset my bowels . . . . . . [.]
66 Causing the discharge of phlegm, they brought on a fever in my [lungs.]
67 They caused fever in my limbs and made my fat quake.

68 My lofty stature they destroyed like a wall,
69 My robust figure they laid down like a bulrush,
70 I am thrown down like a bog plant and cast on my face.

71 The *alû*-demon has clothed himself in my body as with a garment;
72 Sleep covers me like a net.

73 My eyes stare, but do not see,
74 My ears are open, but do not hear.

75 Feebleness has seized my whole body,
76 Concussion has fallen upon my flesh.

77 Paralysis has grasped my arms,
78 Impotence has fallen on my knees,
79 My feet forget their motion.

80 [A stroke] has got me; I choke like someone prostrate.
81 [. .] . . . death, it has covered my face.

82 The dream priest mentions me, but I do not respond.
83 [. . .] . weep, but I have no control of my faculties.

84 A snare is laid on my mouth,
85 And a bolt bars my lips.

86 My 'gate' is barred, my 'drinking place' blocked,

---

r: *ur-ba-ti-i[š* G: *rap-šá-tu ur-ba-ti-iš uš-ni-il-lu*$_4$ 70 G: *ú-lil-tum* **r**: ⌜*ú*⌝*-lil-ti* **i**: *ú-lil-tú an-na-bi-*⌜*ku*⌝ *bu-ba-ni-iš* G: *bu-up-pa-niš* 71 **i**: *a-lu-u* 73 **i**: *i-na-ṭ[a-* 74 **i**: *pi-ta-a, i-še-ma* 75 **i**: *ka-la* 76 **i**: *mi-šit-tú, e-lu* 77 **i**: *iṣ-ṣa-[bat* 78 **i**: *e-li* 79 **i**: *ma-šá-a-ma nam-ši-[, še-pa-a-a* l: *še-pa-[* 80 **i**: *šuk-šú-[* l: *]-nap-pa-qa* **i**: *ú-nap-*^{pa}*paq ma-aq-tíš* 81 **i**: *mu-ú-[* 82 l: *šá-e-lu* 83 l: *i-bak-ku-ú ra-ma-nu* **h**: *-]ú ra-ma-ni, i-šú* 84 **hl**: *-b]a-lu* 85 l: *u, sa-ki-ir* **h**: *si-kir* 86 **h**: *e]-dil, maš-qu-*⌜*ú*⌝*-[a* **i**: *]-ú-a*

MSS				
Ch i l	87	[*á*]*r-kat bu-bu-te*		*ka-tim ur-*⌜*ú*⌝*-*[*d*]*i*
G	88	*áš-na-an šum-ma*		*da-ad-da-riš a-la-'-ut*
	89	^{d}*siriš*(šim) *nap-šat niši*^{meš}		*elī-ia im-tar-ṣu*
G Y	90	*ap-pu-na-ma*		*e-te-rik si-le-e-tum*
	91	*ina la ma-ka-le-e*		*zi-mu-ú-a it-ta*[*k-ru*]
	92	*šīri iš-taḫ-ḫa*		*da-mi iz-zu-*[*ba*]
	93	*e-ṣe-et-tum us-su-qat*$_6$		*a-ri-ma-at maš-*[*ki*]
	94	*ši-ir-a-nu-ú-a nu-up-pu-ḫu*		*ú-ri-iq-tum maḫ-*[*ru*]
	95	*a-ḫu-uz* ^{giš}*irši me-si-ru*		*mu-ṣe-e ta-ni-ḫ*[*u*]
A G	96	*a-na ki-suk-ki-ia*		*i-tu-ra bi-i-tu*
G B	97	*il-lu-ur-tú ši-ri-ia*		*na-da-a i-da-a-a*
G	98	*maš-kan ram-ni-ia*		*muq-qu-ta še-pa-a-a*
	99	*ni-ṭa-tu-ú-a šum-ru-ṣa*		*mi-ḫi-iṣ-tu dan-na-a*[*t*]
G	100	*qin-na-zu id-da-an-ni*		*ma-la-ti ṣil-la-a-tum*
G	101	*pa-ru-uš-šú ú-saḫ-ḫi-la-an-ni*		*zi-qa-ta dan-nat*
	102	*kal u*$_4$*-mu*		*ri-du-ú i-ri-id-da*[*n-ni*]
	103	*ina šat mu-ši*		*ul ú-nap-pa-šá-an-ni sur-riš*
D	104	*ina i-tab-lak-ku-ti*		*pu-uṭ-ṭu-ru rik-su-ú-a*
	105	*meš-re-tu-u-a su-up-pu-ḫa*		*i-ta-ad-da-a a-ḫi-tum*
	106	*ina ru-ub-ṣi-ia*	*a-bit*	*ki-i al-pi*
G	107	*ub-tal-lil*	*ki-i immeri*(udu.nitá)	*ina ta-ba-áš-ta-ni-ia*
	108	*sakīki*(sa.gig-*ki*)*-ia*	*iš-ḫu-ṭu*	^{lú}*mašmaššu*
	109	*ù te-re-ti-ia*	^{lú}*bārû*(ḫal)	*ú-téš-ši*
	110	*ul ú-šá-pi a-ši-pu*		*ši-kin mur-ṣi-ia*
	111	*ù a-dan-na si-li-'-ti-ia*		^{lú}*bārû*(ḫal) *ul id-din*

COMMENTARY

88 *da-da-ru bu-'-šá-nu* 90 *ap-pu-na-ma ma-'-diš*: *si-le-e-tum*: *murṣu* 96 *ki-suk-ku ki-lum* 97 ^{giš}*il-lu-ur-tum is-qa-tum* 98 *maš-kan*: *bi-ri-tum* 100 *qin-na-zu is-tuḫ-ḫu*: *ṣil-la-a-tum ka-ta-a-tum* 101 ^{giš}*pa-ru-uš-šú* ^{giš}*ḫaṭṭu* 107 *ta-ba-áš-ta-nu*: *zu-ú ši-na-tum*

VARIANTS

87 l: sar (= *arqat*!) *bu-bu-tum* **h**: *-k*]*àt bu-bu-ti, ru-*['*-ti* 88 **h**: *da-ab*!*-da-riš* G: *a-la-ut* 89 **h**: *ilī*^{meš} **i**: *elī-ia*$_5$ l: *elī-iá* 90 Y: *i-te-r*[*i-* **h**: *i-te* (erased) *i-te-ri-ik* **i**: *i-ti-ri-ik* l: *i-te-*[*ri*]*k* C: *s*[*i-l*]*i-'-*[91 l: *i-na* 92 **h**: *š*]*e-i-ri* **i**: *ši-ri, i-*[*zu-ba* Y: *i*]*š-taḫ-ḫu*

87 My hunger is prolonged, my throat stopped up.

88 When grain is served, I eat it like stinkweed,
89 Beer, the life of mankind, is distasteful to me.

90 My malady is indeed protracted.

91 Through lack of food my countenance is changed,
92 My flesh is flaccid, and my blood has ebbed away.
93 My bones have come apart, and are covered (only) with my skin.
94 My tissues are inflamed, and have caught the . . . .-disease.

95 I take to a bed of bondage; going out is a pain;
96 My house has become my prison.

97 My arms are stricken—which shackles my flesh;
98 My feet are limp—which fetters my person.

99 My afflictions are grievous, my wound is severe.
100 A scourge has thrown me down, the *stroke* is *intense*.
101 The crop pierces me and the spur is severe.

102 All day long the tormentor torments [me,]
103 Nor at night does he let me relax for a minute.

104 Through twisting my sinews are parted,
105 My limbs are splayed and knocked apart.

106 I spend the night in my dung like an ox,
107 And wallow in my excrement like a sheep.

108 My complaints have exposed the incantation priest,
109 And my omens have confounded the diviner.

110 The exorcist has not diagnosed the nature of my complaint,
111 Nor has the diviner put a time limit on my illness.

---

93 **h**: ⌜*e*⌝*-ṣe-en-te* Y: *-e]n-ti-i*$_{14}$ **i**: *e-ṣe-en-ti us-su-q[at*$_{6}$*/q[àt a-ri-m]at* 94 **i**: *šír-a-nu-u-a, -r]iq-ta* Y: *ú-r[iq-* 95 **i**: *ir-ši* Y: *me-sír* 96 **i**: KU?*-suk-ki-ia, bi-i-ti* G: *bé-e-tu* 97 G: ^{giš}*il-lu-ur-tu*$_{4}$ **i**: uzu.meš-*ia* Y: uzu-*ia* 98 A: *r[a-* **i**: *ra-ma-ni-ia* G: *muq-qu-tú* Y: *m[u-u]q-q[u-* 99 **i**: *šum-ru-ṣu me-ḫi-iṣ-ti* 100 B(**i**): *qin-na-zi* G: *ma-la-a* **i**: *ma-lat* 101 G: ^{giš}*pa-ru-uš-šú* B: *ú-saḫ-ḫi-il-an-ni* G: *zi-qa-tum* **i**l: *zi-qa-ti* 102 **i**: *u*$_{4}$*-me ri-du-u i-ri-da-[* l: *i-rad-[d]a-a[n-ni* 103 **i**: ⌜*i*⌝*-na[p-* 104 l: *i-na ú-tab-lak-ku-ti* 105 l: *meš-re-tu-ú-a, a-ḫi-[t]i* **i**: *a-ḫa-ta* 106 l: *i-na, k[i]-ma* gud 107 l: *ki-ma, [t]a-ba-áš-ta-ni-iá* 108 l: sa.[gi]g-*iá, maš-maš-šú* **i**: *-ma]š-šu* 109 l: *u te-re-ti-iá, ú-t[a]š-š[ám]-ma* 110 l: *a-ši-pa*, gig-*iá* **i**: gig-*ia* 111 **i**: *u a-dan-ni si-li-ti-ia* l: *a-dan-nu si-li-ti-iá*

ABDil

112 *ul i-ru-ṣa ilu* — *qa-ti ul iṣ-bat*
113 *ul i-ri-man-ni* ^{d}*iš-ta-ri* — *i-da-a-a ul il-lik*

114 *pi-ti kimaḫḫu* — *er-su-ú šu-ka-nu-u-a*
115 *a-di la mi-tu-ti-i-ma* — *bi-ki-ti gam-rat*

116 *kal ma-ti-ia* — *ki-i ḫa-bíl iq-bu-ni*

117 *iš-me-e-ma ḫa-du-ú-a* — *im-me-ru pa-nu-šú*
118 *ḫa-di-ti ú-ba-as-si-ru* — *ka-bat-ta-šú ip-pir-du*

119 *i-di* u_4*-mu* — *šá gi-mir kim-ti-ia*
120 *šá qi-rib mu-de-e* — ^{d}*šamas-su-un i-rim*

112 My god has not come to the rescue in taking me by the hand,
113 Nor has my goddess shown pity on me by going at my side.

114 My grave was waiting, and my funerary paraphernalia ready,
115 Before I had died lamentation for me was finished.

116 All my country said, "How he is crushed!"

117 The face of him who gloats lit up when he heard,
118 The tidings reached her who gloats, and her heart rejoiced.

119 But I know the day for my whole family,
120 When, among my friends, their Sun-god will have mercy.

VARIANTS

112 D: šu.II 113 i: ^{d}*iš-tar-ri* 114 l: *ki-ma-ḫu* BD: *er-šu-ú* i: *er-[s]u-u* il: *šu-ka-nu-ú-a* 115 i: *m[i-t]u-ti-ma* l: *mi-tu-tim-ma* Dl: *bi-ki-tum* 116 i: kur-*ia* l:]-*iá* il: *ḫa-bil* 117 i: *iš-me-ma ḫa-du-u-a* l: *im-mi-ru* 118 l: *ḫa-di-t]u* i: *ú-ba-si-ru* D: *-si-r]i* il: *ka-bat-ta-šá* i: *i]p-pir-[d]a* 119 i: u_4*-me* 120 i(l): *qir-bi*

TABLET III

MANUSCRIPTS

Line 1 is preserved as the catch-line on the following manuscripts of Tablet II: ABDil.
Lines 1–61

Symbol		*Lines on* *Obverse*	*Lines on* *Reverse*	*Plates*
Assur				
p	= VAT 9954 (a half-length tablet)	1–30	31–45, 47–61	12
Sippar				
q	= Si 55	22–54		13
Ashurbanipal				
G	= K 3291 (Commentary)		1, 25, 37, 40, 60	15–17

After a gap the 36 lines of the reverse of q follow (Pl. 14), of which 18, 19, 30, 31, 33 are contained on G.

For the rest of the tablet only the 21 lines quoted in G are preserved, which are not necessarily contiguous (the first and second pairs, however, seem to be). They have not therefore been numbered, but have been given the letters a–u for convenient identification. Some of these lines in fact doubtless belong to Tablet IV (see Introduction), but since the dividing-point cannot be ascertained they are all put under Tablet III.

ABDilp G

1 *kab-ta-at qāt-su*   *ul a-li-'-i na-šá-šá*
2 [*a*]*d-rat pu-luḫ-ta-šu*   *ú*-[. . . . .]
3 [×]-*nis-su ez-zi-ta*   *a-bu-ba-ma* [. . . . . . .]
4 ×-*na-at tallakta*(ki.gub-*ta*)-*šú*   i × × × [. . . . . .]
5 ×-*nu murṣa kab-ta*   *ra*-⸢*ma*⸣-[*ni*] *la* i ×[× ×]
6 ×-*ru-ti ma-šá-ku*   *ú-šar-pa-du-ni* [× ×]
7 [*u*]*r-ra u mu-šú*   *iš-te-niš a-na-a*[*s-su-us*]
8 *šuttu*(máš.ge$_6$) *mu-na-at-tú*   *mal-ma-liš šu-um-r*[*u-ṣa-ku*]
9 *iš-ta-nu eṭ-lu*   *a-tir ši-kit-*[*ta*]
10 *mi-na-ta šur-ru-uḫ*   *lu-bu-uš-ta ud-du-*[*u*]*š*
11 *áš-šú ina mu-na-at-ti* ŠID-*du-šu*   GAD ta zu b[i?] eš
12 ⸢*mi*⸣-*lam*!-*me ḫa-líp*   *la*-⸢*biš pu*⸣-*ul-ḫ*[*a-t*]*i*
13 [× ×] × ×   *it-ta-zi-iz*!   *el*[*ī-i*]*a*
14 [× × (×) m]a   *iḫ-ḫa-mu-u*   *šīru-u-*[*a*]
15 [× × × (×)]   *be-el-*[*t*]*u*   *iš-pur-a*[*n-ni*]
16 [× × ×]×   × × ×   × ×[. . .]
17 [× (×)]× ma *a-tam-ma-a* [. . . . .] × šú [. . . .]
18 [×]× *um-ma iš-pu-*[*r* . . . .]
19 *i-qu-lu-ma ul* i-[. . . . .]
20 × ud iš na × ×[. . . . .]
21 *áš-*[*n*]*i-ma*   [*šutta*(máš.ge$_6$)   *a-na-aṭ-ṭal*]
q
22 *ina šutti*(máš.ge$_6$)   *aṭ-*[*ṭu-lu*   *mu-ši-ti-ia*]
23 *iš*-⸢*ta*⸣-*nu eṭ-*[*lu* . . . .]
24 ^{giš}*bi-*[*nu*] *mu-u*[*l*]*-li-lu*   *ta-mi-iḫ ri*[*t-tuš-šú*]
G
25 *làl-úr-alim-ma*   *a-šib nippuri*^{ki}
26 *a-na ub-bu-bi-ka*   *iš-pu-ra-an-*[*ni*]
27 *mê*^{meš} *na-šu-ú*   *elī-ia id-*[*di*]
28 *ši-pat ba-la-ṭi id-da-a*   *ú-maš-ši-' z*[*u-um-ri*]
29 *áš-lu-uš-ma*   *šu-ut-tu*   *a-na-aṭ-*[*ṭal*]
30 *ina šutti*(máš.ge$_6$)   *aṭ-ṭu-lu*   *mu-ši-t*[*i-ia*]
31 *ni-ši-iš batūlta*(ki.sikil)   *ba-nu-ú zi-*[*mu-šá*]
32 *šar-ra-at* la × [bi]š/[ḫ]a ti   *i-liš ma*[*š-lat*]

COMMENTARY

1 *kab-tu dan-nu*   25 *ṭa-a-bi-ú-ṭú-ul-*^{d}*enlil*(be)

VARIANTS

1 G: *a-li-'i*   D: *e-le-e na-šá-šú*   i: *na-šá-šu*   12 Tablet: ⸢*mi*⸣-GIM-*me*   13 Tablet:

1 His hand was heavy upon me, I could not bear it.
2 My dread of him was alarming, it [. . . . . me]

3 His fierce [.] . . was a tornado [. . . . . . .]
4 His stride was . . ., it . . . [. . . . . .]

5 . . the severe illness does not . . [. .] my person,
6 I forget . . . [. .] makes my mind stray.

7 Day and night alike I groan,
8 In dream and waking moments I am equally wretched.

9 A remarkable young man of outstanding physique,
10 Massive in his body, clothed in new garments—

11 Since in waking moments . . . .
12 Clad in splendour, robed in dread,

13 [. .] . . he stood over me,
14 [I . . .] and [my] body was numbed.

15 ["‘. . . .] the lady has sent [me]
16 [. . .] . . . . . . [. . .”]

17 [. .] . . I said [. . . . .] . . [. . . .]
18 [.] . . . sent [. . . . .]
19 They were silent and did not [. . . . .]
20 . . . . . . [. . . . .]

21 A second time [I saw a dream,]
22 And in [my night dream which] I [saw]

23 A remarkable young [man . . . .]
24 Holding in his hand a tamarisk rod of purification—

25 "Laluralimma, resident of Nippur,
26 Has sent me to cleanse you."

27 The water he was carrying he threw over me,
28 Pronounced the life-giving incantation, and rubbed [my body.]

29 A third time I saw a dream,
30 And in my night dream which I saw—

31 . . . a young woman of shining countenance,
32 A queen of . . . ., equal to a god.

---

it-ta-zi-MA 23 q:] ⌜*ram*⌝-*ku ti*-×[This could have followed the text of **p** only if q were written diš guruš; otherwise the two manuscripts must have diverged. 24 q: *mu*]*l-li-lu* 30 q: *i-n*]*a* 31 **p**: *ba*-[*tul-tu* 32 **p**: (following *šarrat*) *u*[*n*

q p

33 *i-ru-ba-am-ma i-ta*[*š-ba*?] × [. . .]× *ma-a* [. .]
34 *qi-ba-a a-ḫu-la-pí* [. . . . .] × × [. . .]

35 *la ta-pal-laḫ iq-ba-a* *ú-šá*-×[. . . . . . .]
36 *me-mu-u šutta*(máš.ge$_6$) *i-ṭul* [. . . . .]

G 37 *iq-bi-ma a-ḫu-la-pí* *ma-gal šum*-[*ru-uṣ-ma*]
38 *a-a-um-ma šá ina šat mu-ši* *ib-ru-u bi*-[*ra*]

39 *ina šutti*(máš.ge$_6$) ^{m}*ur-nin-din-lug$_x$-ga* ⸢din?.tir⸣? [. . . .]
G 40 *eṭ-lu ṭar-ru* *a-pir a-ga-šú*

41 *mašmaššum*(maš.maš)-*ma* *na-ši li*-⸢'⸣-[*um*]
42 ^{d}*marduk-ma* *iš-pu-ra-an*-[*ni*]

43 *ana* ^{m}*šub-ši-meš-re-e*-^{d}*šakkan*(gìr) *ú-bil-la ṣi-i*[*m-ra*]
44 *ina qātē*^{II}-*šú ellēti*^{meš} *ú-bil-la ṣi-i*[*m-ra*]

45 *a-na mut-tab-bi-li-iá* *qa-tuš-šú ip-q*[*í-id*]

46 [*ina*] *mu-na-at-ti* *iš-pu-ra ši-pi*[*r-ta*]
p 47 *it-tuš dam-qa-tu* *niši*^{meš}-*iá uk-t*[*al-lim*]

48 *ina si-li-tu* ⸢*i*⸣?-*ri-ku* muš ×[-×-×]
49 *mur-ṣi ár-ḫi-iš ig*-[*g*]*a-mir* *iḫ-ḫi-pi* ×[. . .]

50 *ul-tu šá be-lí-iá* *lìb-ba-šú i*-[*nu-ḫu*]
51 *šá* ⸢^{d}*marduk*⸣ *rim-ni-i* *ka-bat-ta*-[*šú*] *ip-p*[*a-áš-ḫu*]

52 [*il-q*]*u-ú un-nin-ni-ia* [.] × × [. . . . .]
53 [*nu-um*]-*mur-šu ṭa-a-bu* ×[. . . . .]

54 [*iq-bu-u*] *a-ḫu-la-pí* *m*[*a-gal šu-nu-u*]*ḫ-ma*

55 [× × ×] *a-na šu-pé-e* ×[. . . . .]× te
56 [× ×]× *a-na du-lul* ⸢*ù*⸣ [. . . . .]×

57 [× ×]× *ar-ni* [. . . . .]
58 [× ×]× *in-nit-ta* [. . . . .]

59 [× ×] *šèr-ti* × [. . . . .]
G 60 *e-ga-ti-ia ú-šá-bil šāra*

61 [×] mi id [. . . . .]

COMMENTARY

37 *a-ḫu-la-pi a-di ma-ti* 40 *ṭàr-ru dan-nu* 60 *e-ga-a-ti ḫi-ṭa-a-ti*

VARIANTS

36 Text of **p** probably corrupt; q: × [×] *i-na mim-ma* [37 **p**: *iq-bu-u* G: *iq-ba-a a-ḫu-la-pi*

She entered and [sat down] . [. . .] . . . [. .]
"Speak my deliverance [. . . . .] . . [. . .]

"Fear not," she said, "I [will . . . .]
Whatever of a dream saw [. . . . .]

She said, "Be delivered from your very wretched state,
Whoever has seen a vision in the night time."

In the dream Urnindinlugga, the *Babylonian* [. . . .]
A bearded young man with his turban on his head.

An incantation priest, carrying a tablet,
"Marduk has sent me.

To Šubši-mešrê-Šakkan I have brought prosperity,
From Marduk's pure hands I have brought prosperity."

He (Marduk) had entrusted me into the hands of my ministrant.

[In] waking hours he sent the message
And showed his favourable sign to my peoples.

In the protracted malady . . [. .]
My illness was quickly over and [my *fetters*] were broken.

After the mind of my Lord had quietened
And the heart of merciful Marduk was appeased,

[After he had] received my prayers [.] . . [. . . . .]
And his pleasant [smile] . [. . . . .]

[After he had said,] "Be delivered, you [who are in great] toils!"

[. . .] to extol . [. . . . .] . .
[. .] . to worship and [. . . . .] .

[. .] . my guilt [. . . . .]
[. .] . my iniquity [. . . . .]

[. .] my transgression . [. . . . .]
He made the wind bear away my offences.

---

q: *a-ḫu-lap* G: *šu-nu-uḫ-ma* 39 **p**: om. ᵐ q: *ba*?-[*bi*?-*lam*? For bàd = lug$_x$ cf. *MSL* II. 86[1]. 40 G: *ṭàr-ru* **p**: *a-pi-*[*ir*] 41 **p**: maš.maš-*um-ma* 44 **p**: šu.II.meš [46 **p** in error omits this line, which is reflected in the previous section, which should contain 10 lines, but has only 9. 49 **p**: ⌜*ár*⌝-*ḫiš* 51 **p**: *ri-*[*me-ni-i* 53 q: -*mu*]*r-šú* 60 **p**: [*ù*?] *e-ga-*[*ti-ia*

Si 55 (q), Reverse

1	[× × (×)] × [. . . . .]	
2	[× × (×)] × × [. . . . .]	
3	[× × (×)] *ki-ma* te × [. . . . .] × [. . .]	
4	*[uṭ-ṭè-e]ḫ-ḫa-am-ma ta-⌜a-šú*	*šá i⌝-[kas]-su-u* × [. . . .]
5	*[ud-da]p-pir im-ḫul-la*	*a-na i-šid šamê*^{e}
	a-na i-rat erṣetim^{tim}	*ú-bi[l ṭi-'-a]*
6	*[uš-te]-rid ap-su-uš-šú*	*šu-ú-lu lim-[nu]*
7	*ú-⌜tuk⌝-ku la ni-'i*	*ú-tir é-kur-ri-[iš]*
8	*is-kip la-maš-tu*	*šá-da-a uš-te-e[š-šìr]*
9	*a-gu-ú ta-ma-tu*	*šu-ru-up-pa-a ú-šam-ḫ[ir]*
10	*i-šid lu-ú-tu*	*it-ta-saḫ ki-ma šam-m[i]*
11	*šit-ti la ṭa-ab-tu*	*ri-ḫa-a ṣa-la-[li]*
12	*ki-ma qu-ut-ru im-ma-lu-ú*	*šamê*^{e} *uš-ta-r[iq]*
13	*'ù-ú-a a-a*	*ni-'-u ni-še-eš*
	ú-šat-bi im-ba-riš	*erṣetim*^{tim} *uš-*[× ×]
14	*la-az-zu muruṣ qaqqadi*	*šá* ×*-ú-iš* KAB-×
15	*is-suḫ ⌜ki⌝-ma na-al-ši mu-[š]i*	*elī-ia uš-te-es-[si]*
16	*te-'-a-ti īnā*^{II}*-a-a*	*šá uš-téš-bi-iḫ ši-bi-iḫ mu-ú-[ti]*
17	*ú-šat-bi šār*(im) *bēra*(danna)	*ú-nam-mir niṭ-[li]*
G 18	*uznā*^{II}*-a-a šá uṭ-ṭa-am-mi-ma*	*us-sak-ki-ka ḫa-šik-kiš*
G 19	*it-bal a-mi-ra-šin*	*ip-te-ti niš-ma-a-a*
20	*ap-pa šá ina ri-di um-mi*	*ú-nap-pi-qu ni-[pi-is-su]*
21	*ú-pa-áš-ši-iḫ mi-ḫi-iṣ-ta-šu-ma*	*a-nap-pu-uš* [× × (×)]
22	*šap-ta-a-a šá il-lab-ba*	*il-qa-a* KAL-×-[×]
23	*ik-pur pul-ḫat-si-na-ma*	*ki-ṣir-ši-na ip-[ṭur]*
24	*pi-iá šá uk-ta-at-ti-mu*	*ṣa-ba-riš áš-[ṭu]*
25	*[i]m-šu!-uš ki-ma qé-e*	*ru-šá-šú uš-*[× (×)]
26	*[ši]n-na-a-a šá it-ta-aṣ-ba-ta*	*ištēniš*^{niš} *in-ni-i[b-ṭa]*
27	*[ip-]ti bi-rit-si-na-ma*	*ir-da-šin uš-tam-*[× (×)]
28	*[li]-šá-nu šá in-ni-ib-ṭa*	*šu-⌜ta⌝-bu-lu [l]a i-[li-'u]*
29	*[im-š]u-uš ṭu-pu-⌜uš⌝-ta-šá-ma*	*⌜iḫ⌝-da-ád at-mu-u-[a]*
G 30	*ur-ú-du šá in-ni-is-ru*	*ú-nap-pi-qu la-gab-biš*

COMMENTARY

18 *ḫa-šik-ku suk-ku-ku* 19 *a-me-ra ze-e uz-ni* 30 *la-gab-biš šá a-mat pag-ri*

Si 55 (q), Reverse

4 [He brought] near his spell which binds . [. . . .]
5 [He drove] away the Evil Wind to the horizon,
To the surface of the underworld he took [the Headache,]
6 [He sent] down the Evil Cough to its *Apsû*,
7 The Irresistible Ghost he returned [to] *Ekur*,
8 He overthrew the *Lamaštu*-demon, dismissing it to the Mountain,
9 In the Flood of the Sea he replaced Cramp,
10 He tore up the root of Impotence like a plant.

11 Bad Sleep, the pouring out of slumber,
12 He took far [away] like smoke with which the heavens get filled.

13 Woe and Alas, ...,
He drove away like a rain storm so that it . [. .] the underworld.

14 The persistent complaint in the head which . . like . .,
15 He expelled like a shower in the night, and removed it from me.

16 My clouded eyes, which were cloaked in a deathly shroud—
17 He drove it a thousand leagues away and lightened [my] vision.

18 My ears which were clogged and blocked like a deaf man's—
19 He removed their wax and opened my hearing.

20 My nose, whose [breathing] was choked by the onset of fever—
21 He soothed its affliction and now I breathe [freely.]

22 My raving lips which had . . . . [.]
23 He wiped away their terror and loosed their shackles.

24 My mouth, which was blocked so that talking was diffi[cult,]
25 He polished like copper and . [. .] its dirt.

26 My teeth, which were gripped and held together,
27 [He split] their bond and . . [. .] their roots.

28 My tongue, which was bound and [could] not converse,
29 [He] wiped away its . . . . . . and my speech *became plain*.

30 My throat, which was tight and choking like something inanimate,

VARIANTS

18 G: *uṭ-ṭam-me-ma us-sak-ki-ra* 19 G: *a-mir-ši-na ip-te-te* 25 Tablet: *i*]*m*-SU-*uš*
30 G: *ur-ú-di*

G31 *uš-ṭib-ma i-ra-tu-šá* *ma-li-liš uḫ-ta*[*l*]-×-*šá*

32 [*mal-*]*'a-ti šá ú-tap-pi-qu* *la* [*i-ma*]*ḫ*-⌜*ḫa-ru*⌝ [*šá-a-ra*]

G33 *la-ga-šá i-ši-ir-ma* *i-dil-taš ip-ti*

34 [× ×]-*e-a šá* šu × *un-ni-šú* *ú*-×[. . . . .] × [. . .]

35 [× (×)] × kit ḫar tu *e-liš* *ú-šab*-[. . . . .] × ša[b . . .]

36 [× × × *šá*] *ú-tam-mi-lu* × × *'-iš* ×[. . . . .] ta ši [. . .]

K 3291 (G) Reverse

a *šam-ma-ḫu šá ina un-ṣi it-tar-ru-ú* *ki-ma pi-sa-an-ni ir-rak-su*
un-ṣu bu-bu-tum

b *i-maḫ-ḫar ip-te-en-ni* *ub-ba-la maš-qí-ta*
ip-te-en-n[*i m*]*a-ka-lu-ú*

c *ki-šá-di šá ir-mu-ú* *ir-na-ma ik-ka*[*p*]*-pu*
e-re-e-na: *šur-šu*: *e-ri-na-ti*

d *ú-pat-tin kin-né-e* *a-ma-liš iz-qu-up*
kin-nu-u šadû^{ú}: *a-ma-lu* giš.⌜ù.ku⌝

e *a-na ga-mir a-ba-ri* *ú-ma-ši ú-maš-šil*
a-ba-ri e-mu-qu: *ú-ma-ši ṣal-mu*

f *kīma na-kim-tu*$_4$ *šu-ṣi-i* *ú-ṣap-pi-ra ṣu-pur-a-a*
^{lú}*šu*-⌜*ṣu-ú*⌝: *šá* ^{d}*iš-tar ana išāti*(izi) *ušēṣâ*(è-*a*)

g *it-bu-uk ma-*[*na-a*]*ḫ-ta-šin* ×-×-*šá-šin uš-ṭib*
ma-na-aḫ-t[*a*]: *murṣu* [(×) ×]-*šá-šú*: *qaqqadu*

h *bir-ka-a-a šá uk-tas-sa-a* *bu-ṣi-*[*iš ub-bu-ṭ*]*a*
bu-ṣi: *iṣ-ṣur ḫur-ri*

i *šuk-lul-tu*$_4$ *pag-*[*ri-*]*ia* *iš-ta-at-*×[× (×)]×
šuk-lul-tú: *la-a-nu*

j *im-šu-uš ma-am-mé-e* *r*[*u*]*-šu-uš ú-zak-ki*
ma-ša-šú: *ka-pa-ru*: *ma-am-mu-u*: *š*[*u*]*-uḫ-tu*: *ru-ši-iš*: *ib-bi*

k *du-ú-tum um-mul-tum* *it-ta-pir-di*
du-ú-tu: *bu-un-na-nu-u*

l *i-na i-te-e* ^{d}*nāri* *a-šar de-en nišī*^{meš} *ib-bir-ru*
i-te-e ^{d}*nāri ḫur-šá-an*

m ⌜*mut-tu-tu am-ma-riṭ* *ab-bu-ut-tum ap-pa-šir*⌝
[*ab-bu-ut-t*]*u bi-ri-tu*
(two lines missing)

n [. . . . .] × × [×] × *re-e-mu*

COMMENTARY

31 *ma-li-lum im-bu-bu* 33 *la-ga-ú ši-ik-tum*

31 He restored, and let it *sing* songs like a flute.

32 My wind-pipe, which was swollen so that it could not take [in air,]
33 Its swelling diminished, and he opened its blockage.

34 My [. .] . which . . . . [. . . . .] . [. . .]
35 [. .] . . . . above . . [. . . . .] . . [. . .]
36 [. . . which] was darkened like . . . . [. . . . .] . . [. . .]

Lines quoted in the Commentary

a The greater intestine, which was always empty through lack of food, and was twined like a reed basket,
b It receives food and takes drink.

c My neck, which was prolapsed and slouched in the collar,

d He erected it a mountain and set it up like a *pillar*.

e He made my physique like that of one consummate in strength.

f He made my finger nails scratch like the rash of . . .

g He drove out their fatigue and put to right their . . .

h My knees, which were fettered and [bound like] the *būṣu*-bird's,

i The frame of my body he . . . [. .] .

j He wiped away the gangrene and purged its filth.

k My gloomy appearance was filled with light.

l Beside the River, where the judgement of the people is decided,

m My brow was shaved and my slave mark removed.

n [. . . . .] . . [.] . pity.

VARIANTS

31 G: *i-ra-ti-šá, uḫ-*×-×*-šá* 33 G: *la-ga-a-a-šá i-šír*

o *[ku-nu-uš-k]àd-ru* *i-na pi-⌜šèr⌝-ti a-ba-'a*
[ku-n]u-uš-kàd-ru: *sú-qí qat-nu*
p *[šá] a-na é-sag-íl e-gu-u* *ina qāti-ia li-mur*
e-gu-u ḫa-ṭu-u
q *i-na pi-i gir-ra ākili*(kú)*-ia* *id-di nap-sa-ma* ᵈ*marduk*
gir-ra: ur.maḫ *nap-sa-mu*: *ma-ak-ṣa-ru ša pî sīsî*
r ᵈ*marduk šá mu-kaš-ši-di-ia i-kim as-⌜pa⌝-šú as-suk-ka-šú ú-saḫ-ḫir*
as-suk-ku [ku-u]b-tu: *áš-pu uš-pu*
s *id-d[i. . . . .]-bir*
ki.ḫul-*u bi-ki-tum*
t ×[. . . . .]× *i-na-an-na*
u [. . . . .]× tum × ru
[. . . . .]bit
[. . . . .]×

o I proceeded along the Kunuš-kadru Street—redeemed!

p He who has done wrong in respect of Esagil, let him learn from my example!

q It was Marduk who put a muzzle on the mouth of the lion who was eating me.

r Marduk despoiled my pursuer of his sling and turned aside his slingstone.

TABLET IV(?)

For the literary problem of the relationship of the following lines to the work as a whole see the Introduction.

MANUSCRIPTS

Symbol	*Lines on* *Obverse*	*Reverse*	*Plate*
Assur			
u = VAT 9442	1–15	87–101	18
v = VAT 10538	37–50	..	18
(**v** appears to be the bottom obverse portion of the same tablet as **u**)			
t = VAT 9303	24–46	76–97	18
Sultantepe			
w = SU 1952, 212+291 with 302	31–42	..	18

The line numbering may not be final despite the control which is provided by manuscripts divided into sections of ten lines. The difficulty is the gap on each side of the tablet. If it were possible to equate 14 and 15 by our numbering with 24 and 25, thus assuming an overlap of **u** and **t**, the numbers from 24 to 50 would have to be reduced by ten, and those from 76 to 101 by twenty. Considerations of space and content, however, exclude this idea, and the gap has to be assumed for the obverse, with a corresponding one for the reverse. Our assumption that the gap on the obverse is of eight lines may not be correct. It may be of 18 lines, in which case our numbers 24–50 would have to be increased by ten, and 76–101 by twenty.

u

1 *[be-l]í ú-×-×-×-an-ni*
2 *[be-l]í ú-ṣa-bít-an-ni*
3 *[be-l]í ú-pat-t[in]-an-ni*
4 *[be-l]í ú-bal-liṭ-an-ni*
5 *[ina ḫaš-t]i e-kim-an-ni*
6 *[ina ka-ra-]še-e id-⌜kan⌝^{an}-ni*
7 [× × ×] *ina ḫu-bur iš-du-da-an-ni*
8 [× × (×)]*-ti qa-ti iṣ-bat*
9 *[šá] im-ḫa-ṣa-an-ni*
10 *[^{d}mard]uk ú-šá-qi ri-ši*

11 *im-ḫa-aṣ* *rit-ti* *ma-ḫi-[ṣi]-ia*
12 *ú-šad-di* *^{giš}kakka-šu* *^{d}marduk*

13 × (×) × *gir-ri* *za-[×-i]a*
14 [. . . . . *š]am-ma* *^{d}[mard]uk*
15 [. . . . .]× mu ka ×[. . .]

* * * * *

t

24 [× ×] × ti × [. . . . .]
25 [(×)] × *áš-na-an ⌜ru-uš-šá-a⌝* [. . . . .]
26 *[u]l-tap-pit ḫa-šur-ri ṭāba*(dùg.ga) *elī-šu* ×[. . . . . . .]
27 *[qé]-re-e-ti mār bābili*^{ki} *mu-×*[. . . . . . .]
28 *bīt qí-bi-ri-šu e-pu-šu* *ina qé-re-e-t[i . . . . .]*
29 *i-mu-ru-ma* ⟨*mār*⟩ *bābili*^{ki} *ki-i ú-bal-la-ṭu [^{d}marduk]*
30 *pa-a-tu kāl*(dù)*-ši-na* *ú-šá-pa-a nar-bé-e-[šú]*

w

31 *man-nu-um-ma iq-bi* *a-mar ^{d}šamši^{ši}-šú*
32 *ina lìb-bi man-ni ib-ba-ši* *e-te-eq sūqi*(sila)*-šú*
33 *šá la ^{d}marduk man-nu* *mi-tu-ta-šú ú-bal-liṭ*
34 *e-la ^{d}ṣarpānītum*(e$_{4}$.ru$_{6}$) *^{d}iš-tar-tum a-a-i-tum* *i-qí-šá nap-šat-su*
35 *^{d}marduk ina qab-ri* *bul-lu-ṭa i-li-'i*
36 *^{d}ṣar-pa-ni-tum ina ka-ra-še-e* *e-ṭe-ra am-rat*

v

37 *e-ma šak-na-at erṣetim*^{tim} *rit-pa-šu šamê*^{e}
38 *^{d}šamšu*^{šú} *uš-tap-pa-a* *^{d}girra in-nap-ḫu*
39 *mu-ú il-la-ku* *i-zi-qu šá-a-ru*
40 *šu-ut ^{d}a-ru-ru* *ik-ru-ṣu ki-ri-is-si-in*
41 *[š]á-ki-it-tu nap-šá-tu* *pi-ta-a pu-ri-du*

VARIANTS

31 **t**: *^{d}šam*-PI-*šú* 37 **w**: *ša-ma-mi* 38 **v**: *iš-tap-pa-a* 39 **v**: *i-ziq-qu* **w**: im.meš

1 The Lord . . . . me,
2 The Lord took hold of me,
3 The Lord set me on my feet,
4 The Lord gave me life,
5 He rescued me [from the pit,]
6 He summoned me [from] destruction,
7 [. . .] he pulled me from the *Ḫubur* river,
8 [. . .] . he took my hand.
9 [He who] smote me,
10 Marduk, he restored me.

11 He smote the hand of my smiter,
12 It was Marduk who made his weapon fall.

13 [He] . . . the lion, my . [.],
14 It was Marduk who . . [. . . . .]

* * * * *

25 [.] . golden corn [. . . . .]
26 [I] anointed myself with sweet cedar perfume, upon . [. . . . . . .]

27 The banquet of the Babylonians . . [. . . . . . .]
28 The grave I had made [. . . . .] in the banquet.

29 The Babylon⟨ians⟩ saw how [Marduk] restores to life,
30 And all quarters extolled [his] greatness:

31 "Who thought that he would see his Sun?
32 Who imagined that he would walk along his street?

33 Who but Marduk restores his dead to life?
34 Apart from Ṣarpānītum which goddess grants life?

35 Marduk can restore to life from the grave,
36 Ṣarpānītum knows how to save from destruction.

37 Wherever the earth is laid, and the heavens are stretched out,
38 Wherever the sun god shines, and the fire god blazes,
39 Wherever water flows and wind blows,

40 Creatures whose clay Aruru took in her fingers,
41 Those endowed with life, who stride along,

---

40 v: *ik-ri-iṣ-ṣu ki-ri-is-s*[*in*]

t v w

42 [*a-pa*]*-a-tum ma-la ba-šá-a* ^{d}*marduk dul-la*
43 [× ×] a ta bul × ×   *šu-ut pa-a ku*[*n-na*]
44 [. . . . . . .] × [. . . . . . *k*]*al nišī*^{meš} *li-bíl-ma*
45 [. . . . . *r*]*i-'i kal da-á*[*d-me*]
46 [. . . . .]× *mīlī*(e$_4$.la$_6$)^{meš} *ina n*[*aq*]*-be*
47 [. . . . .] sal *ilū*^{meš} × ×[(×)] ×
48 [. . . . .] *si-ḫi-ip šamê*^{e} ⌜*ù*⌝ [*erṣetim*^{tim}]
49 [. . . . .]× *ri-iṣ-ṣa* × × [(×)]
50 [. . . . .] ši zu? nu šú šú šú

* * * * *

t

76 [× × (×)]-⌜*id-ma šá ina tés-li-ti-ia mu*⌝-×[. . . . . . .]
77 [*ina l*]*a-ban ap-pi ut-ni-ni*   *ana é-sag-í*[*l . . . .*]
78 [*šá ú-*]*ri-du qab-ri*   *a-tu-ra ana* ká ^{d}u[tu.u$_4$.è]
79 [*ina* k]á ḫé.gál   *ḫé-gál-la in-n*[*a-ad-na-an-ni*]
80 [*ina* k]á ^{d}lamma.ra.bi   *la-mas-si iṭ-ṭe-ḫ*[*a-an-ni*]
81 [*ina* k]á silim.ma   *šul-ma-na ap-pa-l*[*is*]
82 *ina* ká nam.ti.la   *ba-la-ṭu am-ma-ḫi-ir*
83 *ina* ká ^{d}utu.u$_4$.è   *it-ti bal-ṭu-ti am-ma-ni*
84 *ina* ká u$_6$.di.babbar.ra   *id-da-tu-ú-a im-me-ra*
85 *ina* ká nam.tag.ga.du$_8$.a   *i'-il-ti ip-pa-ṭir*
u
86 *ina* ká ka.tar.ra   *iš-ta-la pi-ia*
87 *ina* ká a.še.er.du$_8$.ù.da   *up-ta-ṭa-ra ta-ni-ḫi*
88 *ina* ká a.sikil.la   *me-e te-lil-te as-sa-li-iḫ*
89 *ina* ká silim.ma   *it-ti* ^{d}*marduk an-na-mir*
90 *ina* ká ḫi.li.sù   *še-ep* ^{d}*ṣar-pa-ni-tum an-na-šiq*
91 *ina su-pe-e ù te-me-qí*   *ma-ḫar-šú-nu ú-tan-nin*
92 *qut-rin-na ṭa-bu-ú-ti*   *ma-ḫar-šú-nu ú-šá-aṣ-li*
93 *ú-šam-ḫir ir-ba ṭa-'-ti*   *igisê e-ta-an-du-te*
94 *ú-pal-liq le-e ma-re-e*   *ut-ṭab-bi-iḫ sap-di*
95 *at-ta-naq-qi ku-ru-un-nu du-uš-šu-pá*   *karāna* [*i*]*l-lu*
96 ⌜*šēdu*(^{d}alàd)⌝ *lamassu*(^{d}lamma)   *angubbû*(an.gub.ba.meš) *li-bit é-sag-í*[*l*]

97 [× (×)]× *tam-qi-ti*   *ka-bat-ta-*⌜*šú-un*⌝ *uš-par-di*
98 [*ina ma-ka-l*]*e-e de-eš-šu-ti*   *lib-ba-šú-un ú-*⌜*šá-li*⌝*-iṣ*
99 [*sip-pu ši*]*-gar-ri*   *me-di-il* ^{giš}*dalāti*^{meš}
100 [× ×]×· *el-la*   *ḫi-ma-tú ṭuḫ-di áš-na-an*
101 [. . . . . . .]× zi *da-*⌜*mé*⌝*-e parṣi*(garza) *bīti*

VARIANTS

43 *ku*[*n-na*]: **v**: *taš-ta-pa*   44 **v**: *li-be-el-ma*   46 **v**: e$_4$.la$_6$ 87–91 **u** reads *a-na.*
90 **u**: ḫi.li.gar gìr^{II}, *-i*]*q*   91 **u**: *su-up-pe-e u te-m*[*i-*   92 **u**: *qut-rin-ni* dùg.ga.meš

42 Mortals, as many as there are, give praise to Marduk!
43 [. .] . . . . ., who give utterance,
44 [. . . . . . .] . [. . . . . .] may he rule all the peoples,
45 [. . . . .] shepherd of all dwellings.
46 [. . . . .] . floods from the deep,
47 [. . . . .] . the gods . . [.] .,
48 [. . . . .] the extent of heaven and earth.

* * * * *

76 [. . .] . . which in my prayers . . [. . . . . . .]
77 [With] prostration and supplication [. . . .] to Esagil.
78 [I who went] down to the grave have returned to the "Gate of the [Sun Rise."]
79 [In the] "Gate of Prosperity" prosperity was [given me,]
80 [In the] "Gate of the . . Guardian Spirit" a guardian spirit drew [nigh to me,]
81 [In the] "Gate of Well-being" I found well-being,
82 In the "Gate of Life" I was granted life,
83 In the "Gate of the Sun Rise" I was reckoned among the living,
84 In the "Gate of Splendid Wonderment" my omens were very plain,
85 In the "Gate of Release of Guilt" I was released from my bond,
86 In the "Gate of Worship" my mouth inquired,
87 In the "Gate of Resolving of Sighs" my sighs were resolved,
88 In the "Gate of Pure Water" I was sprinkled with water of purification,
89 In the "Gate of Well-being" I communed with Marduk,
90 In the "Gate of Exuberance" I kissed the foot of Ṣarpānītum.
91 I persisted in supplication and prayer before them,
92 Fragrant incense I placed before them,
93 I presented an offering, a gift, accumulated donations,
94 I slaughtered fat oxen, and butchered *fattened sheep*,
95 I repeatedly libated honey-sweet beer and pure wine.
96 The protecting genius and guardian spirit, divine attendants of the brickwork of Esagil,
97 [. .] . libation I made their hearts glow,
98 [With] the succulent [meals] I made them exultant.
99 [The threshold, the bolt] socket, the bolt, the doors,
100 [I . .] . oil, curds, and choicest grain.
101 [. . . . . . .] . . . . . the rites of the temple.

---

93 **u**: *ṭa-'-tú* ⌜*gi-se-e*⌝ 94 **u**: *li-'i am-re-e* ⌜*ú*⌝-[95 **u**: -*t*]*a-na-qi ku-ru-un-na da-*⌜*áš-šu-pu*⌝ **t**: k[ù]? 96 **u**: *li-*⌜*bit*⌝*-te é-sag-gíl*

Colophon of **i**

1 egir-*šú kab-ta-at qat-*[*s*]*u ul a-li-*'[*i*] *na-šá-šu*
2 gin$_7$ sumun-*šú* giš-*ma bà-rì* giš ^{m}*i-di-*^{d}*marduk*(mes) [dumu] ^{m}ta-×-×-a
3 ^{lú}šab.tur *li-g*[*i-m*]*u-u š*[*a*] ^{m}a.šú.u ^{lú}sanga
4 *ša* ir ^{d}*nu-dím-mud lit-bal-šú ša ina šur-qu i-šá-ri-qi šá ina dan-na-nu e-kim*
5 ^{d}*lu*[*gal*]*-gìr-ra dan-dan* dingir.meš *kaš-kaš* dingir.meš *muš-mit* dingir.meš
6 *ina* giš.tukul.meš-*š*[*ú ez-z*]*u-*[*t*]*u liš-gi-iš*
7 *ina* lal-*ṣi* ^{md}30.pap.tu man ^{kur}*aš-šur ina* ^{itu}apin ud.3.kam
8 *lim-m*[e ^{m}*ḫa-ba-ni*? ^{lú}*š*]*á-kin* ^{uru}[*tí*]*l-bar-s*[*i*]*-bi*
9 ner.gál.z[u na.a]n.ur ^{d}*tu-*[*tu*]

3

THE BABYLONIAN *THEODICY*

INTRODUCTION

THE *Theodicy* is an acrostic poem of twenty-seven stanzas of 11 lines each. It takes the form of a dialogue between a sufferer, who exposes the evils of current social injustice, and a friend, who tries to reconcile these facts with established views on the justice of the divine ordering of the universe. Nineteen of the stanzas are preserved either completely or sufficiently for the trend of the argument to be apparent. The other eight are either totally lost or inadequately preserved. The acrostic itself can, however, be restored completely, and it reads:

a-na-ku sa-ag-gi-il-ki-[i-na-am-u]b-bi-ib ma-áš-ma-šu ka-ri-bu ša i-li ú šar-ri

"I, Saggil-kīnam-ubbib, the incantation priest, am adorant of the god and the king." A fair number of manuscripts have turned up both from Assyria and Babylonia, and a commentary from Sippar confirms that this composition received much attention in learned circles of the late periods. The earliest datable manuscripts are from the Ashurbanipal libraries, and the latest is probably m, which gives the impression of being Seleucid or even Parthian. The text itself, as will be shown, was probably written about 1000 B.C. The manuscript tradition is nowhere perfect. Even the Ashurbanipal copies, which are usually impeccable, have two errors (D: 248; C: 276), while the copies from Assur and Babylonian cities have many more corrupt passages (a: 23, 24, 25, 28, 264, 268, 277, 279; **f**: 213; j: 217, 219; m: 285, 286, 288, 289, 290, 294). The Commentary alone seems to be free from error, apart from a trivial slip in the comment on line 1. It is indeed a very thorough piece of work, and one cannot but admire the consummate learning of its author and regret that it has not survived in its entirety. Apart from the manuscripts and Commentary, the poem is attested in two other places.

First, a Late Assyrian fragment of a catalogue of literary texts cites it:

1 [. . . . . *lu-*]*uq-bi-ka*
2 [*ša pî* m. . . . . . . *mār* m. . . .]×*-iddina*(sum) lú.maš.maš lú.um.me.a din.tir.ki

1 [. . . . . let] me tell you"
2 [According to . . . . son of . . . .]×-iddina, the incantation priest, scholar of Babylon.

(K 10802, Pl. 19; Lambert, *JCS* 11. 11.)

Here the first line of the poem is given as the title, and this is followed by the ascription of authorship or editorship, the outline of which can be restored from the rest of the catalogue. The writing of this line is cramped compared with that of the first line, which shows that the name ending in -iddina must have been preceded by that of his "son". What cannot be ascertained is whether Saggil-kīnam-ubbib, the author, or another name, that of an editor, has to be restored. See the discussion by the present writer in *JCS* 11. 5–12. The occurrence of (E)saggil, the Marduk temple in Babylon, in the author's name strongly suggests that he was a citizen of Babylon.

The second attestation comes from a Late Babylonian exercise tablet from Sippar (BM 76479 = A.H. 83–1–18, 1847, *PSBA* 18, pl. IV, col. III) where the name Esaggil-kīna-ubbib is used for writing practice, and is copied out in different orthographies. As these seem to be the only occurrences of the name, it is a plausible assumption that the teacher who assigned the name to the pupil consciously used our author's name.

The sufferer begins the debate by addressing his friend with the greatest respect, a politeness which the two speakers maintain to the end. Then he begins his tale of woe: he was born late to his parents, who soon left him an unprotected orphan (I). Already the chief topics have been adumbrated. Why do the gods not protect those who cannot protect themselves? Why do the powerful oppress such? Why has the first-born advantages over the later child? In reply the friend chides the sufferer with unnecessary despondency, and points out that the death of his parents was nothing more than a sharing in the common lot of mankind. The hard life of the sufferer he counters by asserting that prosperity is always the result of piety (II). The answer of the sufferer (III) shows that he considers that his desperate state has not been appreciated, and so he elaborates this point, stressing that he knows no way out. The friend reiterates that a life of piety will not go unrewarded (IV). Against this the sufferer cites examples of crimes which pay, both from the animal kingdom and from human society (V). The friend now draws on the traditional teaching about the remoteness and inscrutability of the divine mind. What it amounts to is that eventually criminals meet a dire end, and so he warns the sufferer not to be tempted into crime, but to cultivate the gods (VI). This explanation is altogether unacceptable to the sufferer, who describes how his life of dedication to religion has only resulted in his present state (VII). This the friend reckons as blasphemy, and he amplifies his statement that it is a hard thing to grasp the wisdom of the gods (VIII).

After a gap, the friend is trying to point out the joys of a life of simple piety, of performing the duties to society and the gods (XII). In desperation the sufferer retorts that all he desires is to escape from settled life and to live as a vagrant (XIII). The text again breaks off, and when it resumes in XVII the sufferer is emphasizing how easily the richest and the poorest change positions. XVIII and XIX cannot be followed, but in XX the friend is repeating his old contention that piety does pay. The sufferer replies that the unscrupulous are those who become wealthy (XXI). The friend repeats that in the end they are discomfited, but makes a concession to his opponent, since he now insists that the god-fearing never starve, though they may not have an abundance (XXII). The sufferer is still not convinced, and now he contrasts the privileges and arrogance of the first-born as compared with others. He ends with a further assertion that his abject state is the outcome of his piety (XXIII). The friend, however, has an answer to the argument from the first-born, and one which he gives as another example of divine wisdom not being apparent to a superficial observer: the first-born is physically inferior to later offspring, and so the privileges are offset (XXIV). There is no need to seek statistics on the physiological truth or otherwise of this proposition. The writer had none. However, common observation is adequate to show that there is some empirical proof of this idea, and this would be more apparent in the ancient Near East where women commenced childbirth at the earliest possible age, and so before they were fully grown. This argument seems to be accepted by both speakers since it is not disputed, but now the sufferer plays his trump. The rich and the powerful, he says, are always upheld in the false witness which they bring against the poor, and thus they grind them down (XXV). With this the friend is compelled to agree. He explains that lies and false witness are part of human nature as the gods made it (XXVI). Having won his point, the sufferer concludes the dialogue with a plea that his friend contemplate his grief, and that the gods resume their protection (XXVII).

A conclusion, then, has been reached, however pathetic the last stanza may sound. But this conclusion undermines the premisses on which the two argued. Both sufferer and friend began by assuming that the gods were responsible for maintaining justice among men. They end by admitting that these very gods made men prone to injustice. In a sense the real problem has been shelved. The view that the wicked ultimately receive their due was stated, and the practical experience that evil men prosper was set against it. Apparently the author could not resolve the conflict between the deep-seated conviction and actual life, so his way out was to assert a thesis which seemed to him logically irrefutable, and in some way related to the problem. Whatever evil men do, he argues, is done because the gods made them that way. Where the author fails is in not seeing clearly the relationship of this thesis to the main problem.

In both form and content the dialogue is a very original composition. The writer seems to be unique in preaching against the privileges of the first-born, and one wonders if he himself had experienced a selfish elder brother. As a whole, however, there are objections to supposing that the writer mirrors his own life. The downtrodden orphan cannot have been the learned author and incantation priest. If it is supposed that he rose to high rank from a very humble origin, there is the difficulty that his writing betrays no optimism, nor any confidence in the saving power of the gods.

The style was apparently intended to be simple. The author is not carried away by words, but makes an economic use of them to force his points home. Even though he employs repetition to gain emphasis (e.g. 245–50, 267–74), there is nothing like the verbosity of parts of *Ludlul*. The vocabulary contains a fair sprinkling of rare words, e.g. *bēl pāni* (52, 63, 275) 'nouveau riche', *in qá-bal* (189) 'formerly, since', and *qadmu* (251, 276) 'god', but never to excess. The difficulties which the work presents at a first reading are due largely to the constricting influence of metre. Some of the lines are epigrammatic to the extent that their meaning only becomes clear after careful study. Lines of four main stresses are hardly long enough for the development of a smooth chain of reasoning such as the author attempts.

The metrical form of the work is outstanding. Each of the 11 lines of the stanzas begins with the same sign, like Psalm 119. To achieve this a few *tours de force* were necessary. A pseudo-archaic pronoun is used in 25 to provide the required first syllable, and throughout the author allows himself the liberty of using a little of the polyphony of the signs. If a stanza has an initial *bu*, he permits words beginning with the same sign, but pronounced *pu*. The other values of the BU sign, however, *gíd* and *sír*, are not used. The 11-line stanza is unique. That of ten lines is common, and scribes sometimes rule a line after every tenth line of the text even when there are no metrical grounds for so doing, as in *Ludlul* IV(?). The 11-line stanza has a purpose. It is made up of five couplets and an odd line. There is no rule about the position of the odd line in the stanza, though it never occurs at the beginning. Commonly it is reserved for an emphatic statement, though exceptions occur. The individual lines have a metre of four principal stresses, and some of the Babylonian manuscripts (aijl) have the space divided into four columns and distribute the words into their compartments. Other poetic works have their lines divided into hemistichs in some manuscripts, an arrangement technically known as *ṣullupu*,[1] though in fact the division is often made at the wrong point in the line (e.g. *Ludlul* **m**; *Counsels of Wisdom* C). Despite this misuse, there can be little doubt that in origin at least this dividing into hemistichs had metrical significance. It is to be regretted that no Babylonian manuscript of line 238 has survived, which has only three words! Other lines too can only be made to have four principal stresses by unnatural means (72, 235). In 72 the first word seems to have been unusually stressed as if to make it serve for a whole hemistich, and probably the other lines which seem to lack four stresses should be understood as exceptions within four-stress metre, rather than as odd three-stress lines.

The date of composition cannot be earlier than the Cassite period. The name Saggil-kīnam-ubbib is of a type only common since Cassite times (J. J. Stamm, *MVAG* 44. 172), and the language shows plain influence of Middle or Late Babylonian, though some scribes have substituted Standard Babylonian forms:

14, 67, 167	*ṭè-en-ga* (a in 14 corrects to *ṭè-en-ka*)
69, 75, 77	*il-te-en, il-ta-kan, il-ta-qu-ú* (*šaqû*)
129, 130	[*u*]*p-te-ṣi-id*, [*u*]*p-te-eḫ-ḫir*

The question, then, is whether it is Cassite period or later. Von Soden in 1935 suggested

[1] The colophon of such a tablet states: *ki-i pi-i* [giš]*li-u₅-um šá a-na pi-i šá-ṭa-ri ṣu-ul-lu-pu* (*CT* 13. 15) "according to a writing board which was *ṣullupu* in its writing". *ṣlp* here certainly does not mean 'damaged' (G. R. Driver, *Semitic Writing*, p. 10), but is connected with the mathematical *ṣiliptu* 'diagonal' (O. Neugebauer and A. Sachs, *MCT*, p. 171; *MSL* I. 54. 46) and [ku.ú]KU = *ṣa-la-pu-um* "durchstreichen" (*MSL* II. 150. 4). Cf. A. L. Oppenheim, *Dreams*, p. 287[141]. Another occurrence in a colophon is Rm 601 (C. D. Gray, *AJSL* 17. 234 = *Šamaš Religious Texts*, pl. XI): [*gab-ri*] *bābili*[ki] *kīma ṣir-pi* DIRI *šaṭir* (SAR) *ṣu-ul-lu-pi*. In this case the tablet is not written with the lines divided into hemistichs, but it may be assumed that this line was copied from a previous copy, which was so written. Assyrian scribes rarely practise this finesse of the scribal art.

that the author lived not earlier than 800 B.C. (*ZDMG* 89. 166[1]). This is the latest possible date since the *Theodicy* is an established work in the Ashurbanipal libraries. There is no strong reason to compel any date in particular between about 1400 and 800. One consideration which has been urged in favour of a late date within this range is the acrostic. Only four other acrostics have been recovered from Akkadian literature:

(i) DT 83 (T. Pinches, *Texts in the Bab. Wedge Writing*, pp. 15–16 = *PSBA* 17. 133–4), a hymn to Marduk with reference to an unnamed king. The stanzas are of five lines beginning with the same syllable.

(ii) BM 55469 = 82–7–4, 42 (*PSBA* 20. 154–62), a hymn to Nābû, written in honour of Nebuchadnezzar II. It consists of five 10-line stanzas. The lines begin with the same sign and the acrostic reads ^{d}*na-bu-ú*.

(iii) K 8204 (*PSBA* 17. 137–41), a prayer to Nābû in stanzas of four lines. Both the first and last syllables of each line form one and the same acrostic.

(iv) Acrostic hymn of Ashurbanipal to Marduk (last edition *KB* VI/2. 108–17). It is made up of thirty sections of elevated prose, each of which begins with the sign forming the acrostic.

(K 14022 (*ZA* 10. 20; *ABRT* I. 53) is a very small fragment of an acrostic prayer.)

Outside Akkadian there are the Hebrew alphabetic acrostics in the Psalter, Proverbs, Lamentations, and Nahum, and from the Hellenistic period onwards both word and alphabetic acrostics appear in the Semitic and Classical languages (see the literature cited by R. Marcus, *JNES* 6. 109–15). Even if it could be shown that the Biblical examples antedate the seventh century B.C.—and it cannot—it would still seem that the Babylonian word and sentence acrostic is a native invention. Although the two dated examples were written for Ashurbanipal and Nebuchadnezzar II, nothing whatever can be deduced from this about the century in which the acrostic was first used. This approach to the problem of dating the *Theodicy* is devoid of result.

On purely stylistic considerations the writer would place it about 1000 B.C. The language shows a certain reconditeness and a measure of striving for rarity which is characteristic of a group of texts which the writer would place in the late Cassite period (see p. 14). On the other hand, the *Theodicy* is not completely under this influence and uses some colloquial forms instead of the standard literary dialect.

One curiosity which the text displays is that the scribes commonly write "gods" when the context, singular suffixes, or a parallel "goddess" leave no doubt that the personal god is meant (49, 82, 219, 241, 295). In some cases not all the manuscripts have been affected. Scribes of *Ludlul* do the same (II. 12, 25, 33). A similar phenomenon can be observed in personal names. In Cassite-period documents the name *arkāt-ili-damqā* (written egir.dingir-*dam-qa*, &c., see A. T. Clay, *Personal Names of the Cassite Period*, p. 59) has a singular "god". The same name is used ancestrally (cf. *JCS* 11. 1–3) in the Late Babylonian period where it is written, for example, *ár-kát*-dingir.meš.sig$_5$ (V *R* 46. 63) with a plural "gods". The use of the plural "gods" for one deity is documented by A. Jirku in *Altorientalischer Kommentar zum alten Testament*, pp. 18–19.

LITERATURE

TEXT, WITH OR WITHOUT EDITION

1895 J. A. Craig, *ABRT* I. 44–53 (text of a, B, D, i, j (in part only), K 3452, K 8491).

1895 S. A. Strong, *PSBA* 17. 141–51 (text of a (rev.), D, i, j (in part only), K 3452, K 8491).

1895 H. Zimmern, *ZA* 10. 1–24 (text of a, B, D, K 3452, K 8491).

1919 E. Ebeling, *KAR* 160 (text of **f**).

1952 R. J. Williams, *JCS* 6. 2–4 (Geers's copies of H, G, K 13929).

EDITIONS, TRANSLATIONS, STUDIES

1903 F. Martin, *Textes religieux assyriens et babyloniens*, pp. 164–94.

1922 E. Ebeling, *BBK* 1/1.

1923 P. Dhorme, *RB* 32. 1–27.

1925 B. Meissner, *Babylonien und Assyrien* II. 431–2.

1926 E. Ebeling, in H. Gressmann, *Altorientalische Texte zum alten Testament*², pp. 287–91.

1936 B. Landsberger, *ZA* 43. 32–76 (the translation alone was also printed in *JEOL* III. 102–6).

1943 J. J. Stamm, *JEOL* IX. 99–107.

1946 J. J. Stamm, *Das Leiden des Unschuldigen in Babylon und Israel* (*Abhandlungen zur Theologie des Alten und Neuen Testaments*, 10).

1950 R. H. Pfeiffer, *ANET*¹ 438–40.

1955 R. H. Pfeiffer, *ANET*² 438–40.

COMMENTARY ONLY: TEXT

1931 C. J. Gadd, *CT* 41. 40–41 and 44.

EDITION

1933 E. Ebeling, in *Festschrift Max Freiherrn von Oppenheim gewidmet*, pp. 27–34.

1933 R. Labat, *Commentaires Assyro-Babyloniens*, pp. 102–9 and 122–5.

MANUSCRIPTS

With the possible exception of the commentary, all the tablets seem to have been written in four columns.

Symbol	*Lines on* Obverse	*Lines on* Reverse	*Plates*
Ashurbanipal			
B = K 8463	I 1–11	E III 158–69	
E = K 8491+13929	I 69–78	B III 229–36	
B	II 79–88	E IV 237–9	
E	II ..	B IV ..	19, 21–23
(These two pieces are parts of the same tablet.)			
C = K 3452+Sm 147	I 35–45, 47–53	IV 258–89	20, 25
D = K 9290+9297	I 48–80	III 176–91	
	II 125–43	IV 235–69	21, 22
G = K 10301	I 7–17	..	19
H = K 5932	..	III 179–89	22
N = K 1743+10858	..	III 193–211	22
(Probably part of the same tablet as C)			
Assur			
f = VAT 10567	II 185–210, 212–20	III 221–4, 226–55	23
Babylon			
a = BM 34773 (Sp II. 265)	I 3–34	III 193–201	
	II (traces)	IV 261–97	19, 24
l = BM 35405 (Sp II. 988+1001)	I 18–57	IV (traces)	20
m = BM 34633 (Sp II. 116)	I 28–45	III (traces between 232 and 242)	
	II ..	IV 279–97	19, 25
i = BM 40124 (81–2–1. 90)	..	III 139–57	20
j = BM 40098 (81–2–1. 63)	I 55–66	III ..	
	II 131–6	IV 210–27	21, 23
(i and j are probably parts of the same tablet.)			
Commentary (from Sippar)			
k = BM 66882+76506 (82–9–18, 6876+6960+A.H. 83–1–18, 1876)	1–88	*c.* 190–end	26

I

MSS					
B	1	a-š[i]š [. . . . .]		ga-na	[lu]-uq-bi-ka
a	2	[.			lu]-šá-an-ni-ka
	3	[. . . . . .]	× ⌜mu⌝? ×	× [.	]×-šu-uk-ka
	4	[. . . . . .]	šá šum-ru-ṣu	ka-⌜a-na⌝	lud-lul-ka
	5	a-a-na	[bē]l pak-ku	[i]m-ṣu	ma-la-ka
G	6	a-a-iš	mu-du-ú	⌜iš⌝-šá-⌜nin⌝	iš-ti-ka
	7	a-[li	m]un-dal-kúm-ma	ni-is-⌜sa⌝-t[um]	lu-ú-ta-me-šú
	8	a-ga-m[ir-m]a	i-ši-ri	lu[m]-nu	lìb-bi
	9	a-ḫu-ra-[k]u-ma	za-ru-ú	š[i]m-tum	ub-til
	10	a-ga-rin-nu	a-lit-ti	i-ta-ar	erṣet là târi
	11	a-bi u ba-an-ti	i-zi-bu-in-ni-ma	ba-al	ta-ru-u-a

II

MSS					
	12	[n]a-a-a-du	⌜ib⌝-ri	šá taq-bu-ú	i-dir-tum
	13	[n]a-ra-am	saḫ-ḫi-ka	tu-šak-pi-du	li-mut-tum
	14	[n]a-ʾ-[d]u	ṭè-en-ka	tu-maš-šil	la li-ʾ-iš
	15	na-am-ru-tum	zi-mu-ka	uk-ku-liš	tu-še-e-ma
	16	na-a[d]-nu-ma	ab-bu-nu	il-la-ku	ú-ru-uḫ mu-ú-t[u]
1	17	na-⌜a⌝-ri ḫu-bur	ib-bi-ri	qa-bu-ú	ul-tu ul-la
	18	na-a[ṭ]-la-ta-ma	niši^{meš}	mit-ḫa-riš	a-pa-a-t[um]
	19	na-×-šú	bu-kúr en-šú	ul × × ú	ú-šá-áš-re-[e-šú]
	20	n[a]-am-ra-a	be-lu meš-re-e	⌜ú⌝-[da]m-mi-iq-šú	ma-an-[nu]
	21	n[a]-ṭil	pa-an ilim-ma	ra-ši	la-mas-[sa]
	22	n[a]-ak-di	pa-li-iḫ ^{d}ištar(15)	ú-kám-mar	ṭuḫ-[da]

III

23	ku-up-pu	ib-ri lìb-ba-ka	šá la i-qát-tu-ú	na-qab-[šú]
24	ku-mur-re-e	gi-piš tam-tim	šá la i-šu-ú	mi-ṭi-[ta]

COMMENTARY

ina a-mat ^{d}bēl u ^{d}nābû(nà) *liš-lim* 1 *a-š[i]š* ⟨:⟩ *it-pe-šú*: A (! error for MIN): *ma-li-ku*: *ga-na*: *al-ka*: × [2, 3] MIN: *la-mad*: *tap-pu-ú*: *šu-ta-pi*: MIN: *šu-za-pi*: *tap-pu-ú*[:] *šu-ta*[*ṣ-bu-tú* 5] *a-a-na*: *ia-a-nu*: 6 *a-a-iš*: *ia-a-nu-uš*: *mu-du-u*: *tup-šar-ri*: [7] *ni-is-sa-tú*: *ni-iš-šá-tú*: 8 *i-ši-ru*: *a-šá-ri*: *sa-na-qa*: *a-šá-ri*[: *a-lak* 10] NIGÍN: *ta-a-ri*: NIGÍN: *a-lak*: 11 *ba-lu ta-ru-ú*: *ba-lu*: *šá la* × [13] *tu-*⌜*šak-pi*⌝*-du*: *ka-pa-du*: *ṣa-ra-mu*: 14 *la li-ʾ-iš*: *ki-ma l*[*a* 22] *kúm-mu-ri*[:] *pu-uḫ-ḫur*: 23 *ku-up-pi*: *ana kap-pa*: *na-a-ri*: 24, 25 *ku*[-

Sufferer I

1 O sage [. . . . .] come, [let] me tell you.
2 [. . . . . let] me inform you.
3 [. . . . .] . . . . [. . . . .] . . . you,
4 I [. . . .], the suffering, will not cease to reverence you.
5 Where is the wise man of your calibre?
6 Where is the scholar who can compete with you?
7 Where is the counsellor to whom I can relate my grief?
8 I am finished. Anguish has come upon me.
9 I was a youngest child; fate took my father;
10 My mother who bore me departed to the Land of No Return.
11 My father and mother left me without a guardian.

Friend II

12 Respected friend, what you say is gloomy.
13 You let your *mind* dwell on evil, my dear fellow.
14 You make your fine discretion like an imbecile's;
15 You have reduced your beaming face to scowls.
16 Our fathers in fact give up and go the way of death.
17 It is an old saying that they cross the river Ḫubur.
18 When you consider mankind as a whole,
19 . . . it is not . . . that has made the impoverished first-born rich.
20 Whose favourite is the fattened rich man?
21 He who waits on his god has a protecting angel,
22 The humble man who fears his goddess accumulates wealth.

Sufferer III

23 My friend, your mind is a river whose spring never fails,
24 The accumulated mass of the sea, which knows no decrease.

VARIANTS

1 *a-š*[*i*]*š* from k; the first wedge of *š*[*i*]*š* is preserved in the colophon. *ga-na* from k.]-*uq-bi-ka* occurs in the catalogue fragment K 10802 (Pl. 19). 2, 3 *tap-pu-ú* from k belongs to one of these lines. 5, 6 The first words are from k. B: *iš-te-ka* 7 B: *l*]*u-u-ta-me-šú* 8 B: *lu-mun* 9 B: -*t*]*a ub-ti-il* 10 G: *a-lit-tú* a: kur.nu.gi, B: kur.nu.gi$_4$ 11 a: *ta-ru-*LU?-*ú-a*; the LU? is perhaps intended as erased. 13 G: *narāmi*?-]*ia* 14 G: *ṭ*]*è-en-ga tu-maš-ši-la* 15 G: *zi-mi-ka uk-ku-li-i*[*š* 16 G: *ab-b*]*u-n*[*i* 19 l: *na-*×-]*šu* 20 l: en 22 l: ^{d}*iš-tar* 23 a: i la *qát-tu-ú* 24 a: ⌜*ku*⌝-*mur-ri-ma*, i la *šu-ú*

a l	25 *ku-a-šú*	*lu-uṣ-ṣi-iš-ka*	*li-mad*	*a-⌜ma⌝?-[ti?]*
	26 *qú-lam-mu*	*a-na sur-ru*	*ši-me*	*qa-ba-⌜a⌝-[a]*
m	27 *ku-ut-tùm*	*gat-ti*	*ma-ku-ú*	*ḫa-šá-a[n-ni]*
	28 *ku-ši-ri*	*ši-ti-qa*	*e-te-ti-iq*	*mut-tu-[ri]*
	29 *ku-bu-uk-ku*	*i-te-niš*	*ba-ṭi-il*	*iš-di-[ḫu]*
	30 *ku-ú-ru*	*u ni-is-sa-tum*	*ú-qát-ti-ru*	*zi-mu-[ú-a]*
	31 *ku-ru-um*	*sa-ḫi-ia*	*a-na niš-bé-e*	*ni-s[a-an-ni]*
	32 *ku-ru-un-nu*	*nap-šat niši*^{meš}	*ṭa-pa-piš*	*ru-u[q-×]*
	33 *ku-un-nam-ma-a*	u_4*-mu dum-qí*	*a-lak-ta-šú*	*a-lam-[mad]*
	IV			
C	34 *sa-an-qa*	*pi-ia*	*šá-du-ú*	*iš-[. .]*
	35 *sa-ad-ri*	*pak-ka-ku*	*dub-bu-biš*	*t[u- . .]*
	36 *[sa]-ap-ḫu*	*[l]a? ṭè-me*	*te-te-mid*	×*[. . -ka]*
	37 *[sa]-meš*	*ur?-qa-ka*	*nu-us-su-qa*	*t[u-maš?-šil?]*
	38 *[sa-an-t]ak-ku*	*[l]a na-par-ka-a*	*šá taḫ-ši-ḫu*	*na-*×*[. .]*
	39 *[sa-di?]-du*	*[g]*^{iš}*ṣillu*	*ina su-up-pe-e*	*i-*×*[. .]*
	40 *sa-lit-[t]um*	^{d}*iš-tar*	*i-ta-ri*	*i-n[a]* ×*[. .]*
	41 *[sa- . . .]*×	*⌜la šu-te-šu⌝-ru*	*i-rim-mu*	*a-na* ×*[. .]*
	42 *[sakkī?]*	*šá mi-šá-ri*	*qaq-dà-a*	*su-ḫu[r]*
	43 *sap-ṣu*	× × *-ka*	*ta-ḫa-na-at*	*liš-k[un]*
	44 *[sa- . . .*	× *b]é-eš*	*nak-ru-uṭ*	*li-gi-[is]*
	V			
	45 *ak-tam-sak-ku*	*[ru-'u-]ú-a*	*a-ta-ḫaz*	*mi-[ri-iš-ka](?)*
	46 [. . . . .] × bu		*sè-kàr*	*at?-[mi-ka](?)*
C D	47 [. . . . .] × di/ki		*ga-na*	*lu-u[q?-bi-ka](?)*
	48 *ak-k[a-an-nu]*	*sír-ri-mu*	*šá iṭ-pu-pu*	šu × [×]

COMMENTARY

25 *lu-uṣ-ṣi-iṣ-ka*: *uṣ-ṣu-ṣu*: *ši-ta-lu*: MIN: *šá-a-l[u* 27 *makû?*:] *bu-bu-tú*: 28 *ku-ši-ri*: × × ri: MIN: *tak-si-tú*: *nik-[* 29] *ku-bu-uk-ku*: *e-mu-qa*: *i[š?-di?-ḫu?]* × × × × [33] *ku-un-nam-ma-a*: *i-kun-na-a* [35] *dub-bu-bu*: *šá-né-e ṭè-e-me*: DU[37 *tumaššil?*:] SI: *šu-lu-ku*: SI: *ma-šá-lu*: 38 *sa-a[n-tak-ku*: 39 *sa-di-du*(?): *qu-ud-mu-ú*(?):] *ana qu-ud-mu*: *maḫ-ri*: 40 *sa-lit-tú*: *sa-[lim?-tú?* 41] *i-ri-im-mu*: *ana re-e-mu*: 42 *mi-šá-[ri* 43] *sap-ṣu*: *dan-nu*: *ta-ḫa-na-[tú* 44] *bé-e-šú*: *pi-tu-u*: *na-ak-[ru-ṭu*: *re-e-mu*:] MIN: *na-as-ḫu-ri*: *li-[gi-is*:] RIG$_7$: *ge-e-su*: R[IG$_7$: *šá-ra-*]*ku*: 45 *ak-tam-sak-ku*: *ka-ma-su*[: (. . .) *a-ta-ḫaz*:] *a-ḫa-za*: *la-ma-du*: 46 du × [× × ×] × du: *aq-ri*: *si-kìr*: *a-mat*: 48 *ak-k[a-an-nu*: . . . . :] *ana muḫḫi* KAN: *a-la-du*:

25 I will ask you a question; listen to what I say.
26 Pay attention for a moment; hear my words.

27 My body is a wreck, emaciation darkens [me,]
28 My success has vanished, my *stability* has gone.

29 My strength is enfeebled, my prosperity has ended,
30 Moaning and grief have blackened my features.

31 The corn of my fields is far from satisfying [me,]
32 My wine, the life of mankind, is too little for satiety.

33 Can a life of bliss be assured? I wish I knew how!

Friend IV

34 What I say is restrained . . . . [. .]
35 But you [. . .] your balanced reason like a madman.

36 You make [your . . . .] diffuse and irrational,
37 You [turn] your select . . blind.

38 As to your persistent unending desire for . . [. .]
39 [The former] security . . [. .] by prayers.

40 The appeased goddess returns by . [. .]
41 [. . . .] . who did not uphold takes pity on . [. .]

42 Ever seek the [correct standards] of justice.

43 Your . ., the mighty one, will show kindness,
44 [. . . . .] will grant mercy.

Sufferer V

45 I bow to you, my comrade, I grasp your wisdom.
46 [. . . . .] . . the utterance of [your words.]

47 [. . . . .] . . come, let me [say something to you.]

48 The onager, the wild ass, who filled itself with . . [.]

VARIANTS

25 a: ⌜*ku*⌝-*a*-RI *lu-uṣ-ṣi-iṣ-ka* 26 a: ⌜*qú-lam*⌝-*ma*, *sur-ri*, *ši*-MI+I! 27 a: *ku-tùm* 28 a: *ši-te-ti-iq* 30 a: *ku-ú-ri* 31 a: [*s*]*aḫ-ḫi*-[*i*]*a* 35 C: *du-*]*ub-bu-bé-e*[*š* 36 C: *ṭè*?-*m*]*a*? 38 C: *ša* 39 l: *su-up-pe-ia* 40 C: *iš-t*]*a-ṛi*, *ina* 41 C: *i-ri-im-mu* 43 C:]*si*/*r*]*a-šu ta-ḫa-na-tu liš-ku-u*[*n*] 44 C:] × × eš *nak-ru-ṭu* NOTE: *tumaššil*(?) (37), *sa-lit-*[*t*]*um* (40), and *sap-ṣu* (43) are restored from the commentary. 45 C: *a-ta-ḫa-az* 47 Traces on C.

MSS					
CD l	49	*[aq-qà]t-ti-i*	*pak-ki ili*	*ú-zu-un-šu*	*ib-š[i]*
	50	*ag-gu*	*la-bu*	*šá i-tak-ka-lu*	*du-muq ši-r[i]*
	51	*[ak-k]i-mil-ti ìl-ti-i*	*šup-ṭu-ri*	*ú-bil*	*mas-ḫat-s[u]*
	52	*[ak-×-]ti*	*bēl pa-an*	*šá uṣ-ṣu-bu-šú*	*na-ḫa-šú*
	53	*[aq-r]a-a*	*ṣa-ri-ri*	*i-ḫi-ṭa*	*a-na* ^{d}*ma-mi*
j	54	*[ak-]la-ma-a*	*nin-[d]a-ba-a*	*i-liš*	*ú-sap-p[a]*
	55	*[ak-]ru-ub*	*sat[tu]kkē*^{e} *il-tim-ma*	*qí-bi-ti*	× [. . .]
		VI			
	56	*[gi-š]im-ma-ru*	*iṣ [ma]š-re-e*	*a-ḫi*	*aq-r[u]*
	57	*gi-mil*	*na-gab ne-me-qi*	*il-lu-uk*	*li[q-ti]*(?)
	58	*gi-na-ta-ma*	*am-ma-tíš*	*ni-si*	*mi-lik i-lim*
	59	*gít-ma-lu*	*[sí]r-ri-mu*	*ú-ṭu-ul*	*i-n[a ṣēri]*(?)
	60	*gi-*⌜*iš*⌝ *qar-ba-tim*	*ir-ḫi-ṣu*	*i-tar-šú*	*mul-mul*
	61	*gi-ir bu-li*	*la-ba*	*šá taḫ-su-su*	*ga-na bit-ru*
	62	*gi-il-lat nēšu*(ur.maḫ)	*i-pu-šu*	*pi-ta-as-su*	*ḫaš-tum*
	63	*gi-is maš-re-e*	*bēl pa-ni*	*šá gur-ru-nu*	*ma-ak-ku-ru*
	64	*gi-riš*	*ina* u_4*-um la ši-ma-ti*	*i-qa-am-me-šú*	*ma-al-ku*
	65	*gi-ir-ri an-nu-tu-ú*	*i-ku-šu*	*a-la-ka*	*taḫ-ši-iḫ*
	66	*gi-mil du-um-qí*	*šá ili*	*da-ra-a*	*ši-te-ʾ-e*
		VII			
	67	*il-ta-nu*	*ṭè-en-ga*	*ma-nit niši*^{meš}	*ṭa-*⌜*a*⌝*-[bu]*
E	68	*il-lu*	*nu-us-su-qu*	*mi-lik-ka*	*d[am-qu]*
	69	*il-te-en*	*zik-ra*	*mut-ta-ka*	*lut-t[i-ir]*
	70	*il-la-ku*	*ú-ru-uḫ dum-qí*	*la muš-te-ʾ-u*	*ì-l[i]*
	71	*il-tap-ni*	*i-te-en-šú*	*muš-te-mi-qu*	*šá ì[l-ti]*

COMMENTARY

49 *qá[t-tu-u*: × (×)] ×: KAK^{u}: MIN: *um-man-nu*: 50 *ag-gu*: *dan-nu*: 51 *ki-mil-t[ú* . . . . . *ak*?:] *ana*: 52 *bēl pa-ni*: *bēl makkūri*(níg-ga): 53 ^{d}*[ma-me*: ^{d}*]bēlit*(gašan)*-ì-lí bānât*(dù^{at}) *nišī*^{meš}: ma: *banû*(dù^{u}): me: *nišī*^{meš}: 54 *i-liš*: [55 *s]at-tuk-ku*: *gi-nu-ú šá ilī*^{m}[^{eš}: *gi-n]u-ú*: *šá-nu-ú* 57 *gi-mil*: *ana ga-*⌜*ma*⌝*-lu*: *na-gab*: *nap-ḫar*: *il-[lu-uk*: . . .] MIN: *šum*?*-su-ku*: 58 *gi-na-t[a-ma*:] *gi-nu-u*: *a-ba/ma-lu*: *am-ma-tíš*: ⌜*kīma*⌝ *er-ṣe-tú*: *i-lim*: *ki-m[a* . . . 59] *gít-ma-lu*: *dan-nu*: 60 *gi-ši[t*?:]×*-ba-ri*: *qar-bat*: *ta-mir-tú*: *mul-mul*: *šil-taḫ*: 61 *gi-[ir*: . . .] *bit-ru*: *bit-ru-u*: *ba-ru-u*: × ×: 62 *ḫa-áš-tú*: *erṣetim*^{tim}: *ana muḫḫi* ḪAŠ: *šá-ga-šú*: 63 *gur-ru-nu*:

49 Did it pay attention to *the giver of assured* divine oracles?
50 The savage lion who devoured the choicest flesh,
51 Did it bring its flour offering to appease the goddess's anger?
52 [. .] . the nouveau riche who has multiplied his wealth,
53 Did he weigh out precious gold for the goddess Mami?
54 [Have I] held back offerings? I have prayed to my god,
55 [I have] pronounced the blessing over the goddess's regular sacrifices, ... [. . .]

Friend VI

56 O palm, tree of wealth, my precious brother,
57 Endowed with all wisdom, jewel of [gold,]
58 You are as stable as the earth, but the plan of the gods is remote.
59 Look at the superb wild ass on the [plain;]
60 The arrow will follow the gorer who trampled down the fields.
61 Come, consider the lion that you mentioned, the enemy of cattle.
62 For the crime which the lion committed the pit awaits him.
63 The opulent nouveau riche who heaps up goods
64 Will be burnt at the stake by the king before his time.

65 Do you wish to go the way these have gone?
66 Rather seek the lasting reward of (your) god!

Sufferer VII

67 Your mind is a north wind, a pleasant breeze for the peoples.
68 Choice friend, your advice is fine.
69 Just one word would I put before you.
70 Those who neglect the god go the way of prosperity,
71 While those who pray to the goddess are impoverished and dispossessed.

---

pu-u[ḫ-ḫur: 67] × × × × × [× : *ṭ*]*è-e-mu*: 69 *zik-ri*: *a-mat*: *mut-ta-ka*: *mu-u*[*t-tú*: . . . SA]G: *re-e-šú*: ṢAG: *pa-ni*: 70 *muš-te-mu-*⌜*ú*⌝[:

VARIANTS

49 C: dingir.dingir l: dingir].meš *uz-zu-uš-šú* 50 l: *la-*(*a-*)*b*]*e* 51 C: *il-ti-i* l: *šup-ṭu-ru* 52 C: *b*]*e-el* l: *uṣ-ṣu-bu-uš* 53 l: *i-*]*ḫi-iṭ* 55 j: *il-ti-i*]*m-ma* l: *q*]*í-bit* × [56 j: *m*]*eš-re-e* l: *meš*]*-ri* 57 j: *i-lu-uk* 58 j: *ni-s*[*u* 61 j: *bi-it-*⌜*ri*⌝? 62 j: *i-p*]*u-šú*, *ḫa-áš-tum* 63 j: *p*]*a-nu*, *gu-ru-un* 64 j: *ši-ma-tú i-qám-meš* 65 j: -]*šú a-la-ku* 66 j: *d*]*a-a-ra-a* 70 E: *du*]*-un-qí*

72	*il-li-gi-mi-ia-a-ma*		*ṭè-em ili*	*as-ḫ[u-ur]*
73	*il-la-ba-an appi*	*u te-mi-qí*	*e-še-'e*	^{d}*iš-tar-*⌜*ti*⌝
74	*il-ku*	*ša la né-me-li*	*a-šá-aṭ*	*ap-šá-nu*
75	*il-ta-kan*	*ilu*	*ki-i maš-re-e*	*ka-tu-ta*
76	*il-an-nu*	*ku-uṣ-ṣu-du*	*pa-na-an-ni*	*lil-li*
77	*il-ta-qu-ú*	*ḫar-ḫa-ru-ú*	*a-na-*⟨*ku*⟩	*at-taš-pil*

VIII

78	*ki-na*	*ra-áš uz-ni*	*šá tuš-ta-ad-di-nu*	*la mur-qa*
79	*ki-it-ta*	*ta-at-ta-du-ma*	*ú-ṣur-ti ili*	*ta-na-ṣu*
80	*ki-du-de-e ili*	*ana la šu-uṣ-ṣu-ru*	*taḫ-ši-ḫu*	*ka-bat-tuk*
81	*ki-nu-te*	*me-si* ^{d}*iš-ta-ri*	× [. . . . .]	
82	*ki-i qí-rib šamê*^{e}	*šib-qí ilī*^{meš}	[. . . . .]	
83	*qí-bít pi-i*	^{d}*il-ti*	*ul iš-še-*[. . . . .]	
84	*ki-niš*	*lit-mu-da-ma*	*sa-*[. . . . .]	
85	*ki-pi-du-ši-na-ma*	*ana nišī*^{me}[^{š}. . . . .]		
86	*ki-ib-si il-ti*	*šu-ḫu-za*	[. . . . .]	
87	*qé-ru-ub*	*ṭè-en-ši-na*	[. . . . .]	
88	*k*[*i-*×] × [×] × [. . . . .]			

[The stanzas *i-*, *na-*, and *am-* are wanting]

XII

125	[*u*]*b-ba-*[. . . . .]	
126	[*u*]*p-te-eṣ-ṣa*	⌜NE⌝[/-⌜*am-ma*⌝[. . . . .]
127	[*u*]*b-tel-li*	an × [. . . . .]
128	[*u*]*b-te-en-ni*	*li-gi-m*[*a-a* . . . .]
129	[*u*]*p-te-ṣi-id*	*nišī*^{meš} [. . . . .]
130	[*u*]*p-te-eḫ-ḫir*	*šà-*× [. . . . .]
131	[*u*]*p-te-eq*	*ila* [. . . . .]
132	[*u*]*b-te-'-i*	*ḫi-ši*[*ḫ-ta* . . . .]

XIII

133	*bi-i-ta*	*lu-ud-di*	×[. . . . .]
134	*bi-šá-a*	*a-a aḫ-ši-iḫ*	×[. . . . .]

COMMENTARY

75 *-n*]*u*: *ka-tu-u*: *muš-ki-nu*: 76 *il-*⌜*an-ni*: *ana e-lu-u*⌝[: . . . . *lil-li*: *l*]*a ṭè-ma-nu*: 77 *ḫar-ḫa-ri*: *gu-*⌜*zal*⌝*-lu*: MIN: *še-e-rum*: × [79 ŠUB]: *na-du-u*: ŠUB: *e-ze-bi*: *ú-ṣur-tú*: *par-ṣi*[: 82] ×: *qí-rib*: *lìb-bi*: 83 *ìl-ti*: ^{d}*iš-tar*: *šá-*[84] × ru × (×) ri: *nak-lu*: *li-*× × [

72 In my youth I sought the will of my god;
73 With prostration and prayer I followed my goddess.
74 But I was bearing a profitless corvée as a yoke.
75 My god decreed instead of wealth destitution.
76 A cripple is my superior, a lunatic outstrips me.
77 The rogue has been promoted, but I have been brought low.

Friend VIII

78 My reliable fellow, holder of knowledge, your thoughts are perverse.
79 You have forsaken right and blaspheme against your god's designs.
80 In your mind you have an urge to disregard the divine ordinances.
81 [. . . . .] the sound rules of your goddess.
82 The plans of the god [. . . . .] like the centre of heaven,
83 The decrees of the goddess are not [. . . . .]
84 To understand properly . [. . . . .]
85 Their ideas [. . . . .] to mankind;
86 To grasp the way of a goddess [. . . . .]
87 Their reason is close at hand [. . . . .]
88 . . [. . . . .]

Friend XII

125 [I] . . [. . .
126 [I] made white . . [. . .
127 [I] *cared for* . . [. . .
128 [I] looked after the young [ones . . .
129 [I] made the people *prosperous* [. . .
130 [I] gathered . . [. . .
131 [I] gave heed to the god [. . .
132 [I] sought that which was necessary [. . .

Sufferer XIII

133 I will abandon my home . [. . . . .]
134 I will desire no property . [. . . . .]

VARIANTS

73 E: *ap-pi, te-me-qi a-*[75 E: *i*]*l ki-ma meš-re-e* 76 E: *k*]*u-ṣu-du* 77 E: *ḫar-*]*ḫa-ru-um-ma* 79 B: *ki-it-tu* D: *ta-du-ma* ("homoeoteleuton"?) B: *ta-at-ta-du-ú-*[80 B: *ilī*^{meš} *la šum-ṣu-r*[*i*

Dj	135	*pí-il-lu-de-e ili*	*lu-meš*	*par-ṣ[i*	*lu-ka]b-⸢bi⸣-i[s]*
	136	*bé-e-ra*	*lu-na-ak-kis*	*lu-* × × × (×)	*ak-lu*
	137	*bi-ir-ta*	*lu-ul-lik*	*ni-⸢sa-a-ti*	*lu⸣-ḫu-uz*
i	138	*bé-e-ra*	*lu-up-ti*	*⸢a⸣-g[a-a]*	*lu-maš-šèr*
	139	*bé-e-ra*	*ki-di*	*⟨šar⟩-ra-qiš*	*[lu-u]r-tap-pu-ud*
	140	*bi-it-bi-ti-iš*	*lu-ter-ru-ba*	*⸢lu-ni⸣-'i*	*bu-bu-ti*
	141	*bi-ri-iš*	*lu-ut-te-'e-lu-me*	*su-le-e*	*lu-ṣa-a[-a-ad]*
	142	*pí-iz-nu-qiš*	*ana qir-bi*	*lu-t[er . . . .]*	
	143	*bé-e-šú*	*dum-⸢qu⸣* × × [. . . . .]		
		XIV			
	144	*[i]b-ri*	*ub-lam* [. . . . .]		
	145	*[i]p-šit nišī*^{meš}	*la taḫ-ši-ḫu* [. . . . .]		
	146	*[i]b-šu-ú*	*ina ṣur-ri-[ka. . . . .]*		
	147	*[ip]-ru-ud*	*pak-ka-ka* [. . . . .]		
	148	*[ib-(×)]a/šá-a-tú*	*nišī*[^{meš} . . . .]		
	149	*[ib-×]-ma*	nam.ulù [. . . . .]		
	150	*[ib-ba?-t]aq-ma*	*šá-sur-ra* [. . . . .]		
	151	[. . .] lul	*it-ti* [. . . . .]		
	152	[. . . .] pa	*šal-ma-a[t?* . . . .]		
	153	[. . . .] × tú	*lu-ut-*[. . . . .]		
	154	[. . . . .] ×	*ú-gu-um* [. . . . .]		
		XV			
	155	*[ma-* . . . .]	*lìb-ba* [. . . . .]		
	156	[. . . . . .]	× *šá* [. . . . .]		
E	157	[. . . . . .]	× [. . . . .]		
	158	*⸢ma⸣-*[. . . . .]	ri × [. . . . .]		
	159	*⸢ma⸣-[ar-]tú*	*a-na ba-an-ti*	*i-⸢qab⸣-b[i* . . . .]	
	160	*⸢ma⸣-[q]i-it*	*la-mi iṣṣūrāti*^{meš}	*šá id-du-u* [. . . . . .]	
	161	*⸢ma⸣-[la] šum-šu*	*a-a-ú*	*ku-ši-ir* [. . . . .]	
	162	*ma-'-da*	*a-šu-ú ṣēri*	*šá ṣil-/ú-×* [. . . . . .]	
	163	*ma-an-nu*	*i-na bi-ri-šú-nu*	*ir-ta-ši* [. . . . .]	
	164	*ma-ra*	*u mar-tum*	*lu-ba-'i* [. . . . .]	
	165	*ma-la ut-tu-ú*	*a-a i-zi-ba*	lu × [. . . . .]	

VARIANTS

139 i: *bé-e-r]i* × [140 i: *-]bi-ti-šú* 141 i: *lut-*[142 i: *a-na*

135 I will ignore my god's regulations and trample on his rites.
136 I will slaughter a calf and . . . . food,
137 I will take the road and go to distant parts.
138 I will bore a well and let loose a flood,
139 Like a robber I will roam over the vast open country.
140 I will go from house to house and ward off hunger;
141 Famished I will walk around and patrol the streets.
142 Like a beggar I will [. . . .] inwards [. . . . .]
143 Bliss is far away . . [. . . . .]

Friend XIV

144 My friend, [your mind] dwells on [. . . . .]
145 Human activity, which you do not want [. . . . .]
146 In [your] mind there are [. . . . .]
147 Your reason has left you [. . . . .]

* * * * *

Sufferer XV

159 The daughter speaks [. . . . . .] to her mother.
160 The fowler who cast [his net] is fallen.
161 Taking everything, which one [. . . . . .] luck?
162 The many wild creatures which . . [. . . . .]
163 Which among them has [. . . .?]
164 Should I seek a son and daughter [. . . . . .]
165 May I not lose what I find . . [. . . . .]

XVI

E 166	*áš-ru*	*ka-an-šu*	*šá pu-ḫur* [. . . . .]	
167	*áš-šá-ru*	*ṭè-en-ga*	*šu-qu-ru* × [. . . . .]	
168	[× ×] ×	*ka-bat-ta-ka*	*ma-qit še-'* [. . . . .]	
169	(traces)			
D 170–5	wanting			
176	(traces)			

XVII

177	*ma-a*[*l-l*]*e-e*	*i-na* × [. . . . .]		
178	*ma-an-nu*	*i-na* [. . . . .]		
H 179	*ma-a-t*[*a*	. .] × [. . . . .]		
180	*ma-la* × [.]×	*nišī*^{meš}	*šit-k*[*u-* . . . .]	
181	*ma-ar*	*š*[*a*]*r-ri*	*ḫa-líp* [. . . . .]	
182	*ma-ar ka-ti-i*	*u mi-ri-ni-i*	*la-biš*	×[. . . . . . .]
183	*ma-aṣ-ṣar*	*bu-uq-li*	*ṣa-ri-ra*	*i-*×[×]
184	*ma-di-id*	*ru-uš-ši-i*	*na-ši*	×[. . . . . . .]
f 185	*ma-lil ir-qu*	*nap-tan*	*ru-bi-i*	⌜*ú*⌝-[. . . . . .]
186	*ma-ar kab-ti*	*ù šá-ri-i*	*ḫa-ru-bu*	*uk-*[*lat-su*]
187	*ma-qit*	*bēl meš-re-em-ma*	*ni-si*	*t*[*a-* . . . . . .]

XVIII

188	*šu-'-ú*	*ta-mu-u*	*lu-ú* [. . . . .]	
189	*šu-ut*	*maḫ-ra*	*in qá-ba*[*l* . . . .]	
190	*šu-um l*[*a*			*mun?-n*]*i-ir-bu*
191	*šu-ru-uk*	*u*$_4$*-mu* [. . . . .]		
a N 192	[*šu-*			*k*]*a?-bat-ta*
193	*šu-up-ru-us*	*ina* ×[. . . . .]× la mar/rat ×[× ×]		
194	*š*[*u-*		*na*]*m-maš-šu-u*	*i-da-*[× ×]
195	*š*[*u-* . . . .]× *-le-e*		*šá-ni-t*[*a*]	×[×]
196	*šu-*[. . . . .]× ma			*qa-a-a-áš*
197	*šu-*[. . . . .]			^{d}*iš-ta-ri*
198	*šu-um-mu*	*ul-tú u*[*l-*×]*-im?*	*meš-r*[*u*]*-ú*	*u la-pa-nu*

COMMENTARY

188–96 (traces): *iš-tu* × × [. . .] × *ra?-ba-tú*: *rabû*^{ú}: *ip-tum*: *bil-tum*: i ×[196 ff. *qa-a-*]*a-áš*: *qa-a-šú*: ⌜*na-da-nu*⌝: *i-šam*: *šá-a-mu*: *na-da-*[*nu*

Friend XVI

166 Humble and submissive one . . . [. . . . . . .]
167 Your will ever submits [. . . . . .] precious.
168 [. .] . your mind . . . . [. . . . . . .]

* * * * *

Sufferer XVII

181 The crown prince is clothed in [. . . .,]
182 The son of the destitute and naked is robed in . [. . . . .]
183 The watchman of malt . . [.] gold,
184 While he who counted his shining gold in a bushel measure is carrying . . [. . .]
185 The vegetarian [devours] a noble's banquet,
186 While the son of the notable and the rich [subsists] on carob.
187 The owner of wealth is fallen. [His . . . .] . is far away.

* * * * *

VARIANTS

185 H: *ir*]-*qí* 188 H: *t*]*a*?-*mu*?-*u*(ras.?) ú [191 D: [*š*]*u-u*[*r-ru-uk* 194 N: *nam-maššu*]-⸢*ú*⸣ 195 N: *šá-ni-tú* NOTE: *ip-tum* in k must belong to 196 or an earlier line, and *i-šam* must go in 197.

XIX

a f N

199 *ka-*[. . . . .] *ta-šim-tú*
200 *ka-áš-šá-a-ta* *kul-lat né-me-qí* *nišī*^{meš} *ta-mal-lik*
201 *k*[*a* . . . .]*-mu-ti-i* *ru-uq-m*[*a*]
202 [. . . . .] *ú-sa-an-di-i* *ú-bil-lu*
203 [. . . . . *ul*? *ip*?*-p*]*a-rak-ki* *lìb-bi*
204 [. . . . . *š*]*u-ḫu-za* *šap-ta-a-a*
205 [. . . . .]× *šu-ka-mi*
206 [. . . . .] *mi-ḫi-iṣ-ta-šú* *ú-pat-tan-ni*
207 [. . . . .] ⌜*ú*⌝*-pat-ta-a* *pa-ni-šu*
208 [. . . . .] *du-un-qí-ma*
209 [. . . . .]× a *a-ṣa-a-ád*

XX

j

210 [*ri-* . . . . *dub-*]*bu sar-ri*
211 [. . . . . *ma*]*-an-nu*

f

212 *ri-pi-it-ta* *nak-la* *ṣur-ra-ka* *tu-šar-šá*
213 [. . . . .-]*su* *né-me-qú* *tu-ṭar-rid*
214 *ri-id-di* [?] [*te*]*-meš*(!) *šum-me* *ta-aṭ-pil*
215 [. . . . .] *bu-*[*b*]*í-nu* *šaḫ-ḫu-ú* *ni-si-iš tup-šik-ku*
216 [. . . . .]*-áš* *ana ka-bit* *šit-kun*
217 [. . . . .] *pa*[*l*]*-ku-u* *ni-bit-su*
218 *ri-ši* *na-aš-šu* *ba-a-ši* *ṣa-bu-u-šu*
219 *ri-di-ma* *us ilī*^{meš} *ú-ṣur* *ma-si-šu*
220 [. . . . .]*-ma* *a-na da-mi-iq-ti* *na-áš-kin*

XXI

221 [*bu-* . . . .]× *ma-qu-ru* *ḫar-ḫa-ri*
222 [. . . . .]× *ka-li-šú-nu* *is-ḫap-pu*

COMMENTARY

200 *ka-áš-šá-a-*]*ta*: *ḫa-*⌜*am*⌝*-ma-*⌜*a-tú*[:] UR$_4$[:] *a-šá-šú*⌝[:] UR$_4$: *ḫa-ma-mu*: *šá-niš ka-*[*šá-šú*: 201–2]*mu-du-u*: an × × × ri na ka ^{d}*ea*(idim) *u* ^{d}*dam-ki-an-n*[*a* 202]*-ri*: *ú-bil-lu*[:] ⌜*ba-ba-lu*⌝: *na-da-nu*: 203–6 *ka-at-mu*: × × [. . . .]*-bi*: *šal-ba-ba*: *né-me-qa*: SAL: *ra-pa-šú*: BA: *e-peš*[: 206] : *mi-ḫi-iṣ-tum*: *mi-ḫi-il-tum*: *ú-pat-ta-an-ni*: × [208–9] *ed-lu-tú*: *ana e-de-lu*: *ka-šá-me*: *ki-šá-ma*: *ḫar-pi*[: NOTE: The exact positions of *mūdû*, *katmu*, *šalbaba*, *edlūtu*, and *kašāme*, attested in k, cannot be ascertained. 210–11]*-li*: *qar-ra-du*: 212 *ri-pi-it-tum*: *ana ra-pa-du*[: 213 *ṭa-ra-du*: *ra*]*-da-du*: 214 *rid-di*: *ṭè-e-mu*: *me-e-šú*: *e-te-q*[*u*: 215] × × ×: *bu-*[*b*]*í-nu*: SAG: *re-eš*: SAG: *qaq-qa-du*: *šá-niš re-e-šú*[: 216–17]*li-'-u*: 217 *pa*[*l*]*-ku-u*: *tup-šar-ri*: 218 *ri-i-ši na-aš-ši ba-ši ṣa*[- 219 *ri-di-ma*: *ri-*[*d*]*u-a*: *a-lak*: *ú-su*:

Sufferer XIX

199 . [. . . . .] wisdom.
200 You embrace the totality of wisdom, you counsel the peoples.

* * * * *

Friend XX

212 You have let your subtle mind go astray.
213 [. . . . .] . you have ousted wisdom,
214 You despise propriety, you profane ordinances.
215 [. . . . .] head a mitre, the carrying-hod is far away from him.
216 [. . . . .] . is made a person of influence.
217 [. . . . .] is called a savant;
218 He is looked after and obtains his wishes.
219 Follow in the way of the god, observe his rites,
220 [. . . . .] . is counted as righteousness.

Sufferer XXI

221 [. . . . .] . . . . rogues,
222 [. . . . .] . all are cheats.

---

kib-su: *mi-si*: *par-ṣi*[: 221] *ḫar-ḫa-ri*: pi × : *šá-niš ku-lu-ʾ-ú*: 222 *is-ḫap-pu*: *sak-lu*: *gu*[*r*?-

VARIANTS

199 N: *ta-šim-te* 202 N: -]⌜*bi*⌝-*l*[*a*] 205 N: *šu-ka-ma* 206 N: *i-š*]*e-ṭa-ni* 207 N: *pa-*]*ni-šú-un* 208 N: *du-un-*]⌜*qí*⌝-*im-ma* 210 **f**: *du-bu-*]*ub* 212 j: *nak-l*]*i*, *t*]*u-šar-šú* 213 **f**: *tu-ziq*?/*zaq*?-*qip* (miscopied from *tu-ḫiš-šid*?) 214 The *mu* of j has been emended to *meš* in accordance with k. **f**: *ta-aṭ-píl* 216 **f**: *kab-*]*ti šit-ku-un*. This line in j is written over an erased line, probably 217, which is lacking in this tablet. *palkû* from k and *nibītsu* from **f** fit the remains of this erased line. 218 j: *n*]*a-šú ba-ši ṣa-bu-šú* 219 j:] *ì-lí ub*!-*ṣur me-si-šú* 220 i: *ana* sig$_5$-*tim* NOTE: *ri-id-di* (214), *bu-*[*b*]*í-nu* (215), and *pa*[*l*]-*ku-u* (217) are restored from k.

223	*bu-šá*	*kit-mu-s[u]*	× a ši bu	*šá* mu × [. .]
224	[. . . . .] × [. .]× *-ku-nu*			*ḫu-bu[r* . .]
225	[. . . . . ×] × gi ri			*šá* × [. .]
226	[. . . . .] × lu			ta [.] × na
227	[. . . .] × × [. . . . .] × × [. . .] ×			
228	[. . .] tur? u × [. . . . .] ×			
229	[. . . t]i × × [. . . . . .] × [. . . . .]			
230	[. . . n]u a' ú t[i]? × × [.] × × [. . . . .] ×			
231	[. . .]-*ku a-na* × × [.] × bi a-[.] × a šá [. . . . . .] ×			

XXII

232	[. . . . .] i te × [(×)] ×			
233	[. . . . .] × ×		*e-te-*[× × (× ×) z]ig/k]iš	
234	[*ša* × ×]	× pa šu	*ni-*⌜*ip*⌝*-šu*	× [× (×)]×
235	*ša ḫar-ḫa-ri*		*šá taḫ-ši-ḫu*	*bu-na-šu*
236	*ša-am-mé-e*	*pu-ri-di-šú*	*za-mar*	*i-ḫal-liq*
237	*ša la ili*	*is-ḫap-pu*	*ra-ši*	*ma-ak-ku-ra*
238	*ša-ga-šu*	*kak-ka-šú*	*i-rid-di-šu*	
239	*ša la tu-ba-'-ú*	*ṭè-em ili*	*mi-nu-ú*	*ku-šìr-ka*
240	*ša-di-id ni-ir ili*	*lu-ú ba-ḫi*	*sa-di-ir*	*a-kal-šú*
241	*ša-a-ra*	*ṭa-a-ba*	*šá ilī*^{meš}	*ši-te-'-e-ma*
242	*ša šatta*(mu.an.na)	*tu-ḫal-li-qu*	*ta-rab*	*a-na sur-ri*

XXIII

243	*i-na ad-na-a-ti*	*ab-re-e-ma*	*šit-na-a*	*i-da-a-tu*
244	*i-lu*	*a-na šar-ra-bi*	*ul pa-ri-is*	*a-lak-ta*
245	*i-šad-da-ad*	*i-na miṭ-ra-ta*	*za-ru-ú*	^{giš}*elippa*
246	*i-na qí-rib*	^{giš}*dun-ni*	*ra-mi*	*bu-kúr-šu*
247	*i-lak-kid*	*lab-biš*	*ra-bi a-ḫi*	*ú-ru-uḫ-šu*
248	*i-li-iṣ-ma*	*tup-pu-šu-ú*	*pa-ra-a*	*i-rid-di*
249	*i-na su-qí*	*zi-lul-li[š]*	*i-ṣa-a-a-ad*	*ap-lum*
250	*i-šar-ra-ak*	*ter-din-nu*	*a-na ka-ti-i*	*ti-ú-ta*

COMMENTARY

223–4] *šá-niš* ⌜*tup-šar*⌝*-ri*: × ×: *pu-ḫur*: 224 *ḫu-bu-ru*: *ši-kar*: *šá-[ni]š* × [225–34] DÙ: *ma-ga-ri*: DÙ[: × ×] ×*-lu-u*: *ki-kur-r[i*:] × ×: ×[ ] KUR: *šub-tú*: RU: *na-d[u?-u?*: *t]a-bi-ni*: × [ ] *mi-ri-šú*: *né-me-qí*: MIN: d[u?] *ḫi-ṣib-šú*: *dum-qí-šú*: *ḫa-?-ú* [Nothing certainly commenting on stanza XXII is preserved. 244] *i-la*: *e-li*: 245 *miṭ-rat*: *n[a-a-ru* 247 *i-lak-kid*: *la-ka-du*: *la-[ka-tu*(?) 248 *tup-pu-us-su-u*: *tar-din-nu*: *p[a-ra-a*(?)

223 They amass goods . . . .

* * * * *

Friend XXII

235 As for the rogue whose favour you seek,
236 His . . . . soon vanishes.

237 The godless cheat who has wealth,
238 A death-dealing weapon pursues him.

239 Unless you seek the will of the god, what luck have you?
240 He that bears his god's yoke never lacks food, though it be sparse.

241 Seek the kindly wind of the god,
242 What you have lost over a year you will make up in a moment.

Sufferer XXIII

243 I have looked around society, but the evidence is contrary.
244 The god does not impede the way of a devil.

245 A father drags a boat along the canal,
246 While his first-born lies in bed.

247 The first-born son pursues his way like a lion,
248 The second son is happy to be a mule driver.

249 The heir stalks along the road like a bully,
250 The younger son will give food to the destitute.

VARIANTS

233 **f**: *i-te-*[235 *šá*: B: *ša* 236 B: *pu*-AŠ-*ri-*[237 **f**: dingir.meš 238 Ef: giš.tukul- 239 **f**: *ṭè-mi, ku-šír-ka* 240 **f**: -]*ri ili lu ba-aḫ sa-dir a-kal-šu* 241 **f**: *ili* 242 **f**: *ta-ra-bi* 243 **f**: ⌜*i-da*⌝*-a-at* 245 **f**: -*t*]*i za-ru-u* 248 D: RID-*pu-šu-ú* (RID and DUB are identical in some Neo-Babylonian scripts) **f**: -*u*]*s-su-ú* 249 **f**: -*l*]*e-eš*

Df

251	*i-na ma-ḫar qád-mi*	*šá ad-da-mu-ṣu*	*mi-na-a*	*ú-at-tar*
252	*i-na šá-pal*	*áš-bal-ti-ia*	*kit-[m]u-sa-ku*	*a-na-ku*
253	*i-na-a-ṣa-an-ni*	*a-ḫu-ru-ú*	*šá-ru-ú*	*u šam-ḫu*

XXIV

C

a

254	*li-'-ú*	*pal-ku-ú*	*šu-e*	*ta-šim-ti*
255	*[l]i-it-mu-um-ma*	*ṣur-ra-ka*	*ila*	*ta-da-a-a-aṣ*
256	*[l]i-ib-bi ili*	*ki-ma qí-rib*	*šamê*^{e}	*né-si-ma*
257	*le-é-a-us-su*	*šup-šu-qat-ma*	*nišī*^{meš}	*la lam-da*
258	*li-pit*	*qāt* ^{d}*a-ru-ru*	*mit-ḫa-riš*	*na-piš-ti*
259	*li-il-li-du*	*mìn-su*	*ka-liš*	*la* ḪAR-*ri*
260	*li-it-tu*	*bu-ur-šu*	*riš-tu-ú*	*šá-pil-ma*
261	*li-gi-mu-šá*	*ar-ku-ú*	*ma-ṣi*	*šit-tin-šu*
262	*li-il-lu*	*ma-ru*	*pa-na-a*	*i-al-lad*
263	*li-'-um*	*qar-du*	*šá šá-ni-i*	*ni-bit-su*
264	*[l]i-'-id*	*mi-na-a pak-ki ilim-ma*	*nišī*^{meš}	*la lam-da*

XXV

265	*ú-taq-qam-ma*	*ib-ri*	*li-mad*	*ši-ib-qí-i[a]*
266	*ú-ṣur*	*nu-us-su-qa*	*sè-kar*	*at-mé-e-⌜a⌝*
267	*ú-šá-áš-qu-ú*	*a-mat kab-tu*	*šá lit-mu-da*	*šá-ga-š[á]*
268	*ú-šap-pal*	*dun!-na-ma-a*	*šá la i-šu-⌜ú⌝*	*ḫi-bi[l-ta]*
269	*ú-ka-an-nu*	*rag-ga*	*šá an-zil-la-šú*	× [. . .]
270	*ú-ṭa-ra-du*	*ki-i-nu*	*šá ṭè-em ili*	*pu-u[q-qu]*
271	*ú-⌜ma⌝-lu-ú*	*pa-šal-lu*	*šá ḫab-bi-lu*	*ni-[ṣir?-ta?]*
272	*ú-raq-qa*	*iš-pik-ku*	*šá pi-iz-nu-qu*	*ti-'-ut-[su]*
273	*ú-da-na-an*	*šal-ṭu*	*šá pu-ḫur-šú*	*an-n[u]?*
274	*ú-la-la*	*ib-ba-tu*	*i-dar-ri-is-su*	*la le-e-[a]*
275	*ú ia-a-ši*	*it-nu-šu*	*bēl pa-ni*	*ri-dan-n[u]*

COMMENTARY

253] *i-na-ṣa-an-ni*: *na-a-ṣi*[: 255] *li-it-mu-um-mu*: *ana l*[*um?-ni?* 260] *bu-ú-ri*: *ma-ri*: × [
265] *ú-te-eq-qu-ú*: *q*[*a-a-l*]*u*: *ana* × [271] *pa-šal-la*: *ḫu-*[*r*]*a-ṣu*: *ana pa-šá-lu*[:

VARIANTS

253 f: *šá-an*[*-ḫu* 254 f: *šu-'e*[C: *li*]*-gi-mu-ú*[- a: *li-*(×)]*-'-*×[262 a: *li*]-×[

251 How have I profited that I have bowed down to my god?
252 I have to bow beneath the base fellow that meets me;
253 The dregs of humanity, like the rich and opulent, treat me with contempt.

Friend XXIV

254 O wise one, O savant, who masters knowledge,
255 In your anguish you blaspheme the god.
256 The divine mind, like the centre of the heavens, is remote;
257 Knowledge of it is difficult; the masses do not know it.
258 Among all the creatures whom Aruru formed
259 The prime offspring is altogether . . .
260 In the case of a cow, the first calf is lowly,
261 The later offspring is twice as big.
262 A first child is born a weakling,
263 But the second is called an heroic warrior.
264 Though a man may observe what the will of the god is, the masses do not know it.

Sufferer XXV

265 Pay attention, my friend, understand my ideas.
266 Heed the choice expression of my words.
267 People extol the word of a strong man who is trained in murder,
268 But bring down the powerless who has done no wrong.
269 They confirm the wicked whose crime is . [. . .,]
270 Yet suppress the honest man who heeds the will of his god.
271 They fill the [store house] of the oppressor with gold,
272 But empty the larder of the beggar of its provisions.
273 They support the powerful, whose . . . is *guilt*,
274 But destroy the weak and drive away the powerless.
275 And as for me, the penurious, a nouveau riche is persecuting me.

---

263 C: *li-'-ú qar-ra-*[a: *li-i*]*a-a* 264 C: *l*]*i-'-id-ma* a: *-i*]*d?-ma mi-na-a pak-ku ni*[*šī*^{meš} 265 a: ⌜*ú-ta-aq-qa-am*⌝ 267 D: *kab-ti* 268 C: *ú-šap-pa-lu* a: SIG-*na-ma-a* (emended above) C: *du-u*[*n-* D: *i-pu-šú* 269 C: ⌜*ú-kan-nu rag-gu*⌝ 270 C: *-ṭ*]*ar-ra-du ki-na šá ana ṭè-em* 271 C: -]*ma-al-lu-ú pa-šal-la, ḫa-bi-la* a: (last word) bi? × [272 C: -]*raq-qu iš-pik-ki, te-'-*⌜*ú*⌝[- 273 C: *ú-dan-na-nu* 274 C: *i-dar-ri-su* 275 C: *it-nu-šú be-el*

a C

XXVI

276	*šar-ri qád-mi*	^{d}*nar-ru*	*ba-nu-ú*	*a-pa-a-t[um]*
277	*šar-ḫu*	^{d}*zu-lum-ma-ru*	*ka-ri-iṣ*	*ṭi-iṭ-ṭa-ši-na*
m 278	*šar-ra-tum*	*pa-ti-iq-ta-ši-na*	*šu-e-tú*	^{d}*ma-mi*
279	*šar-ku*	*ana a-me-lut-tú*	*it-gu-ru*	*da-ba-ba*
280	*sar-ra-a-tú*	*u la ki-na-tu*	*iš-ru-ku-šú*	*sa-an-tak-ku*
281	*šar-ḫi-iš*	*šá šá-ri-i*	*i-dab-bu-bu*	*dum-qí-šú*
282	*šar-mi*	*meš-ru-ú*	*il-la-ku*	*i-da-a-šú*
283	*šar-ra-qiš*	*ú-lam-ma-nu*	*dun-na-ma-a*	*a-me-lu*
284	*šar-ku-uš*	*nu-ul-la-tum*	*i-kap-pu-du-šú*	*nir-ti*
285	*sar-ri-iš*	*ka-la lum-nu*	*šu-ḫu-zu-šú áš-šú*	*la i-šu-ú i-*RI*-tú*
286	*šar-ba-bi-iš*	*uš-ḫa-ram-mu-šu*	*ú-bal-lu-šú*	*ki-ma la-a-mi*

XXVII

287	*ri-me-na-a-tú*	*ib-ri*	*ni-is-sa-tum*	*ši-te-'-me*
288	*ri-ṣa-am*	*nam-ra-ṣu*	*a-mur*	*lu-ú ti-i-du*
289	*re-e-šú*	*pal-ku-ú*	*mut-nin-nu-ú*	*a-na-a-ku*
290	*ri-ṣa*	*u tuk-la-tum*	*za-mar*	*ul a-mur*
291	*ri-bit*	*āli-ia*	*ú-ba-'-ú*	*ni-ḫi-iš*
292	*ri-ig-mu*	*ul iš-šá-pu*	*iš-šá-pil*	*at-mu-ú-a*
293	*ri-ši-ia*$_5$	*ul ul-lu*	*qaq-qa-ri*	*a-na-aṭ-ṭ[a-al]*
294	*ri-šiš*	*ul a-dal-lal*	*ina puḫur*	*it-ba[-ra-ti]*
295	*ri-ṣa*	*liš-ku-nu*	*ilū*	*šá id-da-[an]-ni*
296	*ri-ma*	*li-ir-šá-a*	^{d}*iš-tar*	*šá* × [. . .]
297	*re-e-um*	^{d}*šamši*^{ši}	*ni-ši i-liš*	*ir-['-e]*

COMMENTARY

276] ^{d}*na-ar-[r]i*: ^{d}*en-líl*: 277 ^{d}*su-l[um-mar*: . . . .] MAR: GAR: *n[a]-šú-u*: 278 *šu-'-e-tum*: *be-el-[tum*: 284] *nu-u[l-la-t]i*: *la kit-tú*: *ki-pí-id*: *ṣu-m[i-rat*: 286]*-na*: *uš-ḫa-ram-ma-mu-uš*: *n[a-ḫar-mu-mu*: 288 *ri-ṣa-a]m-ma*: *ra-a-ṣa*: *a-lak*: *šá-niš* DAḪ: *r[a-a-ṣa* 293 (?) *ul-lu*: *ana e-]lu-u*: 294 *ri-ši-iš*: *kīma ardi*: 295 *šá id-dan-ni*: ŠUB[: *na-du-ú* Colophon: [*ṣa-*]⌜*a*⌝*-tú u šu-ut pî maš-a-a-al-tú* ^{lú}*um-man-nu šá a-š[iš* . . .]

VARIANTS

276 C: *šar*, *na-an-na-*(ras.)*-ru ba-nu-u a-pa-a-t[i* 277 a: *šar-ri!* C: ^{d}*zu-lum-mar ka-ri-ṣu ṭi-iṭ-ṭi-š[in* 278 C: *šar-ra-tú*, *šu-e-tum* ^{d}*ma-m[a* 279 a has a crasis of *lut*+*tú*. C: *a-na a-me-lu-ti it-gu-ra* 280 C: *sar-ra-a-ti la ki-na-a-ti iš-ru-ku-ši sa-at-tak* m: *k]i-na-a-tú* ⌜*iš-ruk?-šú*⌝? 281 C: *ša* m: *i-da-ab-bu-bu* 282 a: *šar-*(ras.)*-mi* C: *šar-ma maš-ru-šu* m: *il-la-ak-ku* 283 m: *-]lam-ma-an-nu* C: *i-lam-ma-nu du-un-na-ma-*⌜*a*⌝ 284 C: *šar-*⌜*ku*⌝*-šu nu-*⌜*ul-la-a-ti*⌝ m: *nu-ul-la-a-tú* 285 C: *sar-re-eš* m: *šu-ḫa-ba!-šú* 286 m:

Friend XXVI

276 Narru, king of the gods, who created mankind,
277 And majestic Zulummar, who dug out their clay,
278 And mistress Mami, the queen who fashioned them,
279 Gave perverse speech to the human race.
280 With lies, and not truth, they endowed them for ever.
281 Solemnly they speak in favour of a rich man,
282 "He is a king," they say, "riches go at his side."
283 But they harm a poor man like a thief,
284 They lavish slander upon him and plot his murder,
285 Making him suffer every evil like a criminal, because he has no *protection.*
286 Terrifyingly they bring him to his end, and extinguish him like a flame.

Sufferer XXVII

287 You are kind, my friend; behold my grief.
288 Help me; look on my distress; know it.
289 I, though humble, wise, and a suppliant,
290 Have not seen help and succour for one moment.
291 I have trodden the square of my city unobtrusively,
292 My voice was not raised, my speech was kept low.
293 I did not raise my head, but looked at the ground,
294 I did not worship even as a slave in the company of my associates.
295 May the god who has thrown me off give help,
296 May the goddess who has [abandoned me] show mercy,
297 For the shepherd Šamaš guides the peoples like a god.

šar-ba-!*iš ta*!*-ḫa-ram-ma-mu-šú ú-bal-lu-š*⟨*ú k*⟩*i-ma* 287 C: *ri-mi-na-*⌜*a*⌝[- m: *ri-me-na-at, ši-te-'-e*

288–92: m offers a divergent order:

289 *ri-ši-šú*	*pal-ḫu*	gír gaz ki *nu-ú*	*a-na-ku*
291 *ri-bit*	*āli-iá*	*a-ba-'u*	*ni-ḫi-iš*
292 *ri-ig-mu*	*ul iš-šá-pu*	*šá-pil*	*at-mu-ú-a*
288 *ri-šá*!*-am*	*nam-ra-ṣu*	*a-mur*	*lu-ú ti-i-du*
290 *ri-ṣa*	*tuk-lat*	*za-mar*	u! *ul a-mur*

(gír gaz ki *nu-ú* is a misreading of *mut-nin-nu-ú*; the same scribe also writes *ul*!*-lu* (293) incorrectly.)

288 C: *ri-ṣa-am-m*[*a* 293 m: *ri-ši-ia, a-na-aṭ-ṭ*[*al* 294 m: u! *ul* 295 a: dingir. dingir m: dingir.meš 296 m: *re*]-⌜*e-mu*⌝, ^{d}15[297 m offers some divergent traces.
Colophon of a: *ba-*[*ri*]

A FRAGMENT OF A SIMILAR WORK

VAT 9943 (Pl. 25), a fragment from Assur, is a Middle Assyrian piece, to judge from the script, and belongs to an unidentified work. It is clearly a dialogue, and the little that remains suggests a debate similar to the *Theodicy*.

LITERATURE

TEXT: *KAR* 340. Cf. F. M. Th. Böhl, *JEOL* VII. 415.

1 traces

---

2 . . .] ⸢*um*⸣-*mu šá* × [. . .
3 . . .]-*nu bēl eṭ-lu* × [. . .

---

4 . . .] *ib-ri tap-pe-e* × × [. . .
5 . . .] *ša ul-tu ṣu-uḫ-ra-ni* [. . .
6 . . .]× -KÁL-*ta iš*-×-× *i-na a*-[. . .
7 . . .] *šá* × te *ni-ta-ka-la ni-qe-e* ⸢it⸣? [. . .
8 . . .]× ⸢lu⸣ *lem-nu gal-lu-ú šu-ú* nu [. . .
9 . . .]× ta UD ma *i-na qa-ti-šu-nu* × [. . .
10 . . .]× a PI ma *lu*(-)*ra-qi* × × [. . .
11 . . .]×-*ia at-ta la-a tu-ka-la-ma-an-ni a-i*[*a-ši*]
12 . . .] a PI ma *lu*(-)*ra-qi a-na-ku*
13 . . .] *at-ta la-a tu-kal-lam-an-ni a-ia-ši*
14 . . .] meš ma *lu*(-)*ra-qi a-na-ku*
15 . . .]× *at-ta la-a tu-kal-lam-an-ni a-ia-ši*
16 . . .]× ma *lu*(-)*ra-qi a-na-k*[*u*]
17 . . . *a*]*t-ta la-a tu-kal-lam-an-ni a-ia-ši*

---

18 . . .] *a-na-ku* a × × *ú-ka-la-mu* × [. . .
19 . . .]× ma × (×) na qa a[t?] × *le-e* [. . .

---

20 . . .] *iz-za-qa-ra* [. . .] × × [. . .
21 . . .] *a-na* × [. . .
22 . . .]× × × [. . .

---

4 . . .] friend, companion . . [. . .
5 . . .] which from our youth [. . .
6 . . .] . . . . [. . .
7 . . .] . . . we eat sacrifices . [. . .
8 . . .] . . he is a wretch and a devil . . [. . .
9 . . .] . . . . in their hands . [. . .
10 . . .] . . . . may I . . . . [. . .
11 . .] my [.] . you indeed do not convince me.
12 . . .] . . . may I . .
13 . . .] you indeed do not convince me.
14 . . .] . . may I . .
15 . . .] . you indeed do not convince me.
16 . . .] . . may I . .
17 . . .] you indeed do not convince me.

---

18 . . .] I . . . they convince . [. . .
19 . . .] . . . (.) . . . . . . [. . .

---

20 . . .] spoke [. . .] . . [. . .
21 . . .] to . [. . .

4

PRECEPTS AND ADMONITIONS

(i) *INSTRUCTIONS OF ŠURUPPAK*

INTRODUCTION

THE *Sumerian King List* and the book of Genesis, as is well known, have a common framework of the early history of mankind: a succession of nine or ten long-lived worthies is brought to an end by a divinely sent flood, which destroys the whole human race apart from one man and his dependants, who are warned and escape in a specially built boat. Since the wickedness of men had incited the divine wrath, some instructions on living are given at the time of the flood in both Hebrew and Sumerian records. In Genesis God gives the commandments on consuming animal blood, and shedding human blood (ix. 4–7), which were developed later into a series of ordinances binding on all mankind. In Sumerian there was a work called The *Instructions of Šuruppak* (SU.KUR.RU^{ki}) *son of Ubartutu*, and consisting of sayings addressed to Ziusudra by his father. Šuruppak appears in one manuscript of the *Sumerian King List* (WB 62, written SU.KUR.LAM) as an extra generation between Ubartutu and Ziusudra. In the other manuscripts and elsewhere these two men are father and son, and it has been suggested that the intruder may have arisen through an epithet of the father ("man of Šuruppak") having been taken wrongly for a proper name (Zimmern, *ZDMG* 78. 21; Jacobsen, *AS* 11. 75[32]). Only one small fragment of the *Instructions* has been published (*PBS* x/1, Pl. iv A), though apparently the greater part is extant in unpublished tablets (Kramer, *JCS* 1. 33[208], and *Or* N.S. 22. 190). In Akkadian VAT 10151 is a small fragment of a version of this text, dating from Middle Assyrian times. (The hesitation of Weidner about the date in *AfO* 16. 211 is unnecessary; the script is typical of the period.) The curvature of the piece shows that the first preserved line is not far from the top of the tablet, and the first few preserved lines are certainly introduction. It is fortunate that the available Sumerian fragment also contains part of the introduction, and this has been restored by Kramer from the unpublished material as follows:

1′ [šuruppa]k.e dumu.ni.ra na.na mu.un.ri.ri
2′ [šuruppa]k.dumu.ubara.tu.tu.ke$_4$
3′ zi.u$_4$.sud.rá dumu.ni.ra na.na mu.un.ri.ri
4′ [dumu].mu na ga.ri na.ri.mu ḫé.díb
5′ zi.u$_4$.sud.rá inim ga.ra.ab.dug$_4$ inim gizzal ḫé.im.ši.ag

6′ na.ri.ga.mu šu nam(!).bí.bar.ri
7′ inim.dug$_4$.ga.mu na.ab.ta.bal.e.dè

1′ [Šuruppa]k offered instructions to his son,
2′ [Šuruppa]k, the son of Ubartutu,
3′ Offered instructions to his son Ziusudra,
4′ "O my [son], instruction I offer thee, take my instruction,
5′ O Ziusudra, a word I would speak to thee, give ear to my word,
6′ My instruction do not neglect,
7′ My spoken word do not transgress." (*JCS* I. 33[208])

What remains of lines 1–6 of the Assyrian fragment corresponds exactly with 2′–7′ of the Sumerian, and this suggests that we are dealing with a simple Babylonian translation of the original text. Publication of all the material must be awaited before anything further can be said, and the interpretations offered of the preserved words are necessarily tentative.

The mysterious person of Šuruppak deserves further consideration. He is somehow not included in most of the manuscripts of the *Sumerian King List*, and the later traditions of *Gilgameš*, XI, and Berossus know nothing of him. A reason for his appearance, and especially in connexion with the *Instructions*, is to be sought in the original setting and purpose of this advice. Since it was wickedness on the part of man that brought the flood, whether gross moral corruption, as in Genesis, or unnecessary noise that kept the gods awake, according to the *Atra-ḫasis Epic*, the admonitions given in this context are obviously intended as warnings to mankind against a repetition of the evil. This is very clear in the Biblical account, and the general nature of the Sumerian sayings does not militate against this view, since the several compilations of Ahiqar sayings are examples of the way in which diverse collections of material can get attached to the same figure. *A priori* the obvious person to have given these instructions was the flood hero himself, and in Genesis Noah was the intermediary. The story in *Gilgameš*, XI, however, must have created a difficulty, for although that account, like the *Atra-ḫasis Epic*, describes the boarding of the ark by all the kith and kin of Uta-napištim, when the waters subside it appears that only he and his wife have survived. Then they are promptly made immortal and are settled on a remote island. If the sayings were pronounced by Uta-napištim, he could not have passed them on to the postdiluvian world. Thus in Berossus he is instructed to write "beginnings, middles, and ends" on tablets, and to bury them in Sippar, where they were found after the flood. The *Instructions of Šuruppak* must have been considered part, if not the whole, of this cache. Berossus, however, in the usual confusion of such traditions, states that there were other people in the ark, who repopulated the earth. This, however, stultifies the burying of tablets, seeing that these people could have spread the teaching. Ovid, however, had a tradition that only two persons were saved, and that they engendered offspring by throwing stones over their shoulders.

Teaching implies two parties, and the Mesopotamian version of a flood hero who had no dealings with men after the flood did not allow him the opportunity of being the teacher. This seems to be the background against which the strange figure of Šuruppak is to be set. He may have been invented solely to provide a teacher, or there may have been a little-known recension of antediluvian history from which he was taken. For some reason there must have been an objection to assigning the duty to Ubartutu.

Zimmern first suggested that this Akkadian fragment might belong to the *Counsels of Wisdom*, and asked if the obverse might not be the lacking commencement. His caution has not been maintained by some later scholars who have unhesitatingly called the *Counsels of Wisdom* "Sayings of Šuruppak". It is now known that only some 6 lines are wanting at the beginning of the *Counsels of Wisdom*, and what remains of 7–19 does not permit the insertion of the more than 18 lines of the fragment from Assur. The unpublished Sumerian material also confirms this decision.

LITERATURE

CUNEIFORM TEXT

1915 E. Ebeling, *KAR* 27.

EDITIONS

1916 H. Zimmern, *ZA* 30. 185–7.
1918 W. F. Albright, *JAOS* 38. 60–65.

RELATION TO SUMERIAN

1947 S. N. Kramer, *JCS* 1. 33[208]
1956 Photographs of two otherwise unpublished fragments of the Sumerian text are given by S. N. Kramer in *From the Tablets of Sumer*, p. 138.

VAT 10151 (Plate 30)

OBVERSE

1 ^{m}*šu-ru-u[p-pa-ak* . . .
2 ^{m}*ut-na-p[u-uš-te* . . .
3 *ma-ri š[u* . . .
4 ^{m}*ut-na-pu-u[š-te* . . .
5 *a-šèr-ti* [. . .
6 *a-ma-at* ×[. . .
7 *mu-ú-ra na-*[. . .
8 *me-ri-ša i-na* ḪI[. . .
9 *e-qe-el-ka* [. . .
10 *ina me-ri-ši-ka* ×[. . .
11 *bīt-ka a-na ri-*×[. . .
12 *qa-ta-te la te-p[u-uš* . . .
13 *ù at-ta qa-t[a-te* . . .
14 *a-na a-me-li mu-u[m-* . . .
15 *a-šar ṣa-al-[te* . . .
16 ⸢*ṣa-al*⸣*-tu a-na* ×[. . .
17 [*ṣa-a*]*l-tu* ⸢*a*⸣-[*na* . . .
18 [× × ×] × [. . .

REVERSE

1 [× ×] × × [. . .
2 *ki-ma ri-*×[. . .
3 *ri-i-ib* ×[. . .
4 *a-ḫe-e la tu-uš-*[. . .
5 *ma-ar-ti a-me-l[i* . . .
6 *bēl e-mu-qi te-*[. . .
7 *eṭ-la la tu-uš-*[. . .
8 *a-kíl kar-ṣi* [. . .
9 *i-na pa-ni la ta-*[. . .
10 *ki-ma sa-ar-ri* [. . .
11 *ki-ma ser-ri i-*[. . .
12 [*a-n*]*a qar-ra-di* [. . .
13 [× ×] ^{d}*šá-maš i-*[. . .
14 [*a-na qar*]*-ra-di* [. . .
15 [× × × (×)] an [. . .

OBVERSE

1 Šuruppak [. . .
2 Ut-napušte [. . .
3 "My son . [. . .
4 Ut-napušte [. . .
5 My instruction [. . .
6 The word which . [. . .
7 A foal . [. . .
8 Arable land in . [. . .
9 Your field [. . .
10 On your arable land . [. . .
11 Your house to . . [. . .
12 Do not be a security [. . .
13 Then you [will be] a security [. . .
14 To a man . . [. . .
15 Where there is a dispute [. . .
16 A dispute . . . [. . .
17 A dispute . [. . .

REVERSE

2 Like . . [. . .
3 Recompense . [. . .
4 Do not . . a foreigner [. . .
5 A man's daughter [. . .
6 A strong man . [. . .
7 Do not . . a man [. . .
8 A slanderer [. . .
9 Do not . . . . . [. . .
10 Like a rebel [. . .
11 Like . . . [. . .
12 To a warrior [. . .
13 [. .] Šamaš . [. . .
14 To a warrior [. . .

(ii) *COUNSELS OF WISDOM*

INTRODUCTION

The *Counsels of Wisdom* is a collection of moral exhortations extending for some 160 lines, if the quantity of missing text has been correctly estimated. Concurring changes of metre and subject matter divide the work into short sections dealing with one topic each:

(*a*) 19–25 Avoidance of bad companions.
(*b*) 26–30 Improper speech.
(*c*) 31–. . . Avoidance of altercations and pacification of enemies.
(*d*) . . .–65 Kindness to those in need.
(*e*) 66–71 The undesirability of marrying a slave girl.
(*f*) 72–80 The unsuitability of prostitutes as wives.
(*g*) 81–. . . The temptations of a vizier.
(*h*) . . .–134 Improper speech.
(*i*) 135–47 The duties and benefits of religion.
(*j*) 148–. . . Deception of friends.

Sections *abdefghj* have four principal stresses to the line; *ci* have three. Seeing that the fragment of the sayings connected with Šuruppak does not in fact belong to this work, the problem of authorship, actual as well as fictitious, has to be considered. The text itself is addressed to someone who is one called "My son" (81). This expression is commonly used in the Wisdom literatures of the ancient Near East, either as a literary fiction whereby the writer puts himself into the shoes of some great man instructing his actual son, or where the paternal relationship is that of teacher to pupil, or, in a work which was read, of writer to reader. The advice given in the section beginning "My son" can have had relevance for very few people, unlike the rest of the *Counsels*, which has a general application. This suggests that we are to construe the text as being in the form of admonitions of some worthy to his son who will succeed him as vizier to the ruler. The case of Ahiqar at once springs to mind. Whether or not Ahiqar can be identified with a figure known from Late Assyrian letters, as suggested by von Soden (*ZA* 43. 1–13), the well-known story is set in the reign of Esarhaddon. It is improbable that a text composed about the reign of Esarhaddon could be represented by three copies or more in the libraries of Ashurbanipal, and by at least one copy at Assur. And then there is no room for a story at the beginning of our text. However, the comparison is suggestive. K 13770 (see p. 106) is the beginning of a text in which a wise man instructs his "son". If this should eventually be shown to be the opening of the *Counsels of Wisdom*, then it would not be attached to any great name, but would be simply advice of "a wise man". However, until something more is known about this fragment speculation is to no purpose.

There is evidence that the *Counsels* enjoyed popularity in some circles. A Late Babylonian tablet of bilingual incantations ends with lines 62–66 of our text. Since 61 is inseparable from 62, and 66 begins a new section, this is certainly a direct borrowing of the text in its present form. A Late Assyrian letter gives a couplet of which the beginnings of the lines are followed by the ends of two other lines in our text, though all in the same context (see note on 143–7). Unfortunately the purpose of the letter is obscure, and we do not know if this was a quotation from memory of a written source, or an oral saying. The short sections and the epigrammatic nature of many of the lines would have made this text suitable for oral repetition, but we do not know definitely if, in part or whole, it enjoyed wide popular repute.

There are a few other fragments surviving which show that a wide range of such literature once existed. The *Instructions of Šuruppak* dealt with disputes; the *Counsels of a Pessimist* offers very similar advice (see note on 137); and section (*d*) uses the same framework as the ethical section of the *Šamaš Hymn* (see note on 60).

The date of compilation is probably later than the First Dynasty of Babylon. Gemser placed it so early, and in this he was followed by Böhl, who assigned a First Dynasty date to the tablet of bilingual incantations (*JEOL* VIII. 670). The only criterion for dating this tablet is the script, and this is typical Late Babylonian (see the whole text in *PBS* I/2. 116). There is nothing whatsoever to compel an early date, and to the present writer the tone and type of piety found in the work—admittedly a personal and somewhat subjective judgement—suggest the Cassite period as the time of composition. The author may have had floating oral tradition as well as literary sermons on which to base himself.

LITERATURE

TEXT, WITH OR WITHOUT EDITION

1901 L. W. King, *CT* 13. 29–30 (text of B).
1902 L. W. King, *STC* II, LXIV–LXVI (text of e).
1906 K. D. Macmillan, *BA* V. 557–62 and 622–3 (text of K 7897).
1916 S. H. Langdon, *PSBA* 38. 105–16 and 131–7 (text of A and C).
1918 H. F. Lutz, *PBS* I/2. 116 (text of f).
1923 E. Ebeling, *KAR* 329 (text of **d**).

EDITIONS, TRANSLATIONS, STUDIES

1876 G. Smith, *The Chaldean Account of Genesis*, pp. 78–80.
1880 G. Smith, *The Chaldean Account of Genesis* (revised ed.), pp. 73–74.
1896 F. Delitzsch, *Das Babylonische Weltschöpfungsepos* (*Abhandlungen der Sächsischen Gesellschaft der Wissenschaften*, Phil.-hist. Klasse, Bd. 17/2), 19, 54–55, 88–89, 111–12.
1902 L. W. King, *STC* I. 201–2.
1906 B. Meissner, *OLZ* 9. 547 (review of Macmillan).
1908 H. Zimmern, *ZA* 23. 367–9.
1909 A. Ungnad, in H. Gressmann, *Altorientalische Texte zum alten Testamente*[1], pp. 98–99.
1911 H. Zimmern, *AO* 13/1. 27–29.
1912 R. W. Rogers, *Cuneiform Parallels to the Old Testament*[1], pp. 175–8.
1913 A. Jeremias, *Handbuch der altorientalischen Geisteskultur*[1], p. 334.
1920 A. Ungnad, *OLZ* 23. 249–50 (edition of f).
1923 S. H. Langdon, *Bab* 7. 216–20 (= *Babylonian Wisdom*, pp. 88–92).
1925 E. Ebeling, *MAOG* I/1. 6.
1925 B. Meissner, *Babylonien und Assyrien* II. 421–2.
1926 E. Ebeling, in H. Gressmann, *Altorientalische Texte zum alten Testament*[2], pp. 291–3.
1926 R. W. Rogers, *Cuneiform Parallels to the Old Testament*[2], pp. 175–8.

1929 A. Jeremias, *Handbuch der altorientalischen Geisteskultur*², p. 472.
1931 B. Gemser, *Spreuken* II, *Prediger en Hooglied* (*Tekst en Uitleg*), pp. 51 ff.
1942 F. M. Th. Böhl, *JEOL* VIII. 670.
1942 S. Du Toit, *Bybelse en Babilonies-Assiriese Spreuke*, 31, 110, 113, 130–63.
1943 T. Jacobsen, *JNES* 2. 163–4.
1950 R. H. Pfeiffer, *ANET*¹, pp. 426–7.
1955 R. H. Pfeiffer, *ANET*², pp. 426–7.

MANUSCRIPTS

	Symbol	Lines on Obverse	Lines on Reverse	Plates
Ashurbanipal:	A = K 8282 and K 7897	I 14–48	III 124–42	
		II 54–83	IV 161–6	27, 29

(Although there is no join, everything points to these two pieces being parts of the same tablet)

	Symbol	Lines on Obverse	Lines on Reverse	Plates
	B = K 3364	I 23–51	II 125–55	28
	C = K 8231	I 66–79	II 80–96	28
	G = K 10652	..	156–66	29
Assur:	**d** = *KAR* 329	12–22	..	29

(The original cannot be found, since the number given by Ebeling, VAT 11556, is false)

	Symbol	Lines on Obverse	Lines on Reverse	Plates
Babylon, 458 B.C.:	e = BM 33851 (Rm 4. 411)	I 7–23	III 126–35	
		II 52–68	IV (Colophon)	27, 29
Nippur:	f = CBS 4507, Rev. 54–58		62–66	29

(An "appendix" to a tablet of bilingual incantations)

Lines 7–51 are so numbered on the basis of computation, and may be one or two digits too high or low. The juxtaposition of 51 and 52 is not certain; there may be a gap or overlapping at this point. Lines 52–96 are numbered correctly, since the approximate numbering computed is made precise by the two wedges on the left of Col. II on A, which mark every tenth line. Lines 124 to the end are also based on computation, but here the margin of error may be as much as 20 lines. Lines 124–55 are in correct sequence, but the juxtaposition of 155 and 156 is uncertain.

The suggestion of Böhl (*JEOL* VII. 415) that *KAR* 343 may belong to this work has nothing to recommend it. The piece is included in Ebeling's *Handerhebung*, p. 140, a more suitable place.

MSS	Line	Text	
e	7	[. . . . .] nu × [×]	
	8	[. . . . . *lik*?]*-tar-ra-bu-k*[*a*]	
	9	[. . . . .] × *bīta*	
	10	[. . . . .] × ḫu ka	
d	11	[. . . . . (*t*)*u*-]*šam-ra-aṣ*	
	12	[. . . . .] *i*-⌜*mar-ru-uṣ*⌝	
A	13	[. . . . .] *amēlu*	
	14	[. . . . .] × ši? kar? ni? × [×]*-ta*	
	15	[. . . . . *i-lap*-]*pi-in ar-ḫi*-[*iš*]	
	16	[. . . . .]×*-tum ul ip-pu-uš*	
	17	[. . . . .]× *i-saḫ-ḫur ul i-paq-qid bīt-su*	
	18	[. . . . . *a-na*] *gal-le-e i-tur-ra-áš-š*[*ú*]	
	19	[. . . . .]×*-zi*	*li-qu-u ši-ṭu-us-su*
	20	[*i-na pi-i*] *niši*^{meš}*-šú-ma*	*ma-sik-ta i-ši*
	21	[*it-ti e-pi*]*š na-mu-ti*	*e tu-uš-ta-mi*
B	22	[× × r]i? i?*-ma la ba-bil šip-ri*	*ana ši-tul-ti e tal-lik*
	23	⌜*i*⌝*-na ṭu-ub-ba-ti-ma*	*ṭè-en-šú-nu taš-šak-kin*
	24	*tuš-tam-maṭ-ṭi ši-pir-ka-ma*	*ú-ru-uḫ-ka te-ez-zib*
	25	*en-qu ba-a-a-šá-a*	*tu-sar-ra-ár ṭè-en-ka*

8 may] they constantly speak well of you; 9] house; 11 you/he distress(es); 12] is distressed; 13] man; 15] is quickly impoverished;
16] . . . does not do.
17 [. . . . .] . wanders, does not govern his house,
18 [. . . . .] will turn [into] a devil for him.

19 [. . . . .] . . who insults him,
20 He has a bad reputation [among] his peoples.
21 Do not converse [with a tale]bearer,
22 Do not consult [with a . .] . . . who is an idler;
23 In (your) good grace you will become as a mind for them,
24 Then you will reduce your own output, forsake your path,
25 And will let your wise, circumspect mind be considered rebellious.

VARIANTS

12 **d**: -]*mar-ra-a*[*ṣ*] 14 e: (end) *-t*]*um* 15 e: *-e*]*n ár-ḫi*[*š*] **d**: *ár-ḫiš* 18 **d**: *i-tur-ra-áš-šu* e: *-tú*]*r-raš-šú* 19 e: *li-qu-*]⌜*ú*⌝ 20 **d**: *i-šu* 21 e: *-t*]*a-mu* 23 ⌜*i*⌝!*-na* from trace on B; trace on A uncertain. e: (end) *-k*]*an* 24 B: *tuš-ta*[-

AB

26 *lu-ú sa-niq pi-i-ka*   *lu-ú na-ṣir at-mu-ka*
27 *bal-tu šá a-me-li*   *lu-ú šu-qu-ra šap-ta-ka*
28 *šil-la-tum ma-ag-ri-tum*   *lu-ú ik-ki-bu-ka*
29 *li-zi-nu e ta-ta-mi*   *ṭè-e-mu la ki-i-ni*
30 *ša e-piš na-mu-ti*   *qa-lil qaq-qad-su*

31 *ina pu-uḫ-ri*   *e ta-ʾ-ir*   *ú-zu-uz-za*
32 *a-šar*   *ṣal-tim-ma*   *e tu-ut-tag-ge-eš*
33 *ina ṣal-tim-ma*   *i-ra-áš-šu-ka*   *šim-ta*
34 *ù at-ta*   *a-na ši-bu-ti-šú-nu*   *taš-šak-kin-ma*
35 *a-na la di-ni-ka*   *ub-ba-lu-ka*   *a-na kun-ni*
36 *ina pa-an ṣal-tim-ma*   *pu-ṭur*   *e tak-pu-ud*
37 *lu-u ṣal-ta-ka-ma*   *na-pi-iḫ-ta*   *bul-li*
38 *ṣal-tu-um-ma*   *šu-ut-ta-tum*   *še-ṭi-tum*
39 *du-ú-ru ab-ru*   *mu-kàt-ti-t[i]*   *ga-ri-š[ú]*
40 *ma-ši-is-su*   *i-ḫa-sa-sa-am-m[a]*   *amēla ub-bar*
41 *it-ti bēl*   *ṣal-ti-ka*   *e [t]ul-tam-me-in*
42 *a-na e-piš li-mut-ti-ka*   *damiqta*   *ri-ib-šú*
43 *a-na rag-gi-ka*   *mi-šá-ra*   *[ki]l-⌜la⌝-áš-šú*
44 *a-na ṣir-ri-ka*   *[ka-ba]t-ta-ka*   *[li-i]m-mir-šú*
45 *lu ḫa-du-ka*   [. . . . . . .]   *šu-t[a-ʾ-i-r]a-áš-šú*
46 *a-a ub-la*   *[lìb-b]a-ka*   [^{mí}]*limuttim*^{tim}
47 *an-ni* × [. . . . . .] *ilī*^{meš} [. . . . *m*]*a*?*-ag-rat*
48 [*l*]*um-nu* [. . . . . .] ⌜*ik-kib*⌝ [. . . . ^{d}]*marduk*
49 × × [. . . . .] × bar
50 [. . . . .] × nu
51 [. . . . .] ×

*   *   *   *   *

e

52 [×] × [. . . . .]
53 *e ta-at-ka*[*l* . . . .]

A

54 *a-mur aḫa ra-b*[*a-a* × ×]   × [. . . . .]
55 [. . . . . . . *-n*]*a-a*   *pi-làḫ u* × [× (×)]
56 [× × × *du*]*n-na-me-i*   *ri-ši-šú re-e-m*[*u*]
57 *ṣur-ru-p*[*a* × ×]*-ma*   *ši-ṭu-us-su-nu e tal-*[*qí*]
58 *šal-ṭi-iš e-li-šú-nu*   *e tug-dan-ni-i*[*ṣ*]
59 *a-na an-nim-ma*   *ìl-šú e-zi-is-su*
60 *ul ṭa-a-bi eli* ^{d}*šamaš*   *i-ra-ab-šú lu*[*m-n*]*u*

VARIANTS

26 B: *lu-u* (bis)   27 B: *am*[*ēli l*]*u*   28 B: *šil-la-tu* [*ma-ag-r*]*i-tu*   29 B: *ta-ta-*]*me*
36 A: *ṣal-ti*   38 A: *še-ṭi-*⌜*i-t*⌝[*um*]   41 A: *e t*[*u-*   42 A: *da-m*[*e-*   B: s]ig$_5$ 43 A:

26 Let your mouth be controlled and your speech guarded:
27 Therein is a man's wealth—let your lips be very precious.
28 Let insolence and blasphemy be your abomination;
29 Speak nothing profane nor any untrue report.
30 A talebearer is accursed.

31 Do not frequent a law court,
32 Do not loiter where there is a dispute,
33 For in the dispute they will have you as a *testifier*,
34 Then you will be made their witness
35 And they will bring you to a lawsuit not your own to affirm.
36 When confronted with a dispute, go your way; pay no attention to it.
37 Should it be a dispute of your own, extinguish the flame!
38 Disputes are a *covered* pit,
39 A strong wall that scares away its foes.
40 They remember what a man forgets and lay the accusation.
41 Do not return evil to the man who disputes with you;
42 Requite with kindness your evil-doer,
43 Maintain justice to your enemy,
44 Smile on your adversary.
45 If your ill-wisher is [. . . .,] nurture him.
46 Do not set your [mind] on evil.
47 . . . [. . . . . .] agreeable [to] the gods.
48 Evil [. . . . . .] an abomination [. . . . of] Marduk.

* * * * *

53 Do not trust [. . . . .]
54 Consider the elder brother [. .] . [. . . . .]
55 [. . . . . . .] . . reverence and . [. .]
56 [. . . the] feeble, show him kindness;
57 Do not insult the downtrodden and [. .]
58 Do not sneer at them autocratically.
59 With this a man's god is angry,
60 It is not pleasing to Šamaš, who will repay him with evil.

---

k[*il*- 54–56 The remains of A and e seem to present variant traditions. 54 (e is followed in the text) A: [. . . . .] × a si šú? × × × [× × ×] 55–56 (A is followed in the text) e: (about the centre)] ú [, and ⌜a⌝ × [× × × (×)] × na a ḫ[u? . . . .] 59 A: *ilu*

A e

f 61 *šu-kil a-ka-lu* *ši-qí ku-ru-u[n-n]u*
62 *e-riš-ti qí-i-ši* *e-pir ù ku-ub-bit*
63 *a-na an-nim-ma* *ìl-šú ḫa-di-iš*
64 *ṭa-a-bi eli* ^{d}*šamaš* *i-ra-ab-šú dum-qu*
65 *šub-šu ú-sa-tu* *gi-mil du-ur* u_4*-mu*

C

66 *amta ina bīti* *e tu-kab-bit*
67 *[ki-m]a* ⸢*áš*⸣*-šá-tim-ma* *la i-be-el ú-ru-u[š-ka]*
68 *[×] šá × [. . ar-d]a-a-ti* *pa-gar-ka la te-eš-ši-[ir]*
69 *[e]l-l[i . . . . i]m?-ka* *l[a] tu-ur-ra-[ad]*
70 *[ina] pi-i nišī*^{meš}*-ka-ma* *[k]i-a-am liq-b[u-ka]*
71 *bīt amtum-ma* ⸢*i*⸣*-[be-]el* *i-sap-pu-uḫ*
72 *e ta-ḫu-uz ḫa-rim-tu* *š[á] šá-a-ri mu-tu-šá*
73 *iš-ta-ri-tu* *šá a-na ili zak-*⸢*rat*⸣
74 *kul-ma-ši-tu* *šá qé-reb-šá ma-'-d[a]*
75 *ina ma-ru-uš-ti-ka-ma* *ul i-na-áš-ši-ka*
76 *ina ṣal-ti-ka-ma* *e-li-ka šá-an-ṣa-at*
77 *pa-la-ḫu u ka-na-šá* *ul i-ba-áš-ši it-ti-šá*
78 *lu-u bīta kaš-šat-ma* *ú-ru-ši ina lìb-bi*
79 *a-na kib-si a-ḫe-e* *ú-zu-un-šá tur-rat*
80 *šá-niš*
a-na bīt ir-ru-bu isappuḫ(bir-*uḫ*) *ul i-bar a-ḫi-is-s[a]*

81 *ma-ri lu-u lìb-ba-šú-ma* *šá ru-bé-e at-ta*
82 *na-aṣ-ra-am-ma* ^{zá}*kunukka*(kišib)*-šú* *lu al-lat*
83 *pi-ti-ma ni-ṣir-ta-šú* *e-ru-ub ana lìb-bi*
84 *[ul-l]a-nu-uk-ka-ma* *a-ḫu-u ul ib-ši*
85 *[ma-]ak-kur la ni-bi* *qí-rib-šú tu-ut-ta*
86 *[a-]na mim-ma šu-a-tu* *in-ka e taš-ši*
87 *[a-]a ub-la lìb-ba-ka* *e-pe-eš pu-uz-ru*
88 *[á]r-ka-num-ma* *a-ma-tu in-ni-iṣ[-ṣi-iṣ]*
89 ⸢*ù*⸣ *pu-uz-ru šá te-pu-šú* *ip-pi-[it-ti]*
90 *i-šim-me-ma ru-bu-u* *ú-×[× ×]*
91 *[b]u-un-nu-šú nam-ru-ti* *i-×[× × ×]*
92 ⸢*ù*⸣ *at-ta ta-ra-*⸢*áš-ši a-ma-tam*⸣ × [. . . . . . .]
93 × × ni ma *šá pî nišī*^{meš} [. . . . .]
94 [×] × ni *qa-lal qaqqadi* su × × [. . . . . . .]
95 [× ×] × × × [. . . . .]

VARIANTS

62 e: *e-riš kit-tú pi-[r]a* A:] *kit-tu e-pi-ir* 63 f: *ina*(aš) Af: *ilu* 64 A: *e-]li* ef: *i-rab-* A: *du-[* 65 f: *šum-šu ú-sa-tú* A: *ú-]sa-ta,* u_4*-m]i* 66 A: *b]i-i-ti* 68 e preserves

61 Give food to eat, beer to drink,
62 Grant what is asked, provide for and honour.
63 In this a man's god takes pleasure,
64 It is pleasing to Šamaš, who will repay him with favour.
65 Do charitable deeds, render service all your days.

66 Do not honour a slave girl in your house;
67 She shall not rule [your] bedroom like a wife.
68 [.] . . [. . slave] girls you shall not go yourself,
69 [If she] ascends your . [. . . .] you will not go down.
70 Let this be said [to you among] your peoples,
71 "The house which a slave girl rules, she disrupts."
72 Do not marry a prostitute, whose husbands are legion,
73 A temple harlot who is dedicated to a god,
74 A courtesan whose favours are many.
75 In your trouble she will not support you,
76 In your dispute she will be a mocker;
77 There is no reverence or submissiveness with her.
78 Even if she dominate your house, get her out,
79 For she has directed her attention elsewhere.
80 Variant: She will disrupt the house she enters, and her partner will not assert himself.

81 My son, if it be the wish of the prince that you are his,
82 If you attach his closely guarded seal to your person,
83 Open his treasure house, enter within,
84 For apart from you there is no one else (who may do this).
85 Unlimited wealth you will find inside,
86 But do not covet any of this,
87 Nor set your mind on double-dealing.
88 For afterwards the matter will be investigated
89 And the double-dealing of which you are guilty will be made [known.]
90 The prince will hear, and will . [. .]
91 His smiling countenance will . [. . .]
92 Then you will render account . [. . . . . . .]
93 . . . . by popular repute [. . . . .]
94 [.] . . contempt . . . [. . . . . . .]

---

part of one of the missing signs. 70 A: *i-n*[*a* 72 A: *ḫa-ri*]*m-ta* 75, 76 A: *i-na*
77 A: *pa-la-a-ḫ*[*u* 78 A: *lu-ú* 80 A writes in two lines, insetting the second half: *u*[*l*.

C

96 [. . . .] ×-*ka-ma* [. . . . .]

* * * * *

A

B 124 [. . . . .] × × [. .]

e 125 [×] × [. . . . .] be li [× ×]

126 × ri × [. . . . .] × ma ti *a-ḫ*[*i* ×]

127 *e ta-kul ka*[*r-ṣi*   *q*]*í-bi ba-ni-ti*

128 *lim-né-e-ti e ta-ta-me*   *da-me-eq-ta ti-iz-kàr*

129 *šá a-kil kar-ṣi*   *qa-bu-ú li-mut-ti*

130 *i-na ri-ba-a-ti šá* ^{d}*šamaš*   *ú-qa-'-ú rēs-su*

131 *e tu-ma-ṣi pi-i-ka*   *ú-ṣur šap-ti-ka*

132 *e-nim-me-e kab-ta-ti-ka*   *e-di-iš e taq-bi*

133 *sur-riš ta-ṭa-mu-ú*   *ta-ra-áš-ši ar-ka-niš*

134 *ù ina sa-naq at-me-e*   *tu-šá-an-na-aḫ ṭè-en-ka*

135 *u*$_4$*-mi-šam-ma*   *ìl-ka*   *kit-rab*

136 *ni-qu-u*   *qí-bit pi-i*   *si-mat qut-rin-ni*

137 *a-na ili-ka*   *šà-gi*$_8$*-gur*$_6$*-ra-a*   *lu-u ti-i-ši*

138 *an-nu-um-ma*   *si-mat*   *ilu-ú-ti*

139 *su-up-pu-u*   *su-ul-lu-u*   *u la-ban ap-pi*

140 *ud-da-at*   *ta-nam-din-šum-ma*   *i-rib-ka kaš-šat*

141 *ù a-na at-ri-im-ma*   *it-ti ili*   *tuš-te-šir*

142 *ina iḫ-zi-ka-ma*   *a-mur*   *ina tup-pi*

143 *pa-la-ḫu*   *da-ma-qa*   *ul-la-ad*

144 *ni-qu-u*   *ba-la-ṭu*   [*u*]*t-tar*

145 *ù tés-li-tú*   *ar-ni*   [*i-p*]*aṭ-ṭar*

146 *pa-liḫ ilī*^{meš} *ul i-še-es-su*   ×[×(×)]

147 *pa-liḫ* ^{d}*a-nun-na-ki*   *ur-rak*   [*u*$_4$*-mi-šú*]

148 *it-ti ib-ri u tap-pe-e*   *e ta-ta-me* × [× ×]

149 *šap-la-a-ti e ta-ta-me* ^{mí}*damiqta* [*ti-iz-kar*]

150 *šum-ma taq-ta-bi-ma*   *i-din* × [× ×]

151 [*š*]*um-ma tu-tak-kil-ma*   *ta-*[× ×]

152 [*u a-*]*na tap-pe-e-ma*   ⌜*ṣi*⌝*-b*[*u-ta e-pu-uš*]

153 [*šum-ma*] *tu-tak-kil ib-ri* [. . . . . . .]

154 [*i-na*] *iḫ-zi-k*[*a*]*-ma* [*a-mur ina tup-pi*]

155 [× (×)] muš × [× ×] × [. . . . . . .]

* * * * *

VARIANTS

129 B: *ša*   130 B: *ina*   131 A: *-m*]*a-aṣ-ṣi*   132 B: *i-nim-me-e*   133 e: *sur-riš šá ta-ta-mu-ú ta-ra*[*š-*   134 e: *ina sa-na-qa u at-me-e*   A: [*i*]*-na*   136 A: [*ni-qu-*]*ú*

* * * * *

127 Do not utter libel, speak what is of good report.
128 Do not say evil things, speak well of people.
129 One who utters libel and speaks evil,
130 Men will waylay him with his debit account to Šamaš.
131 Beware of careless talk, guard your lips;
132 Do not utter solemn oaths while alone,
133 For what you say in a moment will follow you afterwards.
134 But exert yourself to restrain your speech.

135 Every day worship your god.
136 Sacrifice and benediction are the proper accompaniment of incense.
137 Present your free-will offering to your god,
138 For this is proper toward the gods.
139 Prayer, supplication, and prostration
140 Offer him daily, and *you will get* your reward.
141 Then you will have full communion with your god.
142 In your wisdom study the tablet.
143 Reverence begets favour,
144 Sacrifice prolongs life,
145 And prayer atones for guilt.
146 He who fears the gods is not slighted by . [. .]
147 He who fears the Anunnaki extends [his days.]

148 With a friend and comrade do not speak . . [. . .]
149 Do not speak hypocrisy, [utter] what is decent.
150 If you have promised, give . [. .]
151 If you have created trust, you must [. .]
152 [And perform] the wish of a comrade.
153 [If] you have created trust in a friend [. . . . . . .]
154 [In] your wisdom [study the tablet.]

* * * * *

137 A: *lu-ú ma*, *tuš-te-eš-šìr* 139 A: -]*pu-ú su-ul-lu-ú* 140 A: *ta-nam-din-áš-šum-ma* 141 A: *at-rim-*

G
156 . . .]× te ni ×[. . .
157 [*u a-na tap-pe-e-m*]*a ṣi-b*[*u-ta e-pu-uš*]
158 . . .] *šá la na-*[. . .]
159 [*i-na iḫ-zi-ka-m*]*a a-mur ina* [*tup-pi*]
A 160 [*dābib? nu?-ul?-l*]*a?-a-te mu-ta-mu-u* [. . .]
161 . . .]× *na-da-ni mu-pat-te u*[*z?-ni?*]
162 . . .] *ṣa-ru-uḫ-šú be-*[*lum?*]
163 . . .] *tuk-ku-lu na-du-*[*u*]
164 . . .]*-ni la na-da-nu ik-kib* ^{d}*mardu*[*k*]
165 [*u* ^{d}*iš-me-k*]*a-ra-bu mār* ^{d}*en-líl-bàn-d*[*a*]
166 . . .]× ^{d}*é-a ú-sap-pa iš-*[*šèr?*]

157 [And perform] the wish [of a comrade.]
158 . . .] without . [. . .]
159 [In your wisdom] study [the tablet.]
160 [He who speaks(?)] slander and gives utterance to [. . .]
161 . . .] . giving, who spreads [information(?)]
162 . . . the lord] is enraged with him.
163 . . .] to create trust and then to abandon,
164 To [. . . . . .] and not to give is an abomination to Marduk
165 [And Išme-]karābu son of Enlilbanda.
166 . . .] . Ea, he will pray and will [prosper(?)]

COLOPHONS

e: ⋆ ⋆ ⋆ ⋆ ⋆
[. . . . . . .] igi.tab
[. . . . . a ^{m}*ḫ*]*u-ṣa-bi*
[. . . . . *ina*] *sar-tú la i-tab-bal*
[itu . . . . mu.]an.na 7 kám
[^{m}*ár-tak-šat-su* lugal] kur.kur

A: [*ki-ma la-bi-r*]*i ša*$_{12}$*-ṭir-ma* igi.k[ár]

Possible Beginnings of the *Counsels of Wisdom*

The following two fragments are clearly the beginnings of texts belonging to the same category as the *Counsels of Wisdom*. One of them, the first perhaps, could even be the missing first few lines.

K 13770 (Pl. 27):

um-ma-nu i[- . . .	A learned man . [. . .
i-na né-me-qí ×[. . .	In wisdom . [. . .
al-ka ma-r[*i* . . .	"Come, my son [. . .

a-na ur-ti š[á . . .	To the command which [. . .
mil-ki li-m[ad . . .	[Take] in my advice [. . .
la mun-tal-k[um-ma . . .	One who is no savant [. . .
šu-tur a-na d[u . . .	Excelling in . [. . .
[×] × *šá* sag [. . .	
[. . .] × × [. . .	

80–7–19, 283 (Pl. 27):

a-me-lu-tum ša di i[d . . .	Mankind . . . [. . .
ṣab-ti kit-tu ina qa-t[i- . . .	Take hold of truth in [your] hands [. .
iḫ-ḫa-la-ṣi-i [. . .	It slips [. . .
šum-ma e-tab-× [. . .	If . . . [. . .
la tu-uš-ta[- . . .	Do not . . [. . .
ta-SAR-*ri* × [. . .	You must . . . [. . .
[*l*]*a ta-ḫa-á*[*š* . . .	Do not hasten [. . .
[×] × × [. . .	

The first line could be read: *ša ṭi-i*[*ṭ-ṭi* "of clay".

(iii) *COUNSELS OF A PESSIMIST*

INTRODUCTION

This small oblong tablet in shape and matter appears to be an extract from a larger work. It takes the form of an address either to a specific person, or simply to the reader. There is no certainty even that the complete work was a Wisdom text, though the 31 lines might easily be one from a number of similar pieces, a paragraph from some other "Counsels of Wisdom". The sense of the first three lines is lost, but 5–10 unmistakably preach the transitory nature of all human life and activity. Confronted with this situation the writer counsels the reader, or who it may be, to continue the duties of religion, and not to neglect the agricultural tasks. Prostration to the city goddess (not, curiously, the personal god) will result in offspring, and two lines (15–16) are devoted to further instruction on children. Unfortunately neither yields any sense. Suddenly the subject changes to the averting of bad dreams. It is not clear what connexion, if any, is to be understood. Line 19 explains that worry or suffering is responsible for these dreams, and so a carefree attitude to life is recommended.

No positive suggestion can be made about date. It cannot be later than Ashurbanipal, from whose library the tablet comes, nor is it likely to be earlier than the First Dynasty of Babylon.

LITERATURE

TEXT	EDITION
1906 K. D. Macmillan, *BA* v. 624–5.	Ibid., pp. 562–4.

Cf. also: S. Du Toit, *Bybelse en Babilonies-Assiriese Spreuke*, p. 165; A. L. Oppenheim, *Dreams*, p. 227.

K 1453 (Plate 30)

OBVERSE

1 [šumma? . . . .]×-ka-ma i-liš tu-maš-[šal]
2 [. . . . .]× ri × (×) ka ta-×-[×]
3 [. . . . . u]l-ṣa × [× (×)] ⌜ip-pu-uš-ma⌝
4 [. . . . .] × × × [× (×)] × ep-ru-um-ma
5 [. . . . .] × qa r[u] i-gam-mar
6 [. . . . .] i-ta-ri a-na ṭi-iṭ-ṭi
7 [. . . . .]× ^{d}girra i-qam-me
8 [. . . . . ul u]ṣ-ṣi a-na ár-kàt u$_4$-me
9 [. . . . . .] niši^{meš} ib-na-a   ul i-si-it a-na da-riš
10 [a-me-l]u-tum ù ši-pir ib-ba-nu-ú   iš-te-niš i-qat-t[i]
11 [at-]ta a-na ilim-ma   su-pe-e šu-taq-rib
12 lu-u ka-a-a-an šagigurû(šà.gi$_8$.gur$_6$)-ka   a-na ili ba-ni-ka
13 a-na ^{d}iš-tar āli-ka lu-u kan-šá-ta-ma   lid-din-ka pir-'a
14 a-na bu-ú-li kit-pad   e-re-šá ḫi-is-sa-as
15 a-na bu-[u]k-ri u bi-in-ti   šu-[qa]m-me-em ⌜šúm⌝-'-u-diš
16 [bu-u]k-r[a] u bi-in-ta   šu-uš-di-da šar-ma-'
17 [a-a] im-qut a-na lìb-bi-ka   li-mut-tum šit-tum
18 [qu-]⌜ú⌝-lu ù ku-ú-ru   i-du-uk-ka šu-us-si
19 [qu-]⌜ú⌝-lu ù ku-ú-ru   i-ban-ni šu-ut-ta

REVERSE

20 [l]u šuttu(máš.ge$_6$) mu-šal-mu na-at   ú ši kur lìb-bu-uk
21 šu-ut-bi-ma lìb[-ba-ka . . . .] šu-ud-ki
22 ⌜zi-mu-ka⌝ [. . . . . l]u-u ṣu-uḫ-ḫu
23–31 detached signs. Illegible traces of a colophon remain.

1 [If?] you will make your [. . . . . . .] like a god's,
2 [. . . . .] . . . . [.]
3 [. . . . .] makes joy . [. .]
4 [. . . . .] . . . [. .] . is dust,
5 [. . . . .] . . . is finished,
6 [. . . . .] turns to clay,
7 [. . . . .] . fire burns it,
8 [. . . . . does not] continue for eternity,
9 [Whatever] men do does not last for ever,
10 Mankind and their achievements alike come to an end.
11 [As for] you, offer prayers to (your) god,
12 Let your free-will offering be constantly before the god who created you,
13 Bow down to your city goddess that she may grant you offspring,
14 Take thought for your livestock, remember the planting.
15 For your first-born son and daughter . . . .
16 Cause your [first-born] son and daughter to . . . .
17 Do [not] let evil sleep afflict your heart;
18 Banish misery and suffering from your side;
19 Misery and suffering produce a dream,

20 Though the dream makes bad . . . your heart.
21 Let [your] heart be quit of [. . . . .] remove [. . . . .]
22 Your countenance [. . . . .] may [your face] smile.

* * * * *

(iv) *ADVICE TO A PRINCE*

The impression is sometimes gained that ancient Mesopotamian kings were typical oriental despots, following their own whims, and unchallenged within their domains. In contrast the authority of the Hittite kings is known to have been carefully circumscribed by law,[1] and the Hebrew prophets fearlessly denounced their kings for any abuse of power. The *Advice* serves as a salutary corrective to this exaggerated contrast. It sets out to caution a king against the divine retribution which will overtake him should he oppress his subjects. At the end the king's officers are similarly warned. The text is written on a tablet from the libraries of Ashurbanipal, and no duplicate copy has yet been found. The form of the words is peculiar. The writer has imitated the style of omens. The ancient Mesopotamians believed that the future could be ascertained from current events. Not only extraordinary phenomena such as an eclipse or the birth of a physically abnormal creature were considered portents, but even such trivial things as a lizard on a wall were regarded as ominous. The Babylonian scholars had made vast compilations of such occurrences with their interpretations, for example: "If tears flow from both eyes of an ox, some evil thing will overtake its owner." These omens betray no prophylactic interest: the reason for the ox's tears is not sought, and the emphasis is entirely on the destined sequence of events.

This literary form was well suited for warnings to a king. The completely general protasis, "If a king . . .", avoided any insinuations against him, and the stressed apodosis conveyed the warning very effectively. The omen style of this work consists of more than sentences beginning with conditional clauses. The syntax of omens is as loose as that of modern headlines. No ambiguity, however, results, for the material of omens is very stereotyped. In our text the syntax is equally loose, but the wider range of thought and expression causes some uncertainty, and a measure of faith has to be used in translating. Also some of the phraseology is directly borrowed from omens: "his land will rebel against him" (5) and "the *status quo* in his land will change" (6) are frequent omen apodoses. Further, the term "chief officer" (*šūt rēši* 14, 45, 55) is an item of omen vocabulary from the Old Babylonian period onwards,[2] an important observation because in the late period this term is only used among the Assyrians. Palaeographically too this text is related to omens in its frequent use of ideograms where other types of texts would write out the words syllabically.

Böhl believed that an even closer dependence on omens existed. It is known that the first protasis of Tablet 53 of the omen series *Šumma ālu* was, "If a king heeds justice", which differs from the opening words of our text only by its being positive instead of negative. The tablet as a whole is not preserved, but it is improbable that it served as a model for our author. The *Advice* is much more specific and detailed than anything found in omens. It is also curious that the writer departs from omen practice in consistently leaving the "If" unexpressed.

[1] See O. R. Gurney, *The Hittites*, p. 69.

[2] Cf., e.g., *YOS* x. 25. 61.

Both Böhl and Diakonoff place this text in the Late Assyrian period. The aim of the text is clearly to protect the rights of the citizens of Sippar, Nippur, and Babylon from taxation, forced labour, and misappropriation of their property. The Assyrian Sargon II in his inscriptions professes to have done just this for these cities, even using an identical phrase.[1] Böhl therefore suggests Merodach-baladan the Chaldean as the king to whom the priestly classes of these cities were opposed, and who was warned by this writing. Diakonoff considers the Assyrian Sennacherib the most probable king because of his notorious anti-Babylonian policy. Both of these suggestions involve difficulties. The author of this text was seeking to maintain the privileges of the three ancient cities. He writes about the king as though he would be involved in any disaster which might overtake these cities (19–22; 35). Also the writer uses "foreigner" in a way which suggests that the king was, in contrast, a native (9, 40). Neither a Chaldean nor an Assyrian fits into this background. The king concerned need not have been an important figure historically. Indeed the picture of a monarch practising extortion on his own cities and trying to buy foreign aid, whether from Chaldeans, Assyrians, or from any other people, implies a very weak king vainly trying to become great. The loose style of the piece suggests one of the kings of Babylon between 1000 and 700 B.C.

LITERATURE

TEXT

1875 H. C. Rawlinson *et al.* IV R^1 55.

1891 H. C. Rawlinson *et al.* IV R^2 48.

1902 L. W. King, *CT* 15. 50.

EDITIONS, TRANSLATIONS, STUDIES

1875 G. Smith, *Assyrian Discoveries*[4], pp. 96–97 and 410–11.

1876 A. H. Sayce, *Records of the Past* VII. 117–22.

1890 A. Boissier, *Recherches sur quelques contrats babyloniens*, pp. 7–20.

1907 S. H. Langdon, *JAOS* 28. 145–54.

1920 B. Meissner, *Babylonien und Assyrien* I. 65–66.

1937 F. M. Th. Böhl, *MAOG* XI/3: *Der babylonische Fürstenspiegel.*

1946 I. M. Diakonoff, *Vestnik Drevnei Istorii* 1946/4 (cf. *RA* 44. 101).

[1] *šá-kin šu-ba-re-e sippar*[ki] *nippuri*[ki] *bābili*[ki] (e.g. H. Winckler, *Die Keilschrifttexte Sargons*, Atlas, pl. 43, Cylinder, 4).

DT 1 (Plates 31, 32)

1 *šarru a-na di-ni la i-qúl niši*^{meš}*-šú innešša*(sùḫ.me-*a*) *māt-su in-nam-mi*

2 *a-na di-in māti-šú la i-qúl* ^{d}*é-a šàr šīmāti*(nam.meš)
3 *šim-ta-šú ú-ša-an-ni-ma a-ḫi-ta irteneddī*(uš.me)*-šú*
4 *a-na rubî*^{me}*-šú la i-qúl ūmī*^{meš}*-šú ikarrû*(lugúd.da.meš)
5 *a-na ummâni*(um.me.a) *la i-qúl māt-su ibbalakkit*(bal)*-su*
6 *a-na is-ḫap-pi i-qúl ṭēm*(umuš) *māti išanni*(man-*ni*)
7 *a-na ši-pir* ^{d}*é-a i-qúl ilī*^{meš} *rabûti*^{meš}
8 *ina ši-tul-ti ù ṭú-da-at mi-šá-ri irteneddû*(uš.me)*-šú*
9 *mār sippar*^{ki} *i-da-aṣ-ma a-ḫa-am i-din* ^{d}*šamaš dayyān šamê u erṣeti*

10 *di-na a-ḫa-am ina māti-šú išakkan-ma rubî*^{me} *u dayyānī*^{me} *ana di-nim ul iqullu*(me.me)
11 *mārī*^{meš} *nippuri*^{ki} *ana di-nim ub-lu-ni-šum-ma kat*$_{5}$*-ra-a ilqē*(ti)*-ma i-da-as-su-nu-tì*
12 ^{d}*en-líl bēl mātāti*(kur.kur) ^{lú}*nakra a-ḫa-a-am*
13 *i-da-kaš-šum-ma ummānāti*(erín.ḫi.a)*-šu ú-šam-qá-tì*
14 *rubû u šu-ut rēši-šu ina sūqi*(e.sír) *zi-lul-liš iṣ-ṣa-nun-du*
15 *kasap mārī*^{meš} *bābili*^{ki} *ilqē*(ti-*e*)*-ma ana makkūri*(níg.ga) *ú-še-ri-bu*
16 *di-in bābilā'a*(lú.din.tir.ki.meš) *išmē*(giš.tuku)*-ma ana qa-li tur-ru*
17 ^{d}*marduk bēl šamê u erṣeti a-a-bi-šu elī-šú išakkan-ma*
18 *bušâ*(níg.⟨šu⟩)*-šu makkūra*(níg.ga)*-šu ana* ^{lú}*nakri-šú i-šar-rak*
19 *mār nippuri*^{ki} ^{uru}*sip-par bābili*(din.tir.ki) *an-na e-me-da*
20 *a-na bīt ṣi-bit-tim šu-ru-bu*
21 *a-šar an-nam* ⸢*in-né-en*⸣*-du ālu ana bērūti*(sur$_{7}$)*-šu iššappak*(dub-*ak*)
22 *a-na bīt ṣi-bit-tim šu-ru-bu* ^{lú}*nakru aḫû*(bar-*ú*) *errub*(tu-*ub*)
23 *sippar*^{ki} *nippuru*^{ki} *u bābilu*(din.tir.ki) *mitḫāriš*(ur.bi.ta) *ušatbi*(zi!-*bi*)
24 *ṣābī*(erín.meš) *šu-nu-tì tup-ši-ik-ka e-me-da-am*
25 *il-ki ši-si-it* ^{lú}*na-gi-ri e-li-šú-nu ú-kan-nu*
26 ^{d}*marduk apkal ilī*^{meš} *rubû muš-ta-lum*
27 *māt-su a-na* ^{lú}*nakri-šú ú-saḫ-ḫar-ma*
28 *ummāni*(erín-*ni*) *māti-šu tup-ši-ik-ka a-na* ^{lú}*nakri-šú i-za-bil*
29 *ṣābī*(erín.meš) *šú-nu-tì* ^{d}*a-num* ^{d}*en-líl u* ^{d}*é-a ilī*(dingir.dingir) *rabûti*(gal.gal)
30 *a-ši-bi šamê u erṣeti ina pu-uḫ-ri-šú-nu šu-ba-ra-šú-nu ú-kin-nu*
31 *mār sippar*^{ki} *nippuri*^{ki} *u bābili*(din.tir.ki)
32 *im-ra-šú-nu a-na mur-ni-is-qí šá-ra-ki*
33 *mur-ni-is-qí šu-ut im-ra-šú-nu i-ku-lu*
34 *a-na ṣi-mit-ti a-a-bi ir-red-du-ú*
35 *ṣābī*(erín.meš) *šú-nu-tú i-na di-ku-ti um-man māti* ⸢*itti ṣābī*⸣(⸢erín.meš⸣) *šarri ì-de-ku-ú*

NOTE: zi!-*bi* in 23 is an emendation of NAM-*bi*

[1] If a king does not heed justice, his people will be thrown into chaos, and his land will be devastated.

[2] If he does not heed the justice of his land, Ea, king of destinies, [3] will alter his destiny and will not cease from hostilely pursuing him.

[4] If he does not heed his nobles, his life will be cut short.

[5] If he does not heed his adviser, his land will rebel against him.

[6] If he heeds a rogue, the *status quo* in his land will change.

[7] If he heeds a trick of Ea, the great gods [8] in unison and in their just ways will not cease from prosecuting him.

[9] If he improperly convicts a citizen of Sippar, but acquits a foreigner, Šamaš, judge of heaven and earth, [10] will set up a foreign justice in his land, where the princes and judges will not heed justice.

[11] If citizens of Nippur are brought to him for judgement, but he accepts a present and improperly convicts them, [12] Enlil, lord of the lands, will bring a foreign army against him [13] to slaughter his army, [14] whose prince and chief officers will roam (his) streets like fighting-cocks.

[15] If he takes the silver of the citizens of Babylon and adds it to his own coffers, [16] or if he hears a lawsuit involving men of Babylon but treats it frivolously, [17] Marduk, lord of heaven and earth, will set his foes upon him, [18] and will give his property and wealth to his enemy.

[19] If he imposes a fine on the citizens of Nippur, Sippar, or Babylon, [20] or if he puts them in prison, [21] the city where the fine was imposed will be completely overturned, [22] and a foreign enemy will make his way into the prison in which they were put.

[23] If he mobilized the whole of Sippar, Nippur, and Babylon, [24] and imposed forced labour on the people, [25] exacting from them a corvée at the herald's proclamation, [26] Marduk, the sage of the gods, the prince, the counsellor, [27] will turn his land over to his enemy [28] so that the troops of his land will do forced labour for his enemy, [29] for Anu, Enlil, and Ea, the great gods, [30] who dwell in heaven and earth, in their assembly affirmed the freedom of those people from such obligations.

[31, 32] If he gives the fodder of the citizens of Sippar, Nippur, and Babylon to (his own) steeds, [33] the steeds who eat the fodder [34] will be led away to the enemy's yoke, [35] and those men will be mobilized with the king's men when the national army is conscripted.

36 ^{d}*èr-ra gaš-ra* [*a-lik p*]*a-an ummāni*(erín-*ni*)-*šú*
37 *pa-an ummāni*(erín-*ni*)-*šú imaḫḫaṣ*(sìg)-*ma idi* [^{lú}*nak*]*ri-šú illak*(gin-*ak*)
38 *ṣi-in-da-at alpī*^{meš}-*š*[*ú-nu*] *ú-paṭ-ṭar-ú-ma*
39 *eqlēti*^{meš}[-*šú-nu*] ⸢*ú*⸣-*šá-an-nu-ú*
40 *a-na a-ḫe-e*! *ì-šar-ra-k*[*u* . . . . . . ^{d}*ad*]*du i-ḫar-ru-up*
41 *ṣi-bit-ti imm*[*erī*(udu.[nita.meš) . . . . .]× *i-ṣab-ba-tu*
42 ^{d}*addu gú-gal šamê u erṣeti*
43 *nam-maš-še-e ṣēri-šú ina ḫu-šaḫ-ḫi ú-šam-qat-ma*
44 *nīqī*(sizkur.sizkur) ^{d}*šamši ú-šá-gar-šá*
45 *um-ma-an u šu-ut rēši man-za-az pa-an šarri*
46 *a-mat-sun ú-lam-man ṭa-as-sun i-maḫ-ḫar*
47 *ina qí-bit* ^{d}*é-a šàr apsî*
48 *um-ma-an u šu-ut rēši ina* [^{gi}]^{š}*kakki imuttu*(úš.meš)
49 *a-šar-šú-nu a-na na-me-*⸢*e*⸣ [*i*]*k-ka-am-mar*
50 *ar-kat*$_{5}$!-*sun šá-a-ru i-tab-bal ep-šet-sun za-*⸢*qí-qí*⸣*-iš im-man-ni*
51 *rik-si-šu-un ú-paṭ-ṭar-ú-ma nārâ*(zá.na.rú.a)-*šú-nu* ⸢*ú*⸣-*šá-an-nu-ú*
52 *a-na ḫarrāni ú-še-eṣ-ṣu-šú-nu-tì a-na a-de-e i-*[× ×]-*šú-nu-ti*
53 ^{d}*nābû tup-šar é-sag-íl sa-níq kiššat*(šár) *šamê u erṣeti mu-ma-*'-[*ir*] *gim-ri*
54 *mu-ad-du-ú šarru-tú rik-sat māti-šú ú-paṭ-ṭar-ma*! *a-*⸢*ḫi-ta*⸣ *i-šam*
55 *lu* ^{lú}*rē'û lu* ^{lú}*šà-tam ēkurri lu šu-ut rēši šarri*
56 *šá ina sippar*^{ki} *nippuri*^{ki} *u bābili*(din.tir.ki) *a-na* ^{lú}*šà-tam ēkurri izzazzu*^{zu}
57 *tup-šik-ku bītāt*^{meš} *ilī*(dingir.dingir) *rabûti*(gal.gal) *im-me-du-šú-nu-tì*
58 *ilī*(dingir.dingir) *rabûti*(gal.gal) ⸢*i-gu*⸣*-gu-ma ì-né-es-su-ú at-ma-an-šu-un*
59 *là ir-ru-bu a-na ki-iṣ-ṣi-šu-un*

š[*arru a-na di-*]*nim la i-qúl* al.til

NOTE: *a-ḫe-e* in 40 is an emendation of *a-ḫi-a*
the scribe has written ma+kàd in 50 instead of šu+kàd
ú-paṭ-ṭar-ma in 54 is an emendation of *ú-paṭ-ṭar-*GIŠ

[36] Mighty Era, [who goes] before his army, [37] will shatter his front line and go at his enemy's side.

[38] If he looses the yokes of [their] oxen [39] and puts them in other fields [40] or gives them to a foreigner, [. . .] will be devastated [. .] of Addu.

[41] If he seizes [their . . . .] stock of sheep, [42] Addu, canal supervisor of heaven and earth, [43] will extirpate his pasturing animals by hunger [44] and will amass offerings for Šamaš.

[45] If the adviser or chief officer of the king's presence [46] denounces them (i.e. the citizens of Sippar, Nippur, and Babylon) and so obtains bribes from them, [47] at the command of Ea, king of the Apsû, [48] the adviser and chief officer will die by the sword, [49] their place will be covered over as a ruin, [50] the wind will carry away their remains, and their achievements will be given over to the storm wind.

[51] If he declares their treaties void, or alters their inscribed (treaty) stele, [52] sends them on a campaign, or [press-gangs] them into hard labour, [53] Nābû, scribe of Esagil, who organizes the whole of heaven and earth, who directs everything, [54] who ordains kingship, will declare the treaties of his land void, and will decree hostility.

[55] If either a shepherd, or a temple overseer, or a chief officer of the king, [56] who serves as temple overseer of Sippar, Nippur, or Babylon, [57] imposes forced labour on them (i.e. the citizens of Sippar, Nippur, or Babylon) in connexion with the temples of the great gods, [58] the great gods will quit their dwellings in their fury [59] and will not enter their shrines.

(v) *VARIA*

An Akkado-Hurrian Bilingual from Ras Shamra

This text from a town on the Syrian coast dates from the fourteenth century B.C. Though Akkado-Hurrian bilinguals are rare, this is by no means a unique piece, as religious texts in the same two languages have been found at Mari, from the Old Babylonian period (*RA* 36. 1–28). A definitive edition of this piece can only be attempted with a full treatment of both versions, so for the present occasion it must suffice to give a transliteration and provisional translation of the Akkadian only. A detailed study has been promised by E. A. Speiser. The text consists of two sections dealing with one topic each. The Akkadian version of each one is given first and is followed by the Hurrian. The Akkadian is very difficult in a number of passages, and it is not clear if this is a piece of Akkadian literature imported from Mesopotamia, though general considerations would favour this idea. Nor can it be assumed that the two versions are exact equivalents of each other.

LITERATURE

TEXT	EDITION
1955 J. Nougayrol, *Le Palais royal d'Ugarit* III, pl. CVI.	1955 J. Nougayrol and E. Laroche, op. cit., pp. 311–24 (cf. E. A. Speiser, *JAOS* 75.165).

1 *šu-ku-un kaspi*^{meš} *ša ma-mi-ti it-ti ili*^{meš} *te-le-eq-*[*q*]*ì*
2 *ma-mi-tá pí-la-ḫé-ma pa-gàr-ka šul-lim*
3 *tá-me-e a-na na-ri ka-li a-pí-il* ZI
4 *du-ri-iš mar-ḫé-ta-šu māra*(dumu) *ú-ul i-šu*

---

10 ⸢*la*⸣ *mu-du-ú ar-na a-na ili*^{meš}*-šu ḫé-mu-uṭ*
11 *la-a-am-tal-la-ak ḫa-am-ṭì-iš a-na ili*^{meš} *i-na-aš-ši qātē*^{meš}*-šu*
12 × × du *ar-nu-šu al pí-ka ša-qa-tá-ma*
13 *la i-*de_4*-ma amēlu a-na ili*^{meš}*-šu ḫé-mu-uṭ*

The first word of 12 is read *la?-*dir_4*?-tù* by Nougayrol, but *ma-'-du* is suggested by Speiser.

1 Deposit the money for the oath, for you will take it (again) from the god.
2 Respect the oath, and save yourself.
3 He who swears (falsely) in the river ordeal . . heir .,
4 His wife will never have a son.

---

10 One who acknowledges no guilt rushes to his god,
11 Without thinking he quickly raises his hands (in prayer) to the god.
12 . . . his guilt . . . .
13 A man in ignorance rushes to his god.

SU 1952, 15+91+186+350 and SU 1952, 23

A copy of this text is to be published by O. R. Gurney in *STT* II. The two separate pieces apparently belong to the same tablet, which is certainly a Wisdom text. Unfortunately there is not one complete line, and only a small number of complete words, so that a transliteration would be of little use. It is, however, worth describing. The opening section, of not less than about 30 lines, consists of clauses with the verb in the infinitive for the beginning of each line, and *ik-kib* ^{d}*nammu* ends each line, i.e. "to do such and such is an abomination to the god Nammu". After this the text seems to break into ethical admonitions without any such framework. Two adjacent sayings have been identified, one in the *Dialogue of Pessimism*, the other in bilingual proverbs, which suggests that the work is a compilation of traditional material. See *Dialogue of Pessimism* 32–33, and Bilingual Proverbs, BM 38596 obv. I. 13–15.

K 9908

The fragment K 9908 (Pl. 30) may belong to an ethical text:

1 . . .]× *i-ba* ×[. . .
2 . . . *-k*]*a mi-ti ba-liṭ* [. . .
3 . . .]× *-šú* ^{d}*šēdī*(alàd.meš) ×[. . .
4 . . .]× *-kám-ma a-di ūmī*^{meš} *bal-ṭu*: *a-mat la* ×[. . .
5 . . .]× *ni-iš ilī*^{meš} [. . .
6 . . .] *a-na né-e-ri ul* ×[. . .
7 . . .*-z*]*u ina e-peš šip-ri-šú in-na-saḫ m*[*i-* . . .
8 . . .]× *la a-dir di-*×[. . .
9 . . .]× *šá ri-id-di šal-m*[*u* . . .
10 . . .]× *-ru-u giš-par-ra-šú* ×[. . .

5

PRECEPTIVE HYMNS

(i) A BILINGUAL *HYMN to NINURTA*

VAT 10610 is a minutely written two-column bilingual tablet, in script quite unlike tablets written in Assur, where it was found. E. Weidner is undoubtedly correct in assigning its use in Assur to the Middle Assyrian period, and in taking it for an importation from Babylon, or a clever copy of one (*AfO* 16. 199–200). Weidner's further deduction that Tukulti-Ninurta I brought such tablets to Assur in the booty from Babylon is now proved correct by a newly published piece of the *Tukulti-Ninurta Epic* (*AfO* 18. 44. 3–8). The tablet is then one of the few surviving Cassite-period religious tablets.

The text appears to be a hymn to a god whose name is not preserved, though the reference to his entering the temple Ešumeša leaves no doubt that this is Ninurta. The obverse contains ethical injunctions, which are a well-known feature of some Sumerian hymns, and the reverse addresses the god as he enters his shrine in words reminiscent, for example, of *KAR* 15+16, a "Prozessionshymnus zum Ehren der Ninkarrag" (E. Ebeling, *MVAG* 23/1. 52).

LITERATURE

TEXT

1917 E. Ebeling, *KAR* 119.

EDITIONS, TRANSLATIONS

1917 E. Ebeling, *MDOG* 58. 39–40.

1918 E. Ebeling, *MVAG* 23/1. 78–81; *MVAG* 23/2. 79.

1925 B. Meissner, *Babylonien und Assyrien* II. 420–1.

1953 J. J. A. Van Dijk, *La Sagesse*, pp. 114–18.

VAT 10610 (Plate 32)

OBVERSE

1	[. . . . .]	× × [. . . . .]
2	[. . . . . .] × × × ×	*pár-ṣú-šu* di × [. . . . .]
3	[lú] dam.lú.da ná.a	nam.tag.ga dugud[.àm]
4	*ra-ḫu-ú aš-ti a-wi-lim*	*a-ra-an-šu kab-*[*tum-ma*]
5	lú níg.nu.gar.ra gu$_4$ bal.e	lú eme.sig.ga k[ú.(kú).a]
6	*mu-ta-mu-ú nu-ul-la-a-ti*	*a-kil kar-ṣi*
7	lú gaba.ri egir.ra.ni	šu.ḫul bí.in.dù.a
8	*ša ar-ki mi-iḫ-ri-šu*	*ú-ba-an li-mut-ti i-tar-ra-ṣ*[*ú*]
9	lú du$_{11}$.du$_{11}$.ga nu.me.a im.ri.a.šè	mu.un.šub.ba
10	*šá la qá-bi-tam el a-ḫi*	*i-na-ad-du-ú*
11	lú lú.mašdá.e	nam.gú bí.in.ag.a
12	*šá muš-ki-na*	*i-ḫa-ab-bi-lu*$_4$
13	lú.nam.kala.ga si.ga sag.e.éš	bí.in.rig$_7$.ga
14	*en-ša ana da-an-ni*	*i-šar-ra*[*-ku*]
15	a.ša.an.gàr.ra dumu.uru.na.ka	á íb.⸢ta⸣.a[n . . . .]
16	*šá ina ta-aš-qir-ti mār āli-šu*	*ú-ša-*[. . . . . .]
17	aš.daḫ a.šà.ga.tab.ba.na.ka	× [. . . . .]
18	*ar-da-du šá ina eqli tap-pi-šu*	[. . . . .]
19	× × × (×) ki e$_{11}$ la	nam[. . . . . . .]
20, 21	traces	

OBVERSE

3 He who has intercourse with (another) man's wife, his guilt is grievous.
5 One who utters slander, who is guilty of backbiting,
7 Who spreads vile rumours about his equal,
9 Who lays malign charges against his brother,
11 Who oppresses the poor,
13 Who gives the weak into the power of the strong,
15 Who . . [. . .] a fellow citizen with lies,
17 A bully, who, in his neighbour's field . [. . . . .]

REVERSE

1 traces
2 ^{urudu}ùb á.lá × [. . . . . mu.r]a.an.tuku.[ne]
3 *ḫ[a-a]l-ḫal-la-tu a-lu[-ú . . . .]× -tu iz-za-am-mu-[ru-ku]*
4 sizkur.sizkur.lugal.la gu$_4$.niga ud[u.niga] mu.ra.an.gaz.[gaz.e.ne]
5 *ni-iq šar-rim alpī*^{meš} *marûti*^{meš} *i[mmerī*^{meš} *marûti*^{meš}*] up-tál-la-k[u-ku]*
6 guruš á.tuku.bi gešpú lirum.ma mu.ra.an.ra.r[a.e.ne]
7 *eṭ-lu-tu be-el e-mu-qí ina ú-ma-ši u a-ba-ri im-taḫ-ḫa-ṣ[ú × ×]×*
8 dumu nibru^{ki} ildú.ildú.ba ḫé.gál.ta u$_4$ mu.[× ×]
9 *mārū*^{meš} *ni-ip-pu-ru ina il-la-ti-šu-nu ḫi-in-gál-la uš-*[× × (×)]
10 šèr.zu un.sag.ge$_6$.ga me.téš im.i.i.[(×)]
11 *zi-im-ri-ka ni-šu ṣal-mat qaq-qa-di ut-ta-'-a-d[u]*
12 ki.bi.ta igi.zu gar.ra.[zu.dè]
13 *iš-tu aš-ri šu-a-tum pa-ni-ka ina ša-ka-ni-[ka]*
14 ká.gal.ú.zug bar.šèg.gá.bi tu.ra.[zu.dè]
15 *ina a-bu-ul ú-suk-ki sar-bi-iš ina e-re-bi-i-[ka]*
16 sila.dagal.ká.gal.ú.zug.sil$_6$.lá.gál.la dib.bi.da.zu.[dè]
17 *ina re-bit a-bu-ul ú-suk-ki šá ri-šá-ti ma-la-a-at ina ba-i-k[a]*
18 ⌜é⌝.šu.me.ša$_4$ é.an.ki.da.lá.a bal.e.da.zu.[dè]
19 *[ana é-šu-]me-ša$_4$ bītu šá ana šamê*^{e} *u erṣetim*^{tim} *tar-ṣú ina e-re[-bi-ka]*
20 [. . .]× ki.ága.zu igi.lá.e.× [. . .]
21 [. . . . *n]a-⌜ram⌝-ti-ka ina n[a-ṭa-li-ka]*

REVERSE

2 Drum and cymbal [. . . . . . .] sing out to you,
4 Fat oxen and [fat] sheep are slaughtered for you as the king's offering,
6 Athletic young men fight for you with physique and might,
8 The citizens of Nippur by families . . [. .] prosperity,
10 The dark-headed people sing your songs of praise.
12 When [you] set your eyes on this place,
14 When [you] enter the Gate of the Impure like a storm,
16 When you tread the square of the Gate of the Impure, which is full of rejoicing,
18 When you enter Ešumeša, the house which stretches to heaven and the underworld,
20 When [you] behold your beloved [. . . .]

(ii) *THE ŠAMAŠ HYMN*

INTRODUCTION

This composition of exactly 200 lines is one of the largest and most beautiful cuneiform hymns. Unlike most compositions of this kind it seems never to have been used as an incantation, and lacks én ("Incantation") at the beginning. Its content is not suitable for such a purpose. Nearly all the manuscripts contain this one text only, written in four columns, but there is a fragment of a right-hand portion of a tablet (F) which contains parts of the first ten lines preceded by the remains of two other lines. Too little of these is preserved to be able to ascertain the nature of the preceding text, but clearly the hymn was part of a larger whole, a conclusion reinforced by the catch-line of another hymn to Šamaš written at the end on MS. A. Undoubtedly the hymn had a liturgical use and was presumably composed with this end in view.

In the priestly hierarchy of gods as represented in the lists of deities, Šamaš, the sun god, was only of second rank, and in certain periods other gods, such as Marduk in the First Dynasty of Babylon and Ninurta in late Middle Assyrian times, were promoted to a pre-eminent place, but never Šamaš. He was, however, as shown in Chapter 1, always held in respect and occupied an important place in Mesopotamian thought as the god of justice. In this hymn he is praised first as the giver of light throughout the universe (1–20), then as the god who cares for every creature (21–52), the revealer of secrets, and the one who looks after those in especial need (53–82). Now the line of thought turns to justice, and a number of offences against Šamaš are listed, chiefly malpractices in business, with the inescapable retribution stressed. In contrast to each offender the virtuous trader is described, again with stress on the rewards that Šamaš gives (83–127). At this point another section begins, which emphasizes how the all-seeing eyes of Šamaš are watching over those spheres of life which men see least—the poor, the hunters, travellers, even highwaymen and wandering souls in areas remote from human habitations (128–48). This passage ends with a plea of the speaker that Šamaš will curse none of these—the only personal note in the whole hymn. After further praise for the giving of omens (149–55) there is a reference to the monthly festival when beer was libated to him and he granted the wishes of his worshippers (156–66). After a few lines not knit in the context (167–73) there is a renewal of praise for the light of the sun, even as the controlling force in climate and season (174–83). The rest of the hymn is badly preserved; apparently it ended with a conventional plea that Šamaš may be appeased by some other deity, not a worthy conclusion to the elevated thought of the whole.

In subject matter there is no very rigorous arrangement of topics. The same is true of metre. All the manuscripts, except F, have rulings after every second line as though the hymn consisted of 100 couplets. A very superficial study shows that this is a purely mechanical arrangement of the text, since such an obvious couplet as 174–5 is split by the scribes' rulings. An empirical examination shows that the couplet is the most common grouping of lines, but triplets and odd lines are not absent; that in some passages it is difficult to decide how to divide the lines; and that there is no strophic arrangement even in the section which lends itself to such treatment by contrasting a series of good and bad merchants. The individual lines show a similar state of affairs. The general pattern is the standard rhythm of four principal stresses to a line with a caesura after the second. Lines of three principal stresses are unusual (8, 27, 51, 92, 166), and a few lines with so many as six stresses or more occur (105, 118, 150, 157, 178), some of which are scarcely distinguishable from prose.

Almost nothing is known of the history of this extensive hymn. The manuscripts are all Late Assyrian apart from one Late Babylonian piece which appropriately comes from the god's own city of Sippar. There were, however, at least five copies in the Ashurbanipal libraries (E is certainly not part of any other manuscript, but D might conceivably go with C). This abundance of copies suggests that it was a popular text in this period, and this conclusion is confirmed by the exercise tablets **h**, where it is used for writing exercises along with the standard works *Maqlû*, *Ludlul*, the *Epic of Creation*, and the *Era Epic*.

There are three criteria from which a date of composition may be deduced. There is, of course, the usual complication that old material can be incorporated into a late text. The criteria are (i) the state of commerce reflected in the section on merchants, (ii) relationship to literature in general, and (iii) stylistic considerations.

(i) *The state of commerce*

Lines 65–70 speak of merchants risking their lives and capital on the sea. Sea-borne trade via the Persian Gulf is discussed by Oppenheim in "The Seafaring Merchants of Ur" (*JAOS* 74. 6–17), who concludes that this foreign trade was at its height in the Agade Dynasty, continued to flourish on a somewhat smaller scale during the Third Dynasty of Ur and the Isin-Larsa period, and came to an end before the fall of the First Dynasty of Babylon. In any age a work of literature may be composed which reflects conditions no longer prevailing, and in the ancient Orient the habit of literary borrowing continually passed on material from earlier generations. However, the memory of these dangers does suggest a written source going back to the First Dynasty of Babylon.

Lines 103–6 speak of a society in which merchants travelled to remote lands and risked losing the money staked in the enterprise. This suits the Old Babylonian era very well, but such trading was also known in the Cassite period. The terminology used in the elevated style of a hymn is necessarily different from the precise commercial language of business documents, but in 113 and 118 (see the notes on these lines) phrases strongly redolent of Old Babylonian commercial terms occur. It is not known how soon such phrases were forgotten, but their occurrence is another suggestion that Old Babylonian material is contained in the hymn. The use of *tamkāru* is a perplexing matter. In the hymn he is the trader who travels into foreign lands (69, 139), a Middle Babylonian usage. The present state of knowledge does not allow us to say whether the Old Babylonian *tamkārum* personally went on these journeys or merely financed them.

(ii) *Relationships to other literature*

The following instructive list of parallels is documented in the notes:

17, 18 the *vault* of heaven, the corn field—a hymn to Marduk
69 the merchant carrying his capital—*Tukulti-Ninurta Epic*
100, &c., it is pleasing to Šamaš—*Counsels of Wisdom*, &c.
104, 109 he loses his capital—omens
107, 110 to hold the balances—*Šurpu*
117 to take over the estate (lit. enter the house)—*Ludlul*
125 whose mouth says "No"—*Šurpu*
134, &c., there confronts you—an incantation
135 whose family is remote, whose city is distant—*Šurpu*

This list, which does not include any stock epithets, must not be taken as direct borrowings; they are examples of different writers' appropriations from a common store of tradition. The writer could then draw on a strong and well-founded literary tradition. One of the great differences between hymns certainly written in the Old Babylonian period and late compositions is in this very matter. The early texts have a freshness and originality which the late texts lack, as they are more grounded in convention. This criterion does not favour an Old Babylonian date.

(iii) *General style*

Despite what is written under the last heading the *Šamaš Hymn* is no mere cento of clichés or string of epithets. It has a great literary merit and ranks as one of the better products of Mesopotamian religious writing. That, however, cannot blind us to an unevenness of style in certain places. In two cases (17–18, 125, cited above) the text in itself is meaningless, and only becomes intelligible when the literary parallels are studied. In 125 it appears that a stock phrase has been truncated, and in 17–18 some words of the Marduk hymn have been embedded in a totally foreign context. Line 109 (= 104) is not applicable to its present position, and its placing there implies that the compiler did not know to what it refers. Also there is one couplet lacking a main verb (167–8), which has no connexion in substance or grammar with its setting. Line 122 seems to begin a sentence which is never continued. Lines 169–73 also are without a main verb or connexions with their context. This decadent aspect militates strongly against an early date for the present form of the text.

There are two possibilities which could account for the text. Either the hymn is the result of a late reworking of an early text, or it is an original late composition based on early materials. Between these extremes there is a third possibility that an early kernel has been much expanded. As for a date of the present form, the Cassite period would probably be too early. The section on merchants has the clearest claim to be Old Babylonian. Böhl has stressed the difference in style between this section and the rest of the hymn, and has concluded that it was borrowed from a Wisdom text (*JEOL* VIII. 673). Certainly if this section alone had been preserved no one would have guessed that it formed part of a hymn.

LITERATURE

TEXT WITH OR WITHOUT EDITION

1889 R. E. Brünnow, *ZA* 4. 1–35 (text of most of B, and a little of A).

1901 C. D. Gray, *AJSL* 17. 129–45 (full text of A), ibid., p. 242 (text of C) (also published separately as *The Šamaš Religious Texts*).

1923 E. Ebeling, *KAR* 321 obv. 12–17 (= g).

1952 F. Schollmeyer, *AfO* 16. 46 and pls. VII–VIII (text of i).

EDITIONS, TRANSLATIONS, STUDIES

1905 M. Jastrow, *Die Religion Babyloniens und Assyriens* I. 432–6.

1911 H. Zimmern, *Bab. Hymnen und Gebete, Zweite Auswahl* (*AO* 13/1), pp. 23–27.

1912 A. Schollmeyer, *Sumerisch-bab. Hymnen und Gebete an Šamaš*, pp. 80–94.

1915 P. Jensen, *KB* VI/2. 96–107.

1921 A. Ungnad, *Die Religion der Babylonier und Assyrer*, pp. 185–9.

1922 B. Landsberger, in E. Lehmann and H. Haas, *Textbuch zur Religionsgeschichte*[2], pp. 308–11.

1925 E. Ebeling, *BBK* II/1, p. 8 (edition of g).

1925 B. Meissner, *Babylonien und Assyrien* II. 167–8.

1926 E. Ebeling, in H. Gressmann, *Altorientalische Texte zum alten Testament*[2], pp. 244–7.

1930 C. J. Mullo Weir, *JRAS* 1930, 41–42 (edition of g).

1934 A. Van Selms, "Opmerkingen over het religieuze taalgebruik der Šamašteksten", in *MVEOL* I. 21–32.

1942 F. M. Th. Böhl, *JEOL* VIII. 665–80.

1950 F. J. Stephens, *ANET*[1], pp. 387–9.

1953 W. von Soden, in A. Falkenstein and W. von Soden, *Sumerische und akkadische Hymnen und Gebete*, pp. 240–7, 381–2.

1953 K. Tallqvist, *Babyloniska Hymner och Böner*, pp. 122–7.

1955 F. J. Stephens, *ANET*[2], pp. 387–9.

MANUSCRIPTS

Symbol	Lines on Obverse	Lines on Reverse	Plates
Ashurbanipal			
A = K 3182+3187+3312+5121+5459+6823+8232+9356+9699+10587+13430+13794+Sm 311+Sm 1398	I 1–16, 18–56 II 68–85, 89–95, 101–12	III 113–65 IV 169–88, 197–200	33, 34
(K 9356 does not touch the joined pieces, but is almost certainly part of this tablet)			
B = K 3650 and K 3474+8233+Sm 372	I 1–9, 17–58 II 59–70, 82–108	III 141–50, 159–70 IV 179–91, 193–200	35, 36
(K 3650 appears to be the top of the tablet of which the bottom portion is represented by the three other numbers)			
C = Sm 1033 and 83–1–18, 472	I 17–34 II 88–93, 108–19	III 124–36 IV ..	33, 34, 35
(These two pieces appear to be parts of the same tablet)			
D = BM 98631 (Th 1905–4–9. 137)	..	IV 175–9	34
E = K 10866	I 14–20	..	33
F = BM 98732 (Th 1905–4–9. 238)	1–10		33
Assur			
g = VAT 10174 obv. 12–17	143–54		36
h = VAT 10071 rev. 1–2 and VAT 10756 rev. 3–4	138–41		73

(**g** and **h** are exercise tablets containing extracts from the *Šamaš Hymn inter alia.* The two tablets cited as **h** can be taken together as in the literary extracts the pairs of lines on 10756 are the immediate sequence to the pairs on 10071)

Symbol	Lines on Obverse	Lines on Reverse	Plates
Sippar			
i = Si 15	I 21–35 II 68–80	III 106–25 IV 168–85	33, 36

1 *muš-na-m[ir . . . .] šá-ma-mi*
2 *mu-šaḫ-li e[k-li-ti . . . .]* ⌜*e*⌝*-liš u šap-liš*

3 ^{d}*šamaš muš-na-m[ir . . . .] šá-ma-mi*
4 *mu-šaḫ-li ek-l[i-ti . . . . e-l]iš u šap-liš*

5 *[saḫ]-pu ki-ma šu-uš-[k]al-l[i . . . . šá-]ru-ru-ka*
6 *[šá] ḫur-šá-a-ni bi-ru-ti e-ṭ[u-ti-š]u-nu tuš-par-di*

7 *a-na t[a]-mar-ti-ka iḫ-du-ú ilū*$^{meš.u}$ *ma-al-ku*
8 *i-reš-šu-ka gi-mir-šú-nu* ⌜^{d}⌝*í-gì-gì*

9 *pu-uz-ru sat-tak-ku šu-ḫu-zu ba-ri-ru-ka*
10 *ina na-mir-ti ṣīti*(ud.da)*-ka ki-bi-is-si-na in-na-[mar]*

11 *mi-lam-mu-ka iš-te-ni-'-*⌜*ú*⌝*[. . . . .]*
12 *kib-rat er-bet-ti ki-ma* ^{d}*gir[ra*(giš.b[ar) . . . .]

13 ⌜*tuš*⌝*-pal-ki ba-a-bi šá ka-liš [. . . . .]*
14 *šá kul-lat* ^{d}*í-gì-gì nindabê*^{meš}*-šú-n[u]* × × ×

15 ^{d}*šamaš ana a-ṣi-ka kit-*⌜*mu*⌝*-sa te-ni-še-e-ti*
16 × × × × × × × × [(.)] *gi-mir-ši-na mātāti*(kur.k[ur)

17 *[m]uš-na-mir pi-tu-u ek-li-ti ṣir-rit šá-m[a-mi]*
18 *mu-šaḫ-miṭ ziq-nat ur-ri me-reš še-em na-piš-[ti]* ⌜*māti*⌝

19 *šá-di-i bi-ru-ti e-ri-ma šá-lum-mat-ka*
20 *nam-ri-ru-ka im-lu-ú si-ḫi-ip mātāti*(kur.kur)

21 *šu-ra-ta ana ḫur-sa-a-ni er-ṣe-ta ta-bar-ri*
22 *kip-pat mātāti*(kur.kur) *ina qí-rib šamê*^{e} *šaq-la-a-ta*

23 *nišī*^{meš} *mātāti*(kur.kur) *kul-lat-si-na ta-paq-qid*
24 *šá* ^{d}*é-a šàr mal-ku uš-tab-nu-ú ka-liš paq-da-ka*

25 *šu-ut na-piš-ti šak-na mit-ḫa-riš te-re-'e*
26 *at-ta-ma na-qid-si-na šá e-liš u šap-liš*

27 *te-te-ni-ti-iq gi-na-a šá-ma-mi*
28 *[š]u-um-dul-ta er-ṣe-tu ta-ba-'a u*$_4$*-me-šam*

29 *mīl*(⌜e$_4$.la$_6$⌝) *tâmti*(⌜a.ab.ba⌝) *ḫur-sa-a-ni er-ṣe-ta šá-ma-mi*
30 *ki-i* gán × si *gi-na-a ta-ba-'a u*$_4$*-mi-šam*

31 *šap-la-a-ti m[a-a]l-ki* ^{d}*kù-su*$_x$(BU) ^{d}*a-nun-na-ki ta-paq-qid*
32 *e-la-a-ti ša [d]a-ád-me ka-li-ši-na tuš-te-šèr*

VARIANTS

7 B: *m]a-al-ki* 8 F: ^{d}*i-gi*$_4$*-gi*$_4$ 17 C: *-t]u-*⌜*ú*⌝ E: *-l]i-te* 18 E:] × × × *me-ḫer še-em* 20 C: *na]m-ri-ir-ru-ka* 21 A: ki-*ti]m* 24 C: *paq-da-t[a* i: *paq-da-a-ka*

1 Illuminator [. . . . .] the heavens,
2 Who lightens the darkness [. . . . .] in upper and lower regions;

3 Šamaš, illuminator [. . . . .] the heavens,
4 Who lightens the darkness [. . . . .] in upper and lower regions;

5 Your beams like a net cover [. . . . . .]
6 You brighten the gloom of the vast mountains.

7 At your appearing the counsellor gods rejoice,
8 All the Igigi gods exult in you.

9 Your rays grasp secrets unceasingly,
10 With the brightness of your light their path is seen.

11 Your dazzle ever seeks out [. . . . .]
12 [You . . . .] the four world regions like the Fire God.

13 You open wide the gates of all [. . . . .]
14 *You acknowledge* the food offerings of all the Igigi.

15 Šamaš, at your arising mankind bows down,
16 . . . . [.] every land.

17 Illuminator, dispeller of darkness of the *vault* of the heavens,
18 Who sets aglow the *beard* of light, the corn field, the life of the land.

19 Your splendour covers the vast mountains,
20 Your fierce light fills the lands to their limits.

21 You climb to the mountains surveying the earth,
22 You suspend from the heavens the circle of the lands.

23 You care for all the peoples of the lands,
24 And everything that Ea, king of the counsellors, had created is entrusted to you.

25 Whatever has breath you shepherd without exception,
26 You are their keeper in upper and lower regions.

27 Regularly and without cease you traverse the heavens,
28 Every day you pass over the broad earth.

29 The flood of the sea, the mountains, the earth, the heavens,
30 Like a . . . you pass over them daily without cease.

31 In the underworld you care for the counsellors of Kusu, the Anunnaki,
32 Above, you direct all the affairs of men,

---

25 i: *ša*]*k-nu, te-re-'-e* BC: *ta-re-'e* 26 i: om. *šá* A: ⌜*ù*⌝ 27 A: *š*]*a-ma-mi* 28 i: ki-*ti*]*m* Ai: *u*$_4$*-mi-šam* 29 (A)i: ki-*tim* C: *ša-ma-mi* 30 B: *u*$_4$*-me-šam* 32 i: *tuš-te-eš-šer*

ABC i

33 *re-'-u šap-la-a-ti na-qí-du e-la-a-ti*
34 *muš-te-šer nu-úr kiš-šá-ti* ^{d}*šamaš at-ta-ma*
35 *te-te-ni-bir ta-ma-tum rapaštum*^{tum} *šá-di-il-ta*
36 [*šá*] ^{d}*í-gì-gì la i-du-ú qí-rib lìb-bi-šá*
37 [^{d}*šama*]*š bir-bir-ru-ka ina ap-si-i ú-ri-du*
38 [^{d}*laḫ-m*]*u šu-ut tâmti*(a.ab.ba) *i-na-aṭ-ṭa-lu nu-úr-ka*
39 [^{d}*šamaš*] *ki-ma qé-e ka-sa-ta ki-ma im-ba-ri* [*ká*]*t-ma-ta*
40 [*rap*]*-šu an-dùl-la-ka sa-ḫi-ip mātāti*([k]ur.kur)
41 [*l*]*a ta-šu-uš* u_4*-me-šam-ma ul 'a-da-ru pa-r*[*u*]*-ka*
42 [*tuš*]*-ta-bar-ri ina mu-ši-im-ma tu-šaḫ-miṭ* [×]-×
43 ⌜*a*⌝*-na šid-di šá la i-di ni-su-ti u bi-ri la ma-n*[*u-ti*]
44 ^{d}*šamaš dal-pa-ta šá ur-ra tal-li-ka u mu-šá ta-saḫ-r*[*a*]
45 *ul i-ba-áš-ši ina gi-mir* ^{d}*í-gì-gì šá šu-nu-ḫu ba-li-ka*
46 *ina ilī*^{meš} *nap-ḫar kiš-šá-ti šá šu-tu-ru ki-ma ka-a-ta*
47 [*ṣ*]*i-tuk-ka ip-ḫu-ru ilū*^{meš} *ma-a-ti*
48 [*n*]*a-mur-rat-ka ez-zi-ti ma-a-tum saḫ-pat*
49 [*š*]*a nap-ḫar mātāti*(kur.kur) *šu-ut šu-un-na-a li-šá-nu*
50 [*ti*]*-i-di kip-di-ši-na ki-bi-is-si-na na-aṭ-la-a-ta*
51 [*kam-s*]*a-nik-ka kul-lat-si-na te-ni-še-e-ti*
52 [^{d}*ša*]*maš a-na nūri*(zalág)*-ka ṣu-mu-rat mit-ḫur-ti*
53 [*i-na*] *ma-kal-ti ba-ru-ti a-na ri-kis* ^{giš}*erini*
54 [*at-ta*] *mu-ši-mi šá-ilī*^{meš} *pa-še-ru šunāti*(máš.ge_6.meš)
55 [× ×] × *šá rik-sa-a-ti kit-mu-sa ma-ḫar-ka*
56 [*i-na ma*]*ḫ-ri-ka kit-mu-su rag-gu u ke-e-num*
57 [*ul ib-ši šá*] *ur-ra-du ina apsî ba-li-ka*
58 [. . . . . *ṣ*]*e-e-ni u za-ma-né-e tu-šá-pi di-in-šu-u*[*n*]
59 a ×[. . . . .]
60 *i-re-eḫ-ḫi-šu ma-šit-ta* × × ×[. . . . . . .]
61 *tu-tar-ra ṣal-pa šá la-mu-ú* [. . . . .]
62 *tu-šel-li ina ḫu-bur šá di-na ti-iṣ-bu-tú* ×[. . . . .]
63 *ina di-in ki-na-a-ti* ^{d}*šamaš šá taq-bu-u* [. . . . . .]
64 *šu-pu-u zik-ru-ka ul in-nen-nu-u pa-na ul* ×[. . .]

VARIANTS

34 i: *kiš-šá-*]*ta* 35 A: *ti-am*]*at rap-šá-ti šá-dil-t*[*a* i:]×-⌜*ta šá-di-il-tú*⌝ 37 A: *a-na* zu.ab 41 A: *la i-ad-da-r*[*u* 43 A: *ù ana* danna 44 A: *mu-ša* 46 A: nigin

33 Shepherd of that beneath, keeper of that above,
34 You, Šamaš, direct, you are the light of everything.

35 You never fail to cross the wide expanse of sea,
36 The depth of which the Igigi know not.

37 Šamaš, your glare reaches down to the abyss
38 So that the monsters of the deep behold your light.

39 [Šamaš,] you draw in like the cord (of a net), you shroud like a fog,
40 Your covering protection stretches over the lands.

41 You are not dejected during the day, nor is your *surface* darkened,
42 By night you continue to kindle [.].

43 To unknown distant regions and for uncounted leagues
44 You press on, Šamaš, going by day and returning by night.

45 Among all the Igigi there is none who toils but you,
46 None who is supreme like you in the whole pantheon of gods.

47 At your rising the gods of the land assemble;
48 Your fierce glare covers the land.

49 Of all the lands of varied speech,
50 You know their plans, you scan their way.

51 The whole of mankind bows to you,
52 Šamaš, the universe longs for your light.

53 [In] the seer's bowl with the cedar-wood appurtenance
54 [You] *enlighten* the dream priests and interpret dreams.

55 [. .] . of arrangements prostrate themselves before you,
56 Before you the wicked and just prostrate themselves.

57 [There is none] but you who goes down to the deep,
58 [. . . . .] you blaze abroad the judgements on the criminal and law-breaker.

59 . . [. . . . .]
60 It/he pours bruises upon him . . . [. . . . .]

61 You dismiss (to the underworld) the rogue who is surrounded [. . . . . .]
62 You bring up from the underworld river him entangled in a lawsuit . [. . . . .]

63 What you say in a just verdict, Šamaš, [. . . . . .]
64 Your manifest utterance may not be changed, and is not . [. . .]

---

47 A:] × kur   49 A: kur.meš   50 A: *na-aṭ-la-ta*   52 A: *ṣu-um-mu-rat mit-ḫur-tum*
53 A: lú.ḫal-*ti*   54 A: *-š*]*im-me šá-i-li pa-ši-ri*   55 A: *kit-mu-su*   56 A: *ù ki-na*

65 *te-em-mi-id a-na al-la-ki šá šup-šu-qat ú-r[u-uḫ-šú]*
66 *a-na e-bir tâmti*(a.ab.ba) *a-dir a-ge-e ta-nam-d[in* × ×]
67 *ḫar-ra-na-a-ti šá la am-ra ṣa-'-i-da-ta a[t-ta]*
68 [*su*]-*li-i terteniddi*(uš.meš-*di*) *ma-ḫi-ru šá* ^{d}[*šamši*]^{ši}
69 ^{l}[^{ú}*tamkā*]*ru*(dam.gà]r) *na-áš ki-si ina e-de-e tu-še-zib*
70 × [×] × *a-rid* ^{d}*za-nun-ze-e tu-šá-áš-kan kap-pa*
71 *m*[*u-un-n*]*ab-tú-tim u* [*e*]*r*?-*bi ma-ḫa-zi tu-kal-lam*
72 *ḫa*[*r-ra-n*]*a-a-ti šá* ⸢^{d}⸣[*ša*]*maš i-du-ú tu-kal-lam šal-la*
73 *šá i-na pu-uz-*⸢*zu*⸣?-× [×] × × × × × × ×
74 *ab-ka šá ina bīt ṣi-b*[*ít-ti* . . . .]
75 *šá ìl-šú it-ti-šú* [. . . . .]
76 *i-na a-ma-ri te-*× [. . . . .]
77 *te-mid a-na* ^{lú}*ma*[*rṣi* . . . .]
78 *ta-par-ra-as ar-*[*kat* . . . .]
79 *tu-ub-bal* × [. . . . .]
80 *ina erṣet lā târi* (kur.nu.gi$_4$.⸢a⸣) *tuš-*[. . . .]
81 ^{d}*ištārāti*(*iš-tar*.meš) *šab*?-*s*[*a-ti* . . . . . .]
82 *ṣi-ra-*⸢*ta*⸣-*ma* ul tu [. . . . .]
83 ^{d}*šamaš* ⸢*i-na*⸣ *šu-uš-kal-l*[*i-ka* . . . .]
84 *i-n*[*a*] *giš-par-ri-ka la* [. . . . .]
85 *šá a-na ma-mi-ti* × [. . . . .]
86 *a-na la a-dir* ṣa × [. . . . .]
87 *tar-ṣa-at še-et-ka rap-*[*šá-tu* . . . .]
88 *šá a-na al-ti tap-pi-šú iš-šu-*⸢*ú*⸣ [*īnē-šú*]
89 *i-na u*$_4$-*um la ši-ma-ti ú-šá-*× [. . . . .]
90 *kun-na-áš-šu kip-pu zi-ru ú-*× [. . . . .]
91 *iš-šir-šú* ^{giš}*kakka-ka-ma mu-še-zi-bu u*[*l i-šu*]
92 *ina di-ni-šú ul i-za-az-za abī-*[*šú*]
93 *ina pî daiāni ul ip-pa-lu šu-nu aḫḫū*^{meš}-*šú*
94 *ina ḫu-ḫa-ri šá e-re-e sa-ḫi-ip ul i-di*
95 *šá ka-ṣir an-zil-li qar-na-šú tu-bal-la*
96 *e-piš rid-di ka-pi-du e-ni qaq-qar-šu*

VARIANTS

68 i: ⸢*te-er*⸣-*t*[*e-* 69 A: kuš.níg.]zá *i-na* i: *ki-i-s*[*i* 70 B:]⸢*za-nun*⸣-*za-a* 76 i: ⸢*a*⸣-

65 You stand by the traveller whose road is difficult,
66 To the seafarer in dread of the waves you give[. .]

67 It [is you] who patrol the unseen routes,
68 You constantly tread paths which confront [Šamaš] (alone).

69 You save from the storm the merchant carrying his capital,
70 The . [.] . who goes down to the ocean you equip with wings.

71 You point out settling-places to refugees and fugitives,
72 To the captive you point out routes that (only) Šamaš knows.

73 The man in . . . . [.] . . . .
74 The prisoner who [. . . . .] in a jail [. . . . . . .]

75 He whose god [is angry] with him [. . . . .]
76 . . . . . [. . . . .]

77 You stand by the sick [. . . . .]
78 You diagnose [. . . . .]

79 You bear . [. . . . .]
80 In the Land of No Return you [. . . . .]

81 The angry goddesses [. . . . .]
82 You are exalted . . [. . . . .]

83 Šamaš, in [your] net [. . . . .]
84 From your meshes [. . . . .] does not [escape.]

85 He who in taking an oath . [. . . . .]
86 Who does not fear . . [. . . . .]
87 Your wide net is spread [. . . . .]

88 A man who covets his neighbour's wife
89 Will [. . . . .] before his appointed day.

90 A nasty snare is prepared for him . . [. . . . .]
91 Your weapon will strike at him, and there [will be] none to save him.

92 [His] father will not stand for his defence,
93 And at the judge's command his brothers will not plead.

94 He will be caught in a copper trap that he did not foresee.

95 You destroy the horns of a scheming villain,
96 A zealous . . . ., his foundations are undermined.

---

mar 83, 84 B: *ina* 89 A: *š*]*i-ma-tuš* 90 (A)C: *kun-na-áš-šú* 92 A: *di-n*]*i-šu*
93 A: *d*]*a-a-a-ni* 94 A: urudu

B

97 *da-a-a-⸢na⸣ ṣal-pa mi-si-ra tu-kal-lam*
98 *ma-ḫir ṭa-'-ti la muš-te-še-ru tu-šá-az-bal ar-na*

99 *la ma-ḫir ṭa-'-ti ṣa-bi-tú a-bu-ti en-še*
100 *ṭa-a-bi eli* ^{d}*šamaš balāṭa*(ti.la) *ut-tar*

A

101 *da-a-a-na muš-ta-lum šá di-in me-šá-ri i-di-nu*
102 *ú-gam-mar ēkallu šu-bat rubê*^{meš} *mu-šab-šú*

103 *na-din kaspa a-na šid-di ḫab-bi-lu mi-na-a ut-tar*
104 *uš-ta-kaz-zab a-na né-me-li-ma ú-ḫal-laq kīsa*(kuš.níg.zá)

i

105 *na-din kas-pa a-na šid-di rūqūti*(sud.meš) *mu-ter ištēn šiqla a-na še-*×-×
106 *ṭa-a-bi eli* ^{d}*šamaš balāṭa*(ti.la) *ut-*[*tar*]

C

107 *ṣa-bit* ^{giš}*zi-ba-*[*ni-ti e-piš ṣ*]*i-lip-ti*
108 *muš-te-nu-ú* [*a-b*]*a-an ki-i-si* ⸢*ú*⸣-× × (×) [*ú*]-*šap-pal*
109 *uš-ta-kaz-za-ab a-na né-me-li-im-ma ú-ḫal-l*[*aq ki-i-sa*]

110 *šá ki-ni ṣa-bit* ^{giš}*zi-ba-ni-ti ma-'-d*[*a . . .*]
111 *mim-ma šum-šú ma-'-d*[*i*] *qí-šá-áš-šú* [. . .]

112 *ṣa-bit sūti*(giš.bán) *e-piš ṣi-l*[*íp-ti*]
113 *na-din ši-qa-a-ti a-na bi-ri-i mu-šad-din at-ra*

114 *ina la u*$_4$*-me-*⸢*šú*⸣ [*a*]*r-rat nišī*^{meš} *i-kaš-šad-su*
115 *ina la a-dan-ni-šú* ⸢*i*⸣*-šá-al i-raš-ši bil-ta*

116 *makkūr*(níg.ga)*-šú ul i-be-el apal*(ibila)*-šú*
117 *a-na bīti-šú ul ir-ru-bu* [*š*]*u-nu aḫḫū*^{meš}*-šú*

118 *um-ma-ni ki-nu na-din še-em i-na* [*kab-ri*]*m pān*(pi) *ú-šat-tar dum-qu*

119 *ṭa-a-ab eli* ^{d}*šamaš balāṭa*(t[i]-la) *ut-tar*

120 *ú-rap-pa-áš kim-ta meš-ra-*⸢*a*⸣ *i-ra-áš-š*[*i*]
121 *ki-ma mê*^{meš} *naq-bi da-ri-i zēr-*[*šú*] *da-*[*ri*]

122 *a-na e-piš ú-sa-at dum-qí la mu-du-ú* [*ṣi*]*-líp*[*-ti*]

123 *muš-ten-nu-ú šap-la-a-ti ina mas-da-ri šá-k*[*in ina maḫ-ri-ka*]

VARIANTS

103 A: *kas-pa* 104 A: *uš-ta-kaz-za-ab* 107 i: om. giš B: *zi-ba-ni-*]*t*[*a* 108 A: zá.me ku[š.níg.zá 109 i: *uš-ta-kaz-z*[*ab* 110 i: *ki-nim* A: giš ×[111 C: *ma-*

97 You give the unscrupulous judge experience of fetters,
98 Him who accepts a present and yet lets justice miscarry you make bear his punishment.

99 As for him who declines a present, but nevertheless takes the part of the weak,
100 It is pleasing to Šamaš, and he will prolong his life.

101 A circumspect judge who pronounces just verdicts
102 Controls the palace and lives among the princes.

103 What is he benefited who invests money in unscrupulous trading missions?
104 He is disappointed in the matter of profit and loses his capital.

105 As for him who invests money in distant trading missions and pays one shekel per . . .,
106 It is pleasing to Šamaš, and he will prolong his life.

107 The merchant who [practises] trickery as he holds the balances,
108 Who uses two sets of weights, thus lowering the . . . . .,
109 He is disappointed in the matter of profit and loses [his capital.]

110 The honest merchant who holds the balances [and gives] good weight—
111 Everything is presented to him in good measure [. . .]

112 The merchant who practises trickery as he holds the corn measure,
113 Who weighs out loans (or corn) by the minimum standard, but requires a large quantity in repayment,

114 The curse of the people will overtake him before his time,
115 If he demanded repayment before the agreed date, there will be guilt upon him.

116 His heir will not assume control of his property,
117 Nor will his brothers take over his estate.

118 The honest merchant who weighs out loans (of corn) by the maximum standard, thus multiplying kindness,
119 It is pleasing to Šamaš, and he will prolong his life.

120 He will enlarge his family, gain wealth,
121 And like the water of a never failing spring [his] descendants will never fail.

122 For him who does kind deeds and knows no trickery—

123 The man who constantly disguises his intentions with hypocrisy—his case [is before you.]

]*a-ad* 112 i: *su-t*[*i* 113 C: *bi-re-e* 114 C: *á*]*r-rat* 115 C: *i-ra-áš-ši* gu[n 116 C: *a-pal-š*[*u* 118 i: *k*[*i*]*-ni* C: *kab-r*]*i pa-an* 119 A: *ṭa-a-b*]*i* 123 i: ***muš-te-nu-ú šap-la-a-tú***

A C i

124 *šu-ut lum-nu i-pu-šú zēr-šú-nu u[l da-ri]*
125 *[š]u-ut ul-la pi-i-šú-nu šá-kin ina maḫ-ri-ka*

126 *[tu-]šaḫ-maṭ ṣi-it pi-i-šú-nu ta-pa-áš-šar at-ta*
127 *[t]a-šim-me te-bir-ši-na-ti šá rug-gu-gu tu-mas-si di-in-šú*

128 *ma-na-ma ma-am-ma pu-uq-qu-du qa-tuk-ka*
129 *tuš-te-eš-šer te-re-te-ši-na šá šuk-ṣu-ru ta-paṭ-ṭar*

130 *ta-šim-me* ^{d}*šamaš su-up-pa-a su-la-a ù ka-ra-bi*
131 *šu-kin-na kit-mu-su lit-ḫu-šu ù la-ban ap-pi*

132 *a-na ḫur-ri pi-i-šú dun-na-mu-ú i-šá-as-si-ka*
133 *ú-la-lu en-šú ḫu-ub-bu-lu muš-ke-nu*
134 *um-mi šal-la mas-da-ra gi-na-a i-maḫ-ḫar-ka*

135 *šá ru-qat kim-ta-šú né-su-ú ālu*^{u}*-šú*
136 *[ina] šu-ru-bat ṣēri re-'-ú i-maḫ-ḫar-ka*

h

137 *[k]a-par-ri ina te-še-e na-qí-du ina* ^{lú}*nakri*(kúr)
138 ^{d}*šamaš i-maḫ-ḫar-ka a-lak-tu i-ti-qu pu-luḫ-ti*
139 ^{lú}*tamkāru*(dam.gàr) *al-la-ka* ^{lú}*šamallû*(šamán.lá) *na-áš kīsi*(kuš.níg.zá)

B

140 ^{d}*šamaš i-maḫ-ḫar-ka bā'ir*(šu.peš$_{x}$(ḪA)) *ka-tim-ti*
141 *ṣa-a-a-du ma-ḫi-ṣu mu-ter-ru būli*(máš.anše)
142 *ina pu-un-zir-ri* ^{lú}*ušandû*(mušen.dù) *i-maḫ-ḫar-ka*

g

143 *mut-taḫ-li-lu šar-ra-qu mu-ṣal-lu-ú šá* ^{d}*šamši*^{ši}
144 *ina su-le-e ṣēri mut-tag-gi-šú i-maḫ-ḫar-ka*

145 *mi-i-tum mur-tap-pi-du e-ṭím-mu ḫal-qu*
146 ^{d}*šamaš im-ḫu-ru-ka tal-te-me ka-la-ma*

147 *ul tak-li šu-ut im-ḫ[u]-ru-ka ta-×-ta-ti*
148 *a-na ia-a-ti* ^{d}*šamaš la ta-zir-ši-na-ti*

149 *šá ad-[na]-a-ti* ^{d}*šamaš uz-[ni]-ši-na tuš-pat-ti*
150 *pa-ru-ka ez-zu šam-ru nūr*(zalág)*-ka at-ta ta-nam-din-ši-na*

151 *[tuš-te-š]èr te-re-te-ši-na ina ni-[q]í-i áš-ba-ta*
152 *a-na šār erbetti*(im.limmu.ba) *ar-kàt-si-na ta-par-ra-as*

153 *kal si-ḫi-ip da-ád-me u[z]-ni-ši-na tuš-pat-ti*

154 *ma-la kap-pa ni-ṭi-il īnē*^{II}*-ka ul im-ṣu-ú šá-ma-mu*
155 *ma-la ma-kal-ti ba-ru-ú-ti ul im-ṣa-a gi-mir-ši-na mātāti*^{meš}

VARIANTS

126 C: *pi-šú-nu* 127 C: *ta-bir-ši-na-ti, tu-maš-šá de-en-ši-[na* 128 C:] *u ma-am-ma* 129 C: *-š]èr* A: *te-ret-ši-na, šuk-ṣu-ra* 130 C: *su-up-pu-ú su-ul-lu-ú ka-ra-bu* 131 C: *lit-ḫu-ša*; om. *ù* 132 C: *pi-]i-šu* 133 C: *en-š]u* 134 C: *mas-]da-ri* 135 C: *a-lu-šú* 136 C: *re-'-]⌜ú⌝* 138 **h**: *a-lak-ti e-t[e]-qu*

124 The progeny of evil-doers will [fail.]
125 Those whose mouth says "No"—their case is before you.

126 In a moment you discern what they say;
127 You hear and examine them; you determine the lawsuit of the wronged.

128 Every single person is entrusted to your hands;
129 You manage their omens; that which is perplexing you make plain.

130 You observe, Šamaš, prayer, supplication, and benediction,
131 Obeisance, kneeling, ritual murmurs, and prostration.

132 The feeble man calls you from the hollow of his mouth,
133 The humble, the weak, the afflicted, the poor,
134 She whose son is captive constantly and unceasingly confronts you.

135 He whose family is remote, whose city is distant,
136 The shepherd [amid] the terror of the steppe confronts you,
137 The herdsman in warfare, the keeper of sheep among enemies.

138 Šamaš, there confronts you the caravan, those journeying in fear,
139 The travelling merchant, the agent who is carrying capital.

140 Šamaš, there confronts you the fisherman with his net,
141 The hunter, the bowman who drives the game,
142 With his bird net the fowler confronts you.

143 The prowling thief, the enemy of Šamaš,
144 The marauder along the tracks of the steppe confronts you.

145 The roving dead, the vagrant soul,
146 They confront you, Šamaš, and you hear all.

147 You do not obstruct those that confront you . . . .
148 For my sake, Šamaš, do not curse them!

149 You grant revelations, Šamaš, to the families of men,
150 Your harsh *face* and fierce light you give to them.

151 You manage their omens and preside over their sacrifices,
152 To all four points of the compass you probe their state.

153 So far as human habitations stretch, you grant revelations to them all.

154 The heavens are not enough as the vessel into which you gaze,
155 The sum of the lands is inadequate as a seer's bowl.

---

139 **h**: *al-la-ku*, *k*[*i*?-*i-si* 140 **h**: lú.šu.peš$_x$(ḪA) 141 **h**: lú.giš.[b]an.tag.ga 143 **g**: *muš-taḫ-li-lu*, *mu-ṣal-lu-u* 144 **g**: *su-li-i*, *i-maḫ-ḫa-ru* 145 B: lú.úš **g**: *mi-e-tu* 146 **g**: *im-ḫa-ru-ka* 147 **g**: *im-ḫa-ru-ka* 149 **g**: geštu^{II}-*ši-na* 150 **g**: the first sign may be *maš*-. 151 A: *te-ret-ši-na* **g**: siz-kur.sizkur 152 **g**: *šá-a-ri er-bet-ti ár-kàt-si-na ta-pa-ra-as* 154 **g**: *kap-pi ni-iṭ-li*, *im-ṣu-šú šá*-⌜*ma*⌝-*me*

156 *ina* ud.20.kám *re-šá-ta il-la-ta ù ḫi-da-a-ti*
157 *tak-kal ta-šat-ti el-la ku-ru-un-ši-na ši-kar si-bi-'-i ka-a-ri*
158 *i-naq-qa-nik-ka ši-kar sa-bi-'i ta-maḫ-ḫar*

159 *šá la-mu-ši-na-a-ti dan-nu a-gu-ú tu-še-zib at-ta*
160 *el-lu-ú-tum eb-bu-ú-ti sír-qí-ši-na tam-taḫ-ḫar*

161 *ta-šat-ti mi-zi-'-ši-na ku-ru-un-n*[*a*]
162 *ṣu-um-mi-rat ik-pu-du tu-šak-šad at-ta*

163 *šu-ut ik-kam-sa el-let-si-na ta-paṭ-ṭar*
164 *šu-ut ik-tar-ra-ba ik-ri-bi-ši-na tam-ta-ḫar*

165 *ši-na-ma pal-ḫa-ka* [*i*]*š-tam-ma-ra zi-kir-k*[*a*]
166 *tar-ba-ti-ka i-dal-lal a-na da-r*[*iš*]

167 *sak-la-a-ti šá li-šá-na da-bi-bu ṣa-l*[*íp-ti*]
168 *šá kīma erpēti*(im.diri.meš) *la i-šá-a pa-na u b*[*a-b*]*a*

169 *šu-ut i-ba-'u er-ṣe-ti rapaštim*^{tim}
170 *šu-ut ú-kab-bi-su šadê*^{meš} *e-lu-ú-ti*

171 ^{d}*làḫ-mu š*[*u-ut tâm*]*ti*(a.a]b.ba) *šá ma-lu-ú pu-luḫ-ta*
172 *e-ri-ib tâ*[*m*]*ti*(a.a[b.b]a) *šá apsâ i-ba-'-ú*
173 *mi-ḫir-ti nāri šá ir-te-du-ú* ^{d}*šamaš ina maḫ-*⌜*ri*⌝*-k*[*a*]

174 *a-a-ú-tu ḫur-sa-a-nu šá la lit-bu-šu šá-ru-ru-ka*
175 *a-a-ta kib-ra-a-tum šá la iš-taḫ-ḫa-nu na-mir-ta ṣīti*(ud.da)*-ka*

176 *muš-par-du-ú e-ṭu-tum muš-na-mir uk-li*
177 *pi-tu-ú ek-li-ti muš-na-mir erṣetim*^{tim} *rapaštim*^{tim}

178 [*m*]*u-šaḫ-lu-ú* u_4*-mu mu-še-rid an-qul-lu ana erṣetim*^{tim} *qab-lu* u_4*-me*
179 [*m*]*u-šaḫ-miṭ ki-ma nab-li erṣetim*^{tim} *ra-pa-áš-tum*

180 [*m*]*u-kar-ru-ú* u_4*-me mu-ur-ri-ku mušâti*^{meš}
181 [*mu-šab-šu-*]*u ku-ṣu ḫal-pa-a šu-ri-pa šal-gi*

182 [. . . . . .]× gal *sik-kur šamê*^{e} *muš-pal-ku-u da-lat da-ád-me*
183 [. . . . . .]× [*u*]*p-pi sik-ka-ta nam-za-qí áš-kut-ta*

184 [. . . . . . .]× *la ba-bil pa-ni šá-ri-ku ba-la-ṭi*
185 [. . . . . . .] *šal-la ina te-še-e qa-bal mu-ú-t*[*i*]

VARIANTS

159 B: -]*ši-na-ti, a-gu-u* 160 B: kù.me]š *eb-bu-ti si-ir-qí-šú-nu tam-ta-ḫ*[*ar*] 161 A: kaš.tin.na 163 A: *ik-kám-*[164 A: *tam-taḫ-ḫar* 165 A: ⌜*zik-ri*⌝*-*[*ka* 169 A: ki-*tim ra-pa-áš-ti* 170 B: kur.meš-*e el-l*[*u-* i:]×-*tú* 171 i: -]⌜*luḫ*⌝*-tú* 172 i: *ap-sa-a* [*i-b*]*a-'u* 173 i: -]*te-ed-du-ú* 174 i: *ḫu*]*r-sa-a-ni*; om. *šá* 175 D(i): *kib-ra-a-ti* i: om. *šá, iš-taḫ-ḫa-na* D: *iš-taḫ-ḫi-na* 176 D: *e-ṭu-ti* i: *e-ṭu-tú, uk*]*-lu* 177 i: *ek-l*]*i-tú* 178 D: -*š*]*aḫ-lu-u*

156 On the twentieth day you exult with mirth and joy,
157 You eat, you drink their pure ale, the barman's beer from the market.
158 They pour out the barman's beer for you, and you accept.

159 You deliver people surrounded by mighty waves,
160 In return you receive their pure, clear libations.

161 You drink their mild beer and ale,
162 Then you fulfil the desires they conceive.

163 You release the . . . . of those who bow themselves down,
164 From those who regularly bless you, you regularly accept their prayers.

165 They in their reverence laud the mention of you,
166 And worship your majesty for ever.

167 Scoundrels, the informers who speak mischief,
168 Who like clouds have no face nor . .

169 They that pass over the broad earth,
170 They that tread the lofty mountains,

171 The monsters of the sea, filled with fearfulness,
172 The offering of the sea, which moves in the deep,
173 The oblation of the river, which passes, Šamaš, before you—

174 Which are the mountains not clothed with your beams?
175 Which are the regions not warmed by the brightness of your light?

176 Brightener of gloom, illuminator of darkness,
177 Dispeller of darkness, illuminator of the broad earth,

178 Who makes the day to shine, who sends down scorching heat to the earth at midday,
179 Who makes the broad earth glow like flame,

180 Who yet shortens the days and lengthens the nights,
181 [Who causes] cold, frost, ice, and snow,

182 [. . . . . .] . . the bolt of the heavens, who opens wide the doors of the earth,
183 [. . . . . .] . thong, lock-pin, latch, and door handle.

184 Who grants life [. . . . .] . the merciless,
185 [. . . . .] the captive in a struggle of mortal combat.

---

u_1-mi i: *an-qul-lum a-na, qa-[bal* 179 D: ⌜*kīma*⌝, ⌜*er-ṣ*⌝*[e-* i: *ra-pa-áš-tú* 180 i: *mu-ur-ri-ka* B: *mu-š[á-* 181 B: *šu-ri-pu* i: *šal-gu* 182 A: giš.sag.kul Ai: *muš-pal-ku-ú* 183 A: giš.mud giš.gag giš.e_{11} giš.á.suḫ i: *sik-ka-tú nam-za-qu áš-kut-tú* 184 i: *pa-an šá-ri-ka ba-la-ṭu* A: *ba-lá-ṭ[i* 185 A: múru *mu-t[i* i: ⌜*mu-ú-tú*⌝

AB
186 [. . . . . . *ṭ*]*è-me mit-lu-ku ši-tul-ta mil-k*[*u*]
187 [. . . . . . . *a*]*p-pa-ri še-re-e-ti a-na nišī*^{meš} *ra*[*pšāti*^{meš}]
188 [. . . . .]× *ku-us-si-i pa-le-e* t[u × × (×)]
189 [. . . . .]× na *e-mu-q*[*a* . . . . . .]
190 [. . . . .]× *li-šar-*[. . . . . . .]
191 [. . . . .]× r[u . . . .]
B 192 [. . . . .]
193 [. . . . .] *nam-ru šu-bat ta-ši-la-ti-ka*
194 [. . . . .]× pi *nap-tan kib-ra-a-ti*
195 [. . . . . . *šak-ka-n*]*a-ku e-nu u ru-bu-u*
A 196 [. . . . . k]a *bi-lat-su-nu liš-šu-ka*
197 [. . . . .] ra *ina ni-qé-e ḫi-ṣib ma-ta-a-ti*
198 [. . . . . *p*]*arakka-ka li-te-di-iš*
199 [. . . . . *š*]*á la in-nen-nu-u qí-bit pi-šú*
200 [. . . . . *ḫi*]*r-tum ina bīt maiāli*(ki.ná) *liq-bi-ka*

Catch-line on A: [. . . . . . *š*]*amê*^{e} *u erṣetim*^{tim} [. . . . .]

A has an Ashurbanipal colophon (not copied), belonging to type (e) in the classification of Streck, *VAB* VII. 358. B also has a few remnants of an unidentifiable Ashurbanipal colophon.

186 [. . . . .] discretion, consultation, discussion, advice,
187 [. . . . . . .] . . . . to the [wide-spread] peoples.
188 . . .] . throne, royal office . [. . . 189] . . strength [. . .
190–2 wanting
193 [. . . . .] shining, your mirthful abode,
194 [. . . . .] . . a banquet for the world regions.
195 [. . . . .] regent, *enu*-priest, and prince,
196 [. . . . .] . may they bear your tribute.
197 [. . . . .] the wealth of the lands in sacrifice,
198 [. . . . .] may your throne-dais be renewed.
199 [. . . . .] whose utterance cannot be changed,
200 May [*Aia your spouse*] say to you in the bedchamber, ["*Be appeased*".]

Catch-line on A: [. . . . . . of] heaven and earth [. . . . . .]

VARIANTS

186 A: *ṭè-m*]*i, ši-tul-ti* 187 Another possible restoration is *ṣal*[*-mat qaqqadi*]. 188 A: ba]l-*e*
197 A: sizkur, kur.[×] 198 A: *lit-*[

6

THE DIALOGUE OF PESSIMISM[1]

INTRODUCTION

THIS composition is unique in cuneiform, and is a very effective piece. It takes the form of a dialogue between a master and his slave. The master, evidently a man of means, announces to his slave that he is about to engage in some activity, and the discreet slave promptly points out the benefits of the proposed course of action. But the master has already tired of the idea and declares that he will certainly not do the thing, whereupon the slave equally promptly mentions some of the unpleasant consequences which might have followed the realization of the plan. When the master has thus disposed of all the ideas which he can summon, he finally asks the slave what is worth doing. Now the slave takes the initiative and declares that death is the only desirable end.

Quite diverse interpretations of this composition have been advanced. Prior to 1954 most scholars took it as a serious philosophical tractate. Böhl, however, has regarded it as a skit reflecting the Babylonian "Saturnalia", a reversal of social statuses, which took place, he believes, on a day during the New Year festival. Speiser has independently reached the conclusion that it is a burlesque or farce. Many scholars have been won to Speiser's general position. This new interpretation has certainly done good in drawing attention to the satire on the relations of master and slave. The old view seemed blind to the vivid realism of the portrait of these two types, which gives to the piece its timeless appeal. The same types exist today. The writer once worked for an employer whose plans changed as rapidly as the master's in the *Dialogue*, and whose employees' apparently placid assent to the whim of the moment fully equalled the slave's smooth tongue. It would be a serious mistake to regard the slave as a mere yes-man. We are poor students of human nature if we cannot recognize that the slave is laughing up his sleeve from the very start. His final retort is the expression of his real self, which he had seen fit to suppress up to that point.

This piece, then, should be regarded as satire, and can very properly be compared with Juvenal. The outstanding question is how seriously the philosophic content is to be taken. In this connexion comparison with Juvenal is fallacious, since he was using a well-established

[1] Perhaps I may be allowed to point out that my retention of this accepted title has no partisan motive. There is an unfortunate tendency in current Oriental studies for scholars to adopt changes in nomenclature because of the etymological inadequacy of the accepted terminology (an absurd reason), or on other insubstantial grounds. See G. Bolling in *JAOS* 76. 263. The work is in fact a dialogue stressing pessimism, and those who consider that it has no serious purpose are at liberty to understand the title as the "(Humorous) Dialogue of Pessimism".

literary form which demanded denunciation, and so the adoption of a traditional morality. Our author has no known literary antecedents and displays most unorthodox views. Speiser brings three arguments in favour of the view that the content of the discussion is not to be taken seriously: (i) that the blasphemy of the piece is inconceivable in a canonical work, (ii) that the pessimism is merely one side of the debate, and is offset by the equally stated opposite view, and (iii) that various passages are inconsistent with serious purpose.

In answer to the first it must be stressed that 'canonical' in this connexion does not mean 'accepted into a body of sacred literature', but only 'commonly found in late libraries'.[1] As to the blasphemy, Speiser's own dictum, "the Mesopotamian's idea of reverence was plainly not the same as ours" (*JCS* 8. 103), gives a lead. Many things are found in cuneiform literature that are blasphemy by our standards. The *Gilgameš Epic* records a speech in which Gilgameš heaps abuse on the goddess Ištar, and Enkidu later follows suit (Tablet 6). After the flood the gods, who had been deprived of offerings during the destruction of mankind, collected over the sacrificing hero's head "like flies" (*Gilg.* 11. 161), which is scarcely a reverent simile. Also it may be asked in what way the presence or absence of humour affects the nature of blasphemous words. Is irreverence less heinous for being funny? The possibility of a completely nihilistic view of life in ancient Babylonia cannot be peremptorily excluded. There is a famous discussion of the advantages of suicide in Egyptian literature,[2] which is certainly serious. Although no other work of Mesopotamian literature goes so far in denying all values, teaching approximating to this extreme occurs. The sufferer in the *Theodicy* is on the verge of it when he resolves to accept no social responsibilities (lines 133–43), and that dialogue ends not "on a note of hope" (*JCS* 8. 104), but with a desperate plea from the sufferer. See further p. 17.

The second objection is difficult to understand. Pros and cons are freely stated by many dramatists, but that does not prevent scholars from writing on their views of life. In this case there is no possible ambiguity. In each section, excluding the last, the master begins with a burst of enthusiasm for life, and ends in despondency. The slave's words merely reflect the master's changing moods. The final section drives home the pessimistic tone even more forcefully. The whole manner of the writing is dramatic,[3] and the repeated contrast between the initial interest and the final dejection is neither close reasoning nor "outright ambivalence" (Speiser, p. 104), but a dramatic way of throwing the conclusion into relief.

The third objection consists of a variety of interpretations. It is maintained that the slave replies in irrelevant stock phrases. Here, as elsewhere, Speiser underestimates the extent, and exaggerates the importance, of clichés in Babylonian literature. We are in no position to know if the author cites "Go up on to the ancient ruin heaps and walk about" (76) from the *Gilgameš Epic*. It appears at the very beginning and end of the *Epic*, and is presumably one of the latest elements. The words may have been a stock phrase before

[1] Cf. W. G. Lambert, *JCS* 11. 1–14.
[2] *ANET* 405–7.
[3] So already A. Jeremias, *Handbuch der altorientalischen Geisteskultur*², p. 439.

the author of the *Epic* used them, so that the two known occurrences may be dependent on a common source. No one considers the phrase humorous in the epic context. "Perhaps the strongest proof of the mechanical nature of the replies" (*JCS* 8. 105) consists of two plural suffixes which are contained on no manuscript, and one of which rests on a very recondite textual reconstruction.[1] The one certain quotation of a proverb is, *pace* Speiser, very apposite (see note on 83, 84). The point of the last line is not that the master could not live for three days without a slave, but that if the slave were put to death first, as the master had proposed, death is so attractive that the master would soon follow.

There is one real objection which can be raised to taking the text seriously. We may overlook the inconsistency of taking suicide as the ultimate good in life and of not acting promptly upon this attitude. However, if a writer seriously held such views, would he be likely to express them in a witty satire? It can be granted that the dramatic satire gives the views a forcefulness and appeal which any other presentation would have lacked. An answer to the question must be very subjective. In a normal person a desire for death and an abundance of wit would be incompatible, but on any view the writer of this dialogue was an extraordinary person. It is the opinion of the present writer that the work is intended seriously, but with one qualification. It has been argued so far that the text must be one of two alternatives: either a serious rational tractate, or a joke. There is in fact a third possibility, which is adopted here. It is that the writer was in earnest, but owed his outlook to his emotional state. The whole atmosphere of the text is reminiscent of contemporary western adolescents, and particularly those of high intelligence. Extensive study has revealed that many bright youths have sudden changes from exuberance to brooding depression, and that suicide is often in their thoughts, though rarely acted upon.[2] The writer of this piece may well have been of abnormal personality, a genius given to fits of morbid depression. His work should perhaps be studied by a psychologist as well as an Oriental scholar.

Two pieces of evidence suggest that this is a comparatively late composition. The mention of the "iron dagger" (52) excludes the Old Babylonian period, and the early part of the Cassite period. The manuscripts frequently disagree in the division of the text into lines, which suggests that the copying tradition was not so long or so firmly established as that of other literary works.

[1] The prime error of Speiser's exposition of 41 [43] is the assumption that the last word must be the same in the two manuscripts, though the penultimate word in **a** is *mi-nu-u*, but *ri-iq-qa* in e. He then reconciles the first signs of the last word in each manuscript, *ḫi-* and *di-* (on our copy the *di-* is uncertain), by assuming the none too common value *ṭi*. Then for no sound reason he reads an almost unknown word *ḫi-it-tum* (cf. *CAD*, vol. Ḫ, 208) as *ṭi-it-tum*. This is *obscurum per obscurius*, and still leaves the reader wondering how *mi-nu-u ḫi-it*-KU/L[U- . .] can be translated, "what is [in] your beer jug?"

[2] W. D. Wall, *The Adolescent Child* (London, 1948), especially pp. 84–86.

LITERATURE

TEXT WITH OR WITHOUT EDITION

1896 G. Reisner, *SBH*, no. VI, p. 143 (text of e).
1917 E. Ebeling, *KAR* 96 (text of a).
1919 E. Ebeling, *MVAG* 23/2. 50–70 (text of e and C).
1952 R. J. Williams, *JCS* 6. 1–2 (Geers's copy of D).

EDITIONS, TRANSLATIONS, STUDIES

1917 E. Ebeling, *MDOG* 58. 35–38.
1919 C. Bezold, *ZA* 32. 206.
1920 G. B. Gray, *Expository Times* 31. 440–3.
1921 F. M. Th. Böhl, *Stemmen des Tijds* 10/1. 42–55.
1921 É. Dhorme, *RB* 28. 624.
1922 H. Zimmern, *ZA* 34. 87–89.
1923 S. H. Langdon, *Bab* 7. 195–209 = *Babylonian Wisdom*, pp. 67–81.
1925 B. Meissner, *Babylonien und Assyrien* II. 433–4.
1926 E. Ebeling, in H. Gressmann, *Altorientalische Texte zum alten Testament*², pp. 284–7.
1946 T. Jacobsen, in H. Frankfort and others, *The Intellectual Adventure of Ancient Man*, pp. 216–18 = *Before Philosophy*, pp. 231–3.
1947 F. R. Kraus, *JCS* 1. 103.
1948 F. M. Th. Böhl, in G. Van der Leeuw, *De Godsdiensten der Wereld*² I. 162–3.
1950 R. H. Pfeiffer, *ANET*¹, pp. 437–8.
1951 F. M. Th. Böhl, in F. König, *Christus und die Religionen der Erde* II. 493–4.
1951 A. Ungnad, *AfO* 15. 74–75.
1954 E. A. Speiser, *JCS* 8. 98–105.
1955 F. M. Th. Böhl, *Supplements* to *Numen* II (= C. J. Bleeker, *Anthropologie Religieuse*), 47–48.
1955 R. H. Pfeiffer, *ANET*², pp. 437–8.

MANUSCRIPTS

	Symbol	*Lines on Obverse*	*Lines on Reverse*	*Plates*
Assur:	**a** = VAT 9933	1–43	49–86	37
	b = Two unnumbered Assur fragments in the Museum of the Ancient Orient, Istanbul, here given as A . . .1 and A . . .2. They are at present located in cupboard 44, drawers 16 and 10 respectively. Though not quite touching, they are parts of the same tablet.	35–55	56–78	38
Ashurbanipal:	C = K 10523	10–31	75–78	38
	D = K 13830	..	55–65	38
Babylon:	e = VAT 657			38

The Babylonian manuscript differs in order of sections and shows considerable textual variation from the Assyrian copies, which have been followed as the better text. The following table shows the differing orders:

	Assyrian	*Babylonian*
1–9	Visiting the palace	[Not preserved]
10–16	Dining	[,, ,,]
17–28	Hunting	[,, ,,]
29–38	Having a family *and* litigation	Litigation
39–45	Insurrection	..
46–52	Love	Love
53–61	Sacrifice	Sacrifice
	..	Insurrection
62–69	Big business	Big business
70–78	Charity	Charity
79–86	*Summum bonum*	[Not preserved]

a is not a well-written tablet. The signs are usually clear, but there are no less than four erasures (13, 32, 81, 82), one certain omission (74) and another probable (65), also two clear mistakes (22 and 64). Also the vulgarisms *lut-ti*, *it-ti* (63) and the solecism *li-pu-uš* (40) do not suggest a first-class scribe. Under these conditions the editor has adopted readings not agreeing with the traces of **a** in 20 and 28. Similarly the scribe of e cannot escape the charge of carelessness or incompetence, having made two omissions (29′, 33′) and three errors (40, 47, 48).

The manuscripts differ so often from each other in the dividing of the text into lines that no mention of this is made in the apparatus except for a special reason.

a
1 [*arad mi-tan-gur-an-ni*] *an-nu-u be-lí an-*[*nu-u*]
2 [*ši-šìr-ma di-kan-ni-ma* ^{giš}*narkab*]*ta ṣi-in-dam ana ēkalli lu-un-š*[*ur*]
3 [*mu-šur be-lí mu-šur* . . .]× *-mar-ka-ma i-ba-áš-šú-ka*
4 [. . . . .] *ub-ba-la pa-ni-ka*
5 [*e arad a-na-ku ana*] *ēkallim-ma ul a-maš-šar*
6 [*la ta-maš-šar be-*]*lí la ta-maš-šar*
7 [. . . . .]× *-bu-ú i-šap-par-ka*
8 [. . . . . *ša l*]*a ti-du-ú ú-šá-aṣ-bat-ka*
9 [*ur-ra u m*]*u-ši mar-ṣa-ta ú-kal-lam-ka*

C
10 *ara*[*d mi-tan-gu*]*r-an-ni an-nu-u be-lí an-nu-u*
11 *ši-*[*šìr-ma di-kan*]*-ni-ma mê*^{meš} *ana qātē*^{II}*-ia bi-nam-ma lu-up-tu-un*
12 *p*[*u-tu-u*]*n be-lí pu-tu-un sa-ḫi-ru pa-ta-nu pi-te-e lìb-bi*
13 ŠE[. . .]× *pat-ni ili-šú*: *it-ti qātē*^{II} *mi-sa-a-ti il-lak* ^{d}*šamaš*
14 *e* [*ara*]*d a-na-ku pa-ta-nu-um-ma ul a-pa-tan*
15 *la* [*ta*]*-pa-tan be-lí la ta-pa-tan*
16 *bur-ru-ú a-ka-lu ṣu-um-mu-ú šá-tu-ú eli amēli il-lak*

---

17 *arad mi-tan-gur-an-ni an-nu-u be-lí an-nu-u*
18 *ši-šìr-ma di-kan-ni-ma* ^{giš}*narkabta ṣi-in-dam-ma ana ṣēri lu-un-šur*
19 *mu-šur be-lí mu-šur ša amēli mut-tap-raš-ši-di ma-li kar-as-su*
20 *kalbu da-a-a-lu eṣemta i-ḫi-ip-pi*
21 [*ḫa-ḫu-r*]*u mut-tap-raš-ši-di i-qa-an-nun qin-n*[*a*]
22 *ak-kan-nu mur-tap-pi-du* i me × [×] ×
23 *e arad a-na-ku a-na ṣērim-ma ul a-*[*maš-šar*]
24 *la ta-maš-šar be-lí l*[*a ta-maš-*]*šar*
25 *ša amēli mut-tap-raš-ši-di ṭè-en-šú* [*iš*]*-ta-ni-šú*
26 *ša kalbi da-a-a-lu i-šab-bi-r*[*u šin-*]*ni-šú*
27 *ša ḫa-ḫu-ru mut-tap-raš-ši-di i-n*[*a* . . .] *dūri bīt-su*
28 *ù šá ak-kan-nu mur-tap-p*[*i-d*]*u na-mu-*⌜*ú*⌝ [*na*]*r-ba-su*

---

29 *arad mi-tan-g*[*ur-an-ni an-nu-u be-lí an-nu-u*]
30 *lu-ub-ni* [*bīta lu-ur-ši ma-*]*ru*
31 *ri-ši* [*be-lí*] *ri-*[*ši ba-*]*nu bīti* [× × ×]× *-u*
32 [. . . . . K]AL *dal-tu pi-til-*[*t*]*um šùm-šú*
33 [. . . .]× *qa-a-a-lu ši-ni-pat lil-li*
b 34 [. . . .] *lu-uq-mu-ma lu-lu-uš-ma lu-tar-ma*
35 [*a-*]*na pa-an be-el da-ba-bi-ia lud-gul*

VARIANTS

13 This line is written as two lines on C, the second of which begins with *it*[, so the traces following the division mark on **a** are to be interpreted as *it-ti* written over an erasure. 19 C: *a-me-l*[*i* 20 The trace on **a** preceding *daiālu* is not consistent with any writing of *kalbu*. 22 **a** may have begun with *ù*. *mur-tap-raš*!*-pi-du* (a) has been emended. 27 C: *ḫa-ḫur*[- 28 The traces

1 ["Slave, listen to me."] "Here I am, sir, here [I am."]
2 ["Quickly, fetch me the] chariot and hitch it up so that I can drive to the palace."
3 ["Drive, sir, drive . . .] . . . . will be for you;
4 [. . . . .] will pardon you."
5 ["No, slave, I] will by no means drive to the palace."
6 ["Do not drive,] sir, do not drive.
7 [. . . .] . . . will send you [. . . .]
8 And will make you take a [route] that you do not know;
9 He will make you suffer agony [day and] night."

10 "Slave, [listen] to me." "Here I am, sir, here I am."
11 "Quickly, [fetch] me water for my hands, and give it to me so that I can dine."
12 "Dine, sir, dine. Repeated dining relaxes the mind.
13 . [. . .] . his god's repast; Šamaš accompanies washed hands."
14 "No, [slave,] I will certainly not dine."
15 "Do not dine, sir, do not dine.
16 Hunger and eating, thirst and drinking, come upon a man."

17 "Slave, listen to me." "Here I am, sir, here I am."
18 "Quickly, fetch me the chariot and hitch it up so that I can drive to the open country."
19 "Drive, sir, drive. A hunter gets his belly filled.
20 The hunting dogs will break the (prey's) bones,
21 The hunter's falcon will settle down,
22 And the fleeting wild ass . . . [.] ."
23 "No, slave, I will by no means [drive] to the open country."
24 "Do not drive, sir, do not drive.
25 The hunter's luck changes:
26 The hunting dog's teeth will get broken,
27 The home of the hunter's falcon is in [. . .] wall,
28 And the fleeting wild ass has the uplands for its lair."

29 "Slave, listen [to me." "Here I am, sir, here I am."]
30 "I am going to set up [a home and have] children."
31 "Have some, [sir,] have some. [The man who sets] up a home [. . .] . .
32 [. . . . .] . a door called 'The Snare'.
33 [. . . .] . robust, two-thirds a weakling."
34 ["‘. . . .] I will burn, *go* and return.
35 I will give way to my prosecutor."

---

on **a** have not been strictly followed; see Introduction. 30, 31, 41 The restorations are conjectural. 32–33 The Akkadian Wisdom text SU 1952, 15+91+186+350 rev. 4–5 has these lines:

[×] *šá la i*-K[AL × ×] *pi-til-*[*tu*]
[× (×) *l*]*ib-bi* [. . . *ši-n*]*i-pat* [*lil-li*] See p. 117.

ab

36 *[ki-]mi du-gul be-lí du-gul*
37 *ke-e ke-e lu-pu-uš bīta bīta e te-pu-uš*
38 *a-lik i-nanna bīt abī-šú iḫ-te-pi*

In place of 29–38 e has:
1′ *a-na* [. . . . .]
2′ *su-kut be-lí* MIN(*sukut*) [. . . . .]
3′ *e arad a-na-ku ana* [. . . . . . *ul a-sak-kut*]
4′ *la ta-sak-kut be-lí* [*la ta-sak-kut*]
5′ *pi-i-ka ul te-ep-pu-*⌜*uš*⌝ × [. . . . .]
6′ *be-lu di-ni-ka uz-za-zu ina muḫ-ḫi-k*[*a* . . .]

---

ab e

39 *arad mi-tan-gur-an-ni an-nu-u be-lí an-n*[*u-u*]
40 *um-ma sa-ar-tu li-pu-uš ki-mi e-pu-uš be-lí e-p*[*u-uš*]
41 *ša sa-ar-tu la te-tep-šú mi-nu-u ḫi-it-l*[*u-up-ka*]
42 *man-nu i-nam-dak-ka-ma tu-mal-la-a kar-a*[*s-ka*]
43 *e arad a-na-ku sa-ar-tu ul e-pu-uš*
44 *a-me-lu šá sar-tam ip-pu-uš šum-ma di-i-ku šum-ma* ⌜*ki*⌝*-ṣi*
45 *šum-ma nu-up-pu-lu šum-ma ṣa-bit šum-ma ina bīt kil-lu na-di*

---

46 *arad* [*mi-ta*]*n-g*[*ur*]*-an-ni an-nu-ú be-lí an-nu-*[*ú*]
47 *sin-niš-*[*ta*] *lu-ra-am* [(×)] *ra-a-ma be-lí ra-*[*a-ma*]
48 *amēlu šá sinništa i-ram-ma* [*k*]*ūra u nissata i-me-šu*

a

49 *e arad a-na-ku sinništam-ma la a-ra-mu*
50 [*la ta-*]*ra-ma be-lí la ta-r*[*a-ma*]
51 *sinništu bur-tú bur-tú šu-ut-ta-tu ḫi-ri-tum*
52 *sinništu paṭ-ri parzilli še-e-lu šá ik-ki-su ki-šad eṭ-l*[*i*]

---

53 *arad mi-tan-gur-an-ni an-nu-u be-lí an-nu-ú*

D

54 *ši-šìr di-kan-ni-ma mê*^{meš} *ana qātē*^{II}*-ia bi-nam-ma*
55 *niqâ ana ili-ia lu-pu-uš e-pu-uš be-lí e-pu-uš*
56 *amēlu šá niqâ ana ili-šú ip-pu-uš libba-šú ṭāb*(dùg.ga)*-šú*
57 *qip-tu eli qip-tu ip-pu-uš*
58 *e arad a-na-ku* ^{udu}*niqâ ana ili-ia-a-ma ul ep-pu-uš*
59 *la te-pu-uš be-lí la te-pu-uš*

VARIANTS

36 *ki-mi*: om. **b** 39 e: *mu-un-tan-gir-an-ni an-nu-ú* 40 *um-ma*: om. **be** **b**: *sar*[- e: *sar-tam lu-pu-uš* DI! 41 *ša*: om. **be** **b**: *sar-t*[*a* e: *sar-tam-ma ul te-ep-pu-uš ri-iq-qa* × [42 e: *i-nam-din-nak-ma ta-mal-la-a ka-*×*-*×*-k*[*a*] 43 e: *sar-ta-am-ma* **b**: *sar-*]*tam*[44 **b**:]⌜*e-p*⌝[*u-šu* 45 **b**: *n*]*u-up-pu-ul šum*$_4$*-m*[*a* 46 e: *mu-un-tan-gir-an-ni*, ^{d}*bēl* 47 e: mí *lu-ra-mu* DI!*-mi ra-mu be-lu ra-mu* 48 e: *a-me-lu*, *i-ra-mu ku-ú-ri*, sag.pa.KU! The trace at the end of **b** is not the beginning of *i*[*-me-šu*]. 49 e: mí*-am-ma ul* 50 Lacking from e.

36 "So give way, sir, give way."
37 "So, so, I will make a home." "Do not make a home.
38 A man who follows this course breaks up his father's home."

(The preceding section seems to be in some disorder; in particular 35 and 36 are probably from another section dealing with litigation. The end of what appears to be a variant form of this assumed paragraph appears in another manuscript as follows:

2′ "Remain silent, sir, remain silent. [. . . . ."]
3′ "No, slave, I . [. . . . . . will not remain silent."]
4′ "Do not stay silent, sir, [do not stay silent.]
5′ Unless you open your mouth . [. . . . .]
6′ Your prosecutors will be savage to you [. . ."])

39 "Slave, listen to me." "Here I am, sir, here [I am."]
40 "I will lead a revolution." "So lead, sir, lead.
41 Unless you lead a revolution, where will your clothes come from?
42 Who will enable you to fill your belly?"
43 "No, slave, I will by no means lead a revolution."
44 "The man who leads a revolution is either killed, or flayed,
45 Or has his eyes put out, or is arrested, or is thrown into jail."

46 "Slave, listen to me." "Here I am, sir, here I am."
47 "I am going to love a woman." "So love, sir, love.
48 The man who loves a woman forgets sorrow and fear."
49 "No, slave, I will by no means love a woman."
50 ["Do not] love, sir, do not love.
51 Woman is a pitfall—a pitfall, a hole, a ditch,
52 Woman is a sharp iron dagger that cuts a man's throat."

53 "Slave, listen to me." "Here I am, sir, here I am."
54 "Quickly, fetch me water for my hands, and give it to me
55 So that I can sacrifice to my god." "Sacrifice, sir, sacrifice.
56 The man who sacrifices to his god is satisfied with the bargain:
57 He is making loan upon loan."
58 "No, slave, I will by no means sacrifice to my god."
59 "Do not sacrifice, sir, do not sacrifice.

---

51 **a**: *bur-t*]*u* MIN **b**: *bu-ur-tu*]*m bu-*[*ur-t*]*um šu-ut-ta-tú* e: *šu-ut-ta-tum* 52 e: *ta-na-ki-su* gú guruš **a**: g[uruš 53 **b**: [1]*an-n*]*u-ú* e: *mu-un-tan-gir-an-ni an-nu-ú* [d]*bēl* 54 **b**: *a-n*]*a* e: *a-na qa-ti-ia i* 55 e: *ni-qa-a* 56 e: *a-me-lu, ni-qa-a, lìb-ba-šú ṭa-ab*[*-šú*] D: [ud][[u]*niqâ* **b**: *a-na* *libbašu ṭābšu* was apparently lacking from **b**. 57 e: *qí-ip-tu ana muḫ-ḫi qí-ip-tu* D: [1][*q*]*í-ip*[- **b**: [2]*qip-t*[*i* 58 e: *ni-qa-a a-*[*na ili-*]*ia* **b**: [*a*]*-na il*[*i*]*-ia, e-pu-uš* 59 **b**: *te-e*]*p-pu-u*[*š, te*]*-ep-pu-uš* D: [1]*tep*[- e: *be-lí* M[IN

a b D e

60 *ila tu-lam-mad-su-ma ki-i kalbi arki-ka it-ta-na-lak*
61 *šum$_4$-ma par-ṣi šum$_4$-ma ila la ta-šal šum$_4$-ma mim-ma šá-nam-ma ir-riš-ka*

---

62 *arad mi-tan-gur-an-ni an-nu-u be-lí an-nu-u*
63 *um-ma-na lud-din ki-mi i-din be-lí [i-din]*
64 *a-me-lu šá um-ma-na inamdinu*(sum-[*n*]*u*) *uṭṭat-su uṭṭat-su-ma ḫu-bul-lu-šú at-r*[*i*]

65 *e arad a-na-ku u*[*m-m*]*a-nam-ma ul a-nam-d*[*in*]
66 ⌜*la*⌝ *ta-nam-din b*[*e-l*]*í la ta-nam-din*
67 *na-da-nu ki-ma ra-a-m*[*e sin-niš-t*]*i*: *ù tur-ru ki-ma a-la-di ma-ru* [(×)] ×
68 *uṭṭat-k*[*a*] *ik-k*[*a-lu u a-n*]*a ka-a-šá it-ta-nam-za-*[*ru-ka*]
69 *ù ḫ*[*u-b*]*u-*⌜*li*⌝ *uṭṭati-ka ú-ḫal-la-qu-nik-*[*ka*]

---

e has the following recension of 62–69:

29′ *arad mu-un-tan-*⟨*gir*⟩*-an-ni an-nu-ú* [d]*bēl an-nu-ú*
30′ *um-ma epra ana māti*[i] *lu-ú-din ki i-din be-lí i-din*
31′ *amēlu šá epra ana māti*[ti]*-šú i-nam-din uṭṭat-su*
32′ *uṭṭat at-ri e arad a-na-ku epra ana māti*[i] *ul a-nam-din*
33′ *la ta-*⟨*nam*⟩*-di-in be-lí* MIN(*lā tanamdin*) *uṭṭat-ka ik-kal ḫubulli*(ur$_5$.ra) *uṭṭati-ka*
34′ *ú-maṭ-ṭu ana ka-a-šú ana muḫ-ḫi it-ta-na-za-ru-ka*

---

a b e

70 *arad mi-tan-gur-an-ni an-nu-u be-lí an-nu-*[*u*]
71 *um-ma ú-sa-tam ana māti-ia lu-pu-uš ki-mi epuš*[uš] *be-lí epuš*[uš]
72 *amēlu šá ú-sa-tam ana māti-šú ip-pu-uš*
73 *šak-na ú-sa-tu-šú ina kippat*(gi.gam.ma) *šá* [d]*marduk*
c
74 *e arad a-na-ku ú-*⟨*sa*⟩*-tam-ma ana māti-ia ul ep-pu-uš*
75 *la te-pu-uš be-lí la te-pu-uš*
76 *i-li-ma ina eli tillāni*[meš.ni] *labirūti*(libir.ra)[meš] *i-tal-lak*
77 *a-mur gul-gul-le-e šá arkûti*[meš] *u pa-nu-u-ti*
78 *a-a-u be-el li-mut-tim-ma a-a-u be-el ú-sa-ti*

---

79 *arad mi-tan-gur-an-ni an-nu-u be-lí an-nu-u*
80 *e-nin-na mi-nu-ú ṭa-a-ba*
81 *ti-ik-ki ti-ik-ka-ka še-bé-ru*
82 *a-na nāri na-šá-ku ṭa-a-ba*
83 *a-a-ú ar-ku šá a-na šamê*[e] *e-lu-ú*
84 *a-a-ú rap-šú šá erṣetim*[tim] *ú-gam-me-ru*
85 *e arad a-dak-ka-ma pa-na-tú-u-a ú-šal-lak-ka*
86 *ù be-lí lu 3 u$_4$-mi ki-i arki-ia i-bal-lu-ṭu*

VARIANTS

60 To judge from the spacing of the preserved portions, e must have diverged considerably from the Assyrian manuscripts in both 60 and 61. D: *tu-lam-mad-m*[*a* **b**: gi[n$_7$ *kal-b*]*i*, gin.gin-*ak* 61 **bD**: garza *ila*: om. **a** **e**:] *šum-ma mim-ma šum-ma* ×[**b**: *e-riš-k*[*a*] 62 **b**: [1]*a*[*n-nu-*]*ú* 63 **a**: [*um-ma um-ma-*]*nu lut-ti*, *it-ti*, *it-t*[*i*] 64 D: (first sign) i[d? **a**: -]*nam-di-nu*, eš!.bar-*su-ma* 65 **a**: *u*]*m-*⟨*ma*⟩*-nam-ma* (or, *na-t*]*a-nam-ma*?) 67 **a**: *ki-i ra-a-m*[*e* 69 **b** has

60 You can teach your god to run after you like a dog,
61 Whether he asks of you rites, or 'Do not consult your god', or anything else."

62 "Slave, listen to me." "Here I am, sir, here I am."
63 "I am going to make loans as a creditor." "So make loans, sir, [make loans.]
64 The man who makes loans as a creditor—his grain remains his grain, while his interest is enormous."
65 "No, slave, I will by no means make loans as a creditor."
66 "Do not make loans, sir, do not make loans.
67 Making loans is like loving [a woman;] getting them back is like having children [.].
68 They will eat your grain, curse [you] without ceasing,
69 And deprive you of the interest on your grain."

(Another recension of the preceding section is also attested:
29′ "Slave, listen to me." "Here I am, sir, here I am."
30′ "I will loan food to my country." "So loan, sir, loan.
31′ The man who loans food to his country, his grain
32′ Is grain * enormous." "No, slave, I will not loan food to my country."
33′ "Do not loan, sir, do not loan. They will eat your grain,
34′ Diminish the interest on your grain, and curse you without ceasing in addition.")

70 "Slave, listen to me." "Here I am, sir, here I am."
71 "I will perform a public benefit for my country." "So perform, sir, perform.
72 The man who performs a public benefit for his country,
73 His deeds are placed in the *ring* of Marduk."
74 "No, slave, I will by no means perform a public benefit for my country."
75 "Do not perform, sir, do not perform.
76 Go up on to the ancient ruin heaps and walk about;
77 See the skulls of high and low.
78 Which is the malefactor, and which is the benefactor?"

79 "Slave, listen to me." "Here I am, sir, here I am."
80 "What, then, is good?"
81 "To have my neck and your neck broken
82 And to be thrown into the river is good.
83 'Who is so tall as to ascend to the heavens?
84 Who is so broad as to compass the underworld?' "
85 "No, slave, I will kill you and send you first."
86 "And my master would certainly not outlive me by even three days."

---

an aberrant trace before *ú-ḫal-la*[- 70 e: *mu-un-tan-gir-an-ni an-nu-ú* ^{d}*bēl* **b**: ^{1}*an-nu*]-*ú* 71 *um-ma*: om. **b**e e: *ú-sa-tu*, om. *ki-mi*, ^{1}*e-pu-uš* **b**: ^{1}*e-p*[*u-uš* 72 e: *ú-sa-tu*, *māti*^{ti}-*šú* 73 e: *šak-na-a ú-sa-ti-šú ina gap-pat* 74 e: *ú-sa-tu* **b**:]⌜*a*⌝-*na* 75 **b**: ^{1}*tep-p*[*u-uš* e: ^{1}*te-ep-pu-uš*, ^{2}⌜*te-ep*⌝[76 **b**: *e-le*-⌜*e*⌝[C: *e*-[*li-ma* Colophon on **a**: [gi]n_7 sumun-*šú* sar-*ma* igi.kár

* The text is clearly defective at this point.

7

FABLES OR CONTEST LITERATURE

GENERAL INTRODUCTION

FABLES of the type best known from the Aesopic collections never became a literary genre in Babylonian. They circulated in Sumerian,[1] and enjoyed a popularity in the Near East generally.[2] In Akkadian a late collection of popular sayings (Chapter 8) contains some examples, but in traditional literature only one has found a place. This is the fable of *The Snake and the Eagle*, which was preserved as literature because, for some unknown reason, it got incorporated in the *Etana Legend*.[3] The reason for the lack of so well known a type of literature from the Babylonian 'canon' is probably the same reason which we have suggested for the similar lack of Babylonian proverbs: the academicians of the Cassite period, who either developed or suppressed genres of literature, had no respect for anything which circulated orally among the common people.

There is a type of fable which became traditional Babylonian literature, but quite distinct from the Aesopic type. The texts consist of verbal contests between creatures, substances, or other personifications. This contest literature also had a wide circulation in the Near East, and in Mesopotamia a tradition was established by the Sumerians. Such works they called adaman.dug$_4$.ga, though the term included other kinds of texts which a modern scholar would not categorize as 'contest literature'. Most of them follow a stock pattern: a mythological introduction leads up to the meeting of the two contestants, who proceed to the cut and parry of debate. The session is wound up with a judgement scene before a god, who settles the question. The surviving Sumerian texts were written in several cases expressly for kings of the Third Dynasty of Ur, and probably served as court entertainment on festive occasions.[4]

Remains of six Babylonian examples have been found, and these are edited below. In two cases, *The Tamarisk and the Palm* and *The Ox and the Horse*, the introduction is preserved, and it follows the mythological type of the Sumerian contests. Also the fable of *The Snake and the Eagle* in the *Etana Legend* has the same kind of introduction. There is, however, no suggestion that the Akkadian texts are direct descendants of Sumerian originals, and the Sumerian pattern is sometimes broken. *The Tamarisk and the Palm*, which

[1] See E. I. Gordon, *JCS* 12. 1 ff. and 43 ff.

[2] A survey of the fable in the ancient Near East is given by R. J. Williams in *A Stubborn Faith*, ed. E. C. Hobbs, pp. 3–26.

[3] See R. J. Williams, *Phoenix* 10 (1956), 70–77.

[4] A general account of the Sumerian contest fables with a full bibliography and a partial editing of the texts themselves is given by J. J. A. Van Dijk, *La Sagesse*, pp. 31–85.

certainly goes back to Old Babylonian times, and *The Ox and the Horse* have, so far as preserved, only two contestants, as is reflected in the titles, which are known from the ancient lists and catalogues. But the same sources give "The Series of the Fox" as the title of one known fable, and in the surviving fragments no less than three other animals appear: the Wolf, the Dog, and the Lion. Here the old pattern has been expanded, and as a result the work is not a two-sided debate, but centres on the cunning of the Fox. Traces of judgement scenes are found in two of the Babylonian texts: *Nisaba and Wheat*, and *The Fable of the Fox*, but they are not sufficiently complete to allow a comparison with the Sumerian judgements. There is no certainty that a judgement did take place in all the Babylonian texts.

Like Aesopic fables, contest literature spread far, but this development is too extensive to be followed here.[1] Attention, however, should be drawn to the one instance where a Babylonian fable seems to be a lineal ancestor of a Pahlavi dispute: *The Tamarisk and the Palm*. For details see the introduction to this text.

(i) *THE TAMARISK AND THE PALM*

The following entry occurs with other literary titles in Rm 618:

> éš.gàr ^{d}nisaba u ^{giš}gišimmar
>
> The series of Nisaba and the Palm (line 12, Bezold, *Catalogue* IV. 1627)

No such fable is known, but an error has probably occurred. There are two known fables: *The Tamarisk and the Palm*, and *Nisaba and Wheat*. In cuneiform the signs for Nisaba and Tamarisk are very similar, and this suggests that the list has telescoped two titles:

> The series of Nisaba ⟨and Wheat⟩
>
> ⟨The series of the Tamarisk⟩ and the Palm

The Tamarisk would in fact come before the Palm in the title since it leads the debate: it speaks and the Palm replies.

Three very diverse recensions of this work have been recovered. The best recension (A) is offered by two pieces, apparently of the same tablet, from Tell Harmal. They date from the Old Babylonian period and are written in a little-known dialect of Old Babylonian, presumably that of Ešnunna. Unfortunately one piece, which contains the beginning, is small, and the other is very damaged.

A Middle Assyrian tablet (**b**; cf. *AfO* 16. 200), which is a beautiful specimen of calligraphy, offers a variant form of the work. The scribe was unfortunately no master of his craft, and writes both inconsistently and inaccurately. ^{d}*nisaba* is written both with and without the *še* (obv. 16 and rev. 19); *li* appears either with or without the middle row of

[1] Some idea of the extent of the material can be gained from M. Steinschneider's *Rangstreit-Literatur* (*Sitzungsberichte der philosophisch-historischen Klasse der Akademie der Wissenschaften*, Wien, 155/4, 1908), which is restricted to Arabic, Hebrew, and a few of the better-known European languages.

wedges. Twice inexplicable groups of wedges are put down (obv. 10, rev. 1), and twice the same omission is made (rev. 5 and 10). To judge from the curvature of the tablet, a little more than a half of the length of the tablet is preserved. The missing top half of the obverse must have been occupied with the introduction, for the first two surviving speeches are clearly the first round of the debate. On this occasion only are the speakers introduced with the proper formulas; in the following cases the ditto sign is used to indicate that they are to be repeated. As the right-hand edge is broken away it is a matter of some importance for the interpretation to discover, if possible, the amount missing at the right-hand side. The curvature of the bottom edge suggests that very little indeed is wanting, but such a deduction is only approximate. The last section of the obverse offers the only possible direct evidence, since there the other recensions run closely parallel. Line 21 requires *šakin* or another verb, which might be written in three signs. 22, however, if the parallel text can be relied upon, needs *-l*[*i-ia šarratu išatti*] (or, *šarrutu tašatti*), which could not be written in less than seven signs. 24 needs not less than three signs (*a*-[*ma-ḫa-aṣ*]). Thus there is no certainty how much is to be restored, especially as we do not know if the scribe ever resorted to writing on the edge. Something, however, has to be assumed, and previous translators have erred in carrying on the sense from one line to another without indicating a gap. For the most part the text is written in Assyrian dialect, cf. *am-mar*, obv. 20, *e-kal*, obv. 22, &c.

The worst recension is **c**, a curious tablet, perhaps written a century or two after the Middle Assyrian period. At the first glance it has the appearance of a business document. The text is written continuously over obverse, bottom edge, reverse, and is then continued on the left-hand edge. It is neither a library copy nor a school exercise. The suspicion is aroused that it comes from a scribe more accustomed to writing letters and contracts than literature. The signs are clumsily written, often difficult to read, and one in line 9 cannot be identified. The dialect is Assyrian (cf. e.g. *us-ba-at*, 6, *e-za-qa-ap*, 12). The orthography of the text is most peculiar. The scribe writes indifferently "Palm" or "Palms", though one tree is always meant. Grammatical solecisms occur in 2 (*iḫ-ri-ú*, subject *šīmāte*^meš^) and 5 (*a-ši-be*: stative). In 33 ^giš^BAR is an error for ^giš^banšur, and *ma-li-la-ia* in 34 is almost certainly transposed, for *ma-la-li-ia*. The most striking corruptions are at the end; see the notes on 37–41. Throughout the scribe seems to have mangled the composition. Only in one case does he write the proper introduction to the speeches, and here he violently separates "the Palm answered" and inserts "speaking to his brother" between the two Akkadian words (38–39). Elsewhere the change of speaker has to be deduced from the subject matter. The opening speech is of two short lines only (20–21), which is very suspicious. Altogether the tablet shows how bad a poor Assyrian scribe can be, though it is interesting as one of the few specimens of Akkadian literature that have not come from the scribal schools.

A comparison of the three recensions is very instructive. A and **c** have the introduction. **c** enlivens his recension with a heavenly council of which A knows nothing. The first two rounds of speeches are preserved on **b**, and **c** also has the first few speeches, but they have nothing in common. Then with the opening speech of the third round the three recensions are comparatively close to each other, as can be seen by printing them together:

A *bi-nu-um pí-šu i-pu-ša-a-[m]a i-sa-qa-ra-am gi-⌜ši⌝-ma-ra-šu-* ×
b KIMIN
c (nothing parallel)
A The Tamarisk opened his mouth and addressed the Palm,
b Ditto

A *mi-im-ma-ki mu-ta-li-ka-am i-na e-ka-lim ḫu-si-i*
b *ḫu-us-sa mu-tal-li-ki i-na ēkal šarri mi-nu-i[a . . . .*
c *ḫa-sa-ku/ma mu-tal-li-ka ina ēkalli*^{li} MAN *me-nu-ia [š]a-ki-in*
A "Consider what items of your equipment are to be found in the palace.
b "Consider my equipment in the king's palace. What of mine [. . .]
c ". . . the equipment in the king's palace. What of mine is to be found

A *[šu]m-ma i-na pa-šu-r[i-i]a i-ka-al ša-ru-um*
b *i-n]a bīt šarri i-na* ^{giš}*paššūri-ia šarru e-kal i-na ma-la-l[i-ia . . . .*
c *ina ēkalli* MAN *ina* ^{giš}BAR*-ia* MAN *e-ka-la ina ma-li-la-ia* ^{mí}*šar-ru-tu ta-šá-ti*
A It is from my dish that the king eats.
b In the king's house? The king eats from my dish, from [my] goblet [. . . .]
c In the king's palace? The king eats from my . . The queen drinks from my goblet.

A *šum-ma i-na bu-ki-ni-⌜ia⌝ [i-k]a-lu qa-r[a-du*
b *i-n]a it-qu-ri-ia e-ka-lu qar-ra-du i-na bu-gi-ni-i[a . . . .]* ^{lú}*nuḫatimmu qēma i-la-qat*
c (nothing parallel)
A It is from my bread-basket that the warriors eat.
b from my plate. The warriors eat from my bread-basket [. . . .] the baker takes up flour.

A *iš-p]a-ra-ak-ma qé a-ma-ḫa-aṣ ú-la-ba-aš um-ma-nam-ma*
b *iš-pa-ra-ku-ma qe-e a-[. . .] ú-la-ba-áš um-ma-na* × [. . . .]
c *išparā-ku-ma qe-e a-ma-ḫi-ṣ[i]* × [(. .)]
A I am a weaver and beat up the threads. I clothe the troops.
b I am a weaver and [. . .] the threads. I clothe the troops. . [. . . .]
c I am a weaver and beat up the threads . [. .]

A [×] × [× × × *m]a-aš-ma-ša-ak-ma bi-it i-li-im ú-la-al* [. . . .
b × *ša ili rab-maš-maš-a-ku-ma bīt ili ú-da-aš lu e-tel-l[a-ku . . .]*
c *rab-maš-maš-šak ul-la-a[l (. . .)]* giš × *ul pi-ia-ma*
A [.] . [. . .] I am the exorcist and purify the temple [. . . .]
b . of the god. I am the chief exorcist and renovate the temple. [I am] indeed an aristocrat [. . .]
c I am the chief exorcist, I purify [. . .] . . not . . .

A *ša-ni-n]a-am* *ú-ul i-šu i-na i?-li*
b *ša-ni-na* *ia-a ar-ši*
c *ša-nu-ti* × [(. .)] giš ku *ul pi-šu-ma*

A I have no rival among the *gods*."
b I certainly have no rival."
c second . [. .] . . not . . ."

After this speech **c** has a couple of unintelligible lines and then ends. A and **b**, however, continue, and for the following two speeches have some few words in common which are sufficient to show that they followed roughly the same argument. After this the material of A is badly damaged, and no further coincidences can be detected.

What survives of the fable of *The Tamarisk and the Palm* suggests that it followed the pattern of Sumerian fables. It begins with the mythological introduction, which leads up to the planting of the two trees in the first king's courtyard. This introduction is very brief, and is more allusions to myths than a telling of the story. The time referred to is when the gods were giving kingship to men, which occurred twice according to Sumerian history—right at the beginning of civilized life, and again after the flood. It is not clear which occasion the fable refers to, though the statement about the earth groaning (A 2) suits the times before civilized life began better than the post-diluvian world. When the newly appointed king has planted the two trees, he puts on a banquet in the shade of the Tamarisk, and does something else in the shade of the Palm. In this setting the two trees debate their superiority, the one over the other.

Traces of this work can be found in a Pahlavi fable, *The Assyrian Tree*, edited and translated by J. M. Unvala in *Bulletin of the School of Oriental and African Studies* II. 637–78, on which S. Smith commented, ibid. IV. 69–76. A lineal connexion seems certain, though the Pahlavi writer has used other material as well, and employed his work for a quite different purpose. Strabo had heard of a Persian song which enumerated 360 uses of the palm-tree (*Geography* 16. 1. 14), and this could easily have depended for some of its inspiration on our fable. In Greek a fragment of Callimachus preserves a similar work, see H. Diels in *Internationale Wochenschrift* 4. 993–1002.

LITERATURE

TEXT

1917 E. Ebeling, *KAR* 145 (**b**).
1923 E. Ebeling, *KAR* 324 (**c**).
1958 J. J. A. Van Dijk, *Sumer* XIII. 85–89 (A).

EDITIONS, TRANSLATIONS, STUDIES

1917 E. Ebeling, *MDOG* 58. 32–34.
1926–8 S. Smith, *Bulletin of the School of Oriental and African Studies* IV. 69–76.
1927 E. Ebeling, *MAOG* II/3. 1–17.
1950 R. H. Pfeiffer, *ANET*[1], pp. 410–11.
1955 R. H. Pfeiffer, *ANET*[2], pp. 410–11.

MANUSCRIPTS

A = IM 53946 and IM 53975	Plates 39, 40
b = VAT 10102	„ 41, 42
c = VAT 8830	Plate 43

A = IM 53946 and IM 53975

IM 53946 OBVERSE

1 *[i-n]a ú-mi-im ul-lu-tim i-na ša-na-tim ru-qa-tim i-nu-ma*
2 *[šamûm]* ⸢*iz-zi*⸣*-qú ù erṣetum nu-ba-tam i-ta-an-ḫu* ⸢*i*⸣*-lu a-na* ⸢*a-we*⸣*-lu-tim*
3 × *-bu ip-ša-ḫu ù* × *-du-ši-im nu-uḫ-ša-am da-* × *-ni*
4 *[a-n]a šu-te-ši-ir ma-tim gu-šu-úr ni-ši uq-bu ša-ra-am*
5 [×]× am ki ši *a-na ša-pa-ri-im ṣa-al-ma-at qa-qa-di ni-ši ma-da-tim*
6 *[ša-ru-u]m i-na ki-s[al]-li-šu i-za-qa-ap gi-ši-ma-ra-am i-ta-* × *-* ×
7 *[i-za-qa-ap b]i-na-am i-na ṣí-*⸢*il-li bi*⸣*-n[im n]a-ap-ta-nam*
8 *[iškun? i-na ṣí-il-]li gi-[ši-ma-ri-im . . .]* × × bi ×
9 . . .] × × [. . . . .]× ur ×

IM 53975 OBVERSE

1 [×] *sar-ru-um* ×[. . .
2 *gi-ši-ma-ru-um* pi × [. . . . .]× [. .]
3 × × *ša i-ta-la-al-*[× ×] ru [× ×] ad [. . .
4 [× × × ×] *in-bi* × × × [. . .
5 [× × ×]*-šu?-nu?-ma? da-mi-iq* [. . . . .] × × × [. . .
(The rest of the obverse is represented by detached signs and traces.)

OBVERSE

1 In former days, in far-off years when
2 [The heavens] were grieved and the earth groaned at evening time, the gods . .
3 To mankind, they became appeased and *granted* them abundance . . .
4 To guide the land and establish the peoples they *appointed* a king.
5 [.] . . . . to rule the black-headed, the many peoples,
6 [The king] planted the Palm in his courtyard . . .
7 [He planted] the Tamarisk. In the shade of the Tamarisk [he arranged]
8 A banquet; in the shade of the Palm [. . .] . . . .

REVERSE

1 ⌜*a*⌝*-na-di-in* × am la ka am za × × × × *a-na-di-in e-sa*
2 *bi-nu-um pí-šu i-pu-ša-a-*[*m*]*a i-sa-qa-ra-am gi-*⌜*ši*⌝*-ma-ra-šu-*×
3 *mi-im-ma-ki mu-ta-li-ka-am i-na e-ka-lim ḫu-si-i*
4 [*šu*]*m-ma i-na pa-šu-r*[*i-i*]*a i-ka-al ša-ru-um šum-ma i-na bu-ki-ni-*⌜*ia*⌝
5 [*i-k*]*a-lu qa-r*[*a-du iš-p*]*a-ra-ak-ma qé a-ma-ḫa-aṣ ú-la-ba-aš um-ma-nam-ma*
6 [×] × [× × × *m*]*a-aš-ma-ša-ak-ma bi-it i-li-im ú-la-al*
7 [. . . . *ša-ni-n*]*a-am ú-ul i-šu i-na i?-li i-pu-lam*
8 *gi-ši-m*[*a*]*-ru-*[*um a*]*l-ka-am* × × in *ra-bi-a-am*
9 *a-di la* [*a-zi-zu u*]*l i-na-*⌜*qí*⌝ *š*[*a-*]*ar-ru-um*
10 × [× (×)] × × [t]im? la ru li × ḫu × *e-ru la ka-ás-pu*
11 [. . .]× *š*[*a*]*-ar-ru-um i-nu-mi-šu at-ta i-na qa-ti si-ra-ši-i*[*m*]
12 [. . . .]× ⌜*e*⌝*-li-ka ka-am-ru bi-nu-um pí-šu i-pu-ša-am-ma*
13 [*i-sa-qa-ra-a*]*m gi-ši-ma-ra-a-šu al-ki-im i-na ú-mi i-si-nim*
14 [. . . .]*-li ba-ši šum-ma i-na* ×-×*-tim la ṣú-ba-bu bi-nu-um*
15 [. . . .]*-am* la šu ta al UD ma *ar?-nu i-nu-mi-š*[*u*]
16 [*at-ti i-na*] *qa-ti nu-ḫa-ti-im-mi ta-ba-ši-ma i-na pa-ar-ši ù* [*d*]*a-mi-im*
17 [. . . .]×*-ši-id i-na* × × × ⌜*i-pu-lam*⌝ *gi-ši-im-ma-ru-um*
18 [. . .]×*-ni gu-ga-la-ni* gu × ša ša? *in-bu ma-an-ni-im*
19 [. . .]×*-ši-da-am-ma in-bi-ia in-bu ra-ma-ni-ia i-na li-*×-×
20 [. . .]×*-el ša-ar-ri-im* × × ḫi × nam? *ḫi-nu-ia a-na mi-šu-*×[(-×)]
21 [. . .]×*-ri e-ru-i*[*a*] a × × × × × *ki-nim a-na ši-i-im* × × [. .]
22 [. . .]×*-e a-na* × × × × × × × *ar-zu-tim ḫa-*× × [. .]
23 [. . . .]× × [. .] × × × [×] *be-el pa-ar-ṣí* a × [×] iš [. .]
24 [*bi-nu-um pí-šu i-pu-ša-am-ma i-sa-qa-ra-am*] *gi-ši-ma-r*[*a-š*]*u*
25–26 traces

IM 53946 REVERSE

1 traces
2 [. . . .]×*-ti-ni ma-aš-ši* × ×[. . . . .]
3 [. . .]× *qí-bi i-na pí-ki li-im-*×[. . . . .]×
4 [. .] × ×*-pa-ra-ki a-na-ku* ad ba? ×[. . . . .]×*-ra*
5 [*uz?*]*-na-ši-na il-tu-ki i-na* × × [. . . . .]×*-bi*
6 [*i-nu*]*-mi-šu a-na-ku i-na qa-t*[*i* . . . .]
7 [×] × am ša × ma × × [. . . . .]
8 [*i*]*-na ši-li-im* ⌜*a*⌝-[. . . . .] × ×
9 *ši-ik-ka-tum a-n*[*a*] × × × × × × [*i*]*l-ku*
10 [×]-×*-ru bi-nim*

REVERSE

2 The Tamarisk opened his mouth and addressed the Palm,
3 "Consider what items of your equipment are to be found in the palace.
4 It is from my dish that the king eats. It is from my bread-basket
5 That the warriors eat. I am a weaver and beat up the threads. I clothe the troops.
6 [.] . [. . .] I am the exorcist and purify the temple.
7 [. . . .] I have no rival among the *gods*." The Palm
8 Answered, "Come, the great . . .
9 While I am not [present] the king does not libate,
10 . [. .] . . . . twigs not cut up.
11 The king [. . .] . At that time you are in the brewer's hand
12 [. . . .] . are heaped upon you." The Tamarisk opened his mouth and
13 [Addressed] the Palm, "Come, in the time of festivals
14 [. . . .] . is . . . . the Tamarisk, which is no . . .
15 [. . . .] . . . . *guilt*. At that time
16 You are in the hand of the butcher amid offal and blood.
17 [. . . .] . . . ." The Palm answered,
18 ["'. . .] . . our canal supervisor . . . . Whose fruit
19 [. . .] . . . . . my fruit. My own fruit . . . . .

b = VAT 10102

OBVERSE

1 [× ×] × × × × [. . . . .]
2 [×] × × *ka-ia-m*[*a-nu* . . . .]

---

3 [^{giš}*bī*]*nu pî*^{i}*-šu e-*[*pu-uš-ma* . . . .]
4 [*a*]*t-tu-ia šīrū*^{meš} *a-na šīrī*^{m}[^{eš}*-ka* . . . .]
5 *aq-ra dam-qa tu-ba-li* ta-a*[*d-* . . . .]
6 *ki-i amti ša a-na bēlti*^{ti}*-ša ub-*[. . . . .]

---

7 *ut-túr pî*^{i}*-šu e-ta-pal* ^{giš}[*gišimmaru* . . . .]
8 *um-ma i-na ú-ri-ni-ma i-ta-*[P]A *pi-ri-ka* [. . . . .]
9 *ilam-ma ni-sa-aq-ra a-na ḫi-ṭi-ma šīrī*^{meš}[- . . . .]
10 *ul i-di* ^{giš}*bīnu du-muq* × (×) meš *du-muq* ×[. . . . .]

---

11 KIMIN *a-na-ku e-lu-ka a-bu um-ma-ni ka-la-ma* ^{lú}×[. . . .]
12 *ma-la-šu i-šu* ^{lú}*ikkāru i-na pa-pal-li-ia i-ta-ke-ès* [. . . .]
13 *i-na uṭ-li-ia* ^{giš}*marra-šu ul-te-li i-na* ^{giš}*marri-ia* [. . . .]
14 *i-pi-ti nam-ka-ru-ma i-ša-ti eqla as-sà-an-qa* ×[. . . .]
15 *ù a-na nu-ur-bi ša er-ṣe-ti as-na-an* MIN ×[. . . .]
16 *ú-da-aš ù* ^{d}*nisaba šu-muḫ nišī*^{meš} *ú-da-*[*aš*]

---

17 KIMIN *a-na-ku e-lu-ka a-bu um-ma-ni ka-la-ma* ^{lú}*ikkāru* ×[. . . .]
18 *ma-la-šu i-šu šúm-ma-ni tam-ša-ri ṣubāt na-aṣ-ma-di ù e-*[. . . .]
19 ⌜*ri-ik-su*⌝ *ṣubāt le-e ṣubāt ši-da-ti še-ta* ^{giš}*ṣumba*(mar.gíd.da) ×[. . . .]
20 *ša* × × × *ú-nu-ut* ^{lú}*ikkāri am-mar i-ba-šu-ú e-lu* ×[. . . .]

---

21 KIMIN *ḫu-us-sa mu-tal-li-ki i-na ēkal šarri mi-nu-i*[*a* . . . .]
22 [*i-n*]*a bīt šarri i-na* ^{giš}*paššūri-ia šarru e-kal i-na ma-la-l*[*i-ia* . . . .]
23 [*i-n*]*a it-qu-ri-ia e-ka-lu qar-ra-du i-na bu-gi-ni-i*[*a* . . . .]
24 ⌜^{lú}⌝*nuḫatimmu qēma*(zì.da) *i-la-qat iš-pa-ra-ku-ma qe-e a-*[*ma-ḫa-aṣ* . . .]
25 ⌜*ú*⌝*-la-ba-áš um-ma-na* ×[. . . .]
26 × *ša ili rab-maš-maš-a-ku-ma bīt ili ú-da-aš lu e-tel-l*[*a-ku* . . .]

27 [(×)] *ša-ni-na ia-a ar-ši*

---

* The remains of a sign, probably to be considered erased, are visible here.

OBVERSE

---

3 The Tamarisk opened his mouth [and . . . .]
4 "My flesh compared with [your] flesh [. . . . .]
5 My precious, fine climbing-belt you [. . . . .]
6 Like a slave-girl who . [. . . . . . .] her mistress."

---

7 [The Palm] answered with exaggerated utterance [. . . . . .]
8 ". . . your pods with a rod [. . . . .]
9 When we call on a god [. . . . . .] flesh for sin.
10 The Tamarisk does not know the best of . . ., the best of . [. . . . . . ."]

---

11 Ditto. "I am superior to you, a master of every craft. The . [. . . .]
12 All he has, the farmer has cut from my branch [. . . .]
13 He produces his spade from my bosom, and with my spade [. . . .]
14 Opens [. . .,] so that the irrigation canal drinks. I have kept in order the field . [. . . .]
15 And for the moisture of the soil . . . . . [. . . .]
16 I thresh, and corn, on which mankind thrives, I thresh."

---

17 Ditto. "I am superior to you, a master of every craft. The farmer . [. . . .]
18 All he has: leading-reins, whips, the cover of the team, and . [. . . .]
19 Harness, the cover of the oxen, the cover of the . . ., the net, the wagon . [. . . .]
20 . . . . the farmer's equipment, all that exists . . . [. . . ."]

---

21 Ditto. "Consider my equipment in the king's palace. What of mine [is found]
22 [In] the king's house? The king eats from my dish, from [my] goblet [. . . .]
23 From my plate. The warriors eat from my bread-basket [. . . .]
24 The baker takes up flour. I am a weaver, [beating up] the threads.
25 I clothe the troops . [. . . .]
26 . of the god. I am the chief exorcist and renovate the temple. [I am] indeed an aristocrat [. . .]
27 [.] I certainly have no rival."

REVERSE

1 [KI]MIN *i-na gi-zi-na-ki* ni × × ^{d}*sin*(30) *ru-b*[*e-e* . . .]
2 [*a*]-*šar a-na-ku ul a-zi-zu ul i-na-qí*! (tablet DI) *šarru i-na im-*×[. . . .]
3 [*š*]*ul-lu-ḫu šu-lu-ḫu-ia tab-ku e-ru-ia i-na qa-qa-ri-ma e-*×[. . . .]
4 [*i-n*]*a* u_4*-mi-šu* ^{giš}*gišimmaru* ^{lú}*sīrāšû*(šim) *ba-ši-ma irāti*^{meš}*-ki* ka ma ×[. . . .]

---

5 [K]IMIN *al-ki i ni-li-ka a-na-ku ù* ⟨*ka*⟩*-a-ši a-na āl kiš* ×[. . . .]
6 *a-šar ši-ip-ri um-ma-*⟨*ni*⟩ *i-ta-tu-ia* [*l*]*a ma-la-a* [×]× ×[. . . .]
7 *la ma-la-a qàt-ri-ni qa-di-iš-t*[*u*] *mê*^{meš} *is-*[*sa-riq*]*-ma* [. . . .]
8 *i-la-qí-ma i-dal-la-lu-ma i-pa-šu i-si-na*! *i-*⌜*na u*⌝$_4$*-mi-š*[*u* . . . .]
9 *a-na qāt* ^{lú}*ṭa-bi-ḫi ba-ši-ma e-ru-šu i-na pár-ši* [. . . .]

---

10 KIMIN *al-ki i ni-li-ka a-na-ku ù* ⟨*ka*⟩*-a-ši a-na āl* ×[. . . .]
11 *a-šar ḫi-ṭa-ti e-peš-ka bi-nu* ^{lú}*nangāru i-na* ×[. . . .]
12 *ù šu-ú pal-ḫa-ni-ma* u_4*-mi-šám-ma ú-na-ia-da-*[*an-ni*]

---

13 KIMIN *ma-an-nu* el ma × la ú gad pi kur di [. . . .]
14 *na-ša-ku-ma ka-pár-ri ma-ar-te-e ra-bu-ti* ud ×[. . . .]
15 *ú-bi-ta-qa* [*d*]*a-a-ni-ki ki-ma* ^{lú}*atkuppi ša* [. . . .]
16 [*i-n*]*a du-ni e-mu-*⌜*qé*⌝*-ia ra-ba-te lu-uḫ-d*[*i* . . . .]
17 [*lu*] *aš-ku-un-ka a-na ga-me-ri gu-šur* ×[. . . .]

---

18 KIMIN *a-na-ku e-lu-ka* 6-*š*[*u*] *mu-tu-ra-ku* 7-*šu* ×[. . . . .]
19 *a-na* ^{d}*nisaba te-nu-ú a-na-ku* 3 *arḫu du* [. . . . .]
20 *e-ku-tu al-mat-tu eṭ-lu la-ap-nu* ×[. . . . . .]
21 *e-ka-lu šá la ma-ṭa ṭa-bu suluppi* ×[. . . . . . .]
22 $^{\text{ḫi-pí}}$ *šír-šír-ri* [. . . . .]
23 [*l*]*i-ib-li-bi-ia e-dal-la-l*[*u* . . . .]
24 ×^{meš}*-ia* a [(×)] × ra pi li [. . . . .]
25 [×] × × [× ×] × ti × [. . . . .]
26 [. . . . .]× ta[. . . . .]

REVERSE

1 Ditto. "At the place of Sin's offering . . . . Sin the noble [. . .]
2 Where I am not present the king does not libate . . . . [. . . .]
3 My rites are performed, and my twigs are heaped up on the ground . . [. . . .]
4 At that time the Palm is a brewer; your . . . . . [. . . ."]

---

5 Ditto. "Come, let us go, I and you, to the city of Kiš . [. . . .]
6 Where the work of the savant takes place there are signs of me. Not full [.] . . [. . . .]
7 Not full of incense. The prostitute has sprinkled water and [. . . .]
8 She takes and they worship and hold a festival. At that time [. . . .]
9 Is in the hand of the meat-carver. His twigs in offal [. . . ."]

---

10 Ditto. "Come, let us go, I and you, to the city of . [. . . .]
11 Where there are sins, there is your sphere, Tamarisk. The carpenter . . . [. . . .]
12 He respects me and daily praises [me."]

---

13 Ditto. "Who . . . . [. . . .]
14 I lift up. The drovers . . [. . . .] great staves.
15 I split your might like a reed-worker who [. . . .]
16 I shall rejoice in the might of my great strength [. . . .]
17 I made you a master, prevailing . [. . . ."]

---

18 Ditto. "I am superior to you. Six times I excel, seven times . [. . . . .]
19 I am the successor to the corn goddess; for three months . [. . . . .]
20 The orphan girl, the widow, the poor man . [. . . . . .]
21 Eat without stint my sweet date . [. . . . . . .]
22 (broken) . . . [. . . . .]
23 They worship my offshoots [. . . . ."]

c = VAT 8830

1 *ina* u_4*-me*(-)*el-lu-te nišū*^{meš} × *šu-u-te*
2 *nārāte*^{meš} *iḫ-ri-ú šīmāte*(nam.tar.meš)
3 *puḫra iš-ku-nu ilāni*^{meš} *mātāte*^{meš} ^{d}*a-nu* ^{d}*enlil*(be) ^{d}*é-a*
4 ^{d}*e*[*n-lí*]*l u ì-lì id-da-al-gu*
5 *ina be-er-šu-nu a-ši-be* ^{d}*šá-maš*
6 KIMIN *i-it-til-la-at ilāni*^{meš} *rabītu us-*⸢*ba*⸣*-at*
7 *ina pāna*^{na} *šar-ru-tu ina mātāti*^{meš} *ul ba-ši*
8 *u be-lu-tu a-na ilāni*^{meš} *šar-ka-at*
9 giš.×.meš *šarru*(man) *ilāni*^{meš} *ra-mu-ni-šu*
10 *ṣa-lam* sag.meš *iq-bu-ni-šu*
11 *šarru*(man) *ina ēkalli*^{li}*-šu*
12 *e-za-qa-ap* ^{giš}*gišimmarī*^{me}
13 *e-*⸢*il*⸣*-te-šu* KIMIN *ma-li* ^{giš}*bi-nu*
14 *ina ṣi-li* ^{giš}*bi-ni nap-tu-*[*nu*]
15 *ša-ki-iḫ-ma ina ṣi-li* ^{giš}*gišimmari*
16 ur ta za ub te ×[× (×) *šu-*]*ṭú-ub-bu*
17 *pi-it ina* ×[×] *ṭú-u-du šarri*(man)
18 *mar a-ḫi* ú × × × šu × šu lu
19 ^{giš}*bi-nu u* ^{giš}*gišimmarū*^{meš} ⸢it⸣ × × × × lu
20 *um-ma* ^{giš}*bi-nu ma-gal ra-ma* × ×
21 *šúm-ma* ^{giš}*gišimmarum-ma šu-tu-ra* × [(×)] ka
22 *at-ta* ^{giš}*bi-nu iṣṣē*^{meš} *la-a ḫi-še-*[*e*]*ḫ-te*
23 *mi-i-na āru*(pa)*-ka* ⸢*iṣ*⸣ × *la-a* [*in*]*-bi*
24 *at-tu-ú-ia in-bi iṣ* × × e
25 *ša-aḫ-ma e-ka-al* um *ša-nu-ta-šú*
26 *da-me-eq-ti e-qa-bi* ^{lú}*nukarribu*
27 *ni-ma-la-aš ša ar-da u šá ḫa-za-ním*
28 *u-ra-ba še-er-ra* (ras.) ta *inbi-ia*
29 *e-ka-la ra-bu-u in-bu-ia*
30 × *me-e*[*ḫ*]*-ri šarri*(man) la/te *ḫa-sa-ku/ma*
31 *mu-tal-li-ka ina ēkalli*^{li} *šarri*(man)
32 *me-nu-ia* [*š*]*a-ki-in ina ēkalli šarri*(man)
33 *ina* ^{giš}BAR*-ia šarru*(man) *e-ka-la*
34 *ina ma-li-la-ia* ^{mí}*šar-ru-tu ta-šá-ti*
35 *išparā-ku-ma qe-e a-ma-ḫi-ṣ*[*i*] × [(. .)]
36 *rab-maš-maš-šak ul-la-a*[*l*(. . .)]
37 giš × *ul pi-ia-ma ša-nu-ti* ×[(. .)]
38 giš ku *ul pi-šu-ma e-ta-ap-la* [(. .)]
39 *e-za-qa-*⟨*ar*⟩ *a-na a-ḫi-šu* ^{giš}*gišimmaru* [(. .)]

1 In former days the peoples . . . .
2 The Fates dug the rivers;
3 The gods of the lands, Anu, Enlil, and Ea, convened an assembly.
4 Enlil and the gods took counsel,
5 In their midst Šamaš was seated,
6 In their midst was seated the great lady of the gods.
7 Formerly kingship did not exist in the lands,
8 And the rule was given to the gods.
9–10 (untranslatable)

11 The king planted
12 The Palm in his palace;
13 With it he planted . . the Tamarisk.
14 In the shade of the Tamarisk a feast
15 Took place; in the shade of the Palm
16 . . . . . . [. . was] improved
17 Open . . [.] the way of the king.
18 Each other's worth . . . .
19 The Tamarisk and the Palm . . . . . .
20 Thus the Tamarisk, "Greatly . . . .
21 If the Palm excelling . [.] ."
22 "You, Tamarisk, are a useless tree.
23 What are your branches? Wood . without fruit!
24 My fruit . . . .
25 . . . . second
26 The gardener speaks well of me,
27 A benefit to both slave and magistrate.
28 . my fruit makes the baby grow,
29 Grown men eat my fruit."
30 " . the equal of the king . . . .
31 The equipment in the king's palace,
32 What of mine is to be found in the king's palace?
33 The king eats from my . .
34 The queen drinks from my goblet.
35 I am a weaver and beat up the threads . [. .]
36 I am the chief exorcist and purify [. . .]
37 . . not . . . second . [. .]
38 . . not . . ." There answered [. .]
39 Addressing his brother, the Palm [. .]

40 *šúm-ma* ká ni ta di ša *zi-iz* qaq za ×[.]
41 *šúm-ma* na ku/ma ni ḫa *qa-ar*

(ii) *THE FABLE OF THE WILLOW*

In the list of literary texts Rm 618 (Bezold, *Catalogue* IV. 1627), 13 this work is given as éš.gàr giš.asal, and the catalogue K 9717 and Sm 669 (edited in *JCS* 11. 11–12) rev. 14 deals with it:

[éš.gàr] giš.asal: *šá pi-i* ${}^{\text{m}}$*ur-*${}^{\text{d}}$*nan*[*na*] ${}^{\text{lú}}$×[. . .]. ${}^{\text{lú}}$u[m.me.a . . .]

[The series] of the Willow; according to Urnanna the [. . .] . the scholar [of . . .]

The tree name here rendered 'Willow' with R. C. Thompson (*Dictionary of Assyrian Botany*, pp. 292–6) is obscure. Other renderings such as 'Mulberry' (e.g. Salonen, *Landfahrzeuge*, p. 143) and 'Poplar' (A. L. Oppenheim, *Dreams*, p. 273[55]) have been proposed. One certain piece of this work survives: K 8566+13771, in which the Willow speaks and the Laurel replies. K 8413 is included here as very probably belonging to the text since it is certainly part of a tree fable, and in line 7 "with slivers of me" there is reference to ritual appurtenances which are known to have been made of willow in many cases. Since the catalogue only mentions one tree, it may be assumed that several other trees were involved, though no one had a part equal to that of the Willow.

LITERATURE

K 8566 was wrongly identified by George Smith as part of Tablet 8 of the *Gilgameš Epic*, and a translation of it is given in his *Chaldean Account of Genesis* (1876, p. 243; 1880, p. 254). The fragment was copied by P. Haupt and appeared as no. 28 of his *Das babylonische Nimrodepos*. B. Meissner correctly identified it as a fable fragment (*Babylonien und Assyrien* II. 429). K 8413 was recognized as a fable fragment by B. Landsberger.

K 8566+13771 (Plate 44)

1 × × [. . .
2 *lu* ^{giš}*nu-*[*úr-mu-ú* . . .
3 ^{giš}*erenu* ^{giš}*šur*[*mēnu* . . .
4 *i-na ki-ši ù*! (tablet LU) *a-p*[*i* . . .
5 *at-ta-ma lid-di-*× [. . .
6 *lu ṣab-ta-ta bīt ḫi-im-*× [. . .
7 *ina pu-ḫur kul-la-ti* × [. . .
8 *mu-ḫal-liq ma-'-du* × [. . .
9 *lil-lum šá iṣṣī*^{meš} [. . .
10 *ina šat-ti-ka* ^{giš}*ēru*(ma.nu) *īpuš*^{u}[^{š} . . .
11 *šur-šu-ka ul dun-nu-nu* [. . .
12 *ul šá-ru* ^{giš}*ṣilla-ka* [. . .
13 *ul šam-ḫat qim-mat-ka* [×] ri [. . .

---

14 *ag-giš* ^{giš}*ēru*(ma.nu) *īpuš p*[*â-šu*] ^{giš}*ṣarbata*(asal) [*i-tap-la*]
15 *šit-nun-ta ip-*[*pu-šá*] *ú-šam-ris*[*-su*]
16 *kīma* ^{giš}*bīni* [× × ×]× *ul šīr* ×[× × (×)]
17 [*ki-*]*ma* ^{giš}*gišimmari šàr iṣ*[*ṣī*^{me}]^{š} i ni ib [. . .
18 [*ki-ma* ^{giš}*ša*]*ššugi*(m]es.gàm) *sa-pi-in māt a-a-bi* × [. . .

2 Or the pomegranate-tree [. . .
3 The cedar, the cypress [. . .
4 In reed-bed and thicket [. . .
5 You . . . [. . .
6 . . . . [. . .
7 In the sum of everything . [. . .
8 Destroyer of much . [. . .
9 The idiot of the trees [. . .
10 In your . ., Laurel, he made [. . .
11 Your roots are not exceeding strong [. . .
12 Your shade is not abundant [. . .
13 Your top is not luxuriant [. . .

---

14 Angrily the Laurel opened [his mouth and answered] the Willow,
15 Making a controversy he provoked [him,]
16 "Like the tamarisk [. . .] . not flesh . [. . .]
17 Like the palm, the king of the trees, . . . [. . .
18 [Like] the mountain ash, that overwhelms the enemy land . [. . .

19 [× ×]× *šum-su-ku ga-na* [. . .
20 [× ×-*k*]*a ul ir-rak-ka-*[*s*]*a* ×[. . .
21 [*ul-la-*]*nu-uk ul i-šak-k*[*a-na* . . .
22 [*a-na d*]*an-ni u a-ki-i* [. . .
23 [× × × (×)] ^{giš}*marru še-ra-'* [. . .
24 [× × × ×]× *ip-pu-šá* [. . .
25 trace

K 8413 (Plate 44)

1 [. . . . .]×-*ú* ^{giš}*mēsu* ×[. . .
2 [. . . .]× ^{lú}*tamkāru ul* ×[. . .
3 × × [. .]-*ia ul is-sek-ke-ru* [. . .
4 × giš pa × × *la ma-gi-ri i-naṭ-ṭú-*⸢*ú*⸣ [. . .
5 *ú-qar-rad lil-la a-ka-a* ⸢*ú*⸣[- . . .
6 *šá la še-me-e-ša a-ma-ti ú-pat-ta-a* [. . .
7 *ina lu-te-e-a šarra ú-šal-la-mu* [. . .
8 *eli kab-ti ù muš-ki-ni šá-kin* [. . .
9 *a-na e-de-né-e āli ma-an-ga-li* [. . .
10 ^{giš}*dalta ù* ^{giš}*sikkūra i-na-aṣ-ṣu-ru* ×[. . .
11 *a-na šu-zu-ub ú-ri šá-kin* ×[. . .
12 *ki-ma ki-li-li ēkallu zu-'u-na-at* ×[. . .
13 [*i*]*ṣ-ṣur šá-a-ri ana maš-tak šāri i-na-ṭa-lu* [. . .
14 [×] ×[×]e ^{lú}*malāḫu*(má.laḫ$_4$) *i-za-bi-la* [. . .
15 [. . . .] × × [. . . .] *ma-lu-u-ni bi-iṣ*[- . . .
16 [. . . . .]× *du-um-mu-šu* ru ×[. . .
17 [. . . . .]× ⸢bu⸣ × *ni-qa-a* [. . .
18 traces

19 [. .] . overthrown, come, [. . .
20 Your [. .] will not be bound . [. . .
21 [Apart] from you [. . .] does not place [. . .
22 [To] strong and weak [. . .
23 [. . . .] spade the furrow [. . .
24 [. . . .] . makes [. . .

4 They smash the disobedient . . . . . [. . .
5 I make the weak strong, I [. . . . .] the cripple.
6 Without her hearing it I make known the words [. . .
7 With slivers of me they protect the king [. . .
8 To noble and commoner is provided [. . .
9 To a solitary city . . . . [. . .
10 They guard door and bolt . [. . .
11 [. . . . .] . is placed to save the roof.
12 Like a crown the temple is adorned with . [. . .
13 They look at the weather vane for the direction of the wind [. . .
14 [.] . [.] . the sailor carries [. . .

(iii) *NISABA AND WHEAT*

This is the most curious of all the Babylonian fables. It may be listed on a tablet of literary titles, see the Introduction to the fable of *The Tamarisk and the Palm*. Nisaba was the Sumerian grain goddess, later taken over by the Babylonians, and her name is even used in Babylonian as a common noun, 'grain'. Thus there are no obvious grounds for a dispute between Nisaba and a particular kind of grain. The preserved portions of this work do not explain the matter. One large fragment of a tablet from Sultantepe is the only certain portion of the work. A small piece from Sultantepe is also included here since it seems to be part of the same tablet as the large fragment. Less certain is the attribution to this work of a small piece from Assur, which is nevertheless given below.

The first preserved portion of Column I of the main fragment is the conclusion of a speech praying for, or promising, prosperity. Nisaba is probably the speaker. Then Wheat speaks, addressing Nisaba as mistress of the underworld, and accusing her of disseminating hatred in every part of the universe. The basis of this charge is not made clear. The connexion of the grain goddess with the underworld is that plants derive their nourishment from below ground. In *Ludlul* it is stated that underworld demons reach the sphere of men by emerging from the ground like plants (II. 57). The second column is very poorly preserved. The names of several gods are, however, preserved (Ea, the Anunnaki, Anu), and the surviving phrase "Ereškigal answered" (14) in this connexion could be taken as part of a judgement scene, since Ereškigal, as queen of the underworld, is often represented in a judicial capacity. The third column is all but gone, though a substantial part of Column IV is preserved. This is a pure hymn in praise of Nisaba, which suggests that she had won the contest, and that the work is almost concluded.

It is not possible to date the poem more precisely than to give 2000 and 800 B.C. as the extreme limits. The stress on rain as a fertilizing agent (I. 17–18 and 21–22) implies a northern place of origin, rather than southern Mesopotamia, where crops depend entirely on humanly contrived irrigation. The dialect is, however, Standard Babylonian, and not a northern vernacular.

MANUSCRIPTS AND LITERATURE

SU 1951, 173+1952, 100+142	*STT* I. 34	Plates 45, 46
SU 1952, 257	*STT* I. 35	Plate 45
VAT 12995	*KAR* 301	„ 44

SU 1951, 173+1952, 100+142 (Plates 45, 46)

OBVERSE I

1 × × [. . . . .]
2 *li-is-*× [. . . . .]
3 *abi ilāni*^{meš} [. . . . .]
4 *nu-úr* ^{d}*šam[aš* . . . .]
5 *ina ṣi-it* ^{d}*[šamaš* . . . .]
6 *lik-kab-du* × [. . . . .]
7 *is-ra-tum ù* [. . . . .]
8 *p/ši-ir-'u li-ku[-un* . . . .]
9 *p/ši-ir-'u lib-ba-n[i* . . . .]
10 *ša gi-mir zēri*(še.numun) [. . . . .]
11 *ḫur-sa-a-ni liš-ša[k-* . . . .]
12 × × × am ši × [. . . . .]
13 *ki-kur-ri lib-ba-[ni* × × × × ×] × × ×
14 *aširtu*(zag.gar.ra) *li-te-[pu-uš a-na ilā]ni rabûti*(ding]ir.gal.gal)
15 *ina gi-mir du-ru-uš-[ši lib-ba-ši]* ^{mí}*damiqtu*
16 *ša áš-ri ka-ṣu-t[e* × × (×)]*-šá a-šìr-šun*
17 *na-al-ba-áš šamê*^{e} *lib-ba-[tiq a-n]a ši-si-te* ^{d}*ad-di*
18 *imbaru*(im.dugud) *liq-i-ma ur-qit [erṣetim*^{tim}*] lip-pát-qu*

OBVERSE I

3 Father of the gods [. . . . .]
4 Light of Šam[aš . . . .]
5 At the rising of [Šamaš . . . .]
6 Let them be honoured . [. . . . .]
7 The granary and [. . . . .]
8 May the fruit/furrow be secure [. . . . .]
9 May the fruit/furrow be created [. . . . .]
10 Of all plant life [. . . . .]
11 May the mountains . . [. . . . .]
12 . . . . . . [. . . . .].
13 Let the temple base be built [. . . . .]
14 Let the shrine be [made for the] great gods.
15 In all the (temple) foundations let divine approval [be shown.]
16 Of cold places [. . .] . their warden.
17 Let the garb of heaven be rent at the cry of Addu,
18 Let the rain storm pour forth that the vegetation of [the earth] may be brought into being.

19 *nam-maš-še-e* ^{d}*šakkan lik-tam-me-[ra* × (×)]× *ina qir-bé-te*
20 *ab-ra-te liš-te-še-ra li[-ku-na] ma-ti-tan*
21 ^{d}*ad-du li-iḫ-mu-ma li-[ša-az-n]in nuḫša*(ḫé.nun)
22 ^{d}*i-šum ina šub-ti-šú li-i[t-bi]*×*-ma-niš*
23 ^{d}*a-ru-ru ummi ilāni*^{meš} *liš-te-še-r[a ta-]lit-tú*
24 *bu-kúr-tum ù tarbaṣu li-tam-ma-*× *[ḫ]ar-pa-te*

---

25 *kibtu*(še.gig) *pâ-šú īpuš*^{uš}*-ma iqabbi*(dug_4.ga)
26 *a-na* ^{d}*nisaba bēlit*(gašan) *erṣetim*^{tim} *amāta izakkar*(mu-*ár*)
27 *am-me-ni* ^{d}*nisaba tan-da-ḫa-aṣ ina m[a]-a-ti*
28 *[i]t-ti gi-mir zēri*(še.numun) *te-te-pu-šá ṣi-[i]l-te*
29 *[a-n]a-an-ta tab-ta-na-a tu-šá-ḫa-za l[i-m]ut-tú*
30 *[nu-u]l-la-a-te ta-tam-ma-a tu-šá-áš-qa-ra a-ḫ[a-ti]*
31 *[ina bi-r]it* ^{d}*í-gì-gì ù* ^{d}*anunnaki* (600) *taš-ta-ka-na zi-[ru-ta]*
32 [× ×] *apsî tu-šam-ka-ra mál-ma-[liš]*
33 [× ×]UR-*ka taš-tak-kan ina ka-liš kib-ra-a-te*
34 [× × *a]pkalli tu-šab-ba-šá tu-ḫal-la-qa nab-nit*
35 *[iš-me-ma* ^{d}*nisa]ba a-ma-tú ma-ru-uš-tú*
36 [. . . . . . .] dir *mar-ṣi-iš iš-gu-um*
37 [. . . . . . *r]a-ma-nu-uš i-ban-ni ṭè-e-mu*
38 [. . . . .] ud *ú-sap-pa-a a-na ib-ri-šú*

OBVERSE II

1 *libbu* [. . . . .]
2 *e-*[. . . . .]
3 *a-na* [. . . . .]
4 *i-ḫi-*[. . . . .]
5 *ù* [^{d}]*é-a* ×[. . . . .]
6 zu [× r]i ma mu [. . . . .]
7 ^{d}*a-[nu]n-na-ki* ×[. . . . .]
8 bu? [×] × ša × ×[. . . . .]
9 *i[t-ti]* ^{d}*nisaba mārat* ^{d}*[a-nim* . . . .]
10 × [×] ^{d}*a-num ka-bat-[ta-šú* . . . .]
11 *ša* ⸢^{d}⸣*é-a ina apsî* [. . . . .]
12 × [(×)^{m}]^{eš} *in-na-šu-u* [. . . . .]
13 ⸢*it*⸣*-taš-kin šá-lum-ma-tú* [. . . . .]
14 ⸢*e*⸣*-tap-la* ^{d}*ereš-ki-[gal* . . . .]
15 *[a-n]a ilāni*^{meš} ×[. . . . .]
16 *[li-]iš-mu* ×[. . . . .]

(Gap of about four lines)

21 ×[. . . . .]

19 Let the creatures of Šakkan be multiplied [. .] . in the meadow,
20 Let the human race prosper and all lands be [established.]
21 May Addu rumble and [rain down] prosperity,
22 May Išum [leave] his dwelling like a . . .
23 May Aruru, mother of the gods, grant successful procreation,
24 May . . . and sheepfold abound [with] growing ewes."

---

25 Wheat opened his mouth and spoke,
26 Addressing Nisaba, mistress of the underworld,
27 "Why, Nisaba, do you fight in the land?
28 You have picked a quarrel with every plant,
29 You have created conflict and stirred up evil,
30 You speak slander and utter [libel,]
31 You have brought about hatred between the Igigi and the Anunnaki,
32 You set at variance [the . . of] the Apsû without exception,
33 Your [. .] . you have continued to put in every corner of the world,
34 You will anger [. .] the sage, you will destroy creation."
35 Nisaba [heard] the disagreeable speech,
36 [. . . . .] . she cried in distress.
37 [. . . . .] herself she formed a plan,
38 [. . . . .] . she besought her friend.

OBVERSE II

5 And Ea . [. . . . .]
6 . [.] . . . [. . . . .]
7 The Anunnaki . . [. . . . .]
8 . [.] . . . . [. . . . .]
9 [With] Nisaba, daughter of [Anu . . . .]
10 [. .] Anu [. . . . . his] heart [. . . . .]
11 Of Ea in the Apsû [. . . . .]
12 . [.] . were carried [. . . . .]
13 Dread awe was put [. . . . .]
14 Ereškigal answered [. . . . .]
15 [To] the gods . [. . . . .]
16 [Let the . . . .] hear [. . . . .]

22 *e-*× [. . . . .]
23 *is-s*[*i* . . . .]
24 *lìb-b*[*a* . . . .]
25 *man-nu* × [. . . . .]

(End of column)

REVERSE III

1 [× × ×]× ^{d}*ni*[*saba* . . . .]
2 [× ×]× × ma × [. . . . .]
3 [×] × ma *si-*[*i*]*r* × × [. . . . .]
4 × kur *lu-ut-ta-ni-*× [. . . . .]
5 [*š*]*a la* ^{d}*nisaba man-*[*nu* . . . .]
6 [×]× pa d[u] × × [. . . . .]

REVERSE IV

1 [. . . . .] mu [× (×)]
2 [. . . . .] × gal [× (×)]
3 [. . . . . *a-z*]*u-gal-la-tú* ^{d}[*gu-la*]
4 [. . . . .] × × [×]× *mi-e-*[. . .]
5 [*nu*]*-ú-ru e-diš-šu-ú mu-nam-me-*⸢*ru*⸣ *e*[*k-li-te*]
6 *ú-ba-nu zu-um-*⸢*ri*⸣*-iš ina la nap-lu-si i-bar-r*[*u* . .]
7 *ni-ba-at* ^{d}*nisaba i*[*na g*]*i-mir ilāni*^{meš} *ka-*× [. . . .]
8 *li-iš-še-pu ri-gim-šá ši-si-sa a-a* [. . . .]
9 *ep-pe-er-šá li-da-áš-ši-pa eli* × [. . . .]
10 *li-ik-nu-šá* ⸢*ma*⸣*-ti-tan liš-šá-a* [*bi-lat-sin*]
11 *e-ri-šu-šá li-iḫ-tan-na-bu li-ri-*[*ku* . . . .]
12 *pi-ir-ʾu-šá a-šu-ú ṣal-mat qaqqadi li*[*-* . . . .]
13 *ša a-ru-ru ib-nu-ú lik-nu-uš še-p*[*u-uš-šá*]
14 *ga-at-ta-šin li-šaq-qa-a liš-nam-mer z*[*i-mi-šin*]
15 *ab-ra-te ma-la ba-šá-a a-na* ^{d}*nisaba* [. . . .]
16 *bu-ul ṣēri nam-maš-še-e šu-up-pa-a nàr-b*[*é-e-šá*]
17 *i-da-at* ^{d}*nisaba qa-i-šá-at napištim*^{tim} × [. . . .]
18 *la me-na te-niš-e-ti ki-ta-ra-ba* × [. . . .]
19 *ni-bit-sa a-a ip-par-ku zi-kir-šá a-a* [. . . .]
20 *e-nem-me-e kab-ta-te-šá šu-tar-ri-ḫa* [. . . . .]
21 *re-e-ši un-ni-ni ša* ^{d}*nisaba ša id-k*[*u-* . . . . .]
22 *ša* × × ma *iš-ta-kan a-na nap-lu-su* × [. . . . .]
23 *a-*⸢*mu-ram*⸣*-ma* ^{d}*nisaba ki-i šu-qu-r*[*a*? . . . . . .]
24 [*r*]*a-bu-u u ṣe-eḫ-ru ú-zak-ke-r*[*u* . . . . . .]
25 [× ×]× *ta-na-ta-šú ú-šap-pa-*⸢*a*⸣ [. . . . . .]
26 [× × × ×] *mu-de-e šip-ri* ša ud × [. . . . . . .]

REVERSE IV

3 [. . . . .] the great healer [Gula,]
4 [. . . . .] . . [.] . . . [. . .]
5 The shining light that illumines the [darkness,]
6 . . . . through not looking . . . [. .]
7 Nisaba gleams, among all the gods . . [. . . .]
8 May her voice be loud, may her shout not [. . . .]
9 May her sustenance be proved sweet to . [. . . .]
10 May all lands submit and bring [their tribute.]
11 May what she has planted ever sprout luxuriantly, may [. . . . grow] tall.
12 May her offspring, animals and the black-headed race [. . . .]
13 Let what Aruru created bow [at her] feet,
14 May she increase their stature and brighten [their countenances.]
15 Let all the human race, as many as exist, [. . . .] to Nisaba.
16 The creatures of the bush, the wild life, extol [her] greatness;
17 Nisaba is unique, she gives life . [. . . .]
18 Ye men beyond count, continually bless . [. . . .]
19 Let mention of her never cease, may her name not [. . . .]
20 Exalt her solemn utterances [. . . . .]
21 Attention and prayer to Nisaba who . . [. . . . .]
22 Who appointed . . . to be looked at . [. . . . .]
23 Behold Nisaba, how precious is [her . . . .]
24 Great and small speak [. . . . . .]
25 [. .] . her praises, they extol [. . . . . .]
26 [. . . .] craftsmen who . . [. . . . . . .]

27 [× × × × ×]× ú šá ad ×[. . . . . . .]
28 × × [. . . .] ú ni[m/la[m . . . .]
29 *re-e-*×[. . . . .]
30 *mu-šá* [. . . . .]
31 *šá* [. . . . .]

LEFT EDGE

[. . .]× itu.gan ud.11.kám *lim-mu* [^{m}*man-n*]*u-ki-šarri nāgir ēkalli* (lú.600.kur)
[. . . .] × ×

SU 1952, 257 (Plate 45)

(Perhaps part of the same tablet as SU 1951, 173+1952, 100+142)

1 [. . . . .] × [. . . . .]

---

2 [^{d}*nisab*]*a p*[*â-ša īpuš*]^{uš}*-ma* [. . . . .]
3 [. . .]× ḫi × × [×*l*]*e-e* an ×[. . . . .]
4 [. . .] ḫi *tu-šaq-qa-a* ×[. . . . .]
5 [. . .]*-la-an-ni-ma ta-šá-di-ḫa* [. . . . .]
6 [. . *na*]*p-ḫar nab-nit nu-šá-na-a* ×[. . . . . . .]
7 [. . . .]×*-ri-ti niš-tak-ka-na* [. . . . .]
8 [. . . .]× *apsû lit-ta-ad*[- . . . .]
9 [. . . *mi*]*t-ḫa-riš lib-bal-*[. . . . .]
10 [. . . . .]× *šá eš-re-*⌜*e*⌝[*-ti* . . . .]
11 [. . . . . .] ^{d}*šakkan liš-še-en-*[. . . . .]
12 [. . . . . .]× *lib-bi* ×[. . . . .]
13 [. . . . . *na*]*p-ḫar né-e-*[. . . . .]
14 [. . . . . .] *liš-tab-r*[*u-ú* . . . .]
15 [. . . . . . .]*-ta-a* [. . . . .]
16 [. . . . . . .] × a ×[. . . . .]

VAT 12995 (Plate 44)

SIDE I

1 [(×)] *gu-ub-bu* ×[. . .	
2 [*u*]*š-kan-na-áš kul-lat* × [. . .	It/He subjects all . [. . .
3 *a-na šēpē*^{meš} [. . .	to the feet [. . .
4 *i-pu-uš-ku* ^{d}*girra*(giš.bar) [. . .	Girra made for you [. . .

5 ^{giš}*narkabtu da-i-[pa-at* . . .	A chariot which throws [back . . .
6 *liš-na-am-me-er* [. . .	May it brighten [. . .
7 *i-*× × ^{d}*é-a* [. . .	Ea . . . [. . .
8 *be-el-*× *šur-b[u-tum* . . .	Mighty lady [. . .
9 *um-ma-ka* [. . .	your mother [. . .
10 *šamû*^{ú} *ù erṣetum*[^{tum} . . .	Heaven and earth [. . .
11 × *i-na ta-ḫa-z[i* . . .	. in battle [. . .
12–15 traces and odd signs	

SIDE II

2 *kiš-šat* [. . .	The whole of [. . .
3 *be-lu* ×[. . .	Lord . [. . .
4 *man-nu* [. . .	Who [. . .
5 ^{d}*nisaba* [. . .	Nisaba [. . .
6 ×*-ka a-n[a* . . .	

(iv) *THE OX AND THE HORSE*

The fable of *The Ox and the Horse* is given in the list Rm 618 (Bezold, *Catalogue* IV. 1627): éš.gàr *alpi u sīsî* "the series of the Ox and the Horse" (line 14). Only a few scraps of this once extensive work survive, all of which come from the libraries of Ashurbanipal. The biggest piece is part of a two-column tablet and is the "first extract" (*nis-ḫu maḫ-ru-ú*) of the complete work. The colophon, which gives this information, also supplies the first half-line of the work: "When exalted Ištar". The conventional mythological introduction is therefore to be presumed, but the latter portion of it, which is all that survives, describes the rise of the annual flood with the Ox and the Horse looking on. In the debate which follows, the two creatures try to establish the superiority of their lot, the one over the other, and also their superiority in other ways. The Horse must have referred to his prowess in war, since the Ox replies that many instruments of war are made with the help of his leather (A rev.). In another passage (C) the Horse speaks of the elaborate provision made for him. There is no suggestion in the surviving pieces that the two animals discussed their usefulness to the human race. No part of a judgement scene has yet been recovered.

This work probably had no Sumerian original, as the horse did not exist in southern Mesopotamia in the earliest times. It was a rarity during the Old Babylonian period. It only became widespread as a result of the breeding by the Mitanni in Syria and eastern Asia Minor during the early Cassite period. Even then the horse was so valuable that infinite care was taken in rearing and training it. A manual of instruction in this art has survived in the Hittite language, though the author, Kikkuli, was of Mitanni extraction.[1]

[1] Edited by J. A. Potratz, *Das Pferd in der Frühzeit*, 1938.

Also fragments of a related text in Middle Assyrian have been recovered.[1] These prove beyond doubt that horses were better cared for than most human beings. Thus the Horse is not exaggerating in fragment C. The fable probably dates from the Cassite period.

LITERATURE

TEXT, WITH OR WITHOUT EDITION

1899 A. Boissier, *PSBA* 21. 34–46 (text of A).
1902 L. W. King, *CT* 15. 34–37 (text of A, K 8198+8200, C–F).
1914 L. W. King, *CT* 34. 18 (text of G).

EDITIONS, TRANSLATIONS

1876 G. Smith, *The Chaldean Account of Genesis*, pp. 147–51.
1880 G. Smith, ibid., revised edition, pp. 150–4.
1912 C. Johnston, *AJSL* 28. 81–100.
1927 E. Ebeling, *MAOG* 11/3. 27–37.
1949 B. Landsberger, *JNES* 8. 276–7.

MANUSCRIPTS

	Plates		Plates
A = K 3456+DT 43	47	E = K 8199	48
B = K 1835+8198+8200+9116	48	F = K 10916+12029	48
C = K 8197	48	G = Ki 1902–5–10. 32	47
D = K 9834	47	H = K 12042	47

A = K 3456+DT 43

OBVERSE

(About nine lines are missing from the beginning)
1 [×] la šá a ×[. . . . .]
2 [*ša*]-*am-mi* ×[. . . . .]
3 *i-zi*-×[. . . . .]
4 *a-na ma*-×[. . . . .]
5 *šarru* ^{d}*e*[*n-líl* . . . .]
6 *su-pe*-⌜*e*⌝ [. . . . .]
7 *iš-me-m*[*a* . . . .] × [. . . .]

OBVERSE

5 King Enlil [. . .
6 Prayers [. . .
7 He heard and [. . .

[1] E. Ebeling, *Bruchstücke einer mittelassyrischen Vorschriftensammlung für die Akklimatisierung und Trainierung von Wagenpferden*, 1951.

8 *ša-am-m*[*i* . . . .] na [× ×]
9 *kup-pu* [. . . . .]× *-ba nārāti*[^{meš}]
10 *šá pu-ra*[*t-ti* . . . .] *nu-uḫ-*[*šá*]
11 *mi-lu-šá* [. . . . . *idi*]*glat šá* an [× (×)]
12 *ig-dap-š*[*u* . . . .]× *i-šú-ú pa-na* [×]
13 *ṣu-ṣu-*⌈*ú*⌉ [*it-tab-lu*   *im-ta*]*-la qar-ba-a-*[*tum*]
14 *ba-ma-a-t*[*um ub-ba-lu*   *in-g*]*i-ra ta-me-ra-a-*[*tum*]
15 *ḫar-ru n*[*a-at-ba-ku*   *ú-šat-b*]*a-*lu_4 *šadû-ú-'*[*a*]
16 *a-na ta-me-r*[*a-a-ti id-ni-n*]*u*   *in-gi-ru ú-ga-r*[*u*]
17 *áš-rat la me-*[*riš-ti*   *a-na*] *ru-ṭib-ti it-tur*
18 *i-na ki-ši* [*ù a-pi*]   *i-ši-ḫu šam-mi*
19 *šá ḫa-ru-ub-t*[*i erṣetim*]^{tim} *ip-pa-ṭir qí-rib-šá*
20 *mi-rit bu-lim ú-šam-mi-ḫa*   *ap-pa-ta ú-šaḫ-ṣa-ab*
21 *alpu ù sīsû*   *ip-pu-šu ru-'ú-ú-ta*
22 *iṭ-ḫu-ud kár-*[*ra*]*s-su-nu*   *šá-muḫ-ta ri-i-ta*
23 *ir-ši-ma ul-ṣa lìb-ba-šu-nu*   *ip-pu-šá ṣa-lu-ú-ta*

---

24 *alpu pa-a-šu īpuš-ma i-qab-bi*   *iz-za-kár a-na sīsî na-'-id qab-li*
25 *at-ta-aṭ-ṭa-lam-ma*   *dum-mu-qa i-da-tu-ú-a*

8 Plants [. . .
9 Streams [. . . . .] . . rivers
10 Of the Euphrates [. . . . .] abundance
11 Its flood [. . . . .] Tigris . . [. .]
12 They rose [. . . . .] have . . [.]
13 [They removed] the riverside meadows [and flooded] the fields,
14 [They carried off] the elevations and watered the low-lying land,
15 [They swept] away (the soil) of the plain into the depressions and [down the slopes,]
16 [They prevailed] over the low-lying land and watered the ground,
17 The unworked [land] became a bog.
18 In reed-bed [and thicket] the plants grew,
19 The bosom of the barren earth was split,
20 It made pasture flourish for cattle, and produced luxuriant growth.
21 The Ox and the Horse became friends,
22 Their bellies were sated with the luscious pasture,
23 In their pleasure they engaged in a dispute.

---

24 The Ox opened his mouth and spoke, addressing the Horse, glorious in battle,
25 "As I look around, my omens are very favourable.

26	*i-na re-eš šatti*(mu.an.na) *u qí-it šatti*(mu.an.na)	*at-ta-ṭa-al mi-ri-ti*
27	*iḫ-tar-pu-ni mīl*(e$_4$.la$_6$) *kiš-šá-ti*	*it-tag-pu-uš mê*^{meš} *naq-bi*
28	*ṣu-ṣu-ú it-tab*$_x$*-lu*	*ṣi-pa il-tak-nu*
29	*ḫar-ru na-at-ba-ku*	*ú-šat-ba-lu šadû-ú-a-i*
30	*ba-ma-a-tum ub-ba-lu*	*ir-ḫu-ṣa qar-ba-a-tum*
31	*ana ta-me-ra-a-ti id-ni-nu*	*in-gi-ru ú-ga-ru*
32	*áš-rat la mi-riš-ti*	*ir-ri-šá ra-aḫ* [*ki-di*]
33	^{lú}*nangāru mu-du-ú*	*it-ta-rak* K[I.KA]L [× (×)]
34	*i-dak-ku-ku bu-ru-ni-ma*	*ú-qa-a-a-ú* [. . . . . .]
35	*ù sīsû la mār ú-ga-ri*	*i-dar-ri-sa* × [. . . . .]
36	*nu-uk-ki-ir ra-ma-nu-uk*	*i-si* ki × [. . . . .]
37	*e-li-ma ina la* ú × × ×	*ši-ṭu-u*[*s-* . . . .]

38 traces

NOTE: *tab*$_x$ (28) = LU

REVERSE

1	[*i*]*t-ti* × [. . . . .]	
2	*šim-ti u š*[*im-ta-ka* . . . .]	
3	*erû*$^{\text{hi.a}}$ *dan-na*	*mu-*⌜*pa*⌝*-aṣ-ṣi-du* [. . . . . .]
4	*ki-ma ṣu-ba-ti na-al-bu-šá-ku*	*i-na*[*m-* . . . .]
5	*e-la ia-a-ti*	*mār la-si-me* × [. . . . . . .]
6	*šarru šakkanakku e-nu u rubû*	*ul i-ba-'-ú pa-da-na* [. . . .]
7	*alpu pa-a-šu īpuš-ma iqabbi*(dug$_4$.ga)	*iz-za-kár a-na sīsî n*[*a-'-id qab-li*]
8	*at-ta-ma-a e-duk-ku*	*tak-di-ra* [. . . . .]
9	*i-na tāḫāzi-ka mi-i-ni*	[. . . . .]
10	*kal* ^{giš}*narkabtu šug-mu-ra-ku*	*ti-'-ú-ti* [. . . . . .]
11	*i-na maškī*^{meš}*-ia ṣu-ub-bu-ut*	× [. . . . .]
12	*i-na šir'ānī*^{meš}*-ia ṣu-ub-bu-ut*	× [. . . . .]
13	*ú-ṣi mu-un-daḫ-ṣi*	*iš-pa-t*[*a* . . . .]
14	*ez-zu-ti a-ri-ri*	*na-šá-a* [. . . . .]
15	*ka-lu-bu bēlī*^{meš}*-ka*	*šu-ut-* × [. . . . .]
16	*ul tam-mar kib-sa*	*ki-ma dun-n*[*a-mi-i* . . . . .]
17	*pal-ṣa-a-ma i-na-ka*	*ul* × [. . . . .]
18	*ul tal-lak ur-ḫa*	*eli ap-pa*[*-ti* . . . . .]
19	*sīsû pa-a-šu īpuš-ma iqabbi*(dug$_4$.ga)	[*a-na alpi gít-ma-li amāta izakkar* (mu-*ár*)]
20	*i-na rig-me-ia ḫi-i*[*t-* . . . .]	
21	*ka-lu-bu ú-*[. . . . .]	
22	^{giš}*kakkī*^{meš}[. . . . .]	

26 From the beginning to the end of the year I find my pasturage.

27 The full flood has come early, and the subterranean waters have amassed,
28 They have carried away the riverside meadows and saturated the soil,
29 They have swept away (the soil) of the plain into the depressions and down the slopes,
30 They have carried off the elevations and swamped the fields,
31 They have prevailed over the low-lying land and watered the plain,
32 The 'Fertilizer of [the Steppe'][1] ploughs the unworked ground,
33 The skilled artisan . . . . . [. .]
34 Our calves gambol and await [. . . . . .]
35 But the horse, since he does not belong on the plain, tramples . [. . . . .]
36 Change yourself, and stay away from . . [. . . . .]
37 Come up . . . . [. . . . . . ."]

---

[1] A poetic name for the plough.

REVERSE

2 My destiny and [your destiny . . .
3 Strong copper which splits [. . . . . .]
4 I am clothed as with a garment . . [. . . . . .]
5 Without me a runner . [. . . . .]
6 King, regent, *enu*-priest, and prince do not go on the road [. . . ."]

---

7 The Ox opened his mouth and spoke, addressing the Horse, [glorious in battle,]
8 "Are you alone fierce [. . . . . ?]
9 What in your battle [. . . . . ?]
10 I put the finishing touches to the complete chariot, [I . . . . . its] equipment,
11 With my hide [the . . . .] is covered,
12 With my skin [the . . . .] is covered.
13 The warrior's arrows, the quiver [. . . . . . .]
14 Fierce javelins carry [my . . . .]
15 Your masters' battle-axes are [. . . . .]
16 You cannot see the way, [you are like a] weakling,
17 Your eyes stare, but you do not [. . . . .]
18 You do not travel the road, on the reins [. . . . ."]

---

19 The Horse opened his mouth and spoke, [addressing the superb Ox,]

20 "At my neighing . . [. . . . .
21 Battle-axes . [. . .
22 Weapons [. . .

23 × × *mu-šam-qí-tú* × × [. . . . .]
24 [×] (×)*-nu lìb-ba šá la-bi-im-ma* [. . . . .]
25 *i-na e-ber nāri* *š*[*u-* . . . .]
26 *i-na ú-ru-uḫ šadî*^{me} ×[. . . . .]
27 *áš-ṭa-ta-ma alap* *ḫar-ḫa-r*[*u* . . . .]
28 *i-na šip-ri-ka ul iz-z*[*a-az* . . . .]
29 *im-ru-ka tuḫ-ḫu* *qaq-qa-*[. . . . .]
30 *ki-i taš-nun sīsû* ×[. . . . .]

---

31 *alpu pa-a-šu īpuš-ma iqabbi*(dug$_4$.ga) *iz-za-kár ana s*[*īsî na-'-id qab-li*]
32 *áš-šú ḫar-ḫa-ri šá taq-bu-ú* [. . . . .]
33 *nis-ḫu maḫ-ru-ú i-nu-um* ^{d}*iš-tar šur-bu-t*[*um* . . . .]
34 *ēkal* $^{m.d}$*aššur-bān-apli*(šár.dù.a) *šàr kiššati*(šú) *šà*[*r māt aššur*^{ki}]

B = K 1835+8198+8200+9116

OBVERSE

1 [. . . . .]× kar
2 [. . . . .]× ku
3 [. . . . .]× šá
4 [. . . . . *n*]*a-gi-ru*
5 [. . . . . *e-lu*] *ù šap-lu*
6 [. . . . .] NE *šam-mi*
7 [. . . . .]×-⌜*šá*⌝ *du-uš-mu-us-su*
8 [. . . . .]× *ka-li ina ta-a-a-rum*
9 [*i-ša*]*ḫ-ḫu-uḫ* [*d*]*i-im-ta-šú ki-ma mê*^{meš} *na-a-di*
10 [×]× an ma *sīsû ka-bit* iš × × ×
11 [*at-t*]*a ù a-ga-li ta-zab-bi-la tup-š*[*ik-k*]*u*
12 [×]× *ḫar-ra-ni* šá × × tu *tu-qar-ra-ba* im × ×

---

13 [*alpu p*]*a-a-šú īpuš-ma iqab*[*bi*(dug$_4$.[ga) *iz*]*-za-kár ana sīsî na-'-id qab-li*
14 [×] × × × × [×]× ba bi *mu-tum la ki-nu*
15 [. . . . . *šá*]*-na-a mi-na-tu-ka*
16 [. . . . .] *gi-mir ālāni*^{meš}
17 [. . . . .]*-ši-na mātāti*^{meš}
18 [. . . . .*-r*]*e-e-tum*
19 [. . . . .*-ḫ*]*a-at*
20 [. . . . .]× × ^{d}*nisaba*
21 [. . . . . *mê*] *ka-ṣu-ti*
22 [. . . . .]× a *qa-ri-tú*

23 . . which throws down . . [. . .
24 [.] . . the heart of a lion [. . .
25 At the ford of a river . [. . .
26 On the road over the mountains . [. . .
27 You are troublesome, Ox, a chain [. . .
28 In your task there does not stand [. . .
29 Your fodder is bran, the ground [is your bed.]
30 How can you rival the Horse? . [. . ."

---

31 The Ox opened his mouth and spoke, addressing the [Horse, glorious in battle,]
32 "About the chain you mentioned, [. . .

B

OBVERSE

9 His tears drip like water from a waterskin.
10 [.] . . . the Horse, ... is honourable,
11 But you and the riding-donkey undergo forced labour.
12 [.] . road . . . . you bring near . . ."

---

13 [The Ox] opened his mouth and spoke, addressing the Horse, glorious in battle,
14 ["·] . . . . [.] . . . an unreliable man

23 [. . . . .]× *an-na-a* ^{lú}*ikkāru*
24 [. . . . .]× *la áš-ku-uk-ku*

---

25 [*sīsû pa-a-šu īpuš-ma iqabbi*(dug$_4$.ga) *a-na alpi gít-ma-l*]*i a-ma-tú i-zak-kar*
26 [. . . . .] *ṣil-la pa-ši-iḫ*
27 [. . . . .] *ka-la-ma*
28 [. . . . .]× bu ši la
29 [. . . . .]× za *ul ti-i-di*
30 [. . . . .] *e-pir-šú*
31 [. . . . .]× aḫ ru
32 [. . . . .]*-pa-áš-šaḫ*
33 [. . . . .] kal ka
34 [. . . . .]× *pu-ut-ka*
35 [. . . . . *u*]*l-lad*

---

36 [*alpu pa-a-šú īpuš-ma iqabbi*(dug$_4$.ga) *iz-za-kár ana sīsî na-'-id qa*]*b-li*
37 [. . . . .*-i*]*a*
38 trace

REVERSE

1–20 Detached signs next to the right edge
21–22 Missing
23 [. . . . .]× (×) [×]
24 [. . . . .]× ib ru [×]
25 [. . . . .] ud *lu-uk-ru-u*[*b*]
26 [. . . . .]× ku *qí-bi damiqtim*(sig$_5$-*ti*[*m*])

---

27 [*sīsû pa-a-šú īpuš-ma iqabbi*(dug$_4$.ga) *ana alpi*] *gít-ma-li a-ma-tú izakkar*(mu-*ár*)
28 [. . . . . *ik-ru-ṣ*]*u ki-ri-is-su-u*[*n*]
29 [. . . . .] *la zak-ru*
30 [. . . . .]× *šu-ma-a-ni*
31 [. . . . .]*-i i-gir-ka*
32 [. . . . . *a-la-ku*] *ù ta-a-ra*
33 [. . . . .]*-uḫ-ḫu sur-riš*
34 [. . . . .]× *la tur-ra*
35 [. . . . .] *pu-ut lim-nu*
36 [. . . . .] × × × [×] ×
37 trace

C = K 8197

1 [. . . . .] × ⌜*rap*⌝-*šá ú*-× ad/la [. . . . . .]
2 [. . .]× *alpu ra-ma-nu-uš* [. . . . .]
3 [*iš-ten*] *arḫu šá-na-a ù* [*šal-šá*]
4 [. . .] ⌜d⌝*nisaba ḫi-it-bu-ṣa-at i-šeb-bi id*-[. . .]
5 [. . .]× *it-tak-ṣa-ru* ki × [×]
6 [. . .]-*at qud-du-šat ana ilī*^{meš} [× ×]
7 [. . .] *el-li-ni it-pu-ṣa uk-tar-ra-bu*-[*ni*]
8 [. . .] KAL *ḫu-um-ṭám ul ap-pal-la-sa*-[*aḫ*]

---

9 [*sīsû p*]*a-a-šu īpuš-ma iqabbi*(dug$_4$.ga) *ana alpi gít-ma-li a-ma-t*[*ú izakkar*(mu-*ár*)]
10 [× × (×)]-*ku-ma ka-bi-sa-ku a-gu*[*r-ri*]
11 [× × (×)] *šarru ma-li-ku na-di ú-ru*-[*ú-a*]
12 [× × (×)] *šam-me ur-qit erṣetim*^{tim} *i-ḫi-r*[*u-ni*]
13 [× × *š*]*ur-ru-ḫu ú-taq-qa-nu maš-qa*-[*a-a*]
14 [× ×] × *nu-uk-ku-sat šá-muḫ-tum ri-i*-[*tum*]
15 [× ×]×-*ma šu-tu-rat e-lat m*[*i-i-ri*]
16 [*ul in-n*]*ak-kal ši-i-ri* × × [. . . . .]
17 [× × ×]× ri ia [. . . . .]
18 trace

2 [. . .] . Ox himself [. . . . .]
3 [The one] month, the second, and [the third,]
4 [. . .] corn flourishes, the . [. . .] is sated,
5 [. . .] . . . . [.]
6 [. . .] . is holy to the gods [. .]
7 [. . .] . . . they speak a long blessing over [me] when I have been struck down (in sacrifice).
8 [. . .] . I do not fall prostrate in the heat."

---

9 [The Horse] opened his mouth and spoke, [addressing] the superb Ox,
10 "I [. . .] and tread a pavement of kiln-fired bricks,
11 [Close to] king and counsellor my stall is located,
12 [The attendants] make ready [for me] plants, the greenery of the earth,
13 [. .] they look after my magnificent drinking-fountain.
14 [. .] . the luscious herbage is cut small,
15 [. .] . . is superior, the special portion of a foal.
16 My flesh [is not] eaten . . [. . .

D = K 9834

1 × [. . . . .]
2 mu[l . . . .]
3 *ki-ma l*[*um-* . . . .]
4 *ta-reḫ-ḫi* × [. . . . .]
5 *šar-ka u d*[*a-ma* . . . .]
6 *ù šar-ru* ka k[u? . . . .]
7 *ina qu-li-im-ma* [. . . . .]
8 *ù ṭu-du šu-šú-r*[*u*? . . . .]

---

9 *sīsû pa-a-šu īpuš-ma i*[*qabbi*(d[ug$_4$.ga) *ana alpi gít-ma-li a-ma-tú izakkar*(mu-*ár*)]
10 *ep-še-ta ki-ma lim-ni* [. . . . .]
11 *ki-ma ṣe-e-ni ši-ip-*[*ra* . . . .]
12 *ki-ma a-si ú-*× [. . . . .]
13 *im-ri-i tak-*⌜*ka*⌝*-l*[*a* . . . .]
14 [*n*]*a-da-*[. . . . .]
15 × × [. . . . .]

E = K 8199

1 [. . . . .]× × × × [. . . . .]
2 [. . . . .]× *qab-li ù tu-q*[*u-un-tu*]
3 [. . . . .]× *iṭ-ṭi-ra nap-šá-*[*tuš*]
4 [. . . . .]× *-la-ku* la × [×]
5 [. . . . .]× *nu-'-ú-du e-mu-qí-*[×]
6 [. . . . .]× *-nu ti-'-ú-ti ḫi-i*[*ṣ-bi*]
7 [. . . . .]*-ti-šú-nu ra-šú-ni* ri [× ×]
8 [. . . . .]× *-lu i-*× [× ×]

---

9 [*alpu pa-a-šu īpuš-ma iqabbi*(dug$_4$.ga) *iz-za-*]*kár a-na sīs*[*î na-'-id qab-li*]
10 [. . . . .] × × [. . . . .]

F = K 10916+12029

OBVERSE

1 [*in*]*a u$_4$-um* k[i . . . .]
2 [*ša*]*rru u rubû* × [. . . . .]

---

3 [*a*]*lpu pa-a-šú īpuš-*[*ma iqabbi*(dug$_4$.ga) *iz-za-kár ana sīsî na-'-id qab-li*]
4 *ma-'-da a-*[. . . . .]

5 *nap-ḫar ni-š*[*i* . . . .]
6 *ú-pat-ti* iṣ × [. . . . .]
7 *rap-šá-a-tum* × [. . . . .]
8 *en-de-ku ilu u mu*[*š-ta-lum* . . . .]
9 *ana te-né-e* ^{d}*ni*[*saba* . . . .]
10 *el-la šul-lu-*[*ma* . . . .]
11 [*m*]*ir-sa* tak × [. . . . .]

REVERSE

1 × šá × [. . . . .]

---

2 *sīsû p*[*a-a-šu īpuš-ma iqabbi*(dug$_4$.ga) *ana alpi gít-ma-li a-ma-tú izakkar*(mu-*ár*)]
3 × *ru-qu-ti* [. . . . .]
4 *uk-ku-šu-ti* × [. . . . .]
5 [*i*]-*šal-lal-ma* [. . . . .]
6 [×] × pa pa × [. . . . .]
7 [× ×]× × [. . . . .]

G = Ki 1902–5–10. 32

1 [. . . . .] × [. . . . . .]

---

2 [*alpu pa-a-šu īpuš-ma iqabbi*(dug$_4$.ga) *iz-za-kár ana s*]*īsî n*[*a-'-id qab-li*]
3 [. . . . .] lu ú [. . . . . . .]
4 [. . . . .] sur ki × [. . . . . .]
5 [. . . . . *u*]*ṣ-ṣar-ri-*[*ip* . . . . .]
6 [. . . . .] × [. . . . .]

H = K 12042

1 traces
2 [. . *in-n*]*ak-kal šīr-ka* [. . . . . . .]

---

3 [. . . *pa-*]⌜*a*⌝*-šu īpuš-ma iqabbi*(dug$_4$.g[a)[. . . . .]
4 [*ina* u_4-]*me-šu-ma* × [. . . . .]
5 [. . . . .] × *ṭa-a-b*[*i* . . . .]
6 [. . . .]× u[k . . . .]

(v) *THE FABLE OF THE FOX*

In the catalogue K 9717, Sm 669, and K 10802 (edited in *JCS* 11. 11–12) *The Fable of the Fox* is listed in rev. 12:

[éš.g]àr ka$_5$.a: *šá pi-i* ^{m}dù-^{d}*marduk* dumu ^{m}lú.dumu.nun.na lú.u[m.me.a . . . . .]

The series of the Fox, according to Ibni-Marduk, son of Ludumununna, scholar of [. . . . .]

Thirteen tablet fragments of varying size are known, which duplicate each other here and there, and which, in view of a common subject matter and phraseology, can be regarded as the remains of the "Series of the Fox". One of these (BM 55470) is Late Babylonian and contains the last tablet of the series. It alone preserves a colophon, which gives the first line of the work, and records that it is a copy of a *tupgalli* ("monster tablet"). What survives, then, is a handful of scraps from a very long composition, and it is impossible either to arrange the pieces in correct order, or to extract from them the general sequence of events. The Late Assyrian library list *KAV* 142 gives the first line of one of the tablets:

iš-me-ma barbaru šu-dur libba-šú (7–8)
"The wolf heard, fearful was his heart."[1]

This, however, is a stock phrase of the work, and cannot necessarily be identified with the same words in K 6435. 13. Beside the Babylonian piece, two are Middle Assyrian (VAT 10349; VAT 13836); one (A) is of unknown provenance, and the remaining nine are Late Assyrian. A has perhaps least claim to be considered part with the others, since the obverse is unique in being bilingual. If it really belongs here, the bilingual side is probably part of the beginning of the first tablet. The first line, however, is known, and is Akkadian. With the rest, too, no absolute proof can be given that they are all from the same text. Other fables on the same topic could have existed apart from the one listed in the catalogue. This, however, is not probable, but in any case the conclusions drawn will be valid, if not for the one example, then for the genre "Fable of the Fox".

The following is a summary of the contents:

Plate 49 A (Rassam tablet—now lost)

Obv. A drought occurs, about which the Fox complains to Enlil.

Rev. The Lion utters a string of threats to some creature, and then proceeds to put them into effect.

Plates 50, 51 **b** = VAT 13836 with Photo Assur S 6814

Obv., restored by VAT 11193 (Plate 49). The Fox complains to the Wolf that he was misled into taking part in an expedition. At the appearance of the Dog both retire to their holes, and the Dog boasts of his strength and how he is the trusty guardian of flocks. His speech ends with a reference to nefarious activities of the Wolf, supported by the Fox, which he threatens to avenge.

[1] Miss E. Reiner kindly drew my attention to this tablet.

Rev. The Wolf replies in humble, flattering tones and acknowledges the might of the Dog. Now the Fox speaks up and brings a list of accusations against the Wolf: treachery to his friend, incendiarism, and interfering with the property of the Lion. A broken-away speech of the Dog follows.

VAT 11193 rev. "the Wolf".

Plate 52 **c** = VAT 10349

Obv. The Dog is again boasting how he guards both life and property in town and country, and how, at the head of a pack of dogs and bitches, he thwarts the marauding Wolf and Fox. The cat and mongoose likewise live in fear of him. The Wolf now chides the Dog with not performing his natural function, since his family connexions are with fire.

Rev. The Fox replies to the Wolf, defending himself and his parents.

Plate 52 **d** = VAT 10154

Col. A. An uncertain speaker talks about slander.

Col. B. The Dog, following the end of a speech by an unascertained speaker, mentions the subject of attacks on domestic animals.

Plate 53 E = K 3641

Obv. I. In a judgement scene before Šamaš the speaker, probably the Wolf, urges Šamaš not to let off the Fox. In turn the Fox begins to plead.

Obv. II. A speech of the Fox begins, probably addressed to the Wolf.

Rev. IV. The Lion is menacingly threatening the Fox, who attempts to buy him off with flattery.

Plate 53 F = K 8567. The Wolf, or more probably the Fox, denies attacking domestic animals, and accuses the Dog of slander.

Plates 52, 53 G = *KAR* 48, Fragment 3, and K 8570

Col. B. An uncertain speaker denounces the cunning of the Fox, to which the Fox begins his defence.

Col. A. The Dog boasts of his powers.

Plate 53 H = K 6435. The Dog speaks against the Fox and Wolf, the latter of whom replies.

Plate 52 I = K 8577. A speech (of the Fox?) is followed by a reply to him.

Plate 54 Z = BM 55470 (from Babylon) and VAT 11556

Obv. The Dog denounces the Wolf and Fox for combining in slandering him to Šamaš and Enlil, and for demanding his death. At this the Wolf speaks to the Fox.

Rev. The Fox proceeds to worship Enlil in Nippur. Epilogue.

The general conclusions which can be drawn from this scanty material are, of course, provisional, but perhaps not altogether wrong. In the first place the fable centres on the Fox. The cataloguer, who knew the whole, recognized this, and it ends with the Fox praying to Enlil. The use of this animal in a fable is easily accounted for. The cunning of the Fox is proverbial everywhere, and is admired despite its anti-social usage. The fable begins with Enlil inspecting the earth, and, if A obv. in fact belongs to the beginning, a drought ensues, for the alleviation of which the Fox pleads with Enlil. The Fox does seem to have a special connexion with Enlil. Twice in the few surviving fragments the Fox announces that he will sacrifice to Enlil with his whole family (**b** obv. 8; Z rev. 10), and the last words of the text before the Epilogue are, "The Fox prayed to Enlil". In the short Sumerian fable published in translation by Kramer in *Biblical Parallels from Sumerian Literature*, p. 25, it is to Enlil that the Fox addresses his request for horns. The drought must have been ordered by Enlil as a punishment. Perhaps his inspection revealed a state of lawlessness to which he determined to put an end by annihilating all life. Somehow, either this, or something else, must have led on to the dispute. There are three disputants: the Fox, the Wolf, and the Dog. The accusation is that the Fox and Wolf have been raiding flocks. The Dog presents this case, not without sounding a trumpet about his own virtues of dependability and strength. The whole vitality of the work lies in the subtle ways by which the Fox comes out victorious. One ruse of the Fox is only known from statements of the Dog (Z obv.). The Fox and Wolf had together taken their case to Šamaš and Enlil, whether to the two gods in common session or separately is not known, and had demanded the death of the Dog. Such effrontery! Yet the skilled advocacy of the Fox is such that we need not doubt that he handled the case with supreme ability. A second trick is to heap all the blame on to his partner, the Wolf, and to declare himself innocent or misled (**b** obv. 4–8). In addition to this he accuses the Wolf of perfidy and other crimes for which he should be punished (**b** rev. 13–22). The Wolf, however, grasps the deception and similarly accuses the Fox of having led him astray (E obv. I. 14), no doubt with more justice, but too late. A second allegation of that kind will not win credence.

Three features of the work are obscure. First, the position of the Lion. He appears twice (A rev., E rev. IV), and both times is an unchallenged power threatening destruction, in A on an unknown party, and in E on the Fox, who has rashly trespassed on his territory. Also the Fox accuses the Wolf of interfering with the property of the Lion (**b** rev. 22). The Lion then has both might and right on his side, and may have been introduced into the story as an instrument of divine punishment, or just as a dramatic convenience to split up the acts, and to prevent the Fox from gaining too easy a victory. Secondly, the nature of the judgement scenes is obscure. There must have been at least two, as there is the reference to the combined petition of the pair to Šamaš and Enlil, and E preserves one where Šamaš alone sits in judgement. The curious thing about this one is that the tears of the Fox go before "the ray of Šamaš". This gives the impression of an 'advanced' writer who could not conceive of a god in person listening to such a complaint, but substitutes a hypostasis by which the older court scene must have been much altered. Finally, there are several statements about the parentage of the animals which rouse curiosity. As representative examples of their species it is not clear why any allusion should be made to their parents, but this happens in **c** obv. 19–20 and rev. 6, 14–15, and E obv. I. 6–8. In the first example the fire god (or should it be simply 'fire'?) is said to be the Dog's mother, the father is broken off, but his brothers are called "Flames that light up the night". This could be dismissed as poetic imagery, but it is the Wolf who speaks these words, and he is accused by the Fox in **b** rev. 15–18 of setting fire to things, and H 8 perhaps contains a similar allusion. Probably some concrete concept or mythology underlies these statements, but for the present they are obscure.

The "Series of the Fox" is not, then, a typical dispute of the Sumerian type, but a development from it. An empirical study of the remains does not lend any support to the idea that it followed a simple pattern of mythological introduction—dispute—decision of the gods. Indeed the only possible verdict with the Fox would have been condemnation. This is no case of two metals useful in different ways, nor two trees supplying different needs of man. The Fox is an enemy of men, the Dog a friend. There can be no basis for an 'evaluation' debate between this pair, and the composition centres on the cunning of the Fox. Its purpose, then, cannot be serious in the sense that a manual of ethics is serious, that the issues involved were of real concern to the writer and his circle of readers, or rather hearers. On the other hand, it does not follow that it was a burlesque intended to raise a laugh. Probably the cleverly thought-out situations and subtle speeches were intended, like the plays of Shakespeare, to grip the minds of an intelligent audience.

The date of composition may be Old Babylonian or Cassite. Being a development out of a Sumerian form, it is probably not older than the First Dynasty of Babylon, and the Middle Assyrian copies do not allow a date later than the Cassite period. The cunning of the Fox seems to have been a popular theme of sayings both in Mesopotamia and elsewhere (see Ch. 8, Sayings), and there is no need to assume that this sophisticated work is a lineal descendant from a simpler work. The Sumerian dispute and the popular reputation of reynard account for the literary and cultural background.

LITERATURE

TEXT WITH OR WITHOUT EDITION

1902 L. W. King, *CT* 15. 31–33, 38 (text of E, F, G, I, Z).
1915 E. Ebeling, *KAR* 48, no. 3 (G).
1923 E. Ebeling, *KAR* 322 (**d**), 323 (**c**).
1937 G. Meier, *AfO* 11. 363–4, pl. II (A).
1953 E. Ebeling, *LKA* 2 (**b**).

EDITIONS, TRANSLATIONS, STUDIES

1876 G. Smith, *The Chaldean Account of Genesis*, pp. 144–7.
1880 G. Smith, ibid., revised edition, pp. 147–50.
1912 C. Johnston, *AJSL* 28. 81–100.
1927 E. Ebeling, *MAOG* II/3. 17–27.
1950 E. Ebeling, *JCS* 4. 215–22.

A = PINCHES'S COPY OF A FRAGMENT ONCE OWNED BY RASSAM (Plate 49)

OBVERSE

1 *la ti-*× [. . . . .]
2 u_4 bar.dagal.la × [. . . . .]
3 *i-nu-ma* UD × [. . . . .]
4 šèg.kur.ra ba.an.gi_4.[gi_4 . . . .]
5 *zu-un-na ik-ka-li* [. . . . .]
6 ka_5.a dug_4 ma.an.ab.bé: *še-*[*li-bu a-ma-tú i-qab-bi*]
7 šèg.kur.ra u_4.diš.a.kám šèg × [. . . . .]
8 *zu-un-ni māti iš-ten* u_4*-me z*[*u-un-ni* . . . . . .]
9 ka_5.a šà.íb.ba.ke_4 ^{d}en.líl.l[á.ra dug_4 ma.an.ab.bé]
10 *še-li-bu ina ug-gat lìb-bi-šú ana* ^{d}[*en-líl a-ma-tú i-qab-bi*]
11 ^{d}en.líl.lá ù.mu.un mu.un.an.dím!.ma mu.un.da.ab.záḫ[. .]
12 ^{d}MIN *be-lí šá tab-nu-ú la tu-ḫal-l*[*aq* . . . . . .]
13 lú.kúr.ra.mu téš.bi mu.un.da.ab.silim.m[a . . . . . .]
14 lú.gú.šub.ba.mu gìr.zu × [. . . . .]
15 *na-ki-ri-ia ištēniš*^{niš} *is-*× [. . . . .]
16 [. . . . .] × [. . . . .]

REVERSE

1 [. . . . .] × [×] × [. . . . . . .]
2 [× ×] × *apkallu* [× ×] bi a × (×) ki [. . . . .]
3 [*lu*]*-bu-uk* an × ak *lu-dan-nin* [. . . . .]
4 [*lu*]*-dir*!*-ma ti-ik-ka-šu ki-šad-su* [*lu-uḫ-niq*]
5 [×] u sa si *qaqqad-su-ma ul ú-šaq-qa* [. . . . .]
6 [*lu*]*-up-ši-in uznē*^{II}*-šú lu-na-si-ḫa ī*[*nē*^{II}*-šú*]
7 [× ×] × × × *la*?*-li-im-ma na-me-e lu-*× [. . . . .]
8 [× × ×]-⸢*šu-ma*⸣ *a-na qa-at urgulī*(ur.gu.la.meš) *bi-*[*ru-ti*]
9 [*urgu*]*lī*(ur.gu.l]a.meš) *bi-ru-ti li-na-áš-ši-ku šī*[*r-šú*]
10 [× ×]-*ḫu ina pu*!*-ut*! ^{d}*šamaš qu-bu-uḫ da-li*[*l* . . .]

---

11 [*uš-pa-al*]*-si-iḫ-ma nēšu git-ma-lu u ana* KU*-šú iš-*[. . . .]
12 [*e-dir*] *ti-ik-ka-šú ki-šad-su i*[*ḫ-niq*]
13 [. . . . *qaqq*]*ad-su-*⸢*ma ul ú-ša*⸣[*q-qa* . . . . . .]
14 [. . . . .] × [. . . . .]

NOTE: Ebeling in *JCS* 4. 120–1 emends obv. 5 to *zu-un-ni*! *māti*!

OBVERSE

2 When . . . [. . . . .]

4 The rain of the land was withheld [. . . . .]

6 The Fox spoke a word,
7 "The rain of the land for one day, the rain . [. . . . . ."]

9 The Fox in the anger of his heart [spoke a word] to Enlil,

11 "Enlil, my master, do not destroy what you have created!

13 My enemies without exception are reconciled [. . . . .]
14 Those that hate me your foot . [. . . . .]

REVERSE

2 [. .] . pundit [. .] . . . . . [. . . .]
3 [I will] carry off . . . I will strengthen [. . . .]
4 [I will] grip his neck, [I will strangle] his throat,
5 [I will] . . . his head so that he cannot raise [. . . . .]
6 [I will] . . . his ears and pluck out [his] eyes,
7 [. .] . . . . a desolate spot I will [. . . .]
8 [I will deliver] him into the hands of hungry lions,
9 And the hungry lions will tear [his] flesh.
10 [. .] . in the presence of Šamaš . . . worshipper [. . .]

---

11 The supreme Lion [threw] (him) down and . [. .] on his . .
12 [He gripped] his neck and [strangled] his throat,
13 [He . . .] his head so that he could not raise [. . . .]

b = VAT 13836 RESTORED FROM PHOTO ASSUR S 6814 (Plates 50, 51)

OBVERSE (lines 9–13 restored by VAT 11193 obv. (Plate 49))

1 [. . . . .] × × × × × la bi it × [× × × (×)]
2 [. . . . . .] ⸢*i*⸣*-la-as-su-um iš-tu ra-ma-ni-šu-ma ut-ta-*[× × (×)]
3 [. . . . .]× *-mi-i u$_4$-mu mu-sa-ar-ri-ḫu mi-na-a-t*[*i-ia*]
4 [. . . .]*-ir-di lu-ú i-di-ma lu la ú-ṣa-ma lu a-bi-it i-na ḫur-r*[*i-ia*]
5 [. .]× *-ma aq-ra-ti na-pu-uš-te-ia*
ištēn^{en} *ap*!*-ru-sa-ma šanû*^{ú} × × (.)
6 ⸢*e*⸣*-te-riš* ka la [a] ki mu maš re e ti
ki-ma zi-it-te elleti^{ti} *zi-ti* [. . .]
7 ⸢*ù*⸣ *e-nin-na-ma at-ta-ṣi-ma ag-da-me-il na-pu-uš-*[*te-ka*]
8 ⸢*ù*⸣ *a-na-ku ina pu-ḫur ki-im-ti-ia u el-la-a-te-ia* ^{udu}*niqâ lu-qí*
9 [*i*]*z-qur-šu-nu-ti-ma kal-bu bar-ba-ru u ša-a-*[*šu*?]
10 [*lu*]*-ú arkā*^{meš}*-nu-ma ip-pa-ra-su ki-ma su-mi*
ki-ma urpāti(im.diri.meš) *me-ḫa-a i-*×[. . .]
11 *ki-i-ma at-mi ku-uš-šu-di i-tar-ra-ku lìb-bu-šu-nu*
12 *iṭ-ṭa-ar-du-ma e-ru-bu ana ḫur-ri*
ērub(tu) *še-li-bu ana eš-di ḫur-r*[*i*]
13 *ir-bi-iṣ bar-ba-ru i-na qabal ḫur-ri*
ṣa-bit kal-bu bābāni^{meš}*-šu-nu-ma iš-te-ni-'-a* ×[. . .]

---

14 *kal-bu pa-a-šu ip-pu-ša i-lab-bi*
na-dúr elī^{meš}*-šu-nu ri-ig-m*[*a*]
15 *ku-uš-šu-ud lìb-bu-šu-nu-ma i-ma-'-ú ma-ar-t*[*a*]
16 *ga-áš-ra-a-ku e-mu-qí ri-it-ti* ^{d}*zi-i ki-ṣir né-e-ši*
17 *la-a-as-ma-a bur-ka-ia eli iṣṣūrāti*^{meš} *šu-ut a-gap-pi*
18 *a-na ri-ig-mi-ia dan-ni e-ta-na-ab-ba-la-a šadû*^{ú} *ù na-a-r*[*u*]
19 *as-ba-ku-ma pi-iš-nu-qí-iš i-na ma-a-ḫa-ar* ^{udu}*ṣe-e-ni*
20 *ki-i-ma rē'î*^{meš} *ù na-qi-di na-piš-ti-ši-na pa-aq-da-a-ni*
21 [*ṣē*]*ra maš-qa-a ka-*⟨*ia*⟩*-ma-ni-ia ur-ḫa šu-tu-ra-a-ku la-a-ma-a-ku tar-ba-a-ṣa*

22 [*i-n*]*a ti-ri-ik* ^{giš}*kakkē*^{meš}*-ia na-du-ru-*⟨*ti*⟩ *a-na-*^{sa}*saḫ né-e-*×
23 [*a-n*]*a ri-ma-ti-ia ig-ru-ru nim-ru mi-di-nu la-a-bu-ú šu-ra-a-nu*
24 [*ul*] *ip-pár-ša iṣ-ṣu-ru su-la-a ul eš-ši-*[*ir*]
25 [*i-na p*]*í-it-qí-ia ša-ar-ra-a-qu mi-li-iḫ-ta ul eš-ku*[*n*]

NOTES

6 *pat*!*-ti* is a possible reading of the tablet. 9 VAT 11193 has two lines: [*i*]*z-qur-šu-nu-ti-m*[*a* . . . × × × *kal-b*[*u* . . . 10 VAT 11193: *ur-pa-*[11 On VAT 13836 *ki-i-ma* is not

OBVERSE

2 [. . . . . . .] he runs, with himself he . . [. . . . .]
3 [. . . . . .] . . . a demon that ruins [my] limbs.
4 [. . . .] . . had I known, I would not have gone out, but would have stayed in [my] hole.
5 [. .] . . my precious life
One I . . ., a second . . .
6 I asked . . [.] . . . . . .
Like a *pure* portion, my portion [. . .]
7 And now I have departed and spared [your] life,
8 And I will offer a sacrifice with all my kith and kin.
9 [He] called them, the Dog, the Wolf, and . . [.]
10 Later they will be divided like *garlic*,
Like clouds which . . [. . .] the storm,
11 Like pursued fledgelings their hearts will thump."
12 They were driven off and entered their holes:
The Fox entered the bottom of his hole,
13 The Wolf crouched inside his hole,
The Dog kept guard of their entrances and sought . [. .]

---

14 The Dog opened his mouth as he bayed,
Fearful to them was his bellow,
15 Their hearts were so overcome that they secreted gall.
16 "My strength is overpowering, I am the claw of the Zû-bird, a very lion.
17 My legs run faster than winged birds,
18 At my terrible bellow the mountains and rivers dry up.
19 I sit like a beggar in front of the sheep,
20 Their lives are entrusted to me as to a herdsman and shepherd.
21 I am sent on the regular round of the [open] country and drinking-place; I encompass the fold.
22 With the clatter of my fearful weapons I extirpate . . . .
23 At my roars the leopard, tiger, lion, and wild cat take to flight,
24 The bird does [not] fly, and does not make its way.
25 [In] my pens the robber does not ravage.

written at the edge; either a space was left at the beginning or [*ù*] is to be restored. VAT 11193 writes *ki-ma* against the edge. 12b VAT 11193: *e-[ru-ub*

26 [× ×] ×-e bar-ba-ru i-šu-ṭa-ni-ma
sa-ra še-la-ba ú-bi-la × × [×]
27 [lu-ú-na-]ki-is um-ma-ti-šu-nu-ma na-piš-ta-šu-nu lu-ú-b[al-li]
28 [× × ×]-ar-ra-ḫu e-lum [. . . . .]

REVERSE

1 [iš-me-ma bar-b]a-ru a-mat kal-bi
na-dúr lìb-ba-šu ×[. . . . . .]
2 [. . . . . . .] mug-dáš-ru bēl i-di pi-ta-[an bur-ki]
3 [. . . . . . .] ki-na-a-ti-šu muš-tàk-ši-du ka-l[u . . .]
4 [. . . . .] it-ti-ka š[ak]?-nu muš-tàk-ši-du la-a bu[. . .]
5 [. . . . .] i-na še-ti-ka [ku-u]p-pu-lu la-si-mu ḫa-muṭ [. . .]
6 [ra-ma-t]a-ma ki-ma ili pu-luḫ-ta u[z]-za
ina la-a zērē^{meš} [. . . . .]
7 [a-na mārē]^{meš}-ia la pa-da-a ṣi-bit-ka
dan-nu ḫur-ba-áš-ka ×[. . . . .]
8 [× ×]×-ku pí-še-er-ta-šu-nu ṣi-bit-ka am-ra-ku
ú-ma-e-ra-ni še-li-b[u . . . .]
9 [uš]-ti-la-an-ni a-na ba-ab kal-bi mu-ṭa-ar-ri-du ú-[ma-mi]
10 [u]l i-še-ta-an-ni dan-nu ḫur-ba-áš-ka šá e-ta-na-da-ru i-lid bīti-[ia]
11 [ù] a-di-ra-tu-ka it-ta-áš-ka-na a-na pa-ni-⸢ia⸣ ar-kiš

---

12 ⸢e⸣-tap-la ⸢še⸣-li-bu-um-ma i-bak-ki ṣar-piš
na-an-gul lìb-ba-šu [m]a-li di-im-t[a]
13 [iz]-⸢za⸣-qár-ra a-na ša-šu-nu-ma
at-ta bar-bar ṣa-lam [ṭa]-píl-ti
14 ⸢e-pí-iš⸣ lim-né-ti na-ki-su na-piš-ti tap-pí-šu
15 [am]-mi-⸢ni⸣ a-na ki-rim a-pi ug-gu-li ta-za-ar-ru nab-li
16 [i-n]a ^{giš}kišti ša ša-bu-la-at tu-qa-at-ta-ar qu-ut-ra
17 [×]× bu-ri ša iṭ-ṭe-e ^{d}girra(bil.gi) tu-ša-ḫa-az
18 [i-na] ú-tu-un pa-ḫa-a-ri im-me-ti ú-ḫu-la ta-ṣer-ru-u[p]
19 [× ×] kal-ba ma-a-ṣi lìb-bi-šu ú-gi-ra-a ia-a-ši
20 [an-nu]-ú de-en ilim-ma kal-bu li-mut-ta-šu li-× ×[. . .]
21 [li-na]-ki-is ia-a-ba-am-ma li-ni-ir i-na ^{giš}kakkē[^{meš}-šu]
22 [at-t]a ta-al-pu-ut ma-ku-ur ur-gu-le-e ḫi ×[. . . . .]
23 [am-m]i-ni ia-a-ši mār la ma-am-ma-na-ma tu-mar-ra-ṣa-ni [. . . . .]

---

24 [kal-bu pa-a-]šu i-pu-ša i-qa-bi
na-dúr elī-šu-nu ríg-[ma]
25 [kuš-šu-ud] lìb-bu-šu-nu i-ma-'-ú ma[r-ta]
26 [. . . . .] šamê^{e} la-a ip-ru-sa su-[. . . .]
27 [. . . . .] × × la-a iš-ta-na-a e-[. . . . .]

26 [. .] . . the Wolf has outraged me
And has brought the truce-breaking Fox . . [.]
27 [I will] butcher their hosts, I will extinguish their life.
28 [. . .] . . . god [. . . . .”]

REVERSE

1 The Wolf [heard] the word of the Dog,
His heart became fearful, . [. . . . . . .]
2 [“. . . . .] O mighty one, endowed with strength, fast runner,
3 [. . . . .] his associate, who . . . all [. . .]
4 With you there is [. . .], you who . . . . . . [. . .]
5 [. . . . . .] in your net is enmeshed the fleet, the swift, [. . .]
6 [You sit] like a god, (clothed) in awe and dread.
Without offspring [. . . . .]
7 Your hold on my [children] is merciless.
Your terrible horror . [. . . . .]
8 I [. . .] their release; I have experienced your hold.
The Fox sent me [. . . . .]
9 [He] made me go up to the gate of the Dog, who drives away wild [animals.]
10 Your terrible horror, which the youngsters of [my] house constantly fear, does not
11 [And] fear of you comes upon me both from in front and behind.” [miss me,

---

12 The Fox answered, weeping bitterly,
His heart grew incensed, and his tears were profuse;
13 He addressed them,
“You, Wolf, are an image of backbiting,
14 An evil-doer, who cuts his friend’s throat.
15 Why do you spread flame to the glowing reed . .?
16 Send up smoke from the parched thicket?
17 Set ablaze [.] . the pitch wells?
18 Ignite constantly the alkali [in] the potter’s kiln?
19 [. .] the Dog at his pleasure has started a lawsuit against me.
20 This is the verdict of the god, “Let the Dog . . [. . .] his evil.
21 [Let him] butcher the enemy and let him kill them with [his] weapons.”
22 [You] have touched the property of the Lion . . [. . . . .]
23 Why do you aggravate me, a nobody [. . . . .?”]

---

24 [The Dog] opened his [mouth] as he spoke,
Fearful to them was his bellow,
25 Their hearts [were so overcome] that they secreted gall.

REVERSE OF VAT 11193 (Plate 49)

1 [× ×] ab × [. . .
2 [× k]a [. . .
3 [*ina l*]*a-a* ⸢ri⸣/ḫu ×[. . .
4 [*ri-*]*ṣu-ši-n*[*a* . . .
5 [*p*]*a-aḫ-ru-ma* [. . .
6 ⸢*e*⸣*-ša-am-ma* r[a . . .

---

7 *barbaru* [. . .
8 *iḫ-du* [. . .
9 ⸢*lu*⸣ *ib-ri* × × [. . .
10, 11 traces

c = VAT 10349 (Plate 52)

OBVERSE

1 [. . . . .] × [. . . . .]
2 × [. . . . . . .]× ṣi na [a]n mi [. . . . . .]
3 *a-šar* × × da/ša ti *a-na-ku* ×[. . . . .]
4 *na-gi-ir āli-ia* [. . . . .]
5 *na-an-za-aq up-pi ù* ^{giš}*sikkatu* [. . . . .]
6 *i-na re-eš ṣa-al-li nab*[- . . . .]
7 *i-na qa-an-ni bu-ú-li ù* um/dub ×[. . . . .]
8 ⸢*ki*⸣*-i il-qí bar-ba-ru ḫa-an-*[*ṭiš* . . . .]
9 ⸢*ki*⸣*-i la-a im-mi-lik še-li-bu-um-*[*ma* . . . . . .]
10 *ga-na le-e-pu-uš pi-i-ia aḫḫū*^{meš}*-ia up-*[. . . .]
11 *na-ba-a-tu kal-ba-a-tu ki-ma kakkab ša*[*mê*^{e} . . . .]
12 *li-ik-ki-su da-a-nu li-*[*d*]*u-ku* [. . . . .]
13 *kal-ba-a-tu ki-ma ku-un-ši-il-li li-m*[*a-áš-ši-ra* . . .]
14 ⸢*ù*⸣ *a-na-ku šal-ma-su-nu sa-pa-a-na* [. . . . .]
15 [*i-ṭ*]*a-pí-il šu-ra-a-nu ḫu-ur-ra-ša ku-*[*un-nu-un*]
16 [*ù*] *ši-ik-ku-ú i-na na-aṣ-be-e* al da/ša na ×[. . . .]

---

17 [*iš-m*]*i-ma bar-ba-ru a-ma-a-at* [*kal-bi*]
18 [*ul i*]*m-lik lìb-ba-šu-ma e-pal* [*kal-ba*]
19 [*k*]*a-lab um-mu a-lit-ta-ka* ^{d}*girra*(bil.gi) *ba-n*[*u-ka* . . .]
20 *aḫḫū*^{meš}*-ka nab-lu mu-ḫa-mi-ṭu mūšâti*[^{meš} . . . . . .]
21 *ù at-ta mê*^{meš} *nap-ša-at nišī*^{meš} × mu × [. . . . .]
22 *ab-bu-ut ti-du-ú ú-sa-a-ti-ka* [. . . . .]
23 *ib-ni-ka-ma* ^{d}*en-líl a-na ri-ṣu-ut* [. . . . .]
24 [*n*]*a-a-ši-ma da/ša-pa-ru-ú* [. . . . .]
25 × × × *ni-ip-pa-lis-ma* ×[. . . . .]
26 [× × ×] × [× ×] nu ×[. . . . .]

OBVERSE

3 Where there is . . . . there am I . [. . . . .]
4 [I am] the sergeant of my city [. . . . .]
5 [I am] the latch of the door-thong and lock-pin [. . . . . .]
6 [I . . . .] . at the head of the sleeper,
7 [I . . . .] at the cattle pens and . . [. . .]
8 When the Wolf has hastily seized [. . . . .]
9 When the Fox has been indiscreet [. . . . .]
10 See, I will open my mouth and my brothers will [*assemble*,]
11 The glistening bitches like stars in the sky [. . . .]
12 Though the mighty slash and kill [. . . . .]
13 The bitches will [tear apart . . . .] like a teasel,
14 And I [know how] to overwhelm their bodies.
15 The wild cat spreads slander, crouching in his hole,
16 [And] the mongoose in the sewers . . . . [. . . ."]

---

17 The Wolf [heard] the word of [the Dog,]
18 Indiscreetly he answered [the Dog,]
19 "Dog, your mother who bore you is Fire, [your] father [. . .]
20 Your brothers are Flames that set alight the night [. . . . . .]
21 Yet you . . . [. . . . .] water, the life of the peoples.
22 The championing which you know, your kind deeds [. . . . .]
23 Enlil created you for the help of [. . . . .]
24 As for us . . . . [. . . . .]
25 . . . we saw . [. . . . .]

REVERSE

1 [. . . . .] × [. . . . .]
2 [. . . . . .] × × × × × [. . . . . . .]

---

3 [*e-tap-l*]*a še-li-bu-um-ma i-ba*[*-ak-ki ṣar-piš*]
4 [*na-a*]*n-gul lìb-ba-šu* [*ma-li di-im-ta*]
5 *iz-za-aq-qa-ra* [*a-na bar-ba-ri*]
6 *abul a-bi-ia u ga-an-*[*g*]*u-r*[*i-ta-šu* . . . . .]
7 ⸢*e*⸣*-ta-an-šu im-da-*× [. . . . .]
8 *ḫu-ur-ri i-di-*⸢*i*⸣ *ma-ia-a*[*l* . . . .]
9 *i-da-at ḫu-ur-ri* ru × × [. . . . .]
10 *a-bi ul* × × [. . . . .]
11 *um-mi a-na tar-ba-ṣ*[*i*] × × [. . . . .]
12 *a-na-ku ri-i-ma ul ú-šab-ra* × × [. . . . . .]
13 *i-na qí-ni-ka bar-bar ib-ba-ni* [. . . . . . .]
14 *a-bu ba-nu-ka il-ta-ḫaṭ* × [. . . . .]
15 *um-m*[*i*] *a-lit-ta-ka ú-da*/*ša-*[. . . . .]
16 *a*[*t-ta*] *tar-bi-s*[*u*]*-nu tu-*× [. . . . .]
17 [×] × [×] × a [×]×*-nu tu-*[. . . . . . .]

(End of Tablet)

REVERSE

---

3 The Fox answered, weeping [bitterly,]
4 His heart grew incensed [and his tears were profuse;]
5 He addressed [the Wolf,]
6 "The 'city gate'[1] of your father and [his] larynx [. . . . .]
7 They have become weak and have . [. . . . .]
8 He knows the hole, the bed [. . . . .]
9 The sides of the hole . . . [. . . . .]
10 My father does not . . [. . . . .]
11 My mother . . [. . . . . . .] to the sheep pens.
12 I shall not have mercy . . [. . . . .]
13 In your kin, Wolf, was born [. . . . . . .]
14 The father who begat you stripped off . [. . . . .]
15 The mother who bore you . . . [. . . . .]
16 You, their offspring, have . [. . . . .]

[1] An expression for the mouth or throat as the organ of eating.

d = VAT 10154 (Plate 52)

Column A

1 . . .]×-*kàt-su*
2 . . .]×-*m/puk-šu*
3 . . .] *arkat-su*

---

4 . . . *i*]-*zak-ka-ra*
5 . . .] *lim-né-e-ti*
6 . . .] ⌜*a*⌝-*ḫi-ti*
7 . . . *su*]*r-ra-a-ti*
8 . . .]-*e ši-ri*
9 . . .] *la kit-ti*
10 . . .] × *ma-mit*
11 . . . *d*]*i-nu*
12 . . . *u*]*š*?-*šá-ab*
13 . . .]-*sak-ku*
14 . . .] × *bītu-ú-a*
15 . . .] *bēl e-mu-qí*
16 . . .]-*na-a-ti*
17 . . .]-*ši*
18 . . .]×

Column B

1 × × [. . .
2 *ki-šá-ma ina* × [. . .
3 *id-lul* × [. . .
4 *en-qa* × × [. . .
5 *la-pit makkūr*(níg.ga) × [. . .
6 *pa-kid ši-ga-ri* × [. . .
7 *at-ta tal-pu-ut* × [. . .

---

8 *kalbu pa-a-šú* × × [. . .
9 *ina dal-ti* × e × [. . .
10 × × × × [. . .
11 *d*[*a*]*l-ḫa* zu nu [k]ur? ru [. . .
12 *pu*[*ḫā*]*du la li-'u alpu* × [. . .
13 *ka-par-ru ina ši-iḫ-ṭ*[*i* . . .
14 *ik-tar-ru-ú* × [. . .
15 *ta-ad-du* ka × [. . .
16 × ku ap tar ⌜mu/ik⌝? ba? [. . .
17 × i mi lu bu ul [. . .
18 [×] × × × [. . .
19 [. . . . .] × [. . .

E = K 3641 (Plate 53)

OBVERSE I

1–2 traces
3 *ina* i[š . . . .]
4 a × [. . . . .]
5 ad × [. . . . .]
6 *a-bi* × [. . . . .]
7 *ummi* na bu [. . . . .]
8 *e-muq a-b*[*i-ia* . . . .]
9 *al-su-um* [. . . . .]
10 *e-lu nap-šá-a-ti* [. . . . .]
11 *at-ta ina* u_4*-me-šu-ma ta-az-za-zi* × [. . . . . .]
12 *ti-di šar-ra-qu muš-te-pi-šu ta-*× [-×]
13 *šá rag-ga u me-šá-ri qí-bit-su e-z*[*i-ib*]
14 *iš-tu i-lam-ma šēlibu ú-ma-'-ir-a-ni a-a-*[*ši*]
15 *ina kib-sa kar-ra iš-ku-nu ina še-pi-i*[*a*]
16 *e-nin-na ina qí-bi-ti ub-bu-rat na-piš-ti*
17 ^{d}*šamaš ina de-e-ni-ka mur-tu-du-u a-a ú-ṣi*
18 *en-qu muš-te-pi-šu li-du-ku še-li-bu*

---

19 *šēlibu an-ni-tú ina še-me-šú iš-ši re-ši-šú ana pān* ^{d}*šamaš i-bak-ki*
20 *ana pān šá-ru-ri šá* ^{d}*šamaš illiku*(gin-*ku*) *di-ma-a-šú*
21 *ina di-ni šu-a-ti* ^{d}*šamaš la tu-ub-bar-an-ni*

OBVERSE II

1 × [
2 *a-*× [
3 *iš-*[

---

4 *šēli*[*bu*
5 *bar-b*[*ar*

REVERSE IV

1 *a-rid* ^{giš}*qīšti-ia ul ú-ta-ra ana arki-šú*
2 *ù šal-miš ul uṣ-ṣi-ma ul im-mar* ^{d}*šamšu*^{šú}
3 *at-ta a-a-ú la li-'-u a-mi-l*[*am*]
4 *šá ina ug-gat libbi-ia-ma uz-za-at pāni-iá ti-še-ra ana ma*[*ḫ-ri-ia*]

5 *lu-kul-ka-ma ul a-sa*[*p-pid-ka*]
6 *lu-ul-'-uṭ-ka-ma ul tap-pa-rik* × [. . . . .]

OBVERSE I

6 My father . [. . . . .]
7 My mother . . [. . . . .]
8 The strength of [my] father [. . . . .]
9 I ran [. . . . .]
10 *Upon life* [. . . . .]
11 You in that time stand . [. . . . .]
12 You know the thief, you . [.] the sorcerer,
13 He has forsaken the commandment of right and wrong.
14 Since the Fox appeared and sent me
15 They have set . . in the way at my feet.
16 Now by the command I myself am arraigned.
17 Šamaš, do not let the persecutor escape from your judgement.
18 Let them kill the wise one, the sorcerer, the Fox."

---

19 When the Fox heard this he lifted his head, weeping to Šamaš,
20 His tears came before the ray of Šamaš,
21 "Do not arraign me, Šamaš, in this judgement.

REVERSE IV

1 He who goes down to my thicket does not get out again,
2 Nor does he escape to see the light of the sun.
3 Who are you? A feeble man
4 That you make your way to my presence in my fury of heart and ferocity of countenance.
5 I will eat you and not lament [you!]
6 I will devour you without your resisting . [. . . . .]

7 *lu-ú-ṣu-ub dām*(úš)*-ka-ma ul ú-*×-×[. . . . . . .]
8 *lu-mal-li-iẖ šīrī*^{meš}*-ka-ma* ×[. . . . .]
9 *i-bak-ki šēlibu* ×[. . . . .]
10 *i-na-ṭal pa-ni-š*[*ú ù ar-ki-šú* . . . .]
11 *at-ta nē*[*š* . . . .]
12 *ka-šid* ×[. . . . .]
13 *ez-zu* ×[. . . . .]
14 *dan-nu* ×[. . . . .]
15 *bēl* ×[. . . . .]
16 *i-*×[. . . . .]
17 × [. . . . .]

F = K 8567 (Plate 53)

1 . . .] × [×] × × [× (×)]
2 [*ul a*]*s-suk šīra dama*(úš) *ul aṣ-ṣu-*[*ub*]
3 [*maš*]*-ki ul áš-ru-uṭ a-na e-re-me ul ú-*[*tir*]
4 [×]× *na-ka-ru ka-sa-ku ana-*[*ku*]
5 [× (×)]× *aẖ-te-bil a-zab-bil šèr-*[*ta*]
6 . . . *u*]*l-tu ul-la-nu-um-ma kalbu a-ẖi-ta* [*iq?-bi?*]
7 . . .]× *i-lit-ta-ni šu-bat ki-na-a-t*[*i* . .]
8 . . .]× *ì-si-in-na ana-ku šá* ^{d}*en-l*[*íl*]
9 [*ul in-na-suk*] *šīrum-ma ul in-na-ṣu-ub damū*(úš)$^{\text{me[š]}}$
10 . . .]× n[a] × ra *na-piš-ti ul ú-k*[*ar-ri*]
11 . . .] ⌜*i*⌝*-še-li šin-ni* [. .]
12 . . . *q*]*u-mu ka-si* [. .]
13 . . .]*-e ma-li kal damī*$^{\text{m[eš]}}$
14 . . .] × [(×)] *ia-a-š*[*i*]

---

15 . . .] *kuš-šu-*[*ud*]
16 . . .] × × [. .]

7 I will suck your blood and not . . [. . . . . . .]
8 I will tear your flesh and . [. . . . .”]
9 The Fox weeps . [. . . . .]
10 He looks before [him and behind . . . .]
11 “You, Lion, [. . . . .]
12 Conqueror . [. . . . .]
13 Savage . [. . . . .]
14 Mighty . [. . . . .]

2 [I did not] bite the flesh, nor did I suck the blood,
3 I did not tear the skin, nor [cause] a festering sore.
4 [.] . enemy, I am bound.
5 [If . .] . I have done injury, I will bear the punishment.
6 . . .] since the Dog [has spoken] slander,
7 . . .] . our children, the abode of truth [. .]
8 I am the [. . . of .](-)Isinna of Enlil.
9 Flesh [has not been bitten,] nor has blood been sucked.
10 . . .] . . . . I have not endangered life.
11 . . .] teeth are sharp [. .]
12 . . .] . . is bound [. .]
13 . . .] . is full of every kind of bloodshed.
14 . . .] . . me.”

---

15 . . .] overcome.

G = *KAR* 48, FRAGMENT 3, and K 8570 (Plates 52, 53)

(VAT 10148, from which the *KAR* copy was made, cannot be found.)

KAR 48, Fragment 3, Column B, and K 8570

KAR | K

1 × × × *barbaru* ×[. . .
2 *ir-ru u kip-pu* ×[. . .
3 *ḫi-ri-iṣ lìb-bi* ×[. . .
4 *i-ba-áš-ši ina pi-i-*[*šú*] × [. . .
5 *qí-i-pa nu-ul-la-te-šú* ×[. . .
6 *ul ti-de-e en-qu ka-l*[*i* . . .
7 [*ša*] *ina kár-ras šēlibi i-ba-áš-šú-u* ×[. . .
8 [*šar*]*-raq ṣēri šēlibu mut-taḫ-l*[*il* . . .
9 [*ú*]*-šaṭ-ṭi-iṭ ḫi-ir-ṣi ina šá-pal rē'î mu-*×[. . .
10 [*ina k*]*a-lu ru-ub-ṣi kib-su-šú* šu ut na ma ×[. . .
11 [*n*]*i-it-ta i-dàg-ga*[*l*] *i-še-'a* [. . .
12 × mut *ṭè-me ana*[1] *nāqidim-ma* × × a a am ×[. . .
13 × mi *lip-par-ka* u s[ar] *ṣa-bit* ×[. . .
14 [*u*] *ina* u_4*-me-šu-ma šēli*[*bu*] *na-q*[*í-da* . . .
15 [*ana u*]*m-ma-ni iq-ta-*⌜*bi*⌝ *mi-na*[*-a* . . .
16 [× ×] × × aḫ *kalbu na-qí-dam-ma* [. . .

---

17 [*e-tap-la šēli*]*bu na-an-gul* [*lìb-ba-šú*]
18 [. . . . .] *suk-ku-k*[*u* . . .
19 trace

KAR 48, Fragment 3, Column A

1 . . .]*-ni*: *kuš-šu-ud*
2 . . .]^{meš} *ṣi-ri-iḫ-ti*
3 . . .]*-bi-'-i pir-ti*
4 . . .]× *e-ri-i ki-šá-di*
5 . . .] *ki-ṣir par-zil-li*
6 . . . *ú-*]*ṣu mul-mul-lum ka-li-ši-na ṣu-pur*
7 . . .]× ru *i-še-'i* i ti *mar-ti*
8 . . .]× e *ḫab-bur la li-qé-e i-lit-ta* ad nu ni
9 . . .]*-li ti-rik a-le-e ra-mi-mi*
10 . . .]*-du-ru ti-bu?-ú ik-t*[*u-um*]
11 . . . *il*]*-li-ka barbaru ḫa-an-ṭ*[*i-iš*]
12 . . .] × e ma ×[. . . . . .]
13 . . .] × × [. . . . . .]

[1] The sign *ana* is written very small and the scribe may not have intended it to be read.

1 . . . . . Wolf . [. . .
2 Bowels and intestines [. . .
3 The determination . [. . .
4 In [his] mouth there is . [. . .
5 Believe me, his blasphemy . [. . .
6 You do not know the wise one . . [. . .
7 [What] is in the Fox's heart . [. . .
8 The Fox is the thief of the open country, the prowler [on . . .
9 He burrows under the herdsman . . [. . .
10 [In] every pen is his path . . . . [. . .
11 He watches the burglar, he looks at [. . .
12 . . . . the shepherd . . . . . [. . .
13 . . . . [.] he takes . [. . .
14 [And] at that time the Fox [. . . . .] the shepherd.
15 He said [to the] craftsman, "What [. . . . . . .?"]
16 [. .] . . . the Dog the shepherd [. . . . ."]

---

17 [The] Fox [answered, his heart] grew incensed,
18 [. . . . .] deaf [. . .

H = K 6435 (Plate 53)

1 [. . . . .] × [. . . . . .]
2 [. . . . .]× *ḫi-si* ×[. . . . . . .]
3 [. . . . .] *ú-sa-tú* i[d . . . .]
4 [. . . . .]× *ú-tar-ru* ×[. . . . . . .]
5 [. . . . . . . *m*]*ur-ru-u na-du-u la* ×[. . . . . .]
6 [. . . . . .]*-tu-u ka-su-u mu-up-*×[. . . . . . .]
7 [*šēlibu u ba*]*rbaru šá iš-šu-ku du-muq* [*šīri*]
8 [. . . . .] *tag-ra-a* ^{d}*girra*(giš.bar) *ni-iḫ* [. . . . . . .]
9 [. . . .] *tu-šar-i-ba šul-li-ma bēl ṣi-*×[. . . . . .]
10 [. . . .] *ḫur-ru mu-ṣu-ku-nu ul ib-*[. . . . .]
11 [. . . .]× *maškī*^{meš}*-ku-nu li-ru-ba z*[*u-* . . . .]
12 [. . . .]× *nap-ṭi-ku-nu li-kil-lu* [. . . . .]

---

13 [*iš-me-ma ba*]*rbaru šu-dur* [*libba-šu* . . . .]
14 [. . . . . . .] *ap-sa-a* [. . . . .]
15 [. . . . . . *ši*]*t-nun-ta* ×[. . . . .]
16 [. . . . . *u*]*l ur-ra*[*-ad* . . . .]
17 [. . . . .] me ×[. . . . .]

I = K 8577 (Plate 52)

1 [. . . . .] × × [. . . .]
2 [. . . . . g]iš.meš × [. . . .]
3 [. . . . .] ⌜*i*⌝*-šid-su* ×[. . . . .]
4 [. . . . . ^{m}]^{eš} *lìb-ba-šú ḫi-pi* [. . .]
5 [. . . . .]×*-li* ú kur la ×[. . . .]
6 [. . . . .]× *i-na sa-ḫa-r*[*i-šu*]
7 [. . . . . . *nēšu*? *g*]*ít-ma-lu pa-nu-uš-šú i-z*[*i-iz*]

---

8 [. . *pâ-šu īpuš-ma iqab*]*bi*(dug$_4$].ga) *ana šēlibi amāta* [*izakkar*]
9 [. . . . .]×*-ka ana maḫ*[*-ri-*×]
10 [. . . . .] × [. . .]

Z = BM 55470 (82–7–4. 43) and VAT 11556 (Plate 54)

(VAT 11556 is a reverse flake of which the first column duplicates and restores the obverse of BM 55470, and the second column the reverse.)

OBVERSE AND COLUMN A

BM

1 *[kalbu pâ-šu īpušamma] i-qab-bi*
2 *[na-dúr elī-šu-n]u rig-ma*
VAT 3 *[kuš-šu-ud lìb-ba-šu-nu-ma i-]ma-'-ú mar-ta*
4 × × × × [. . . . .]× *limuttu*^{tú}
5 *en-qu* ×[. . . . .]× *-ta i/uḫ-te-ra-a*
6 *qa-a-a-lu* × ×[. . . . . .] *e-piš e-ni-ti*
7 *ba-bil pa-ni* × × [(.)]× *ṣi-lip di-nim-ma*
8 × × × *ni-ir-ta* × [(.)]× *mi-ku-ú ra-ta-tu*
9 *šá zēra ik-ṣa ig-[m]i-lu ṣi-bu-us-su ul ik-šú-ud*
10 *bu-un-nu zēr nu-ul-la-ta i-ban-ni*
11 × × *qa-a-a-la-tu i-še-'-a mi-iḫ-ṣa*
12 *ṣābu la muš-šu-ru i-saḫ-ḫur di-na*
13 *šēlibu ù bar-bar ša iš-šu-ku du-muq šīri*
14 *pa-a e-da iš-šak-nu-ma im-taḫ-ḫa-ru* ^{d}*šamaš u* ^{d}*enlil*(50)
15 *ù a-na kalbi rē'î-ši-na iš-te-ni-'-ú mar-ṣa-a-ti*

OBVERSE

1 [The Dog opened his mouth] as he spoke,
2 [Fearful to them] was his bellow,
3 [Their hearts were so overcome] that they secreted gall.
4 ". . . . [. . . . .] . evil
5 The wise one . [. . . . .] . . . . . .
6 The powerful . . [. . . . . .] doer of iniquity,
7 He who pardons . . [.] . a miscarriage of justice.
8 . . . murder . [.] . neglect and trembling.
9 One who spares an insolent offspring does not achieve his wish;
10 Kindness begets a blasphemous offspring.
11 The powerful . . seek (to impose the penalty of) a blow,
12 The warrior not released strives after a verdict.
13 The Fox and the Wolf who bit the best of the flesh
14 Came to an agreement and petitioned Šamaš and Enlil,
15 They sought the discomfiture of the Dog, their herdsman:

VARIANTS OF VAT 11556

9 *ig-me-lu* 11 *qa-a-a-la-a-ti* 13 *u barbaru*

BM VAT

16 ⌜*ul*⌝-*la-nu-um-ma a-a ib-ba-ši li-mut kalbu*

17 [× ×]× *in-na-ad-ru-ma la it-ta-du-ú šal-mat-su-un*

---

18 [*bar-ba*]*r an-ni-ta i-na še-mé-e-šu*

19 [*i-zak-k*]*a-ra a-na šēlibi ina ḫur-ri*

20 [. . . .] *ib-ru-ut-ka mi-ḫu-ú a-bu-bu*

21 [. . . .] × × × -*tu ḫur-ba-šu*

22 [. . . . .]-*ṣu-ka* ib × ×

23 [. . . . . *k*]*a-bit el*[*i* . . .]

24 [. . . . .] × [. . . . . .]

REVERSE AND COLUMN B

BM

1 [. . . . .] ⌜*i-na*⌝ [. . . . .]

2 [. . . . .] × × ra ma a × × × × × × ×

3 [. . . . .] *a-na ṣe-e-ni*

VAT 4 [. . . . .]× *i-pé-eš a-ḫi-tú*

5 [. . . . .]× *ú-ṣa-am-ma ana bīti-šú i-šas-si bāb*

6 [. . . . .]× *tum-ma-al ù gemé uzu-mú-a*

7 [. . . . .]× *pi-ta-nim-ma*

8 [. . . . . *giz*]*illâ*(gi.iz]i.lá) ^{dug}*egubbâ bīta lu-uš-bé-ʾ-ma*

9 [. . . . .]×-*nu ar-ki-ku-nu liṭ-ṭar-rid*

10 [*ù a-na-ku ina*] *pu-ḫur kim-ti-ia ana* ^{d}*enlil*(50) *be-li-iá niqâ lu-uq-qí*

11 [. . . . . .]×-*su šēlibu ú-sap-pa* ^{d}*en-líl*

12 [. . . . . .]-*gab ul i-zi-ba*

13 [. . . . . .]× na ga *ul ú-rab-ba-a*

14 [. . . . . .] *ikrib*(sizkur) *pi-i ba-la-ṭa mu-ḫur*

---

15 [. . . . .] ⌜*e*⌝-*nu-ma* ^{d}*en-líl ina māti iš-ku-nu pi-qit-tú*

16 [. . . . .] zag.til.la.bi.èš

17 [. . . . . *tu*]*p-gal-li* gaba.ri ká.dingir.ra.ki

18 [. . . . .]× gin$_7$ ka im.gíd *ṣar-pa šá-ṭar* $^{m.d}$*marduk-šu-mi-u-ṣur*

19 [. . . . . ^{d}*nāb*]*û-na-din-ip-ri* a ^{m}*ku-du-ra-nu* in.sar

20 [. . . . .].àm mu.šita.bi.im

VARIANTS OF VAT 11556

6 ⌜*uzu-mú*⌝-*a*^{ki} The division between 8 and 9 occurs after *egubbâ*. 10 ^{d}*en-líl bēli-i*[*a* . . . *lu-u*]*q-qa* 15 A trace of the Assur colophon remains.

16 "At this let not the Dog live; let him die!
17 [Since .] . he became enraged, but did not throw down their . ." "

---

18 When the Wolf heard this,
19 He spoke to the Fox in his hole,
20 [". . . .] your friendship is a storm, a hurricane.
21 [. . . .] . . . . dread

REVERSE

3 [. . . . .] to the sheep
4 [. . . . .] . the utterance of slander
5 [. . . . .] . went out and called to his temple, "Door!
6 [. . . . .] . Tummal, and slave girl of Uzumua,
7 [. . . . .] . open for me!
8 [. . . . .] let me bring a torch and pitcher into the temple.
9 [. . . . .] . . let it be expelled behind you,
10 [And I] will sacrifice to my lord Enlil [with] my assembled family."
11 [. . . . .] . . the Fox prayed to Enlil.

12 [. . . . .] . did not leave out,
13 [. . . . .] . . . did not increase.
14 [. . . . .] prayer receive health.

(Colophon)
15 [Tablet . . . . of] "When Enlil made an inspection in the land".
16 [. . . . .] completed.
17 [. . . . . . . according to] a monster tablet, an original of Babylon,
18 [. . . . .] . according to a baked copy. This document belongs to Marduk-šumi-uṣur,
19 [. . . . .] Nābû-nādin-ipri descendant of Kudurānu wrote (this).
20 [. . . . .] is the number of lines.

(vi) *THE FABLE OF THE RIDING-DONKEY*

The list Rm 618 (Bezold, *Catalogue* IV. 1627) has the following entries:

6 *e-nu-ma pu-rat-tu iš-šá-a* "When the Euphrates lifted up"
7 *a-ga-lu an-ni-tú ina še-me-e-šú* "When the Riding-donkey heard this"

The second of these lines certainly refers to a tablet of *The Fable of the Riding-donkey*; any tablet but the first. In every other case where a fable is entered in a list it is given as a series (éš.gàr), and only here is a single tablet from such a work included. Probably *The Fable of the Riding-donkey* consisted of two tablets only, which was not enough to be reckoned a series. Line 6 suggests itself as the first line of a conventional mythological introduction, and so could be the first tablet. Line 7 will then be the second and last. Only one fragment has yet been recovered, K 8592.

LITERATURE

TEXT	EDITION
1902 L. W. King, *CT* 15. 37.	1927 E. Ebeling, *MAOG* II/3. 37–38.
	1956 A. Salonen, *Hippologica*, 69.

K 8592 (Plate 53)

OBVERSE: odd signs and traces

REVERSE

1	[× × (×)]-*ka ana* [. . .	
2	[(×)]×-⌜*la*⌝-*ta-ma ul* [. . .	You . . . not [. . .
3	[*zi*]-*iq-tu ù qin-na-zu* ×[. . .	Spur and scourge . [. . .
4	⌜*e*⌝-*ri-iš e-ma-ta-ma* ×[. . .	You are like an *eagle* . [. . .
5	*ki-ma la ba-bil šip-ri* [. . .	Like an idler [. . .

6	*a-ga-lu an-ni-t*[*a ina šemêšu*]	[When] the Riding-donkey [heard] this
7	*ag-giš il-si-m*[*a* . . .	He cried in his anger and [. . .
8	*rig-mi ú-sad-dir-ma* [. . .	He continued shouting and [. . .
9	*i-pu-uš-ma pa-a-š*[*u* . . .	He opened his mouth [. . .
10	*ki-ki-i i-na il-lat* × (×)[. . .	"How among the family of . . [. . .
11	*ù ia-a-ši* ra × × [. . .	And as for me . . . [. . .
12	*ma-lil ir-qu ù* ×[. . .	The vegetarian and . [. . .
13	*da-k*[*i i*]*s-se-e-a d*[*a-* . . .	. . . my *cheek* . [. . .

(vii) *VARIA*

SU 1952, 138+169+181A–D (Plate 55)

This text reads like a speech from a fable. Someone or something speaks boastfully of his powers and attainments. As such it may be an extract from a fable, but it may be complete in itself, and so a different kind of text altogether. Due to the poor state of preservation and difficulties in some passages only detached phrases could be translated, and as this would have little purpose a translation has been dispensed with. The joins of two of the fragments as indicated on the copy are uncertain; they are therefore given here separately after the main piece. The copy has been printed before in *STT* I. 37.

OBVERSE

10 traces
11 [× × ×]-*šú-nu a-nam-b*[*i* . . .
12 [*a-na e-p*]*eš pi-ia kakkabāni*^{meš} ×[× ×] ma? na a ṭ[u . . .]
13 [× ×] *ina par-sik-ti mun-du-d*[*a-k*]*u ma-a-mi* bu KU[. . .]
14 × × ×-*pu-la šá-qa-a u šap-l*[*a-a*]
15 *rap-šá né-me-qi ilu ul* ⌜*i*⌝-*lam-*[*mad*]
16 *ba-ra-ku-ma mu-da-a-ku-*[*ma*] *a-mu-*[*ra?-ku?*]
17 *kul-lat gi-mir né-me-qí a-*[. . .] × [. . .]
18 *ni?-ra-a-ḫa-*⌜*ku*⌝ *um-ma* ⌜la/at/ṣi *ni-su*⌝-*ú*(-)[. . .]
19 ⌜*a*⌝*?-dan-nu si-iḫ-ru* × (×) *a-na la-ma-di mar-*[*ṣu?*]
20 *ú-paṭ-ṭar ki-iṣ-ri-šú* [×]×-*a ú-tar-ra-*×[. . .]
21 *am-mar ni-*[. . .]× ⌜ša/da⌝ *mu-ṣa-šú* ×[. . .]

REVERSE

22 ⌜*a*⌝-*šas-s*[*i*] ×-*ra-ku* [(×)] *a-*[. . .]
23 *a-bar-ri* ^{uzu}*tērta*(ur$_5$.úš) *šá la* ⌜*i*⌝-*du-u* ^{d}[*šamaš?*]
24 *maš-maša-ku-ma a-nam-bi mar-*[*ṣi-iš*]
25 *a*[*lam-*]*dím-*⟨*ma*⟩*-a u sa-gig-ga* × × *mu-d*[*a-ku*]
26 [× ×] mi? *ug-ga-li-tu-šú murus-su* ×[. . .]
27 [× ×]-*e a-pa-*⌜*áš*⌝-*šaḫ-ma i-nap-pu-uš* [. . .]
28 [× ×]× *ú-šal-lam-ma a-s*[*a*]-⌜*a*⌝ *ú-*×[. . .]
29 [× ×]× *a-šak-kan-ma i-ba*[*l-lu*]*ṭ ma-*[*ar?-ṣu?*]
30 [*ul i-*]*ḫa-kim ilu ma-am-*×[. . . . . .]
31 [× ×]×-*tu a-a-i-tu* × × šuk lu [. . .]
32 [× × ×]× *ki-še-ra* ×.meš *li-qa-*×[. . .]
33 [. . . . .]× *uk-ku* [. .]× a bu ti ×[. . .]
34 [. . . . . .u]s ×[. . .] ru i tu p[u? . . .]
35 [. . . . . . .]-*iš-šú a-na ṣeḫri*(lú.gina) t[a . . .]

36 [. . . *ú-z*]*u-un-šú lip-ta-ta-a liṭ-ṭu-l*[*a i-na-a-šú*]
37 [. . . . . . .]× *ia-a-ti* ⌜*e*⌝?*-šá-tu-u-a li*(! tablet TU)*-iz-ka-ma* ×[. . .]

PIECE A

1]× u ×[
2]×*-ti šá-qa-a* [
3]× *da-ád-me na-*[
4 *m*]*u-da-at* [
5]*-pu-*KUR *šá-qu-u* [
6]× *e-te-ni-*×[
7]× *ku-kal-la-k*[*u*
8 *u*]*ṣ-ra-tum* ×[
9]× pi nu [
10]× ×[

PIECE B

1]× [
2]× an za ×[
3] *qa-bu-ru-u*[*m*
4] *ab-rak-ka-*[*ku*?
5 i]k? *su-um-me* [
6]× diš ×[
7] *e-til aḫḫī*^{m}[^{eš}
8] *šamû*^{ú} *u erṣetim*^{tim} [
9 *ma*]*-an-za-az*(-)[
10]× [

Sm 1420+1729 (Plate 43)

This fragment is similar to the preceding piece, and is clearly not a fable of the usual type. One may even suspect that it is a god who speaks, perhaps Ea or Marduk.

Column A: traces

Column B

1 traces
2 . . .]×*-su ilāni*(dingir.dingir) *ana kul-lat ka-l*[*i* . . .
3 *a-na* [*zi*]*k-ri-šú ú-*[. . .
4 *a-šá-red qar-rad ši-i-ḫi e-tel ri-*[. . .
5 *kun-nu ina šamê*^{e} *pu-ug-g*[*ul* . . .
6 *ra-bi ina er-ṣe-ti ṣi-r*[*i*? . . .
7 *aplu*(ibila) *kun-nu-ú šá* ^{d}*en-líl i-lit-ti* ×[. . .
8 *šá-nin* ^{d}*a-nim qar-ra-du* [. . .

---

9 *a-sa-ku-ma bul-lu-ṭa a-l*[*i-'*. . .
10 *na-šá-ku šam-mi kul-lat-su-nu a-ni-is-*×[. . .
11 *es-ḫe-ku su-ḫi-i šá ši-pat* ×[. . .
12 *na-šá-ku maš-da-ra ša* [. . .
13 *a-nam-din bul-ṭa a-na ba-*[. . .
14 *el-lu rik-si si-im-*[*me* . . .
15 *rap-pu ṣi-in-di* ^{lú}[*marṣi*? . . .
16 *i-na ni-iš īnē*^{II}*-i*[*a* . . .
17 *i-na e-peš pi-*[*ia* . . .
18 *ri-mi-na-ku gam-ma-*[. . .
19 [×] ŠE ti ×[. . .
20 trace

8

POPULAR SAYINGS

THE common people of Babylonia and Assyria undoubtedly had a store of anecdotes, which were freely passed from mouth to mouth. The only collection of such material is preserved on VAT 8807, a large Assyrian tablet from the sixth year of Sargon II (716 B.C.). Unfortunately only a few traces remain of the obverse, but the reverse is preserved almost completely. Two small fragments from the Ashurbanipal libraries (K 5797, K 13247) also belong to this collection. A single saying of a similar kind is preserved on two pieces of a Late Babylonian exercise tablet (BM 53309 and BM 53555).

The material of the Assyrian tablet is short anecdotes arranged to some extent by community of subject matter (III. 5–16 are four sayings against the pig) or connected by a common phrase ("the city moat" occurs in two juxtaposed sayings III. 42–47). The stories are partly short animal or insect fables, which serve for amusement, though a moral might be extracted from some, and partly about humans. Here one can detect satire in the fowler trying to catch fish in his bird net (III. 42–43). The male prostitute apparently makes a witty remark about the unsatisfactory nature of his financial arrangements with the pander, and the street prostitute apparently makes a display of cleverness (IV. 3–7). The two sayings which expose corruption and deceit in lawsuits (IV. 8–14) seem intended to comfort the afflicted rather than to warn off possible offenders. Direct moral exhortation is completely absent.

The popular nature of the sayings is apparent not only from the content, but also from a comparison with other literatures. The Ahiqar sayings, and especially the Aramaic recension, present the same mixture of similar material, and one of the sayings even turns up in Greek dress in Aesop (III. 50–54). This connexion with the popular sayings of the post-Assyrian world, which probably circulated through the medium of Aramaic, suggests that the Assyrian tablet contains things which were in use in the late period, rather than older material which survived in written form. This conclusion is confirmed by the language, which is Late Assyrian dialect:

III. 31 *ú-ra-di-i-šú*
38, 41 *taš-ḫi-iṭ, ta-laq-qa-ta* (3rd fem.)
51 *an-a-a-ma* (from *ne'û*; the Sultantepe Gilgameš fragment *STT* I. 15 (*JCS* 8. 91) has a marked preference for the *a* vowel)
55 *e-rab*

The syntax is marked by an abundance of subordinate clauses introduced by *ki-i*, a phenomenon first appearing in Middle Babylonian (S. J. Bloch, *Or* N.S. 9. 343–6). A very late date is compelled by *lapān* (III. 19 and 32), which does not appear until Late Babylonian and Late Assyrian. It is always possible that old material could have been incorporated, but the collection as we have it is probably not much older than the tablet on which it is written.

An interesting question is whether there was a whole genre of such literature, and, if so, what was its relation to what are called in this book 'proverbs'. The unilingual Sumerian proverbs contain material similar to VAT 8807, but it is not possible with present knowledge to affirm whether the bilingual proverb collections took over some of this type of 'proverb' or not.

LITERATURE

TEXT WITH OR WITHOUT EDITION

(*a*) 1919 E. Ebeling, *KAR* 174 (VAT 8807). Plates 55–57.
1952 E. Weidner, *AfO* 16. 80 (K 13247). Plate 55.

(*b*) 1896 T. G. Pinches, *PSBA* 18. 258 (BM 53309 and 53555). Plate 57.

EDITION

(*a*) 1927 E. Ebeling, *MAOG* II/3. 39–53.

(*b*) 1939 J. Nougayrol, *Mélanges Dussaud* I. 73–74.

VAT 8807 (Plates 55–57)

REMAINS OF OBVERSE: I: 1 . .]×; 2 . .]ú; 3 . .]×
II: 1–6 traces

7 *ki-i* tar ×[. . . . .]

---

8 *an-na-bu* ×[. . . . .]
9 te ma bu [. . . . .]
10, 11 traces

(Gap of about ten lines)

22 [. . . . .] × × [. . . . .]
23 [. . . . .]× za tu[m . . . .]
24 [. . . . .] su ma ×[. . . .]

(End of column)

OBVERSE II

8 The hare . [. . . . .]
9 . . . [. . . . .]

* * * * *

REVERSE III (3–7 restored by K 5797; 42–49 by K 13247, Plate 55)

1 ^{lú}× sa [. . . . .] šú × [. . . .]
2 *ilu* [. . . . . *li-m*]*ut-ta iš-te-ni-'-*[*e*]

---

3 ^{lú}t[u/l[i] × *ḫa-at-tu-ú ba-ab* kur [ku]r? *šu-n*[*u*]
4 *a-na šá*[*-ma-'*]*i ba-šá-a uz-na-a-š*[*u*]

---

5 *šaḫû* [×]× *ul i-ši ṭè-e-ma*
6 *ra-bi-i*[*ṣ ina* × (×)]×*-me ik-ka-la ku-ru-um-ma-tu*
7 *ul i-*[*qab-bu-*]*ú šaḫû me-nu-ú ku-ba-du-ú-a*
8 *i-qab-bi* [*a-na lib*]*bi-šú šá-ḫu-ú tuk-la-ti*

---

9 *šaḫû u*[*l i-š*]*i ṭè-ma šu-ú-ma*
10 *še-am* ×[. . . . .]× *i-na diqar šamni*^{meš}
11 *ni-ḫu ki-i* [× × ×] *be-la-šú šá-ni-iṣ*
12 *be-la-šu e-zib-š*[*u . . . iš-t*]*a-gi-is-su* ^{lú}*ṭābiḫu*

---

13 *šaḫû la qa-šid* [. . . . *mu-bal-l*]*il ar-ki*
14 *mu-ba-ḫi-iš su-qa-ni* × [*mu*]*-ṭa-an-ni-pu bītāti*^{meš}

---

15 *šaḫû la si-mat ēkurri la amēl* [*t*]*è-me la ka-bi-is a-gur-ri*
16 *ik-kib ilāni*^{meš} *kāl-a-ma taḫ-da-a*[*t il*]*i ni-zir-ti* ^{d}*šamaš*

REVERSE III

1 The . . man [. . . . .] . . [. . . .]
2 The god seeks evil [. . . . .]

---

3 The . . man, ...
4 Directs his attention to heaven.

---

5 The [.] . pig has no sense;
6 Lying [in . .] . . he eats his food.
7 They do not [say,] "Pig, what respect have I?"
8 He says [to] himself, "The pig is my support!"

---

9 The pig himself has no sense;
10 . [. . .] corn [. .] . in the oil pot.
11 When at leisure [. . .] he mocked his master,
12 His master left him [. . .] the butcher slaughtered him.

---

13 The pig is unholy [. . . .] bespattering his backside,
14 Making the streets smell . polluting the houses.

---

15 The pig is not fit for a temple, lacks sense, is not allowed to tread on pavements,
16 An abomination to all the gods, an abhorrence [to (his) god,] accursed by Šamaš.

---

17 *pi'āzu ti-bu-ú šá ina* ×[× × t]i × × ru
18 *a-na šikkê* [. . . .] × [.] × šu

---

19 *pi'āzu la-pa-an šik-ke-e ina* ⸢*ḫur-ri*⸣ *ṣēri e-ru-ba*
20 *um-ma mušlaḫḫu iš-pur-an-ni šul-mu*

---

21 *šēlibu lìb-ba-šú nu-ḫu-ub-ma su-ul-le-e né-ši i-ba-'a*
22 *a-na su-ul-le-e bar-ba-ri i-ḫaṭ qer-bi-tu*
23 *ina ba-ba-at āli ina* ⸢*qé*⸣*-re-bi-šu ú-ṭar-ri-du-šú kal-bi*
24 *a-na šu-zu-ub napšāti*^{meš}*-šú šil-ta-ḫi-iš ú-ṣi*
25 *ša la i-du-ú a-mir-šú bēl bir-ki i-*× [×] × ×

---

26 × an × × *šat-ti* ^{d}*addu i-ra-mu-um* × × [× ×] ×
27 an × × *a-na* ^{d}*enlil*(be) [. . . . .]
28 *um-ma a-na-ku ki-i* × × ⸢a ma⸣ × [. . . . . .]

---

29 *kalbu ina muḫḫi sin-niš-ti-šú ki-i* [*e-lu-ú*]
30 *pa-ni-šú ṣu-uḫ-ḫu lìb-ba-šú* ×[. . . . . .]
31 *a-na ú-ra-di-i-šú ina ni-*[*r*]*u-ub-ba-ti* ×[. . . . . .]

---

32 *šikkû la-pa-an kal-bi ina nam-ṣa-bi* [*e-tar-ba*]
33 *kal-bu ki-i iš-ḫi-iṭ-ma ina bāb nam-ṣa-bi* [. . . .]
34 *šikkâ iš-tu nam-ṣa-bi ú-*⸢*šá-aḫ*⸣*-*[*li-iq*]

---

35 *al-ti ag-ri ag-ri šá amti* aḫ ×[. . . . . .]
36 *ša ina bīt tap-pat-ti aḫātu ummu* [. . . . . .]
37 *ša ḫa-pi-ir in-di* is? [. . . . . .]
38 *gaš-riš ki-i taš-ḫi-iṭ* [. . . . . .]
39 *ina bī*[*t*] *la-qit ḫa-ru-pi ki-i te-*[. . . . . .]
40 *a-di* u_4*-um bal-ṭa-tu a-na pi-*[. . . . . .]
41 *ta-laq-qa-ta* ka × [. . . . . .]

---

42 ^{lú}*ušandû ša nūnī*^{meš} *la i-šu-ma iṣṣūrāti*[^{meš} . . . .]
43 *na-ši ka-tim-ta-šu ḫi-rit āli ṭi-*[*bi-ma*]

---

44 *šēlibu ina ḫi-rit āli iš-ta-'i-ru* ×[. . . . .]
45 *bar-ba-ru ina irti-šú ki-i e-la-a šulmu*^{mu} *ana* [*ka-a-ši*]
46 *ù šu-ú a-na bar-ba-ri ki-a-am i*[*p-pal*]
47 *um-ma šikaru*^{meš} *ṣab-ta-ni-ma ul a-li-'i* [. . . . .]

---

48 *pi-a-zu*! *ša ina qer-ba-a-ti i-laq-qa-tu* pi ×[. . . . .]
49 *a-na nam-bu-*⸢*ba*⸣*-ti a-ki-lat enib ṣip-pa-a-ti šá-ni-iṣ-*[*ma*]

---

50 *ni-ni-qu ina m*[*u*]*ḫḫi pēri ki-i ú-š*[*i-bu*]

VARIANT

43 K 13247: *ka-tim-ta-šú*

17 A lusty mouse which in . [. .] . . . .
18 To the mongoose [. . . .] . [.] . .

---

19 A mouse, out of the way of a mongoose, entered a snake's hole.
20 He said, "A snake-charmer sent me. Greetings!"

---

21 The fox with . . . heart was seeking the 'way of the lion',
22 For the 'way of the wolf' he was exploring the meadow land.
23 As he approached the city gates, the dogs drove him away;
24 To save his life he departed like an arrow.
25 Unconsciously a runner, seeing him, . . [.] . .

---

26 . . . . . . Addu bellows . . [. .] .
27 . . . to Enlil [. . . . .]
28 "I, like . . . . . [. . . . . ."]

---

29 When a dog [mounted] his wife
30 His face was glowing, and his heart . [. . . . . .]
31 To get down . . . . [. . . . . .]

---

32 A mongoose, out of the way of a dog, [entered] a drain-pipe.
33 When the dog jumped [it got wedged] in the opening of the pipe
34 And let the mongoose escape from the pipe.

---

35 Wife . . . . slave girl . . [. . . . . .]
36 Who, in the house of a concubine, sister, mother [. . . . . .]
37 . . . . [. . . . . .]
38 When she jumped mightily [. . . . . .]
39 In the house of a gatherer of carob-pods when she [. . . . . .]
40 So long as she lives . . . [. . . . . .]
41 She will gather . . [. . . . . .]

---

42 The fowler who had no fish, but [had caught] birds,
43 Holding his bird net jumped into the city moat.

---

44 The fox moved around in the city moat . [. . . . .]
45 When the wolf came upon him (he said,) "Greetings to [you!"]
46 The former replied to the wolf,
47 "I am drunk; I cannot [. . . . ."]

---

48 The mouse who gathers . . [. . . . .] in the meadows
49 Mocks the wasps who eat the fruit of the orchards.

---

50 A *mosquito*, as it settled on an elephant,

51 *um-ma ta-lim id-[k]a an-a-a-ma ina ši-qi mê*^{meš} *e-ra-[aq-ma]*
52 *pe-e-ru a-na ni-ni-qi ip-[pal]*
53 *ki-i tu-ši-bu ul i-di-ma ka-la-ka mi-[i-nu]*
54 *ki-i ta-at-bu-ú ul i-de-e[-ma]*

---

55 *barbaru šá e-rab āli la i-du-[ú]*
56 *e-nin-na [ina]* ⸢*su*⸣*-qa-a-ni šaḫê*^{meš} *ú-ṭar-[ra-du-šú]*

---

57 *kalbu la-a e-ri-ib bī[ti]*
58 *ra-b[i-i]ṣ ina bīt ruq-qí ir-ti* × × × × [. . . .]

---

59 *amēlu ḫu-ub-bu-lu ra-*× [. . . . .]
60 *a-n[a] ma-mit ilāni*^{meš} *ba-ab* ×[. . . . .]

---

61 [×] × na.^{lú}ni.× *a-na ṣi-il-t[i* . . . .]
62 [× (×)] šá [i]m *ina bīt* ⸢*tarbaṣi*⸣? ḫi it ta[b? . . . . . .]
63 [× ×] × × *ina* × × [. . . . .]
64 [× × ×] ⸢ú⸣ *ina* za × [. . . . .]

---

65 [. . . . .] × × × × [. . . . .]

REVERSE IV

1 *a-na āl ku-ú-ti ki-i il-li-ku*
2 *ina ti-ib še-e-ri ina bāb ḫa-za-an-ni ig-ru-šú*

---

3 *sin-niš-a-nu ina bīt áš-tam-me ki-i e-ru-ba*
4 *ni-iš qa-ti ki-i iš-šu-ú um-ma ig-ri šá an-za-ni-nu*
5 *at-ti lu miš-ru-um-ma ana-ku lu meš-lu*

---

6 *ka-*⸢*az*⸣*-ra-tu pit-qu-u[t]-tu muṭ-ṭap-pi-la-at šar-rap-ti*
7 *ina qí-bit* ^{d}*ištar*(išdar) *šum-*⸢*su-kàt*⸣ *al-ti kab-ti*

---

8 *ṣap-par-ru-ú ina bāb de-*⸢*e*⸣*-ni ú-šu-uz*
9 *im-na ù šu-me-la kàt-*⸢*ra*⸣*-a ú-pa-qa-ad*
10 *i-di ḫi-bíl-ta-šú* ^{d}*šamaš qu-ra-du*

---

11 *šaḫ-šá-aḫ-ḫu ina pān ru-bé-*⸢*e*⸣ *[i-da-]bu-ba zi-ra-a-te*
12 *i-qab-bi ni-kil-tùm-ma i-tam-ma-a a-*⸢*ḫi-i*⸣*-ta*
13 *ru-[b]u-ú ina taḫ-sis-ti-šu ú-sal-la* ^{d}*šamaš*
14 ^{d}*šá-maš lu-ú ti-i-di da-mi niši*^{meš} *ba-'-i qa-tuš-šú*

---

15 *sīsû ti-bu-ú ina m[u]ḫḫi a-ta-ni pa-re-e ki-i* ⸢*e-lu-ú*⸣
16 *ki-i šá ra-ak-bu-ú-ma ina uz-ni-šá ú-làḫ-ḫa-áš*
17 *u[m-ma m]u-ú-ru šá* ⸢*tu-ul-li*⸣*-di ki ia-ti lu la-si-im*
18 *a-n[a i-me-r]u za-bíl tup-šik-ki la tu-maš-šá-li*

---

51 Said, "Brother, did I press your side? I will make [off] at the watering-place."
52 The elephant replied to the *mosquito*,
53 "I do not care whether you get on—what is it to have you?—
54 Nor do I care whether you get off."

---

55 A wolf who did not know the entrance of the city—
56 Now the pigs drive [him out along] the streets.

---

57 A dog, not allowed indoors,
58 Lies in the house of . . . . [. . . .]

---

59 A man in debt . . [. . . . .]
60 At the oath of the gods . . . [. . . . .]

---

65 [. . . . .] . . . . [. . . . .]

REVERSE IV

1 When he went to the city of Cutha
2 They took him to law at break of dawn in the magistrate's gate.

---

3 When a male prostitute entered the brothel,
4 As he raised his hands in prayer, he said, "My hire goes to the promoter.
5 You (Ištar) are wealth (*mešrû*), I am half (*mešlu*)."

---

6 The discreet street prostitute slanders the . . . woman.
7 At Ištar's command the noble's wife gets a bad name.

---

8 The sycophant stands in court at the city gate,
9 Right and left he hands out bribes.
10 The warrior Šamaš knows his misdeeds.

---

11 The maligner speaks hostile words before the ruler,
12 Talking cunningly, uttering slander.
13 The ruler, thinking it over, prays to Šamaš,
14 "Šamaš, you know. Hold him responsible for the blood of the people."

---

15 When a lusty stallion was mounting a jenny-ass,
16 As he was mating he whispers in her ear,
17 "Let the foal which you bear be a swift runner, like me;
18 Do not make it like an [ass] which suffers hard labour."

---

19 *ina* [*s*]*u-ú-qí* ⸢*ku*⸣*-za-zu a-na ṣi-i*[*l*]*-te ki-i il-li-ku*
20 *ḫa-mit za-re-e ka-pi-ṣu a-na mu-kin-nu-ú-te il-su-ú-ni*
21 *ḫa-me-tu* KU.KIL *it-ta-ad-du-ú bi-re-e-ti*
22 ⸢*i-na*⸣ *pu-ut eqli ina bāb ḫur-ri pi-a-zi n*[*a*]*-ku-ú-sa na-kis*

---

23 [*it-*]*tu-tú* ⸢*a-na zu*⸣*-um-bi iḫ-ta-dal pu-un-zir-ru*
24 [*ṣu*]*rarû*(em]e.dir) *e*[*l*]*i pu-un-zi-ir-ri*
25 [*i*]*t-ta-ši-iš a-na* [*i*]*t-tu-ú-ti*

---

26 [× ×] zi im × ri × [. . . . .]
27 [× ×] × × × eme.dir × × × × × × ×
28 *um-ma* ub [×] *dam-qu tap-pu-ú-šú ki-i e-mu-ru*

29]˙bir.ra.bi.gin$_7$ ab.sar ba.an.è
30 *tup-pi* $^{m.d}$*ninurta-ú-bal-liṭ-su* lú.a.ba
31 šà.bal.bal ^{m}*gab-bi-ilāni*$^{meš.ni}$*-ēreš*(kam-*eš*) lú.× × meš
32 × × × [. . .] × itu × [. . . . .]
33 [*lim*]*-mu* ^{m}*ṭāb-ṣilli-ēšarra*(dùg.ga.gi[š.g]e$_6$*-é-šár-ra*) ^{lú}*šá-kìn* ^{uru}*libbi-āli*
34 mu.6.kám ^{m}*šarru-kēnu*(gi.na) *arkû*^{ú} *šàr māt aš-šur*$^{ki!}$

19 As the wood-wasp went along the street to a lawsuit
20 The . . . summoned the . . . sand-wasp to witness.
21 The spiders threw the sand-wasp in fetters,
22 And on the edge of the field in the entrance to the mouse's hole he was cut to pieces.

---

23 The spider spun a web for a fly.
24 A lizard was caught
25 On the web, to the spider's disadvantage!

---

26 [. .] . . . . . [. . . . .]
27 [. .] . . . lizard . . . .
28 " . [.] when he saw his good friend."

BM 53309 (82–3–23. 4344+4473) and BM 53555 (82–3–23. 4595) (Plate 57)

1	^{lú}*ušandû*	The fowler
2	*še-e-tú*	cast
3	*id-di-ma*	his net and
4	*im-taḫ-ḫar*	persistently prayed
5	^{d}*šamši*^{ši}	to Šamaš,
6	^{d}*šamši*^{ši} ud.20.kám	"Šamaš, the twentieth day
7	*u*$_4$*-mu-ka nam-mar*	is your bright day;
8	× × × × ×	. . . . .
9	× ×*-ú-a*	my . . ."

VARIANTS

2 *še-e-ti* 9 pa pa [

9

PROVERBS

(i) BILINGUAL PROVERBS

THE word 'proverb' is used here in a traditional and convenient way to refer to a particular genre of Sumerian literature. Proverb tablets are made up of numerous short, mutually independent sections of very diverse nature. Some are proverbs in the English sense: short pithy sayings. Mixed in, however, are anecdotes, extracts from works of literature, short fables, and a great deal of material which is not yet understood. These texts are available most extensively in unilingual Sumerian tablets of the Old Babylonian period, though one or two small bilingual tablets of the same date (N–3395, UM 29–15–330, and BE unnumbered) show that Akkadian translations were already being made. Two Middle Assyrian bilinguals from Assur (VAT 10251 in the *Assyrian Collection*, and VAT 10810) are evidence that proverbs, like other traditional literature, had been moulded in a particular cast during the Cassite period, and from the late period both Assyrian and Babylonian copies of bilinguals have survived in quantity. The late tablets are for the most part very fragmentary. On them there is nowhere any explicit mention of a series of proverb tablets in the late libraries, but in two cases where the end of a tablet is preserved (K 4207 and K 5688) an odd line of Sumerian is appended, apparently serving as a catch-line, and so proving that some of the tablets at least were arranged in a sequence. Only one other tablet has the end preserved (Sm 61), and here two complete Sumerian proverbs without Akkadian renderings appear. These do not seem to be catch-lines, and this tablet probably did not belong to a series. It is, moreover, a tablet of two double columns only, whereas most of the Assyrian fragments belong to tablets of four or six double columns. In the Assyrian tablets there is only one case of duplication, but it is striking. Six fragments, one of them Middle Assyrian, overlap or can be placed in relation to each other, so providing a considerable part of one group of proverbs. This has been called the *Assyrian Collection*. For the rest, the pieces are cited by their museum numbers. The five Neo-Late-Babylonian pieces duplicate neither each other nor the Assyrian material.

The comparison of the late bilingual copies with the Old Babylonian unilingual material promises to be one of the most instructive lessons in literary history, but for the present only a few indications can be given. The Sumerian proverb collections were first taken in hand by S. N. Kramer, and now his talented pupil E. I. Gordon is continuing the work. All that is written here on this subject is obtained from Gordon, who most generously placed his unique knowledge of this whole subject at the writer's disposal. The excavations at Nippur have yielded by far the greater part of the Old Babylonian material, which can be arranged into large stock collections, smaller groups of proverbs excerpted from the larger collections, and "extra-canonical" tablets, which often contain proverbs found in the large collections, but not in the same order. In some of the collections the proverbs are carefully arranged by the first words, or by community of subject. Outside Nippur, Old Babylonian copies of Sumerian proverbs have been found at Susa and Ur, and enough is known to affirm that the same proverbs were copied in different places, but until the Ur texts are published it cannot be ascertained whether the Nippur grouping and arrangement into collections was widespread or purely local.

Connexions between the Nippur Sumerian and late bilingual editions are sometimes striking, sometimes completely absent. E. I. Gordon has so far traced thirty-four individual proverbs common to both groups of material. What is more significant is that whole groups of proverbs in the same sequence are carried over from the unilinguals to the late bilinguals. *STVC* 3+4, an "extra-canonical" Nippur tablet, is the most striking case. Three Assyrian bilingual fragments, which seem to be parts of the same tablet, reproduce sequences from it: K 4327+4605+4749, K 15227 and 80–7–19. 130. K 4605 has one proverb not in *STVC* 3+4, and K 15227 adds extra material at the beginning of one. K 4327 adds a variant form of one of the proverbs. The circulation of variant forms of the same proverb is well known in Hebrew literature (e.g. Proverbs xi. 14: "Through lack of direction a people falls, but success comes from a large number of counsellors", and Proverbs xxiv. 6: "By direction you make war for yourself, but success comes from a large number of counsellors"), and this is exactly the phenomenon in K 4327, except that the variant forms are found together. The collection of textual variants is more endemic to Babylon than Israel. Apart from these differences the three Assyrian fragments follow *STVC* 3+4 with only slight verbal differences. The other duplications between Old Babylonian and late copies are not so impressive, but generally the important fact is that the concurrences are frequent in some tablets (nine in BM 38283; five in Sm 61), though completely lacking from others. Nothing duplicating any part of the *Assyrian Collection* has yet been found. This suggests that the Cassite scribes and editors drew on material not copied in Old Babylonian Nippur, and presumably obtained it from other towns, unless it is of later date. There is one indication of textual work in the Akkadian translation: BM 38596. III. 7 gives the variants *a-ar* and *ia-ar*.

Langdon confidently believed (*AJSL* 28. 218) that the Sumerian is a translation from the Akkadian; Meissner (*MAOG* III/3. 24) hesitated to commit himself. This view cannot any longer be sustained. Even in the bilinguals one tablet (K 4347+) has several proverbs without an Akkadian version. However, since Semitic influence on the Sumerian language is known from very early times (see A. Falkenstein, *CRR* II. 13) it is, of course, possible that some proverbs in the unilingual collections may have been Semitic originally, and may have passed into Sumerian at a very early date.

Seeing that this is Sumerian literature the question may be asked whether it should have any place in a corpus of Babylonian Wisdom literature. Apart from the general impossibility of drawing a clear line of demarcation between Sumerian and Semitic culture in the southern part of Mesopotamia, there is evidence of the influence of Sumerian proverbs on Babylonian texts. The *Dialogue of Pessimism* quotes one (83–84) in Akkadian, and another appears in the Amarna letters (see note on *Assyrian Collection* IV. 14–21). An exercise tablet quotes a third in Akkadian (p. 280). A fourth is incorporated into an Akkadian text (p. 117). Two more are quoted in another exercise tablet (p. 267).

The difficulties of Sumerian proverbs are well known. In addition to the usual problems of grammar and lexicon which any Sumerian text may present, there is the frequent obscurity of content. Proverbs serve for a fixed occasion, and because of their epigrammatic nature are only meaningful against that background. We only know the proverbs out of their context, and in many cases we can only guess at the point. Many English proverbs would be difficult if not connected with a particular circumstance. In parts of England, for example, "Many mickles make a muckle" is well understood as enjoining thrift, but hardly anyone could define 'mickle' or 'muckle'. In fact they are phonetic variants, and this form of the proverb is a corruption of "Many a little makes a mickle".

The study of Sumerian has advanced considerably since scholars like Barton and Langdon, admirable pioneers in their way, translated largely by guesswork, and were often completely wrong. Even with the latest grammatical and lexical helps equally wild renderings can still be made.[1] This is no reflection on the care of the translators, but a commentary on the difficulties of the material. In these circumstances the writer, who is no trained Sumerologist, has avoided littering his book with bad guesses, and has left many proverbs untranslated. The aim has been to present a reliable text for specialists to work upon, and only to hazard a translation when it seems that the approximate sense is more or less certain. A further reason for this decision is that several thousands of unilingual Sumerian proverbs are now being prepared for publication by E. I. Gordon. Whatever the difficulties in this material, it cannot but throw much light on these texts generally. This, then, is no time to attempt a definitive interpretation of the bilinguals, and the comments have been kept to a minimum.

To meet the special needs of these difficult texts the arrangement found elsewhere in this book has been modified. The translations are interspersed with the comments, and the literature on the unilinguals has not been cited. Gordon's editions of the Sumerian Collections should always be consulted. The literature on the bilinguals is given with the individual texts, but note that (i) now antiquated or otherwise useless editings are not necessarily cited if reference is made to them in the works listed; (ii) to facilitate the finding of references, and to collect stray comments on single proverbs, certain references

[1] J. J. A. Van Dijk, *La Sagesse*, p. 10, translates the first three lines of *KAR* 103: "Quand ⟨l'ombre⟩ de l'éclipse s'étend, ⟨pareillement⟩ au seigneur et au roi elle annonce la main de dieu." The lines are in fact only the end of a proverb (*Assyrian Collection* IV. 25–26), and mean, ". . . you have seen, you will praise (your) god and salute the king"! This is an unpleasant reminder of the pitfalls which beset even the careful scholar, in which class J. J. A. Van Dijk belongs.

are given immediately under the translations of the proverbs concerned. However, only editions, translations, or comments of value are handled this way.

THE *ASSYRIAN COLLECTION*

This group of proverbs, which was written on a single tablet of four columns, appears to have enjoyed some popularity in Assyria. Of the six pieces from which a considerable part can be reconstructed, five are from the libraries of Ashurbanipal, and attest the presence of at least three different copies there. The other piece was found at Assur, and both script and orthography (*šap-ta-i*[*a*, (ii) 16) suggest a Middle Assyrian date, though E. Weidner did not include it in his study of Middle Assyrian literature from Assur (*AfO* 16. 197–215). All five pieces belong to the same textual family, as the division into columns occurs at the same points, within a few lines, in all the copies. For convenience this has been called the *Assyrian Collection*, though the title must not be interpreted to mean that the proverbs or their redaction originated in Assyria. No doubt they came from Babylonia, like the rest.

B. Landsberger has suggested (orally) that the text is not a simple collection of proverbs, but a dialogue between the Amorite, as he reads the first word, and his wife, who each adopt the garb and manners of the opposite sex and proceed to woo one another.

The connexion of the first five pieces listed below was discovered by T. Jacobsen, to whom the writer is obliged for the information. The sixth piece the writer identified himself.

MANUSCRIPTS

A=K 2024+2951+2983	Plates 58, 59
b=VAT 10251	„ 58, 59
C=K 7638	Plate 59
D=K 8206	Plates 58, 59
E=80–7–19. 286	Plate 59
F=80–7–19. 289	„ 58
(D, E, and F may be parts of the same tablet)	

LITERATURE

The text of A and D was previously published by T. J. Meek, *RA* 17. 122–3 and 157; that of **b** by E. Ebeling, *KAR* 103. **b** has also been edited by J. J. A. Van Dijk, *La Sagesse*, pp. 9–11. Much of A was edited by B. Meissner in *MAOG* III/3. 24–30, and the whole by J. Pereman, *The Book of Assyro-Babylonian Proverbs*, pp. 189–216.

(i)

A

1	[Sumerian column lost]	*[a]-ḫ/mur-ru-ú*
2		*[a-n]a aššati-šu i-qab-bi*
3		*[at]-ti lu eṭ-lu*
4		*[a-na-k]u lu ar-da-tu*
5		[. . . .] × *a-na eṭli*(guruš) *at-tu-ru*
6		[. . . . . *l*]*u si-ni-šu*
7		[. . . . .]× *zi-ka-ru*
8		[. . . . . .]×*-ti-ka-ma*
9		[. . . . . .]×*-ti-ka-ma*
10		[. . . . . . .]*-at-ma*
11		[. . . . . . .]*-gu-u*
12		[. . . . . . .]*-ku-u*
13		[. . . . .]*-ú*
14		[. . . . .]×

* * * * *

(i a)

[Sumerian lost]	1	traces
	2	. . .] an
	3	. . .]×*-an-ma*
	4	. . .]× *ni-qí-i*
	5	. . .]×*-in-ma*
	6	. . . *-k*]*al-lim*
	7	. . .]×*-'-a*
	8	traces

* * * * *

(ii)

b

1	[× (×)] × [.	. . . .]
2	[×] da zu [.	. . . .]
3	[×] gig [.	. . . .]
4	gíd.da.[muše]n nu.me.[a	. . . .]
5	ba.an.u[r$_4$	. . . .]
6	nam.me.[a	. . . .]
7	igi.mu ur.a	[. . . . .]
8	é.gar$_8$.mu ^{d}lamma	[. . . . .]
9	íb.ga ša$_6$.ga	[. . . . .]

MS		Sumerian	Akkadian
b	10	en.šár.ra.kám	× [. . . . .]
	11	a.ba	*man-*[*nu* (. . . . . . .)]
	12	dam la.la.mu ḫé.em	*lu* × [. . . . .]
	13	šà.mu nam.kù.zu	*lìb-bi* [. . . . .]
	14	lipiš.malga.mu	*sur-ri* [. . . . .]
	15	bar.mu nam.nin.a	*ka-bat-t*[*i* . . . .]
	16	nundum.mu ša$_6$.ša$_6$	*šap-ta-i*[*a* . . . .]
	17	mu.un.dug$_4$.dug$_4$.a	*man-nu* [. . . . .]
	18	a.ba nitalam igi.íla.mu ḫé.em	× [. . . . .]
A	19	a.ba gar.ra a.b[a g]ál.la	*man-nu gi-it-ru-nu man-nu ša-ru*
	20	a.ba úr.mu ga.an.na.ab.urù	*a-na man-ni uṭ-li a-na-ṣar*
	21	níg ki e.da.ág	*ša ta-ra-am-mi*
	22	ù ⸢šudul⸣ al.kúš.ù.dè.en	*ù ni-ra tu-šá-aṭ*
	23	ud.da ir.pag an.ag.en	*u$_4$-ma ta-kap-pu-ud*
	24	dingir.zu níg.zu	*ìl-ka ku-u*
	25	ud.da ir.pag nu.an.ag.en	*u$_4$-ma ul ta-kap-pu-ud*
	26	dingir.zu níg.nu.zu	*ìl-ka la-a ku-u*
	27	ù.e.dè.ná.dè.en	*it-ti-ka lu-uṣ-lal*
	28	dingir zi.ga kú.e	*i*[*l*]*a ša ni-siḫ-ti šu-kíl*
	29	da.da.ri ù.bí.dug$_4$	[*šit-pá*]*r-ma i-lu*
	30	dingir.zu ri.a.zu ḫé.a	[*lu*] *na-ra-ar-ka*
	31	giš.tukul ù.⸢bí.i⸣.e	$^{gi[š}$*kakku* . . . . .]*-ma*
	32	dingir á.daḫ.zu ḫé.a	*il*[*u lu ri-ṣu-k*]*a*
	33	za.e ab.gam.gam.dè.en	*a*[*t-ta* . . . .]
	34	an.ta ḫé.en.dù	*tap-p*[*u-ú* . . . . . .]
	35	[l]ú.ša$_6$.ga.zu.šè	*ša a-n*[*a dam-qi-ka lemutta*]
	36	níg.ḫul ba.e.dù	*te-pu*[*-šu a-na lem-ni-ka*]
	37	[l]ú.ḫùl.zu ta an.ag.en	*mi-n*[*a-a te-ep-pu-uš*]
D	38	[l]ú.numún.z[i].zi.dè kù.dun.bi	*ša* × [. .] *e*[*l* . . . .]
	39	[×].gi.ga.gin$_7$.nam	*ta-tu*[*r-š*]*ú ki-ma* × [. . . .]
	40	[l]ú.kù.dím.ma kù.dun.bi	*ša kás-*[*p*]*a ip-pu-*[*šu*]
	41	[(×)]×.KU.ra.gin$_7$.nam	*ta-tur-š*[*ú*] *ki-ma a-*× [. .]
	42	[á.d]aḫ.zu níg.tuku.nu.me.a	*ri-ṣu-ka ul maš-*[*ru-ú*]
	43	[dingir].ra.àm	*i-lu-um-*[*ma*]

VARIANT

19 **b**: *gi*[*t-ru-nu*]

AD F

44	[sig] kala.ga	*ṣe-ḫe-er r[a-bi]*
45	dingir ⸢á.daḫ⸣.zu na.nam	*ilum-ma r[i-ṣu-ka]*
46	lú.kúr.r[a AN.]a babbar.ra.a	*na-ak-r[i . . . .]*
47	su.me.a [z]á ḫé.em	× × [. . . . .]
48	me.dè.en A[N].⸢a⸣ babbar.ra.a	[. . . . .]
49	su.me.a níg.kala.ga ḫ[é.em	. . . .]
50	su.lú.kúr.ra zá [. . . .	. . . .]
51	ud.da AN.a an.ga.× [. . . .	. . . .]
52	níg.kala.ga ḫé.em.× ×[. . . .	. . . .]

* * * * *

(iii)

D

1–8	traces and detached signs	
9	[. . . . . . lugal.]la	*a-a iz-ziz ma-ḫar ili u šarri*
10	[. . . . . na]m.en.bi	*e-zi-bu-šu ilū^{meš}-šu*
11	[. . . . . .] níg.bi	*be-lu-ta-šu ud-da-pár*
12	[. . . . . .].in.nu	*ìl-šu la-a šu-u*
13	[. . . . .]na.gá.aḫ × im	*na-an-duq er-šú ṣu-bat bal-ti*
14	[. . . . .]× múd an.mu$_4$	*nu-'-ú ú-lap da-me la-biš*
15	[. . . .]× kur ḫé.en.gul.e	*eli a-a-bi-ni mātu li-ab-bit*
16	[. . . .].me.a bàd sig$_4$.zil.lá	*eli lim-ni-ni dūru šá i-qú-pu*
17	[. . .]×.bi ki lú.kúr.me.a	*lim-qut er-ṣe-et na-ak-ri*
18	[. . .]šè ḫé.en.lá.e	*li-ir-[t]e-si i-na gim-[ri-šá]*
19	[. . .]× ḫi ud ag.ag an ul	an × [(×)] *pe-e* da [. . . .]
20	[. . .] × ⸢ga⸣.an.du$_7$	× [×] e a s[u? . . . . .]
21	[.	. . . .]× e na ×[. . . .]
22	[.	. . . . .] × × × [. . . .]

* * * * *

(iv)

A

1	[. . . .] × šud$_x$(KA×ŠU) ×[. .	. . . .]
2	[. . . .].gin$_7$ ì.[. . .	. . . .]
3	[u]r$_5$.bi dingir.ra.gin$_7$.nam	[. . . . .]
4	[l]ugal.ra	[. . . . .]
5	[K]U/[k]i.nu.me.a	[. . . . .]
6	[š]à.zu nam.ša$_6$.ga	[. . . . .]
7	ḫé.en.dib bar.da níg.ge si.sá	[. . . . .]
8	izkim.igi ḫé.me.a	[. . . . .]

9	nam.á.dah̯.é.gal.zu.šè	[. . . . .]
10	lugal.zu níg.nu.zu h̯é.a	[. . . . .]
11	ᵈutu an.na.ab.bé	[. . . . .]
12	apin ù.un.h̯ul.pà.da	[. . . . .]
13	ᵈutu an.nà.nà.bi na.nam	[. . . . .]
14	un lugal nu.me.a	[. . . . .]
15	udu sipa.bi in.nu	[. . . . .]
16	un ugula nu.me.a	[. . . . .]
17	a gú.gal.bi in.nu	[. . . . .]
18	erín nu.bàn.da nu.me.a	*ṣābu* [*ša la-a la-p*]⌜*u-ut-te*⌝-[*e*]
19	a.šà engar.ra in.nu	*eq*[*lu ša la-*]*a ik-ka-r*[*i*]
20	é en.bi nu.nam	*bītu ša la-a bēli*
21	munus nitá nu.tuku	*sinništu ša la-a mu-ti*
22	en.e h̯é.tuku lugal.e h̯é.tuku	*bēla ri-ši šarra ri-ši*
23	šagub ní.te.bi	*šakkanakka pi-làh̯*
24	ud.da á.tuku ní.te dingir.ra	*u*$_4$*-ma né-me-el pa-la-ah̯ ili*
25	mu.ni.in.lá	*ta-ta-mar*
26	dingir ár.ag.en ù lugal.ra ba.an.na.ab.bé	*ila ta-na-ʾ-ad ana šarri ta-kar-rab*
27	lú.tur šud$_x$(KA×ŠU) ù.bí.gi	*ṣih̯-ra* [. . . . .]
28	níg.šár.ra an.ni.e	*mìm-ma li-*[. . . . .]
29	[u]r.tur.ra ninda ù.bí.šub	*ana mu-ra-ni* [. . . . . .]
30	[ku]n.da.ra.an.gùn.gùn.nu	*li-kan-*[*zi-ib-ku*]
31	[lú].tur.ra íb.ù.dam.za	*tu-ta-z*[*a-am ṣih̯-ra*]
32	[é]r	*ú-*× [. . . . .]
33	[ì.š]éš.šéš	*a-na* [*mu-ra-ni*]
34	[ur].tur.ra	*ku-si-*[*ip-ta* . . . .]
35	[ninda] ⌜ù⌝.bí.šub	*ul-*[*te*?]-
36	[× × u]n.ša.ra.ab.tùm	*bi-l*[*a* . . . . .]
37	[. . . . .]un h̯i.li.a	ud [. . . . .]
38	[. . . . .]×.za.za.àm	la[. . . . .]
39	[. . . . .] ba.dúru.nu	×[. . . . .]
40	[. . . . . u]n.h̯ul.×	[. . . . .]
41	[. . . . . .] × [. . .	. . . .]

*   *   *   *   *

VARIANTS

18 C: nu.tuku.a   24 C has a ruling after this line.   25 **b**: mu.ni.lá   26 **b**: šu.an.na.ab.bé

i. 1–7. [A low] fellow/[An A]morite speaks [to] his wife, "You be the man, [I] will be the woman. [Since . .] . I became a man [. . . . .] . female [. . . . .] . male."

The section apparently refers to transvestite practices, which are first known in the ancient Near East from their condemnation in Deuteronomy xxii. 5. Later references to these rites in Syria and Asia Minor are more abundant (see S. R. Driver, *Deuteronomy*, p. 250), though there seems to be no clear evidence for them at any period in Mesopotamia. Thus the alternative 'Amorite' could be supported on the assumption that these people were notorious for this perversion, as were the men of Sodom, Corinth, and Bulgaria, and the women of Lesbos, for other things. B. Landsberger also supports this alternative with the fragment 79–7–8. 245 (Plate 58):

1 . . .].ni.íb.[× ×]

---

2 . . . mar?]ùru dam.a.ni
3 . . .].ab.bi.a
4 . . .] × giš.tukul.la
5 . . .] × bal

He suggests that this may be part of the text under consideration, and may belong in the gap immediately below the present context.

ii. 4–6. He went fowling without a bird trap. He caught nothing (lit. There was not).

4. gíd.da.mušen = *ár-rum šá iṣṣūri* (*CT* 19. 48. II. 7), on which see B. Meissner, *AS* 4, no. 10.
5. On ur_4 = *ašāšu, ešēšu*, see the note on *Theodicy* 1.

ii. 7–12. My eye is a lion, my figure is a protecting angel, my *hips* are absolute charm. Who will be my voluptuous spouse?

ii. 13–18. My heart is wisdom, my reins are counsel, my liver is lordliness, my lips speak pleasant things. Who will be my chosen spouse?

These two similar courting sayings are distinguished in that one invites a dam, the other a nitalam. Both terms can be used for either sex, though the writer probably used them to distinguish between a man and a woman. The phraseology is reminiscent of Song of Songs iv. 1–5.
8. é.gar_8 = *lānu* and *gattu*, *MSL* IV. 36. 93–94.
14. It is assumed that the mu is misplaced, and that the line should read lipiš.mu malga.

ii. 19–20. Who is *miserly*? who is opulent? For whom shall I reserve my vulva?

B. Meissner, *MAOG* III/3. 24.

Again a saying about prospective marriage. Meissner assumed a contrast between 'miserly' and 'liberal', though it is not certain that the words will bear this interpretation. gar is certainly 'lay up', see the note on K 4347+. II. 45, but, like *gitrunu* (cf. *Theodicy* 63), it may only indicate the possession of great wealth. In that case the two parts of the first question will be parallel rather than antithetic.

ii. 21–22. Whom you love—you bear (his) yoke.

B. Meissner, *MAOG* III/3. 25.

ii. 23–26. When you exert yourself, your god is yours. When you do not exert yourself, your god is not yours.

A. Poebel, *GSG*, § 422.
B. Meissner, *MAOG* III/3. 25.

T. Jacobsen, in H. Frankfort *et al.*, *The Intellectual Adventure of Ancient Man*, p. 204 = *Before Philosophy*, p. 219.

"Your god is yours" (cf. iii. 12 below) involves the same idea as 'having a god' (cf. *Theodicy* 21 and note), i.e. being successful. The whole understanding of the proverb then depends on obtaining the exact sense of ir.pag = *kapādu*. In Akkadian *ṣarāmu* and *ṣamāru*, a metathesized form, are approximate synonyms of *kapādu* (cf. Comm. on *Theodicy* 13 and 284; *Šamaš Hymn* 162; v *R* 36, I. 56–57 (= *á.A* II_4, 58–59); passages cited by Klauber, *PRT* Glossar s.v. *ṣarāmu*; *Tukulti-Ninurta Epic* v (II), 16–17; E. Ebeling, *Handerhebung*, 106. 13: ⌜*e-ma*⌝ *a-kap-pu-du lukšud*^{ud}, in place of the usual formula *ema uṣammaru lukšud*). Meanings of the Arabic *ḍamara* are equally valid for Akkadian: 'think of', 'determine upon a thing', 'apply oneself to'. Hitherto translations of the Akkadian roots *ṣrm*/*ṣmr* and *kpd* have tended to centre on 'thinking' and 'desiring' to the exclusion of 'striving', which is nevertheless common. *ṣrm* is the opposite of *aḫam nadûm* 'be negligent' in the Mari letters (*TCL* 23. 62. 7–8; *TCL* 24. 77. 18–19), thus 'be diligent', and in many contexts *kapādu* is best rendered this way: e.g. *KAR* 327 obv. 7 *ak-pu-ud a-na né-me-li* "I have striven after gain"; *Tukulti-Ninurta Epic* v (II), 13 *i-na-an-na ku-pu-ud ana šar*$_4$ *kaš-ši-i* "Now occupy yourself with the Cassite king". The proverb may be an exhortation to work to achieve success, or may imply that success is readily available, like "Seek, and ye shall find". Whichever is meant, a parallel is found in a Cassite-period seal inscription (L. Delaporte, *Cylindres orientaux de la Bibliothèque Nationale*, no. 297 = *RA* 16. 84–85): *ak-pu-ud lu né-mi-lu ú-tú-lu du-un-qu su-pe-e* ^{d}*mard*[*uk*] *li-ib-ba-šu-nim-m*[*a*] *lu-mur du-un-qa ša-kín*!*-šu li-bur* "I have made my effort. Now let an increase in wealth, flocks, divine favour—things for which I have prayed to Marduk —come about. May I experience divine favour, and may he who is granted it live long."

ii. 27–28. "Let me lie with you!" "Let the god eat (your) ration."

B. Meissner, *MAOG* III/3. 25.

Meissner took this proverb as a commentary on Oriental lethargy, but while *ṣalālu* can indicate lying down for rest, "with you" is unexplained. There is no reason for disassociating this phrase from *ṣalālu ina sūn* and *ṣalālu eli*, all referring to sexual intercourse. This then naturally refers to a man's approach to a prostitute (cf. Genesis xxxviii. 16), against which interpretation the disregard of gender in *it-ti-ka* is no sufficient evidence. The second half is more ambiguous. The zi.ga is that which is paid out by a big economic concern, such as a temple, and in this case the occurrence of "god" strongly suggests a temple. The situation may then be the following: a man to whom the temple owes a certain zi.ga requests the services of one of the temple prostitutes. She demands that he dedicate his zi.ga to the god as payment. With *ša ni-siḫ-ti* cf. *ša ni-is-ḫa-tim* (*Laws of Ešnunna*, ed. Goetze, *AASOR* XXXI, § 2).

ii. 29–30. Gird yourself! (Your) god is your help.

B. Landsberger, *MSL* v. 198.

The restoration of the Akkadian is based on *RA* 12. 74. 15–16:

á.kár mer da.da.ra.dè da.da.zu ur$_5$.šè ḫé.en.gub.gub.bu
ap-luḫ-ta ez-zi-ta ina šit-pu-ri-ki li-la-bi-ib a-bu-bu

Cf. also *STT* I. 70 obv. 3: *mu-tu šá kak-ki šit-pu-ru-ma uz-za lab-šu*, and *TCL* 3. 21: *a-na i-tap-lu-us ni-ṭil ēnē*^{II} *šit-pu-rat pu-luḫ-tu* for *šapāru* B, 'gird'.

ii. 31–32. [*Unsheathe*] your sword! (Your) god is your help.

B. Meissner, *MAOG* III/3. 26.

The general sense of the proverb is clear, and the translation attempts to convey this, rather than to recover the damaged word. If i is correctly read, one might think of i = *amāru* (*RA* 17. 199. I. 7) "Let your weapon be seen", or i = *banû* (ibid. 6) "Polish your weapon".

ii. 33–34. When you are humiliated, let (your) friend act.

B. Meissner, *MAOG* III/3. 27.

ii. 35–37. Seeing you have done evil to your friend, what will you do to your enemy?

A. Poebel, *GSG*, § 421.

B. Meissner, *MAOG* III/3. 27.

ii. 38–39. The profit of the . . . . is like . . .

ii. 40–41. The profit of the silversmith is like . . .

It is tempting to restore the end of 38: *e*[*l-pi-ti*] (= numún), but it is difficult to restore the trace b[a/z[u to equate zi.zi.

ii. 42–43. It is not wealth that is your support. It is (your) god.

B. Meissner, *MAOG* III/3. 27.

ii. 44–45. Be you small or great, it is (your) god who is your support.

B. Meissner, *MAOG* III/3. 27.

iii. 9–12. . . . . may he not stand in the presence of (his) god and king; his gods will forsake him, his lordship will be driven out, and his god will not be his.

Cf. ii. 23–26 above.

iii. 13–14. The wise man is girded with a loin-cloth. The fool is clad in a scarlet cloak.

B. Meissner, *MAOG* III/3. 42.

iii. 15–18. Let the land be destroyed on top of our enemies, let the tottering wall fall on our antagonists, let the country of the foe be completely bound.

B. Meissner, *MAOG* III/3. 42.

The Sumerian lá suggests the meaning 'bind' for *rasû*. This word occurs again in *PBS* I/2. 129. 10 (= J. Laessøe, *Bît Rimki*, 40. 46) [*ši*]-*i li-ir-te-si-ma ana-ku lu-bi-ib*. Here the contrast with *ebēbu*, and also *rusû* 'magic spells', imply a magic rather than a literal binding. It also occurs in *STT* I. 77. 21: *ú-ra-as-sa-an-*[*ni*], in a context of words for binding.

iv. 3–5. B. Meissner, *MAOG* III/3. 28, read [á]š.bi.

iv. 9–11. As a support to your palace, though your king knows nothing, Šamaš will speak to him.

iv. 14–15. A people without a king (is like) sheep without a shepherd.

iv. 16–17. A people without a foreman (is like) water without a canal inspector.

iv. 18–19. Labourers without a supervisor (are like) a field without a ploughman.

iv. 20–21. A house without an owner (is like) a woman without a husband.

B. Meissner, *MAOG* III/3. 28–29.

T. Jacobsen, in H. Frankfort *et al.*, *The Intellectual Adventure of Ancient Man*, pp. 202–3 = *Before Philosophy*, pp. 217–18.

From the Amarna period Rib-Addi of Byblos four times quotes a proverb of this type to the Egyptian king: "My field is like a woman without a husband because it lacks a cultivator" (*eqli-ia aššạta ša lā muta mašil aššum bali īrišim*: *VAB* II. 74. 18–19; 75. 15–17; 81. 37–38; 90. 42–44). This is a combination of lines 19 and 21 of our text.

iv. 22–23. Recognize (? lit. 'have') the overlord; recognize (do.) the king; respect the vizier.

B. Meissner, *MAOG* III/3. 29.

The grammar of en.e and lugal.e is difficult. If they are integrated in the sentence syntactically, they can only be vocative or the object of tuku, but not subject. It seems as if the e must be e "des Lokativ-Terminativs der unmittelbaren Nähe" in A. Falkenstein's terminology (*AnOr* 28, § 31), though tuku is not usually construed this way. The use of e as a vocative element is very rare (T. Jacobsen, *JNES* 5. 133[9]).

iv. 24–26. When you have seen the profit of reverencing (your) god, you will praise (your) god and salute the king.

B. Meissner, *MAOG* III/3. 30.

Cf. *Ludlul* II. 26–28 and note for the idea of profit in religion, and the juxtaposition of the king and god.

iv. 27–30. Refuse a boy's wish and he will . . . . Throw a sop to a puppy and he will fawn on you.

iv. 31–36. Vex a boy and he will weep. Throw a sop to a puppy and *he will bring it back to you.*

K 4160+13184 (Plate 60)

LITERATURE (for K 4160 only)

Text: T. J. Meek, *RA* 17. 132.
Translation: T. Jacobsen, in H. Frankfort *et al.*, *The Intellectual Adventure of Ancient Man*, p. 203 = *Before Philosophy*, p. 218.

1 [é.gal dug$_4$.ga.a.n]i an.na.gin$_7$ nu.gam.da
ēkallu qí-bi-is-sa ki-ma qí-[*bi-it* ^{d}*a-nim*]

2 [lugal ^{d}utu.gin$_7$] inim.a.ni zi.da
ul na-da-at šarrụ ki-ma ^{d}[*šá-maš a-mat-su ki-na-at*]

3 [dug$_4$.ga.a.ni nu . . . ka.t]a.è.a.ni šu nu.bala.e
qí-bi-is-su ul iš-šá-na-an ⸢*ṣi-it pi-šú*⸣ [*ul ut-tak-kar*]

---

4 [é.gal an.na.gin$_7$ d]ug$_4$.ga.a.ni zi.da
ēkallu ki-ma ^{d}*a-nim qí-bi-is-s*[*a ki-na-at*]

5 [lugal ^{d}utu.gin$_7$ níg.si.sá ki ba.]ág níg.ne.ru ḫul ba.gig
šarru ki-ma ^{d}[*š*]*á-maš mi-šá-ra i-ra-am* [*rag-ga i-zi-ir*]

---

6 [é.gal . . .š]à.bi lú.en.bi rab.kala.ga
ēkallu × [×] × × *qí-rib-šá šarru bēl* [. . . .]
7 [. . . . . .] gúr.ru.da ḫul.gál
la ×[. . . . . .]×*-bi-ib* [. . . .]

---

8 [. . . . . . s]u.bi.šè na.me sag nu.gá lugal šà.bi
ēkallu [. . . . .]× *zu-um-ri man-m*[*a* . . . .]
9 [. . . . . . s]ig$_5$.na lú šúr.a.ni bàn.da.a
×[. . . . . *na*]*m-ri-ir-ri um-*[. . . .]
10 [. . . . . . .]× šir.bur.aš ba.ab.×.×
[. . . . .] ga ti ×[. . . .]

---

11 [. . . . . . dug$_4$].ga zi.da [. . . .]
[. . . . .] × × [. . . . .]
12 [. . . . .]× ki ×[. . . . .]
13 [. . . . .] un [. . . . . .]

1–3. The command of the palace is like Anu's: it may not be set aside. Like Šamaš', the king's word is sure, his command is unequalled, and his utterance cannot be altered.

For "like of An" in the Sumerian, the Akkadian repeats "command": "like the command of Anu". This phenomenon occurs again in the Akkadian of BM 38596. I. 9.

4–5. The command of the palace, like Anu's, is sure. Like Šamaš, the king loves righteousness and hates evil.

For the command of Anu cf., for example, *Enūma Eliš* IV. 6: *ši-mat-ka la ša-na-an sè-kàr-ka* [d]*a-num*.

K 4207 (Plate 61)

LITERATURE

Text: B. Meissner, *MAOG* III/3. 56 (based on a copy of Delitzsch).
Edition: B. Meissner, *MAOG* III/3. 30–32.
J. Pereman, *The Book of Assyro-Babylonian Proverbs*, pp. 179–88.

OBVERSE: odd signs on the left side
REVERSE I: 1 an[; 2 gub.b[a; 3 du.gá ×[; 4 ab.šu[
REVERSE II

1 × × × × ga.an.× × [(×)] [Akkadian

---

2 ní.e.tuku ù.ni.ḫúl.le[.(×)] lost]
3 ur [giš]mar.gíd.da
4 ab.ta.×.a.gin$_7$

5	KA.tur.r[a] ma.da	
6	im.di.šè al.⌜e⌝	
7	[tù]n.e.tag$_4$.a.ta sag.a[b]	
8	(*vacat*)	
9	tùn.e.tag$_4$.a.ta níg.g[ú]	
10	[í]d.da ní.te e.ba[l]	
11	KA.zu.šè gar.ra.ab	
12	(*vacat*)	
13	igi a.ra.du$_8$	
14	me.šè mu.da.gin.a	
15	gur nu.me.a.ta	×[. . . . .]
16	ḫar.ra.an gur nu.me.a.ta	*ina* ⌜*la*⌝ *ka*-[*šá?-di?* . . .]
17	gin.na na.an.du.un	*a-lik e ta*-⌜*al*⌝-*l*[*i-ik*]
18	dingir.nin.zu.šè	*ana ili be-lí*-[*ka*]
19	lú šà.gar an.tuku.a	*bi-ru-ú-um*
20	é.sig$_4$.al.ur$_5$.ra in.bùru.dè	*bit a-gur-ri i-pal-la-aš*
21	šu lú.ab.sìg.gi.da.šè	*ana qá-at na-si-ki-i*[*m*]
22	lag ab.ta.lá.e.en	*ki-ir-ba-na tu-m*[*a-al-la-a*]
23	a.su$_6$.ma.ke$_4$	(*vacat*)

13–14. He/She looked at you. Where will he/she go with you?
17–18. Go—or do not go—to the god your lord.
19–20. A hungry man breaks into a building of kiln-fired bricks.
21–22. Would you place a lump of clay in the hand of him who throws?

(The subscription to the tablet is not intelligible.)

K 4327+4605+4749 (Plate 60)

LITERATURE

K 4327: Text: II *R* 8, no. 3.
Edition: J. J. A. Van Dijk, *La Sagesse*, p. 7.

K 4605: Text: T. J. Meek, *RA* 17. 146.
Edition: B. Meissner, *MAOG* III/3. 39–41.

(K 15227 and 80–7–19. 130 may be parts of this tablet; see Introduction, p. 223.)

OBVERSE I

1	^{ka}[^{š}kašbir.a]	[. . . . .]
2	g[a].a[n].n[ag]	[*lu-uš-t*]*i*-⌜*ma*⌝
3	zag.gal.la ⌜ga.tuš⌝	*ina rab-ba*-⌜*a*⌝-[*ti*] ⌜*lu-šib*⌝

4	ḪÁŠ a.ra.[an.BU.nam]	
5	lú.še.[giš.ià]	
6	[b]í.í[b.íl.íl.i]	

OBVERSE II

1	traces	

2	[u]r$_5$ ama.mu	[. . . . .]
3	[nin$_9$].bàn.da.mu	[. . . . .]
4	[×] ba?.ag.e	[. . . . .]
5	[×]×.a mà.e	⌜*ul-la-a*⌝[. . . . .]
6	[lú.dí]m.ma mu.un.da.lá	*ṭe-e-ma ma-ṭ*[*a-ku*]
7	[te.mu] mu.na.ab.ḫa.za	*le-ti ú-ka*[*l-ši*?]

8	[uḫ].e gada ba.lá	*ana par-šá-'-i ki-tu-u ta-ri-is-s*[*u*]
9	[num].saḫar.ra	*ana la-am-ṣa-ti*
10	[× r]in.na ba.×	*i-aš-rin-na ma-ḫi-si*
11	[mu]š.dam.kur$_4$.ra	*ana pi-ṣal-lu-ri*
12	[š]utum	*šu-tu-um-mu*
13	[a]n.na.dù	*e-pu-us-si*

14	[a].rá.bu^{mušen}	*a-ra-bu-ú*
15	[×] u$_4$.á.ba.ka	*šá ina si-ma-ni-šá*
16	nu.un.kú	*la in-nak-ka-lu*

17	im.ma.an.ri.ri	*ul-ta-aq-qí-tam-ma*
18	šaḫ.ni ba.an.šum	*iṭ-ṭa-ba-aḫ šá-ḫa-šú*

19	[im.ma.an.]ri.ri	
20	[giš.ni ba.an.til]	*ig-da-mar i-ṣi-šú*

OBVERSE III

1	[z]á.kín sír.r[a. ×]	*ta-*×[. .]
2	al.ri.ri.e	*ki-ma e-re-e* ×[× (×)]

3	ka ba.lá	*šá pi-šu ma-ṭú*
4	dam.bi gi.in.na	*aš-ša-as-su a-mat*

5	ka.mu mu.lu.da	*pi-ia it-ti amēlī*^{meš}
6	an.da.ab.sá.e	*iš-šá-na-an-ni*

7	ka.mu mu.lu.da	*pi-ia it-ti amēlī*^{meš}
8	an.da.ab.šid.e	*im-ta-na-an-ni*

REVERSE IV

9	[u$_6$.di.kalam.m]a.ra	*ana tab-rat ma-a-ti*
10	[uru.ni.ta? . .]è	*ina āli it-ta-ṣi*
11	[al.di.di.dè.en]	*a-tal-lak*
12	[nu.kúš.ù.dè.en	*ul*] ⌜*a*⌝*-na-aḫ*
13	[ì.di.di.dè.en	*a-da-a*]*l-ma*
14	[ù nu.tu$_9$.tu$_9$.me.en	*ul a-ṣa*]*l-lal*
15	[ti.la lul.la	*ba-laṭ sar-r*]*a-ti*
16	trace	

REVERSE VI

1	níg.ú.nu.un.kú	*š*[*á* . . .
2	am.kur.ra.k[e$_4$]	
3	níg.a.nu.un.[nag]	
4	maš.dà.edin.n[a.ke$_4$]	
5	gu.du.šè nu ×[×(×)]	
6	TAR.šè ×[. . .]	
7	(*vacat*)	
8	àm ×[. . .	
9	gu [. . .	
10	u$_8$[. . .	
11	dam ×[. . .	
12	im ×[. . .	
13	ḫul [. . .	
14	ka [. . .	

OBVERSE I

1–3. Let me drink [diluted] beer, let me sit in splendour.

This is restored from *STVC* 3+4. I. 31 and Sumerian Collection III. 155.

4–6. This is restored from *STVC* 3+4. I. 33–34 and Sumerian Collection III. 74, but note that the proverb *STVC* 3+4. I. 32 and Sumerian Collection III. 156 is missing here.

OBVERSE II

2–7. The Sumerian is restored from Collection I. 143, where, however, mà.e appears immediately after lú.dím.ma.

8–13. Linen is stretched out for the flea; . . . is woven for the fly; the store house is built for the lizard.

B. Landsberger, *Fauna*, 115 and 131.

The Sumerian is contained in *STVC* 3+4. II. 18–21, which reads ba.e.si for the verb in 10, and [^{g}]^{i}kid.aš.rin for the preceding word. E. I. Gordon compares this with ^{gi}kid 'reed-mat'. The Sumerian reading of é.gi.na.ab.du$_7$ comes from *PBS* v. 106 rev. IV. 21: [šu].tu.um = é.gi.na.ab.du$_7$ = *šu-tu-um-mu*.

14–16. A duck which is not eaten at the right time.

B. Landsberger, *JNES* 8. 257[46].

The Sumerian is contained in *STVC* 3+4. II. 22.

17–18. He . . . and slaughtered his pig.

19–20. He . . . and used up his wood.

The Sumerian of the first of this pair occurs in *STVC* 3+4. II. 23, but at this point the tablet breaks off and it is not known if the second of the pair followed.

OBVERSE III AND REVERSE IV

1–2 = *STVC* 3+4. III. 3–4, but the second line reads al.UL.UL.UL.×. This proverb also occurs in Sumerian Collection III.

3–4. The wife of a man who cannot talk well is a female slave.

The Sumerian is found in *STVC* 3+4. III. 5–6, and in Collection III. 174.

5–6. My mouth makes me comparable with men.

7–8. My mouth gets me reckoned among men.

Only the first of this pair of variants occurs on *STVC* 3+4. III. 7–8 (also Collection III. 186). The use of eme.sal (the unilingual form has, however, lú) suggests that a woman may be speaking. The Akkadian form *iš-šá-na-an-ni* is unintelligible.

9–10. For a spectacle to the land he left the city.

STVC 3+4. III. 9–10 offers: u$_6$.di un(kalam!).di.dè.en uru.ni mu.un.è.e.

11–14. I walk about, but do not become tired. I keep moving, but do not take rest.

The Sumerian occurs on *STVC* 3+4. III. 11–14 and in Collection I. 174. Is it a riddle?

15–16. The Sumerian can be restored in full from *STVC* 3+4. III. 15–17 and Collection III. 54.

REVERSE VI

1–4. It is the wild ox in the underworld that eats no grass; it is the gazelle in the open country that drinks no water.

The first part is preserved on *STVC* 3+4. IV. 39, and the whole in Sumerian Collection I. 30: níg.ú.nu.kú am.kur.ra.ka/kam níg.a.nu.nag maš.dà.kur.ra.ka/kam. In the unilingual form both animals are pictured in the underworld. Also the proverb ends with line 4 in Collection I, whereas the bilingual copy has two extra lines. Unfortunately the end of the proverb and the sequence is lost from *STVC* 3+4 in the broken-away beginning of column V.

K 4347+16161 (Plates 61–63)

This is a six-column tablet from the Ashurbanipal libraries, of which no duplicate has yet been found. Either this tablet, or an antecedent copy on which it is based, was copied from a damaged original, and the scribe very faithfully reproduced this. When he wrote on one line what was split between two in his original, the dividing point on the original was marked with the pair of wedges used in commentaries to separate words quoted from the comments on them (II. 8; III. 16). In III. 30–44, where the original was badly damaged, the scribe copied out exactly what he saw, and left blank spaces marked "broken" where nothing remained. The three upright wedges in III. 43 are undoubtedly not the numeral 'three', as taken by S. Langdon (*AJSL* 28. 225), but are all that remained of a sign containing three verticals. Apparently for III. 45–49, and certainly for IV. 4–6 and V. 41–42, no Akkadian translation had been handed down.

LITERATURE

The first copy appeared in II *R* 16. Further pieces were later joined to the top of the tablet, and the second copy, by S. Langdon in *AJSL* 28. 234–41, presents a more complete text, though in accuracy it marks a retrogression. The copy now given has one further addition: K 16161 has been joined as the Akkadian column of III. 55–60, a join discovered by B. Landsberger.

EDITIONS IN WHOLE OR PART

M. Jäger, *BA* II. 274–305 (reviewed by R. E. Brünnow, *ZA* 8. 125–31).
S. Langdon, *AJSL* 28. 219–30.
B. Meissner, *MAOG* III/3. 32–39.
J. Pereman, *The Book of Assyro-Babylonian Proverbs*, pp. 41–142 (quotes all previous translations).
R. H. Pfeiffer, in *ANET*, p. 425.
A. Falkenstein, *IF* 60. 125–9.

OBVERSE I

1	[Sumerian	[. . . . .] ×
2	column	[. . . . .]×-*ma*
3	lost]	[. . . . . .] *ú-la-pa*
4		[. . . . .]-KUR
5		[. . . . . . . -]*ša-am*
6		[. . . . .]×-*an*
7		[. . . . .]-*am*
8		[. . . . .]×
9		[. . . . .]×

OBVERSE II

	Sumerian	Akkadian
1	traces	
2	[×] × ḫé.en.×.ri	× [. . . . .]
3	[×] × × g[i.n]a	× × [. . . . . *k*]*i-nim*
4	× × × × × × ×	e × [. . . . .]×-*ki-il*
5	[.] NE? (×) kám	× [. . . . . . .]×-*tuk*
6	[traces	[(×)]×-*ni-i ta-maḫ-ḫa-aṣ*
7	of	[*i*]*na li-pi-i*
8	Sumerian]	× × *eš-bu*: *ta-šam-miṭ*
9		*li-pa-a la ta-ak-kal*
10		*u da-ma la te-te-eṣ-ṣi*
11		*sà-ar-t*[*a*]
12		*la te-pu-u*[*š*]
13		*pu-luḫ-ta* [*ili*]
14		*la ik-kal-k*[*a*]
15	[Sumerian	*a-ma-ta la tu-lam-man*
16	lost]	[*n*]*i-*⌜*is*⌝*-sà-tú ana libbi-ka*
17		[*la ta-š*]*ad-da-ad*
18		[*le*]*-mut-ta*
19		[*la*] *te-ep-pu-uš*
20		[*dan-n*]*a-ta da-ri-ta*
21		[*l*]*a ta-liq-qí*
22		[*z*]*u-qa-qí-pu a-mi-lam iz-qu-ut*
23		[*mi*]*-na-a il-qí*
24		[*mu-na*]*m-gi-ru a-mi-lam uš-mit*
25		[*mi-na*]*-a ut-ti-ir*
26		[. . .] *zu-qa-qí-pu*
27		[. . *mu-na*]*m-gi-ri*
28		[. . . . . .*-n*]*a šu-mi*
29		[. . . . . . .] *zi-ir-ma*
30		[. . . . . . .] *ra-am*
31		[. . . . . . .*-g*]*i-ru-tú*
32		[. . . . . . .*-p*]*u-uš*

33		[. . . . .]×-*ti*
34		[. . . . .]×-*ma*
35		[. . . . .]×-*as*

36		[. . . . .] × ×
37		[. . . . . *r*]*i-ṣi*

38		[*ku-u*]*ṣ-ṣu le-mun*
39	[. . . . .] ×	*um-ma-a-tum ṭe-ma i-šá-a*

40	[nu.um.me.d]a.ná al.peš$_4$.a.	*ina la na-ki-mi-i e-rat-me*
41	[en?.e.š]e nu.kú.da.a.ni	*ina la a-ka-li-me*
42	[a]l.kur$_4$.re.en.e.še	*ka-ab-rat*

43	um.me.da.ná.a	*na-a-ku šu-nu-qa*
44	ga.ṣub(KA×GA) íb.ta.an.šub	*ú-ša-ad-da*

45	ga.gar mu.da.an.kar	*lu-uš-kun ik-ki-mu*
46	ga.an.diri.ga	*lu-ut-tir-ma*
47	a.ba mu.ra.an.sum	*man-nu i-nam-din*

48	túl.a.nu.gál.la al.bal.bal	*ḫi-pí eš-šú*
49	su.in.a.še.nu.a al.ḫi.ḫi	*ma-šá-ak la sun-*$^{ḫi\text{-}pí}$

50	a.ri.a.šè dingir.bi	*a-na* ⟨*na*⟩*-me-e i-lu-šú-nu*
51	gi$_4$.gi$_4$.dè	*i-tu-ru*
52	é.šub.šè	*ana bīti na-di-i*
53	akkil ga.an.tu	*i-te-ru-ub ik-kil-lum*
54	ga.an.tuš níg.ne.ru	*áš-šab rag-gu*
55	nu.libir.ra geštú.ga.ri.im	*ul ú-lab-bar ḫa-as-su*
56	gašam kù.zu	*um-ma-na em-qa*
57	[k]ù.zu.ba (ras.) lugal.bi	*ša né-me-eq-šú bēl-šú*
58	[geš]tú.ga na.ri.ga	*la ḫa-as-su*
59	[ù] lú kal.la	*ù mám-ma aq-ra*
60	[× (×) ge]štú.ga.na	*ša be-el-šú*
61	[. . . . .]× zu.LU.a	*im-šú-šú*
62	[. . . . . . l]e.en	*ib-ba-aš-ši ḫi-šiḫ-ta-šú-ma*
63	[sag . . . . . í]l.la	*in-na-ši ri-is-su*

64, 65 traces

OBVERSE III

1	[. . . . .]	*ṣil-li mu-ka-aš-ši-di*
2	×[. . . . .]	*ik-ka-aš-šad*

3	giš.gi ×[. . . . . . .]×	*it-bal-mi a-pu*
4	šám g[i.b]i	*ši-im qa-ni-šú*
5	ù šà.túm.ma šá[m ú.b]i.	*ù qir-bé-e-tum*
6	e.ne.e.⌜še⌝	*ši-im šam-mi-šá*

7	á.gál ì.kú.e	*ik-kal li-'-u*
8	šám á.bi	*ši-im i-di-šú*
9	ù á.nu.gál.la	*ù la li-'-u*
10	šám gina.bi.e.še	*ši-im [šè]r-ri-šú*

11	⌜šà.mu⌝ sag.kur	*lìb-b[i (×)]×-bi*
12	[. . . m]u sag.kúr	*bi-ki-ti* ×[. . .]×
13	[. .]× × zé.en	*ši-ta-la* [. . . .]

14	[g]al$_4$.la.mu al.ša$_6$	*ú-ri-mi da-m[i-i]q*
15	un.gá e.dè.	*ina ni-ši-ia*
16	ti.il ba.ab.dùg:en.e.še	*gu-um-mu-ra-an-ni*

17	dù.a.bi al.ša$_6$	*ana ka-la da-mi-iq*
18	ù túg.níg.dára ba.an.tu	*u ú-la-pa la-bi-iš*

19	igi gu$_4$.da gin.a	*pa-an al-pi a-li-ki*
20	mud.šè bí.íb.ra.ra	*ina up-pi ta-rap-pi-is*

21	dùg.mu an.ta.túm.túm.mu	*al-la-ka bir-ka-a-a*
22	gìr.mu nu.kúš.ù	*la a-ni-ḫa še-pa-a-a*
23	lú.sag.dù.dù.nu.tuku.a	*la ra-áš ta-šim-ti*
24	adaman mu.un.ús.e	*ip-pi-ra ri-dan-ni*

25	anše.dussa.a.na.me.en	*a-ga-la-ku-[ma]*
26	anše.giga.šè ab.lá.e	*ana pa-re-e ṣa-an-d[a-ku]*
27	giš.gar šu.gi.me.na.nam	*nar-kab-ta a-n[a-aš-ši-ma]*
28	gi.ú.kin	*šu-ú-[ra]*
29	ab.íl.íl.e.en	*a-za-bi-[il]*

30	*ḫi-pí*	
31	u kud.da	
32	te ab ri ×	*ḫi-p[í]*
33	an × e.ne	
34	× kin	

35	gig a.nu.zu nu.me.a	*si-im-me*
36	šà.gar.ra kú.e	*la-a*

37	nu.me.a	
38	giš la	
39	kù.babbar.ra	*bi-pí*
40	giš ×	
41	guškin.bi	
42	a × gar × ú mu	
43	šà kám × šub.da	
44	mu.un.túm.túm.mu	*bi-pí*

45	dinig.mu	
46	túg.àm ri.ta	
47	gá.e gú.e	
48	ḫúb.íl.mu	
49	abzu ri.ri	

50	é.a esir.è.a	*ina bī*[*t* . . . .]
51	sig$_4$ al.ùr.ra.ta	⌜*ù*⌝ [. . . . .]
52	al.tuš$^{bi\text{-}pí}$	[. . . . .]
53	im.ma lag sag.gá	[. . . . .]
54	ugu.mu al.bi.iz.	[. . . . .]
55	e.dè.e.še	⌜*i-na*⌝[*-at-tu-uk-mi*]

56	mu.im.ma sum.sar	*šad-dag-da šu-*[*ma*]
57	im.ma.an.kú.e	*a-ku-ul-*[*ma*]
58	mu.àm	*šat-t*[*a*]
59	šà.mu al.gír.gír.e	*lìb-bi iṣ-ṣa-r*[*ip-ma*]

60	gi.duru$_5$.diri.ga.×	⌜*a-ma*⌝[. . . . . . .]
61	ab.u$_5$ ×[.]	[Akkadian
62	ù gi.KA [×]	lost]
63	gù mu.un.zu[.×]	
64	igi nu.mu.ni.in.×[.×]	

65	× × ùr.ra K[U.×.(×)]	
66	[×(×)]× du ×[.×.(×)]	

REVERSE IV

1	[×]× bu ní.te.ni × ×	[Akkadian
2	ur.ÉŠ.re á.mu in.è.a	lost]
3	zú ba.an.kud.dè.en	

4	mušen in.na.ab.bé	[Akkadian
5	ur$_5$.bi an.na.k[e$_4$]	column
6	ù su.bi mi.in.bar.re.e[n]	blank]

7	ti.la ša.du$_{11}$.ba.ta	*bu-luṭ šá am-šá-l[a]*
8	ud.da an.ga.me.a	*u$_4$-mi-šam-m[a]*

9	giš.gu.za itu.ab.ba.è	*ki-ma ku-us-si a* ×[. .]
10	suḫ an.di ne.íb.	*ti-iq-ni*
11	sìr.sìr.re.en	*tu-taq-qá-n[u-ma]*
12	ù ti.mu	*ù a-na ṣi-l[i-ia]*
13	al.gurud.da	*ta-nam-d[a-aš-šú]*

14	giš.gu.za lú.ra dingir.ra.a.ni	*ki-[m]a ku-us-[si . . .]*
15	^{d}ša.ḫa.an al.me.a	*šá ìl-šú ^{d}ša-ḫ[a-an]*
16	ér im.ma.an.šéš.šéš	*ta-pa-ak-ka-[a-šú]*
17	kuš.bi an.še.tab.tab.bé.en	*tu-ṣar-ra-a[p mašak-š]ú*
18	ù izi an.na.ab.ús.e	*u i-šá-tú tu-šá-aḫ-ḫa-za-šú*

19	íd.da.šè bí.gar.re.en.na	*ina na-ri tab-ba-aš-ši-ma*
20	a.zu ú.šà.lu.úb.zé.da	*mu-ka da-ad-da-ru*
21	an.ga.àm kiri$_6$.šè	*ap-pu-na-ma*
22	gar.re.en.na.zu	*ina ki-ri-i tab-ši-ma*
23	zú.lum.zu	*su-lu-up-pa-ka*
24	zé an.ga.àm	*mar-tum*

25	dim$_6$ ù.mu.⟨ni⟩.in.ag.a	*áš-šar-šu-ma*
26	ù e.ne níg.ù.tu.ud.da.	*šu-ú šá al-ti-šú-ma*
27	ni na.nam	*a-ma-aš-ša-as-su-[ma]*
28	šu.su.ub ù.mu.ni.in.ag.eš	*šu-⌜ú⌝*
29	e.ne sig$_4$ an.ga.àm	*li-bit-tum-ma*

30	ḫén[bur s]i.nu.sá	*ḫab-bur-ru la i-šá-r[u]*
31	ab.[sí]n.e	*še-er-⌜ú⌝*
32	na.an.ni.íb.tu.ud	*a-a ú-[lid]*
33	še.numun na.an.ni.íb.dím.ma	*zi-ra a-a i[b-ni]*

34	še.nim.ma	*še-um ḫa[r-pu]*
35	si ì.sá.sá.e.dè	*iš-še-[er]*
36	a.na.àm	*mi-nam-[mi]*
37	ì.zu.un.dè.en	*ni-i-[di]*
38	še.si.ga	*še-um up-pu-l[u]*
39	si ì.sá.sá.e.ṣe	*iš-še-er*
40	a.na.àm	*mi-nam-mi*
41	ì.zu.un.dè.en.e.še	*ni-i-di*

42	ga.nam ga.ug$_5$.ga.en.dè.en	*pi-qa a-ma-at-man*
43	giš.en ga.an.kú	*lu-ku-ul*

44	ga.nam ga.ti.li.dè.en	*pi-qa a-bal-lu-uṭ*
45	giš.en ga.bí.íb.gar	*lu-uš-kun*

46	a.gigrí.dè	*iṭ-ṭi-ib-bu-*[*in-ni*]
47	zi.mu ma.da.lugúd.da	*ik-te-ru na-pi*[*š-ti*]
48	ku$_6$ nu.mu.ni.in.dib.ba	*nu-na ul a-bar*
49	túg.mu	*ṣu-ba-a-t*[*i*]
50	ú.ugu.da.[a]n.dé.e	*uḫ-tal-li*[*q*]

51	mu.lu è.⌜e.dè⌝	*mu-lu-u ú-áš-*⌜*šú*⌝
52	nagar bí.íb.SAR.dè.e.×	*nam-ga-ri ip-pat-ti*

53	uru giš.tukul.a.ni	*a-lu šá kak-ka-šú*
54	× [×]× la gi [(×)]×	*la dan-nu*
55	[. . . .]×[. . . .]	*na-ak-ru*
56	[. . . . .]	*ina pa-an a-bu-ul-li-šú*
57	[. . . . .]	*ul ip-paṭ-ṭar*

REVERSE V

1	[Sumerian	[*m*]*a-ti-ma-a*
2	lost]	*kal-bu*
3		*a-na* × (×) bi
4		kit [(× ×)]×
5		*ul ú-*×-×*-ši*

6	[. . . . .]	*lu* [. . . . .] *zi-ri*
7	[. . . . .]	*u*[*l* . . . . .]×*-ru*
8	[. .]× ⌜ra⌝ ×[. . . .]	ku × × × [(×)]-*ka*
9	×.bí.íb	[*p*]*i-it*

10	im.šu.nigín.na.gin$_7$	*kīma ti-nu-ri*
11	libir.ra.ta	*la-bi-ri*
12	kúr.kúr.ru.zu	*ana nu-uk-ku-ri-ka*
13	al.gig	*ma-ri-iṣ*

14	GIŠ.gin.ne mu.un.íl	*tál-lik taš-šá-a*
15	a.šà lú.kúr.ra.[e.še]	*e-qé-el nak-ri*
16	ì.du.un.í[l]	*il-lik iš-šá-a*
17	a.šà.zu lú.kúr.ra	*e-qé-el-ka nak-ru*

18	[na]m.lugal.la	*šar-ru-*[*t*]*u*
19	[(×)]× ba.è.a.ke$_4$	*a-*[×(×)]
20	[× (×)]×.KU.àm	*ki-ma* ×[. . . .]×

	Sumerian	Akkadian
21	[. . . . .].àm	*e-mi* ×[. . .]×
22	[. . . . . . . tag?.]ge	*u ḫi-il-la la*?-*pit*
23	[Sumerian	*bu-uq-li na-'-pi*
24	lost]	*meš-ṭú-ú ul uḫ-ḫur-šú*
25		*[k]u-uz-pa*
26		*[la] ta-kul*
27		[(×)×]*-lil-ta*
28		[. . . . .]× bar?

29: missing 30:]×*-sa* 31:]×*-diš* 32:]×-×*-e* 33:]*-lu-lu* 34: *l*]*i-'-i* 35:]×*-ma-mi-i*
36:]*-pit-ti*

	Sumerian	Akkadian
37		*[mi-n]a-a ana kip-pa-ti*
38		*[ta]-kap-pap*
39		*[ana] ri-gim šá-ḫi-i*
40		*[k]às-pa ta-šá-qal*
41, 42		(*vacant*)
43		*[bu]r i-me-ri a-saḫ-ḫur*
44		*[e-q]í-il id-ra-ni*
45		[× ×].kám *a-di šalši-šú*
46		*[le]-mu-un*
47		[. . . .]×*-ti*
48		[. . . . .]×*-it*
49		×[. . . . . . .]×
50		×[. . . . . . .]*-ti*
51	[traces of Sumerian]	×[. . . . . . .]*-ti*

52 traces

53–55 traces

	Sumerian	Akkadian
56	[. . .]× kù.babbar.ra ×	[traces
57	[. . .]× ir/sa lá.àm	of
58	[. . .] giš × × ×	Akkadian]
59	[. . .]× ab.di.di.en	

REVERSE VI

	Sumerian	Akkadian
1	[Sumerian	[. . . . . *t*]*um*
2	lost]	[. . . . .]×*-ši*
3		[. . . . .]×*-ti*
4		[. . . . .]⌜*lu-ma*⌝

ii. 9–10. Eat no fat, and there will be no blood in your excrement.

Cf. R. Labat, *TDP* 132. 12 ff. *š. ina* KU-*šú dama i-te-ez-zi* "If through his anus (or, in his excrement) he voids blood". *tezû/teṣû* 'cacare' (*ZA* 41. 222; *MAOG* XIII/2. 41. 29) is a secondary root formed from *ezû* (*MSL* II. 151. 19)/*eṣû* (Comm. *Šumma izbu* 529).

ii. 11–14. Commit no crime, and fear [of (your) god] will not consume you.

ii. 15–17. Slander no one, and then grief [will not] reach your heart.

Cf. note on *Advice to a Prince* 46; *CT* 16. 19. 53–55: inim šà.bi.šè ba.an.bu.i = *a-ma-ta ana lìb-bi-šú iš-du-ud*, and *Gilgameš* 9. I. 4: *ni-is-sa-a-tum i-te-ru-ub ina kar-ši-ia.*

ii. 18–21. Do [no] evil, and then you will not experience lasting misfortune.

ii. 22–25. A scorpion stung a man. What did it get? [A common] informer brought about a man's death. What benefit did he receive?

B. Landsberger, *JCS* 9. 123.

The restoration [*mu-na*]*m-gi-ru* and its interpretation are Landsberger's; cf. *Ludlul* I. 86. For *minâ ut-ti-ir* see *Theodicy* 251 and note.

ii. 38–39. Winter is evil. Summer has sense.

For the frequent contrast between *kuṣṣu* and *ummātum* see B. Landsberger, *JNES* 8. 248–53.

ii. 40–42. Has she become pregnant without intercourse? Has she become fat without eating?

A. Falkenstein, *IF* 60. 127.

This translates the Akkadian. The persons of the Sumerian are difficult. -a.ni is third, but -en second or first. The spacing also requires a sign between al.peš$_4$.a and [e.š]e. This might well be -en provided that the a, which is curiously written over the last vertical of peš$_4$, can be explained as part of the root and not an affix. On e.še, which is used quite commonly with proverbs, see the article of Falkenstein just cited. Landsberger and Jacobsen by their rendering of the corresponding *-mi* with "they tell" imply a derivation from e 'speak' (*JNES* 14. 15).

ii. 43–44. Intercourse brings on lactation.

Reading of KA×GA from *MSL* III. 120. 273: ṣu-ub KA×GA *na-ṣa-bu. nadû*, as used for throwing off sweat (cf. *Ludlul* II. 66 and note), is the appropriate word for giving suck.

ii. 45–47. If I put things in store, I shall be robbed. If I squander, who will give to me?

F. Thureau-Dangin, *AnOr* 12. 310–11.

For gar = *šakānu* 'put in store' see *CT* 39. 33. 62 = *Or* 31. 64: *amēlu šû bu-ša-a iraššì-ma e-ki-a-am lu-uš-kun i-qab-bi* "that man will acquire property and will say, "Where can I store it?" " Cf. also IV. 45 below, and *Assyrian Collection* II. 19. The form mu.ra.an.sum has curiously the second person infix: "Who will give to you?"

ii. 48–49. He dug a well in which was no water. He *tanned* a skin without . . .

For ḫi.ḫi = 'tan'(?) cf. *á.A* V$_2$. 20: [$^{\text{he-e}}$ḪI] = ×*-a-mu ša* su, and *Ḫarra* 11a, 5–8 su.al.ḫi.a and su.nu.al.ḫi.a (Akk. lost).

ii. 62–63. Cf. *Theodicy* 218.

iii. 1–2. My shadow—my pursuer—is being pursued.

Many other renderings are possible, but without the Sumerian it is impossible to decide between them.

iii. 3–6. Does the reed-bed take the price of its reeds, and the meadow the price of its grass?

A. Falkenstein, *IF* 60. 128[1].

The possible sense of *wabālu* 'be worth' (Oppenheim, *JNES* 11. 131) would give the rendering, "The reed-bed is worth, &c.". Cf. the English 'fetch' (a price).

iii. 7–10. The strong man lives off what is paid for his strength (lit. arm), and the weak man off what is paid for his children.

A. Falkenstein, *IF* 60. 128.

The sale of children by their parents to ward off starvation is documented and discussed by A. L. Oppenheim in *Iraq* 17. 69–89.

iii. 14–16. My vagina is fine; (yet) according to my people (its use) for me is ended.

B. Meissner, *MAOG* III/3. 33.
A. Falkenstein, *IF* 60. 125.
CAD, vol. G, 29.

This again translates the Akkadian. The Sumerian has been construed in different ways. T. Jacobsen suggests (*CAD*): "My vagina is fine, (yet) among my people it is said of me, "It is finished with you." " I.e. an old prostitute is defending her ability to continue her profession.

iii. 17–18. He/It is altogether fine, and clothed with a cloak/bandage.

A. Poebel, *GSG*, § 572.
B. Meissner, *MAOG* III/3. 33.

Meissner took this as a reflection on the prestige obtained from good clothes. T. Jacobsen (orally) suggests that it is connected in content with the preceding one, and that gal_4 has to be understood as the subject. In this case túg.níg.dára will be the sanitary napkin.

iii. 19–20. Do you strike the face of a moving ox with a *strap*?

The translation of *uppu* is very difficult. The drum *uppu* is a loan from the Sumerian ([kuš])ùb (*KAR* 16 rev. 15–16; *CT* 11. 17. 56). It is, however, uncertain if this has anything to do with the piece of door-fastening equipment ([giš])mud (*CT*. 40. 12. 10, and 21, &c.) = *uppu*. The translation 'key' (e.g. Sidney Smith, *RA* 21. 80) is inconsistent with its being the object of *patû* 'open' (E. Ebeling, *Or* N.S. 17, pl. 37. 8 = *Parfümrezepte und kultische Texte aus Assur*, pl. 37 = *Stiftungen und Vorschriften für assyrische Tempel*, p. 24). The determinative giš need not be taken too seriously, as in the passage just quoted those of the temple-doors were of gold. If, however, the door-*uppu* can only be a wooden or metal part of a lock, this will make no sense in the proverb, where this article is presumed to be in the hand of a person meeting an ox. Perhaps *uppu* is the name of the thing which moves the bolt in the door. In primitive and simple locks this is a simple thong of leather or some other substance, which has been proposed for the rendering of *uppu* (A. Heidel, *Gilgamesh Epic*[2], p. 131). In more elaborate locks this was replaced by a handle which moved the bolt when the key was turned. 'Handle' too has been proposed for *uppu*: A. Salonen, *SO* VIII/4. 130 and *Landfahrzeuge*, p. 97. Door thongs were certainly known even in late times in ancient Mesopotamia (cf. *ebil sikkūri, ebil aštarru*: *Or* N.S. 19. 153[1]), and the many literary passages which give the names of three or four parts of the lock must surely include that part which actually moves the bolt. If this suggestion is correct, ***uppu*** is originally a thong, from which, via the door lock, the meaning 'handle' was obtained.

iii. 21–24. My knees are in constant motion, my feet are tireless, (yet) a half-wit pursues me with trouble.

The complaint of an overworked slave or labourer? or of a beast of burden as in the following proverb? 21–22 are stock phrases, cf. *STC* II. LXXVII. 29 = E. Ebeling, *Handerhebung*, p. 131; IV R^2 9. I. 38–39 = *LSS* II/4. 2.

iii. 25–29. I am a riding-donkey, (yet) I am yoked to an ass, I draw a chariot, and suffer the crop.

B. Meissner, *MAOG* III/3. 34.
G. Meier, *ZA* 45. 211.
A. Salonen, *Hippologica*, pp. 68–69.

For the reading giga for anše.(šú).MUL cf. A. Salonen, *Hippologica*, p. 74. The identification of *šūru* as a driver's stick was established by G. Meier, *ZA* 45. 212.

iii. 35–37. A wound without a doctor (is like) hunger without food.

This appears to be complete in itself, and of the same type as the group of four in the *Assyrian Collection* IV. 14–21. The original from which this tablet derives may have been so damaged at this point that the dividing line was not visible. The first line is reminiscent of curse formulas (e.g. *CH* 28r. 57–60); kú.e may be a form of the infinitive kú.a, cf. A. Falkenstein, *AnOr* 28, § 42. 1b.

iii. 50–55. I live in a house of pitch and baked brick, (yet) a lump of clay falls upon my head.

A. Falkenstein, *IF* 60. 127.

iii. 56–59. Last year I ate garlic; this year my inside burns.

A. Deimel, *ŠL* 399. 165.

Deimel's rendering is confirmed by the newly found Akkadian version.

iii. 60–64. B. Meissner, *MAOG* III/3. 35.
iv. 4–6. B. Meissner, *MAOG* III/3. 36.

iv. 7–8. The life of last night (is the same as) every day.

iv. 9–13. Like a seat of the month Tebet, which you adorn and put at my side.

B. Meissner, *MAOG* III/3. 36.

iv. 14–18. Like a seat of a man whose god is Šaḫan: you lament it, burn its leather, and set it on fire.

B. Meissner, *MAOG* III/3. 36.

iv. 19–24. When you are in the river, the water around you absolutely stinks. When you are in a plantation, your dates are gall.

A riddle?

iv. 25–29. B. Meissner, *MAOG* III/3. 37.

iv. 30–33. Let the furrow not bear a bad shoot; let it produce no seed (rather).

šer'u (*MSL* I. 152–9) is of course the subject, cf. *AMT* 12, no. 1, 52 = *JNES* 14. 16 and 17. 56: *še-er-ḫu ḫab-bur-ra* (ù.tu).

iv. 34–41. Will the early corn thrive? How can we know? Will the late corn thrive? How can we know?

A. Falkenstein, *IF* 60. 126.

iv. 42–45. Should I be going to die, I would be extravagant (lit. eat). Should I be going to survive, I would be economical (lit. store).

F. Thureau-Dangin, *AnOr* 12. 307–10.

A. Falkenstein, *ZA* 45. 178–9; *IF* 60. 129.

Thureau-Dangin took the first Sumerian verb to be erroneously copied for ga.ug$_5$.ga.dè.en, under the influence of the preceding ì.zu.un.dè.en. Falkenstein considers this emended form doubtful, and accepts that the Sumerian verbs in 42 and 44 are first person plural: "Should we (my family) be going to die, I would &c."

iv. 46–50. They pushed me under the water and endangered my life. I caught no fish and lost my clothes.

iv. 53–57. The enemy does not depart from before the gate of a city whose weapons are not powerful.

v. 10–13. Like an old oven, it is hard to replace you.

J. J. A. Van Dijk, *La Sagesse*, p. 8.

v. 14–17. You went and plundered enemy territory. The enemy came and plundered your territory.

v. 23–24. For dried green-malt spreading does not come too late.

B. Landsberger, *MSL* I. 199[1].

In brewing, the grain was first encouraged to germinate, and then dried to prevent this process continuing. *na'āpu* 'dry' is a known root: von Soden, *GAG*, § 106c, also the noun *ni'pu* 'dry wood' occurs (*Diri* III. 9 = *AS* 4. 85; *Ḫarra* VI. 72 = *MSL* VI. 57; *á.A* III/5. 72 = *CT* 12. 14. 11). However, according to A. L. Oppenheim (*Beer*, p. 15) *nâpu* is the technical term for drying the green-malt by roasting it in a kiln. The alternative to this was spreading in the sun, for which the root *šeṭû* is used. This process supplied a common simile in Late Assyrian royal inscriptions, where enemy troops are slaughtered and lie thick on the ground like spread malt (*kīma buqli ašṭi/ašṭaṭi*, e.g. *TCL* 3. 134 and 226). The difficulty in the proverb is that if green-malt has been dried or roasted, there would seem to be no reason for spreading it at all. However, the point of the proverb may lie in just this.

v. 37–38. What [will you] bend to a circle?

v. 39–40. Do you pay out money [for] a pig's squeak?

v. 43. I am seeking an ass's foal.

K 5688 (Plate 60)

LITERATURE

Text: v *R* 20, no. 5. Edition: E. I. Gordon, *JAOS* 77. 78.

1 gu.⸢du⸣	[*qin-na-*]*tum*
2 še$_{10}$.dúr.ru	*zu-ru-ut*
3 KA.ge inim.diri.ga	*pu-ú ba-ba-nu-tú*
4 ba.ab.tùm	*ub-lam*
5 [× (×) s]al.la.a.ni	

For *z/ṣarātu* 'break wind' see BM 98743. 10 below, *ZA* 41. 222; and cf. Arabic *ḍaraṭa*. Apart from this passage *babbanû* seems only to occur in Late Babylonian documents with the meaning 'of good quality'. See the passages quoted by M. San Nicolò and A. Ungnad, *Neubab. Rechts- und Verwaltungs-urkunden*, Glossar, and E. Ebeling, *Glossar zu den neubab. Briefen.*

1–4 appear in Sumerian Collection IV. 61.

K 7654 (Plate 60)

LITERATURE

Text: T. J. Meek, *RA* 17. 154.

1 traces	
2 ^{giš}má.ad[dir	. . . .]
3 zabalam^{ki}.a ba.d[a.an.s]ù	[. . . . .]
4 ^{d}utu larsam^{ki}.ma	^{d}*ša*[*maš* . . . .]
5 a.ba mu.da.an.zé.er	*šá man-*[*ni* . . . .]
6 gá.e šeš.mu ga.gin.na.kam	*ana-ku ana* ⸢*a*⸣-[*ḫi-ia* . . . .]
7 šeš gá.gin$_7$ ì.ti	*a-ḫi ki-m*[*a ia-ti* . . . .]
8 gá.e nin.mu ga.gin.na.kam	*ana-ku ana* ⸢*a*⸣-[*ḫa-ti-ia* . . . .]
9 nin gá.gin$_7$ ì.ti	*a-ḫa-ti k*[*i-ma ia-ti* . . . .]
10 ⸢a⸣.e.šub.ba lugal.gi.na	*e-zu-u*[*b* . . . .]
11 [d]am ildú.bi	*mu-tú* [. . . . .]
12 [na]m.ninnu.àm geštú.ga.a.ni	*ḫa-an-š*[*á-a* . . . .]
13 [nu.m]u.ni.in.nigin.e.e.še	*u*[*l* . . . .]
14 [. . . . .]× gú zi ×	[. . . . .]
15 traces	

2–5 = Sumerian Collection I. 89.
10–13: A. Falkenstein, *IF* 60. 125.

K 7674+11166+13568 (Plate 64)

LITERATURE

Text of K 7674: T. J. Meek, *RA* 17. 155.

OBVERSE II

1	[. . . . .] × × [. .]	⌜*ù*⌝ *bit* an ×[. . . . .]
2	[. . . . i]gi? ag.a[g]	*su-up-p*[*e-e*]
3	[šu ḫé.en.]da.ab.gi$_4$.gi$_4$	*li-šal-l*[*i*]*-mu-k*[*a*]
4	[.]×.bi	*sa-l*[*i*]*-mi-iš*
5	[ḫé.en.]túm.túm.mu	*l*[*i*-×-×(-×)-*k*]*a*
6	traces	

REVERSE III

1	zag šu × [. . . . . .]	
2	me.a a.ba an ×[. . . .]	[Akkadian
3	ur ša.ra.a[b.×]	lost]
4	za.za.a ša.ra.da.ab.lá[l]?	
5	[×].da.ši.in.gi.me.en	
6	⌜á⌝.kúš.ù.zu	
7	im.mi.ni.in.[d]úb.dúb.bu	
8	gu$_4$.ab kab ×[. . . . . .]	
9	usàn dúb ×[. . . . . . .]	
10	e lu ma al [×]	
11	ka ra gál bi ni giš ḫé? ×	⌜*ru-uṣ-ṣu-na ši-te-em-mi*⌝
12	ús.si.il.lá	*ú-sa a-di ne-e-er ši-iḫ-ma*
13	× lá lu ḫé.na.da.e	*is-ḫu-uk li-ma-al-lu-ú*
14	[× (×)]× dun.dun e ḫi a zu	*sa-ḫa-a-nu*
15	[× × (×)] a ba.an.du$_8$.du$_8$.u$_8$	*šu-ub-tuq*
16	[. . . giš.KIB].gal sag.kal	*ilu i-lik mar-ma-ḫu-ti*
17	[. . . . . g]i.na tag.tag.ga	*ṣi-ḫi-iš qit-rad-ma*
18	[. . . . . . .]× ab.bé.na.a	*le-é-um-ma liq-bu-ka*
19	[. . . . .]× le	*ur-ru-uk nap-šá-ti*
20	[. . . . .] ne	*rit-pu-uš ṣur-ri*
21	[. . . . . g]a	*ḫe-se-e a-ma-ti*
22	[. . . . .]×	*na-zaq la ṣa-la-li*
23	[. . . . .]×	*maš-re-e*
24	[. . . . .]	*ka-bat qaqqadi ú-al-lad-ka*

25	[Sumerian	[. . . . . . *š*]*i*?-*ik-ra*
26	lost]	[. . . . . . *i*]*m*? *ṣi-iḫ-ti*
27		[. . . . . . .] × ×

12. There are several ways of connecting the Akkadian signs. ús may well be represented by ***ú-sa***, but ús.si.il.lá = ***nēru*** (*ŠL* 211. 65 and *MSL* I. 89. 51).
16. Restoration after *Ḫarra* III. 131.

19–24. Long life begets for you a sense of satisfaction; concealing a thing—sleepless worry; wealth—respect.

B. Meissner, *MAOG* III/3. 41.
CAD, vol. Ḫ, 177a.

K 8216 (Plate 63)

LITERATURE

Text: T. J. Meek, *RA* 17. 158.
Edition: B. Meissner, *MAOG* III/3. 43–44.
J. Pereman, *The Book of Assyro-Babylonian Proverbs*, pp. 170–6.

1	. . .]ag.a	*e-nu-ma taḫ-bi-lu*$_4$
2	. . .]túm	^{íd}*idiglat ub-ba-lu*
3	. . .]bal	*e-nu-ma ta-ḫab-bi-tu*$_4$
4	. . .]tag$_4$	*šamû*^{ú} *e-zi-bu-ka*
5	. . .]me	*iš-tu taḫ-li-qu ri-ma-ta*
6	. . .]a.ta	*iš-tu iṣ-ba-tu-ka*
7	. . . g]ùn.nu.un	*kīma kal-bi tu-ka-an-za-ab*
8	. . .]en	*tu-uš-te-gir*
9	. . .]⌜e.še⌝	*pal-ga ul ta-šá-ḫi-iṭ*
10	[Sumerian	*šadâ*^{a} *ta-na-áš-ši*
11	lost]	[*ina*? *qa*]*nî*? *šu-qal-lu-la ul ta-li-ʾ-i*
12		[× ×]× ku *ner-ru-bat*
13		[. . .]× *ṣa-bat-ka-ma*
14		[. . . . . . .]× × *ib-ni-ma*
15		[. . . . .]×

1–4. When you commit a crime, the Tigris will bear away (the guilt?). When you *pass over*, the gods (? lit. heaven) will forsake you.

CAD, vol. Ḫ, 5a.

The rivers and river water played a prominent part in ancient Mesopotamian purification rites, and the first sentence may allude to this. The last line is rendered "rain forsakes you" in *CAD*. This assigns a more natural meaning to *šamû*, but *ezēbu* surely implies that the party forsaken has been enjoying the company of *šamû*. In Palestine and Syria loss of rain might well be a thing to be commented upon, but hardly in Sumer. The nearest parallel for 'heaven' = 'the gods' is the Rabbinic Hebrew *šāmayim*.

5–7. When you have escaped, you are a wild bull. When you have been caught, you fawn like a dog.

8–9. You are lame (lit. twisted) and are unable to hop over a ditch.

Jumping ditches was forbidden on the unpropitious seventh of Teshrit: *palga là i-šá-ḫi-iṭ* (*KAR* 178 rev. IV. 43 = R. Labat, *Hémérologies et Ménologies d'Assur*, p. 114).

10–11. You lift a mountain, but you cannot hang [from(?) a re]ed(?).

A. Heidel, *AS* 13. 32.
E. I. Gordon, *JAOS* 77. 69.
A riddle?

12. See note on *Sayings* III. 31.

K 8315 (Plate 64)

LITERATURE

Text: S. Langdon, *AJSL* 28. 243.
Edition: B. Meissner, *MAOG* III/3. 44.
J. Pereman, *The Book of Assyro-Babylonian Proverbs*, pp. 167–9.
A. Falkenstein, *IF* 60. 124.

1	[. . . .]× ù.um.U	diš ×[. . . .]
2	[zá.za].gìn.a	*uq-ni-*[*ma*?]
3	[lú].dub.sag.gá	*maḫ-ra-*[*a*]
4	[i]zi an.kú.e	*i-šá-tum ik*[*-kal*]
5	nu.ub.bé	*ul i-qab-*[*bi*]
6	lú.egir.ra	*ar-ku-*[*ú*]
7	me.a lú.dub.sag.gá.e.še	*a-li šá maḫ-*[*ri-i*]
8	edin.na ninda.dingir	*ṣe-ru a-ka-*[*al ili*]
9	[š]à ba.gar.re	*lìb-bi* ×[. . . .]
10	×.ba me.e[n	. . . .]
11	[(×)]× e ×[. . .	. . . .]

1–2. The Sumerian is in Collection II. 46, where the first line appears as ti.ba un.U.

3–7. Fire is consuming an aristocrat. The proletarian does not say, "Where is the aristocrat?"

The Sumerian is contained in Collection III. 189. Falkenstein proposes the translation, "Fire is consuming the aristocrat" is not what the proletarian says. He says, "Where is the aristocrat?" This allusion to class distinction is paralleled in the *Dialogue of Pessimism* 77. The *šá* before *maḫ-*[*ri-i*] is unexplained.

K 8338 (Plate 64)

LITERATURE

Text: S. Langdon, *AJSL* 28. 243.
Edition: S. Langdon, *AJSL* 28. 232–3.
J. Pereman, *The Book of Assyro-Babylonian Proverbs*, pp. 163–7.

1	li n[e	. . . .]
2	èn.tar.re.šè bir.bir.re	[. . . . .]
3	gú.šeš.gal.la an.bu.i	*mu-qal-li*[*l* . . . .]
4	ní.balag a.šà.ga.gin.na	*ku-ub-bu-ru šá eqla*
5	^{kuš}a.ga.lá ba.šè.$suru_5$	*ina a-la-ki-šú na-ru-uq-q*[*a*]
6		*šu-qal-lu-lu*
7	[l]ú.lul.la	*sar-ru*
8	[gal_4].la ba.ab.ús	*mur-te-ed-du-ú ú-ri*
9	[l]ú.nu.gi.na	*la ki-nu*
10	[^{gi}]^{š}šu.kin.bi min.àm	*ši-it-ta ni-ig-gal-la-šú*
11	[dam].nu.íl.la	*mu-taš-šu-ú áš-šá-ti*
12	[dumu].nu.íl.la	MIN *ma-ri*
13	[× n]í.ba.a	*s/šar-ru la mu-taš-šú-u*
14	[nu.í]l.la	*ra-ma-ni-šú*
15	[. . . . .]	*šu-ili-šú da-mi-i*[*q*]

4–6. The Sumerian as preserved on UM 29–16–53. III. 10 = Ni 4073. III. 5 has balag, not dúb (the sign forms are distinct), and šu.šè.$suru_5$.
7–10. In the Sumerian Collection I. 158 a proverb similar to 7–8 occurs.

11–14. There is a man who supports a wife. There is a man who supports a son. An outlaw/The king is a man who does not support himself.

This translates the Akkadian. The nu in 11 and 12 has no parallel in the Akkadian, and E. I. Gordon ingeniously suggests that the *-la* in 11 and 12 has got misplaced on the wrong side of the dividing line. Cf. Sumerian Collection I. 153; III. 9, and Ni 9752. II. 9–10.

K 9050+13457 (Plate 64)

	Sumerian	Akkadian
1	[. . . . .]×	[. . . . .]
2	[. . . . .] di	z[i] a ×[. . . . .]
3	[. . . . . . . sig$_5$].ge	*sur*(! tablet ḪU)-*riš ú-da*[*m*]-*m*[*a-aq*]
4	[. . . . . . . ḫ]ul.un	*za-mar ú-gal-*[*lal*]
5	[. . . . . . .] ne di	*it-ti šu-a-ri* × [(×)]
6	[. . . . .]× nu du$_9$.na	[*it-t*]*i la áš-r*[*i*?]
7	[. . . . . .]× lá.a.ke$_4$	mut [×] li 'a li [×]
8	[. . . . . .]× dù.dù.un	*la ten-né-ed-di*[*l*]
9	[. . . . . .]× ul.la.ta	*ana q*[*é-r*]*e-et áš-tam-me*
10	[. . . . . r]e.en	*la ta-ḫa-áš-ma*
11	[. . . . .]×.da	*šum-man-na*
12	[. . . . .]×.e	*la te-en-né-'-i*[*l*]

3–4. . . . now he does a good deed, now an evil deed.

For the contrast between *dmq* and *gll* cf. *Ludlul* II. 34 and p. 16.

5–12. With rejoicing . . with an unsubmissive person . . . . . . you will not be barred. Do not hasten to a banquet in the *inn*, and you will not be bound with a halter.

5. Cf. *Malku-šarru* VIII. 154: *šu-a-ru* = *mi-l*[*u-lu*] (*CT* 18. 31 rev. 7).

9. *aštammu*: see the note on *Sayings* IV. 4. For the reading *q!erētu* see *MSL* V. 11.

K 11608 (Plate 64)

LITERATURE

E. I. Gordon, *JAOS* 77. 71–72.

Lines 7–10 and 11–13 can be restored from Sumerian Collection IV. 11 and 12 respectively as follows:

7 lú.[dìm.ma.mu]
8 ki na.a[n.ba.al]
9 èm.ú.[gu.dé.a.mu]
10 nu.un.p[àd.dè.en]

11 máš ⌜a⌝.[a]
12 lú ba.ni.i[n.e$_{11}$.dè]
13 kaš$_4$.a s[u.búru]

K 15227 and 80–7–19. 130 (Plate 65)

Though not touching, these two pieces appear to belong to the same tablet, and can be taken together. The columns are numbered on the assumption that these two pieces form the reverse of the same tablet as K 4327+4605+4749; see Introduction, p. 223.

LITERATURE (on 80–7–19. 130 only)

Text: S. Langdon, *AJSL* 28. 242.
Edition: S. Langdon, *AJSL* 28. 232.
B. Meissner, *MAOG* III/3. 45.
J. Pereman, *The Book of Assyro-Babylonian Proverbs*, pp. 157–60.

COLUMN V

1	⸢a⸣[.ba . . .	
2	a.b[a . . .	
3	× [. . .	
4	šà.mu [. . .	. . . .]
5	giš ḪA [. . .	. . . .]
6	^{d}[utu . . . .] × × ×	^{d}*šamaš ul ú-×-[×]*
7	[. . . . . .]×.le.e	
8	[agrig šu.d]im$_4$.ma	*a-ba-rak-ku sa-an-qu*
9	[sa.KU kala.g]a me.en	*is-ḫa-an dan-na-tu*
10		*ana-ku*
11	[gu$_4$.kúr.ra] ú kú.kú	*alap na-ka-ri šam-me ik-k[al]*
12	[gu$_4$.ní.]ba.a	*alap r[a]-ma-ni-šú*
13	[ú.šim.]e ba.ná	*bi-ri-iš ni-il*

COLUMN VI

1		. . .] ^{d}[MIN]
2	. . .	× *ṣ]a-al-mi rab-bu-ti*
3	. . .	*b]ìt* ^{d}MIN
4	. . .]	*ú-ṃa-al-lu-ú*
5	[u$_4$.da ga.ti.e]	*ištēn u$_4$-ma lu-ub-lu-uṭ*
6	[gu$_4$.gin$_7$ ^{túg}BU.n[un.]túg.tu]	*alpu šu-um-ma-nam*
7	[bí.in.lá]	*id-di*

COLUMN V

1–3, 4–7 occur on *STVC* 3+4. IV. 31–32 and 33–34. The latter of the two is apparently fuller in the bilingual form; in Sumerian it also occurs in Collection III. 166.

8–10. The stewards are suppressed. I am brawny arms.

I.e. When the cat is away, the mice will play. The Sumerian is restored from *STVC* 3+4. IV. 35–36 and Collection III. 59. For *isḫu* see B. Meissner, *AS* 4, no. 6.

11–13. A foreigner's ox eats plants; one's own ox lies in green pastures.

R. H. Pfeiffer, *ANET* 426.

The Sumerian is restored from *STVC* 3+4. IV. 37–38 and Collection II. 93 (first noted by A. Falkenstein, *OLZ* 40. 225). The point of the contrast between ú kú.kú (cf. *PBS* 1/2. 126. 10–11 = *OECT* VI. 52. 19–20) and ú.šim.e ná (cf. *KAR* 375 rev. III. 37–38 = V *R* 52b. 60–61) is not really clear.

COLUMN VI

1–7. Of this proverb only lines 5–7 are contained on *STVC* 3+4. V. 36–38, from where the Sumerian has been restored. For the *šummannu ša alpi* see *Fable of Tamarisk and Palm* B obv. 18 and note.

K 16171 (Plate 64)

	Sumerian	Akkadian
1	[. . . . . . .] × [. . . . .]	
2	[. . .]× a.ge$_6$ a [. . . . .]	[Akkadian lost]
3	[. . .] lá.a [. . . . .]	
4	[. . .] a gi ⌜a⌝ [. . . . .]	
5	[. . . m]u.ni.in.K[A ? . . . .]	
6	[. . .] ḫé.em kù.g[i . . . .]	
7	trace	

Sm 61 (Plate 65)

LITERATURE

Text: S. Langdon, *AJSL* 28. 242.
Edition: S. Langdon, *AJSL* 28. 231–2.
B. Meissner, *MAOG* III/3. 44–45.
J. Pereman, *The Book of Assyro-Babylonian Proverbs*, pp. 145–56.

	Sumerian	Akkadian
1	[.	*ma*]-⌜*am-ma*⌝-*an a-a i*-× × (×)
2	[šà.]gidru[.ka]	*a-na libbi ḫa-aṭ-ṭi*
3	[ià] si [× (×)]	*šam-nu ša-pi-ik-ma*
4	[lú.n]a.me nu.un.z[u]	*ma-am-man ul i-di*
5	[sum.m]a.ab lugal.la.ke$_4$	*na-da-nu šá šarri*
6	[dùg.g]a sagi(šu.sìla.du$_8$).ke$_4$	*ṭú-ub-bu šá šá-qí-i*

7	[su]m.ma.ab [lug]al.la.ke$_4$	
8	[š]a$_6$.ga agrig.a.ke$_4$	*dum-mu-qu šá a-ba-rak-ku*
9	nam.ku.li níg.u$_4$.diš.kám	*ib-ru-tum šá u$_4$-ma-ak-k*[*al*]
10	nam.ge$_4$.me.a.aš	*ki-na-tu-tu*
11	níg u$_4$.da.rí.kám	*šá da-ra-a-t*[*i*]
12	du$_{14}$.da	*ṣa-al-tu*
13	ki.nam.ge$_4$.me.a.aš.ke$_4$	*a-šar ki-na-tu-ti*
14	eme.sig kú.kú	*kar-ṣi a-ka-li*
15	ki.nam.luḫ.šè ì.gál	*a-šar pa-ši-šu-ti ip-pa-aš-ši*
16	gir$_5$ uru.kúr.ra.àm	*u-bar-ru ina āli šá-nim-ma*
17	sag.gá.àm	*re-e-šú*
18	zá.kín nu.un.urù.me.en	
19	nam.dub.sar.ra ama.gù.dé.ke$_4$.e.ne a.a.um.me.a.ke$_4$.eš	

2–4. If oil is poured inside a staff no one will know.

The Sumerian appears as Collection I. 107 and elsewhere, but with line 3 as: *ià* ḫé.en.dé.

5–6. Giving pertains to a king, doing good to a cup-bearer.

7–8. Giving pertains to a king, showing favour to a steward.

L. W. King, *First Steps in Assyrian*, p. 294.

A. Poebel, *GSG*, §§ 699 and 709.

The first of this pair of variants appears as Sumerian Collection III. 85, where .ab is appended to both sum.ma and dùg.ga in some of the copies, and where dumu precedes sìla.šu.du$_8$.a.kam (var. šu.sìla.du$_8$.a.kam). For the reading sagi cf. *ZA* 52. 119[59]. It seems best to take the sum.ma(.ab), &c., as infinitives, with the Akkadian and Poebel, though the .ab is unexplained. A similar phrase commonly appears in incantations: ša$_6$.ga zíl.zíl.li.bi za.a.kám = *bu-un-nu-u du-um-mu-qu ku-um-ma* (*CT* 17. 21. 96–97, &c., &c.).

9–11. Friendship lasts for a day, business connexions for ever.

12–15. There is quarrelling among colleagues, and backbiting among bishops.

These two proverbs occur in this sequence as Sumerian Collection III. 17 and 18, being connected by nam.ge$_4$.me.a.aš. For *kinātu* see note on *Ludlul* I. 87. For line 10 one Sumerian copy offers: ki.nam.šeš.gal.la.šè ì.gál, i.e. "among 'big brothers' ".

16–17. A resident alien in another city is a slave.

The latest discussion of *ubāru* is by J. Lewy, *HUCA* 27. 59[250].

18. I/You do not keep a millstone.

19. The scribal art is the mother of orators and the father of scholars.

BM 98743 = Th 1905–4–9. 249 (Plate 65)

1	[. . . . . .]×	× × × [. . . . . . .]
2	[. . . . . .]×	*lu-u na-ki*[. . . . .]
3	[. . . .]× × dè	*la tu-kab-*[. . . . .]
4	[. . . .].ag.e	*ṣu-bat am-*[. . . . .]
5	[níg u_4.b]i.ta	*šá ul-tu u_4-um pa-*[*ni*]
6	[la.ba.g]ál.la	*la i-ba-aš-šu-*⸢*ú*⸣
7	[ki.sikil].tur	*ár-da-tum ṣi-ḫir-t*[*um*]
8	[. . . .]×.ta	*ina su-u*[*n*]
9	[. . . . .]×	*mu-ti-*[*šá*]
10	[. . . . .]×	*iṣ-r*[*u-ut*]

5–10. A thing which has not occurred since time immemorial: a young girl broke wind in her husband's bosom.

A variant form of this proverb occurs in Sumerian Collection I. 12, where lines 8–10 read: úr.dam. na.ka $še_{10}$ nu.ub.dúr.re. There does not seem room for the negative in the Akkadian. A fragment apparently dealing with a similar topic, though not proved to be proverbs or bilingual, is K 4539 (Pl. 65):

1 traces
2 [× ×]× *ra-a* ×[. . .
3 [(×)]× i ba li a ×[. . .
4 [*š*]*a-am-ni* [. . .
5 *ú-ṣú-ra-at ni-ši* ×[. . .
6 *zi-ka-ru* [. . .
7 *a-na ar-da-ti* [. . .
8 *ar-da-tum* [. . .
9 *eṭ-lu a-na ar-d*[*a-ti* . . .
10 ⸢*li*⸣?*-il-qí a*[*r*?*-da*?*-tum*? . . .

VAT 10810 (Plates 67–68)

(Middle Assyrian)

OBVERSE

1	. . .]× ma.nu	*ni-ḫi* ×[. . . . .]
2	. . .]nam.silim	[. . . . .]
3	. . .].i.ra.ni mu.na.dug_4	*la* šid rat *a-na za-e-r*[*i*? . . . .]
4	. . .] bal	*i-nak-kár* [. . . . .]
5	. . .]× du ḫé? za la lum	*im-*× li ba × uš [. . . .]
6	. . . ^{g}]^{iš}mar.gíd.da	*la lam-du-um-mi* ^{giš}*eriqqu*(mar.gíd.d[a])
7	. . . kas].kal.bi	*la mu-du-ú ḫar-ra-*[*an-šu*]

8	. . .]×.du.ú	*a-ka-a i-ṣu kal-ba-tu* ni [×]
9	. . .]×.iš	*a-di it-tal-la-ku it-ti um-me* [×]
10	. . .]ti	*kal-lat-mi te-pu!-ši e-mi-ta*
11	. . .]lá	*ù a-na ka-a-ši*
12	. . .]×	*ip-pi-ša-nik-ki-im-ma*
13	. . .]×	*aš-šum* IT-*bu-us ki-ša-da aš-šum i*[-. .]
14	. . .]	*maš-ka il-*×[. .]
15	. . .]	*i-ši* NUN *qá-qá-du ana nam-*×[. .]
16	. . .]	[(×)]× *pi-ik* × [. .]
17	. . .]	[*mu*?]-*tál-lik-ta* [. .]
18	. . .]	*bi-tu-mi a-a i-*× × × [. . .]
19	. . .]	*ni-šu-um-mi ú-*× × [. . . .]
20	. . .]	*ṣi-iḫ-ra-šu-m*[*a* . . . . . .]
21	. . .]ZA	*ina bu-bu-ti-ma i-*[. . . . . .]
22	. . .]×.az.gi	*en-bu* du ×[. . . . .]
23	. . .]×.bi	*da-bi-lum di-ib-*×[. . . . . . .]
24	. . .]×.un	*ul* ú bu ṣi ×[. . . . .]
25	. . .]	*ki-ri-is-su-um-m*[*i* . . . .]
26	. . . .	. . *g*]*ul*?-*li* ×[. . . . .]

27 traces

REVERSE

1–2 odd signs and traces

3	[Sumerian	. . .] é *ḫi-pi* [. . . . .]
4	lost]	. . .]× ta *ḫi-pi* [. . . . .]
5	. . .]×	[. .]× im [. . . . .]
6	. . .]×.ki.in.×	*ša qá-qá-*[×] × [. . . .]
7	. . .]×.li	*a-a-um-ma a-na a-la-*×[. . . .]
8	. . .]×.di.il	*ù šu-ú a-na la* ki uš? [. . . .]
9	. . .]×.be	*it-ta-nam-d*[*i*?]
10	. . .]× ú ḫi	*iš-tu iḫ-li-qú* ša ḫi ×[. .]
11	] × × pa ku	*aš-bu ú-dan-na-nu ir-ri* ×[. .]

12	. . .]da di bu × × tab $^{\text{ḫi-pí}}$	*šal-mu ku-nu-uk-ku-ú a-ḫa* × [. .]
13	. . .]× nu.da.ta.[l]á.lá	*ra-ma-ni-šu* su × ku × [. . .]
14	. . .] ba lum × al.ti	
15	. . .]× gal × × [×]× × gál	(×) × an mi × *be-e-el* [. . .]
16	. . .] × × × [. . .]	*ù bīta* ú [(×)]× ti ib nu [. . .]
17	. . .]×	*em-qú* [. . . .]
18	[Sumerian	[×] ra ú? di *uṣ-ṣa-ḫi-ir* [×]
19	lost]	[× (×)] × × ma ša ra × [. . .]
20		[× (×)] ne ud *ša la e-mu-*[*qi* . .]
21		[× (×)]× *ka-ri* la ×[. . . .]

22 trace

OBVERSE

6–7. The unlearned is a cart. The ignorant is his road.

"If the blind lead the blind . . ."

10–12. Bride, you have . . . your mother-in-law, and women will do the same to you.

13. Is IT-*bu-us* an error for *ik!-bu-us*?

23. The objection to reading *ṭa-bi-ḫum* is that the value *ḫum* is not yet attested in Middle Assyrian.

BM 38283 = 80–11–12. 165 (Plate 66)

OBVERSE

[ka$_5$.a dam.a.ni an.na.ab.bé]
[gá.nu unug^{ki}(.ga) garàš^{sar}.gin$_7$ zú ga.àm.gaz.e.en.dè.en]
[kul.aba^{ki} ^{kuš}e.sír.gin$_7$ gìr.me.a ga.àm.ma.ab.si.ge.en.dè.en]
[uru.šè geš'u.GAR.uš nu.te.a.ba]
[uru.da ur.re ara(KA×ŠED) àm.da.gi$_4$.gi$_4$]

1	[gi$_4$.in.tum.ma.a]l	[. . . . .]
2	[gi$_4$.in.tum].ma.al	*g*[*i$_4$-in-tum-ma-al*]
3	[tuš.zu.š]è ga.nam.ma.da	*a-na* ×[. . . . . . .]
4	[ur]u.a níg.ḫul.a	*mim-ma lim-*[*nu i-na āli*]
5	ara(KA×ŠED) an.da.ab.gi$_4$.gi$_4$	*iš-ta-*[*ag-ga-am/mu*]
6	níg.gú.kud.kud.du	*a-na mu-ka-a*[*b- . . . ki-ša-di*]
7	gú nam.ba.an.kud(! tablet gam).e.en	*ki-ša-da a-a ik-k*[*a- . . .*]
8	^{d}nin.giš.zi.da.ra	*a-na ^{d}nin-giš-z*[*i-da*]
9	ga.ti na.an.ab.bé.en	*bu-lu-uṭ a-a iq-q*[*a-bi*]
10	ká.na ṅam.mu.ni.íb.dib.bé.en.zé.en.	*ba-ab-šu e tu-uš-bi-a-ni*[*-iṅ-ni-mi*]
11	e.še	

12	šu.gi$_4$.gi$_4$.ra	*a-na mu-ter gi-mil-l[i]*
13	šu {ḫé} ḫé.en.gi$_4$	*gi-mil-lum li-túr-š[ú]*
14	^{d}ḫum.ma	ŠU-*m[a]*
15	[l]ú.inim.gar.ša$_6$.ga.ra	*šá i-gir-re-e dam-q[í]*
16	[ša$_6$.]ga ḫé.en.na.gar	*da-ma-qu liš-kun-[šú]*

17	[× ×]× uga.gin$_7$	*ši-bu ki-ma* [. . . .]
18	[× (×)]× [š]u?.ba.an.ti	*sír-qí* la ni? [. . . .]
19	[. . . . .]× in? ag.ni	da bi ×[. . . . . . .]
20	[. . . . . .]×.da	la ×[. . . . .]
21	[. . . . .]× ×	×[. . . . .]

REVERSE

1	[^{d}en.líl.]le	^{d}[*en-líl*]
2	[uru nam.tar].áš.dug$_4$.ga.šè	*a-n[a āli šá ši-ma-tu-šú ar-rat]*
3	[ḫa.ba.an.š]i.íb.íl.e	*lip-[pa-lis]*

4	[igi].baḫár.e	*nap-lu-u[s pa-ḫa-ri]*
5	im.šèg.gá mu.un.ši.íb.íl.e	*a-na zu-un-ni* ×[. .]
6	^{d}en.líl.le	^{d}*en-líl*
7	uru nam.tar.áš.dug$_4$.ga.šè	*a-na āli šá ši-ma-tu-šú a[r-rat]*
8	ḫa.ba.an.ši.íb.íl.e	*lip-pa-[lis]*

9	engar.igi.urù.a	*ik-ka-ru šá i-nam* ×[. . .]
10	a.na.àm ag.na	*mi-nam ip-pé-[eš]*

11	u$_4$ šú.uš.ru im nu.šèg.⸢šèg⸣?	*u$_4$-mu i-ru-up-ma šá-mu-ú u[l iz-nu-un]*
12	im al.šèg ^{kuš}e.sír.ra [nu.du$_8$.a]	⸢*ša*⸣*-mu-ú iz-nun-ma še-na ul i[p-ṭur]*
13	^{íd}idigna.a inim.ba nam.b[ir.re	^{íd}*id]iglat i-na qí-bi-ša* ×[. . .]
14	a.gàr nu.si.s[á	*ú-g]a-ri ul im-[la-a]*

[This proverb is also contained in bilingual form on BE Unnumbered, see p. 274. From it in the Akkadian *ip-ṭur* has been restored, and the following variants are also offered: *ú-mu*, *i-di-ig-la-at*, *qí-bi*-RA-AM *iš-ta-ra ú-ga-ra*, *ú-ma-al-li*. In the Sumerian nu.du$_8$.a has been restored from this source, and the following variants are offered:]al.šèg (for nu.šèg.⸢šèg⸣), [^{kuš}e].sír, [^{íd}idig]na, (end)].si.]

15	[× . .] × [(×)].⸢a⸣	[× ×]× *ip-ti* [. . .]
16	[. . . . .] a [×]	×[. . .] *zu-un-n[i* . . .]
17	[. . . . .] nu.bi.iz	*a-n[a . . u]l i[t-* . . .]

18	[^{d}en.líl.]le	^{d}*en-l[íl]*
19	[. . . . . . .]×.mu	*a-na* ×[. . . . .]
20	[. . . . . . .]×.ḪAB	*ú*-×[. . . . .]

OBVERSE

1–5. This is restored completely from Sumerian Collection II. 69, and is given here because of its importance for piece Z of *The Fable of the Fox*, reverse 5–10. E. I. Gordon translates the proverb: "The fox said to his wife, "Come, let us crush Uruk (with our) teeth as (if it were) a leek; let us strap Kullab upon our feet as (if it were) a sandal." When they had not yet come within a distance of 600 GAR from the city, about(?) the city the dogs began to howl. All the slave-girls (of(?)) Tummal with (the cry) "(Go) home! Go along!" howled menacingly(?) about(?) the city."
6–11. In Sumerian Collection I this "proverb" appears, but split into three: 6–7 = I. 3; 8–9 = I. 4; 10 = I. 5. The e.še does not appear.

12–16. May kindness be repaid to him who does a kindness. May Ḫumma grant favour to him of whom favour is predicated.

The Sumerian appears in Collection VI (CBS 14139+UM 29–13–361 obv. I. 1–3), though with gál for gar. Ḫumma was the deified Eannatum of Lagaš as worshipped in Nippur (T. Jacobsen, *AS* 11. 98–99; S. N. Kramer, *BiOr* 11. 172[19]). See *ZA* 52. 131 for the reading Ḫ!um-ma, not L!um-ma.

REVERSE

4–8. The glance of the potter is turned in the direction of rain. May Enlil glance at the city whose fate is a curse.

This and the remains of the preceding proverb belong to a group which differ from each other only in the professional name in the first line. Four are contained in the Sumerian Collection XIV, and two on unclassified tablets of Sumerian proverbs. Beside 'potter', 'farmer' (engar), 'shepherd-boy' (kabar = sipa.tur), and GÀR(?).sar occur. The unilingual form lacks im.šèg.gá, which was probably added as a gloss to explain the purpose of the potter, &c., raising his eyes. áš.dug$_4$.ga is also lacking from the unilingual form.

9–10. The Sumerian is on Ni 9752 obv. III. 8 and Ni 4210+4444a obv. II. 9.
11–14 = Sumerian Collection III. 149, and appears elsewhere in Sumerian tablets of proverbs, where, however, the final verb is nu.si.si. Cf. *YOS* X. 22. 23 and *RSO* 32. 193. 66–67.
15–17. Ni 4210+4444a may offer this proverb as:

ki.a . [. . . .] . .
bar.rim$_4$.m[a . . .] nu.um?.bi.iz?

BM 38486 = 80–11–12, 370 (Plate 66)

OBVERSE

1 trace

2 [. . . . .]× erín.bi.šè	[. . . . .]
3 [. . . . .]× na × ge.me.a.aš e.ne	*re-du-*⌜*ú*⌝ [. . . . .]
4 [× × (×)]× in.×.a.ni sù si.sá sù	*ak-lu šar-r*[*u* . . . .]
5 [× × (×) ḫ]a.an.tag lú.še.še.ga	*da-a-a-nu* [. . . . .]

6	[× × (×)] ku/šu igi na.an.du$_8$.du/mèn	*qar-ra-du šá* ×[. . . . . .]
7	×[× (×)]×.ri mu.un.ag.ag.e.še	*i-*× bi a ×[. . . . .]
8	u[r.sag.k]ala.ga a.ge$_6$.a gaba gi$_4$.gi$_4$.a	*qar-ra-du-ú da[n-nu-tu . . . .]*
9	[× us]u.tuku ^{d}giš.bar.ra al.ḫun.gá.e.še	*u be-el e-m[u-qí . . . . .]*
10	ne [m]è.a ur.sag.e.ne	*an-nu-ú ta-ḫa-*×[. . . . . .]
11	ne [× m]è.a lú.záḫ.e.ne	*an-nu-ú* × × × [. . . . . . .]
12	šu[.na nu].dù.dù ka.bi inim bal.bal.e	*ina q[a-ti-š]u ul ip-pu-u[š . . . .]*
13	a [× ×] in.ga.ḫúl ní.te.na	× × × *mu-uḫ-ḫi* [. . . . . . .]
14	g[a.nam] in ⌜ka⌝ ud.⌜di zalág⌝.ge.e.dè	*tu-ša* lu ra mi [. . . . . . .]
15	[× ×] × × [×] × tuku.bi	*mi-[i]n-di a-na ma-*×[. . . .]
16	[. . . . .] × [×]×.nam	*ur-ra-šu ki-i ša* ×[. . . . . .]
17	[. . . . .]×.nam	*ma-ti-ma ki-i* ×[. . . . . . .]
18	[. . . . .]	*ú-šam-ši-ma mu-ú-š[ú? . . . .]*
19	[.	× ×]× × na šú ×[. . . . . .]
20	trace	

REVERSE

1	traces	
2	[. . . . .]×.e.še	traces
3	× × [(×)]× lu me.a šub × ⌜gú⌝?	*ra-aṭ mu-sa-re-e* ×[. . . . .]
4	⌜e⌝ × [×] × × li šu gar.r[a] × [×]	×*-za e-mi ni-is-sa-[tu . . . .]*
5	× [(×)] bal.bal.[(×)]	*iš-tu i-te-nu-ú* ×[. . . . . .]
6	níg × [× ×]× su sa.a nam × ×	*ši-ri u da-mu ni-*×[. . . . .]
7	umuš dingir.r[a n]u.zu a.rá dingir.ra n[u].×.×	*ṭe$_4$-em ili ul il-lam-mad* [. . . .]
8	[n]íg.nam dingir.ra pàd.da × × ba [×]	*mim-mu ili a-na a-*[. . . . .]
9	l[ú] gír.bi gù.dé.a SAR.bi × [g]i$_4$.gi$_4$	*šá ar-ḫi-iš is-su-[ú . . . . .]*
10	èri nu.gi.na i.[b]í.za × e [. . .] × ×	*[ar-d]u la ki-nu i-*×[. . . . .]
11	áš.bal.dag.gi$_4$.a.ke$_4$ lugal × [×] × ×	*[ar]-rat ba-ab-t[im . . . . . .]*
12	gemé igi.bi tùm.ma nin.a.ni di.di	*am-tum šá pa-nu-[šá bab-lu . .]*
13	su lugal.a.ni ḪUR.ra.ab	*e-el be-l[í-šá . . . .]*
14	dumu? lugal.a.ni di.bi.ri ba.an.ús	dumu?.me *be-l[í-šá . . . . . .]*
15	×.ḫul.a.šè záḫ.e.dè	*lu-m[u-un . . . .]*
16	× × × e sig$_5$.ga ḫul.bi	×[. . . . .]

17 [. . . .]× su nu.dùg.ga.ke$_4$	×[. . . . .]
18 [. . . .]	[. . . . .]
19 traces	

OBVERSE

8–9. Can strong warriors resist a flood? and mighty men quieten the fire god?

9. For usu as the reading of Á.KALA see *JAOS* 65. 225. 47.

REVERSE

6. Cf. note on BM 56607 B 16 below.

7–8. The will of a god cannot be understood, the way of a god cannot be known. Anything of a god [is difficult] to find out.

See *Ludlul* II. 36–38.

BM 38539 = 80–11–12, 423 (Plate 67)

1 traces	
2 [. . . . .]× e ×	[. . . . .]
3 [. . . . .]× addir ×	[. . . . .]
4 [dam.nu.gar.ra tu]ku.a.mu.d[è	. . . .]
5 [dumu.nu.gar.r]a tu.ud.⌜da.mu⌝.dè	×[. . . . .]
6 [dam.nu.gar.ra] ⌜é⌝.a.ti.la	*á*[*š-ša-tu* . . . .]
7 [á.sìg.á.sì]g.ga diri.ga	*a-sa*[*k-ki* . . . .]
8 [. . . . g]ù ba.na.an.dé.e	*is-su-ú* [. . . . . . .]
9 [. . . .]× ú.da na.an.SAR.SAR	*i-ta-ti-šú* ×[. . . . .]
10 [. . . . .]× na.an.×.e?	*pa-ru-ú* ×[. . . . . .]
11 [. . . . .]× da?.šè na.an.ag.e	*ina še-pi-šú l*[*a* . . .]
12 [. . . . .]× × ⌜ù⌝.gù ba.an.dé.e	*tu-ut-ta-ma* [. . . . .]
13 [. . . . da?.r]í.šè al.gar	*ta-nam-di-ma ana d*[*a-riš*? . . .]
14 [. . . . . .]× × ab.ta.si.eš	*ṣu-ḫu ut-ti-ir*? ḫa ba ni[. . .]
15 [. . . . . .]× ḪUR ×	*šá i-sa-an-*[*ni-qu*(. .)]
16 [. . . . . . s]u.ub.bé	*i-na-aš-ši-q*[*a* . .]
17 [. . . . . . .]×.e.NE	*e*-RIM [. . . . . .]
18 [. . . . .].da	*šá e-gi-i e*-RIM [. . . .]
19 [. . . . . d]é.a	
20 [. . . . .]×.ka	*ar-ki-šú i-k*[*a-* . . . .]

21	[. . . . .]×.sù	*e-lip tel-mun* ×[. . . .]
22	traces	

4–7. By marrying a spendthrift wife, by begetting a spendthrift son, ⟨I got solace for my unhappy heart and confirmed it.⟩ A spendthrift woman in the house is worse than all devils.

Lines 4–5 are the first two-thirds of Sumerian Collection I. 151, and are incomplete without the third line (šà.nu.dùg.ga ma.a.ḫun ma.an.gar) which has been added in the translation. It was, however, lost from some editions in the Old Babylonian period, as the two lines without the third appear in Sumerian Collection XIV (CBS 14139+UM 29–13–361 rev. III. 5–6). Then on to this incomplete proverb Sumerian Collection I. 154 (also Collection XIV, ibid. 13–14) is added without a separating dividing line.

12–13. You find something, but it gets lost. You throw something away, but it is preserved indefinitely.

BM 38596 = 80–11–12, 480 (Plate 69)

OBVERSE I

1	traces	
2	[. . . . .].ke$_4$	*mu-ša-ak-li-la-at*
3	[. . . . šu . . . d]u$_7$.ù.a	*pil-lu-de-e šá ilī*[meš]
4	[. . . . .]×.ke$_4$	*mu-ša-ti-rat sak-ke-e šar-ru-tú*
5	[. . . . . í]b.diri.ge.e.a	*a-na aḫ-rat u$_4$-mi*
6	[^{d}en.líl en.]gal.e	*^{d}en-líl be-lu ra-bu-ú*
7	[a.na].gin$_7$.n[am] nam.bí.in.ag	*ki-ma mi-ni-i i-pu-uš-ma*
8	[su]ḫuš.a.ni.šè	*iš-di-ša*
9	in.bu$_5$.bu$_5$.a.gin$_7$ bí.in.SAL	*ki-ma iš-di pe-e ú-qal-lil*

10	mi.in.ga.ab.ag.ag.e	*da-pa-nu* GI*-bu-ú*
11	× × bi sag ab.bu.i.dè	*su-un-gu-ru a-ba-ku*

12	ka.bí.a inim bal.bal.e	*um-mul ra-ma-ni*
13	ní.àm sag ba.ab.ag.ag.e	
14	igi.a šà.ga ab.tu.tu.dè	*pa-ni a-na qí-ir-bi tur-ru*
15	nam.lú.u$_x$(gàl).lu nu.ni.me.a	*ši-i la a-me-lu-tùm-ma*

[The Akkadian Wisdom text SU 1952, 15+91+186+350 rev. 2–3 incorporates the translation of the last proverb: *pa-ni qa-me š[un?-nu?-u? um-mul] ra-ma-nu pa-na [ana qer-bi t]ur-ru ši-i la a-me-lu-tù[m-ma]*. See p. 117. The exercise tablet Leiden 853 (formerly P 206, cf. *OLZ* 16. 204 ff.) II. 1 ff. quotes the Akkadian of lines 10–15, agreeing with BM 38596 as far as preserved, except that the dividing line between 11 and 12 is missing (von Soden). See Pl. 68.]

OBVERSE II

1	trace	
2	si[p]a.da × un ×[. . . .	. . . .]
3	šà.túm.šà.túm.⸢ma⸣?.šè	[. . . . .]
4	× ḫi in.ra.ra.e.a	×[. . . . .]
5	ú.kú a.nag e.dùg.ga.ta	*mu-uš-t[e-'i ri-tú maš-qí-tú]*
6	an.da.ab.kin.kin.e.a	*ṭa-a[b-tú]*
7	lú.šul/šaḫ.a.šè šu.ni in.ag.eš	*ana amēli qá-a-ti ut-tir* ×[. .]
8	lú.tùr.ra igi àm.da.bar.bar.re.e.a	*mu-še-š[è]r tar-ba-ṣi mut-*×[. .]
9	^{giš}gidru šu in.da.[a]b.kar.re.eš.a	*[ḫ]a-aṭ-ṭa-šú i-ki-im-m[a]*
10	ú.na.nam.na.×.×.ke$_4$	*š[am]-mu ⸢ṣi⸣-ḫa-a-ti*
11	a.gàr.ta ba.×.×.bé.eš	*ina ú-ga-ri i-tab-lu*
12	lú.im.ta.[b]a.nu.me.a.	*si-im-ḫu tar-ba-ṣu rap-šú*
13	ke$_4$ tùr.d[agal b]í.íb.ta.an.[tu]r.re	*uṣ-ṣa-aḫ-ḫe-er*

14	ḫu e × × × ga.šè	ḫu iš ru *ana* di gu še × ×
15	la × × × × àm	[l]a i [. . . . .]
16	kúš? úr? búr šita? ta?	× ×[. . . . .]
17	[b]ar.šè la zu da ru [(×)]×	× [. . . . .]
18	× ni e? ur$_5$.gin$_7$ × × ×	× [. . . . .]

REVERSE III

1	[(×)]× bi níg.g[ig? . . . .]	traces
2	× × da ×[. . . . . .]	traces
3	[. . .] × × [.]× ×	*a-na na-ka-as na-pi[š-ti]*
4	[. . . . .]×.ab	*ul ú-ma-a[k]*

5	u[r.sag.g]an.ni.meš.a	*a-n[a] qar-ra-di git-ma-lu-ti*
6	šà.diš.e in.da.an.gál.la.eš.a	*ša [i]š-ten lìb-ba šak-nu*
7	a.ba sag mu.un.gá.gá	*man-nu-ú a:ia-ar {ar}*

8	lú.al.ti.la áš.	*ša áš-bi e-pu-uš*
9	a.na.ne.eš aš.ag.ab	*ṣi-bu-ti*
10	[l]ú.nu.ti.la ×	*ša la áš-[bi]*
11	[e]me.sig.šè dug$_4$.ga.ab	*a-k[u]l* ×[. . . .]
12	nam.lú.⸢u⸣$_x$(gà[l]) [. . .	. . . .]
13	ur ×[.	. . . .]

REVERSE IV

1	a.na.àm × × ì.meš	*ma-ti* ma × (×)
2	a.na.àm × × ì.meš	*ma-ti* kal

	Sumerian	Akkadian
3	a.na.àm × [(×)] × ×	*ma-ti* (×) da bi ta a [×]
4	[. . .]×.[g]ur.re.⌜e⌝.eš	*i-tu-ra-*[*nim*]
5	é.ki.tuš nam.é.gi$_4$.a.[k]e$_4$	*ú-ru-uš k*[*a*]*l-*⌜*lu*⌝*-*[*ti*]
6	šà.ba šà.ḫúl.la b[í].⌜si ?.a⌝?	*šá lìb-ba-šu im-lu-ú* [*ḫi-du-tú*]
7	u$_5$ ^{giš}ḫa-šur ×[. .	× (×)]× ^{giš}ḫ[a] × × ×
8	× × × bi ×[. .	. . . .] ḫa × ×
9	[×] ⌜šà⌝ nu.[u]b.×[. .]	× × (×) ⌜ul⌝ iš × ×
10	[× ×]× × e ba.ni.in.×	× × × (×) id [×]*-tum*
11	[. .] × [.].kam	*i-na* mi/gi[g] × × (×) da [(×) t]um
12	[. . . .]×.ga	*i-lam-mi*(-)[*n*]*i*
13	[. . . . .]×.ke$_4$	*ù ši-*⌜*i*⌝
14	[. . . . . .]×.la.ke	*tu*/*šar-ra-ḫa*(-)*a-*[*tu*]*m*?
15	[. . . . .].ke$_4$	*i-ma-al-la du-u*[*l*?*-lu*]*m*?
16	[. . . . .]×	*a-na bi-i*[*t* . . . .]
17	trace	

I. 2–9. . . . she who carried out in full the ordinances of the gods, she who multiplied the rules of kingship for ever; how did Enlil the great lord react? He despised her foundations like foundations of chaff.

There is some as yet obscure relationship between 5–9 and Sumerian Collection III. 37: ^{d}en.líl.le a.na.àm in.ag in.bu$_5$.bu$_5$ ^{urudu}šukur in.na.an.sì kuš mi.ni.ib.te.e.

For "like foundations of chaff" the Sumerian has "like (those) of chaff". Cf. K 4160. 1 above and note.

I. 12–15. To converse with a blazing face, to become downcast, to concentrate one's attention on oneself—that is not human nature (as it should be).

The scribe omitted the first line of the Akkadian rendering, part of which can be restored from the Sultantepe text. The Sumerian has main verbs in place of the Akkadian infinitives: "A blazing face converses, one is downcast, the face is turned inwards." The concept of "humanity" is found in other Sumerian texts, see J. J. A. Van Dijk, *La Sagesse*, pp. 23–26.

III. 3–4. Cf. *Era Epic* v. 9: *a-na na-ka-si ul ú-ma-ak.*

III. 5–7. Who will go against mighty warriors who have one purpose?

CAD, sub voce *gitmālu.*

III. 8–12. Perform the wish of the one present. Slander the one not present. Mankind . . . .

BM 56607 = 82–7–14, 989 (Plate 70)

(from Sippar)

COLUMN A

1	traces	
2	[.	× × (×)]×*-ra-nu-tum*
3	[.	× (×)]× *ḫu-bu-ul-lum*
4	[.	×]× ni *zi-ra-a-nu*

5	[.	*an*]*a ḫu-bu-ul-li te-el-qí-ma*
6	[. . . . .]×	*ana bu-ṣa-ṣe-e ta-nam-din*

7	[. . . . .].gar	*a-ga-rin-nu en-ṣe-et*
8	[. . . . . . .]× [a]l.dùg.ge	*ši-ka-ri ina mi-nu i-ṭi-a-ab*

9	[ba.an.d]u_8.du_8 íd.da ì.diri.ge	*pa-at-tu-ú ina na-a-ri iq-qí-lip-pu*

10	[$munu_4$] nu.me.a.ta	*iš-tu la bu-uq-li-*
11	[. . . d]a?.kú.ù × (×)	*ma li-ku-la*
12	[$munu_4$ n]u.me.a.[ta]	*iš-tu la bu-uq-li-*
13	[. . . .]× bi[r . .	*m*]*a li-is-sà-pí-ḫa*

14	[. . . . .]	× ^{giš}*gišimmari sà-ar-ri*
15	[.	×] × × na šá ab bi
16	[.	*suk?*]*-ka-al-li*
17	[.	× (×)]× *na-pa-a-ši-im*
18	[.	. . . .]× ku ni
19	[.	. . . . .]× iš *qá-ti*
20	[.	. . . . .]*-an-ni*
21	[.	. . . . . .*-a*]*n-ni*
22	trace	

COLUMN B

1, 2	traces	
3	za.a.ra ×[× ×]× × × g[i]	*a-*[. . . . .]
4	ù [t]ukumbi	*ù* [*šum-ma*]
5	lú.ulù nu.e.da.an.gi	*a-wi-lum tu-u*[*p-pa-al* . . .]
6	ki ^{d}utu di.ku_5.ta	*it-ti* ^{d}*ša*[*maš da-a-a-ni*]
7	za.ra gá.gá.e.še	*ir-te-ma* [. . . . .]

8 en.e.níg.e.pag.a	*a-di ša-ra-[ḫi?-ka]*
9 nam.ša$_6$.ga dingir.zu.ta	*ina du-uq-qú ša ì-l[í-ka]*
10 šeš.ra ù.ne.sum	*ana a-ḫi i-d[i-in]*
11 nin.ra na.ab.šèr.re.en	*ana a-ḫa-ti e ta-*× [. .]
12 šu.sa.a.še.ni.ḫu.šè ag.a.ab	*sa-la-at-ka e* × [. . .]
13 lú.zu.a.zu.šè ag.a.ab	*mu-da-ka ku[n?-ni?]*
14 nam.ša$_6$.ga.bi ZU.za al.gál	*du-um-qí šú-ú e-l[i . . .]*
15 ki.na.me.šè nu.gin.e.še	*e-ša-am-ma ul i[l-lak-mi]*
16 su.su.àm sa.sa.àm	*ši-i-ru ši-i-ru-[ma . . . . . .]*
17 lú.bar.ra lú.bar.ra.àm	*na-ka-rum na-[ka-rum-ma]*
18 lú.kú[r].ra lú.kúr.ra.an.ga.àm	*a-ḫu-[ú a-ḫu-ú-ma]*
19 ki im mu × tam.ma.àm	× ×[. . . . .]
20 × (×) ⌜le⌝.en kíd.du.à[m	. . . .]
21 [× ×] × e [. . . .	. . . .]
22 trace	

COLUMN A

7–8. The mother brew is bitter. How is the beer sweet?

For the brewing term *agarinnu* see A. L. Oppenheim, *Beer*, p. 24. 5, and note 63.

9. The bucket floats in the river.

ba.an.du$_8$.du$_8$ = *pattû*: von Soden, *Or* N.S. 16. 70–72.

10–13. Since he has no green-malt, let him use up. Since he has no green-malt, let him squander.

li-is-sà-pí-ḫa is apparently II/2, though this normally has a passive force. *akālu* 'eat up' or 'use up' is also found in K 4347+, IV. 43.

COLUMN B

8–15. So long as you are *thriving*, with the prosperity (coming) from your god give to (your) brother; do not . . . . (your) sister; . . . . your family; . . . . your acquaintances. (Then) this prosperity will stay with you and will not go elsewhere.

ZU.za in 14 is perhaps an error for su.za "in your body".

16–18. Flesh is flesh, blood is blood. Alien is alien, foreigner is indeed foreigner.

Cf. BM 38486 rev. 6: su sa.a = *ši-ri u da-mu*; also *MSL* I. 43. 23–24: nu.nu.ne nu.sa.ne = *ši-ir-šu da-mu-šu*, followed by nu.bar.bar.ra = *li-biš-tu a-ḫi-tu*. Probably *damu* is to be restored in our passage. See also B. Landsberger, *JCS* 8. 32, I. 12–13 = II. 10–11: *ša za-ra a-ḫi-tim la ši-ir āl ^{d}a-šur*, and note 7 thereto. In Hebrew Judges ix. 2 is similar.

N–3395 (Plate 71)

The piece from Nippur presents extraordinary interest and difficulties. The surface is worn and in parts very difficult to read. The scribe, too, was none too skilled, and writes the same signs in different ways even in the same line, as *al* in 11 (cf. also *na* in 5, 11, 12, with 16). The date may be Old Babylonian (note the form of the *nu*), though the possibility that this is a copy of an Old Babylonian tablet made in the Cassite period cannot be ruled out. In either case the value *ṭé* (15) is unexpected.

OBVERSE (?)

1 traces	
2 × × × [(×)] × ri ×	[. . . . .]
3 × du$_8$.bi.ib níg.nu.gar.re	× ×[. . . . .]
4 na? × × × gàr.ri.in.nam	*a-na ša-ḫi-i-im* ×[. . . .]
5 di.bi.da! an.ša$_4$.an^{ki}.na	*i-mi-ir an-ša-ni-*[*im*]
6 × (×) × mar.ḫa.ši^{ki}	*ma-ar-gi$_4$ pa-ra-aḫ-*[*še*]
7 × × (×) me.luḫ.ḫa^{ki}	*šu-ra-an me-luḫ-*[*ḫa*]
8 am!.si.ug/úg sa$_{12}$.ti.um^{ki}	*pi-i-ir ša-ad-di-*[*im*]
9 ^{giš}asal ḪI garàš^{sar}.gin$_7$	*ša ṣa-ar-ba-tam ki-ma ka*[*rāšim*]
10 šab.(or, pa ib.)šab.ba	*i-ḫa-ra-*[*ṣu*]
11 ^{giš}al im.ì.dar?.a gar.ra	*al-lum ša i-na ṭi-ṭim na-*[*du-ú*]
12 ^{d}nin.kilim.ma uru.na	*ši-ku* tu? *a-*(ras.?)-*l*[*i*?]

REVERSE (?)

13 ka níg ba ur gur š[à] × a	*im-ṣa* a pa? šúm? áš × ša ×[.]
14 [(×)]× ul en gin$_7$ × ×	*ki-ma ka-aš-*× an [.]
15 [×] × nu.ús	*ṭé-ma-am ú-ul ṣa-ab-*× [.]
16 [(×)]× ki nu.(ras.).lá	*a-na i-nim ú-ul i-qá-*[*al*]
17 [×] × a tùn? ḫur?	*qá-aq-qá-r*[*a*?*-a*]*m*? × × [×]
18 [SAL.kar.]kid gi × × × × × ru	*ḫa-ri-im-tum ša i-na*? × gi × × (×) mu ut ×[.]
19 [× ×] × × ka? na.an.gar	
20 [×]×.gin$_7$ × × (×) [g]ar.r[a]?	× (×) ma *i-me-rim*? tum ri × × × ša tum × [×]
21 [× (×)]× × × (×) na? ab? × × × ba	*ša-⌜ri⌝-ú-um ša ka-ak-ka-šu*? *wa-ṣi-a* ša ni? × [×]

22 [×] × × × × šú.a	*ša i-na la-aḫ-ta-nim ù* × × [×]
23 [× (×)] × ki umún ka šu.du$_8$.a	*ap-pa [i]b-bir-ru* [×]
24 [×] e.gi.LU.dè	× × × (×) PI-*lum ša i-na* ir × [× (×)] *ik?-kum?* ši?[. . . . .]
25 [. . .]×.e.ne	× × × × [. . . . . . .]

5–10. The donkey of Anšan, the . . . . of Paraḫše, the cat of Meluḫḫa, the elephant of the steppe, (are the creatures) which bite off a willow(?) as though it were a leek.

5. Cf. di.bi.da = *e-me-ru* (*Izi-išātu* C IV. 35).
6. A reading *ku-ar-gi$_4$* is just possible, though 'cock' fits badly among the other animals. Paraḫše is an uncontracted and metathesized form of Parašî, a district in the neighbourhood of Persia, on which see E. Weidner, *AfO* 16. 20. The name has a curious resemblance to the Semitic word for 'flea', even to the extent that the guttural may appear before or after the *š*.
7. On the much-discussed location of Meluḫḫa see E. Weidner, *AfO* 16. 6–11.
8. *šaddûm* here must bear the meaning 'open country', as shown by A. Heidel for several passages in the *Gilgameš Epic* (*JNES* 8. 233–5). There were no mountains around Mesopotamia on which elephants roamed. The writing sa$_{12}$.ti.um occurs again in *ZA* 51. 52, and *JAOS* 77. 71. 4. 9.
9–10. The simile of the leek is a stock phrase, found again in Sumerian Collection II. 69 (see BM 38283 beginning), and *CT* 17. 29. 13–14.

11–12. A spade put in the ground (is like) a mongoose in its city.

15. A part of *ṣabātu* is no doubt correct, though the traces are not helpful.
16. For *īnu* = 'skill' cf. H. Winckler, *Die Keilschrifttexte Sargons*, Atlas, pl. 43 Cylinder, 38: ***pi-it*** *ḫa-si-si li-'i i-ni ka-la-ma*, also ibid. 74.

UM 29–15–330 (Plate 68)

(Old Babylonian)

OBVERSE (?)

1 ⌜ninda.ni⌝ × × [. . . . .]
2 *a-ka-šu lu* PI × × × ma ×

---

3 ninda.ni gìr.pad.du.DALLA ḫé.a
4 zi.ni ḫé.×
5 *a-ka-šu lu da-du-ma*
6 *li-ip-si-iq-šu*

REVERSE (?)

7 dingir.kú.kú.me.en an.na.dím? (×) zu
8 *a-na-a-ku lu* × × × *i-di-ma*
9 × × ×-*am*

---

10 a × (×) × × × × × tu

---

11 an a ni a? zum × × × i im ×
12–13 traces

1–6. A group of three proverbs of this type occurs in Sumerian Collection I. 41–43, and no. 42 = 3–4. The traces in line 1 are too doubtful to allow the assumption that this is the end of no. 41; it may be a fourth of the type. The Akkadian *a-ka-šu* (= *akāl-šu*) is a valuable indication of actual pronunciation. For *pasāqu*, if this is the root, see *Reisner Vocabulary* III. 35–36 (*ZA* 9. 163).
7. Cf. Commentary on *Šumma izbu* 22: dingir.kú = bad$^{mu\text{-}ta\text{-}[nu]}$meš.

BE UNNUMBERED

This is an Old Babylonian exercise tablet from Babylon itself, but known only from a transliteration of A. Falkenstein as communicated by F. Köcher. It contains two bilingual proverbs, the first of which duplicates and restores BM 38283 rev. 11–14, q.v. The other reads:

10	. . .].bi?	*eṭ-lum ú-ua**
11	. . .].dug$_4$	*iq-bi-ma*
12	. . . b]a.da.sù	*e-li-pa-šu iṭ-ṭe$_4$-bu*
13	. . .]× bí.dug$_4$	*a-la-li iq-bi-ma*
14	. . . b]a.da.kud	*si-ka-an-šu it-te-eš-bi-ir*
15	. . .]	*ú-ua* ù a-a-ru*
16	. . . bí].dug$_4$	*iq-bi-ma*
17	. . .]×.šè	*e-li-pa-šu a-na ki-ib-ri*
18	. . .].te	*iṭ-ṭe$_4$-ḫi*

* Transliteration: KU

A man said, "Alas!" His boat sank. He said, "Hurrah!" His rudder broke. He said, "Alas!" and "Aiaru!" His boat came to the side.

The Sumerian alone is preserved in *STVC* 3+4. IV. 26–30:

PA.a bí.in.dug$_4$ má ba.d[a.an.sù]
a.la.la bí.in.dug$_4$
^{giš}gi.muš ba.da.an.kud
guruš.e u$_8$.àm ⌜u$_8$⌝.àm.di
^{giš}má ki.bi ba.te

and in a shorter form in Collection III. 179:

ù.ua.àm (v. ù.ua.PA) bí.in.dug$_4$
^{giš}má ba.da.an.su
a.la.la bi.in.dug$_4$
^{giš}gi.muš ba.da.an.kud

Proverbs Incorporated in the Lexical Series

(i) *Diri-Si* v. 183–7:

àm.tu.tu	*i-ru-u*[*m-ma*]
nu.si.sá	*ul i-ša-*[*ar*]
íb.ta.è	*uṣ-ṣi-ma*
nu.šilig.ga	*ul i-ka-*[*la*]
níg.ga.lugal	*makkūr*(níg.ga) *šarri*

It entered, but was not in good order. It will go out and not cease: something belonging to the king.

Apparently a riddle, with a clue added.

(ii) *Nabnītu* M, 73 (II *R* 62, no. 3 rev. IV. 64):

gú.ki gú.an.ta an.ag.a	*e-li-tu šá-pil-tu i-na-aṭ-ṭu*

Cf. *CT* 18. 49. II. 18–20:

gú.bala gú.ki.ta diri	*i-li ig-rù*
gú.bala gú.ki.ta	*ša e-li-t*[*u*]
al.ag.a	*šap-li-tu i-n*[*áṭ-ṭu*]

and *Nabnītu* L, 174 (II *R* 30, no. 1 obv. II. 4):

gú^{gud} gú.ki.ta an.ag.a	*e-li-tum pi-tú*

Sumerian Collection III. 181 and *STVC* 3+4. v. 15 offer: gú.bala gú.ki.ta al.ag.e. E. I. Gordon takes the gú.bala to be the turning edge of a tablet, and extracts the undoubtedly correct general sense of "topsy-turvy".

(ii) BABYLONIAN PROVERBS

There is every indication that proverbs circulated in the Akkadian language, but it is a curious phenomenon that they do not seem to have become a part of stock literature. The only surviving tablets written with collections of Babylonian proverbs are an Old Babylonian fragment, and two pieces found in the old Hittite capital at Boghazköy, one of which has part of a Hittite rendering. The late libraries, from which our knowledge of traditional Babylonian literature usually comes, have so far yielded not a single piece of Babylonian proverbs. The nearest approach to such is a Late Babylonian exercise tablet which has four Babylonian proverbs among a hotchpotch of extracts used for writing exercises. This lack in the late libraries can hardly be explained by the accidents of discovery. Any day an odd piece may turn up, but it is most unlikely that the general position will be altered. Babylonian proverbs are not a genre in the traditional literature of the Babylonians and Assyrians. The reason can be suggested. The codifiers of traditional literature during the Cassite period were very academic scholars, who may well have frowned on proverbs which were passed around among the uneducated. These scholars already had a vast traditional genre of proverbs, Sumerian with Babylonian translations, which formed the proper study of the educated. Some of the bilingual proverbs in their Babylonian translation do in fact turn up in Akkadian texts (see the introduction to Bilingual Proverbs), so that the line between the two kinds is not rigorous.

The existence of a body of oral proverbs in Babylonian is shown by their occurrence in letters, works of literature, and elsewhere. Some are expressly given as proverbs (*têltu*), while others can be safely identified from a knowledge of them in other contexts. Caution must be used, however, in making identifications of proverbs not confirmed in these ways. It must not be assumed that a person who dictated a letter was incapable of coining similes himself. Writers of literature have every liberty of using epigrammatic phrases if they wish, and need not always be quoting proverbs.

CBS 14235 (Plate 70)

This piece from Nippur is written in a script and orthography which suggest either an Old Babylonian date, or a Cassite copy of an Old Babylonian text. One curious feature is the occurrence of different forms of the same sign even in adjacent lines (*am* in A 2 and 3; *an* in B 11 and 14). This same phenomenon occurs in the bilingual Nippur fragment N–3395 above. The identification of this piece as proverbs has been made purely from the contents. There are no lines, as in the bilinguals, to separate the individual proverbs.

LITERATURE

A copy is given by L. Legrain as *PBS* XIII. 11, who also edited it ibid., p. 46. Elsewhere only extracts have been quoted: B. Meissner, *Babylonien und Assyrien* II. 424, R. H. Pfeiffer, *ANET* 425.

COLUMN A

1 traces
2 . . .-*t*]*e-di-a-am*
3 . . .]-*ra-am*
4 . . .]-*lum-ma-ti-šu*
5 . . .]×-*me ṭé-mi-im*
6 . . .]×-*am-ma-an*
7 . . .]×-*gi*
8 . . .]×-*aš*
9 . . .]-*ša-ár*
10–15 traces

COLUMN C

1 *ṣe-e-*×[. . .
2 *i*-PI-×[. . .
3 *i-ša-a-ḫu/ri* ×[. . .
4 *ú-še-el-*[. . .
5 *a-na ma-a-k*[*a-* . . .
6 *ši-ni-šu i-m*[*a-* . . .
7 *ù at-ta* ×[. . .
8 *i-na* UD-[. . .
9 *ú-*× × ×[. . .

COLUMN B

1 trace
2 *un-ne-*×-×[. . .
3 *i-li-iq-qi*$_4$ *a-*PI-×[× × (×)]
4 *a-šar ṣi-*×*-tim ub-ba-*×[(×)]
5 *eṭ-ṭer i-ṣa-bat i-na pa-ni šar-ri-im*
6 *ú-qí?-ip? a-na me-si*$_{12}$*-im ú-la-ba-ak*
7 *ša-am-mi-ma*
8 *ù a-wi-lum a-di la i-na-ḫu*
9 *ú-ul i-ra-aš-ši mi-im-ma*
10 *ma-an-nu-um mi-nam a-na ti-ša-nim*
11 *i-na-an-di-iš-šu*
12 *ša ša-di-i i-te-ni-ti-ip? im?-ma-ni eprum*
13 *ša la i-šu-ú šar-ra-am ù šar-ra-tam*
14 *be-el-šu ma-an-nu-um*
15 *šu?-ú-ma lu ú-ma-mu lu ra-bi-iṣ* × ×
16 traces

5 He takes away, he seizes, in the king's presence
6 He . . to . . . he anoints
7 With oil.
8 And a man, so long as he does not toil,
9 Will have nothing.
10 Who will give him anything
11 For . . .?
12 He who frequently *puffs* at mountains is counted as dust.
13 He who has not king and queen,
14 Who is his lord?
15 *He* is either an animal or one who lies . .

Bo 3157 (Plate 72)

This is part of a four-sided prism, of which an uncertain amount of the height remains, and about a half of the width is preserved, since it has been broken roughly through the middle of two of the sides. Thus the lower portion of one face is well preserved, and parts of the two faces on either side. That on the left, however, is blank, which suggests it as the last column. That on the right has some script, but only a narrow strip, which merits no further attention here. It is not clear whether the order of the columns was clockwise or anticlockwise. The scribe ruled lines between certain sections of the text, but in most cases he then wrote the following line of signs over his ruling, so that it can only be seen where there is a gap in the writing. In some cases, e.g. that below line 6, it clearly serves to mark the division between proverbs, as in the bilinguals, but there is no ruling to separate 4 and 5, though they are not part of one proverb. Since this and the following piece come from Boghazköy, they must date from *c.* 1300 B.C. They have every appearance of being copies of Babylonian proverb collections.

LITERATURE

Text: E. Weidner, *KUB* 4. 40.
Edition: E. Ebeling, *MAOG* IV. 21–23.
R. H. Pfeiffer, *ANET* 425.

1 trace
2 [×]× ×[× ×] × ri i[d]? × ka × × [. . .
3 [(×)]× *nu?-ú-ri-ka* × *a-ma-ka ta-ra-ab-*× *ú-*×[. . .
4 [*š*]*u-up-li ú-ul e-n*[*e*]*-eḫ-ma ṣú-mi ú-ul at-r*[*u*(× ×)]
5 [*m*]*u-uš-šur še-tum ú-ul i-še-eṭ bi-ir-*[*tum*]
6 *al-te-qi qa-ta-ta i-bi-is-sú-ú ú-ul i-qa*[t_6*-ti-*×]
7 *ta-al-li-ik mi-i-nu tu-ši-*⌜*ib*⌝ *mi-i-*[*nu*]
8 *ta-az-zi-iz mi-i-nu ta-tu-ra-am mi-i-*[*nu*]
9 *šum-ma-ma-a-an la a-li-ka i-da-a-ia ma-an-nu-um-ma* ⌜a⌝ [×]
10 × × re e lu? ma *la-am il-pu-uš šum-ma-ma-*⌜*a*⌝*-an la i-zi-ir-*[×]
11 *ma-ti-ma-a-an ki-ma ni-ši-im ú-ši-ib e-le-ni* × [×]
12 *a-ḫa-ia a-li-ka-a-tum pí-ia la-a ki-ma ni-ši at-te-ni-*[*bu?-ub?*]
13 × giš ⌜*ke?-e*⌝*?-ma ni-iš ú-ši-ib a-ku-ul e-le-ni* [× ×]
14 [*i*]*b-ri-mi la na-aṣ-ṣi-ir pí-r*[*i*]*-iš-ti-ia* × (×) *lu-ú* [× ×]
15 × ma *lu-ú mar-tum ib-ri-mi na-aṣ-ṣi-ir pí-ri-i*[*š-ti-ia*]
16 [× (×)]× *-ú i-kal-li pu-um-ma a-na-ku lu-ú a-k*[*u-ul?*]
17 [× ×] × *ni-ši da-bi?* × [×] × × a me × [×]
18 [× × *-t*]*a-ti ú-ši-ib* ti? ti? × *li-ib-bi* [× ×]

4. My well does not tire (of giving water); my thirst is not excessive.
5. The net is loosed, but the fetter is not slack.
6. I have gone shares in business; loss is unending.

These are well-known commercial terms, see e.g. *MSL* I. 40–41 and 145; ibid. 39. 22–25 and 144.

7–8. You have gone. So what? You have stayed. So what? You have stood. So what? You have returned. So what?

Is there perhaps a slight reflection of this proverb in *Sayings* III. 53–54, where the Elephant replies to the Mosquito?

14–15. *na-aṣ-ṣi-ir* stands for *nāṣir*, the participle. Cf. von Soden, *GAG*, § 20 d. For the reading *pirištu*, not *piristu*, see R. Borger, *BiOr* 14. 190[1].

Akkado-Hittite Bilingual

Bo 4209+4710 (Plate 72)

LITERATURE

Text: E. Weidner, *KUB* 4. 97 (Bo 4209 only: *KUB* 4. 9).
Edition: E. Ebeling, *MAOG* IV. 23–25.

	Akkadian	Hittite
1	traces	
2	[× ×]-*tum* [. . .	
3	[. . .] a ad? a li × [. . .	
4	[×] ud a [. .] a ša ši ma [. . .	
5	^{giš}*ašūḫu*(ù.ku) *še-eg-ga-tum* [(× ×)] [. . .	
6	*ša te-ri-in-na-ta iš-*[*ku*?-*nu*?]	[. . .
7	*in-bu pa-an ša-at-ti*	×[. . .
8	*mu-ut-ḫu-mu ni-is-sà-a-t*[*i*]	*ar-*[. . .
9	*ra-a-ṭum ša a-na m*[*u-ḫu*]*r ša-a-ri*	pa$_5$ *aš-ma* × ×[. . .
10	*me-e ku-uz-bá ub-bá-*[*al*]	*dam-me-tar-wa-an-ti*(-)[. . .
11	*as-sà-an-nu-ú du-*[*na*?-*mu*?-*ú*?]	sal.kab.nun.n[a . . .
12	*ša i-na is-*×[. . .]× *še-ti-e-*⌜*ú*⌝	*na-aš-kán*(-)[. . .
13	*it-tum* × ×[. . .	
14	*ma-*×[. . .	
15	trace	

6. *terinnatu*: see *AfO* 11. 234; *Ḫarra* III. 83; *Era* IV. 41.

7–8. Prematurely ripe fruit is produce (bringing) grief.

B. Landsberger, *JNES* 8. 257.

Landsberger argues that *šattu* in this context is "the right time of year". Cf. *in-bi pa-an šat-ti* in Rm 287 (*RA* 53. 136) and *kirî pa-an* mu.an.na (*KAR* 104. 16–17). *mut-ḫu-um-mu* = *enib ki-re-e* (*LTBA* II. 2. 243), cf. B. Meissner, *MAOG* 1/2. 39–40.

9–10. An irrigation ditch (running) in the direction of the wind brings a copious supply of water.

11–12. Ebeling takes *assannu* as a form of *assinnu* 'male prostitute' (see *Sayings* IV. 3 and note) and reads line 12: *ša i-na b*[*it*] *aš-*[*tam-me zi-ka-ru-t*]*am še-ti-e-*⌜*ú*⌝ and renders it, "der im Fr[auen]ha[us nach Männlichkei]t sucht". The parallel he quotes (*CT* 39. 44. 16–17: *ás-sé-e-ni-iš na-ak zi-ka-ru-ta ḫu-uš-šu-uḫ-šu*) does not, however, support his suggestion, for there the male prostitute has an urge not for manliness (*zi-ka-ru-ta*), but homosexual intercourse (*na-ak zi-ka-ru-ta*). The restoration, furthermore, does not fit the space or traces. Provided that *assannu* is a form of *assinnu*, the restoration *dunnamû* in 11 is very plausible. The Hittite column unfortunately does not offer any light.

Proverbs contained in the Late Babylonian exercise tablet

BM 56488 = 82–7–14, 864 (Plate 71)

(from Sippar)

LITERATURE

Text: B. Meissner, *ZA* 7. 27–29. Edition: G. Dossin, *RA* 22. 116.

Rev. IV. 1–3
. . .] × × *ki-ma ú-lu šam-ni ina pi-i nišī*^{meš} *as-mat*

. . .] . . like fine oil it is fitting in the mouth of the peoples.

Rev. IV. 4–7
ša ul-tu ú-ri im-qu-tú gi-sal-le-e [. . .]×*-it*

What/he who fell from the roof [. . .] . . the roof fence.

CAD, vol. G, 97 restores [*i-laq-q*]*ì-it*.

Rev. IV. 8–10
[×] × × zi *kak-ku* × (×) tin ^{d}*en-líl ri-ṣu-šú*

Rev. IV. 11–22 (written twice)
bītu šá ^{d}*mes-an-ni-pàd-da i-pu-šu na-an-na la-qí-it zi-i-ri uš-tal-pit*

The temple which Mesannipadda built, Nanna, whose seed was cut off, destroyed.

The Sumerian original of this has been discovered and published by E. I. Gordon in *BASOR* 132. 27–30: é.babbar me.silim.e mu.un.dù.a an.na.né.lú.numun.til.til.la šu.ḫul mu.un.dù.a. The interchange between Mesilim (Old Babylonian) and Mesannipadda (Late Babylonian) raises, but does not settle, the question of whether the two names stand for one person. See *ZA* 52. 129[87].

Proverbs quoted in letters and elsewhere

TCL 22. 5 = *ARM* 1. 5 (see von Soden, *Or* N.S. 21. 76).
10. *as-sú-ur-ri ki-ma te-el-tim ul-li-tim*
11. *ša um-ma-a-mi ka-al-ba-tum*
12. *i-na šu-te-pu-ri-ša ḫu-up-pu-du-tim*
13. *ú-li-id*

Just like the old proverb which goes: "The bitch in her search for food gave birth to a poor litter."

This comes from a letter of Šamši-Addu, king in Assyria *c.* 1700 B.C., to his son Iasmaḫ-Addu, regent in Mari. The point illustrated by the proverb is that the son is not really coming to grips with the enemy, but is using up his energies on fruitless manœuvres in the same way as a bitch shortly to give birth spends herself in the search for food. At least this seems to be the best explanation yet offered (it is von Soden's), though the sense of *šu-te-b/pu-ri-ša* and the exact sense of *ḫu-ub/p-b/pu-du-tim* is not, perhaps, finally settled.

R. F. Harper, *ABL* 403 obv. 4–7 (see L. Waterman, *Royal Correspondence of the Assyrian Empire* I. 278–9 and III. 148–50; W. F. Albright, *JAOS* 38. 64; S. Langdon, *Bab* 7. 214–15 (= *Babylonian Wisdom*, pp. 86–87); B. Meissner, *AfO* 10. 361; R. H. Pfeiffer, *ANET* 426).

4. *ina tel-te šá pî nišī*^{meš} *šá-ki-in*
5. *um-ma kalbu šá* ^{lú}*paḫāru*(baḫár)
6. *ina libbi utūni*(udun) *ki-i i-ru-bu*
7. *a-na libbi* ^{lú}*paḫāru ú-nam-baḫ*

The popular proverb says: "When the potter's dog enters the kiln it will bark at the potter."

This is from a letter sent by a Late Assyrian king, almost certainly Esarhaddon. He addresses some "pseudo-Babylonians", and this proverb commences his communication to them. The point of the proverb seems to be that the dog inside the kiln is really in a very vulnerable position to bark at its master. The letter goes on to explain that these pseudo-Babylonians have been complaining against the king's servants. The king probably used the proverb with the implication that these people were in danger of receiving much harm at his hands, and were in no position to raise complaints against trusted servants. This proverb is also known from the Syriac and Arabic versions of the Ahiqar saying:

My son, you have been to me like the dog that came to the potter's oven to warm himself, and after he was warm he rose up to bark at them. (Syriac; F. C. Conybeare, J. Rendel Harris, A. S. Lewis, *The Story of Aḥiḳar*[2], p. 125.)

O my son, you have been to me like the dog that was cold and it went into the potter's house to get warm. And when it had got warm, it began to bark at them, and they chased it out and beat it, that it might not bite them. (Arabic; op. cit., p. 158. 14.)

Ibid. 13–15 (literature as for the previous proverb).

13. *i-na tel-tim-ma šá pî šá-ki-in*
14. *um-ma sinništu ḫa-ṭi-tú ina bāb bīt* ^{lú}*daiāni*(di.kud)
15. *pî-šá al-la šá muti-šá da-an*

The oral proverb says: "In court the word of a sinful woman prevails over her husband's."

Here the king continues his reply to the pseudo-Babylonians, and accuses them of thinking that by their smooth speaking they will get their own way with him.

R. F. Harper, *ABL* 555 rev. 3–6 (see A. L. Oppenheim, *BASOR* 91. 38).

3. *eṭlu šá si-bat*
4. *né-ši iṣ-bat-u-ni ina nāri*
5. *iṭ-ṭu-bu šá si-bat še-li-bi*
6. *iṣ-bat-u-ni ú-se-zib*

The man who seized the tail of a lion sank in the river. He who seized the tail of a fox escaped.

If this is really a proverb, its point eludes us.

R. F. Harper, *ABL* 652 rev. 9–13 (see F. M. Th. Böhl, *MAOG* XI/3. 48–49; R. Labat, *Le Caractère religieux de la royauté assyro-babylonienne*, p. 222; A. L. Oppenheim, *BASOR* 107. 9[6]; R. H. Pfeiffer, *ANET* 426).

9. [*š*]*a qa-bu-u-ni am-me-ú*
10. [*m*]*a-a ṣilli*(giš.ge$_6$) *ili a-me-lu*
11. [*u*] *ṣilli* [lú]*a-me-le-e*
12. [*a*]*-me-lu*: *šarru*: *šu-ú*
13. [*qé*]*-e mu-uš-šu-li šá ili*

As people say: "Man is the shadow of a god, and a slave is the shadow of a man"; but the king is the mirror of a god.

It is not clear whether the last clause is an addition of the flattering writer, for he was addressing the Assyrian king, perhaps Esarhaddon, or whether it is really part of the proverb. *qê muššuli* "reflecting copper" is presumably Akkadian for 'mirror'. The difficulty of the proverb lies in lú *a-me-le-e* [*a*]*-me-lu*, and though the rendering given makes best sense, 'slave' is *amēlūtu*, not *amēlu*.

R. C. Thompson, *Prisms of Esarhaddon and of Ashurbanipal*, p. 24. 25 = R. Borger, *Asarhaddon* 58. 25 (see A. Schott, *MVAG* 30/2. 90[2] and B. Meissner, *AfO* 10. 362).
šēlibu(ka$_5$.a) *la-pa-an* [d]*šamaš e-ki-a-am il-lak*

Where can the fox go out of the presence of Šamaš?

This is put in the mouths of Esarhaddon's enemies, who thereby admit that they cannot escape from him. One wonders if this alludes to a then well-known fable in which the Fox and Šamaš were enemies.

T. Bauer, *ZA* 40. 257. 29–30 = R. Borger, *Asarhaddon* 105. 29–30 (see B. Meissner, *AfO* 10. 362).
29. *ki-ma li*[*l-li* . . .] ×*-a arki niqī*(udu.sizkur.meš) *ta-ra-muk mê*[meš]
30. *ki-*⸢*i*⸣ [. . . . . .] × *ar-ki za-na-an šamê*[e] *ta-šá-kan na-an-ṣa-bu*

Like a fool [. . .] . . you perform your ablutions after sacrifice; like [. . . . . .] . you put in a drain pipe after it has rained.

C. Bezold and E. A. Wallis Budge, *The Tell el-Amarna Tablets in the British Museum*, no. 61 = *VAB* II. 252. 16–19 (see W. F. Albright, *BASOR* 89. 29–32; R. H. Pfeiffer, *ANET* 426).
16. *ki-i na-am-lu*
17. *tu-um-ḫa-ṣú la-a*
18. *ti-qà-bi-lu ù ta-an-*⸢*šu*⸣*-ku*
19. *qa-ti amēli*[lì] *ša yu-ma-ḫa-aš-ši*

When ants are struck, they do not take it (passively), but bite the hand that strikes them.

This extract from an Amarna letter more Canaanite than Akkadian has a proverbial form, but it is possible that it was coined by the chieftain who dictated it.

CRITICAL AND PHILOLOGICAL NOTES ON CHAPTERS 2–8

Chapter 2. *Ludlul*

TABLET I

43. Cf. *Theodicy* 295.

šá-da-šu i-[*mid*]: the phrase *šadâšu emēdu* is well known as a euphemism for 'to die' (Landsberger, *MAOG* IV. 320; see recently Salonen on *ana šadê rakābu*, *ArOr* 17/2. 316); it is, however, only one of a number of similar idioms, the others being:

tubqāti emēdu (*Epic of Creation* IV. 113; *Era* I. 17);
šaḫāti emēdu (K 9759. 10 = Thompson, *Gilg.*, pl. X; *Ludlul* I. 91);
puzrāti emēdu (*KAR* 29 obv. 9; *KAR* 307 rev. 25 = Ebeling, *Tod und Leben*, p. 37; *Šurpu* IV. 100; *CT* 35. 18. 7; *ABRT* I, p. 59, K. 8961. 7 = *BA* V. 360).

There are also occasionally compound expressions:

šaḫāt šadêšu emēdu (*TCL* 3. 150)
puzur šaḫāti emēdu (*KAR* 58 obv. 43)

A study of these passages in their contexts makes it evident that the phrases do not normally signify 'die', but rather 'go away', 'disappear', or something similar, and that must be the meaning which *šadâšu ī*[*mid*]—*si vera lectio*—must bear in our passage.

44. A similar passage for *naparkû* is *KAR* 14. I. 10–11. The nuance of this verb 'cease work' is documented by Goetze, *JAOS* 65. 223, and 'desert' (in a military sense) in *ARM* 15. 241.

45. The context requires that the verb in this line should have the general sense 'depart' or the like. The verb, and the restoration of the first sign, can be provided from *JTVI* 26. 153. 13–14:

[šul] ᵈinanna.bi *eṭ-lu* [*šá*] ᵈ*iš-tar-šu*
[. . . s]i.il.la *is-li-tu-uš*

The Sum. equivalent of *salātu* here is the verb sil, which, also written sil, síl, and sil_7, has precisely the required meaning in the following passages:

CT 17. 5. 35–36:] gidim ab.si.il.lá = [*še*]*-e-du ud-da-pa-ru*
Nabnītu J, 354: síl = *né-su-u*
356: níg.síl.síl.lá = *nu-us-su-ú* (*MAOG* 1/2. 52. 294 and 296)

The relationship of this to the well-known verb *šalātu*, *salātu* 'cut, split, undo (a bolt)', which also corresponds to the Sum. sil, may be as follows. The basic idea will have been that of separation, which developed on the one hand into the intransitive *islit* 'he departed', and on the other into the transitive *išlut* (*KAR* 389 obv. II. 29–30 = *Or* 39–42. 102) or *islut* (cf. *su-lu-ut*, *AfO* 16. 300. 18) 'he severed'. The Arabic *salata* 'cut' is a cognate, and in one form this has the meaning 'slip away stealthily'.

46. *iprud* occurs with a similar meaning in *Theodicy* 147, in *ABL* 1237. 5–8, where it appears to denote the final 'disappearance' of a meteor (see Weidner in *RSO* IX. 300, and von Soden in *Or* N.S. 15. 428), and in the *Tukulti-Ninurta Epic*, BM 98731 obv. 17, 18 (*AfO* 18. 46):

[*i*]*ḫ-ḫi-is-ma i-ni-'* it × [
ip-ru-ud ṭar-di-iš ki-ma × [
He withdrew and turned . . [
He fled as a refugee like . [

Von Soden (loc. cit.) wishes to connect the astronomical passage with a transitive verb *parāṭu*, but it is simpler to assume that *prd* in Akkadian has the sense 'flee' as well as 'fear'. The Syriac *p^e^rad* 'fugit' can be quoted as confirmation, and also to show the connexion between the Akk. meanings and the Hebrew and Arabic *prd* 'be separate'.

47. Cf. Tablet III k with Commentary, from where the comment here is restored.

51. This use of *nuppuḫu* with *tērētu* shows that the well-known phrase *dalḫā tērētūa* has often been misunderstood. The *tērētu* are not the omens themselves, but the viscera of the sacrificial animals on which they were based. This agrees with the circumstances of this institution. The omens *per se* are clear and unambiguous: "if a certain configuration of the organs occurs, then such and such will happen". It is easy to understand that often the state of the viscera could not be related to any known omen protasis, which was taken as showing that Šamaš, the god responsible for the omens (see *Šamaš Hymn* 151 with note), was angry with the inquirer and would not answer.

52. Cf. K 2765. 8–9, p. 288. The *bārû* and *šā'ilu* were the priests who diagnosed the root of any trouble and provided the appropriate ritual for dissolving it. If recourse to them was without avail, the case was incurable. Cf. II. 6–9 and 110–11, and *SBH* 1–3 (= 4), 52–55. The same concept lies behind *SBH* 1–3 (= 4), 18–19 = Witzel, *Tammuz-Liturgien*, p. 268:

e.ne.èm.mà.ni a.zu nu.un.tuku	šim.mú nu.un.tuku
a-mat-su ba-ra-a ul i-šu	*šá-i-la ul i-šu*
"His Word has no diviner,	has no dream priest."

[The choice of terms in the Akk. is undoubtedly the result of the pair *bārû* and *šā'ilu* being expected in such a context. The almost identical couplet *BRM* IV. 11. 9–10 renders the same Sum. with *asû* and *bārû*, the first of which is certainly a more accurate translation.]

The general sense of the line under consideration is beyond question the same: these people failed to provide a cure. The obscurities lie in *it-ti* (preposition or 'omen'?) and the last three signs *ul* UD KUR. They are commonly construed as (*alakti*) *ul par-sat*. There are three possibilities with this. (i) "My 'way' has not been determined with (= by? or, at the place of?) . . .." This is satisfactory sense, but meets a serious objection in that *alakta parāsu* is a common phrase meaning 'block the way', and it is doubtful if it could be used in a totally different sense. (ii) "My way to(!) . . . has not been blocked", i.e. "I kept on consulting." Again the sense is adequate, but "the way is not blocked" is at the best a very indirect way of implying frequency of going, and *itti* is not the right preposition; one goes 'to' (*ana*) someone. (iii) "The omen of . . . does not determine my way." The objection raised against the first explanation holds good for this too, but the difficulties of taking *itti* as a preposition are overcome, and no better interpretation can yet be offered. This whole context is taken over in an inscription of Nabonidus: *it- ti*^lú^*bārî* ^lú^*šā'ili*(en.me.li) *a-lak-tú ul par-sat at*!*-til*!*-ma ina šat mu-ši šutti*(máš.ge$_6$) *pár-da-at* (*Anatolian Studies* VIII. 62. 1–2).

53–54. Cf. K 2765. 6–7 (p. 288).

53. For *egirrû* (from Sum. enem.gar) 'an ordinary but ominous experience' cf. Landsberger, *MAOG* IV. 315–19, and Oppenheim, *AfO* 17. 49–55.

55. *šīr ilī*: the same description of Gilgameš was given by the scorpion folk: 9. II. 14. Cf. also *AfO* 18. 50, F 8. *šamšu*: Tukulti-Ninurta I and Aššur-naṣir-pal II call themselves *šamšu* (*ša*) *kiššat nišī* (e.g. *KAH* II. 58 obv. I. 3; *AKA* 208. 8).

56. The reading on **m** *lim-niš* is grammatically difficult, but that of k: *li-i*]*m-ni* can be taken as *limni* for *lemun* (*metri causa*): "It is difficult for curing." *libbu kaṣāru* is best taken in the same sense as *kiṣir libbi* 'anger', as e.g. *YOS* X. 44. 63: *ki-ṣi-ir libbi ili pa-ṭe-er*. For *paṭāruš* cf. *GAG*, § 66 f.

57. Just as there are two senses of *ṣullû*, 'pray' and 'show hostility', so we may perhaps presume on a second *teslītu* 'hostility', though it is not attested elsewhere.

58. For *ušaḫḫazu nullâti* cf. King, *STC* I. 211. 18–20 (quoted on *Counsels of Wisdom* 28).

59. It is tempting to emend *šumma* to *umma*, as the sense is certainly 'saying', but if there is a corruption in the text, it must be an early error, since it appears both in the Nineveh and Sultantepe copies.

61. *šá ki-ma*: cf. *MSL* IV. 175. 270–1: dam = *ma-a*: *ki-*[*ma*] and *ša ki-*[*ma*].

62. Cf. *Šamaš Hymn* 117. The entering is certainly for the purpose of taking over.

67. The meaning of *pâ iteddi* is suggested by the idioms *pâ ištēn šuškunu*, *ana pî ištēn turru*, and *pâ ēda šakānu* (*Fable of Fox* Z obv. 14). Cf. especially *pû nenpušu VAB* II. 104. 51. *iteddi* looks like IV/3 stative of *wedû*.

68. *na-an-ḫu-uz-zu*: cf. A Finet, *L'Accadien des Lettres de Mari* (*Académie Royale de Belgique, Classe des Lettres et des Sciences Morales et Politiques, Mémoires*, Tome 51/1), p. 277; R. Borger, *Asarhaddon*, p. 104, note on II. 6.

69. The Commentary explains *napraku* as *pirku*, and *pirki itti* x *dabābu* = 'verleumden' (Ebeling, *Glossar zu den neubab. Briefen*, p. 180).

70. The verb may be I/1 perfect of *ešē'u*/*ašā'u*, or IV/3 stative of *še'û*/*ša'û*. The former has been adopted here, from the verb attested in *Malku-šarru* IV. 235–7:

sa-ḫa-pu = *ṣa-ba-tu*
e-še-'-ú = ,,
a-ḫa-zu = ,, (*LTBA* II. I. XIII. 105–7)

and in *Diri* II, where [la.ab]DU.DU = *a-ḫa-zu* (21), *ba-ba-lum* (24), and *e-še-'u* (25) (*MAOG* III/3. 47). Though not apparently known elsewhere, this might well be a word whose rarity made it attractive to the author. *apātiš* is taken, though not with complete certainty, as a defective writing of *appātiš*.

71. The comment *ḫa-šik-ku* = *suk-ku-ku* is given again on III, Si 55 rev. 18, and appears as *Malku-šarru* IV. 12.

71–72. Cf. *Theodicy* 292–3.

šá-pu-tum: von Soden has collected occurrences of verbs *ša*/*eb*/*pû* (*ZA* 43. 261; *ZA* 47. 10–11; *BiOr* 10. 11) to which must now be added *RB* 59. 242 ff., 7 (cf. *Or* N.S. 26. 316) and *Fable of Nisaba and Wheat* IV. 8. The meaning 'be silent' may be correct for Old Akkadian (so Gelb, *MAD* III. 279) and Old Assyrian, but 'be loud' or 'bellow' is required for several literary passages in the Babylonian tradition: the verb is used of a bull in *BRM* IV. I. I. 3 (Speiser, *ANET* 104, reasonably conjectures 'bellowed'); in the *RB* 59 passage *iš-š*[*a*]*-pu* occurs after a line in which the supplicant is said to bray like a young donkey, and precedes a line in which his voice is compared to a wild ox's, and to that of two lamentation priests; in *Theodicy* 292 the parallelism demands a meaning such as 'be loud'; it is most improbable that Ištar would be spoken of as a goddess "whose cry is silent" (*KAR* 57 obv. I. 3+duplicates = E. Ebeling, *MVAG* 23/2. 3 and *Tod und Leben*, p. 50. 31); the contexts of the fable passage and of that under discussion require a similar meaning. There is reason for asking if the II stem in such examples as *mušebbi saḫmašātim* really belongs to the root *špw* 'be silent', as there seems to be no evidence for a specific connexion of these II forms with sound.

A possible restoration of 72 is [*l*]*a še-*[*ma-ta*].

73. *qaq-qar-*[*šu*]: cf. note on *The Tamarisk and the Palm*, A, IM 53975 rev. 2.

75. *it-te-'-*[*i*]: perfect of *ne'û*.

76. *šadāḫu* is used again of the arms in Sm 28+83 (*RA* 28. 138–9; *LSS* N.F. I. 93–99) rev. IV. 11–12 (collated):

á.bi.šè SUD.g[e.e]š mu.un.ši.in.gar.ra
a-na i-di-šu šá-da-ḫa i-šak-kan

In the context it is certain that *šá-da-ḫa* is a good quality of the arms, probably 'strength'. The relation of this sense to 'go (in procession)' is obscure, but a similar problem exists with *išdiḫu*, 'perambulation' and 'profit'.

77. See *ḫalālu* A in *CAD*.

79. *ki-ma-ti*: this form of *kīmtu* is attested in the list *CT* 18. 7. II. 12. *kīmtu* is sometimes fem., as in the etymology of Hammurabi as *kim-ta ra-pa-áš-tum* (V *R* 44 a–b 21).

80. Cf. K 2765. 12 (p. 288). Cf. *uznā*^{meš}*-šu tar-ṣa*, used of a sheep (Ebeling, *Tod und Leben*, p. 42. 11; *ZA* 43. 253). A tempting emendation is *ú-ba!-na-a-ti*.

81. *i-ṣa-pu-ra*: there is *zapāru* 'be evil', *ṣabāru* 'seize', *ṣab/pāru* 'chatter', and *ṣuppuru* 'scratch' (see note on III f). In addition there is quite a number of occurrences of *ṣapāru* with the eye: *STT* I. 28. II. 9: *īnā*$^{II.meš}$*-ia aṣ-ṣa-nap-rak-kám-ma* "I keep blinking at you"; *īn-šú šá šumēli i-ṣap-par* (*TDP* 72. 8; 74. 29); *i-in-šu ša i-mi-tim/šu-me-lim iṣ-ṣa-pa-ar* (*AfO* 18. 65. 24 and 26); ŠID = *ṣe-pe-ru ša īni* (*RA* 16. 201 = *BRM* IV. 33. 1). Oppenheim (*AfO* 18. 65[17]) deduces the meaning 'wink' from the use of the root with stars ('twinkle') in C. Virolleaud, *L'Astrologie chaldéenne*, Ištar 1. 3.

85. Cf. *Counsels of Wisdom* 18 and note.

86. The meaning 'denounce' for *nugguru* is established by Landsberger in *JCS* 9. 123–4. A form which may be related to this root *ngr* is in *LKA* 112 obv. 2 = *RA* 50. 30: *mu-ra-še-e šá ina bīt amēli i[b]-ta-na-k[u-u i-da]m-mu-mu it-ta-nam-gi-ru* "a wild cat which persistently wails, howls and hisses(?) in a man's house". For *lbb* cf. Tablet III, Si 55 rev. 22 and note.

87. For *kinātu* 'colleague', which also appears in Aramaic, see *ZA* 49. 178 and *LTBA* II. 1. III. 51–54 restored by *Igi.duḫ.a* = *tāmartu* (Short Version) 291–4 (*AfO* 18. 84):

lú.ku.li	= *eb-ru*
lú.an.ta	= *tap-pu-u*
lú.×.×	= *ta-li-mu*
lú.ù.il (v. lú.kù.sikil)	= *ki-na-a-tu*

Cf. also *Maqlû* III. 115 (IV. 65): *ib-ru tap-pu-u ki-na-at-tu*.

89. *šūpû* is not necessarily always 'glorious', but can be 'manifest'; the distinction between them is not always easy to make in particular passages. *šūpîš* "publicly" and *šarqiš* "furtively" are contrasted in *KAR* 92 rev. 29 = *LKA* 144 obv. 14–15, and J. Laessøe, *Bīt Rimki*, p. 39. 33.

90, 94. *ṭapiltu*: see note on *Counsels of Wisdom* 28.

90. Cf. *um-ma-nu* = *pu-ḫur nišī*^{meš}, *LTBA* II. 1. VI. 35.

91. Cf. note on 43.

92. Cf. K 2765. 11 (p. 288), and the note on Bilingual Proverbs BM 56607, B, 16–18.

93. *qa-ab* ^{mí}*dameqti-ia*: cf. *MAOG* IV. 314; *AfO* 14. 148. 160–1; and *ZA* 4. 256. 20.
pi-ta-as-su ḫaš-ti: this same phrase occurs in *Theodicy* 62, where it is explained by the Commentary (q.v.). This passage justifies the interpretation that a literal lion pit is not meant, though we may be unable to accept the etymology from the Sum. ḫaš. For similar names of the underworld see Tallqvist, *SO* 5. 4, p. 3.

96. *aḫulap* is said by a person in distress, or by the priest representing him, when divine help is sought, and the deity replies in the same word as a guarantee that help is coming. In English there is no one translation which can cover both uses, and the commentator's *adi mati* "How long?" can only apply to the first. Cf. III. 34, 37, 54.

97. For *lā amātu* see note on *Counsels of Wisdom* 28.

99. The monstrum *ú-zu-'u-zu* is scarcely more than a scribal error, for the verb is stative where the phrase occurs in Esarhaddon: *a-na ṣi-in-di ù bir-te zu-'-ú-zu* (R. Borger, *Asarhaddon*, p. 15 Fassung c: D). Literally: "they were divided between the bond and fetter". The otherwise obscure phrase has plenty of attention in a vocabulary:

lú.ab.ta.kur$_4$.ra	= *ṣi-in-du bir-tum*
umbin.bir.bir.ri	= ,, eme.gal
bar.bar.ri	= ,, eme.sukud.da
PAB+E$^{pa.ap}$.nir$^{ni.ir}$.tag.ga	= ,, eme.suḫ.a
nin$^{ni.in.du}$du$_8$.ma	= ,, eme.te.ná
na.ri.KU	= ,, ,, (*ZA* 9. 159 ff., IV. 10–15)

Cf. also *Erim.ḫuš*:

II. 132–3 bar = *ṣi-in-du*
bar.bar.ri = *bi-ir-tú* (*CT* 18. 44. II. 51–52)
VI. 195–6 umbin = *ṣi-in-du*
bir.bir.ri = *bi-ir-tú*

and *MSL* IV. 119. 1–2: lú.nu.lú kúr.bar.bar = *ṣi-id-du-um ù bi-ir-tum* "Crethi and Plethi (and) the mob".

100. There is a possibility that the *ú* in *ak-mu-ú* should be taken with the second half of the line to form a verb *ú-man-di-lu*, but obscurity still prevails.

101. For ᵈ*alāla* see *BASOR* 103. 11–14, and especially *VAB* VII. 56–58, 102–3. Cf. now *Era* III. 18 (ed. Borger and Lambert, *Or* N.S. 27. 141): *ri-gim* ᵈ*a-la-la ina qir-bé-ti ú-šá-dáš-šá*.

102. The context requires the verb to be taken causatively, but no examples of this are given by Heidel in *AS* 13. 34–37. However, with the quadriliteral verbs the causative and passive meanings are not distinguished as clearly as modern grammarians would like. *liš-ḫar-miṭ* occurs in *Maqlû* I. 33 in a passive sense. Heidel (*AS* 13. 61–62) emends all the manuscripts to *liḫ!-ḫar-miṭ*. But the same form *liš-ḫar-miṭ* occurs in *Era* I. 34 (misread *šú-ḫar-miṭ* by F. Gössmann) again in a passive sense. Note also the variants *li-iḫ-ḫar-mi-im* and *liš-ḫar-*[× - ×] (*Epic of Creation* I. 139, &c.); *mut-taḫ-li-lu* and *muš-taḫ-li-lu* (*Šamaš Hymn* 143).

105–6. With the Commentary on these lines cf. that on *Šumma izbu* 157: *qí-ta-a-a-u-lu* = *bi-ki-tú*.

107. Cf. *ZA* 43. 15. 37: *ki-ma su-um-me*, and K 225. 94: *su-um-meš*; usually the phrase is *kīma summati*.

108, 110. The verb is *ṣrp*; the *ṣ* is proved by e.g. *KAR* 177 rev. III. 13: *ṣu-ru-up libbi*, and the *p* by Tablet II. 42, reading of l: *ú-*⌜*ṣar*⌝*-ra-pa*. The root has three main groups of meanings: (i) 'press' as in the *Sennacherib Prism* VI. 30–31 (*OIP* II. 47): *ši-na-te-šu-un ú-ṣar-ra-pu* "they held back (not "passed", cf. Arabic *ṣaraba* 'keep in (urine)') their urine"; Thureau-Dangin, *Rit. acc.* 22. 8: *ta-ṣar-rap* "you will rub" (the new drum skin with certain chemicals). (ii) 'oppress', e.g. *JTVI* 26. 153. I. 9–10:

. . .] e *eṭ-lu ša ni-is-sa-tú*
. . .] si.ga *zu-mur-šú iṣ-ru-pu*

K 225. 150: *ṣur-ru-up šu-us-suk*; *SBH*, no. 2 obv. 30: *un-na-aš*, with a translation variant *ú-ṣar-rap*. (iii) 'emit (groans)', with the word for groan expressed, in the III/1 (IV R^2 54. 21a; *DP* 10, pl. XII. IV. 19) and II/1 (K 225. 144), but with no word for groan, in the II/1 in Tablet II. 42. Connected with this last sense is *ṣarpiš* 'bitterly' (of weeping).

109. It is tempting to connect *šubrâ* with *šutabrû* 'continue, be steady' (*ZA* 43. 308); cf. Ebeling, *Handerhebung* 132. 50: *a-ḫu-lap kab-ta-ti-ia šá uš-ta-bar-ru-ú dím-ti u ta-ni-ḫi*. There seem, however, to be no cases of the verb without the *t*.

110. For *usukku* (part of the body) see Meissner, *AS* 4, no. 7, Kraus, *Physiognomatik*, p. 34[52], and Jensen, *OLZ* 32. 851. It is well known that it is part of the face in the neighbourhood of the cheek, but distinct from it. An important passage is Rm 98. 9 and 11 (*CT* 40. 27 = *Or* 39–42. 164) where the sequence occurs: *šūr īni, kappi īni, usukku, lētu* "eyebrow (*MVAG* 40/2. 22[1]), upper eyelid, . . ., cheek". This confirms Jensen's translation 'lower eyelid'. Three other passages in which the *usukkā* are connected with weeping are *LKA* 142. 25:

[× ×]*-ši-ru īnā*[meš]*-ia di-im-tú ina ú-suk-ki-ia ul ut-tak-ki-ru*

OECT VI, pl. XIX, obv. 9–10:

ér.ra unú.bi nu.è.du ér
ina ú-suk-ki-šú šá dim-tim la ib-ba-lu$_4$
"With his lower eyelids which never dry of tears"

and K 9387, Col. B, 5–9:

mur-ṣu ka-li-šú-nu a-[. . .
ki-ma zu-'-ti ina nak-kap-ti na-á[*š-* . . .
ki-ma di-im-ti ina ú-suk-ki na-á[*š-* . . .
ki-ma ú-pa-ṭi ina nap-pa-ši na-á[*š-* . . .
[*k*]*i-ma gi-šu-ú-ti ina nap-šá-ti* [*na-áš-* . . .

(Cf. S. H. Langdon, *BE* 31, pl. 48. 12–16.) The sense of *ṣurrupu* in this context is difficult to determine. As shown in the note on 108, *ṣrp* has nuances intimately connected with weeping, but it is difficult to apply them with eyelids as subject. Probably 'press' is the sense intended, that the constant flowing of tears resulted in the wrinkling of the skin immediately below the eyes.

APPENDIX TO TABLET I

K 2765 (Pl. 19) seems to be part of a prayer, but it offers so many parallels to the first tablet of *Ludlul* that it deserves a place here. The numbers in brackets refer to the parallel lines in *Ludlul*.

OBVERSE

1 × × × × [. . .
2 *la ṭu-ub lìb-bi* × [. . .
3 *ṣur-ru-up lìb-bi* × [. . .
4 *dím-tú šu-ḫu-za-at* [. . .
5 *a-dam-mu-um ur-ru qaq-*[*da?-a?* . . .
6 *ina pi-i sūqi*(sila) *u gir-ri le-m*[*un egirrū'a?*] (53)
7 *at-til-ma ina šat mu-ši šu-ut-t*[*i pardat?*] (54)
8 *ú-šab-ri* ^{lú}*bārâ*(ḫal) *ter-ti d*[*al-ḫat*]
9 *áš-al* ^{lú}*šā'ila*(en.me.li) *a-lak-ti ul* [*par-sat*] (52)

REVERSE

10 *ik-kil-man-ni ib-ri tap-pu-u a-*[. . . (82)
11 *ki-i šīr a-ḫe-e e-zi-q*[*a?* . . . (92)
12 *šá gi-mir nišī*^{meš} *āli-ia tur-ru-*[*ṣa uzunāti?*] (80)
13 *šá ta-li-me-ia suk-*× [. . .
14 *a-na ta-ba-ak napišti-ia ik-*[*pu-ud?* . . .
15 *ina pān ti-ri u na-an-za-z*[*i* . . .
16 *ina pān* ^{d}*šamaš da-a-a-ni* × [. . .
17 *tuš-šu šu-ḫu-zu* [. . . (58, 69)
18 *ú?-še?* × × × [. . .

TABLET II

1. *a-na ba-laṭ*: for the meaning 'to the next year' cf. *MSL* v. 65. 193–4: mu.tin/ti.šè = *a-na ba-laṭ*, and *MDOG* 91, pp. 76–77. 6, 10, 23, 29, 31 (von Soden).
a-dan-nu e-te-eq: this is a common phrase in the *KAJ* texts, e.g. 11. 9, and also occurs in the Tell Billa documents 1–4 (*JCS* 7/4). For a literary use cf. *KAR* 169 obv. IV. 12: *u_4-mu iq-ta-tu-ú i-te-ti-iq a-dan-nu* (*Era*, ed. F. Gössmann, p. 19).

3. For the reading *zapurtu* see von Soden, *Or* N.S. 20. 158–60. Despite the *p ú-ta-ṣa-pa* must be from *waṣābu* = daḫ 'increase', not *eṣēpu* = tab 'double'. Cf. *RA* 33. 56[1]; *Or* N.S. 16. 75.

4. *id-di-na pa-ni-šú*: cf. *JAOS* 61. 256; *BBSt*, p. 121. 15.

5. *ú-šá-qa-a ri-ši-šá*: the traces of *ú-* on **i** are not such that *i-* is absolutely excluded, the reading of A. But in any case the idiom 'pay attention' is *rēša šuqqû* (*MAOG* IV. 299[3]; *JAOS* 61. 254), and Witzel (*Or* N.S. 4. 115) is correct in insisting that *i-šaq-qa-a* can only mean 'is high', not 'raises'. The parallelism of the previous line too shows that a preterite is required, and so the text of A must be emended to *ú-šaq-qa-a* with C. J. Ball, *The Book of Job*, p. 14. Errors of this kind do occur: 7: *ú-šá-pi*, G: *i-šá-pi*; 103: *ú-nap-pa-šá-an-ni*, **i**: ⌜*i*⌝*-nap-*[.

6–7. See note on I. 52, and cf. IV R^2 22, no. 2. 8–16 = *OECT* VI. 44:

uzú!.e máš.a.ta si nu.mu.ni.íb.sá.e
ba-ru-ú ina bi-ri ul uš-te-šir-šú
ensi.e še.e.ta i.bí.a nu.mu.un.na.an.bad.dè
šá-i-lu ina mu-uš-šá-ak-ka ul i-pi-te-šú

⌜níg⌝.gig.ga.bi.šè zír.ág.lá.a.ta nu.sid.dè
⌜a-na⌝ ma-ru-uš-ti-šú ina ṣi-in-di ul i-na-aḫ
[lú.maš.maš] inim.kù.ga.aš nu.mu.ni.íb.te.en.⌜te⌝.en
a-ši-pu ina š[i-ip]-ti ul ú-pa-áš-šá-aḫ-šú

The clergy mentioned were, of course, just as essential in illness as the *asû*. Cf. Ungnad in *AfO* 14. 252, and Labat, *TDP* 170. 14: [lú]*asâ* [lú]*āšipa* [lú]*bārâ* [lú]*šā'ila šu-ud-di* "to inform the . . .". The *ma/uššakku*-offerings are connected with the *šā'ilu*-priests again in Langdon, *Etana* (*Bab* 12) 34. 37: *ig-dam-ra maš-šak-ki-ia* [mí]*šā'ilātu*[meš]. Cf. A. L. Oppenheim, *Dreams*, p. 222. The purpose of the U in AF, but lacking from EGi, is not apparent.

8. For the *zaqīqu* cf. A. L. Oppenheim, *Dreams*, pp. 233–6; with *puttû uzna* cf. Harper, *ABL* 355 rev. 19; *ARM* III. 39. 17–18; *ARM* v. 17. 6′; *Era* v. 56. The BA.BI of **i** appears to be a misreading of the sign BAL.

11. *ridâtu* 'persecution' occurs in *eṭim ridâti*: *KAR* 184 obv. 36 and 45 = E. Ebeling, *Tod und Leben*, pp. 85–86, and *Maqlû* III. 147. *ippēru* = *mānaḫtu* (Commentary) also appears as *Malku-šarru* IV. 205.

13. This hardly refers to grace at an ordinary meal, but to a cultic meal. Cf. *KAR* 55 obv. 14–15 = E. Ebeling, *MVAG* 23/1. 23: *ina* [giš]*paššūr ma-ka-le-e ilī*[meš] *rabûti*[meš] *šùm-ka az-kur*.

14. *enû* ordinarily means 'change', but this context, where prostration is obviously meant, suggests 'bend', cognate with the Hebrew *ḥānâ*.

16. For the *eššēšu*-day cf. Landsberger, *LSS* VI/1–2. 111, and Langdon, *Bab. Menologies and the Semitic Calendars*, p. 150.

19. Does the suffix on *a-kal-šú* refer to *ilu*, or to the subject of *iz-ku-ru* and *i-ku-lu*? A comparison with *BA* v. 640. 3–10 = *OECT* VI. 22 with *RA* 9. 66 obv. and IV R^2 10a. 28–31 suggests that there was an offence in eating—even in error—"for oneself" (*ana rāmānišu*) what presumably should have been dedicated to a god. *Šurpu* II. 77 may refer to the same thing.

20. On the *masḫatu*-offering see F. Blome, *Die Opfermaterie in Babylonien und Israel*, p. 350[19], and L. F. Hartman and A. L. Oppenheim, *Beer*, p. 52[97]. The reading of A, *mas-ḫas*, results from the dropping of the final vowel from the suffixed form (*masḫas-su*, *masḫat-šu*) and the shortening of the doubled consonant. Cf. *CT* 6. 37a. 9 = *VAB* v, no. 35 [*i-n*]*a-di-iš* for *inaddin-ši*. Cf. *Theodicy* 51.

21. *im-ḫu-ú*: other examples of this word (R. Borger, *Asarhaddon*, p. 42. 41: *im-ma-ḫu-ma*; Labat, *TDP* 134. 34: *libba-šú ma-ḫu*; Witzel, *Tammuz-Liturgien*, pp. 230–2 B 4–8: ḪAR.mu al.è.dè = [. . *šá im-*]*ma-ḫu-ú*: *ik-ka-mu-ú*: // urú.me.e ḪAR.mu al.è.dè = [*ina*? *p*]*a-ra-aṣ māti šá im-ma-ḫu-ú*) are clearly related to *maḫḫûtu* 'a distraught state', but that gives a very inadequate sense here. The explanation of the Commentary may take it as a loan from the Sum. maḫ; the translation adopted is conjectural.

22. Cf. *RA* 9. 66 obv. 7 = *DP* 14. 46–48: [*ki-*]*ma ša nīš*(mu) *ili-šú kab-tu qà-*[*al-liš* . . .; *PBS* I/1, no. 14 obv. 25: *niš*!*-ka kab-tu qa-liš* [*a*]*z-za-kar* (collated; a loose piece of the tablet wrongly placed in the copy and photograph has now been lowered to its correct position); *VAB* VII. CXCI. 3–4: *ša ni-iš šumi-*[*ka*] *rabâ*[a] *qa-liš iz-kur-ú-ma*.

24. *tašīmtu* here, and in *TCL* 3. 81 and 93, *CT* 16. 15. 9, is that practical wisdom which enables a man to make the best of his circumstances.

26. The Babylonians had no hesitation in demanding a practical return from their religious observances, and so the word 'profit' (*nēmelu*) is commonly used in this connexion. Cf. *Theodicy* 74; *Assyrian Collection* (Bilingual Proverbs) IV. 24–26; a personal name declares, "There is profit in righteousness" *né-me-lu-kit-ti-ì-ba-áš-ši* (J. J. Stamm, *MVAG* 44. 313); in a ritual a recited incantation ends: "May whatever I am doing be profit; may it succeed" *mim-mu-ú ep-pu-šu lu-ú né-me-lum-ma liš-lim* (H. Zimmern, *BBR Ritualtafeln*, no. 45, II. 13–14).

29. *ú-šar/ú-šá-ri*: A. Salonen takes this as II/1 of *šâru* 'know' (*JNES* 9. 110), but R. Borger prefers *šurru* "sich herabneigen" (*Asarhaddon*, p. 104 note on I. 32).

30. The orthography of k *šu-ú* is paralleled in *CT* 22. 129. 5: *šu-ú*, *CT* 22. 146. 9: *šu-ú*, and in personal names it is even written *šu*: *ᵈnābû-mukîn-šu* (*AJSL* 34. 125, no. 31. 6). See E. Ebeling, *Neubab. Briefe*, p. 72, n. 5 (*Abhandlungen der Bayerischen Akademie der Wissenschaften*, Phil.-hist. Klasse, N.F. Heft 30).

34. For the root *gll* 'commit an offence' see *CAD* sub voce *gullulu*.

35. The meaning of *mussuku* 'give a bad reputation to' occurs again, and in contrast with *dmq*, in *VAB* VI. 143. 26: *šu-ú-um-ni dam-qá-am i-na a-li-ni tu-ma-sà-ku* (similarly 38); cf. also *PBS* 7. 42. 24: *ma-si-ik-tam a-na da-mi-iq-tim tu-ta-ra. masiktu* likewise = 'bad reputation' in *Counsels of Wisdom* 20, which is a line closely paralleled in *Era* I. 53: *šum-suk ina pî nišīᵐᵉˢ-šú-ma qa-lil qaqqad-su*. In the *Statue of Idri-mi* 4 [× × (×)] *ma-ši-ik-tú it-tab-ši* could be taken in the same way: a bad reputation in his city caused him to flee, though the gap prevents a certain interpretation. *TCL* 3. 226 *āl ta-nit-ti-šu ú-ma-si-ik-ma ú-šaṭ-pi-la na-gu-šu* is to be translated "I made his glorious city a byword and covered his district with shame". Cf. *Sayings* IV. 6–7, where *ṭpl* and *msk* are used together again, and see the note on *Counsels of Wisdom* 28 for *ṭpl*. The association of *msk* with the idea of blasphemy is clear from the Middle Assyrian *Harem Regulations*: *i-na ṣa-al-ti-ši-na šu-*[*um il*]*i a-na ma-šik-te ta-zak-ru-u-ni* (*AfO* 17. 279. 57). There is no reason to connect this verb with (*m*)*usukku* 'one ritually impure', a Sum. loan.

37. Five examples of AN.*zanunzû* are preserved. In two it is a designation of the ocean, on which sailors sail: *Šamaš Hymn* 70; and which has fish in it: K 4872 (V *R* 50) II. 36–39, restored by K 4922+K 11953 (Gray, *Šamaš Religious Texts*, pl. XIV = *AJSL* 17. 237)+K 4997 (unpublished). Both texts have been collated; Kunstmann, *LSS* N.F. 2. 78⁴, cites these lines in an unsatisfactory way.

36 AN!.[za.nu].un.zu.ta sùḫ.sùḫ.ḫa bí.in.[gar]
[*ina* AN.*z*]*a-nu-un-zi-i te-šá-a iš-ku*[*n*]
38 ×.[×].sùr.ra.bi a.gu.la.aš ba.an.t[u]
sur-ra!*-ni-šu ana mêᵐᵉˢ rabûtiᵐᵉˢ ut-tir*

[Note: 36. For *ta* K 4872 has another sign, perhaps a badly written *un*. 38. The first sign (on K 4872) is not certainly NUN.]

"In the deep he created confusion,
He turned his water channels to great waters."

(The fish are mentioned in the following lines.) Twice it refers to subsoil water conceived as a subterranean ocean (cf. *JCS* 7. 16⁴⁴): (Sargon II) *ina qi-rib* AN.*za-nun-ze-e kāra ib-ni-ma* (*RA* 10. 84. 15–16), and *Malku-šarru* II. 51–54:

la-i-ra-nu = *mêᵐᵉˢ pa-ši-ru-ti*
AN.*za-na-an-zu-ú* = *mêᵐᵉˢ šap-lu-tum*
(var. [AN.*z*]*a-nu-zu-ú*)
a-sur-rak-ku = ,,
a-ru-ru = ,, (*ZA* 43. 236)

Finally in the *Ludlul* passage the contrast with the previous line shows that it refers, directly or indirectly, to the underworld gods. In many ways it is similar to *apsû*, and the question is whether the emphasis is greater on the group of gods, making it a synonym of *ᵈanunnaki*, or greater on the abstract cosmic concept. Numerically the passages favour the second alternative, but five examples is hardly sufficient to decide the matter. The answer to this question would also settle between the alternatives *ᵈzanunzû* or *anzanunzû* for the reading. In the absence of more evidence we are holding to the reading of Meissner (*MAOG* XI/1–2, p. 26).

41. *ṣi-bit ap-pi*: cf. *ZA* 31. 268; *Or* N.S. 19. 150¹.

42. *pi-it pu-ri-di* is the time taken to part the legs when taking a stride. To 'open the knees' is a Sum. expression for walking: dùg mu.un.bad.bad.du (*Enmerkar and the Lord of Aratta*, 317). For *ṣurrupu* see the note on I. 108.

43. *ki-i pi-te-e ù ka-ta-mi*: this phrase also appears in *Izi-išātu* C IV. 31: di.di.bi.gub.ba = *pi-tu-u ù kut-tu-mu* (*MAOG* XIII/2. 35. 31). The Sumerian "walking and standing" can only be found in the Akkadian when it is realized that there is an ellipsis of *purīda*: *pitû* (*purīda*) = 'open the legs', i.e. 'walk', and *kuttumu* (*purīda*) = 'close the legs', i.e. 'stand'. Thus the whole phrase is another way of saying *ina pīt purīdi*. The commentator's "day and night" is far from clear. Bezold (*Glossar*, 230b) apparently understood it to imply opening and shutting the eyes, but more probably the commentator was thinking of the gates of heaven being opened to let Šamaš commence his daily perambulation across the sky, and being closed on the other side when he had passed through them.

44. The IM of **i** is clearly an error for *lam*, but interesting because in Neo-Babylonian script these signs are very easily confused, though not so easily in Neo-Assyrian. This implies a Neo-Babylonian copy somewhere in the tradition. A similar error occurs in a manuscript of the *Theodicy* (248, D).

48. For šà.zu = *qirba lamādu* cf.:

Gudea Cyl. A I. 28: šà.bi nu.zu; IV. 21: šà.ga.ni nu.mu.zu (said about dreams)

Enki and Ninhursag (*BASOR* SS. no. 1) 217: šà.ba ba.ni.in.zu!?

SBH, nos. 1–3 (= 4) 64–69 = Witzel, *Tammuz-Liturgien*, p. 270; cf. p. 166. 36–37:

e.ne.èm.mà.ni . . . . šà.bi a.ba nu.un.zu.zu

a-mat-su . . . . qí-rib-šú man-nu i-lam-mad

e.ne.èm.mà.ni šà.bi nu.un.zu.àm . . . . .

a-mat-su qí-rib-šá ul il-lam-mad . . . . .

CH 28r. 57–60: *ṣí-im-ma-am mar-ṣa-am ša . . . . asûm qí-ri-ib-šu la i-lam-ma-du.*

49. Cf. *Theodicy* 275.

50. *nenšuru* 'set out, be set in motion'(?): cf. R. Borger, *Asarhaddon*, p. 88. 17 and the literature there given. The root and precise meaning are still obscure.

51–57 are taken up in Tablet III (Si 55 rev. 5–10), and the two passages restore one another.

52. Cf. gab.kur.ra.[šè] = *ana i-rat er-ṣe-tim* (IV R^2 30, no. 2 obv. 22–23 = Witzel, *Tammuz-Liturgien*, p. 230). More references to this and *irat kigalli* are given in *VAB* IV, Glossar.

54. Cf. *CT* 16. 1. 25; *CT* 17. 7. 15–16; *CT* 17. 25. 1–2.

55. Cf. *CT* 17. 12. 5.

56. For *šuruppû* cf. Labat, *TDP* 159^{272} and *JCS* 9. 12. Poebel (*AS* 9. 28^1) discusses *nwš* as a verb of motion, and identifies it with *namāšu*. An example in a continuous text is K 2546 obv. 13 = *PSBA* 37. 195: *it-ti šāri lil-li-ku it-ti me-ḫe-e li-nu-šu.*

57. In similar contexts *kīma urqiti* occurs:

Šurpu VII. 5–6:

dù.dù ú.šim.gin$_7$ ki.a mu.un.d[ar]

aḫ-ḫa-zu ki-ma ur-qí-ti er-ṣe-ta i-pi-ṣ[i]

"The *aḫḫāzu*-demon cleaves the ground like grass."

K 4872 (V *R* 50) II. 29, restored by K 4997 (unpublished):

maš.giš.ra ú.šim.gin$_7$ edin.na ba.ra.bí.in.[. .]

i'-i-lu ki-ma ur-qí-ti ina ṣe-ri a-ṣi [. .]

"The *ī'ilu*-disease (cf. *CAD*, s.v. *ē'elu*) comes forth from the plain like grass."

The figure of the plant is kept up in the parallel line in Tablet III (Si 55 rev. 10), q.v. The idea is that these demons come up out of the underworld through a crack in the ground, just as plants grow. For *pêṣu* 'split' see *JRAS Cent. Sup.*, pl. VIII. 24: *i-ša-at a-pi-im ša da-na-ta-am i-pe-e-ṣú* "A fire of reeds that cracks the ground", and *Malku-šarru* I. 112: *pe-e-ṣu* = *li-tu-u*, also von Soden, *GAG*, § 98 o.

59. For *te'û* see note on Si 55 rev. 16.

60. *i-na-i-lu*: there are two derivatives of the root *n'l* which have connexions with water or liquid: ***ni'lu, nīlu***:

(i) *ŠL* 579. 280k: *ni'lu* (*ša mê*) = A.KAL (e_4.la_6, Akk. *illu*)

(ii) *ZA* 5. 80. 7: *par-sa-ku-ma ni-'-lu ul a*-[. .]

(iii) K 225. 166: *a-na šat-ti ni-'-li-šú* [. . .

((ii) and (iii) probably refer to weeping)

(iv) *CT* 39. 44. 9 and 45. 26: *ni-il-šú bul-lul* "is spattered with his own semen".

and *nā'ilu* or *na'īlu*, pl. *na'ilātu*:

(i) *Malku-šarru* II. 63–66:

na-[*i*]-*lu* (v. *na-'i-lu*) = *il-l*[*u*]
na-i-lu („) = UD-*ri-tú* (v. *ḫi-ri-tum*)
na-i-lu („) = *ḫar-ru* („)
na-i-lu („) = *is-su-u* (*ZA* 43. 236)

(ii) E. Ebeling, *Bruchstücke einer mittelassyrischen Vorschriftensammlung*, p. 33 'O' rev. 7 and p. 34: *na-i-la*-[*t*]*e* = '(wässrige) Niederung'.

(iii) *ABRT* I. 79. 14: *lik-la-ku-nu-ši na-'-i-lu ša* K[I . . .

(iv) *JNES* 15. 144. 11: ᵈ*kù-bu*ₓ(sud) *na-i-lu* ᵍⁱˢ*erini*

(v) *KAV* 218 A III. 15 . . .] šu.bar.r[a]⸢ù⸣ ná ki [. . . = 21–22 ᵈ*šamaš šu-ba-ru-ta u na-i*-[*la*] *šá er-ṣe-ti i-ša-ka*-[*an*]

The etymological relation of these forms to *na'ālu* 'lie down' is complicated. The Sum. ná suggests that in *KAV* 218 *na-i*-[*la*] = 'rest', but 'rest' does not suit *na'ilu* (iii) or (iv). In (iii) it is something which can restrain demons, and in (iv) it is involved in what the deity does to a cedar-tree. In (i) and (ii) it is a watercourse or piece of boggy land. *ni'lu* or *nīlu* is perhaps best rendered 'flow', and the usual view that 'semen' is a meaning derived from *na'ālu* in the sense 'lie with sexually' is at least doubtful. In the passage under discussion *na'ālu* is clearly 'flow' or something similar. In view of the Arabic *nahala* 'drink a first draught' and *manhalun* 'watering-place', the Hebrew *nēhēl* is rendered 'lead to a watering-place and cause to rest there'. This explains the connexion between the Akk. meanings 'lie down to rest' and 'be flowing'.

61. Cf. *CT* 17. 10. 50. The implications of the latter half are stated in K 2599+3069. I. 13: *ú-ram-mi ki-šá-di qaq-qa-di na-šá-a ul a-li-'i.*

62. The restoration of *irti* is suggested by the series *ana marṣi ina ṭeḫêka*, where the section on the *irtu* immediately precedes that on the *tulû*, and in particular by *š. ina irti-šú maḫiṣ*ⁱˢ*-ma* (*TDP* 100. 4).

iṭ-ṭe$_4$*-ru*: the verb *ṭerû* 'strike' is documented in Meissner, *AS* I, p. 49, and E. Ebeling, *Glossar zu den neubab. Briefen*, pp. 90–91 (*dirû* II). The first radical is proved to be *ṭ* by the passage *a-ṭè-ru-u līt-su* (*KAR* 71 rev. 4 = *MAOG* V/3. 32).

63. Cf. the commentary entry *BRM* IV. 20. 69 = *AfO* 14. 260: *ra-'-i-bi mur*-[*ṣu*]; for the meaning see ibid. 267.

64. Cf. Labat, *TDP* 110. 9′: [*š. rēš libbi-šú*] *i-ḫa-am-maṭ-su*; similarly 178. 12. *TDP* 112. 30′–31′: *š. rēš libbi-šú êm*; similarly 146. 62′.

66. Cf. *CT* 38. 50. 46 = *Or* 51–54, 60: [*š. kal*]*bu* [*ana*] *pān amēli uḫ-ḫa iddi*(šub-*di*). *uḫḫu* 'spittle' is a loan from the Sum. *úḫ*, cf. *Diri* I. 117–23; it is also used for a waste product in metallurgy, cf. *Diri* VI. 82. The restoration *šuddû* is suggested because *nadû* is the verb normally used for spittle, sweat, and breast milk.

la'ābu, and the nouns *la'bu, li'bu*, is difficult. In *CH*, § 148 if a woman is afflicted with this complaint her husband is allowed to marry again, though he must support his first wife in a separate place. It seems then to be a lasting complaint of which there is no cure. See the passages quoted in G. R. Driver and J. C. Miles, *The Babylonian Laws* II, p. 227.

67. For *pitru* in a similar context see *KAR* 80 rev. 27 = E. Ebeling, *MVAG* 23/1. 30: *pit-ri-ia*$_5$ *ú-tab-bi-ku.*

69. Cf. *CT* 17. 20. 70–71 and *CT* 17. 25. 36 = *KAR* 368. 8–9.

70. *būppānu* = *būn pāni*: *ZA* 42. 162. Cf. *LKA* 291, 1 S., 6: *bu-up-pa-ni-ia ta-bu-uk-an-*[*ni*].

71. This line seems to contain a variant on the stock cliché túg.gin$_7$ ba.an.dul = *ki-ma ṣu-ba-ti ik-tum*. Cf. *Tukulti-Ninurta Epic* III (IV), 24: *'-ur-ti šarri dan-ni ki-ma a-le-e zu-mur-šu ik-si*.

73–74. These lines have interesting literary connexions. Their substance appears first in a Sumerian incantation, which later turns up in bilingual form (see Falkenstein, *LSS* N.F. I. 52):

igi.ni bad.bad lú igi.nu.un.bar.ri
i-na-a-šú pi-ta-ma man-ma ul ip-pal-la-as
geštu^{II}.ga.ni ×. dè lú.a.šè* nu.tuk.tuk
uz-na-a-[*šú* . . .] *man-ma ul i-šim-me*
[* So K 3705 (collated).]

Later the phrase appears in Jeremiah (v. 21), whence it is quoted in the New Testament.

77–78 are identical with *PBS* I/I. 14 obv. 10–11:

mun-ga iṣ-ṣa-bat i-di-ia$_5$
lu-'-ti im-ta-qut eli [*bi*]*r-ki-ia*$_5$

Thus *iṣ-ṣa-*[*bat*] of **i** is vindicated against *iṣ-bat* of C. Derivatives of *magāgu*/*maqāqu* are often used with *idu*; e.g. *BBSt*, p. 36. 45: *qat-su lim-gu-ug*.

79. *na-mu-ši-šá*: cf. Bauer, *Das Inschriftenwerk Assurbanipals* II, p. 1, note on II. 21, and *CT* 41. 46 obv. 13: du.du.ur.ḫi = *na-mu-ši-šu-um* (*MSL* IV. 124) (*CT* 19. 45, K 264 obv. 6–7 is similar).

80. *nuppuqu*: cf. von Soden, *Or* N.S. 20. 165–6, to which must now be added Labat, *TDP* 228. 92–94; 230. 118–19; also perhaps *DP* 14, p. 50. II. 5: *i-na-paq* belongs here. Is the verb perhaps connected with *ni-ip-*KU (*TDP* 84. 34), an unidentified part of the throat?
ma-aq-t[*i-i*]*š*: in *Šurpu* IV. 73–74 *maqtu* parallels *marṣu*, *kasû*, and *ṣabtu*.

81. Cf. *LKA* 63 rev. 21: *me-lam-mu iq-du-tu bu-ni-šu-nu e-tar-mu*; and *BiOr* 11. 82, II. 5–6: *pa-ni-šu li-iḫ-ri-im* (OB. incantation).

83. *ra-man ul i-ši*: similar phrases are:

kimu nu.mu.un.dib	ní.mu nu.mu.uš.tuku.mèn
ṭè-e-me ul ṣab-ta-ku	*ra-ma-ni ul ḫa-sa-ku* (IV R^2 19b. 47–48)

K 225. 157: *ṭè-em-šú ul ḫa-sis ma-ši ra-ma*[*n-šú*].

85. *si-kir* (v. *sa-ki-ir*) is best taken as infinitive: *sekēr* "the blocking of".

86. *bābu* and *mašqû* are presumably poetic words for the mouth. Cf. *Fable of Fox* C rev. 6, where *abullu* is used for the gullet of the fox; and F. Thureau-Dangin, *Rit. acc.*, p. 56. 93, where *bābu* is used for the mouth of a jar.

87. The variant of **h** *ru-*[is the Assyrian form of *ur'udu*, *ru'tu*. Cf. *ZA* 33. 18. 7, and Landsberger, *Fauna*, p. 99, where the dropping of an initial *a* in Assyrian tablets is documented.

88. *šumma* is taken as II/1 stative of *šâmu* 'fix'; cf. 28.
daddariš: this simile is used also in *ZA* 4. 254. 6; *ZA* 5. 80. 10: kaš.tin.nam (for this writing cf. L. F. Hartman and A. L. Oppenheim, *Beer*, p. 41[27]) *šá nab-la-ṭí a-na da-da-ri bit-nu-u*; and *RB* 59. 242 ff., 29: *i-wi da-da-ar-šu* (*-šu* = *-šum*, cf. *GAG*, § 67 g, *Or* N.S. 26. 317).

89. The *šá nab-la-ṭí* cited in the last note could be taken as evidence for reading *nab-laṭ* here, in *Theodicy* 32, and in *KAR* 256 obv. 6: [*na*]*p-*KUR *nišī*^{meš}. However, *nap-šat* is shown to be better by:

CH 27 rev. 11–12: ^{d}*ašnan na-pi-iš-ti ni-ši*
Fable of Fox C obv. 21: *mê*^{meš} *nap-ša-at nišī*^{meš}
Sumer III. 11, 10: *a-na ša-di-im na-pí-iš-tì ni-ši*

and by the phrase *napišti māti* (e.g. *Šamaš Hymn* 18).

90. Cf. *ZA* 45. 208. 20: *si-li-'-ta-šu ú-ta-ar-ri-ik-ma*.

91. Cf. *LKA* 28. 6: *pa-nu-u-a it-tak-ru.*

93. For *esēqu* see G. R. Driver and J. C. Miles, *The Babylonian Laws* II, p. 263[1]. Strictly *armat*, not *ārimat*, is required for the translation adopted.

94. On *šir'ānu* see J. V. Kinnier Wilson, *Iraq* 18. 140–1. Note also that there is evidence that the ideogram for *šir'ānu* (sa) also stands for *damu* (BM 56607 (Bilingual Proverbs) note on B 16–18).

ú-riq-ta appears to be a *hapax legomenon.* Though it could be a part of the body (cf. *KAR* 154 rev. 4: *a-ri-ik-ta ša* ú[r?), which would require a restoration *maḫ-*[*ṣa-at*], more probably it is the name of a complaint, and this allows the restoration *maḫ-*[*rat*] or *maḫ-*[*ru*], which suit the space better.

95. Cf. K 2599+3069, I. 15: [*mar?-ṣ*]*a?-ku ina* [giš]*erši šá* ⌜*ši*⌝*-ig-ge-e ú-qat-ta* u_4*-me.*

For the use of *aḫāzu* cf. *Theodicy* 137 and *VAB* VII. 24. 1–2, &c.: *e-ḫu-uz mar-qí-tú.*

97. Cf. Labat, *TDP* 152. 52: *ubānāt*[meš] *qātē*[II]*-šú u šēpē*[II]*-šú am-šá ina-da-a-ma.*

98. The medical texts commonly use *maqātu* in the I/1, I/2, and II/1 with reference to a large variety of parts of the body without it being apparent which complaint is meant in terms of modern medical knowledge.

99–101. Similar passages are *BA* V. 639. 9–18 = *OECT* VI. 21–22, and K 4636. The *qinnazu*, *ziqtu*, of which *ziqatu* is a poetic form, and *ištuḫḫu* (for the reading see *JCS* I. 168[12] and *JNES* 9. 108) are all instruments for urging on a horse: A. Salonen, *Hippologica*, pp. 150–61. Cf. *Gilg.* VI. 54 and *Fable of the Riding-donkey*, rev. 3.

100. The variants *ma-la-ti* and *ma-lat* construe the obscure *ṣil-la-a-tum* as a singular; *ma-la-a* as a plural. It has been derived here from *ṣalû* = Arabic *ṣalâ* 'wound in the back'.

The Commentary seems to be related to *Ḫarra* 11. 262 (with *Ḫargud*): kuš.[usàn] = *qin-na-zu* = *il-tuḫ-ḫu.*

101. Cf. K 2599+3069, I. 12: *ú-ni-iš irti*(gaba)*-ia ú-sa-ḫi-la mi-na-te-ia.*

104. Cf. Labat, *TDP* 124. 18: *rík-su-šú ir-mu-ú*, and the Commentary (Dougherty, *GCCI* II, no. 406. 7): *ri-ik-su-šú*: *šír-a-nu-šú*, and *KAR* 196 obv. II. 53: *meš-re-e-tu lip-te-ṭi-ra li-ir-mu-ú* sa.meš.

105. Cf. *CT* 3. 2. 14: *a-ḫi-ta na-an-di-i-ma.*

106–7. Cf. IV *R*[2] 22, no. 2. 16–20: gud.gin$_7$ kar.mud.d[a.na] e.da.šub
ki-ma al-pi [*ina*] *i-di-ib-ti-šú na-di-ma*
udu.gin$_7$ murgu.ba ⌜e.da⌝.lú.lú
ki-ma im-me-ri ina [*ta-ba-áš*]*-ta-ni-šu bu-lul-ma*

107. Cf. *OB.Lú*, Part 7. 5: lú.lum.ba.ná.a = *ša* ⌜*i*⌝*-na ta-ba-aš-ta-ni-*⌜*šu*⌝ *bu-ul-lu-lu* (*SLT* I. I. 5); *BA* X. 108. 3.

The Commentary also appears in T. G. Pinches, J. N. Strassmaier, and A. J. Sachs, *Late Babylonian Astronomical and Related Texts*, no. 1577 rev. IV. 13: *ta-bar-ta-ni* = *ze-e ù* kàš.

108–11. This is no literary fiction; an actual case occurs in the letter *ABL* 391 obv. 7–12: *ka-a-a-ma-nu šarru be-lí i-qab-bi-ia ma-a a-ta-a ši-ki-in murṣi-ia an-ni-ia-u la ta-mar bul-ṭe-e-šú la te-pa-áš ina pa-ni-ti ina pa-an šarri aq-ṭi-bi sakīkē*(sa.gig*-ke-e*)*-šú la ú-šá-aḫ-ki-me* "The king my lord keeps on saying, "Why do you not grasp the nature of this my complaint and cure it?" Previously I spoke before the king but he did not inform me of his complaints."

For the meaning of *sakīkū* see J. V. Kinnier Wilson, *Iraq* 18. 140–1.

114–16. Cf. K 225. 146–7: *làl-la-ru-šú dím-ta-šu i-ṣip-*[*šú*]
ana nu-bé-e-šú mar-ṣu-ti ip-ḫu-ra sa-lat-[*su*]
"His hired mourner doubled the tears for him,
His family assembled for the bitter lamentation."

This is another case of a sick man's funeral rites being carried out in anticipation of his death.

114. For *ersû* (a quadriliteral) *see CAD* sub voce. This new verb shows that *šukānū* (also *TCL* 3. 391 and *AKA* 247. 30) are precious things put in the grave.

119–20. These lines are a crux. The last word of 119 can be either *kim-ti-ia* or *dím-ti-ia*. Since *gimru* can only have the meaning 'all' the former is better, and as a parallel to *mūdû* 'friends' in 120. This word can also be 'scholars', but it is 'friend' in I. 91. The *šá* in 119 can only be expressive of the genitive, but that in 120, because of the preposition before *mūdê*, must go with the verb. *ina qirib/qirbi* would have been more usual, but *ša qirib* as a preposition is not possible. The writer may have written *qirbu(m)* as a locative. In the group AN.UD-*su-un* the suffix demands an antecedent, and this can only be *mūdê*. Thus ᵈ*šamas-su-un* is demanded against *ilu-ut-su-un*, since one cannot speak of the divinity of his friends. The form *šamas-su-un* may seem strange, but that is only because it is most unusual to find a third person suffix on *šamšu*. Grammatically no exception can be taken to it. As to the meaning, in this poem the monolatry of Marduk is so strong that it may be assumed that he was meant by "their Sun". The verb may be *i-kil* (is dark), *i-rim* (covered or had mercy), *i-qìr* (is precious), or *i-ḫap* (purifies). Two considerations make for *i-rim*. One is that metre requires a trochee at the end. The other is that the *šá* at the beginning requires a subjunctive. The sign KIL is only preserved on two manuscripts, Bi, and it must be one of many examples in the manuscripts of *Ludlul* where the endings of verbs are not written. Thus there is only a choice between *i-ḫap* and *i-rim* (have mercy). In the translation it is assumed that the writer put *irimmu*.

B. Landsberger suggests, orally, the readings *i-ṭi* and *i-kil*: "The day of all my family is darkened." This raises a factual difficulty that in the rest of the poem the family gloat over the sufferer and do not share his grief. Grammatically line 120 is difficult because the verb should be subjunctive *íkilu*, which is not a trochee. The idea is supported, however, by the Sumerian 'Poem of the Righteous Sufferer' (*Vetus Testamentum, Supplements* III. 170 ff.) 68:

dingir.mu kalam.e u_4 ba.zalag mà.ar u_4 ma.ku_{10}.ku_{10}
"My god, the day shines bright over the land, for me the day is black."

TABLET III

1. The comment also occurs twice in the Commentary on *Šumma izbu* (71, 175).

3, 4. Cf. R. Borger, *Asarhaddon*, p. 97. 12–13: *šarru šá tal-lak-ta-šú a-bu-bu-um-ma ep-še-ta-šú* [*la*]*b-bu na-ad-ru*.

6. For *rpd* of mental wandering cf. *Theodicy* 212. In omens *ú-rap-pad* is said of the result of a complaint (e.g. *CT* 37. 40. 23, "It makes him wander"), and there is a disease *rapādu* (e.g. *ASKT*, p. 83. 20), perhaps a fever which brings delirium.

7. Cf. *VAB* VII. 252. 12: *ur-ra u mūša*(ge_6) *a-na-as-su-us*.

8. *munattu* (from the root *nwm*) is the early-morning period of light sleep and waking, as in *Era* V. 43. Cf. *Malku-šarru* VI. 208–10:

	mu-na-ma-tu	= *mu-na-at-tum*
	[*š*]*e-ep* u_4*-me*	= ,,
	[*š*]*e-ep* u_4*-me a-lik-tú*	= ,,
Also *Erim.ḫuš* II. 261–3:	[máš].ge_6	= *šu-ut-tum*
	×.li	= *ḫi-il-tum*
	×.UD.ra	= *mu-na-at-tum*

Also in *CT* 23. 20. 22 note *ina šutti*(máš.ge_6) *u mu-na-at-ti*. A. L. Oppenheim (*Dreams*, p. 225) thinks of some kind of dream for *munattu*, but in all the passages where the meaning is plain 'waking time' is clearly correct. In the *Era Epic* it is the time when the author speaks what he had seen in the vision. In our passage *šuttu munattu* parallels *urra u mūšu* in 7.

15. Cf. 26, 42. The phrase *MN išpuranni* is the standard formula with which messengers and representatives announce their senders, and one borrowed from Sumerian. Cf. *Enmerkar and the Lord of Aratta* (ed. S. N. Kramer) 177, 379, 516; it occurs in many Sumerian or bilingual incantations, see *LSS* N.F. I. 25.

In Akkadian two most interesting examples occur in the Mari letters (*TCL* 23. 90. 19; *TCL* 24. 40. 13), which show that this was no mere literary convention.

21, 22. Restored from 29, 30 and *Gilg.* I. v. 26: *šuttu*(máš.ge$_6$) *aṭ-ṭu-la mu-ši-ti-ia.*

25. làl-úr-alim-ma occurs again with the same explanation in BM 32574 rev. 2–3 (King, *STC* I. 217):

làl! : *ṭa-a-bi* : úr : *uṭ!-lum* : a[lim . . .
mu-ṣu-ú šá-niš nippuru^{ki} : *šul-mu* × [. . .

Both by King and Poebel (*PBS* IV, p. 42[1]) the second line was read *šá šar*(MAN), thus making the figure "offspring of the king of Nippur". This, however, is not probable since it requires an unexpected value of MAN for a Late Babylonian tablet, while *šá-niš* is a frequently met word in this tablet and others of the category. No doubt the connexion with Nippur was established by some play on the values of signs. Elsewhere this name occurs in the list of Cassite-period names, with the same interpretation, in V *R* 44, II and III (see the discussion on this list by Lambert, *JCS* 11. 5–7). Twice the name occurs in Cassite administrative texts (*BE* 15. 44. 10 and 168. 12—Stamm, *MVAG* 44. 236). In these latter three instances there are no grounds for connecting the persons with the figure of *Ludlul.* There have been suggestions to restore the name in a manuscript of the *Sumerian King List* (*AS* 11. 72[17]) as an antediluvian king of Larsa, but against this must be urged that it seems to be no genuine Sumerian formation, but a Cassite invention after the pattern of such Akkadian names as *ṭāb-ṣilli-adad* (*MVAG* 44, § 32).

āšib nippuri was apparently an officer, since it appears in *Lú* = *amēlu* I. 134: lú.tuš.a.nibru^{ki} = *a-šib ni-ip-pu-ri* (*AS* I. 81. 61) placed between *šandabakku* and *guennaku.* (Reference provided by T. Jacobsen.)

26. See note on 15 above.

27, 28. Cf. *LKA* 102 rev. 3–4: ^{giš}*bi-nu ana mê*^{meš} *tanaddi*(šub) *ina tinūri*(nindu) *tesekker*(úš-er) *zumur*(su)-*šú tu-maš-šá-'.*

33. A. L. Oppenheim (*Dreams*, p. 189) proposes a restoration *i-taz-zi-iz*, but the form should be *ittaziz* (A. Poebel, *AS* 9. 80 and 83; von Soden, *ZA* 50. 165).

35. *lā tapallaḫ*: this common phrase is used to introduce supernatural messages again in *VAB* VII. 116. 47 and 346. 24; IV *R*^{2} 61. II. 16; Thureau-Dangin, *Rit. acc.* 144. 434.

39. *Nin-din-lug*$_x$*-ga* is a goddess attested in the Fara texts and onwards (Kraus, *JCS* 3. 70–73), and the name form Ur-^{d}xyz is a very common type of Sumerian name. There was, however, a person bearing the name *Ur-Nindinlugga* who lived in the vicinity of Nippur in the time of Adad-šum-iddina (King, *BBSt*, no. 3, pp. 7–18 *passim*), and the name is given in the Cassite-period name list V *R* 44, II and III (see the note on 25) with the interpretation ^{m}*amēl-*^{d}*gu-la* (II. 9). No great antiquity then is implied in it.

40. Since the sign TAR has the value *dar*$_x$, if at all, in Old Akkadian only (Gelb, *MAD* II, p. 67), 'bearded' must be *ṭarru*, not *darru*. Meissner's statement that *ṭ* is possible (*AS* I. 43) is an understatement.

42. Cf. note on 15 above.

43. The name Šubši-mešrê-Šakkan is both very rare itself, and there seem to be no examples of the type with other deities' names instead of Šakkan. Outside *Ludlul* the only other occurrence appears to be in K 9952, an historical epic(?) about Cassite times, and here the last element is broken, but what remains seems strongly in favour of Šakkan (Pl. 12).

Obv. 1 . . .] × ar [. . .
2 . . .] li 'a × [. . .
3 . . .] × *-ia ina nārî*(zá.na.rú.a) [. . .
4 . . .] × *-ka tu-kil* × [. . .
5 . . .] × *-ka urû*(šeš.unug-*ú*) *arad ēkalli iš-riq* [. . .
6 . . .] *i-pu-šu im-me-du* × [. . .
7 . . .]*-šú iš-ta-ra-an* × [. . .
8 . . .] ⌜*i*⌝*-du-ú i-bar-ru-ú lìb-b*[*i* . . .
9 . . .] ad *maš-maš šarri ip-*[. . .

10 . . . *i*]*t-ti* ^{d}*nir*-× [. . .
Rev. 1 . . .] × × × *mār* ^{m}*šá-g*[*a-rak-ti*- . . .
2 . . .] *maḫ-ri i-pi-qí-id* [. . .
3 . . .] × × *ga-du qin-ni-šú* [. . .
4 . . .] × *gi-mir-tú* × × [. . .
5 . . .]-*la-ka pa-qir-a-nu i*-× [. . .
6 . . . *ú*]-*bi-lu-nim-ma še-re-e-ti in*-[. . .
7 . . .]-⌈*bur*⌉-*ia-áš ana* ^{m}*ki-lam-du*-^{d}*marduk ki-i* × [. . .
8 . . .] ×-*ni ul ad-bu-u*[*b* . . .
9 . . .] × *ba-ni-ka* ^{m}*šub-ši-maš-ru-ú*-^{d}*ša*[*kkan* . . .
10 . . .] *it-ta-na-áš-šú* nu t[e? . . .
11 . . .] × nu *i-te-ez* × [. . .
12 . . . *it-t*]*a-ṣu-u be-lí a-ma-ti-ia* × [. . .
13 . . .] × ⌈*ke*⌉-*e* × × [. . .

It is possible that this very Šubši-mašrû-Šakkan is the hero of *Ludlul*. Unfortunately the historical context of this fragment is too obscure to throw any light even on the exact time of the historical events. Thompson in the *editio princeps* (*PSBA* 32. 19) made the error of reading ^{d}gìr *Nergal*, and curiously this has never been corrected. In Akkadian at least ^{d}gìr—Sumuqan—is to be read *Šakkan*, cf. *PSBA* 20. 156. 5: *bu-ú-lu*$_4$ *ša-ak-ka-an*.

54. What appears as a variant in the Commentary in line 37 (*šūnuḫ*) is apparently the text of **p** in this parallel line.

Si 55 REVERSE

5–10. These lines take up Tablet II. 51–57.

13. *u'a a'a*, *per se* mere groans, are personified into demons of illness, as in *Maqlû* VII. 131 and *Šurpu* IV. 85.

14–15. Cf. *CT* 17. 26. 78–79:

sag.gig šèg.ge$_6$.gab.ba.gin$_7$ ḫa.ba.ra.an.zi.[zi]
mu-ru-uṣ qaq-qa-di šá ki-ma zu-un-ni mu-ši kit-mu-ru li-in-[*na-siḫ*]

Von Soden in *Or* N.S. 20. 266–7 argues for 'persistent' rather than 'causing pain' as the meaning of *lazzu*, since the root is also used of rain.

16. For *te'û* 'cover' cf. von Soden, *Or* N.S. 24. 140–3. A further passage is K 2599+3069. II. 6: *te-'a īnā*^{II}*-a-a ul ú*-[. For *šbḫ* see von Soden, loc. cit.

17. This is a variant of *nesû šār bēri*, which occurs frequently in incantations. The writing with IM is the commonest, and E. Ebeling (*Tod und Leben*, p. 142^{b}) correctly explains this as a play on ideograms for šár. Often IM 1 is written (*LKA* 110 rev. 2; *LKA* 125 rev. 4; *LKA* 127a rev. 5; *RA* 48. 84 rev. 9; *KAR* 55 obv. 20; J. Laessøe, *Bît Rimki*, p. 58. 86), which is to be read the same as IM alone. Once apparently IM 2 is found (*RA* 48. 182. 19: *šār* II *bēri*—transliteration only). The proper ideogram šár occurs in *OECT* VI, pl. VI obv. 12 (cf. p. 105), and K 11804. 7 (unpublished), where the sign form ( ) is distinguished from the ordinary ḪI ( ). This distinction between ḪI and šár in Late Assyrian script also occurs in the *Gilgameš Epic* (XI. 65–69).

18. The comment on this line is the same as that on I. 71 (see note there).

19. This *amīru* 'ear wax' is probably to be derived from *amāru*, *emēru* 'be full' (Labat, *TDP* 118^{213}).

22. For the IV stem of *lbb* see I. 86, *RA* 12. 74–75. 15–16, and S. Smith, *First Campaign* I. 25.

25. Cf. *OECT* VI. 54. 28–29: zabar.gin$_7$ níg.su.ub.ta ḫé.em.ta.su.ub
ki-ma qé-e ma-áš-ši lim-ta-ši-iš

The same simile, in almost identical words, also appears in *CT* 17. 23. 184–5 and *ASKT*, pp. 98–99. 54.

The second half is paralleled in *CT* 17. 23. 182–3:

kù.babbar.sig$_5$.gin$_7$ mu.sír.bi ḫu.um.ta.zalág

ki-ma ṣar-pi ṣur-ru-pi ru-uš-šu-šú lit-tan-biṭ

The sense of *ruššu* 'dirt' is established by Oppenheim in *Or* N.S. 19. 133, and other derivatives of the root *'rš* 'be dirty' are *aršu* and *urrušu* 'dirty'. The reading of the Sumerian is established by *Dimmer* = *dingir* = *ilu*, Tablet 3. 92: me.zé.er = mu.sír = *ur-ru-šum* (*MSL* IV. 35). A possible restoration of the end would be *uš-*[*tan-biṭ*].

27. suḫuš = *ir-di*! in *PBS* XII/1, no. 7 obv. 20–21 confirms *irdu* as a phonetic variant of *išdu*, which is to be compared with *irdudu*, a variant of *išdudu* (*GAG*, § 30 j).

28. *šutābulu* appears to be an ellipsis for *šutābulu amāti.*

29. The root *ṭpš* to my knowledge occurs again only thrice, in the phrase quoted on line 100 of Tablet IV(?), II *R* 60. I. II. 14, and II *R* 47. 18. A verb *ḫadādu* occurs only in the present in omens *iḫaddud*. There is a little uncertainty about the reading *iḫdad*, and the different stem vowel is a further difficulty, but the meaning of *ḫdd* "roar, rumble, chatter" (*CAD*, sub voce) suits this context very well.

30. See note on II. 80 for *nuppuqu. lagabbu* appears to be a *hapax legomenon* in literature, though it is attested in lists as a loan from the Sum. lagab 'block'.

31. The syntax of this and the preceding line is clear: there are two main verbs connected by *-ma. ur'udu*, qualified by a relative clause, is the object of the first, and the object of the second is expressed by the feminine suffix on the verb. The smoothest and most natural construction is to assume the same subject for both verbs (i.e. Marduk), and also the same object; this then makes *irātuša* a second object of the final verb. The similar line in *ASKT*, p. 122 = *OECT* VI, pl. XIX obv. 15–16:

gaba.a.ni gi.gíd i.lu.zé.eb.bi.da.gin$_7$ ér

ina ir-ti-šú šá ki-ma ma-li-li qú-bi-i i-ḫal-lu-lu$_4$

suggests that the final verb is *ḫll*, and this is once used in the II stem causatively (*CAD*, sub voce), by which our passage would read *uḫ-tal-lil-šá*. The traces, however, are not in favour of this. In other respects this passage is only superficially similar. The simile of the flute is not surprising as medical texts refer to the wind-pipe, or some part of it, as 'the flute of the lungs' (gi.gíd *ḫa-še-šú*/ḫar.meš-*šú*: *KAR* 199. 14 and *AMT* 2. 7. 8, &c.). *irātu* are a special kind of songs (*JRAS* 1921, 183; Ebeling, *BBK* I/3. 6).

32. *mal'ātu* (*ma'latu*) is discussed by von Soden in *Or* N.S. 24. 139–40. *ūtappiqa* is derived from *epēqu* and *šāru* is restored from the similar phrase *KAR* 151 obv. 39: *up-pu-uq-ma* IM *là imaḫḫar*(igi-*ḫar*).

33. *lagā'u* occurs also in: *ASKT*, p. 122 = *OECT* VI, pl. XIX obv. 11–12:

šu.um.du.um si.kúr.e šub.ba.a.ta ér

ina šap-ti-šú šá la-ga-a na-da-a

R. Labat, *TDP* 64. 54′: *šumma liq pî-šú šá-bu-ul la-ga-a* šub.šub

MSL I. 88. 24: ḪAR.in.nu.bi = *la-ga-šu*

Ḫarra 10. 355: la.ga.gir$_4$ = *la-ga ki-i-ri*

In his unpublished commentary to *Ḫarra*, Landsberger interprets the last reference as 'slag of the furnace', comparing the Commentary *la-ga-ú* = *ši-iK-tum* with *ši-iK-tu* in a metallurgical context in *ZA* 36. 190. 11. This suggests 'blisters' for the first two passages, and some similar swelling for the example under consideration.

a. Cf. *Ḫargud* D (to *Ḫarra* 15) 58: [uzu].šà.maḫ = šU-*ḫu* = *ir-ru kab-ru*. For *arû* 'defecate', 'vomit(?)' cf. Küchler, *AB* 18. 108. The comment on this line is a repetition of that on II. 44.

c. *ir-na-ma*: the explanation of the commentator comes from *Syl.* B, I. 124 (*MSL* III. 106) or a related source (cf. *Ḫarra* 3. 493): [e.ri.in] $^{\text{muš}}_{\text{muš}}$a.na = *šur-šu*. The final *e-ri-na-ti* is obscure. While it is not inconceivable that the "root" of the neck could be spoken of, there is a much better alternative, which is in addition attested in other Akkadian texts.

Cf. *Erim.ḫuš* II. 47–49:

[giš].az.lá = *ši-ga-ru šá kal-bi*
[giš].az.gú = *ši-ga-ru šá ki-šá-di*
[giš].az.bal.lá.e = *e-ri-in-nu* (*CT* 18. 44. I. 47–49)

Ḫarra VI:
196 giš.az.bal = *na-ba-ru* [= *na-bar-tum šá nēši—Ḫargud*]
198 giš.az.lá = „
201 giš.az.bal = *ši-ga-ru*
203 giš.az.bal = *e-ri-in-nu*
204 giš.ma.nu = „
204a giš.KA.dù = „
205 giš.ma.nu = *ši-ga-ru*

Lú = amēlu IV: 197 lú.éš.lá = *šá e-ri-na lab-šu* (*MAOG* XIII/2. 46. 14)

I *R* 43. 34–35: *e-ri-in-nu bi-ri-tu id-du-šu-ma* (= *OIP* II. 87–88)

Now it is known that *šigaru* in these passages is 'neck stock' (see E. I. Gordon, *Sumer* XII. 80–84) it is clear that *erinnu* is some similar object put on the neck of wild animals and captives. The quotation from *Lú = amēlu* suggests that it may have been an article of dress also, and this is the best explanation of *ir-na-ma*.

d. Cf. Strassmaier, *Nabonidus* 441. 5–6: *gušūrū a-ma-lu-tum pi-ti-nu-tu*, and *VS* 5. 11. 9–10: *ḫu-ṣa-bi a-ma-lu*-KI!. Also, as suggested by von Soden in *Or* N.S. 25. 245, *a-b/ma-lu* explaining *kinnû* in *Theodicy* Commentary, 58, may be connected. This raises doubts as to whether *amalu* is a particular kind of tree, as might be deduced from the Commentary, since in the lists giš.ù.ku = *ašūḫu* (a variety of cedar). Perhaps it means 'straight' or 'straight beam'. The comment on *kinnû* also appears in *Malku-šarru* VIII. 22; cf. *CAD*, sub voce *ginnû*.

e. Cf. *Hymn to Ninurta* rev. 6–7 (p. 120) and note.

f. This is an extremely difficult line, and the explanation attempted is only tentative. The first half is paralleled in *ZA* 4. 258. 12–13 (collated):

ki-i na-ak-mi šu-ṣu-ú lu-šèr ⌜*a*⌝-[*na* . . .]
ki-i RI.RI-*ti lut*!-*tag*!-*giš*! *i-na k*[*a-ma-a-ti*]

This couplet perhaps means that the writer wishes to forsake society and wander like a person suffering from an incurable contagious disease. RI.RI-*ti* is perhaps to be read *miqti* or *miqitti*.

The comment, that *šūṣû* is one whom Ištar has taken out "to fire", perhaps implies one whose skin is inflamed, and since Ištar is the cause one could imagine a venereal disease. The same complaint may be indicated in *OB.Lú* Tablet A 234: lú.izi.da.gur.ra = *ša iš-tu i-ša-*[*tim*] *i-*[*tu-ra-am*], see *AfO* 18. 69. *nakmu* and *nakimtu* are certainly diseases in IV R^2 28*, no. 3 obv. 11 = E. Ebeling, *MVAG* 23/2. 22. 50: *li-še-ṣi nak-ma u na-kim-ti ša zumri-ia* (is *AMT* 107. 2. 18 *muruṣ na-kam-ti* related?). Two lexical sections deal with it:

Nabnītu 22. 174–9:

gi_4 = *na-ka-mu*
KA.nig.dug_4.ga = „
lú.giš.ga.KA.SAR = *na-ak-mu*
níg.lú.úr = „
níg.lú.úr.sù.ud = „
á.kum = *na-ki-im-tum* (*CT* 12. 48. III. 6–11)

OB.Lú Tablet A 27–28:

lú.giš.gi.sag.kéš = *na-ak-*⌜*mu*⌝
[SAL].lú.giš.gi.sag.kéš = *na-*gi_4*-im-tu*[*m*]

The last passage shows that *nakmu* can also be the person suffering, and *na-*gi_4*-im-tu*[*m*] raises doubts whether the root is *nkm*, and not *ng/qm*. A further related lexical passage is *OB.Lú* Tablet B v. 25–27:

lú.umbin.na = *na-di-il-la-nu-um*
lú.umbin.na = *mu-na-ak-ki-mu-um*
lú.umbin.na = *mu-su-uk-ka-nu-um*

The last entry here is no doubt derived from *(m)usukku* = ú.zug "a person who is sexually unclean, who is dangerous to the community because he is under a sexual taboo" (T. Jacobsen, *JNES* 5. 132[9]). The II form of *munakkimum* may be taken causatively, 'one who spreads . . .'. A word which may be related, though it is very obscure, is *ni/ne-ki-im-tum* in OB. omen texts (*YOS* x, no. 6. 3–4; no. 20. 7; no. 36. I. 43 and II. 11, 14, 22, 35, 39; *CT* 5. 4. 23–24; *CT* 3. 2. 12 = *LSS* 1/1. 42 and 50 'bubble'? in the last two passages).

The interpretation of this material can best begin with the second half of the line, where there is either a cognate accusative, or more probably a denominative verb, since these are commonly in the II form (*GAG*, § 88 g). This *ṣuppuru* (see note on *Ludlul* I. 81) may be a *hapax legomenon* in Akkadian (cf., however, *Fable of the Fox* G, Col. A 6), but the juxtaposition with *ṣu-pur-a-a* and the Arabic *ẓafara* 'scratch someone with the finger-nails' leave little doubt that the meaning is 'scratch'. This connects with the Sumerian equivalent of *munakkimum* 'man of the finger-nail', and there is evidence elsewhere that a certain skin complaint was connected with scratching, as though the finger-nails had caused it: sa.umbin.ag.ag = *ri-šu-tum* 'rash, inflammation' (*Antagal* E d 6; cf. A. Goetze, *JCS* 9. 12, and von Soden, *Or* N.S. 25. 148). Again this connects with the definition of *šūṣû*.

h. The commentalso appears in *Ḫargud* B_4. 263: [bu]ru$_5$.us^{mušen} = *bu-ṣu* = *iṣ-ṣur ḫur-ri*, and the bird had presumably an ungainly walk. Landsberger (*Fauna*, p. 79) believes that the comment is unreliable and prefers *būṣu* 'hyena'. The restoration is based on K 9917 rev. III. 4: *šá in-ni-ib-ṭa bir-ka-*[*a-šú* . . . (to be published in "Hymns to Marduk in Paragraphs", no. 2).

j. Elsewhere *mammû* is apparently 'ice' (*ZA* 42. 159), but here the commentator's *šuḫtu* 'verdigris, rust(?)' (*Or* N.S. 22. 209) must be approximately correct. *ru-šu-uš* is best taken as 'dirt' as in line 25 above, though the commentator regarded it as *ruššu* 'shining'.

k. The same comment is made on I. 47.

l. It is uncertain whether this line is to be taken literally or not. The following line m reads more like poetic imagery. So far as we know the sufferer had not actually been made a slave.

m. *muttutu* appears to be a variant form of *muttatu*. For *abbuttu* see Szlechter, *ArOr* 17/2. 402–6, and G. R. Driver and J. C. Miles, *The Babylonian Laws* II, pp. 226–7.

o. Kunuš-kadru ("Bow, fierce one!") was a processional street in Babylon, and Landsberger first noted its occurrence here (*MAOG* IV. 299[4]). The references to it are collected by Unger in his *Babylon*, p. 109, and *RLA* I. 358. The comment on it occurs also in one of the texts dealing with the topography of Babylon (Unger, *Babylon*, p. 235. 15 = Taf. 45).

p. For the idiom *ina qāti amāru* see R. Borger, *Asarhaddon*, p. 103. 19, and *AfO* 18. 118; and E. Reiner, *JNES* 15. 149. 51′.

r. *aspu* and *assukku* have been identified by B. Landsberger as 'sling' and 'slingstone'. Cf. Commentary on *Šumma izbu* 264–6:

as-suk-k[*u*] = *a-bat-ti as-pu*
as-suk-k[*u*] = [× *-u*]*z-qu*
as-suk-ku = [*kir*]*-ban-nu* (cf. *CT* 31. 39. 29)

aspu occurs again in *Ḫarra* 11. 108 as the equivalent of kuš.dal.til, and *assukku* in *Ḫarra* 10. 504: [im].dugud = *as-suk-ku* (= *kir-ba-nu*—*Ḫargud*). See *AfO* 18. 378–9.

TABLET IV(?)

10. See note on II. 5 for the more common idiom of *rēša šuqqû* 'pay attention'. Here, and in *JRAS* 1929, 764. 2: *di-im-tu tum*$_4$*-tal-an-ni rēšī*^{meš}*-ia šu-uq-qí*, it signifies the lifting of a head bowed in grief (cf. *Theodicy* 293). A similar passage is *AMT* 52. 1. 13: *mu-še-qa-at ri-ši-šú*.

Though grammatically subject of both verbs in the sentence, Marduk is placed at the beginning of the second clause to avoid saying plainly that he was responsible for all the ills. In the two following sentences, which speak of the recovery, the subject, Marduk, is placed in the most emphatic position, as last word, and in the first of them *mḫṣ* is twice used to emphasize that the smiting was actually done by others, or by Marduk on the sufferer's behalf.

25. Cf. *VAB* IV. 154. 48: *aš-na-an ru-uš-šá-a.*

27. For *q!erētu* see note on K 9050+ (Bilingual Proverbs).

31, 32. These lines stress the surprising recovery from the hopeless state. Either they say, "Who could have imagined that this man would recover?" or more probably, "What man in such a state would expect to recover?" For *amār šamšišu* see 89 below and II. 120, and perhaps line o above should be compared for *etēq sūqi.*

40. Cf. *Theodicy* 277. The variant *ik-ri-iṣ-ṣu* is probably a simple error under the influence of the following word.

41. *šakittu napšatu* is taken as a variant of *šiknat napišti*; cf. *CH* 27r. 18: *ša-ak-na-at na-pí-iš-tim.*

42. Cf. K 225, 227 for *dulla.*

43. Cf. E. Ebeling, *Handerhebung* 60. 10 *ša pa-a šak-nu*, with the variant of K 6179+82-5-22, 496: *šu-ut pa-a šak-nu.*

48. For *siḫpu* see the note on *Šamaš Hymn* 5.

78–90. Of the eleven Esagil gates mentioned, eight are known from other passages (the material is collected by Unger in his *Babylon*, chs. 16 and 19, and in *RLA* I. 357–8; some comments are added by Weissbach in *ZA* 41. 260–2), but the nam.ti.la, ka.tar.ra, and a.še.er.du$_8$.ù.da appear only in this context. There can be no question that the names are to be read as Sumerian, as in *VAB* IV. 124. 51 ká ḫi.li.sù is interpreted as *bāb ku-uz-bu.* The variant of this, ḫi.li.gar (**u**), has no support elsewhere. The sù does not make any important difference to the meaning, as in *Nabnītu* R, 208–9 ḫi.li and ḫ[i.li].sù = *ra-a-šu.* The gate in 80 is also written ^{d}lamma.a.ra.bi and ^{d}lamma.ar.r[a.bi], but the second element remains obscure (*ZA* 41. 297).

90. Kissing the feet of a deity is commonly attested (e.g. *MVAG* 44. 55. 13; *OECT* VI, p. 42. 7–8; *KB* VI/2. 108. 11; *RA* 18. 31 rev. 8; *ZA* 43. 17. 54; IV *R*^{2} 55, no. 2 rev. 3). The most interesting examples are from the Mari letters, where Kibri-Dagan in Terqa twice urges his master to come to Terqa to kiss the foot of Dagan (*ARM* III. 8. 26 and 17. 16), and once alludes to instructions he has received about this rite (ibid. 41. 7).

92. Cf. R. Borger, *Asarhaddon*, p. 5. VII. 4: *ṣe-li qut-rin-nu.*

93. *etandu* is Assyrian for *itmudu*, see *Bab* 7. 233[2] (von Soden).

94. *sap-di* seems to be otherwise unknown, and is probably corrupt. A similar sounding word is *šapṣu* 'fattened sheep' (*Ḫarra* 13. 75, *JNES* 4. 160), but the otherwise identical line R. Borger, *Asarhaddon*, p. 5. VI. 37–39, has *as-li.*

96. The an.gub.ba.meš are well attested as astronomical phenomena (*RA* 16. 155; *RLA* I. 108; *ŠL* IV/2, p. 9), but they also existed on earth. In the line under consideration it is not clear if they are another name of the *šēdu* and *lamassu*, or distinct minor deities. The Akkadian reading is certainly *angubbû*, cf. the OB. ritual from Mari: ^{d}*la-ta-ra-ak ù ilānu*^{meš} *an-gu-ub-bu-ú uš-ša-bu* (*RA* 35. 5. II. 2–3). Cf. also R. Borger, *Asarhaddon*, p. 90, § 59. 14: [^{l}]^{ú}*pa-ši-ši an-gub-bé-e na-ṣir pi-riš-ti* "the *pašīšus* of the *angubbû* spirits who keep secrets", where it is the *angubbê* and not the priests who keep the secrets. See H. Winckler, *Die Keilschrifttexte Sargons*, Atlas pl. 24 no. 50. 13 (edited by A. G. Lie, p. 76), restored by and correcting ibid., pl. 36 no. 76. 2: . . . (certain priests) *la-med pi-riš-ti* an.gub.ba!.meš "who learn the secrets of the *angubbû*". In *VAB* VII. 268. 27 (cf. ibid. 414): [^{lú}*pa*]-*ši-šu* LÚ an.gub.ba.meš, the LÚ may

be either *amēl* ("the man/men of the *angubbû*"), or perhaps an error. The *angubbû* were certainly not human. *KAR* 142 obv. II. 21–24 preserves four of the names of the 7 an.gub.ba.meš *šá* é × [. . .: ^{d}*qu-du-mu*, ^{d}nar, ^{d}sig$_7$.sig$_7$, ^{d}kala.ga.dib.ba. Other names are collected by Tallqvist, *SO* VII. 24–25.

98. Restored after *PBS* XII/1, pl. VI. 6–7: níg.kú.šár.šár.ra.bi = *ina ma-ka-le-e du-uš-šú-tú*, and *CH* 3. 33–34: *mu-de-eš-ši ma-ka-li el-lu-tim.*

99. Restored after *VAB* IV. 258. 13: *sip-pu ši-ga-ri me-di-lu u* ^{giš}*dalāti*^{meš} *ì-gu-la-a ú-ṭah-hi-id-ma.*

100. For the dialectical form *ḫimātu* see *CAD*, sub voce *ḫimētu*. The use of grain in these dedications is also attested in King, *BBSt*, p. 124. 33–34: *ina* làl geštin *u masḫata*(zì.mad.gá) *ú-ṭaḫ-ḫi-da* giš.si.gar.meš; cf. also IV R^2 54. 54a: *ṭu-pu-uš áš-na-an.*

COLOPHON OF i

2. giš stands here for *šaṭir*, and occurs elsewhere in colophons for different derivatives of the root *šṭr* (*SBH*, pp. xi–xiii; *Anatolian Studies* IV. 98). Its use is difficult to explain. Perhaps it was connected with sar = *šaṭāru* through the common value mu: giš = mu$_9$, sar = mú.

3. See note on *Theodicy* 72 for *ligimû* 'son'.

9. = *tākil-ka ul ibâš* ^{d}*tutu*, cf. *ZA* 36. 204. 26.

Chapter 3. *Theodicy*

1. The probable reading *āšiš* is participle of *ašāšu, ešēšu*. There are four roots 'šš in Akkadian: (i) 'lay foundations', (ii) 'experience distress', (iii) 'rage' (of a storm), and (iv) 'catch (in a net)'. The third occurs in *abūbu āšišu* (K 5983: C. Bezold, *Catalogue*, p. 753; *AOTU* I. 316, 349; *OECT* VI, pl. XXI; *TCL* 15. XLVII. 16 = C. Frank, *Kultlieder*, p. 43; *SBH*, no. 34. 7–8) and in *a-šá-šú* = *ra-'-i-bu* (*LTBA* II. 2. 271). The verb 'catch' occurs both in literature (*Sayings* IV. 25; *KAR* 375 obv. II. 15–16; *SBH*, p. 130. 22–23), and in lexical texts (*Nabnītu* Tablet J 137: [. . .] = *a-šá-šu ša* mušen; *Erim.ḫuš* II. 117: [ù]r.ri = *e-še-šum* (*CT* 18. 43. II. 36); *Erim.ḫuš* III. 157: [. . .] = *a-šá-šú šá ḫa-ṭa-me*; VAT 8573. 1 = *Ḫarra* 18 (Pl. 73): á.mušen AŠ.ur$_4$.ri = [*e-še*]-*šu*). The same word also has the more general sense of the Sumerian ur$_4$ 'gather, collect', as seen in the comment on 200, and in *ZA* 4. 252. I. 10 and 12: *a-ši-ši šu-ka-a-mu* "(Nābû), the acquirer of learning". In the passage under discussion *āšiš* apparently has a meaning derived from this last usage: 'scholar'; at least so it was understood in the Commentary.

2. For the restoration of the Commentary cf. *CT* 41. 43 rev. 11 = R. Labat, *Commentaires*, p. 114: *šu-ta-ḫu-ú* = *šu-taṣ-bu-tu.*

3. Landsberger proposed *š*]*á-šu-uk-ka* (cf. *šá-as-suk-ku*! = *tup-šar-ru*, *LTBA* II. 11. I. 11 = *Malku-šarru* IV. 11) for the last word, but the word proposed is not *šaššuku*, and the other line of the pair strongly suggests a verb with suffix.

4. [*a-rad-ka*] might be restored.

5. For *mala . . . maṣû* 'have the capacity to meet the requirements of', cf. *Šamaš Hymn* 154–5; E. Ebeling, *Handerhebung*, p. 21[44]; *LKA* 23. 2 S., 6–7; IV R^2 9 obv. 52; *Era* IV. 138. The Assyrian form *ammar . . . maṣû* also occurs (*JAOS* 61. 266[84]).

6. *išti* for *itti* 'with' disappeared from Old Akkadian between the end of the Agade Dynasty and the Third Dynasty of Ur (*MAD* II. 26 and *GAG*, § 114 l).

8. For the Commentary cf. *CT* 41. 30. 5 = R. Labat, *Commentaires*, p. 58:

a-šá-ri : *a-la-ku* : *šá-niš a-šá-ri* : *sa-na-qu*

9. *aḫurrû* 'youngest son' is also attested in *Malku-šarru* I. 140: *a-ḫu-ru-u* = *ṣi-iḫ-ru*; and in *LKU* 43. 13–15:
[m]d*en-ki-ušum* lúurúki.ú *bu-kúr* md*sin*(30)-[. . .
[*l*]*i-i-pi riš-tu-ú ḫi-ru-ú* si ? [. . .
[m]d*sin*(30)-*abu*(ad)-*ilī*meš-*ēreš tup-pu-us-su-ú a-ḫu-ru*-[*ú* . . .

Cf. *Era* IV. 101: *u*4-*mu ub-til-la-an-ni ši-ma-ti*. The form *ubtil* must be accented *úbtil* to conform with the trochaic line ending, and this agrees with its being from *b'l*, as middle weak verbs do not keep the stress on the supposedly long syllable, e.g. *tuštámit* (F. Gössmann, *Era*, p. 75). This derivation, first proposed by B. Landsberger, ad loc., has been championed by F. Gössmann, *Era*, p. 55. This phrase cannot, however, be separated from *šīmtu ubil*, in which phrase the verb also appears as *ub-lu* (R. Borger, *Asarhaddon*, p. 54, note on 19, and *AfO* 18. 116). In view of this it is best to regard *ubil* as *ūbil* (from *wabālu*), and *ubtil* as a second perfect formed on the analogy of *ipqid* : *iptaqid*, or of *imūt* : *imtūt*.

10. *agarinnu ālitti* is a variant form of *ummi ālitti*, required for the acrostic, though it does occur elsewhere (R. Borger, *Asarhaddon*, p. 115, L 8). This, and the corresponding *abu ālidu*, are very common in religious texts and imply physical as opposed to adoptive parenthood.
i-ta-ar is tentatively taken as I/1 perfect of *a'āru* (*GAG*, § 106 f). Usually it is construed with *ana*, though the possibility of its taking a simple accusative cannot be excluded. It is not certain that the Commentary takes *târu* as the root.

11. *ta-ru-u-a*: see note on *Counsels of Wisdom* 45.

13. The meaning given to *saḫḫu* is conjectural. The known words *saḫḫu* offer nothing relevant. For the Commentary cf. *Malku-šarru* VIII. 17: *ṣa-ra-mu* = *ka-pa-du*, and the note on *Assyrian Collection* (Bilingual Proverbs) II. 23–26.

18. *mitḫāriš* is often used when speaking of the whole of mankind, e.g. *Šamaš Hymn* 25, and line 258 below. It is "alike" in the sense of omitting none; similarly *malmališ* in *Nisaba and Wheat* I. 32.

19. For the restoration of the end cf. *ZA* 4. 38. 4 = *BA* V. 321: *ú-dam-mi-iq ma-gi-ri-i ú-šá-áš-ra ki-na*; cf. Thureau-Dangin, *Rit. acc.*, p. 135. 259.
enšu in this line, *ītenšu* in 71, and *itnušu* in 275 are not expressions for physical weakness, but for impecuniosity. Cf. *Antagal* E b 19: sig = *en*-[*šu*] *ša muš*-[*ke-ni*] (*CT* 19. 48. II. 19); *Laws of Ešnunna*, § 39: *šum-ma awīlum i-ni-iš-ma bīs-su a-na kaspim it-ta-di-in* "If a man is hard up and sells his house for silver"; *BIN* VII. 53. 27–29 = *MCS* II. 9: 1 gín *kaspam li-ša-bi-lam la e-ni-iš* "let him send me one shekel of silver that I may not become impoverished"; *BIN* VII. 22. 7–9 = *MCS* I. 16–17: *ù* 10 ma.na *kaspam it-nu-šu-ú at-ta ú-la ti-di* "And you did not know that he was bankrupt by 10 minas of silver". Closely related to this sense is the more general 'sparse': *i-iṣ bu-bu-tam it-nu-uš a-ka-lam* (*BiOr* 11. 82. A, 9–10).

20. *namrû*, from the root *marā'u* (cf. *MAD* III. 182), is, like the cognate Hebrew *m*e*rī'*, normally used for fattened animals in the phrase *ša namrâti* 'for fattening' (*JNES* 11. 132). Here it is a jibe at the plumpness of the wealthy in the same spirit as when Amos called the opulent Samaritan ladies "cows of Bashan".

21. *lamassa* or *ila rašû* is a common expression for being successful: *Assyrian Collection* (Bilingual Proverbs) ii. 23 and iii. 12. The idea is discussed by F. R. Kraus in *ZA* 43. 109, and by T. Jacobsen in H. Frankfort *et al.*, *The Intellectual Adventure of Ancient Man*, pp. 203–7 = *Before Philosophy*, pp. 219–23, and *ZA* 52. 138[108].

22. The Commentary appears to depend on *Erim.ḫuš* V. 51–53:
gú.gar = *pu-uḫ-ḫu-ru*
gú.gar.gar = *gur-ru-nu*
šu.ul.la = *ka-ma-ri* (*TCL* 6, no. 35, II. 1–3)

23. The commentator took *kuppu* as a variant form of *kappu*, but in *JNES* 15. 134. 63 they are written together as though different words: *kup-pu* (v. *ku-pu*) *kap-pu*.

24. Cf. *Malku-šarru* II. 50: *gi-ip-šu* = *a-gu-ú* (*ZA* 43. 236). For *miṭītu* cf. *šá la i-šu-u mi-ṭi-tú* (R. Borger, *Asarhaddon*, p. 90, § 59. 7), the passages cited in *ARM* XV. 227 (add to the references VI. 30. 3) and E. Ebeling, *Glossar zu den neubab. Briefen*, pp. 146 and 266. For this nuance of *mṭ'* see *Maqlû* III 119–20.

25–26. This is stock phraseology, cf. *Era* V. 5 and 17.

25. The archaizing *ku-a-šú* was necessitated by the acrostic. The Commentary goes back to *Erim.ḫuš* I. 11–13:
èn.tar = *šá-a-lum*
èn.tar.tar = *šit-a-l*[*um*]
[èn].tar.a.ri.a = *uṣ-ṣu-*[*ṣu*] (*KBo* I. 44 obv. 11–13 = *CT* 18. 47, K 214 = *CT* 19. 8, Rm II. 587)

27. *gattu* in *Ludlul* II. 69 is feminine, but here masculine. *katāmu* has meanings other than 'cover', though perhaps derived from 'cover (with a net)', cf. *Maqlû* III. 162–4. Note *Era* IV. 11: *a-ku-u bēl e-mu-qí i-kàt-tam*; *ZA* 43. 18. 69: *bēl bir-ki ik-tùm-mu-šú-ma*. 'Overtake' or 'overwhelm' suits these occurrences.
makû is distress of some kind; cf. *BBSt*, p. 36. 44: *lu-up-nu ma-ku-ú u le-me-nu*; A. L. Oppenheim, *Dreams*, p. 323, 82–5–22, 538. 6.

28. *mut-tu-*[*ri*]: restoration and meaning are very uncertain. *mutturu* may be II/1 infinitive of *watāru*. Cf. the lexical excerpt given in the note on line 127.

29. With the Commentary cf. *Malku-šarru* I. 64: *ku-bu-uk-ku* = *e-mu-qu*; and in *Antagal* VIII. 61–62 *e-mu-qu* and *ku-bu-uk-ku* appear together (II *R* 36, no. 3, I. 55–56).

31, 32. The parallelism of *nesû* and *rêqu* is also found in *ZA* 4. 252. 18 = A. Falkenstein and W. von Soden, *Sum. und akk. Hymnen und Gebete*, p. 263: *kib-ri ru-uq-šú ni-si-iš na-ba-l*[*i*] "The coast is far from him, the dry land is remote from him". For a metaphorical usage note *JRAS Cent. Sup.*, pl. III. 4: *pa-ra-as ár-ka-tú ni-sa-an-ni* "I am far from getting to the root of the matter", and the personal name *ṣi-iḫ-ti-ru-qá-at* "Laughter is remote" (*MVAG* 44. 287). The ablative sense which the suffixes have on *rêqu* and *nesû* fits the general picture of Akkadian, where verbal suffixes are used much more loosely than in the other Semitic languages.
ku-ru-um appears to be construct state of *kurummatu*. For *napšat* see the note on *Ludlul* II. 88.
ṭa-pa-piš: this and *iṭ-pu-pu* in 48 are clearly not from *dabābu* 'speak'. In 48 the action is involved in a wild ass's trampling down the fields (cf. 60), and here it parallels *ana nišbê*. In *á.A* III_4. 164 si = *ṭa-pa-pu* (*CT* 12. 9. III. 4), and it is explained by *AN* VIII. 15–17:
ṭa-pa-pu = *š*[*e-b*]*u-u*
ṭa-pa-pu = [*ma*]*-lu-ú*
ṭa-pa-pu = ⌜*a*⌝*-pa-rum* (*CT* 18. 23, K 5566 = *CT* 18. 14. 73–75)
It appears to mean 'satisfy one's hunger, take one's fill', cf. Arabic *ṭaffa* 'be within reach'.

33. *ku-un-nam-ma-a*: in a question not introduced by an interrogative word the writer consistently marks the question with an unnaturally stressed vowel, as here and in 49, 51, 53, 54, 65. Cf. *SO* XIX/I. 6. This stress resembles the Latin *-ne*.
alaktašu alammad: cf. *Maqlû* I. 14, &c.

34. *sa-an-qa pi-ia*: see note on *Counsels of Wisdom* 26.

39. The restoration in text and Commentary is based on *Malku-šarru* III. 68–70:
qu-ud-mu = *maḫ-*[*ru*]
ul-lu-ú = *maḫ-*[*ru-u*]
sa-di-du = ,, (B. Meissner, *Supplement*, pl. 24, Rm II 200 A)

43. The acrostic is responsible for the irregular spelling *sap-ṣu*.

44. Commentary: cf. *Ea* II. 73–74: ^be.e^BAD = *be-e-šu*
pi-tu-ú
and *Malku-šarru* V. 80: *nak-ru-ṭum* = *re-e-mu*.

48. See the note on *Dialogue of Pessimism* 22 for *akkannu*. Here only one animal is meant, and so the question arises whether both names should be considered synonyms, or whether one is the noun and the other, in this use at least, is an epithet. In origin *akkannu* is apparently an adjective of Hurrian derivation which is applied to horses; see *AASOR* 16, no. 99. 1–5, K. Balkan, *Kassitenstudien*, p. 33, and Salonen, *Hippologica*, p. 27. A similar case is *LKA* 101 obv.(!): *ak-kan-ni ṭar-du sìr!-ri-mu ṭar-du*. Again one animal is meant.

The verb of this line is discussed in the note on 31–32.

49. The restoration, which appears to be the only one possible, gives the noun *k/qattû*, equated with lú.KA.gi.na in *Ḫarra* II. 352, thus 'one who may be relied upon' or 'guarantor'. A [lú]*kát-te-e* occurs, but in a broken context, in *JTVI* 29. 87. 34 and 37.

50. *dumuq šīri*: cf. *Fable of Fox* Z obv. 13; *OIP* II. 112. 81: *du-muq áš-na-an*.

51. Cf. *Ludlul* II. 20.

55. The *-e* after sá.dug$_4$ is peculiar, unless the sentence is interrogative (see note on 33). If the second *ginû* has been restored correctly in the Commentary, it is possible that the commentator took the *ginû* not as 'regular offering', but as 'young animal' (cf. *ginû* C 'baby'—*CAD*, vol. G, 83), so that *šanû* would be 'foal'.

56. *gišimmaru* is certainly a compound noun from *giš*+*immaru* (cf. *CAD*, sub voce), and it is possible that *iṣ mešrê*, which also occurs as a name of the palm in *OIP* II. 109. 10, is an attempt at etymology. As a name of the palm it is already Sumerian: *Ḫarra* III. 273: giš.níg.tuk. In the *Fable of the Tamarisk and Palm* c 39, the palm addresses "his brother", and it is possible that the writer is consciously imitating some such passage in addressing his friend as a palm.

57. In view of *liqtu* 'gold' (*ZA* 43. 75), if this is the correct restoration, *illuku* must be the article of jewellery rather than the garment.

For the Commentary cf. *Erim.ḫuš* V. 44–45:

[gu]gú = *na-ag-bu-ú*
gú[di.ir]diri = *nap-ḫa-ri* (*TCL* 6, no. 35, I. 44–45)

58. It is best to take *gi-na-ta-ma* as the adjective, though von Soden actually thinks of *ginû* 'baby' (*Or* N.S. 25. 244). "You are immovable" will mean "What you say cannot be gainsaid". The Commentary is not clear. *ammatu* 'earth' also appears in the second line of the *Epic of Creation*, with an Assyrian variant *abbatum*. It may be a cognate of the Hebrew [a]*dāmâ*.

60. *gi-iš* is taken as the participle of *gêšu* 'gore' (cf. *CAD*). The Arabic *ǵaḥš* is 'young ass, colt, gazelle'. Commentary. Cf. *Malku-šarru* III. 12: *mul-mul-lu* = *šil-ta-ḫu* (*LTBA* II. 1. x. 52).

62. For the reading *gillatu* (not *qillatu*) see *CAD*, sub voce *gullulu*. For the latter half of the line cf. *Ludlul* I. 93 and note.

63. For the Commentary see the note on line 22.

67. Cf. R. Borger, *Asarhaddon*, p. 104. II. 5: *ina qí-bit* [d]*marduk šar$_4$ ilī*[meš] *i-*[*z*]*i-qam-ma iltānu ma-nit bēl ilī*[meš] *ṭa-a-bu*; and *Malku-šarru* III. 174: *ma-ni-tú* = *šá-a-ru* (*LTBA* II. 1. XI. 140). B. Meissner's argument from the first passage, that *manitu* is masculine, has since been ignored, but not answered (*MAOG* 1/2. 38–39; *AfO* 6. 108); cf. *AfO* 18. 116.

68. For the restoration *damqu* cf. *Era* I. 108 and *VAB* IV. 232. 18: *šá mi-lik-šú dam-qu*; also *AfO* 17. 133. 17; *YOS* X. 13. 15; &c.

70. Note the Late Babylonian *muš-te-mu*!-⌜*ú*⌝ in the Commentary; the opposite is seen in *šu-ú* for *šumu* in *Ludlul* II. 30, k, on which see the note.

71. *i-te-en-šú*: see the note on 19.

72. *ligimû*, literally 'palm shoot' (*MSL* I. 194), is also 'child' or 'offspring' in *Malku-šarru* I. 142: *li-gi-mu-u* = *ṣi-iḫ-ru*; ibid. I. 153 [*l*]*i-g*[*i*]*-mu-u* = *ma-ru*.

73. Cf. *YOS* I. 38. 37: *ina te-mi-qí ik-ri-bu ù la-ba-a-nu ap-pi.*

74. For *nēmelu* see the note on *Ludlul* II. 26.

76. Cf. K 10499. 4: . . .]× *pa-na-an-nu-ú lil-l*[*u* . . . This shows that there are here adjectives *pānânû* and *elânû* 'the man in front' and 'the man above'. For *kuṣṣudu* cf. *Á-Tablet* 58–60:

á.šu.gìr.kud = *ku-uṣ-ṣu-du*
[á].šu.gìr.kud = *us-su-lum*
á.šu.gìr.kud = *pu-us-su-lum* (*CT* 19. 16 obv. 8–10)

The juxtaposition of *lillu* and *kuṣṣudu* occurs again in *igi* = *x*, App. A 11′–12′:

. . .] = *lil-lum*
. . .].kud = *ku-uṣ-ṣu-du*

77. For this *ḫarḫaru* see *CAD*, sub voce *ḫarḫaru* B. The Commentary is related to *CT* 37. 24. III. 2–4:

lú.ur.tab.ba = *ḫa-*[*ar-ḫa-ru*]
lú.*aš-bal-tum* = *gu-*[*zal-lu*]
lú.ur.KA×GA = *še-er-*[*ru*]

78. *mur-qa*: the commonest use of *mrq* in Akkadian is in Late Babylonian deeds of sale, where *murruqu* is used for 'be responsible' (for complying with the terms of a contract), and especially in the phrase *pūt aḫameš ana murruqu* "there is a mutual responsibility for insuring . . .". Instead of *murruqu*, *mu-ur-qu* does occur rarely: *BRM* II. 32. 18; ibid. 55. 18; *VS* 15. 12. 16; ibid. 39. 52; ibid. 49. 24. This may be behind *Erim.ḫuš* IV. 148–9:

nam.mud = *mu-ur-qu*
nam.mud.zé.eb.ba = *ṭu-ub-bu*

ul mur-ru-uq occurs as a technical term in commentaries (*CT* 41. 28 obv. 9; *CT* 41. 29 obv. 17; *CT* 41. 33 obv. 3; ibid. rev. 5), much like *ul i-di*, and probably meaning 'uncertain'. Of direct relevance for our passage is *Erim.ḫuš* VI. 98–100:

$^{u.muš}$KU = *mur-qu*
KA$^{di.im.mu}$ḪI = *pa*[*q*]*-q*[*u*]
a.rá = *a-l*[*ak-tum*]

This takes *murqu* for a noun (umuš also = *ṭēmu* and *milku*), and *lā murqu* will then be a negated noun like *lā amēlu* 'no gentleman' and *lā mār āli* 'foreigner'.

82. For *qirib šamê* cf. 256 (with note). The reading *šib-qí* is possible (see *ZA* 49. 176), but *me-ki* is not excluded.

127. In the context it is not certain that *bullû* 'extinguish' is the verb. A homophone seems to exist in *Alam-lānu* Fragment A, 29–32: [×].dùg.ga = *mut-tu-ru, ma-ḫa-ru, na-šu-ú, be-lu-ú* (*CT* 18. 39. I. 23–26); and in *Nabnītu* K, 135: si.giš = *pi-lu-u* (*CT* 19. 43. III. 7). si.giš in the same tablet also = [*e-nu-u*] *šá nu-up-pu-š*[*i*] (111 = *CT* 19. 42. II. 24) and *pa-du-u* (121 = *CT* 19. 42. II. 34).

129. The *pṣd* here cannot be the same as *pṣd* 'split (rocks)'. Cf. *á.A* II$_1$. 6′–7′: $^{di.ig}$NI = *di-šu-ú, ba-nu-ú, pu-uṣ-ṣu-du.* This suggests a beneficial action, as perhaps also in *MSL* III. 133. 25.

130. *šà-g*[*i-gur*$_6$*-ra-a* might be restored; cf. *Counsels of a Pessimist* 12 and note.

137. For *bīrtu* 'way' see *Maqlû* III. 3; for this use of *aḫāzu* see note on *Ludlul* II. 95.

139. For the restoration cf. H. Winckler, *Die Keilschrifttexte Sargons*, Atlas pl. 7 no. 13. 7–8 = ed. Lie, p. 30. 189–90: *ir-tap-pu-du* [*šar*]*-ra-qiš*. Here the restoration of one sign is required by the space, and provided by a similar passage ibid., Atlas pl. 26 no. 56. 12. For *bēru* see note on *Advice to a Prince* 21.

141. For *ne'ellû* cf. *Malku-šarru* V. 75: *i-te-'e-lu-ú* = *sa-ḫa-ru* (*CT* 18. 22. II. 24), and von Soden, *Or* N.S. 20. 156–8.

142. For the meaning of *piznuqu* 'beggar' cf. *Fable of Fox* B obv. 19. The last word should perhaps be *pānū'a*; cf. BM 38596 obv. I. 14 (Bilingual Proverbs).

147. *iprud*: cf. note on *Ludlul* I. 46.

166–7. For *ašru* and *aššāru* in the same context cf. *naiādu* and *na'du* in 12 and 14.

183. Malt was spread out in the sun to dry, or was dried in a kiln. One learns from this passage that a man watched it, to drive away dogs and birds if it was in the sun, or to prevent it from being overheated in a kiln. Cf. L. F. Hartman and A. L. Oppenheim, *Beer*, p. 15. In view of the unskilled nature of the job it was no doubt very poorly paid.

184. The contrast with the previous line shows that *mādid ruššî* was a highly paid worker, or a man who, because of his doing this, would be wealthy. As a substantive *ruššû* is only known as a red garment: *Ḫarra* 19. 174 and *Ḫargud* B_5. 12: túg.ḫuš.a = *ru-uš-šu-u* = *lu-bar eb-bi*. *ruššû*, however, is a very common epithet of gold, and it is probable that in this context, contrasted with *ṣariru*, it is used as a noun, 'red gold'.

185. Cf. *Fable of the Riding-donkey* rev. 12: *ma-lil ir-qu*, and the Commentary on *Šumma izbu* 423: *ma-la-lu* = *a-k*[*a*]-*lu*. As in the book of Daniel, to live without eating flesh was a sign of poverty.

189. *in qá-bal* 'formerly, since' is known elsewhere only lexically: *Malku-šarru* III. 90–92:

in qá-bal = *iš-t*[*u* u_4-*um*]
iš-tu ru-qá = *iš-t*[*u* × ×]
iš-tu ul-la = *iš-t*[*u* × ×]

Also in *MSL* IV u_4.ta/da = *i-na qá-bal* and *iš-tu* u_4-*um* (149. 26–27; 176. 281–2; 142. 319–20).

188–96. Commentary: *iptu* 'abundance' seems to be confined to Late Babylonian royal inscriptions. Cf. *VAB* IV, Glossar.

196. Commentary: cf. *Malku-šarru* IV. 188: *qa-a-šu* = *na-da-nu* (*LTBA* II. 2. 211).

198. *šummu*: a noun formed from *šumma* 'if', i.e. a section of a text beginning with *šumma*; it is also found in H. Zimmern, *BBR*, p. 96. 15: *ḫi-im-mat šum-mi u mi-šá-ri*. Cf. B. Landsberger in *Symbolae Koschaker*, p. 220[5]. See also 214 below.

200. Cf. note on *Counsels of Wisdom* 78.

202. The first *ú* may be the last sign of a preceding word, so that the shortened form *sandû* would occur. On such see note on *Ludlul* II. 87.

206. For *miḫil/ṣtu* 'script' ('wedge' or 'sign'?) cf. A. Falkenstein, *WO* I. 179[28], and *STT* I. 70 rev. 5. For the Commentary see *Antagal* VIII. 76–78:

$^{ge.e}$U = *mi-ḫi-il-tum*
gú.gú = *mi-ḫi-iṣ-tum*
si = *mi-iḫ-ṣa-tum* (*CT* 18. 36. II. 4–6).

210. *dubbu* also occurs in *YOS* II. 150. 11: *du-bu-um*.

212. Cf. *YOS* X. 44. 59: *ḫarrān ri-pi-it-tim*, and *KAR* 454 obv. 32: *ḫar-ra-an ri-pí-it-ti*.

214. *riddu* 'what is proper' is from *redû*, *irdu* 'be suitable', to be distinguished from *redû*, *irdi* 'drive, &c.'. In the Mari letters it has been read *ri-it-tum* (*ARM* 15. 251). See also note on *Šamaš Hymn* 96.
šummu: cf. note on 198.
taṭpil: for the meaning cf. *a-me-ru a-a iṭ-pil* "let not the reader profane it" in colophons (*CT* 14. 9 rev. 17; ibid. 28, K 4345 rev. IV. 4).

215. This line states the blessedness of those who follow the speaker's advice. The *tupšikku* (from the Sumerian dub.sig 'brick board') was an aid to carrying bricks and clay, and became a byword for menial toil. Nabopolassar describes how he once participated, at least for a moment, in the construction of a temple: *libnāti ù ṭi-iṭ-ṭam i-na qá-qá-di-im lu az-bi-il tu-up-ši-ka-a-tim* (v. adds *ḫurāṣi ù kaspi*) *lu ú-dar-rig-ma* (*VAB* IV. 62. 66–70). This suggests that the *tupšikku* covered the head, perhaps like a hood. The *šaḫḫû* (Sumerian šà.ḫa) was also "put on" (e.g. *KAR* 184 obv. 38: túg.šà.ḫa mu_4.mu_4), but its use was limited to ritual. The sense of the line then seems to be that those who perform the duties of religion by

wearing the *šaḫḫû* are spared the menial toil of wearing the *tupšikku*. The comment explains a word for head, and the vocabulary citation is preceded by *bu*-× -*nu*, which could be regarded as an explanation of the previous illegible word (cf. the scheme of the comment on 200). However, in general the commentator has no fixed procedure and seems to have accommodated his methods to the needs of individual passages. The tablet j contains]-*nu* as the end of the second quarter of the line, and it is probable that this is the word in the Commentary. The only possible known word is that in *Ḫarra* 15. 9 (*PBS* XII/1, no. 7 rev. 19 and II *R* 24, no. 1 rev. 25) with *Ḫargud*: uzu.a.za.ad = *bi-bé-e-nu* = *qaq-qa-du* (cf. *bi-bé-en* KA, F. R. Kraus, *Physiognomatik*, pl. 25 obv. 10′). One difficulty in accepting this identification is that although the traces favour *bu*-[N]E-*nu*, the value *bí*, apart from the petrified letter formula *qí-bí-ma* and archaizing Late Babylonian royal inscriptions, is rare. It does, however, occur in all periods, if rarely: OB. omens *ra-bi-a-na* (*YOS* X. 31. X. 37); Cassite-period flood tablet *ra-bí-tam* (*BE* Ser. D V/1. 6; cf. Barton, *JAOS* 31. 30–48, and E. I. Gordon, *JBL* 75. 336); Late Babylonian *Era* IV. 40 *bí-la-ti-šú*. The *bu*- instead of *bi*- is another difficulty, and the restoration is therefore only tentative.

218. The whole line occurs, with slight verbal differences, in Bilingual Proverbs, K 4347, II. 62–63.

219. Cf. E. Ebeling, *Handerhebung*, p. 60. 24: *ir-di us-ki*. *usu* is a loan from the Sumerian uš (ús) = *redû*. *mēsu* = *parṣu* (Comm.) is also *AN* VIII. 49.

220. *naškin* seems to be intended for IV/1 stative of *šakānu*, which would ordinarily be *naškun*.

223. *kamāsu* 'collect', cf. *RA* 17. 108. 93; *AJSL* 47. 23[4]; *ARM* 15.

235. *būnū* or *bunnū* is probably an ellipsis for *būnū namrūti*, a common phrase (e.g. *Counsels of Wisdom* 91) for 'smiling face' and so 'approval, consent'. It is used again without *namrūti* in *Fable of Fox* Z obv. 10, and in E. Ebeling, *Handerhebung*, p. 22. 26–1: *šá qa-bé-e-ia li-pu-uš* "let them do what I command", with a variant *šá bu-ni-ia li-pu-šú* "let them do what I approve".

236. The first two words are very difficult. The variant of B could be read *sūqa*(e.sír) *ina ri-di-šú* "as he goes along the street", and *šammê* could easily be a variant form of *sammû* 'musical instrument' or 'praise' (*ZA* 42. 155), influenced by the acrostic. Cf. *KAR* 76 rev. 8 = *ArOr* 21. 405: *muš-šir eṭ-lu ina sammî* (zà.mí) *ri-bit li-ti-*[*iq*] "Let go of the young man; let him cross the square with (playing of) the lyre", and R. Borger, *Asarhaddon*, p. 50. 37: *it-ti* [lú]*nāri ù* [giš]*sammî ina ri-bit ninua*[ki] *e-te-et-ti-iq* "with singer(s) and playing I traversed the square of Nineveh". These two possibilities do not support each other. If e.sír is read, only *ša-am-mi* remains of the first word.

239. *ša lā*: cf. note on 251.

240. *baḫû* is documented by von Soden in *Or* N.S. 24. 380.

241. For the concept of the *šāru ṭābu* and similar expressions see E. Unger, *Babylon*, pp. 128–35, and A. L. Oppenheim, *Dreams*, pp. 233–5.

244. *šarrabu* (*PB*, no. 3098; *SO* VII. 462) was a minor deity of the Nergal type, or possibly a demon. Cf. IV R^2 34, no. 2. 2 = *AfO* 10. 2: *a-me-ni dib-bu-ku-nu a-na ša šar-ra-bé-e maš-lu* "Why are your words like a demon's?" Similarly ibid. 7.

245. The restoration of the Commentary is based on *Malku-šarru* II. 41: *miṭ-ra-tum* = *na-a-ru* (*ZA* 43. 235).

248. Commentary: cf. *Antagal* III. 9–11: bulùg.gal = *šeš-gal-lum*
ús.sa = *tar-din-nu*
dub.ús.sa = *tup-pu-su-u*
(*CT* 18. 32. I. 9–11). In *BBSt*, p. 67. 19 ff. *terdinnu* is clearly 'second son': *mār-šu rabî*[i] . . . *mār-šu ter-din-nu* . . . *mār-šu šal-šá-a-a*. Cf. *JNES* 8. 271#.

249. *zilullîš*: cf. *Advice to a Prince* 14; Landsberger, *ZA* 43. 76; Jacobsen, *Studia Orientalia Ioanni Pedersen Dicata*, p. 182[37]. *zilullû* is a loan from PA.GIŠGAL, pronounced zilulu, and also rendered into Akkadian

saḫḫiru. In Sumerian zilulu is 'head worker', and it is easy to understand how 'bully' was derived from this. *ilu saḫḫiru* occurs twice in omens (*TDP* 4. 37; *AfO* 18. 72, F. 3. 9), but its meaning is not clear.

251. *qadmu* here and in 276 is nothing but a common noun for 'god'. Cf. *CT* 25. 18 rev. II. 9–10:

qa-ad-mu = *i-[lu]*
di-gi-ru-ú = MIN : *ḫi-li-pu-ú*

This gives excellent sense in both passages. In 276 Narru, or Enlil, is "king of the gods", and translations such as "king from (*sic*!) of old" (A. Heidel, *Gilgamesh Epic*, p. 138) show how impossible the passage is otherwise. Here the *qadmu* bowed down to is obviously the personal god. The attempt to make it a human tormentor ("the leader"?) removes all logic from the line. No one expects to benefit from submitting to such a person. In origin *qadmu* (also *qudmu*) is a particular god (*PB*, no. 1711; *SO* VII. 437). Cf. *ul-liš qàd-mi-šu*: K 225. 103, and *qá-ad-mi-iš*: *AKF* I. 21. 3.

ad-da-mu-ṣu: cf. *Malku-šarru* 4. 127–9:

da-ma-ṣu = *ka-na-šu*
da-ka-mu(v. *-šu*) = ,,
ti-id-mu-ṣu = ,,

(*LTBA* II. 1. XIII. 14–16 = ibid. 12. II. 3–5). Cf. also *ZA* 4. 256. 17: *da-ma-ṣu ba-la-ṣu ù ut-nin-šú*.

Syntactically the line has a relative clause without an antecedent, which acts as a *casus pendens* before the main clause. A relative clause with a personal *ša* and without an antecedent is very common: "He who . . .", but the impersonal: "The fact that . . ." is not rare. Cf. *ša mārī*[meš] *ši-ip-ri* [lú]*qa-ta-na-ya*[[ki]] *a-di i-na-an-na ta-ak-lu-ú am-mi-nim ta-ak-la-š[u-nu-ti]* "As to your having kept back the messengers of the Qatanaya until now, why have you held them back?" (*ARM* I. 15. 6 ff.). Middle Babylonian examples are cited in *SO* XX. 146–7. Note also 239 above, where, however, the existence of a preposition *ša lā* 'without' rather alters the case. There *ša lā* may be a conjunction 'unless'.

mi-na-a ú-at-tar: cf. *Šamaš Hymn* 103 and Bilingual Proverbs K 4347, II. 25.

252. For *ašbaltu* see note on 77 and *RA* 16. 167. III. 50–51:

[i.di.im]BAD = *áš-bal-[tu]*
BAD = *ú-la-[lu]*

The suffix need not be taken as a possessive genitive. The first stanza does not allow the assumption that the sufferer owned even a very poor grade of slave. "My" must mean "with whom I come into contact".

254. Cf. *LTBA* II. 2. 30: *šu-'-u* = *šar-ru*, and *Malku-šarru* I. 9 (*OECT* IV. 59): *šu-e-tum* = *be-el-tum* (= comment on 278).

255. *litmum-ma* = *litmun-ma*: *GAG*, § 33 h. With *li-it-mu-um-mu* in the Commentary cf. *li-šá-rik-šum-mu* (*YOS* I, pl. XXV. 23).

Aro (*SO* XX. 141; cf. von Soden, *GAG*, § 158 e) takes a stative+*ma* followed by a present as usually a consecution: e.g. *pal-ḫa-ku-ma ul a-ṭe-eḫ-ḫa-a* (*Gilg*. I. III. 35) "I was afraid and so did not approach". However, this is unlikely in *Gilg*. 2 (OB.), I. 4: *ša-am-ḫa-ku-ma at-ta-na-al-la-ak*; not "I was magnificent and therefore walked about", but "In my magnificence I walked about". Cf. also C. D. Gray, *AJSL* 17. 227 (= *Šamaš Religious Texts*, pl. IV), 20: *ṣe-eḫ-ra-ku-ma aḫ-ta-ṭi* "in my youth I sinned". The stative, according to its nature, expresses the circumstances in which the action of the second verb takes place. Often the circumstances are also the cause of the action, but not always.

256. Cf. Gudea Cyl. A VII. 4 (cf. ibid. IX. 2): en.na šà.an.gin$_7$.sud.du.ni "The lord, whose heart is remote like the heavens".

258. *mitḫāriš*: see note on 18.

259. *mìn-su* and *la* ḪAR-*ri* are difficult. The interrogative *minsu* 'why?' (R. Borger, *Or* N.S. 27. 147) is well known in certain literary texts, but in this context even a rhetorical question seems impossible. The

line seems to state the general rule which is exemplified in 260–3. Thus *mìn-su* is taken as *mensû* 'leader', 'first'. The normal form of the word is *massû*, derived from the Sum. máš.sag 'leading goat'. Since, however, the ancients confused this with *massû* = maš.su(d) "mit fernem (weitem) Blick" (*MSL* II. 103–4), it is legitimate to compare *mé-en-su-ú* in the prayer of Tukulti-Ninurta I (*KAR* 128 rev. 23 = maš.su(d) in 22) and *mìn-sa-a* in *KAR* 158. I. 40 as evidence of *mensû* 'leader'. The example in Tukulti-Ninurta's prayer is probably a Middle Babylonian form, a form thus not unexpected in the *Theodicy*.

260. Commentary: cf. *á.A* VIII$_1$. 37–38: $^{ma.ar}$ZUR = *ma-a-rum*
$^{a.mar}$ZUR = *bu-ú-rum* (*CT* 12. 10. I. 26–27)

265. *šibqu*: see note on 82. The comment also appears as *Malku-šarru* IV. 97: *ú-te-qu-u* = *qa-a-lu* (*LTBA* II. I. XII. 126).

266. Cf. *BA* V. 394. 45: *at-mu-šu nu-us-su-uq-ma sè-kàr-šú šu-šur*; *SSS* XIV, p. 23. 19: *at-mu-šu na-as-qu-ma.*

267. Cf. *ARM* V. 4. 13: *š*]*a pa-ra-ša-am la-am-du.*

270. Cf. *VAB* IV. 252, I. 1: *ša a-na ṭè-me ilī*^{meš} *pu-ú-qu*; similarly *RA* 11. 109. 21 and *OECT* I. 33. 14.

271. Commentary: cf. *Malku-šarru* V. 168: *pa-šal-lu* = *ḫu-ra-ṣu* (*LTBA* II. I. XV. 15).

275. The same pattern is seen in *Ludlul* II. 49; for *itnušu* see note on 19.

276. *qadmu*: see note on 251.
Narru is not, of course, the river goddess. This name of Enlil is also found in the variant form Larru in the name ^{d}la.ar.ru.níg.du.al = ^{d}*en-líl-kudurri-ú-ṣur* (V *R* 44. III. 54 = *JCS* 11. 13). The interchange of *l* and *n* is discussed by von Soden in *Or* N.S. 25. 241–3, who concludes that it is due to foreign influence. In Late Babylonian times the honourable name of Sin-liqi-unninni (see *JCS* 11. 4) was again used, but corrupted to Sin-niq-unninni (e.g. *VS* 6. 40. 3). Narru may be listed in the god lists (note ^{d}*na-ar*[. . , *ZA* 31. 110. II. 10), but the scribe who wrote the variant *na-an-na-*(ras.)*-ru* evidently did not know it.

277. Cf. *CT* 25. 33. 16: ^{d}KA^{zu}.lum.GAR^{mar} = ^{d}*é-a.* ^{d}*zu-lum* (*Epic of Creation* VII. 84) may be a shortened form of this name.

278. For *šu'ētum* see note on 254. Mama, or Mami, is a name of *bēlit-ilī*, the mother goddess, of which Aruru (258) is another form.

279. Cf. *Epic of Creation* VII. 39: *na-si-i*[*ḫ*] *it-gu-ru da-ba-ba*; H. Zimmern, *BBR*, p. 198. 14 (top) and 8 (bottom): *it-gu-rat lišāni.* The Latin *perversus* offers a semantic parallel to this nuance of *egēru.*

280–4. Cf. E. Ebeling, *Handerhebung*, p. 132. 57: *ina sur-ra-a-ti u la ki-na-a-ti i-kap-pu-du-ni lem-né-e-ti.*

283. A. L. Oppenheim has collected the examples of *amēlu* used in connexion with another more specific noun in *Or* N.S. 17. 25[4] and 19. 129[1]. Cf. *Fable of Fox* E rev. 3.

284. *nullâtu* is commented upon in *Counsels of Wisdom* 28.

286. Cf. *Epic of Creation* I. 138, &c.: *šar-ba-ba* (v. *-biš*) *liš-*(v. *li-iḫ-*)*ḫar-mi-im*; and *CT* 23. 10. 13: *bi-li kīma la-'-me*, *BA* V. 386. 18 and 387. 21: *tu-bal-li la-'-meš.*

287. For the reading *ši-te-'-me* see note on 70.

288. The comment *ra-a-ṣa* = *a-lak* is the only Akkadian evidence for *râṣu* as a verb of motion. In Hebrew *rûṣ* is 'run'.

289. See note on *Fable of Nisaba and Wheat* IV. 21. The corruption of m: gír.gaz.ki.*nu-ú* for *mut-nin-nu-ú* is clearly a mistake of sight, not of hearing. This is also the case with RID for *tup* in D, 248.

292. For *iš-šá-pu* see note on *Ludlul* I. 72–73. The reading of m (*šá-pil*) is probably superior to that of a (*iš-šá-pil*), which appears to have been attracted to the preceding *iš-šá-pu.*

293. Cf. *Epic of Creation* II. 86.

Chapter 4. Precepts

(i) *INSTRUCTIONS OF ŠURUPPAK*

OBVERSE

2. For the form *napuštu* see *Fable of Fox* B obv. 5 and note.

5. *wašāru* = 'instruct', cf. Landsberger, *Belleten* 14. 261[82]; for *ašertu* see Kramer, *BASOR* 79. 25–26.

12, 13. The usual phrase 'be a security' is *qātāte leqû*, e.g. *MSL* I. 40–41 and 145.

(ii) *COUNSELS OF WISDOM*

18. Cf. *BBSt*, pp. 62–63. 29–31: ^{d}LA[MMA]-*šú a-na gal-le-e . . . li-tur-šú.*

20. Cf. note on *Ludlul* II. 35.

21, 30. *e-piš na-mu-ti*: von Soden in *Or* N.S. 24. 388–9 proposed 'joker' for this expression. In the context it is doubtful if a simple humorist would merit condemnation. A question prior to deciding the meaning of the phrase is whether we have an abstract from *nu'u* 'fool', 'boor', 'low fellow'. Writings such as *na-'-ú-ti* and *nu-'u-tú* hardly settle the matter, since the difficulty remains that *ex hypothesi* the abstract is often written with *m*, but the simple noun never. [Too little is known of the $^{lú.me}$*na-mu-ti* of Ugarit, 'peasantry' according to A. E. Speiser, *JAOS* 75. 164[71], to bring them into the discussion.] Until more evidence is available it is best not to be influenced by the possible connexion with *nu'u*. The phrase only occurs in connected texts in these two passages, but it has much attention in lexical series:

Nabnītu Tablet E:

127 a.kud.di = *e-pi-šu ša na-mu-ti*
128 a.kud.du$_{11}$.du$_{11}$ = ,, *ša* ,,
129 a.kud.lál = ,, *ša* ,,

Lú = *amēlu* Tablet 4. III (*MAOG* XIII/2. 41. 17–21 = *RA* 17. 195, K 1904-10-9. 66. II):

240 a.kud.du$_{11}$.du$_{11}$ = *e-piš nu-mut-te* (v. *na-'-ú-ti*)
241 di.du$_{11}$.du$_{11}$ = *muš-tar-ri-ḫu* (v. *muš-ta-mu-ú*)
242 za.ra.du$_{11}$.du$_{11}$ = *muš-ta-lu* (v. *muš-ta-mu-ú*)
243 èš.ta.lú = *šu-u*
244 inim.bal.bal = *mu-ta-mu-ú*
(*muṣiḫḫu* and *aluzinnu* follow)

Igi.duḫ.a = *tāmartu* (Short Version) 279 (*AfO* 18. 84):

⌜lú⌝.dumu.sila.dù.dù = *e-piš nu-'u-tú*

The group from *Lú* = *amēlu* are all persons using their voices in some capacity. *eštalû* is a singer, *aštalûm* in the Mari letters (A. L. Oppenheim, *JNES* 11. 134). More support for 'joker' can be obtained from *OB.Lú* Part XII. 8–12 (*SLT* 7 obv.), where only the Akk. is preserved: *a-lu-zi-in-nu*, ⌜*e-pi*⌝*-iš na-mu-tim*, [*k*]*u-lu-*[*l*]*u-ú-um*, [*mu*]-⌜*ṣi-iḫ*⌝*-ḫu-um*. However, *RA* 16. 166. II. 8–10 = *CT* 18. 29. II. 3–5 has a different interpretation of a.kud.lál:

a.kud.lál = *mu-pi-gu-ú*
a.kud.lál = *a-kíl kar-ṣi*
kar.ta.AŠ.AŠ = *da-bi-bu*
(*aluzinnu* follows)

Here 'slanderer' is the meaning assigned to a.kud.lál and *ēpiš namūti* in the *Counsels* is best suited with this rendering. 'Joker' may not be absolutely wrong, since an Aristophanic type of humour makes abundant use of slander.

23. For the phrase *ina ṭubbāti*, the meaning of which is still not completely certain, see the material assembled by A. L. Oppenheim, *Dreams*, p. 286[127]. In *KAR* 306 rev. 17–18 and 29–30 *ṭubbātu* appears as the opposite of *ṣaltu*, cf. C. Frank, *Kultlieder*, p. 38.

26. This is a common topic in Akkadian: *ZA* 43. 96. 4–5:

[*šumma na*]-*ṣir pi-šu ka-ba-tu nišī*[meš] *na-mur* : gar-*šú*
[*šumma šap-t*]*a-a-šú sa-an-qá ṭè-em ili* gar-*šú*

Also there are proper names like *saniq-pî-ištar* (J. J. Stamm, *MVAG* 44. 232–3); cf. *sa-ni-iq-qá-bu-ša* (*VS* 8. 69 and 70. 1). Cf. also *Šurpu* II. 40; *Theodicy* 34.

28. *šillatum* and *magrītum* are part of the Akkadian stock of terms for sinful speech, which is extraordinarily rich. Cf. *AN* IX:

100 *nu-ul-la-tum* = [*šil-la-tu*]*m*
101 *mi-gir-tum* = „
102 *pa-ri-tum* = „ *pa-ru*!-*tum* in *Malku-šarru* IV. 245 (*LTBA* II. 1. XIII. 115)
103 *nu-ul-la-tum* = *la qa-bi-*[*tum*]
104 *ma-ag-ri-tum* = „
105 *taš-ši-tum* = „
106 *i-nim-ma* = *la a-ma-tum*
107 *tu-uš-šu* = *mi-iq-tum* (*CT* 18. 6 end)

The only other addition from the lexical texts is *LTBA* II. 2. 406: [*a*]-*tir-tú* = *šil-la-tú* (v. ibid. 3 rev. VI. 2: *zil-la-tum*). For the individual terms note:

nullâtu (= *la kit-tú*, Comm. to *Theodicy* 284)

B. Landsberger (*MAOG* IV. 320; *Kleinasiatische Forschungen* I. 325) proposed as an etymology the ethnic adjective *lulli'u* "Lull(um)äisch", and is followed by von Soden (*Or* N.S. 25. 243). Whether correct or not, there is certainly a contraction; cf. *OB.Lú* Tablet A 121: lú.níg.nu.gar.ra = *ša nu-ul-li-a-tim*. The Sumerian equivalent suggests that in origin it is simply a negative word like *lā amātu* and *lā qabītu*, which took a bad meaning. Cf. the English 'naught', which in one period developed the meaning 'wickedness', now surviving only in 'naughty'. The word is feminine plural, and no singular has yet been found.

šillatu

This has been connected with *šlh* in the Aramaic of Daniel iii. 29, but its derivation is unknown. Examples are collected in *AfO* 14. 271. The equation [in]im.é.gal = *šil-la-tú* (*Erim.ḫuš* I. 282: *CT* 18. 48. IV. 21; cf. A. L. Oppenheim, *Dreams*, p. 283[110]) suggests a meaning 'seditious speech': "word of (i.e. against?) the palace"; cf. the equivalent of *ša ta-aš-ši-tim* below.

magrītu (*migirtu*)

Despite the root *gerû*, *magrītu* is always a spoken offence. Note especially *JTVI* 29. 86. 12, where *ma-ag-ri-tum* is a command to plunder Ekur. Cf. also *VAB* VI. 215. 12–14: *ma-ag-ri-a-tim ša a-na e-ze-nim la na-ṭa-a id-bu-ub* "He spoke slanders which are not fit to be heard"; S. Smith, *Babylonian Historical Texts*, pl. IX. 17: *i-ta-mi ma-ag-ri-ti*; *STC* II. LXVIII. 18–20: *ú-šaḫ-ḫa-zu nu-ul-la-a-tum a-mat su-uš-tum* (= *surtum*, *AKF* I. 75) *i-dab-bu-bu i-qab-bu-ú ma-ag-ri-tum mi-il-ki la ku-šir im-tal-lik i-te-ep-šú sur-ra-a-tum*; *VS* 10. 214 rev. VII. 8–9: *ú-ša-ar-ri-ir-ši am-ma-ag-ra-tim qú-ul-lu-li-im ta-ar-ši-a-tim* "he corrupted her for blasphemy, cursing, and backbiting"; Grammatical Treatise 2NT–344 obv. 6 (cf. *Nabnītu* 4. 268–9 = *CT* 12. 37. III. 36–37): lú.sikil.dù.a di.da.kam = *ša ma-ag-ra-a-ti i-ta-mu-ú*; *AfO* 18. 74. 25: *ma-ag-ri-a-tim i-ta-wi*; K 225. 174: *šap-ti taq-bi-i ma-a*[*g-ra-tim*].

parītum, *parūtum*

Cf. B. Landsberger, *Belleten* 14. 267, and W. von Soden, *Or* N.S. 25. 145.

lā qabītu

Cf. E. Reiner, *JNES* 15. 142. 54'; VAT 10610 obv. 10 (p. 119); *AfO* 12, pl. XIII. 39–44, where *qabītu* and *lā qabītu* explain *anna* and *ulla*, and also inim.nu.gar.ra = *la qa-b*[*i-tú*] *nu-la-tú*.

tuššu (pl. *tuššātu*: IV R^2 17 rev. 21 = *OECT* VI. 49), *taššītu*

These two words appear to be from the same root, though this need not be *ešû*. Examples: *tuššu Ludlul* I. 69; K 2765. 17 (p. 288); *TCL* 3. 93; *ZA* 43. 15. 32; *Šurpu* II. 41; *CT* 18. 48. IV. 22: [k]úr.dug$_4$.ga = *tu-uš-šú*; A. L. Oppenheim, *Dreams*, p. 278[73]; *OB.Lú* Tablet A 123: l[ú.níg].di.é.gal.la = *ša ta-aš-ši-tim*; K 225. 175: *taš-ši-tú az-za-kir-ma*; &c.

inimmû

The presence of this word in the list is curious, since it is a loan from the Sum. inim 'word', and never seems to have a bad sense. See note on 132, and *OECT* VI. 69 rev. 3.

lā amātu

This occurs again in *Ludlul* I. 97, R. Borger, *Asarhaddon*, p. 105. 24, and in a contracted form *la-ma-[tu]* in *LTBA* II. I. XII. 123 and in the *Tukulti-Ninurta Epic* V (II), 12: *ù ki-ma tu-še la-mat šá arki-šá ta-at-tar-ka-su na-šu-ú pu-ul-ḫa-at-ka* "And like a slander, a blasphemy which is attached behind it, they bear your fear". (*rakāsu arki*—*BMS*, no. 53 obv. 7; *CT* 16. 12. 42–43; *CT* 39. 2. 99; *AMT* 96. 7. 3—when said of demons has the same meaning as *rakāsu itti*, to attach to a person inescapably.) Here the idea seems to be that the kings bear the fear of Tukulti-Ninurta like a blasphemy, which, once it has been uttered, cannot be escaped from. A difficulty is the *-ša* on *arki-ša*, since it is hard to decide what its antecedent may be.

miqtu

This appears to be an ellipsis for *miqit pî*, as in the *Middle Assyrian Laws* (*KAV* 1), § 2 (in a context with *šillatu*), *PBS* VII. 60. 9. Cf. also *CT* 38. 39. 15–16: [*ma-q*]*á-at* KA; *CT* 38. 21. 6: šub KA.

atirtu

The idea of the root would only suggest exaggeration, but in the following examples much more is implied: *Belleten* 14. 226. 39 and 44: *qá-bi* (v. *-bi$_4$-i*) *wa-ta-ar-tim* (" "Lügen" wird durch "Zuviel sagen" umschrieben", p. 264); *ARM* I. 47. 10–12: *ištēt a-wa-tum ki-it-tum* [*ú*]*-ul i-ba-aš-ši* [*k*]*a-lu-ši-na wa-at-ra-*[*a*]; *ARM* IV. 58. 19; *ARM* V. 71. 9 and 23; *Šurpu* II. 17: *i-qab-bu-u ut-ta-ru*.

Other terms of the same general meaning, though not listed above, are *aḫītu*, literally 'foreignness' (*Fable of Fox*, D Col. A 6, F 6, Z rev. 4; *Sayings* IV. 12), *ṭapiltu*, literally 'filth' (*Ludlul* I. 90 and 94, *Fable of Fox*, B rev. 13, B. Meissner, *MAOG* XI/1–2, p. 47), and *masiktu* (see note on *Ludlul* II. 35).

It is impressive to find so many terms covering roughly the same idea, and impressive to find them side by side so frequently in texts, as well as in the lexical series. A purely philological approach can only assign approximate meanings; the real significance of these terms can only be found by a study of the ethical ideas involved in the concept of sinful speech (see p. 18).

29. The verb *lezēnu* is documented by von Soden in *Or* N.S. 20. 269, where he derives it from *aluzinnu*. A further example may be *RB* 59. 242 ff. obv. 26: *ma-la al*!*-z*[*é*!?*-nu*?*-k*]*u*? (collated).

31–36. These lines seem to lie behind a section of the Arabic *Ahiqar* (ed. F. C. Conybeare, J. Rendel Harris, and A. S. Lewis, 2nd ed., p. 137. 54): "And stand not betwixt persons quarrelling, because from a bad word there comes a quarrel, and from a quarrel there comes war, and from war there comes fighting, and thou wilt be forced to bear witness; but run from thence and rest thyself." A similar passage occurs in Menander the Egyptian (*RB* 59. 65. 20). A prototype of the whole passage can be seen in *VS* 10. 204 rev. V. 17–20 = J. J. A. Van Dijk, *La Sagesse*, pp. 103–6.

31. *uzuzza* is taken as the infinitive, qualifying the end purpose of *tā'ir*: "Do not go with reference to standing."

33. *šim-ta* is unexplained.

36. For *kapādu* see the note on *Assyrian Collection* (Bilingual Proverbs) ii. 23–26.

38. The metaphor of a concealed pit is also found in *SBH*, p. 7. 38–40: the word of Enlil is bul.bul.àm i.bí nu.bar.bar.[re] = [*š*]*u-ut-ta-tum šá la nap-lu-si*. *šeṭû* 'spread (for drying)' is assumed to have a more general meaning 'spread (a cover over)'. From the same root comes *nūn maš-ṭe-e* (*Epic of Creation* IV. 137) 'a dried fish', cf. *Ḫargud* D, 45 (to *Ḫarra* 15): [uzu].×.min.tab.ba = *šīr ma-áš-ṭe-e* = *šīru ab-lu*: *šīr ab-lu-tu* (*ZA* 33. 18. 5).

39. The adjective from *abāru* 'strength' is known elsewhere lexically: *á.A* IV$_4$. 288: [KA]L = *wa-ab-rum.* The II stem of *katātu* is also found in the lists: *Erim.ḫuš* II. 126: gu$_4$.ud.BUL.BUL = *ku-ut-tu-tú* (*CT* 18. 44. II. 45), but the III/2 stem is more common (see *ZA* 44. 305). The idea of the metaphor is exactly paralleled in the name of a wall built by Sennacherib: bàd.níg.erím.ḫu.luḫ.ḫa *mu-gal-lit za-ma-a-ni* (*OIP* II. 113. 6–7).

40. Cf. *CT* 31. 8. 22–23: *ḫa-si-su šá ummāni*(erín-*ni*) *ḫarrāni-šá ma-ši-ta i-ḫa-sa-as-ma itâr*(gur)-*ma ina* [giš]*kakki nakir*(kúr)-*šá i-sa-kip*, and *RA* 22. 142 rev. I. 5: *ma-ši-tam ḫa-sa-su.*

45. *šu-t[a-'-i-r]a-áš-šú* is taken as III/3 imperative of *warû.* In the I/3 it is common in religious texts for a god caring for his people. Also *tārû* 'guardian' (*Theodicy* 11, v *R* 35. 14) and *tārītu* 'wet nurse' are connected, participles of the secondary root *tarû.*

56. *dunnamû*: cf. p. 18[1].

60, 64. *ṭāb eli šamaš* occurs again thrice in the *Šamaš Hymn* (100, 106, 119), and is implied in an inscription of Kudur-Mabug: *ša e-li* [d]*šamaš la ṭa-ba ú-la e-pu-uš* (*RA* 11. 92. I. 6–7). In the Aramaic *Ahiqar* there are also reminiscences of it: *rḥymh lšmš* (VI. 92), *yqyr* [*qdm*] *šmš* (VI. 93, A. Cowley, *Aramaic Papyri,* p. 215). These three last passages favour an impersonal interpretation ("it is pleasing" rather than "he . . ."), and the aphoristic nature of the phrase explains its grammatically abrupt entry in the *Šamaš Hymn.*

61–62. There is a striking parallel in the Ugaritic 2 *Aqhat* v. 19–20 (C. H. Gordon, *Ugaritic Manual,* p. 182): *šlḥm ššqy ilm sad kbd* "Give food, give drink to the godhead, serve(?) and honour". In lines 29–30 this instruction is put into effect in the same words. There is nothing impossible in a view that our text depends ultimately on the Ugaritic epic, or is connected in some other way, but coincidence is equally possible. Where the epic has *ilm* the Akkadian manuscripts differ. One Babylonian manuscript offers the translatable *e-riš-ti qí-i-ši* "Grant what is asked", but in other respects this is an inferior manuscript. The better manuscripts attest *e-riš kit-tú*, either imperative "ask for *kittu*", or object of the verbs of the line "him that asks for *kittu*". *kittu* 'justice' is not intelligible in the context, and Böhl's citation of the Hebrew *ṣ*[e]*dāqâ* 'justice', and later 'alms' (*JEOL* VIII. 670[28]), does not prove that *kittu* underwent the same development. The difficulty of *kittu* remains.

63. *ḫa-di-iš* with the shortened form of the suffix can only be a scribal vagary. Metre requires *ḫadîšu.*

65. *šubšu* (for *šubši*) probably results from a crasis with the following word. *šumšu* (f) is no doubt a yet closer approximation to actual speech. *gimil* may be either imperative of the verb, as assumed in the translation, or construct state of the noun *gimillu*: "a service (to be continued) for all time".

68. *pagru* may have the meaning 'self' here. Cf. *Maqlû* VII. 23 (= *CT* 23. 10. 26); A. Finet, *L'Accadien des Lettres de Mari,* § 18 c; *Anatolian Studies* v. 110, and *Akkado-Hurrian Bilingual* 2 (p. 116).

72. *šāri* is literally 3,600, the peak of the sexagesimal system.

74. The choice between *kul-ma-ši-tu* and *zir-ma-ši-tu* is still undecided. Poebel (*AS* 14. 41[h]) proposed a Sumerian derivation: kul.ma.ši "seed upon me". *ša qerēbša ma'ada* is literally "whose being approached (sexually) is much". A close parallel is the Middle Assyrian *ša la-a qa-ra-ab-ša-ni* (*AfO* 17. 276. 47) "(a palace woman) with whom intercourse is not possible", literally "whose being approached is not".

76. For *šanāṣu* see the note on *Sayings* III. 11.

78. Here and in 140 a derivation from *kašāšu* has been assumed for a very ambiguous group of signs. The only other plausible suggestion is *bi-lat* "she is mistress", but *be-lat* would be expected. For *kašāšu* cf. *Theodicy* 200 and Commentary, where it is explained by *ḫamāmu* 'master'. Cf. also *CH,* §§ 117–18.

80. *šanîš* for introducing a variant text is also used in *KAR* 307 obv. 23. The syntax of the line is very irregular, and since the vocabulary is characteristic of omens the line should perhaps be construed as omen style: "Into the house she enters—it will be disrupted (bir-*aḫ*)—her partner will not assert himself."

81. Cf. *GAG*, § 160 e.

87, 89. *puzru* 'stealthy crime' seems only to occur in this context.

88. Only the II stem of *eṣēṣu* has been found elsewhere.

91. *bunnū* (*būnū*) *namrūtu* is usually the look of favour which a god shows to his servants.

92. *amāta rašû* is 'to be involved in litigation': *CH* 25r. 3–5: *a-wi-lum ḫab-lum ša a-wa-tam i-ra-aš-šu-ú*, and in omen apodoses: *Or* 51–54, p. 50. 10, &c., *ZA* 43. 104. 13–17. See also Exodus xxiv. 14: *mî ḇa'al deḇārîm yiggaš alêhem.*

130. *qu''û rēš* is used most frequently of a person waiting on a god (E. Ebeling, *Handerhebung*, p. 62. 27; *JRAS Cent. Sup.*, pl. III. 4; *PSBA* 20. 157 rev. 8; *OECT* I, pl. 25. 14; *MVAG* 44. 195). In Middle Assyrian legal texts *ri-ša a-na qa-'u-e* explains the purpose of sheep being entrusted to someone (*AfO* 10. 16[112] and 150). The closest parallels to our passage are *Anatolian Studies* v. 106. 132: *ana ag-gi lìb-bi den-líl ú-qa-a-'-u re-e-šú*, and *LKA* 31 rev. 12: *deraᵣₐ ina šip-ṭi šaq-qaš-ti ú-qa-'-a rēs-su.* There is clearly no great difference between the simple verb and the phrase with *rēš*. Thus in the passage from the *Zû Myth* (*CT* 15. 39. II. 17) *ú-qa-a-a ri-ši u₄-mi* those translators who take *ri-ši u₄-mi* as 'dawn' are wrong. Zû was simply awaiting a 'time' suitable for his robbery.

132. Things said alone and in secret were as effective as a public utterance. Cf. *LKA* 31 rev. 11 and 13: *šá a-na šarri ina lìb-bi-šú i-kap-pu-du mílemut[tu], šá a-na šarri ina lìb-bi-šú i-ta-mu-ú nu-ul-la-a-ti.*
e-nim-me-e kab-ta-ti-ka is found again in the fable of *Nisaba and Wheat* IV. 20, and a similar expression occurs in the *Epic of Creation* VI. 22: *ki-na-a-ti a-ta-ma-a* (v. *ta-ta-a-ma-'*) *i-nim-ma-a it-ti-ia.* While *kabtāti* is clearly not an adjective agreeing with *inimmê*, since it has the suffix, the parallel *kīnāti* proves that it is fem. pl. of the adjective *kabtu*, and not a poetic form or pl. of *kabattu* 'liver'. The most satisfactory explanation of these passages is that *inimmê* and *kabtāti/kīnāti* are in apposition: "words, solemn/reliable things".

133. Despite the variant with *šá*, it is not inconceivable that a relative clause should occur without *ša* even when the relative particle would embrace the antecedent ("that which").

134. Cf. *OIP* II. 105. 75: *ú-ša-ni-ḫu ú-lam-me-nu ka-ras-si-in* "They strained and did themselves harm."

136. Cf. *TDP* 80. 7: *ikrib qí-bít pî-šú*, and ibid. 222. 48: *qí-bít-ka ana dsin.*

137. Cf. *Counsels of a Pessimist* 12.

140. See note on 78.

143–7. Cf. *ABL* 614 rev. 8–9: *[p]a-laḫ ilānimeš da-ma-qu ul-lad*
[p]a-laḫ da-nun-na-ki ba-la-ṭu ú-tar

Unfortunately the context of the letter is too obscure to be certain how these words come to be quoted. See Introduction.

149. *šaplâti*: see note on *Šamaš Hymn* 123.

150–3. Cf. E. Reiner, *JNES* 15. 142. 53′: *aq-bi-ma e-ni ú-ta[k-kil-ma] ul addin*(SUM-*in*) "I promised, but then did differently; I let people t[rust (in me), but then] I did not give."

(iii) *COUNSELS OF A PESSIMIST*

1. *iliš muššulu*: cf. *Ludlul* II. 31; *Epic of Creation* I. 137.

6. *târu ana ṭiṭṭi*: cf. *Gilg.* 11. 118 and 133; *Era* I. 74 (*a-na ṭi-iṭ-ṭi* restored from VAT 10071 rev. 8 (pl. 73)), *SEM* 117. II. 7.

9. For *sâtu* 'remain over' cf. *Era* I. 145; *TCL* 3. 176; *KAR* 196 obv. II. 59: *ki-ma pi-sa-an-ni šur-di-i a-a i-si-tu mu-ú-šá.*

10. Restored after *Gilg.* OB. 3. IV. 7: *a-me-lu-tum-ma ma-nu-ú u$_4$-mu-ša mi-im-ma ša i-te-ni-pu-šu ša-ru-ma* "As for mankind, their days are numbered. Whatever they do is wind."

12. The reading gur$_6$ for kár comes from *Nabnītu* K, 139–40 (*CT* 19. 43. III. 11–12):

$^{\text{gu-ru}}$ÍL = *na-šu-ú*
$^{\text{MIN!}}$GÁN = *na-šu-ú*

The term for free-will offering was taken over as a loan, as is shown by the phonetic complements in *Counsels of Wisdom* 137, *LTBA* II. I. XII. 112, *BBSt*, pl. 26 rev. 12, H. Winckler, *Die Keilschrifttexte Sargons*, Atlas, pl. 25, no. 53. 6. See *JCS* 2. 75. In Sumerian, however, it is a phrase applying generally to "what his heart carries (him) to", as explained by A. Poebel, *AS* 14. 93, and is not specifically an offering. Cf. the proverb igi.íl.la.zu dam tuku.ba.ni.ib šà.ge.guru$_7$.zu tuku.ba.ni.ib "Take a wife according to your choice, have a child according to your heart's desire" (translation of S. N. Kramer, *CRR* III. 81 no. 40), a further confirmation of the reading gur$_6$. This general sense is rendered into Akkadian *bibil libbi*, a translation going back at least to the inscriptions of Lipit-Ištar, where šà.ge.túm.a in the Sumerian texts corresponds to *bí-bí-il li-i-ba* in the Akkadian. From this idiom the verbal phrase *wabālu libbu* originated, basically 'to desire' rather than 'ponder'.

15. Both reading and sense of *šu-[qa]m-me-em* are doubtful.

22. Perhaps restore: *zi-mu-ka [lu-u nam-ru pa-nu-ka l]u-u ṣu-uḫ-ḫu.* Cf. *Sayings* III. 30.

(iv) *ADVICE TO A PRINCE*

1. Tablet 53 of *Šumma ālu* in the Assur recension begins *šumma*(diš) *šarru*(bára) *ana di-nim i-qul* (*KAR* 394. III. 21, cf. *AfO* 11. 359–60). The same protasis appears on Sm 772 obv. 16 (*CT* 40. 9), a piece of uncertain location within the series *Šumma ālu*: [*šumma šarru ana*] *di-nim i-qul palâšu*(bal.bi) *a-ri-ik-ta i*[*m-mar*].

3. *a-ḫi-tu* must be 'hostile action' here and in 54, though elsewhere 'hostile speech', 'slander' is more common; see note on *Counsels of Wisdom* 28.

6. *ṭēm māti išanni*: see note on *Dialogue of Pessimism* 25.

14. *zi-lul-liš*: cf. *Theodicy* 249 and note.

16. *ana qa-li tur-ru*: *qa-li* has been taken hitherto as *qâli* 'to heed', but Böhl's rendering of *ana qa-li iṣḫiru*(tur-*ru*) "sie ihm zu gering waren, darauf zu achten" does not give good sense. A king is entitled to dismiss a trivial lawsuit. *ana qalli turru* is a better interpretation of the signs: "he turns it into a frivolous (lawsuit)".

19, 24. *e-me-da*(*-am*): see note on 32 below.

21. Cf. *SBH*, no. 41 obv. 11–12: ka.nag.gá sur$_6$.bi.ta ba.da.ḫa.lam

ma-a-ti ina [*bi-ru*]*-ti-šú uḫ-tal-liq*

The sign groups ki.dù(sur$_7$) and ki.gal(sur$_6$) leave no doubt as to the sense of *bīrūtu, bērūtu*: 'totality', 'full extent'. It is difficult to separate this abstract from the adjective *bīru, bēru*, discussed by von Soden in *Or* N.S. 16. 442–3. It is used of subterranean waters, mountains (e.g. *Šamaš Hymn* 6 and 19), regions (*VAB* IV. 146. 26; *KAH* II. 60. 100; 61. 48), and the open spaces (*Theodicy* 139). 'Vast' or 'extensive' suits all the occurrences, and though an adjective *bēru* 'choice' certainly exists, ^{giš}*šu-úr-mi-ni ni-is-qí bé-e-ru-tim* is best taken as 'enormous' trees in I *R* 58. IX. 6–7 = *VAB* IV. 118. 41. Their choice quality is already expressed in *ni-is-qí*.

23. The emendation zi!-*bi* was proposed by Diakonoff.

24. *tupšikku*: see note on *Theodicy* 215.

32. *šá-ra-ki*: here, at least, and probably also in *e-me-da*(*-am*) in 19 and 24 an infinitive is used instead of a finite verbal form. This is not customary in omen style, but two further examples occur in the inscriptions of Adad-nirari II: *ma-ḫa-ri* and *na-sa-ḫi* (*KAH* II. 84. 33 and 35 = *MAOG* IX/3. 16). In other

Semitic languages this use of the infinitive is well established: in South Arabic (Maria Höfner, *Altsüdarabische Grammatik*, § 54), in the Hebrew infinitive absolute, and in other dialects of Canaanite (C. H. Gordon, *Ugaritic Manual*, § 9. 25; J. W. Wevers, *Zeitschrift für die alttestamentliche Wissenschaft* 62. 316; W. L. Moran, *JCS* 4. 163–72 and *JCS* 6. 76–80). It is worth noting that the Canaanite form has the ending *-i*: *qatāli*, and this is shared by the three Akkadian examples.

44. Von Soden in *Or* N.S. 20. 153 establishes the existence of a quadriliteral verb *nagaršû* for this passage and *Enūma Eliš* III. 129, and suggests a meaning 'durcheinanderlaufen'. Animals dying of hunger were apparently considered offerings to Šamaš.

46. For *amāta lummunu* see Bilingual Proverbs K 4347+ II. 15 and *BiOr* 14. 7–8.

52. The parallel *ḫarrānu* suggests á.dù = *adû* 'Tagewerk' (also 'Arbeitspensum'), on which see *MSL* I. 232. The lack of the verb, however, does not allow the exclusion of *adû* 'treaty' as a possibility. Diakonoff restores the verb *i-*[*na-du*]*-šú-nu-ti.*

55. It is very curious that a shepherd should be thought a likely person to become a supervisor of a major temple in one of the most important cities in Babylonia.

58–59. The *Tukulti-Ninurta Epic* describes how the gods forsook their cities in the time of Kaštiliaš III (*AfO* 18. 43. 32–47).

(v) *VARIA*

Akkado-Hurrian Bilingual

1. Nougayrol explains this line as referring to money which is deposited with the judges when a person appeals to the river ordeal. He, however, takes *šukun* as construct of a noun *šuknu.*

2. For the use of *pagru* as a reflexive pronoun see the note on *Counsels of Wisdom* 68.

3. Nougayrol reads ZI *innasaḫ*, but the use of an ideogram for a verb is quite unexpected in this text. A suffix would suit the metre better: *kali apilšu* "his son is held back", i.e. he has no children. ZI could also be read *kēnu.*

11. *la-a-am tal-la-ak* separated "before you go" gives little sense, and the rest of the text is written in the third person, apart from the latter half of 12, and the Hurrian of that phrase apparently lacks any second-person element. Also the Hurrian of this phrase does not contain the verb 'go', which is known. Thus a crasis has been assumed of *lā imtallak* "he does not take counsel with himself", cf. *Gilgameš* XI. 168, *KAR* 298 rev. 17.

Chapter 5. Hymns

(i) NINURTA BILINGUAL

OBVERSE

5–10. See note on *Counsels of Wisdom* 28. *me/iḫru* 'equal (socially)' and *nadû* 'lay a charge' are paralleled in *CH*, § 200, §§ 1 and 2.

13–14. Cf. *CH*, § 34; *CH* I. 37–39 and 24r. 59–60; H. Winckler, *Die Keilschrifttexte Sargons*, Atlas pl. 43, Cylinder, 50; *VAB* VII. 226. 11; *LSS* II/4, pl. IV. 11 = E. Ebeling, *Handerhebung*, p. 128; *DP* 24. 118. 28–29.

18. *ar-da-du*: *LTBA* II. 1. VII. 36 = *OECT* IV. 60. 19.

REVERSE

4. The reading niga is based on *MSL* II. 83. 690. Cf. *JNES* 4. 156[7].

6–7. It is not clear whether *ú-ma-ši* and *a-ba-ri* here are concrete objects (rendered "maillon" and "ceinture" by Van Dijk), or just words for 'strength'. Cf. *Ludlul* III e and von Soden, *ZA* 51. 144. The Commentary on *Šumma izbu* 495–7 explains *ú-ma-šu* with *la-a-nu*, *rit-tum*, and *e-mu-qu*. These lines show that one form of athletics at least was practised in ancient Mesopotamian cult.

14–19. Cf. *KAR* 18 rev. 8–9.

18. The reading *é-šu-me-ša*$_4$! is established by Jacobsen in *ZA* 52. 103[19]. It is Ninurta's temple in Nippur.

(ii) *ŠAMAŠ HYMN*

2, 4. *eliš u šapliš* are to be taken quite literally; in his journey through the underworld Šamaš visited the *nišī*^{meš} *šaplâti*(ki.ta)^{meš} (E. Ebeling, *Tod und Leben*, p. 54. 29). This shows that *elâti* and *šaplâti* are not primarily geographical terms, but are to be understood with an ellipsis of *nišī*.

5. [*saḫ*]-*pu*: the basic meaning of *sḫp* seems to be 'stretch out' (intransitive); 'cover' is a natural development of this, and hence 'overwhelm'. For the first meaning cf. *LKA* 109 obv. 12 restored by 83–1–18, 477 (*RA* 48. 8): *e-ma šamê*^{e} *saḫ-pu* "so far as the heavens stretch". Also there is *si-ḫi-ip šamê*^{e} (*ZA* 42. 163[1]; *AfO* 16. 5. 31 and *AfO* 16. 19; *Ludlul* IV(?). 48; W. J. Hinke, *A New Boundary Stone of Nebuchadnezzar* (*BE* Series D, vol. 4), p. 144. 14 = *SSS* XIV, p. 22), *si-ḫi-ip da-ád-me* (*Šamaš Hymn* 153; *JRAS Cent. Sup.*, pl. II. 15), and *si-ḫi-ip* kur.kur (*Šamaš Hymn* 20), where *siḫpu* = 'extent'. No hostile action is necessarily implied in the transitive use of *sḫp*, cf. *Gilg.* 9. II. 8: *gal-tu mi-lam-mu-šu-un sa-ḫi-ip ḫur-sa-a-ni* "their dread dazzle covers the mountains". See also line 40 below.

6, 19. For the meaning of *bēru* see note on *Advice to a Prince* 21.

7. *malkū* in this hymn means the Anunnaki; see also 24 and 31.

10. ud.da: cf. B. Landsberger, *JNES* 8. 252[30].

17, 18. These lines are almost untranslatable. The difficulties are: (i) the uncertain syntactical position of *ṣirrit šam*[*āmi*], (ii) the obscure *zik*-KUR *ur-ri*, (iii) the lack of any kind of connexion between *mēreš še'em napiš*[*ti*] ⌜*māti*⌝ and the sentence, or even with the whole context. Some explanation of the difficulties comes from the Marduk Hymn K 8292 and K 8236 (*ZA* 4. 39–40), which are now joined by K 6906, which fits between them. K 3459 (*ZA* 4. 36) is a duplicate:

5 *muš-te-šir nārāti*^{meš} *ina qí-rib šadî*^{i}
6 *mu-pat-tu-ú bu-ur kup-pi ina qí-rib ḫur-sa-a-ni*

7 *na-ši-ir mīl*(e$_4$.la$_6$) *ḫé*-⌜*gál-li*⌝ *a-na gi-mir kal da-ád-me*
8 [× × × ×]× ta *erṣetim*^{tim} *rapaštim*^{tim} *dš-na-an*

9 [*mu-šá-a*]*z-nin na-al-ši ina ṣir-rit šá-ma-mi*
10 [× × (×)]× *šá-a-ri ti-iq me-e e-lu qar-ba-a-ti*

11 [× × *i*]*š-pik-ki ṭuḫ-di a-na mi-riš še-em ú-ga-ri*
12 [× × *ṣ*]*i-im-ri ku-bu-ut-te-e iš-pik-ki ta-at-tu-r*[*u*]

5 Who directs the rivers inside the hills,
6 Who opens the bowls of the springs inside the mountains,

7 Who lets loose a flood of bounty for absolutely all habitations,
8 [. . . .] . . the broad earth with corn,

9 [Who sends] down showers from the *ṣirrit* of the heavens,
10 [Who . . .] . the winds and downpourings upon the fields,
11 [Who . . . a]bundance and plenty to the low-lying land planted with corn,
12 [Who . . . su]perfluity, profusion, abundance, wealth.

Here two of the offending phrases occur, but now in a proper context, and it is hard to escape the conclusion that the *Šamaš Hymn* in this passage has become contaminated with this Marduk Hymn, or a literary antecedent of it. It is significant that in 18 E has one variant reading, *meḫer*, which is not just orthographic, and this is preceded by some uncertain remains which, when allowance is made for the possibility that some of the wedges were intended as erased, nevertheless cannot be reconciled with the text of the other manuscripts.

Other occurrences of *ṣirrit šamê* are given by Goetze in *JCS* 9. 8–14, where two duplicates of one passage offer as variants *zi-ku-ra-at ša-me-e* and *kakkab ša-me-e*. Cf. also *ṣi-ri-it a-bu-bi*, *KAR* 306 rev. 25 = C. Frank, *Kultlieder*, p. 38.

21. *šu-ra-ta* is taken as III/1 stative of *a'āru*.

22. The meaning of *šql* 'suspend' is not common in Akkadian, but it occurs in the gloss *a-la-lu šá-qa-lu* added to the aphorism ^{d}*en-lil ṭēmi*(umuš-*mi*) *nišī*^{meš} *u milik*(galga!) *nišī*^{meš} *ina sikkati*(giš.gag) *il-lal-ma* "Enlil will hang the plans and counsels of men on a peg" (*CT* 31. 39 obv. I. 18–20). The picture here is that of Šamaš holding up the earth like a pan of balances.

30. With the incomplete word the question is whether Šamaš or the places he traverses are to be compared. A reading *sa*-×-(×)-*si* is also possible.

41. *pa-r*[*u*]!-*ka* is the only possible interpretation of the traces and space, and is to be preferred to the *lectio facilior pa-n*[*a*]-*ka*. This word occurs again in 150, where the palaeographically uncertain *maš*?- of an exercise tablet is not to be chosen against the clear *pa-* in the Nineveh copy. The only known word which may be compared is *pāru* 'skin' (*Malku-šarru* II. 237 (*ZA* 43. 242): *ba-a-ru* (v. *pa-a-ri*) = *maš-ku*; H. Winckler, *Die Keilschrifttexte Sargons*, Atlas pl. 43 Cylinder, 33). It is uncertain, however, if a meaning 'surface' can be assumed.

49. Cf. IV R^2 20. I. 24.

53, 54. The seer's bowl was a vessel holding water on to which oil was poured, and oracles were derived from the shapes which it assumed on the surface of the water. An object of cedar in the hand of the officiating priest was essential, though the part it played in the ritual is not clear. Instructions for this ceremony are preserved in H. Zimmern, *BBR Ritualtafeln*, nos. 1–20. 117–26 and no. 24. *mu-ši*/[*š*]*im-mi* looks like *šemû* II/1, but this stem of the verb is not otherwise attested.

55. Böhl (*JEOL* VIII. 676) restores [*ra-ki-s*]*u*.

60. *ma-šit-ta* is taken as a variant form of *mišittu*; cf. *RA* 44. 16. 4: *ma-ši-it-ti*.

61. *târu* here probably implies going to the underworld, even if the missing half of the line did not expressly state so.

62. A common Akkadian metaphor speaks of persons in mortal danger as though they were in the grave, e.g. *Ludlul* IV(?). 6, 7, 35, 36.

67. Cf. *Maqlû* III. 4: *ṣa-a-a-di-tum šá ri-ba-a-ti* (said of a sorceress), and *Theodicy* 141, 249. In Ugaritic also *ṣw*/*yd* has the sense 'walk about'.

68. Šamaš is referred to in the third person again in 72, 100, 106, 119, and 143.

69. Cf. *Tukulti-Ninurta Epic* II (v), 9: *na-a-šu ki-i-su tamkārū*^{meš}. *kīsu*, a leather bag whose mouth was drawn in with a string (*AMT* 88. 3. 13–14: *kima kīsi šá tamkāri gab-bi šir'ānī*^{meš}*-ia il-du-dam-ma ra-ka-su-um-ma ir-ku-us*), was the purse in which the travelling merchant carried his money, and so can be used for capital invested in such an enterprise. In 108 it is the trader's bag in which the weights were carried, and the phrase *aban*/*abnī kīsi* is the exact equivalent of the Hebrew *aḇᵉnê ḵîs* (Proverbs xvi. 11).

70. For [d]*zanunzû* see the note on *Ludlul* II. 37.

71. *munna/erbu*, *errēbu*, and *arbu* 'fugitive' are all found. If this line is correctly restored, a form *erbu* also exists. The thought is paralleled in *KAR* 55 obv. 7: *muš-ti-šir ur-ḫi mun-nar-bi.*

90. For *kippu* 'Schlinge' see von Soden, *Or* N.S. 26. 317, and A. L. Oppenheim, *Dreams*, p. 286[130].

93. The otiose *šunu* is a stylistic feature common in the *Epic of Creation.*

96. Cf. *OECT* I, pl. 25. 12: *e-li šu-ub-ti-šú kit-ti ul e-pú-uš-ma e-ni qá-qá-ar-šu* "He did not build it on its firm resting-place, and a subsidence of the ground occurred." This leaves no doubt that *e-piš* RID-*di ka-pi-du* is an evil person. For the meaning of *kpd* see the note on *Assyrian Collection* (Bilingual Proverbs) II. 23–26. A reading *šid-di* gives no sense, whether taken as 'region', as in 103 and 105, or 'curtain'. F. J. Stephens's derivation from the Sumerian šid 'reckoning' (*ANET* 388[4]) is not convincing. *riddu* = 'what is proper' (*Theodicy* 214 and note), and gives just the opposite meaning to that required. However, in an inscription of Esarhaddon *riddu* is used in a bad sense; the passage is, however, obscure (see the discussion of R. Borger, *Asarhaddon*, p. 41. 23). Perhaps *riddu* is a word used in its original sense and also for the opposite.

98–99. Akkadian does not distinguish between 'present' and 'bribe'. The receiving of presents by judges was little different from the payment of lawyers' fees in the modern world, and as such is not condemned (cf. J. J. Finkelstein, *JAOS* 72. 77–80). Here blame is put on a judge who accepts the fee, but then fails to secure satisfaction for his client, and a judge who takes up the poor man's case without charge is praised. For *enšu* see the note on *Theodicy* 19.

100. For *ṭāb eli šamaš* see the note on *Counsels of Wisdom* 60.

102. Cf. *CAD*, vol. G, 30 for *gummuru* 'control'.

103. *mi-na-a ut-tar*: see note on *Theodicy* 251.

103–6. *ḫulluqu kīsa* occurs again in omen protases: *KAR* 423 obv. III. 21–22:

mār tamkāri ina ḫarrān illiku kīssu uḫal[laq] rēqūtsu itâr

dumu lú.dam.gàr *ina* kaskal du-*ku* kuš.[níg].zá!-*su* zá[ḫ] sud-*su* gur.ra (cf. *KAR* 428 obv. 15) and *KAR* 423 rev. I. 59–60:

mār tamkāri ina māti rūqte illak [. . .] *kīssu uḫallaq rēqūtsu itâr*

dumu lú.dam.gàr *ina* kur sud-*te* du-[*ak* . .] kuš.níg.zá-*su ú-ḫal-laq* sud-*su* gur.r[a and *KAR* 423 rev. I. 61–63:

mār tamkāri ina māti rūqte [*illak* . .] *šumma kīssu urakk*[*is* . .] *mimma aqru iliqqi ana šarri i*[*târ* . .

dumu lú.dam.gàr *ina* kur sud-[*te* du-*ak* . .] bad-*ma* kuš.níg.zá-*su ú-rak-k*[*i-is* . .] *mim-ma aq-ru* ti-*ma ana* lugal g[ur.ra . .

There can be no question then that 103–6 refer to travelling merchants, and *šiddu* is therefore '(foreign) region'. The failure of such merchants would consist in not making the hoped-for profits, and worst of all in losing the money risked in the venture. Clearly 104 states this. The Akkadian root *kzb* (cognates are found in Hebrew, Arabic, and Aramaic) is well known in the sense of 'fawn' (*kunzubu*), but a meaning 'lie', 'deceive' needs to be substantiated, since the indubitable examples in the Amarna letters could be explained as Canaanisms. Cf. *Antagal* III:

266 [×.(×)].× = *ku-un-zu-bu*
267 [ku]n.gùn.gùn.nu = MIN *šá kal-bi*
268 KA.gùn.gùn = MIN *šá a-ma-ti* (*CT* 18. 34. IV. 21–23)
* * * * *
287 [pi.il].pi.il = *pa-ru-ú*
288 [KA].è.dè = MIN *šá pi-i*
289 KA.gùn.gùn = *pu-ú pur-ru-šú* (*CT* 18. 35. IV. 38–40)

Von Soden (*Or* N.S. 22. 206) in commenting on examples of the root *prš* in the Mari letters assigns to it a meaning 'flatter', and denies any connexion with the root *prṣ* 'lie'. However, if *prš* and *prṣ* are separate roots, as seems probable, a connexion in meaning is established by *Šurpu* II. 63: *bar-ru pa-ar-šú pi-i-šu* with the Commentary: [*pa-ar-šu*]: *da-bi-bu par-ri-ṣu* (*AfO* 12, pl. 14. 23). In the other Semitic languages *kḏb* is not merely used for factual inaccuracies, but in Arabic covers the 'deception' of an animal that ceases to give milk, and in Hebrew the 'deception' of a water course that dries up (Jeremiah xv. 18). In Akkadian *kunzubu* 'fawn' is only another aspect of *kunzubu* "of a word", i.e. 'lie'. The Sumerian gùn.gùn 'variegated' fits into the picture of that which lacks an abiding, trustworthy characteristic. In the III/2 the only other occurrence seems to be *ZA* 4. 250, K 3183. 13–15, and *KAR* 351 15–16:

[*muš*]-*tak-zib šap-la-a-ti ka-ṣi*[*r* . . . . . .]
[. . .]-*ši-ru ṣa-ri-iḫ* × [. . . . .]
[*muš-tak-zib ša*]*p-la-a-ti mu-ta-mu-ú* [. . . . .]
[Who spr]eads misleading hypocrisies, who instiga[tes . . . .]
[. . .] . . . cries out . . [. . . . .]
[Who spreads misleading hypocris]ies, who utters [. . . . .]

A literal translation of *uštakazzab ana nēmelimma* would perhaps be "he experiences unreliability in the matter of profit". Cf. von Soden, *GAG*, § 94 e.

105. *CT* 31. 35. 9 at first sight seems to be a close parallel: *mār tamkāri ina ḫarrān illiku ina ištēn šiqli ištēn manā uttar* (dumu dam.gàr *ina* kaskal du-*ku ina* 1 gín 1 ma.na *ut-tar*). Closer examination, however, suggests that the similarity between *mu-tir* and *ut-tar* is a coincidence.

107–8. The fraudulent use of two standards of weights and measures is commonly attested in the ancient Near East; cf. *CH*, § P, and the discussion of G. R. Driver and J. C. Miles, *The Babylonian Laws* I, pp. 180–4; also *The Story of Aḥiḳar*[2] (F. C. Conybeare, J. Rendel Harris, and A. S. Lewis), p. 61, no. 50, and a Sumerian Nanše hymn (S. N. Kramer, University Museum, *Bulletin*, Philadelphia, XVI/2, p. 33). The wording is paralleled in *Šurpu* VIII. 67: *zi-ba-nit la kit-ti ṣa-ba-tu*, cf. II. 42.

109. This line is not really a logical sequence to the preceding pair, since it properly refers to travelling merchants, while the preceding pair refer to merchants generally.

111. *ki šá-áš-šú* "like gold" is also a possible interpretation.

112–19. *šīqāti ana birî* and *ina kabri pān* are adaptations of OB. business terms expressing standards of measurements for grain: *ši-i-iq me-še-qí-im bi-ru-ú-im* "measured in the small (lit. hungry) measure" and *ši-i-iq me-še-qí-im ka-ab-ri-im* "measured in the large (lit. fat) measure". There is a divergent form of the latter: *i-na ka-ab-r*[*i-im*] *i-na me-še-qum* (passages are cited by A. Goetze, *JCS* 2. 85–86). These parallels provide the restoration of 118, where the adverbially used *pān*, a term never employed for specific amounts (B. Landsberger, *WO* 1. 375–6), takes the place of *i-na me-še-qum*.[1] The root *šêqu* is also known from *Antagal* N II. 5: šu.ùr = *še-e-qu šá ma-*[*da-di*] (*CT* 19. 25, K 4309 obv. 5+*CT* 19. 36, K 13618. 3).

113. *šuddunu* is the common term in OB. loan contracts for demanding repayment.

115. ⌜*iš*⌝-*šá-al* is also possible, but the line remains obscure. In the immediate context *ina lā adannišu* parallels *ina lā ūmešu*, but as a commercial term *adannu* is the date on which repayment of a loan has to be made, and this suits the larger context. Either the parallelism between 114 and 115 is a coincidence, or the writer did not recognize the commercial sense of *adannu*. 'Guilt' is a guess at the meaning of *biltu*, since 'burden' and 'guilt' appear to have been related ideas, for the verbs *našû* and *zabālu* are used with both; cf., e.g., *GCCI* II. 406. 5–6: šu.gá.gá = *na-še-e bi-il-tú* and *na-še-e še-er-ti*.

117. Cf. *Ludlul* I. 62.

[1] I have Professor A. L. Oppenheim to thank for referring me to these commercial terms as explanatory of the hymnal passages.

118. *umme'ānum kēnum* is a common expression in the Cappadocian tablets, but there it is more legal ('established') than moral.

123. *šaplâtu* and other derivatives of *špl* have a bad sense: *Counsels of Wisdom* 149, K 3183 (quoted on 103–6 above), and passages cited by F. R. Kraus, *ZA* 43. 111. 'To speak with a low voice' (A. L. Oppenheim, *Or* N.S. 16. 211[1]) is not established for *šaplâti tamû*, despite the opposite *elīta šasû*. *šaplâtu* are things which the mouth speaks though the heart is thinking differently, i.e. hypocrisy. This line is therefore no sequence to 122, which is left in the air as an incomplete commencement.

ina masdāri = *maldāriš*; cf. *Counsels of Wisdom* 141: *ana atrimma* = *atriš*.

125. *ulla* 'no' may be a form of the old negative *ula*, though it is attested in Sumerian (*RA* 11. 144. 4 and *Erim.ḫuš* III. 90 (*AfO* 7. 273. II. 30)); its opposite is *anna* 'yes'. The bad sense of *ulla* in this line apparently comes from a stock phrase which has been truncated. Cf. *Šurpu* II:

6 *a-na an-na ul-la iq-bu-u a-na ul-la an-na iq-bu-u*
56 *pi-i-šú an-na lìb-ba-šú ul-la*

Another witness to the abbreviation of this phrase is a passage from the inscriptions of Esarhaddon: *nišī*[meš] *a-šib lìb-bi-šu an-na ul-la a-ḫa-meš e-tap-pa-lu i-dab-bu-ba sur-ra-a-*[*t*]*i* (R. Borger, *Asarhaddon*, p. 12. 3a). Thus "no for yes, and yes for no" (i.e. lies) could be shortened to "yes no", or even to "no" and still retain the meaning 'lies'.

127. *mussû* or *muššû* 'decide' (A. Falkenstein, *LKU*, p. 13) is no doubt the same root as *mesû* 'wash', a metaphor arising from the water ordeal.

132. Cf. *CAD*, vol. Ḫ, 253a (d). The reading *ḫur*!-*ri* is by no means certain.

133. Cf. p. 18, note 1.

134. *imaḫḫarka* in this context does not imply any action on the part of the subject, but only that the subject is under the watchful eye of Šamaš. Note the subjects in K 8051 (Pl. 33):

1 . . .] × × × × [. . .
2 . . .] × *šá* mu.1.kám u_4-*ma* × [. . .
3 . . .] × [. . .] × *ana* è-*e* × [. . .
4 . . .] ⌜*i*⌝-*maḫ-ḫar*-⌜*ka*⌝ *qan appāri*(ambar) *ab-lu qa-mi-tú* giš[. . .
5 . . . *i*]-*maḫ-ḫar-ka nāru a-bil-tú atappu*(pa$_5$.lá) *si-k*[*ir-tú* . . .
6 . . . *i*]-⌜*maḫ-ḫar*⌝-*ka būl*(máš.anše) *ṣēri nam-maš-ti-ki šu-ut na-*[*piš-ti šak-nu*]
7 . . . *i*]-*maḫ-ḫar-ka ṣal-mat qaqqadi šu-ut* ma ka × [. . .
8 . . . *mim-ma i-maḫ-*]*ḫa-ra* [d]*šamaš ana ia-a-ti i-ziz-*[*za-nim-ma* . . .
9 . . . *ia-*]*a-ši arad-ka mār*(dumu) *bārî*(lú.ḫal) *qu-u*[*l* . . .
10 . . . du]b.dub *li-kun ma-ḫar* [. . .
11 trace

See also line 68 above. In view of this, the usual interpretation of this line as *um-mi-sal-la maš-da-ra* "with eme.sal-prayer and regular offering" becomes doubtful, especially as the class of persons given in 133 are those who would be least qualified in eme.sal, and would be unable to afford a *mašdarû*.

135. Cf. *Šurpu* IV. 33: *šá āl-šú ru-u-qu ḫarrān-šú ni-sa-*[*a*]*t*.

136. Cf. R. Labat, *TDP* 70. 15: *eṭimmu šu-ru-bat ṣēri iṣbat-su*.

143. Cf. *Malku-šarru* VIII. 35: *mu-ṣal-lu-u* = *sa-ar-ru*.

145. i.e. the souls of bodies not buried and not provided with offerings.

146–50. The exercise tablet g offers the Assyrian form of suffix in 150: -*ši-na*, but its *im-ḫa-ru-ka* in 146 and 147 is neither regular Babylonian, nor Assyrian.

150. See the note on 41 above.

151. Šamaš is particularly the god of omens; it is he who "writes the omen inside the sheep" (*ina libbi immeri ta-šaṭ-ṭar šīra*, E. Ebeling, *Handerhebung*, p. 48. 110).

154–5. These lines say that just as a diviner peers into his bowl to find knowledge, so Šamaš scans the whole universe, but finds it too small to occupy his gaze. Cf. the similar thought in Isaiah xl. 15–17. *niṭil īnēka* = "that into which your eyes look"; cf. *šurubat ṣēri* 136 above, "that which is feared on the steppe".

156. The twentieth day of the month was the festival of Šamaš, whose mystic number was twenty (*CT* 25. 50. 10); see B. Landsberger, *Der kultische Kalender* (*LSS* VI. 1/2), pp. 137–8, and BM 53309 (p. 220) with notes.

167–73. These lines lack a main verb, and while 169–73 are a coherent group of lines apparently leading up to something, 174 ff. form no logical sequence. Apart from lacking a main verb, the couplet 167–8 does not fit into the context.

173. *miḫirtu*: for this reading rather than *miširtu* see B. Landsberger, *JNES* 8. 259[54].

174. Cf. W. J. Hinke, *BE*, Series D, vol. 4. 144. 14–15 = *SSS* XIV, p. 22. 14–15:
ša-ru-ru-šu ka-la si-ḫi-ip šá-ma-me nap-ḫar kin-né-e u kal da-ad-me lit-bu-uš-ma

183. The renderings of the names of the parts of the lock are very tentative. For *uppu* see the note on Bilingual Proverbs K 4347, III. 19–20.

Chapter 6. *Dialogue of Pessimism*

1. *arad*: vocative, see *GAG*, § 62 j; for a phonetic writing cf. *ka-lab*, *Fable of Fox* C obv. 19.
mitanguranni: the Babylonian variant *muntangiranni*, seemingly a deviation from the II/2 imperative, should warn us against attaching too much importance to the I/3 form. Ungnad (*AfO* 15. 74–75) rightly stresses that *magāru* is often a virtual synonym of *šemû* 'hear (with a disposition to obey)', and while there may be some special nuance in this form suggestions such as 'obey me', 'agree with me', or 'oblige me' emphasize an incidental implication to the exclusion of the main idea.
annû bēli annû is evidently the conventional answer of slaves, as in the *Cuthean Legend of Naram-Sin* (*Anatolian Studies* V. 108, 169) a pacifistic king is instructed to reply *an-nu-u be-lí* to an aggressor. The Akkadian 'yes' is *anna* (*GAG*, § 124 a), and there is no evidence of its ever having a long *u*, so that the demonstrative pronoun is to be recognized in this phrase: "this-one-here (am I)".

2. *šēšer*: literally "make straight (the way)". The phrase *šūšuru ḫarrāna* also occurs with an ellipsis of *ḫarrāna* in the Mari letters: *ARM* XV. 188, e.g. *ARM* I. 121. 10–11: *a-na qa-ab-ra-a*[ki] [*u*]*š-te-še-er* "he has gone to Qabrâ".
lunšur: the nouns *māširu* 'wagon' (Salonen, *Landfahrzeuge*, p. 35), and *mašartu* and *tamšaru* 'spur' (Salonen, *Hippologica*, pp. 154–6) are well known, but the existence of a verb *mašāru* 'drive' has been doubted by Salonen (*Landfahrzeuge*, p. 35[1]). This passage, however, demands such a verb, perhaps a denominative, and its existence has been recognized by Ebeling and Langdon (ad loc.), Bauer (*Das Inschriftenwerk Assurbanipals*, p. 3 on IX. 105), and Schott (*ZA* 42. 141[2]).

5. *ē* = 'No', cf. J. J. Stamm, *MVAG* 44. 175.

8. *urḫa*, *ḫarrāna*, or *padāna* is no doubt to be restored.

11. This passage throws welcome light on the dining habits of the Babylonians. Hand washing in the performance of rituals is commonly mentioned, and so it preceded of course cultic meals, cf. the curious fragment IV R^2 13, no. 2:

šu.zu šu.luḫ.ḫe šu.zu zalag.zalag.ga
qa-ti-ka mi-si *qa-ti-ka ub-bi-ib*
dingir.aš.aš.e.ne šu.ne.ne šu.luḫ.ḫa šu.ne.ne zalag.zalag.ga
*ilū*meš *ta-li-mu-ka qa-ti-šú-nu li-im-su-u qa-ti-šú-nu lu-ub-bi-bu*
gišbanšur.sikil.la.ta ú.sikil ì.kú.e
ina pa-áš-šu-ri elli *a-ka-lu ella a-kul*
dugti.gi$_8$.dù.zalag.zalag.ga a.sikil.la.ta nag.ab
ina dug*tigidî ellitim*tim *mê*meš *ellūti*meš *ši-ti*
di.lugal.e dumu.dingir.ra.na geštu.zu ḫé.a
a-na di-in šarri mār ili-šú lu-ú ú-zu-un-ka
. . .].zu: *di-in-šú a-mat-su li-mad*
. . .]×.a.ni bar.ra.ab
. . .]-*šú pu-ru-us*
. . .] muḫ *liq-bi*
. . .].ub.bé

In the divine court of Esagil there was a minor god Nādin-mê-qātı to assist with this rite (E. Unger, *Babylon*, p. 259). From the passage under discussion it is clear that hand washing preceded formal meals, though this was no doubt for a cultic rather than a hygienic reason. The early occurrence of the rite is shown by a bilingual lamentation (M. Witzel, *Tammuz-Liturgien*, p. 376. 28), where reference is made to the invaders' "unwashed hands" in much the same spirit as the Hebrews thought of "uncircumcised Philistines".

As well as with a singular suffix *-amma*, the form *bīn* also occurs with a plural suffix: *bi-in-na-an-na-ši-i-ma* (*YOS* VI. 40. 5). No satisfactory etymology of the form has been suggested, and a root *bânu* 'give' is unproven. The OB. letter passages *AJSL* 32. 270, no. 2. 12 and ibid., no. 5. 7, 11, 28 are to be corrected from *i ba-in*, &c., to *i-di!-in*, &c. C. H. Gordon's derivation from the Persian imperative element *bi*+*innamma* (= *idin-am-ma*) (*Or* N.S. 22. 230) is clearly impossible since it occurs in Ninevite *Gilgameš Epic* (VI. 94). Cf. *ZA* 50. 181[4].

12. *sa-ḫi-ru* may be a noun *saḫīru* 'a round of', but it cannot be an auxiliary verb, as then it would have to be infinitive: *saḫāru*.
pitê libbi: cf. *it-tap-šar kab-ta-tum* (*Gilg*. OB. 2. III. 19).

14. In most dialects the paranomastic infinitive is equipped with the adverbial *-um*+*ma* (*GAG*, § 150 a).

16. The exact implications of *eli amēli illak* are a matter for surmise.

19. Philologically there is no evidence whatsoever for the meaning 'hunter' for *muttaprašširu*, but in the context this meaning seems the only one possible.

20. Cf. *kal-ba ka-si-is eṣemta*: *JTVI* 29. 84. 13 = *MVAG* 21. 94. Hunting dogs are executed very finely on the reliefs of Ashurbanipal (H. Schäfer and W. Andrae, *Die Kunst des Alten Orients* (1925), p. 569).

21–27. The statements about the *ḫaḫḫuru*-bird are very obscure. Unless *muttaprašširi* is used in 21 in a sense differing from that in 19, then in 21 it must surely be a possessive genitive: "the *ḫaḫḫuru* of the hunter", which requires that the bird be a bird of prey such as the falcon. Whether the Babylonians used such birds can be suggested from an Assyrian relief in the Louvre (*Encyclopédie photographique de l'art, Le Musée du Louvre* I, p. 318), where in a scene of bird shooting the smaller figure, probably an attendant (cf. the other portion of the same relief: no. 118829 in the British Museum, C. J. Gadd, *The Assyrian Sculptures*, pl. V), holds an arrow or spear in one hand, and a fluttering bird in the other. Two interpretations are possible. Either it is one of the fallen birds from which the attendant has drawn the arrow and which is now attempting to fly away, or it is a hunting bird taking off from the trainer's wrist. If the latter alternative is correct, it is certain evidence that hunting birds were known in ancient Mesopotamia. If the former is correct, the relief offers no evidence on this matter. On the assumption that this passage does refer to falcons or similar birds, *iqannun qinna* will indicate good sport, and *in*[*a* . . .] *dūri bītsu* the reverse. The Semitic cognates strongly favour "build a nest" for *qanānu qinna*, but as it is also used for animals (R. Borger, *Asarhaddon*, p. 107 Rand), humans (*ARM* I. 18. 23. 29), and snakes (*KAR* 389b obv. I. 9) something more general such as 'settle down' is equally possible. The most obvious failure of a trained falcon or other such bird is flying off when released and not returning to its trainer. Perhaps *in*[*a* . . .] *dūri bītsu* implies that the bird at once flies back to its roost, and *iqannun qinna* that it remains in the game area to which it has been taken.

22. The animal *akkannu* 'wild ass' (see note on *Theodicy* 48) is well known in Akkadian literature (*Gilg.* 8. II. 8; *STT* I. 15 obv. 2 and rev. 7–8 = *JCS* 8. 92–93; *LKA* 95 rev. 12 and 20) and in *LKA* 101 obv.(!) it is expressly called "the hunted onager" (*akkannu ṭardu*). Presumably it is the creature represented on the reliefs of Ashurbanipal (H. Frankfort, *The Art and Architecture of the Ancient Orient*, pl. 112). The reference in 28 *namû* [*na*]*rbassu* must imply failure or difficulty in catching the creatures. In the Sultantepe *Gilgameš* fragments there is also a mention of the *namû* as the habitat of the *akkannu* (*STT* I. 15 obv. 2 and rev. 1, cf. *JCS* 8. 92–93), but it is hardly possible to distinguish *namû*, *šadû*, and *ṣēru* in such contexts (see A. Heidel, *JNES* 8. 233–5). *Theodicy* 60 indicates that these animals were in the habit of making incursions into cultivated areas, and that would naturally give rise to pursuit, and with most likelihood of success since the quarry had come so close to civilization. One can imagine that attempts to chase or corner such swift beasts in open country would be much more difficult, and perhaps that is the implication of 28.

25. *ṭēnšu ištanīšu*: the meaning 'lose one's senses' for *ṭēma* or *milka šanû* is well established (B. Meissner, *MAOG* XI/1 and 2, no. 61), but it is altogether inappropriate here. This phrase can bear another meaning deriving from *ṭēmu* 'news': *ARM* II. 24 rev. 16: *ṭe₄-em ḫa-am-mu-ra-bi i-ša-an-ni-ma* "the news about Hammurabi is different", or "Hammurabi's position has changed"; similarly *ARM* I. 103. 9 and IV. 80. 4. Also this is a frequent phrase in omens, e.g. *mi-lik ma-a-tim i-ša-an-ni* (*YOS* X. 31. VI. 21–22); umuš kur man-*ni* (e.g. *CT* 40. 33. 17). This phrase goes back to a Sumerian idiom, as shown by J. J. Finkelstein in *JBL* 75. 330[8], and whatever the origin of the phrase it implies a change for the worse in the state of the city or land to which it refers. This is obviously the sense of the phrase in the passage under discussion, where the uncertainty of hunting is being stressed. See *Advice to a Prince* 6.

29–38. It can hardly be doubted that 35 and 36, perhaps also 34, are intrusions in their present context. They seem to be related to 1′–6′ of e, since they deal with litigation. What remains of the section refers to having a family, not to building a material house. In *CH* 16r. 80 *bītam epēšum* also means "set up a family" (*ANET* 175, § 191) rather than "erect a building". This twofold sense of building a house also occurs in Hebrew, where David's offer to build God a house is met with the answer that God will build David a house, i.e. the Davidic dynasty (2 Sam. vii. 5–11). Exactly the same words are used there as here (*bānâ bayiṯ*), and the pun probably arose from a folk-etymological derivation of *bēn* from *bānâ*. Line 67 refers back then both to this section and to that on love. 33, and perhaps 32 also, are probably the disadvantages of having a family as stated by the slave, though now out of place. If *daltu* is a correct interpretation of 32, then it may well be a punning comment on the house. 33 most probably states the disappointments of parenthood: *qaiālu* has the meaning 'strong': it follows *rabû* and *pungulu* equating kur₄ in *á.A* I₂. 4 (*MAOG* XI/1 and 2. 101); it equates *šarru ekkēmu* in II *R* 47. 12; it explains *epiq* and *ṣūpi* in the Commentary to *Šumma izbu* 271c. *lillu*, on the other hand, is well known for 'weak (in mind or body)'. The line thus seems to say that a son may turn out two-thirds a weakling; cf. *Gilg.* 9. II. 16: *šit-ta-šu ilu-ma*.

34. *lu-lu-uš-ma*: it is tempting to emend this to *lu-ku*!-*uš-ma*, from *akāšu*. *lu-tar-ma* has been taken as a dialectical form of *lutūrma*. Von Soden in *JCS* 2. 301 has collected a number of similar forms from Late Assyrian texts, such as *áš-par* for *ašpur*. *lu-tar-ma* occurs in **a** only, which elsewhere shows Assyrian dialectical forms.

35. *dagālu pān* = 'be in respectful submission to'. The literal sense 'look at the face of' is completely forgotten, for in the Assyrian Laws a married woman under certain circumstances must 'look at the face' of her absent husband for five years (A, 36. 91).

38. For the syllabic use of *nanna* cf. *AfO* 11. 73[32] and *AnOr* 27, no. 13.
bīta ḫepû can hardly be separated from *bīta suppuḫu*, which is said of a wife (*CH* 7r. 41 and 8r. 8) and of sons (*RA* 27. 153. 35–36), who do it during the lifetime of their father. This can only refer to breaking up the family circle; cf. *Šurpu* II. 53: *qin-na pu-ḫur-ta ú-sap-pi-ḫu.*

1′–6′. The language is paralleled in *KAR* 71 obv. 1–13, an incantation to be said by someone about to engage in litigation (cf. E. Ebeling, *MAOG* v/3. 30); the rubric is inim.inim.ma *uz-zi nu-uḫ-ḫi* (11), and 7 reads *ár-ku su-ku-ut ku-ru-u la* inim.inim.[ma].

41–42. The idea that one must expect to fight to get food and clothing is curiously paralleled in the *Era Epic* I. 52: *a-šib āli lu rubû ul i-šeb-bi ak-la* "a person who stays in the city (in contrast to one who goes out to battle), though he be a noble, does not get enough food".

42. *i-nam-dak-ka* in **a** is an Assyrian form: Ylvisaker, *LSS* v/6, § 27 (a).
tu-mal-la-a kar-a[s-ka]: *ma-li ka-ra-ás-ka* was the advice of Siduri to Gilgameš (Meissner Tablet III. 6).

45. *nuppulu*: cf. Langdon ad loc.; *AOB* I. 118[6]; *AfO* 11. 223. 38.

56. *libbašu ṭābšu*: this is a common formula in Late Babylonian letters (passages cited by E. Ebeling, *Glossar zu den neubab. Briefen*, p. 120), but its apparent absence from one of the best manuscripts throws doubt on its authenticity here. Unlike the Hebrew *ṭôḇ lēḇ* it does not indicate mirth, but rather satisfaction, as when in Old Babylonian business documents it is the usual phrase for expressing the satisfaction of the contracting parties with the terms of the contract: šà.ga.ni al.dùg = *libbašu ṭāb.*

57. Cf. Proverbs xix. 17: The man who is kind to the poor lends to Yahweh, who will repay him his reward.

60. The suggestion of this line implies a reversal of the usual practice, by which the devotee takes the part of the dog: *ki-i mu-ra-ni* ^d*tu-tu a-la-su-um ur-ki-ka* (E. Ebeling, *Handerhebung*, p. 92. 11 and 12).

61. The *ila* on **b** removes the doubt about the meaning of *la ta-šal*; *ša'ālu* is commonly used of consulting a deity.

63. **a** in this section has some peculiar forms of *nadānu*; *lutti* and *itti* may reflect a colloquial pronunciation with the dropping of the final consonant and an interchange of dentals. The imperative *itti* is most unexpected as the normal Assyrian form is of course *din.*

32′. Speiser proposes to insert *uṭṭat-⟨su ḫu-bul-lu-šu⟩ at-ri*, but the Babylonian recension differs so much from the Assyrian in this section that a restoration of this kind is uncertain.

34′. Adverbial uses of *ana/ina muḫḫi* are attested from the late periods (M. San Nicolò–A. Ungnad, *Neubab. Rechts- und Verwaltungsurkunden*, Glossar p. 85; E. Ebeling, *Glossar zu den neubab. Briefen*, p. 128; also once in the *Era Myth*, v. 44).

71. *usâtu*: this word only occurs in the plural (cf. 73), and it is of interest that three other words meaning 'kindness' which are listed with *usâtu* in *RA* 17. 201 and *CT* 18. 29 are also fem. plurals: *ta-li-ma-tú, ta-ḫa-na-tú,* and *a-zi-ba-tú.*

73. While the sense of the line, that Marduk notices good deeds, is obvious, the exact significance of gi.gam.ma or *gap-pat* is unknown. gam, but not gi.gam.ma, is common enough for *kippatu*, which may be a god's symbol, but it is not apparent how good deeds could be placed in this mysterious object. The variant *gap-pat* is certainly no ordinary plural of *kappu* 'hand', but may be a strange writing of *kippat.*

76. This line could be a borrowing from the first and last paragraphs of the Nineveh *Gilgameš Epic*: I. 16 and XI. 303.

77. *arkû* and *pānû* are to be understood as referring to the social scale: poor and nobles, cf. K 8315 (Bilingual Proverbs). In *ABL* 815. 4 ([lú]*uruk*[ki]*-a-a maḫ-ru-tu u ár-ku-tú*) the writer employs almost identical terms in stressing that a petition from the people of Uruk was supported by the whole population. Here the author not only uses the phrase to cover all who lie in the mounds, but obtains an added sting from the very fact that both high and low are now alike mere bones.

83, 84. These lines are a direct quotation of what is presumed to be a proverbial saying. They also occur in Sumerian in *Gilgameš and the Land of the Living* (*JCS* I. 10. 28–29):

lú.uzu.da an.šè nu.mu.un.da.lá
lú.dagal.la kur.ra la.ba.an.šú.šú

The couplet also appears in a Sumerian proverb collection (cf. Kramer, *JCS* I. 35). In the context of the epic the words are addressed by Gilgameš to Utu in a speech eloquent with the fear of death and the consciousness of man's puny powers. It is then altogether appropriate in this context, where the slave uses it to support his suggestion of suicide by affirming with it the futility of human endeavour. The general tenor of the saying is apparent, but the exact rendering is problematic. The first half might be an affirmation that men cannot get to heaven, but the Sumerian lá can hardly bear that sense. kur may be either 'land' or 'underworld'. The lines may refer to a somewhat incomprehensible concept found in other passages, that certain things had their roots in the underworld, and reached to heaven with their uppermost limits. A clear statement of this idea is found in IV R^2 27, no. 2 = *OECT* VI. 16. 8–11:

kur.gal [d]en.líl.lá im.ḫur.sag gú.bi an.da ab.di.a zu.ab.kù.ga.bi
suḫ.bi : uš.uš.e : úru.úru.e
šá-du-ú rabû[ú] [d]MIN *im-ḫur-sag šá ri-šá-a-šú šá-ma-mi šá-an-na*
ap-su-u el-lim šur-šu-du uš-šú-šu

Note also *Papnigingarra Hymns* VI. 25–30 (*JRAS Cent. Sup.*, pl. IX):

bi-tum lu na-ši re-e-šu ša-ap-la-nu-um šu-ur-šu-šu
er-ṣe-ta-am lu ta-am-ḫu
ke-e-eš bi-tum lu na-ši re-e-šu ša-ap-la-nu
šu-ur-šu-šu er-ṣe-ta-am lu ta-am-ḫu
e-le-nu-um zi-ik-ku-šu li-iš-nu-nu ša-ma-i
ša-ap-la-nu-um šu-ur-šu-šu er-ṣe-tam lu ta-am-ḫu

IV R^2 26, no. 4. 43–44:

e.ne.èm.zu sa.pàr.maḫ an.ki.ta ša.mu.un.lá
a-mat-ka sa-pàr-ra ṣi-i-ru šá ana šamê[e] *u erṣetim*[tim] *tar-ṣa-at*

and *Era* I. 150–3:

a-li [giš]*mēsu šīr ilāni*[meš] *si-mat šàr gi-mir*
iṣ-ṣu el-lu it-qú ṣi-i-ru šá šu-lu-ku ana be-lu-ti
šá ina tam-tim rapaštim[tim] *mê*[meš] I ME *bēru i-šid-su ik-šu-du*
šu-pul a-ra-al-[*li*]
qim-mat-su ina e-la-a-ti em-de-tu šamê[e] *šá* [d][*a-nim*]

Hymn to Ninurta, rev. 18–19 (p. 120) is a further example. These examples, which could easily be multiplied, show that the idea of greatness, whether applied to gods, temples, a god's net, or a mythical tree, is expressed in terms of filling the whole universe: based on the underworld and reaching to heaven. The proverb under discussion affirms that man, unlike these other great things, does not stretch in this way. In the magic of an incantation, however, this power was possible: *ar-ka-ku-ma kīma šam*[*ê*[e]] *kīma erṣetim*[tim] *rapšāku*[[ku]*-ma*] (*KAR* 62 obv. 1–2 = *MAOG* V/3. 22).

86. For *kī* and the subjunctive as an oath formula see *GAG*, § 185 k. Since it has the form of a subordinate clause, there has no doubt been an ellipsis of a main clause, see *Or* N.S. 6. 355–7.

arki-ia: "when I am dead", as in *CH* 10r. 19, &c.: *wa-ar-ki a-bi-šu* "when his father is dead"; Job xxi. 21: *aḥ*[a]*râw* "when he is dead".

Chapter 7. Fables

(i) *THE TAMARISK AND THE PALM*

A

IM 53946 OBVERSE

1. The mimation in *ú-mi-im* is very curious.

2. Cf. *i-ta-an-ḫu ālāni*[meš] in the story of the *Slaying of Labbu* (*CT* 13. 33. 1; cf. A. Heidel, *The Babylonian Genesis*[2], pp. 141–3). The exact force of *nubattam* is not clear.

4. *šu-te-ši-ir* is the ordinary imperative form, though here it must be intended for the infinitive. In another Tell Harmal tablet, however (*Sumer* XI, pl. VI. 4), the normal infinitive *šu-te-šu-ur* occurs. The reading *uq-bu* is not certain. It is suggested by *iq-bu* in **c** 10, and would be from a root *wqb*. Otherwise *i-bu* (= *ibbû*) 'they nominated' is possible.

IM 53975 REVERSE

2, cf. 13. The form *gi-ši-ma-ra-(a-)šu(-×)* is curious. Elsewhere in the literary introductory formulas *s/zaq/kāru(m)* takes *ana*, not an accusative, see the material collected by Sonnek, *ZA* 46. 225–35. Thus the *-šu* must correspond to *ana*, and is presumably the shortened form of the ending *-šum*, though in the other few occurrences it is suffixed to the noun without ending: *qá-qá-ar-šu-um* (*BIN* IV. 126. 13 = *Or* N.S. 25. 142), *qaq-qar-šú* (*Era* IV. 143, *KAR* 196 rev. II. 31), *da-da-ar-šu* (*RB* 59. 239 ff., 29 = *Or* N.S. 26. 317).

3. *muttalliku* 'moving' is used here for 'movable object', but elsewhere it has several specialized usages: *muttalliku* 'movable stove' (*Ḫarra* 10. 338 and 340, cf. *Or* N.S. 26. 127–8), *muttalliktu* 'door' (*CT* 18. 4. IV. 35), *muttalliktu* 'cattle' (= *bu-lum*, Commentary to *Šumma izbu* 482), *muttalliktu* 'mobile troops' (*ARM* XV sub voce).

4–5. *šumma . . . šumma*, which is lacking from **b** and **c**, is difficult, as the usual sense 'either . . . or' is obviously wrong here. The Tamarisk is not claiming one of two alternatives, but both. *šumma* as used in oath formulas is also impossible, since it has a negative sense.

4. The OB. *bukinnum* for *buginnu* is paralleled in *kirrum* for *girru* (*CAD* sub voce *girru*). The impression given by **b** obv. 23–24 that *buginnu* is a kneading-trough is now corrected.

5. *a-ma-ḫa-aṣ* is *maḫāṣu ša ṭamê* (*CT* 12. 42. I. 41 = *Nabnītu* 21. 41), i.e. beating up the weft threads to the cloth already formed by means of the 'reed', which is shown by this passage to have been made from tamarisk wood. Cf. the Hebrew *tqʿ* in Judges xvi. 14.

14. Is *ṣú-ba-bu* an OB. form of *ṣumbabû* (*Ḫarra* 3. 91), a botanical term?

b

OBVERSE

5. The reply of the Palm (8) refers to an action done to the pods(?) of the Tamarisk with a rod, no doubt of palm wood. This suggests that *tu-ba-li* here is the noun *tubalû*, a rope article (= giš.KU.lá.gišimmar in *Ḫarra* 3. 408), which B. Meissner has plausibly translated 'climbing-belt' (*Babylonien und Assyrien* I. 205). An excellent picture of such an aid to harvesting dates is to be found in a mural from the palace of Zimri-Lim in Mari (reproduced in *Studia Mariana*, frontispiece). Thus each tree boasts that the fruit of the other can only be secured with the help of one of its own products.

11. *a-bu um-ma-ni* is obviously the correlative of *mār ummâni*, though it seems to be unattested otherwise. The two words are to be construed as a compound noun (see A. Ungnad, *Grammatik des Akkadischen*, § 24 m), and so count as one construct before *ka-la-ma*: "master-craftsman of everything".

15. On *nrb* see von Soden in *Or* N.S. 24. 390–3.

18. *šummannu* here is *šum-man-nu šá alpi* (*CT* 12. 37. IV. 46–48 = *Nabnītu* 4. 375–7), cf. A. Salonen, *Hippologica*, pp. 163–4.

21. *mi-nu-i*[*a*, cf. **c** 32 *me-nu-ia*, is a very unusual use of the interrogative pronoun.

22. From **c** 34 it is clear that *ma-la-l*[*i-ia* is a drinking-vessel. The only known word is *malallû* (from the Sumerian má.lal), a pole connected with boats, and the boat itself (A. Salonen, *SO* VIII/4. 36). Salonen conjectures that this is the word used here for 'cup', compares the English 'vessel' for a similar semantic development, and cites an obscure omen passage: *TCL* 6, no. 9 obv. 17 = *RA* 19. 143.

23. For *itquru* cf. *AfO* 12. 344; *WO* 1/5. 370 (giš.liš); *Iraq* 13. 29; *Or* N.S. 19. 17[2].

27. Cf. *GAG*, § 81 j for *ai* as a strong negative.

REVERSE

1. See *CAD*, sub voce for *gizinakku*.

7. *qatrinnu* is an Assyrian form of *qutrinnu*.

8, 23. *i*/*e-dal-la-lu* in such obscure contexts could also be derived from *alālu*.

18. The succession *x*, *x*+1 is a figure of speech also found in Hebrew and Ugaritic literature, see C. H. Gordon, *Ugaritic Manual* (*AnOr* 35), p. 36.

19. It is not clear in what way the Palm succeeds to the grain goddess, nor is the "three months" clear, though the fable of *The Ox and the Horse* has a similar allusion (C 3).

22. *šír-šír-ri*(-)[is perhaps 'chain', which occurs as *šeršerru* (*MSL* II. 150. 15) and *šeršerratu* (*MSL* I. 137).

C

1–6. The syntax of these lines has been confused by the previous translators, who have made the people in 1 dig the canals in 2, and brought the Fates of 2 into the syntax of 3. If the line division is kept as marking the clauses, a much clearer picture emerges.

1. *u*₄*-me*(-)*el-lu-te* is a crasis for *ūmē ullûte*. The obscure line end is no doubt a corruption of mu.meš *ru-qa-te*.

2. In the incantation to the river goddess (*STC* I. 200–1; *KAR* 254 and 294; *LKA* 124 and 125; *STT* I. 72 rev. 77–86; CBS 344) it is the great gods who dug the river: *e-nu-ma iḫ-ru-ki ilū*[meš] *rabûti*[meš].

3–6. This heavenly council, which has no parallel in the OB. version, has plenty of parallels elsewhere, e.g. *KBo* I. 12 obv. 3–4 = *Or* N.S. 23. 213: (Without Šamaš) [d]*a-nu ù* [d]*en-líl i-na ša-me-e pu-uḫ-ra ú-ul ú-pa-aḫ-ḫa-ru* [*m*]*i-lik ma-a-tim ú-ul i-ma-al-li-ku*. A more complete parallel is contained in the Hittite *Gilgameš* text *KUB* 8. 48, where Anu, Enlil, Ea, and Šamaš debate the fate of Enkidu and Gilgameš (see *ANET* 85). Cf. also *Advice to a Prince* 29–30.

4. The problem is whether Enlil, which is the only satisfactory restoration, is consulting with peoples (*ni-ši*) or gods (*ì-lì*). It is difficult to imagine Enlil asking or taking the advice of men, and so the latter is to be preferred. The sign *ši* has the value *lì* again in 11 and 31. *iddalgu* for *ittalku* = *imtalku* is an orthography abundantly paralleled in the Akkadian texts from Boghazköy.

6. The so-called *Vorschlagsvokal* had a certain vogue among Middle Assyrian scribes as here *i-it-*, and *e-il-te-šu* in 13 below. See the examples from the *Middle Assyrian Laws* in *BBK* 1/4, pp. 5–6; note also *LKA* 62 obv. 7: *i-iš-mu-ú*; *Tukulti-Ninurta Epic* V (II), 30: *ú-uṭ-ṭí e-en*; the latest example from Assyria is perhaps *STT* I. 38. 17 and 46: *a-aṭ-ab-ba-aḫ*.

7–8. The idea that kingship was given to men by the gods is expressed in the antediluvian section of the *Sumerian King List*, with the related text *PBS* v. 1. ii. 88–89, and in the *Etana Myth* (*BRM* iv. 2. i. 11–14).

For the clash in gender between *šar-ru-tu* and *ba-ši* cf. *GAG*, § 132 g, h.

9–13. The context and A leave no doubt that these lines should first state the appointment of a king, and then describe his planting of the Tamarisk and Palm, which is done in 11–13 (cf. A obv. 6–7). Thus 9–10 should cover lines 4–5 in A. However, these lines are hopelessly corrupt. *ṣa-lam* sag.meš is derived from *ṣalmāt qaqqadi* in the OB. text. The two *-ni-šu* at the ends of 9 and 10 appear to be intended as suffixes, but as *ni-ši* 'peoples' appears twice in the OB. recension, it is probable that the Assyrian scribe was mistaken, if he did in fact take these words as suffixes. Also *iq-bu* may be an alteration of *uq-bu*, as we have read the OB. text.

15. Pfeiffer's emendation *ša-ki-im*!*-ma* has been adopted in the translation.

18. *mar* is taken tentatively as the shorter form of *ammar* (Ylvisaker, *LSS* v/6, § 15 c), though the wedges could be read *iṣṣī*^{me}.

37–38. The first six signs of these two lines are a dittography of *ú*!*-ul i*!*-šu*(*-ma*), as the OB. copy reads (rev. 7), and a very clear example of the scribe's inability to read his original.

39. Cf. *Theodicy* 56 and note.

40–41. Here again monstrous corruptions have obscured the text, but the scribe was correct in copying a double *šumma*, since this occurs in the OB. version in another passage (rev. 4), though there the Assyrian scribe understood enough of his original to see the problem of the repeated *šumma*, and omitted them. Here he seems to have understood nothing, so he retained them.

(ii) *THE FABLE OF THE WILLOW*

The Sumerian reading of giš.A.TU.GAB.LIŠ is given in *Proto-Diri* 161: $^{\text{a.sa.ar}}$giš.⌜A.TU⌝.GAB.LIŠ = *ṣa-ar-ba-*[*tum*] and *Diri* ii. 241: $^{\text{a.sal}}$giš.A.T[U.GAB.LIŠ] = *ṣar-ba-tú*.

K 8566+13771

10. The last two signs could also be read *qaq-d*[*à-a*.

12. Bezold (*Glossar* 101b) apparently read this passage *gar-ru* 'spreading', but the derivatives of the root *grr* do not favour this interpretation. Here it is taken as a metaphorical use of the root *šr*' 'be rich' or 'be luxuriant'.

18. For *šaššugu* see *Ḫarra* 3. 210; R. C. Thompson, *Dictionary of Assyrian Botany*, p. 104; and A. Salonen, *Landfahrzeuge*, pp. 143–4. Its wood was used for chariots. A reading [× × m]es *gamlu*(zubu) is also possible.

K 8413

1. There seems not enough space for the restoration [^{giš}× *pâ-šu i-p*]*u-šam* ^{giš}*mēsa* [*i-tap-la*].

7. *lutê ṣarbati* occur in rituals as chips of wood, which were burnt (W. G. Kunstmann, *LSS* N.F. ii. 66). The *ludû, luddu* which occurs in the *Cuthean Legend of Naram-Sin* (*Anatolian Studies* v. 98 ff. 65, 70, 83; cf. ibid. vi. 163) is probably the same thing, perhaps "for earmarking animals".

13. Cf. *Ḫarra* 4. 10–15:

giš.dib.dib	=	*maš-tak-tum*
giš.ki.lá	=	,,
giš.ki.á.lá.bi	=	*a-ṣar-ru*
giš.úḫ	=	*iṣ-ṣur šá-a-ri*
giš.im.šeš	=	,,
giš.im.á.lá	=	,,

In this context *maštaktu* apparently means 'sign-post', so the meaning 'direction' has been assumed for *maštaku*.

16. Cf. *Erim.ḫuš* II. 112–14 (*CT* 18. 43. II. 31–33):

šu.su.ub = *du-um-šum*
šu.gan.zí.ir = *da-ma-šum*
šu.bu.lu.ga = *da-ra-su*

(iii) *NISABA AND WHEAT*

OBVERSE I

7. *isratu* occurs also in the Commentary on the name Asaru, the first word of *Enūma Eliš* VII, where the *A* is explained as *is-ra-tu* (V *R* 21, no. 4 obv. I. 4; *STC* II. LI. I. 4). It is now known to occur in the text itself of *Enūma Eliš* (*STT* I. 10). In both contexts *isratu* obviously has agricultural connexions. The root *'sr* is used for imprisoning, hence the conjecture that *isratu* is the place where grain is stored.

13. Cf. *Malku-šarru* I. 280: *ki-kur-ru-u* = *šu-ub-tum* (*OECT* IV. 64. IV[a]. 50); *AfO* 8. 219; *Sumer* V. 63–64; and Commentary on *Theodicy* 225–34.

17. Cf. *Malku-šarru* II. 106: *na-al-ba-aš šamê[e]* = *er-pe-e-tu* (*ZA* 43. 238), and *AfO* 7. 115–16.

18. *liq-i-ma* is probably related to the Hebrew and Arabic root *qy'* 'vomit', but in Akkadian the only other possible occurrence seems to be *Šurpu* III. 63: *nāru šá-a-nu u nāru qà-ayu* "to urinate in the river and spit(?) in the river".

21. *ḫamû*: cf. *CAD*, sub voce *ḫawû*.

22. The presence of Išum in this context of fertility is not easily explained. With Šubula, a form of Nergal, he is said to be god of the Tigris and Euphrates (*ABRT* I. 58. 11), but since the fertility described has its origin in rainfall rather than in irrigation, this is an unsatisfactory explanation. In the *Era Epic* Išum is said to make his weapons lighten, and to be a torch which the gods follow (I. 5 and 10). The writer clearly bases this on an etymological connexion of *išum* and *išātu* 'fire', thus making Išum god of lightning, and as he follows Addu, god of thunder, in this context a similar interpretation is attractive. The restoration of the line is based on *Era Epic* I. 133 and 170; II. 1; III. *KAR* 169 rev. I. 44.

23. Cf., e.g., *VAB* IV. 84. 19 bottom: *šu-te-ši-ri ta-li-it-ti*.

24. The verb is probably *amāru, emēru* 'be full' (*TDP* 118[213]), though the trace is difficult. For *ḫaruptu* 'recently matured sheep' (usually *ḫurāptu*) see Landsberger, *AfO* 10. 156.

30. *nullâtu, aḫītu*: see note on *Counsels of Wisdom* 28.

32. *mál-ma-*[*liš*]: see note on *Theodicy* 18.

REVERSE IV

7. *nibû* is used primarily of stars; cf. *Fable of Fox* C obv. 11.

8. *li-iš-še-pu*: see note on *Ludlul* I. 72.

9. *ep-pe-er-šá* is taken, doubtfully, as equivalent to *eper-ša*.

16. *šu-up-pa-a* = *šūpâ*.

18. As *la me-na-te* would be expected, an haplography of *te* may have occurred.

20. See note on *Counsels of Wisdom* 132.

21. Cf. *ABRT* II. 17. 23: *be-let re-e-ši ut-nin-ni*, and the phrase *rēšu mutninnû* (*Theodicy* 289; R. Borger, *Asarhaddon*, p. 4. 27 and 12. 16; *VAB* VII. 64. 95 and 300. 6). The usual identification of this with *rēšu* 'head', whether in the sense of 'slave' or 'chief man', is unsatisfactory. A homophonous root *r'š* must exist, an approximate synonym of *utninnu*. This may also occur in *Nabnītu* 4. 232:níg.me.gar = *ri-šá-a-tu* (*CT* 12. 34. I. 48), since in *Nabnītu* A, 173 níg.me.gar = *qa-a-lum* (*MAOG* 1/2. 54. 22) 'pay attention'. The Hebrew *rʿš* 'quake' and the Arabic *rʿs* 'tremble' may be related.

23. *a-mu-ram-ma*: for the retained *u* in the imperative with ending cf. *a-ku-li* (*LKA* 153 rev. 3 and 4), and *su-ḫu-ri-ma* (J. Laessøe, *Bît Rimki*, p. 38. 10).

LEFT EDGE

Cf. *Bab* 7, pl. v. III. 14–15: lú.nimgír é.gal; lú.600.kur.

(iv) *THE OX AND THE HORSE*

A

OBVERSE

12–20 and the corresponding 27–31 describe the rise of the annual Mesopotamian flood, and its effect on the land. Strabo gives a clearer account of what happens: "the Euphrates floods in the beginning of the summer, starting with the spring, when the snow of Armenia melts, so that inevitably it becomes a lake and deluges the cultivated land, unless the inrushing and overflowing water from the river is distributed by a network of ditches and canals, as with the Nile in Egypt, hence the canals. They need, however, a great deal of attention, for the ground is deep, soft, and yielding, so that it is easily carried away by the currents and leaves a bare plain, while the canals get filled and their mouths are readily blocked with the mud" (*Geography* 16. 1. 9). *ṣuṣû*, *qarbātum*, *bāmātum*, *tāmerātum*, and *ugāru* are all names of ground whose top soil may be carried off by the water, though their differentiation is impossible with available knowledge.

14. *ba-ma-a-tum* (= 30): the meaning 'high place' which *bāmâ* has in Hebrew is certainly not correct in Akkadian; cf. Landsberger, *JNES* 8. 276[91], and *še-e ba-ma-tim ša su-ḫu-um*[ki] (*Symbolae Koschaker*, 103, § D, 2).

15 (= 29). The juxtaposition of *ḫarru*, *natbaku*, and *šadû* is frequent in Neo- and Late Assyrian royal inscriptions, e.g. *ḫar-ru na-at-ba-ku šá šadê*[e] (Ashur-naṣir-pal II; *AKA* 272. 53). This combination has proved too much for previous translators, who have tried to find some mountainous connexion. It is, however, quite irrelevant in a southern Mesopotamian scene, with the Ox and the Horse surveying the rising flood. Even in Assyrian royal inscriptions it has been doubted whether *šadû* is always 'mountain' (A. Heidel, *JNES* 8. 235), and *ḫarru* is commonly used for a low-lying piece of ground, or a wadi or irrigation canal. The feminine *natbaktu* is used in Middle Babylonian letters (*MAOG* x/1. 44–58) for "ein Wasserlauf mit starken Gefälle" (von Soden, *ZA* 51. 149). In epic contexts Heidel has shown (loc. cit.) that *šadû* is sometimes a synonym of *ṣēru* 'plain', and *šad(d)ū'ā'u*, as the adjective formed from it, can be presumed to have the same possibility: 'belonging to the plain'. Thus the translation will be: "They (the waters) caused the hollows and slopes to carry away (the soil) belonging to the plain."

18. *apu* and *kīšu* are a common pair in the *Era Epic*: I. 113; *KAR* 169 obv. IV. 41; *LKA* 11 rev. III. 21; IV. 149.

19. *CAD*, vol. Ḫ, 97b suggests the emendation *ki-rim*!*-šá*; cf. *CT* 15. 49. III. 48–49 = 58: *ṣēru pal-ku-ú ú-li-id id-ra-na ib-bal-kat ki-ri-im-šá*. Here, however, the *-šá* refers to Nisaba. The unemended text *qirib-ša* must have substantially the meaning of *kirim-ša*.

24. *na'id qabli* is used of the horse again in *Gilgameš* 6. 53.

28. *ṣi-pa*: the root *ṣapû* 'steep in water' is used in OB. letters for saturating the soil (passages collected by Landsberger in *MSL* I. 255 and *JNES* 8. 276[90]). A plural adjective *ṣi-pu-tum* occurs in *Ḫarra* 23 for 'steeped malt', Oppenheim, *Beer*, pp. 24. 28 and 26. 4. The root is unrelated to the Arabic, Hebrew, and Aramaic *ṣb'* 'dye', but may be a cognate of the Syriac *ṣap̄î* 'purgavit', '(spongia) bibere fecit' (Brockelmann, *Lexicon Syriacum*², p. 635). The first of these two meanings also appears in Akkadian: *TDP* 124[220], *AMT* 61. 2. 3 (cf. *RA* 26. 87[5]).

32. Cf. *CT* 18. 6 rev. 48 = *AS* 1, p. 73: *ra-aḫ ki-di* = *e-pi-in-nu*. The idea of the plough fecundating the earth is also found in *Maqlû* VII. 26: (*ki-ma*) [giš]*epinnu erṣetim*[tim] *ir-ḫu-ú*.

33. ki.kal is perhaps 'hard ground', cf. Landsberger, *JNES* 8. 277[92].

34. *idakkuku*: cf. O. R. Gurney, *Anatolian Studies* VII. 134. 17, and *LKA* 62 obv. 7.
It is not clear why *bu-ru-ni-ma* has a plural suffix.

REVERSE

10. For other translations see *CAD*, vol. G, 31b, and A. Salonen, *Landfahrzeuge*, p. 125.

13, 14. Leather thongs were used to attach heads of arrows and spears to the shafts.

17. Cf. *Ludlul* II. 73 and note.

29. For *tuḫḫu* 'bran' cf. *á.A* VIII$_1$. 151: du-ud-da = GAB = *tuḫ-ḫu šá ḫa-*$^{bi\text{-}pi\ eš\text{-}šu}$ (*CT* 12. 11. III. 18); see also *OLZ* 25. 342, and *WO* I. 373[74].

B

OBVERSE

9. The restoration [*i-ša*]*ḫ-ḫu-uḫ*, which seems inescapable, can be explained from the Arabic *saḥḥa* 'pour forth (water)', 'flow down (tears)', and the Syriac *šaḥ* 'liquefactus est', 'macruit' (Brockelmann, *Lexicon Syriacum*[2], p. 768). The correspondence of the Akk. *ḫ* with the Arabic *ḥ* is irregular, but other cases are well attested (Brockelmann, *Grundriss* I, pp. 127–8), and the second meaning given to the Syriac is similar to the common sense of *šaḫāḫu* in Akkadian: 'lose one's strength'; cf., e.g., *Papnigingarra Hymns*: *i-sà-ḫu-ḫu ri-ig-mi-iš-ka* (of the gods in council: *JRAS Cent. Sup.*, pl. VI. II. 6), from which a passage in the *Zû Myth* can perhaps be restored: [*ri-ig-mi-i*]*š?-su i-li is-sà-aḫ-ḫi-iḫ-ḫu* (*RA* 35. 20. 23 = *RA* 46. 88) = -]*i?-šu ilī*^{meš} *i-šaḫ-ḫu-ḫu* (*CT* 15. 40. 5). An unnoticed occurrence is *Gilgameš* I. IV. 26: *ul-taḫ-ḫi-iṭ*, for which K 2756d offers the unconvincing variant *ul-taḫ-ḫi*; however, the unpublished duplicate BM 37263 (80–6–17, 913) reads *ul-taḫ-ḫa*. Cf. *Ludlul* II. 92.

11. Cf. K 4347+ III. 25–29, Bilingual Proverbs.

C

3. Are these three months, as restored, the same three months to which the fable of *The Tamarisk and the Palm* refers (**b** rev. 19)?

15. See *MSL* I. 75. 1–6 for *eli'ātu* 'Vorzugsanteil'.

16. Cf. below H 2.

F

9. Cf. fable of *The Tamarisk and the Palm* **b** rev. 19.

H

There is no absolute proof that this piece belongs to the fable of *The Ox and the Horse* rather than another fable. However, it is put here because the surviving phrase in line 2 also occurs in C 16.

(v) *THE FABLE OF THE FOX*

A

This fragment is only known from a copy of Pinches made in 1888. The copy was among his personal papers which, on his death, were passed on to Weidner, for whom Gerhard Meier edited it in *AfO* 11. Professor Weidner kindly made over the original copy to the present writer, and it is reproduced in this work. There is some uncertainty about the text, as the original cannot be found. Pinches's note "H. Rassam, Esq." on the sheets shows that this fragment was at some time in the hands of this excavator. Other tablets of his private collection were presented to the Museum at Hove, and these have recently (1954) been entrusted to the British Museum. The fable fragment, however, is not among them. There is no doubt concerning the excellence of Pinches as a copyist, but it has to be remembered that in the case of copies made for his private study, as distinct from those made for the British Museum, he usually made a quick copy where a modern scholar would probably make a transliteration, in order to ascertain the contents. If he then decided to publish the text, this preliminary copy was thoroughly collated. The copy of the fable fragment is clearly not finished. At the ends of lines at the bottom of the reverse he puts his customary crosses, but the marginal notes to which they refer are not entered. The writer has in his possession some of Pinches's corrected copies, and in the preliminary draft whole signs were omitted or seriously miscopied, but were later corrected. A second uncertainty is that in some of his copies Pinches transcribed Babylonian into Assyrian script. In his copy of Reisner, *SBH*, now in the possession of the writer, he adds variants in Assyrian script and in one place prefaces them with the note, "Trans. by me from Bab." Also corrections of *um* to *mes* and *si* to *kil* in a copy in Assyrian script show that the original was Babylonian. In the case of the fable copy there are no unequivocal indications of the original script. KAL in rev. 4 is almost certainly an error for *dir*, and some Neo-Babylonian or Late Babylonian scripts could explain this mistake. However, the non-standard Assyrian forms of *mu* (obv. 14, but not 13, &c.), *li*, and *tu* could be taken as proof of an Assyrian original.

OBVERSE

11. The negative has apparently dropped out before the last verb.

12. Cf. *Enūma Eliš* I. 45.

REVERSE

6. Ebeling connects [*lu*]-*up-ši-in* with *ps/ṣ/šm/n* 'cover', but this is hardly a sufficiently violent action.

10. *qu-bu-uḫ*: cf. *CAD*, sub voce *gubbuḫu*, and O. R. Gurney in *Proceedings of the British Academy*, XLI. 28.

11. The restoration [*uš-pa-al*]-*si-iḫ* is uncertain, since a suffix would be expected with it. [*ip-pa-al*]-*si-iḫ*, however, is no adequate preliminary for the following violent action.

b

Grammatically this Middle Assyrian tablet is very peculiar. The scribe mixes Assyrian and Babylonian forms, as in *napi/uštu*:

Obv. 5: *na-pu-uš-te-ia*	Obv. 20: *na-piš-ti-ši-na*
Obv. 7: *na-pu-uš*-[*te-ka*]	Obv. 27: *na-piš-ta-šu-nu*
	Rev. 14: *na-piš-ti*

napuštu is a Middle Assyrian form (cf. *Instructions of Šuruppak* obv. 4, and *CT* 18. 30. IV. 9: *ut-na-púš-te*) contrasting with the Babylonian *napištu*, and the Old Assyrian *napaštu* (also the sheikh Abi-samar, *ARM* I. I. 11′). The most curious example is obv. 20, since the singular form is used with a plural verb.

Obv. 26: *še-la-ba*	Obv. 12, rev. 12: *še-li-bu*(*-um-ma*)

Note, however, *še-la-bu* (R. Borger, *Asarhaddon*, p. 107, Rand). *as-ba-ku-ma* (obv. 19) seems half-way between the Babylonian *ašbāku* and the Assyrian *uspāku*. Orthographically the tablet shows the abnormal plene writings found also in the *Middle Assyrian Laws* (cf. J. Aro, *SO* XIX/11).

OBVERSE

3. For *sarāḫu* see Ebeling, *JCS* 4. 218, ad loc., and *AOB* I. 53.

10. The peculiar meš in *arkā*^{meš}*-nu-ma* is paralleled in 14 below. The simile *ki-ma su-mi* is not clear, and the existence of *sūmu* 'redness, red spot' (*YOS* X, p. 11[72]) should be noted.

11. The same simile is used in the *Annals* of Sennacherib: *ki-i ša at-mi summati*^{mušen} *kuš-šu-di i-tar-ra-ku lib-bu-šú-un* (*OIP* II. 47. 29–30).

14. *labû*, describing the noises of certain animals, is also attested in *AfO* 14. 146. 102 and Labat, *TDP* 158[271].

16. The same figure of Zû and the lion occurs again in an OB. Narām-Sin legend:

ki-ma né-e-ši-im-mi na-ḫi-ri-im ta-ba-aš-ši
ba-aš-mu-um-mi pi!*-i-ka* ^{d}*zû*(im.dugud) *ṣu-up-ra-ka* (*AfO* 13. 51 rev. II. 2–3)

18. The drying out of a mountain at the uttering of a loud voice is part of Hebrew prophetic imagery (Amos i. 2).

21. The ending on *ka-⟨ia⟩-ma-ni-ia* is the adjectival ending, not the first person suffix. Elsewhere in this text and other Middle Assyrian documents *-ia* is written where other dialects would have *-a*. Cf. 17 above: *bur-ka-ia*, and *KAH* II. 60 obv. I. 11: *ri-ia-ú*.

22. The explanatory *sa* in *a-na-*^{sa}*saḫ* is a phenomenon known in Middle Babylonian, see J. Aro, *SO* XX. 25–26. Examples also occur in Sultantepe tablets.

23. The writing *mi-di-nu* is significantly that used in the inscriptions of Tiglath-Pileser I; cf. Landsberger, *Fauna*, p. 84.

24. Unlike the animals, the birds show their fright by not moving.

25. *b/pitqu* 'sheepfold' also occurs in the Middle Assyrian law tablet F (cf. M. David, *Symbolae Koschaker*, p. 139. 4), the *Era Epic* v. 8, and an Assyrian treaty (*AfO* 8. 18[7]).

26. *i-šu-ṭa-ni-ma*: there seems to be a confusion between *šâṭu-išûṭ* 'bear (a yoke)' and *šâṭu-išêṭ* 'insult', since the form is that of the first, but with the meaning of the latter. This also happens in R. Borger, *Asarhaddon*, p. 57. v. 3: *i-šu-ṭu-ma e-tap-pa-lu zi-ra-ti*. In Hebrew there is the same confusion between verba mediae iod and mediae waw.

REVERSE

6. The restoration is based on *Malku-šarru* I. 78: *ù-uḫ šu-ul-lu-šu* = *šá uz-za pu-luḫ-ta ra-mu-u*.

12. *na-an-gul*: cf. B. Meissner, *AS* IV, pp. 47–48.

13. Cf. *ṣalam damiqti* (*VAB* IV. 128. 30); *ṭapiltu*: see note on *Counsels of Wisdom* 28.

15. In the *Atra-ḫasis Epic* there occurs the *kirimmu* of the *ṣēru*, which gives birth to plants (*CT* 15. 49. III. 49 and 58), and it is possible that here *kirimmu* 'bosom' is used for 'centre'. However, other readings than *rim* are possible, though nothing clear emerges from them.
ug-gu-li: this is taken as II/1 stative of *ngl* (see above note on 12) 'glow'. There are cases of the first radical of verba primae *n* dropping in the II/1: *ib-ru uṣ-ṣi-ra qú-ra-du ši-me-a* (*CT* 15. 1. I. 2), and *uṣ-ṣi-ri* (*Ištar and Ṣaltu* VI. 18), both imperatives of *nṣr*.

18. For *uḫūlu* see R. C. Thompson, *Dictionary of Ass. Chemistry and Geology*, p. 15. This substance may have been used not for pottery, but for glass, but our knowledge of the potter's techniques is so limited that the allusion is obscure.

22. Cf. **d**, Col. B 5 and 7. The last word may be the scribal note *ḫi-p[í*.

23. *mār la ma-am-ma-na-ma*: this phrase is used of usurpers in historical texts; e.g. *KAH* I, no. 30 obv. 26.

c

OBVERSE

5. Cf. *Šamaš Hymn* 183 and note.

7. For *qannu* see *Or* 17. 285[3], and Ebeling, *Glossar zu den neubab. Briefen*, p. 189.

10. Restore perhaps *up-[taḫ-ḫa-ru]*.

12. On the assumption that the endings are regular the subjects of the preceding and following lines cannot also be the subject here. *da-a-nu* appears to be the subject, and in Assyrian *d'n* is well known as the equivalent of the Babylonian *dnn*. The difficulty still remains that *dânūtu* would be expected as the plural "mighty men".

13. The restoration is based on *OB.Lú* Tablet B I. 7: [lú.túg.ŠI.GAG.giš.gišimmar.ùr.r]a = *ša i-na ku-un-ši-li-im i-ma-aš-ša-ru*; and *Ḫarra* 19. 195: túg.BAR.síg.ùr.ra = *šá ina kun-šil-li maš-ru*. The *kunšillu* is the carding instrument, cf. *JCS* 8. 93[107a].

15. See Landsberger, *Fauna*, pp. 86–87, for *šurānu*.

16. The mongoose (Landsberger, *Fauna*, pp. 110–11) again appears as frequenting the sewers in *Sayings* III. 32–34. *naṣbu* is from *nṣb* 'suck', cf. E rev. 7 and note.

21. Cf. the parallels cited in the note on *Ludlul* II. 89.

REVERSE

6. *abullu* for 'throat' should be compared with *bābu* in *Ludlul* II. 86, on which see the note. For *ganguritu* see *CAD*, sub voce *gagguritu*.

7. ⌜*e*⌝*-ta-an-šu* is taken as an Assyrian form of *enēšu*.

13. *qi-ni-ka* appears to be *scriptio defectiva* for *qinni-ka*.

d

COLUMN A

6. *a-ḫi-ti* 'slander': cf. note on *Counsels of Wisdom* 28.

COLUMN B

4. *enqu* is an epithet of the Fox: E obv. I. 18; G Col. B, 6; Z obv. 5.

5, 7. Cf. **b** rev. 22.

E

OBVERSE

15. A very confusing line. *karru* can hardly be 'mourning garment' or 'knob'; the loan from the Sumerian kar, as in *CT* 16. 12. 10–11, perhaps with the meaning 'robbery', is worth consideration. The first *ina* could well be dispensed with; cf. Ebeling, *Handerhebung*, p. 108. 16: [*ki*]*b-sa i-ša-ra šu-kun ina šēpē*^{II}*-ia*$_5$, similarly *JNES* 15. 144. 5, and the stock phrase in Late Babylonian letters: *ḫarrāna ana šēpē . . . šakānu* (E. Ebeling, *Glossar zu den neubab. Briefen*, p. 100). Cf. also *Gilg.* III. 18 (Assyrian version).

REVERSE

3. See *Theodicy* 283 with note.

7. For *nṣb* 'suck' see F 2, 9, and *Or* N.S. 16. 451–2; *JCS* 4. 220.

8. *malāḫu* 'pull apart': see *JCS* 4. 219.

F

8. This important line is unfortunately defective. The Fox, if it is he who speaks, is giving his credentials. The one problem is whether the lady Ninisinna or some other deity, or whether the town Isin is meant. According to Chiera, *Sumerian Religious Texts*, 6. III. 36 and IV. 10, Ninisinna is a daughter of Enlil. Then it is not clear if the mention of Enlil is to be related to the Fox direct, or only through the deity or town in the line.

G

COLUMN B

2. Cf. von Soden, *Or* N.S. 26. 317.

5. *nullâte-šu*: cf. note on *Counsels of Wisdom* 38.

8. Cf. *Šamaš Hymn* 143.

9. *ḫirṣu* here must have the sense of *ḫirīṣu* A in *CAD*.

11. *nittu* = burglar: *Or* N.S. 19. 129[1] and *Erim.ḫuš* V. 71–74:

lú.é.U.U.ru = *ni-it-tum*
lú.lul.la.ga = *ra-bi-ṣu*
lú.IM.zu (v. +tuk) = *šar-ra-qu*
lú.šu.ḪA = *sar-ru-um* (*TCL* 6. 35. II. 21–24 and *CT* 19. 13, K 7331 rev. IV. 8–11)

COLUMN A

5. *ki-ṣir par-zil-li* = very iron.

6. *ṣu-pur*: see note on *Ludlul* III f.

Z

OBVERSE

6. For *qa-a-a-lu* (cf. *qa-a-a-la-tu* in 11) see note on *Dialogue of Pessimism* 33.

8. For *ratātu* 'tremble' cf. *á.A* I_2. 327–9:

tu-kuBUL = *ra-a-du*, *ra-ta-tu*, and *ta-ra-rum*

Also in *Šurpu* II. 58 *râdu* and *ratātu* occur in juxtaposition.

10. See note on *Theodicy* 235 for *bunnu*.

13. Cf. *Theodicy* 50 and note.

14. See note on *Ludlul* I. 67.

17. If the text is correctly read *šal-mat-su-un*, cf. **c** obv. 14. A reading *šal-lat-su-un* 'their plunder' is also possible.

REVERSE

5–10. See BM 38283 (Bilingual Proverbs) as restored at the beginning by Sumerian Collection II. 69. Tummal (on this reading, rather than Ebmal, see *BASOR* 132. 29[18]) was a shrine in Nippur, the history of which is recorded on *PBS* v, no. 6. Uzumua '(the place where) the flesh grew' is also a name for Nippur, or for a part of it (*JNES* 5. 136[13]). It is curious that in the proverb Uruk and not Nippur is mentioned, but the relations between the Fox and the "Slave girls of Tummal" in both proverb and fable are hardly a coincidence. In the fable the Fox is preparing to worship Enlil in one of the Nippur shrines, and orders the female slaves to prepare the place for him.

8. Cf., e.g., Thureau-Dangin, *Rit. acc.* 140. 343: níg.na gi.izi.lá *ina* šà é *uš-ba-'*.

10. Cf. **b** obv. 8.

12–14. This seems to be the epilogue; the writer asserts his integrity in handing on what he had received, like the writer of the *Era Epic* (v. 43–44): *a-a-am-ma ul iḫ-ṭi e-du šu-mu ul ú-rad-di ina muḫ-ḫi* "He did not leave out one line, nor did he put one in addition." The concluding line is an invitation to the pious reader.

COLOPHON

The tablet was written by the same scribe who wrote the *Toothache Incantation* (*CT* 17. 50), where the colophon runs: gaba.ri im.gíd.da *šá a-na* ka *šá-ṭar ṣar-pa la-bi-ri-im šá* m.d*marduk-šúm-uṣur*(šeš) m.d*nābû*(nà)-*na-din-ip-ri* a *ku-du-ra-nu* in.sar (a photograph of this tablet is given in R. C. Thompson, *Devils and Evil Spirits* II). The fable tablet was copied from a baked tablet, which in its turn was based on a Babylonian monster tablet (*tupgallu*), which must have contained the whole series. The only other tablet based on a *tupgallu*, and in that case itself one, is the huge god list of Middle Assyrian date, K 4349. Its colophon reads: *a-na pi-i tup-gal-li* libir.ra [m]*ki-din-*d*sin*(30) a.ba dumu *su-ti-e* a.ba man in.sar igi.kár (*CT* 24. 46).

(vi) *THE FABLE OF THE RIDING-DONKEY*

For the rendering of *agalu* see A. Salonen, *Hippologica*, pp. 67–70.

3. Cf. *Ludlul* II. 99–101 and note.

5. Cf. *Counsels of Wisdom* 22.

12. Cf. *Theodicy* 185 and note.

(vii) *VARIA*

SU 1952, 138+169+181A–D

13. For the *parsikti*-measure see B. Landsberger, *WO* I. 373–6.

25. The two medical series mentioned in this line also occur together in *KAR* 44 obv. 6: *sa-gig-ú alam-dím-mu-ú*; see J. V. Kinnier Wilson, *Iraq* 18. 130–1.

Chapter 8. Sayings

COLUMN III

7. The plural on the restoration *i-[qab-bu-]ú* is difficult. *kubādu*, for *kubātu*, also occurs in a Harper letter (293 rev. 4; cf. *ZA* 43. 111).

11. *šanāṣu* 'mock' is also found in 49 below, *Counsels of Wisdom* 76, *VAB* VII. 214. III. 10, and lexical texts; cf., e.g., *Nabnītu* A, 160–2 (*MAOG* 1/2. 54. 9–11):

ka.ur$_5$ = *šá-na-ṣu*
ig.ki.šè.gar = ,,
šà.dím.ma = ,,

14. *mu-ba-ḫi-iš* stands for *muba'iš*.

16. In the *Tale of the Poor Man of Nippur* (see note on IV. 2 below) the following line occurs three times: *ana be-lí-ka taḫ-da-at ilī*^{meš} *ki-a-am qí-ba-áš-šú* (66, 111, 137). Purely from the context one would expect it to mean, "Speak thus to your master (who is) an abomination of the gods". On this basis *taḫ-da-a[t il]i* has been restored.

19–20 illustrate presence of mind.

21. *nu-ḫu-ub/p-ma*: elsewhere there seems to be no evidence for an Akkadian root *nḫb/p*, but it has to be assumed here. In Syriac *n^{e}ḥaḇ* = 'was lean', and the Arabic *naḫiba* = 'be timid'.
sullû nēši, sullû barbari mean a sheep killed by a lion or a wolf, see *Ḫarra* 13. 40–41 (*JNES* 4. 158):

udu.sila$_4$.ur.maḫ = *su-le-e né-e-šu*
udu.sila$_4$.ur.bar.ra = *su-le-e bar-ba-ri*

The Sumerian antecedent, however, has udu.sila.ur.bar.ra (*SLT*, no. 46 obv. II. 34), and in the context of *á.A* III$_5$ (*CT* 12. 15. IV. 20) line 175 must certainly be restored: [$^{si.la}$KUD] = *su-lu-ú šá* ur.bar.ra. Also among the equivalents of [^{s}]$^{i.la}$KUD in *MSL* III. 220 both *šu-lu-um* (road) and *su-lu-um* ("Fährte des Wolfes") appear. sila$_4$ in *Ḫarra* must stand for sila.

24. Cf. *ZA* 43. 18. 71: *šil-ta-ḫiš ú-ṣi-ma*, and *Gilg*. 9. I. 17: *ki-ma šil-t[a!-ḫi* (collated).

25. Cf. *LTBA* II. 2. 397: *bēl bi-ir-k[i]* = *la-si-mu*.

29. Cf. *ZA* 43. 18. 70: *ki-ma lil-li-di šaḫî ṣe-eḫ-ru šá ina muḫḫi sin-niš-ti-šú e-lu-ú*.

31. *nerrubāti* has been discussed recently by von Soden in *Or* N.S. 25. 249–50. He derives it from *nerrubu* (*'rb*) 'flee', but the context is too broken here to decide on its meaning. The word also occurs in bilingual proverbs K 8216. 12, an even more broken passage.

32–34. Mongooses apparently lived in drain-pipes: *it-tu-ru a-na šik-ki-im-ma it-ta-ṣu-ú ina nu-un-ṣa-ba-a-ti* "They turned into mongooses and emerged from the sewers" (R. C. Thompson, *Gilg*., pl. 59. 14).

35–41 are completely obscure, except that *la-qit ḫa-ru-pi* (39) presumably refers to one of the poorest of the population. Cf. *Theodicy* 186.

42–43. A satire on those who cannot adjust themselves to the needs of a new situation.

44–47. A fox in a moat is obviously in difficulties, and the wolf's greeting is no doubt sarcastic. The fox's indirect invitation to the wolf to come down to have some beer is probably a trick to induce him to come down into the water, just as in the Aesopic fable the fox persuades a goat to descend into the well, into which he himself has fallen, to taste the sweet water.

iš-ta-'i-ru: cf. *AfO* 17. 314 D, 8: *lu-u šá as-kup-pa-a-ti téš-te-ni-'-i-ra* "Or who constantly frequent thresholds".

šikaru[meš] *ṣab-ta-ni-ma*: literally "beer has seized me", cf. *CT* 15. 49. III. 8: *la i-ṣa-ba-ta-ni ši-tu* "sleep does not seize me", i.e. "I cannot sleep".

48–49. Cf. B. Landsberger, *Fauna*, p. 132. *šá-ni-iṣ-[ma]*: see note on 11 above.

50. A free rendering of this fable turns up in Greek in Aesop (B. E. Perry, *Aesopica* I, no. 137): *κώνωψ ἐπιστὰς κέρατι ταύρου καὶ πολὺν χρόνον ἐπικαθίσας, ἐπειδὴ ἀπαλλάττεσθαι ἔμελλεν, ἐπυνθάνετο τοῦ ταύρου εἰ ἤδη βούλεται αὐτὸν ἀπελθεῖν. ὁ δὲ ὑποτυχὼν εἶπεν "ἀλλ' οὔτε ὅτε ἦλθες ἔγνων, οὔτε ἐὰν ἀπέλθῃς γνώσομαι."* A further rendering into Greek choliambics is found in Babrius, no. 84. *ni-ni-qu* is a *hapax legomenon*, but the Greek and the context suggest 'mosquito'.

COLUMN IV

2. *ti-ib še-e-ri* seems to occur also in the *Tale of the Poor Man of Nippur* (*STT* I. 38; *Anatolian Studies* VI. 150 ff.) 98.

3. Cf. *Ḫargud* B_6, 133 (II *R* 51, no. 2 rev. 5+*CT* 18. 16, Rm 360. 5): [lú].ur.SAL = *[a]s-sin-nu* = *sin-niš-⸢a⸣-[nu]*.

4. The meaning of *anzaninu* can only be discussed in connexion with *s/šusapīnu* and *napṭa/uru*, as the following lexical entries show: *LTBA* II. 1. VI. 20–21 = *LTBA* II. 2. 356–7:

an-za-ni-nu = *nap-ṭa/ṭu-ru*
su-sa-bi/pi-nu = ,,

Erim.ḫuš V. 75–77 (*TCL* 6, no. 35 obv. II. 25–27):

sag.gigrí = *šam-ḫu-tú*
nimgir[ni.gír].si = *šu-sa-pi-in-nu*
níg.mud.BAD[1] = *an-sa-mul-lum*

In origin *anzaninu* (or *ansamullu*) and *s/šusapīnu* are presumably foreign words. A. Van Selms, *JNES* 9. 73, attempts to derive the latter from *šusuppu*, a garment, but this is not convincing. The usual starting-point for obtaining the meaning is the Syriac and Jewish Aramaic *šôš[e]ḇînâ* 'friend of the bridegroom', 'best man', and this meaning has been freely assumed for *susapīnu*, from which *šôš[e]ḇînâ* is certainly derived. There are, however, two factors which require modification of this view: (i) in Sumerian religious texts one passage mentions seven nimgir.si lying with Inanna (passage quoted by A. Falkenstein, *ZA* 45. 170[3]), and in another a god addresses Inanna: "nimgír.si.zu ḫé.me.en = *su-sa-pi-in-ki ana-ku*" (*SBH* 69, obv. 16–18). Here then the *susapīnu* is on intimate terms with women, not men. (ii) In the passage under discussion the *anzaninu* seems to be the proprietor of the *bīt aštammi*, whether this be a brothel, an inn incidentally serving the purpose, or even a temple of Ištar (see the discussion of T. Jacobsen in *JNES* 12. 184[68]). Also in *Erim.ḫuš* above *šusapinnu*, *ansamullum*, and *šamḫūtu* ('prostitution') are given in one section.

This apparently conflicting evidence can be reconciled if the custom of *ius primae noctis* is assumed to lie behind the institution. The existence of this custom in ancient Mesopotamia is known from the OB. *Gilgameš Epic* (2. IV. 22–34), as pointed out by A. Schott (*OLZ* 36. 521), and it may be reflected in the *History* of Herodotus (I. 199), who, however, only says that women had to offer themselves once in their lifetime, and does not specify any particular occasion in the life of a woman. One may very tentatively reconstruct the history of this institution as follows. In early times reflected in the Sumerian religious texts the nimgir.si himself performed the *ius primae noctis*. By the OB. period the *susapīnu* conducted a

[1] Is this "he who opens the vagina"? mud = *biṣru*.

kind of social centre (*bīt aštammi*, or *bīt emûtim* in *Gilg.*) in which he arranged, on behalf of the bridegroom, for someone else to do the necessary act, and doubtless ran other similar lines of business. Since there is also a reference to feasting in the *bīt aštammi* (Bilingual Proverbs, K 9050+), eating and drinking also took place there, though in what connexion is unknown. Much later, in Jewish and Christian circles where the custom of *ius primae noctis* had died out, the *šôšᵉbînâ* continued as the friend and assistant of the bridegroom. The *kasap susapīnūtu* in a text from Ugarit (*Mission de Ras Shamra* VI, *Le Palais royal d'Ugarit* III, p. 147. 15) is obviously money paid for the services of the *susapīnu*, but by whom and in what connexion is not clear. The *napṭa/uru* is mentioned more frequently than either of the other two names (see von Soden, *ArOr* 17/2. 371; A. Goetze, *The Laws of Eshnunna* (*AASOR* 31. 98 and 110)), but his function in society cannot be deduced from the passages. From the equation níg.giš.tukul.úr = *nap-ṭa-rum* (*AfO* 14, pl. VII. II. 11) phallic connexions have been suggested (*AfO* 17. 78). In Hittite texts the feminine *napṭartu* is a wife of secondary status, see A. Goetze, *Kleinasien*[2], p. 94.

The point of line 4 seems to be that the male prostitute does not keep the money paid for his services. The "You" in line 5 is fem., and must refer to Ištar (on whose behalf the *anzaninu* operates?), but apart from the play on words the rest of the line is obscure.

6–7. *masāku* = 'have a bad reputation' (note on *Ludlul* II. 35), as does *ṭapālu*, cf. *ṭapiltu* 'defamation' (*Ludlul* I. 90 and 94; *Fable of the Fox* B rev. 13). The sense of the saying seems to be that by spreading slanders the cunning prostitute makes respectable women appear like herself.

8–10. The juxtaposition with 11–14 leaves no doubt that the *ṣap-par-ru-ú* is a miscreant, and this is confirmed by *im-na ù šu-me-la*. The giving and receiving of presents was no offence in itself (see note on *Šamaš Hymn* 98–99), but the emphasis on their multiplicity here implies that they are being used to pervert justice. Thus *ḫibiltu* must be 'wrong done by him' rather than 'wrong done to him'. Although the same words are used in the *Tale of the Poor Man of Nippur* (see note on IV. 2 above) 40, there they have the other sense: [*mi*]-*nu ḫi-bíl-ta-ka-ma kat-ri-a na-ša-*⌜*ta*⌝ "What wrong has been done you that you are bringing a present?" (cf. *Proceedings of the British Academy* XLI. 39). For the root *ṣpr* see the note on *Ludlul* I. 81.

11. *šaḫšaḫḫu* 'slanderer': cf. W. von Soden, *Or* N.S. 16. 457–8 and 18. 403.

12. *a-ḫi-i-ta*: cf. note on *Counsels of Wisdom* 28.

14. Cf. Genesis ix. 5.

19. The *kuzāzu* is known as an insect which tears with its jaws (B. Landsberger, *Fauna*, pp. 132–3; *CAD*, vol. Ḫ, sub voce *ḫanzizītu*), and this is no doubt the reason why the *ḫamītu* is eventually cut to pieces, though "the mouse's hole" is not clear. Mice also bite things to pieces. The *ḫamītu*, provisionally rendered 'sand-wasp' with Landsberger, *Fauna*, p. 133, may be an insect which glows like the fire-fly in view of the passage *TDP* 12. 61: *šumma ḫa-mi-tu šá kīma kakkabi ṣa*[*rḫu*].

21. The KU.KIL may be the same as the KU.KUR.KIL = *an-zu-zu* = *ḫa-di-lu* (*Fauna*, p. 37, A 52; cf. 138–9).

25. [*i*]*t-ta-ši-iš*: cf. note on *Theodicy* I.

28. Cf. *Gilg.* 7. III. 39: *dam-qu* ᵈ*gilgameš tap-pa-a ú-šar-šu-ka ka-a-šá.*

29–34. The colophon comes from the Gabbi-ilāni-ēreš school, but the writer Ninurta-uballiṭsu is not so well known as his contemporary Nābû-zuqup-kīna. See D. J. Wiseman, *Iraq* 17. 9.

BM 53309 and BM 53555

These two pieces are certainly parts of one exercise tablet, and there are remains of three columns, in each of which a short writing exercise was repeated, apparently throughout the length of the column. The left-hand column contains mathematics, and is not dealt with here. The centre column has the saying, and the right-hand column cannot be understood. The scribe does not always form the signs correctly.

The point of the saying is unfortunately lost with the defective end.

The twentieth day of each month was the festival of Šamaš; cf. *Šamaš Hymn* 156 and 83–1–18, 237 (Pl. 57):

én. ᵈ*šamaš* ud.20.kám u_4*-um-ka nam-ru*
ud.20.kám *nam-ru é-babbar-ra nam-*[*ru*]
kīma ud.20.kám *nam-ru ni-i*[*ṭ-li-ka*]
kīma é-babbar-ra n[*am-ru*]
ni-iṭ-li-ši-na [. . . . .]
tu_6.é.nu.[ru]

A comparison of these three passages suggests that the twentieth day was the occasion for asking favours of Šamaš, when he could least refuse.

nam-mar in line 7 stands for *nam-ru*, probably representing a colloquial form. Cf. in the Sultantepe *Gilgameš* tablet *STT* I. 15 rev. 8 *nam-mar*, for *nimru* in the Nineveh copy.

ADDENDA

"The pace of discovery shows no sign of abating." The truth of this part of the opening sentence of the Preface has been amply vindicated during the printing of this book. Before the proofs were returned several new pieces of Wisdom tablets were discovered, and most were worked into the body of the text concerned. However, the several new fragments identified since the proofs were corrected can only be given here as Addenda. The following notes purpose only to draw attention to important additions and corrections resulting from the new fragments. Insignificant orthographical variants can be seen on the copies and are not mentioned here.

Chapter 2 — *Ludlul* I

The "lost" beginning of *Ludlul* has in fact been available since 1906! K 9810 (*BA* v. 389–90), now duplicated by *LKA* 24 (VAT 10522), preserves the first dozen lines on its obverse, and some remains of the last line, and the catch-line of Tablet II, on its reverse. The identification of these two pieces has been made by Mr. Erle Leichty, now (1959) a student of the Oriental Institute, University of Chicago, to whom every credit is due.[1] The following text is based on a new copy of K 9810 (Pl. 74) and collations of VAT 10522 kindly made by F. Köcher and indicated by exclamation marks.

As anticipated, the opening section consists of a hymn of praise to Marduk. After two repetitive couplets introducing the god, his attributes are described in couplets, the first line of which stresses his greatness and severity, and the second his merciful aspects. In the words of the Apostle, we are invited to "Behold the goodness and severity of God". This is a very appropriate introduction to the following monologue, which describes in much detail Marduk's severity to his slave, followed by his mercy.

Both copies preserve in part the thirteen lines. VAT 10522 has rulings after every tenth line, as does the Assur fragment which preserves the end of the tablet (VAT 11565, see p. 30). If the latter could be found it would probably join VAT 10522 back to back.

1	*[lud-lul] be-lu_4 né-me-qí*	*ilu [muštālum?]*
2	*[mu?-ṣa?]-bít mu-ši*	*mu-pa-áš-š[ir ur-ru]*
3	[^{d}]*marduk bēl né-me-qí*	*[ilu mu]š?-t[a?-lum?]*
4	*[mu?-ṣ]a?-bít mu-ši*	*mu-pa-áš-šir ur-r[u]*
5	*[š]á ki-ma u_4-mi me-ḫe-e*	⌜*la*⌝*-mu-u ug-gat-su*
6	⌜*û*⌝ *ki-i ma-ni-ti še-ri*	*za-aq-šú ṭābu*(dùg.ga)
7	*uz-zu-uš-šú la ma-ḫar*	*a-bu-bu ru-ub-šú*
8	*mu-us-saḫ-ḫir ka-ras-su*	*ka-bat-ta-šú ta-a-a-rat*
9	*šá naq-bi qātē^{II}-šú*	*la i-na-áš-š[u]-u šá-ma-'u*
10	*rit-tuš rab-bat*	*ú-k[aš]-šú mi-tu!*
11	^{d}*marduk šá naq-bi qātē^{II}-šú*	*la i-na-šú-u šá-ma-'u*
12	*[ra]b-bat rit-ta-šú*	*ú-ka-áš-šú m[i-tu]*
13	[× ×] × × [×]	× × × × ta a [× ×]

VARIANTS OF VAT 10522

4 *]-tu* 5 *u_4-me* 6 *ma-nit meš-ri-* × *za!?-aq!-šú* 7 *]-zu-[u]š-šu, maḫ-ri* 8 *]-us-saḫ-ḫir ka-*⌜*ra*⌝*-su*
9 *na]q-be qātē^{meš}-šú, i-na-áš-šú-u* 10] × × × × *ú-ka-áš-šú* 11 *ša naq-be qātē^{meš}-šú*

1 I will praise the lord of wisdom, the [deliberative?] god,
2 Who lays hold on the night, but lets free the day,
3 Marduk, the lord of wisdom, the [deliberative god,]
4 Who lays hold on the night, but lets free the day,
5 Whose fury surrounds him like the blast of a tornado,
6 Yet whose breeze is as pleasant as a morning zephyr,

[1] See *Or* N.S. 28. 361–3.

7 His anger is irresistible, his rage is a hurricane,
8 But his heart is merciful, his mind forgiving,
9 The . . of whose hands the heavens cannot hold back,
10 But whose gentle hand sustains the moribund,
11 Marduk, the . . of whose hands the heavens cannot hold back,
12 But whose gentle hand sustains the moribund,

NOTES

8. *mussaḫḫir*, apparently a *hapax legomenon*, can be I/3, II/2, or II/3 participle of *saḫāru*. In the context the I/3 ("constantly turns") and II/2 used reflexively ("turns himself") are both possible.

9. Cf. *SBH* no. 13, rev. 19–20=*SBP*, p. 92:

umun šu.aš.ni an.e nu.íl.e
šá be-lu ti-ri-iṣ qa-ti-šú šá-mu-ú ul ina-aš-šu-ú

The close parallel unfortunately does not clarify the obscure *naqbi*.

10. Soft hands are also mentioned with reference to healing: *[l]i-bal-liṭ-ka* ^{d}*gu-la ina rab-ba-*⌜*a*⌝*-ti qātē*^{meš}*-šá* (BM 98584+98589 rev. v. 7). *kâšu* in the simple stem is well attested with two meanings: (i) 'tarry, be late' (in lists and late letters, see *AfO* 10. 141[2], and E. Ebeling, *Glossar zu den neubab. Briefen*, p. 116), and (ii) 'be kind' (in lists and literary texts, see note on line 226 of the Ištar Prayer appearing in *AfO* 19/1). The Syriac *kōš* 'be quiet, stay' is to be compared, and the two meanings in Akkadian are no doubt from the same root, the second perhaps having the implication of 'slow to anger'. The II stem seems to occur only here, and used with *mītu*, 'one in mortal danger', it may mean 'delay', and so 'keep alive'.

Line 64. Cf. *ur-rid še-du-uš-šu* in *MVAG* 21. 86. 18 and 88. 3, 7.

Lines 75–76. A fresh collation of **m** by O. R. Gurney yields the reading *a-ga-áš-gu-u* (not *a-saḫ-ḫur qu-u*; his copy on Pl. 2 is to be corrected). From other occurrences of this word in colophons (only *KAR* 203 rev. III. 28 is published) he concludes that it means "inexperienced person" or something similar. Fresh collation of the following line gives: *ki/qí-ta-×-um*, and the uncertain sign is not *at*. The emendation *ki-la!-at-ta* is now even more improbable, though the correct reading is still to be sought.

Line 120. The reverse of K 9810 provides . . .] × še ma [. . . from the middle of the line.

Ludlul II

VAT 10569 (Pl. 74), a reverse flake, is a new fragment. The complete tablet was apparently written in four columns of about 70 lines each, and contained the first two tablets of *Ludlul*, the only case of two being written together. The beginnings of lines 50–60 can be restored from rev. III:

50 *m[ur-*	56 *it-ti* ⌜e_4⌝[.la_6
51 *i[m-*	57 *it-ti u[r-*
52 *iš-[tu*	58 *in-ni[n-du-ma pu-ḫur-šú-nu*
53 *šu-lu* [	59 *i-ni-r[u?*
54 *ú-tuk-[ku*	60 *bu-n[a-ia i-ki-lu*
55 *la-maš-tu[m*	

The line numbering of this scribe, as indicated by the ten marks for 50 and 60, is one digit higher than usual. The significance of this is not apparent.

Rev. IV contains the ends of the last four lines of Tablet II, and of the catch-line of Tablet III. In 118 the variant *ul-pir-d[u]* is most curious. The much disputed reading of the last word of the tablet is now settled by the new variant *i-ri-im*, which confirms the view defended on p. 295.

Ludlul III

Two new pieces have come to light, copies of which will be found on Pl. 74:

VAT 11179 (ll. 11–25 on obv.; 16 unidentified lines on rev.)

BM 54821 (82–5–25, 1150: ll. 29–44 on obv.; ll. 19–33 of q rev. on rev.)[1]

Lines 12 ff. The following restorations and corrections come from VAT 11179 obv.: 13: *[i-r]u-ba-am-ma i[t-ta-*. 14: [×-]×*-šu-ma iḫ-[ḫa-mu-u.* 15: *[um?-]ma be-el[-tu.* 16: [×-]× mi × ×[. . .

[1] D. J. Wiseman drew my attention to this as a literary fragment.

17: [*a*/*ta*?-*na*]*r-ram-ma a*-[*tam*-. 18: [*a-na*?] *šarrum-mi* (v. of **p**: [*ana*? *šar*]*ru-um-ma*) *iš-p*[*u*-. 19: [*i-q*]*u-lu-ma* ul lum [(v. of **p**: ul i? []). 20: [*na*?-*ḫiš*] *iš-mu-nin-ni* [(correct *na* of **p**). 21: [*dš-ni-m*]*a šu-na-ta* [. 22: [*ina šut*]*ti*(má]š.ge$_6$) *aṭ-ṭu-lu* [. 23: [*ištānu*] *ram-ku* ×[(correct *eṭ*-[*lu* on p. 48).

Lines 30–33. BM 54821 shows up the omission of a line in the reconstructed text of this passage. The two previously known copies, **p** and q, are so damaged that it was not apparent that both either omit a line or wrote two lines in the space of one at this point. Particularly misleading is **p**, since its rulings after every tenth line give no hint of any missing line. After 30 the text should read:

30a *iš-te-e*[*t*] *batūltu*(ki.sikil) *ba-nu-ú zi*-[*mu-šá*]
31 *ni-ši-iš la*(-)×-[*ḫ*]*a-ti* *i-liš ma*[*š-lat*]
32 *šar-rat nišī*^{m}[^{eš} . .] × [. . .]× *ma-a* [. .]
33 *i-ru-ba-am-ma i-ta*[*š-ba*? . . .] × × [. . .]

VARIANT 31: BM 54821 *ni-šiš*

30a A certain young woman of shining countenance,
31 . . . ., equal to a god,
32 A queen of the peoples [. .] . [. . .] . . . [. .]
33 She entered and [sat down . . .] . . [. . .]

Line 34. BM 54821 confirms the reading of G: *iq-ba-a*, "She spoke (my deliverance) [. . ."

Line 36. The reading of q can now be restored from BM 54821: *ù ina mim-ma* [. . ., but the line still gives no sense.

Line 37. *iq-bu-u* (**p**) is confirmed by *iq-bu-ú* of BM 54821.

Si 55 (q) rev. 21 ff. The rev. of BM 54821 offers the following points of interest: 21: a new error: *ú-šá*!-*dš-šiḫ*. 25: *im-šu-uš* proves the emendation adopted correct, and the restorations in 27 and 28 are also on the new fragment. 29 is to be restored *im-šu-uš*. 32: the new fragment has a text divergent from q: *lu-'-i šá* [. *lu'u* occurs elsewhere only in *CT* 28. 25. 32–33, where it stands between *šaptu* and *lišānu* (see Holma, *Körperteile* 31; references provided by B. Landsberger). Here, as a variant to *mal'atu*, its meaning "throat" is clear, and it is certainly a cognate of the Hebrew *lōaʿ* in Proverbs xxiii. 2.

End of tablet. It is regrettable that the 16 partially preserved lines on the rev. of VAT 11179 cannot be identified. Line 10′ could be line a quoted in the Commentary.

Line m. This line also occurs on K 9724. 10 (Pl. 17), but this fragment does not belong to the text of *Ludlul.*

CHAPTER 3

Theodicy 52, &c. *bēl pāni* occurs outside the *Theodicy* in a bilingual incantation: *ArOr* 21. 363. 47*.

Theodicy 206. For *miḫiṣ*/*ltu* see also B. Landsberger in *Proceedings of the 23rd International Congress of Orientalists*, p. 125.

CHAPTER 4 — *Counsels of Wisdom*

Thanks to F. Köcher **d** has now been found: its number is VAT 10357, and a copy is given on Pl. 75. A more complete trace of line 11 is the only new thing brought to light; the obvious corrections of Ebeling's copy have been justified.

Line 28. For *miqit pî* (p. 313) see also *Or* N.S. 16. 204, and for *atirtu* and *wtr* see A. Falkenstein in *BiOr* 11. 114 and his *Die neusumerische Gerichtsurkunden* II, p. 39.

VAT 17157 (Pl. 75), a fragment from Babylon, is an important addition to the manuscripts. Its first column contains the ends of lines 39–53, and supplies the following corrections and restorations to the text as given on p. 100 (g = VAT 17157):

40 g: *ub-bat* "destroys", as a variant to *ub-bar* "lays the accusation".

44 g: *ka*]-*bat-ta-šú lim-mir-šú*, a variant to *ka-ba*]*t-ta-ka*. "Let his liver be bright for him" gives an inferior sense in the context, which stresses the need for the reader to act on behalf of his enemies.

46 g: *šá-ni-ti* "hostility" (see note on line 64 of the second prayer to Marduk, edited by W. G. Lambert, in *AfO* 19/1) is a variant to *limuttim* "evil".

47–51 can be restored with the help of the new fragment as follows:

47 *an-ni-* × [(. . . . . .)] × *eli ili ma-ag-rat*
48 [*l*]*um-nu* [. . .](-)*za-ri ik-kib* ^{d}*marduk*
49 × × [. . . . .] × *ma-ru-uš-ti tur-ri ik-kib* ^{d}*ninurta*(maš)
50 . . .] × *-ti ili i-raš-ši ár-na*
51 . . .] ^{d}*en-líl* ^{d} × - × - ×

VARIANTS: 47 A: *ilī*^{meš} 50 B: *á*]*r-nu*

Column II of g has the beginnings of 15 lines, but they duplicate no part of the text preserved elsewhere. Lines 6′ and 9′ of these 15 are the refrain which occurs in lines 59 and 63 of the previously known text. The section 53–65 already has some variants in 54–56 which show that widely differing recensions existed, and probably g has a different form of this part of the work rather than additional material to be inserted before line 53. In 6′ and 9′ g agrees with f (in line 63) in reading *ina annîmma*, not *ana annîmma.*

Column III of g contains the beginnings of lines 123–33. It provides a few as yet unimportant new signs for lines 124–6, and a few new orthographic variants for lines 127–33. The writing *ri-ib-ba-a-ti* in 130 leaves no doubt that this is the word which occurs in OB. economic texts, and which Kraus discusses at length in *Ein Edikt des Königs Ammi-ṣaduqa von Babylon*, pp. 88–97.

Chapter 5

The first line of the *Šamaš Hymn* may be given as a catch-line at the end of a long prayer to Marduk (appearing in *AfO* 19/1), K 3175+ and K 9430: *muš-na-*[*mir g*]*i-mir šá-ma-me.*

New text material is provided by the first preserved extract on the exercise tablet BM 65461 (82–9–18, 5448+AH 83–1–18, 2116), of which the second extract has been quoted by King in *STC* II. 34. The new extract (symbol j) covers lines 163–71. In 166 j offers a probably better text:] × *ši-na ana da-ri*[*š*], and its variant in 167 *saḫ-maš-tu*[*m*] deserves consideration along with *ṣa-l*[*ip-ti*]. In 170: *el-lu-ti*, it goes with B in reading "pure" as against "high". It is not clear whether in 171 the defective sign is an incomplete *ša* or *šu-ut.*

Chapter 6

Dialogue of Pessimism 12. The use of *saḫāru* as an auxiliary verb has been noted in late letters by Ylvisaker, *LSS* v/ 6. 30[3].

Dialogue of Pessimism 21, 27. It is certain that birds of prey were trained by the Babylonians, like falcons. See passages in *CAD*, vol. I, sub voce *iṣṣūru.*

Dialogue of Pessimism 51. In *CAD*, vol. Ḫ, p. 218, sub voce *ḫubullu* B, it is suggested that *Malku-šarru* IV. 137 is somehow related to this line. While it is not easy to guess just what the compiler of the lexical text was thinking about, it is not certain that there is any allusion to our text.

Chapter 7

A. Sachs points out that *mḫṣ* in *The Tamarisk and the Palm* (p. 153; p. 156. 5; p. 158. 24; p. 162. 35) may simply be "weave" rather than "beat up (threads)".

P. 169. 18. The first verb in this line, as Miss E. Reiner has pointed out, should be *liq-tur*!*-ma*, and a scribal error must be assumed. Passages justifying this correction are cited in *CAD*, vol. I, sub voce *imbaru.*

P. 180. 9. The meaning assigned to *šaḫāḫu* here (see p. 333) occurs lexically in *šaḫāḫu ša dīmti* (quoted in *CAD*, sub voce *dīmtu*).

P. 200. 20. Cf. *STT* I. 14, rev. 10: [*a-n*]*a šá-ru-ru šá* ^{d}*šamaš il-la-ka* [*d*]*i-ma-*[*a-šú*].

P. 207. Another duplicating fragment is K 8714 (Pl. 54), which offers a noteworthy variant for line 17: *id-du-u.*

A fragment belonging to an otherwise unknown fable was identified too late to be dealt with here. It is VAT 13837, published in photograph only by P. Gössmann, *Das Era-Epos*, p. 114. The two contestants seem to be *ḫa-ma-ni-ra* and *eš-qa-pi-zu.*

Chapter 9

New literature on the bilinguals is appearing in almost every volume of *CAD*, where the proverbs are often quoted in full, and often with original interpretations. E. I. Gordon's publication of the Sumerian proverb collections is so far represented by *JAOS* 77. 67–79 and *JCS* 12. 1–21 and 43–75.

P. 236. 10. This line is to be read: [gi.kid.aš.ni]gín.na and *i-aš-nigín-na*, see *MSL* VII, p. 26.

INDEX OF PUBLISHED TEXTS

INDEX OF WORDS DISCUSSED

LIST OF CUNEIFORM TABLETS

In this list "goes with" means "is part of the same tablet as".

Except where otherwise stated the copy given on the plates referred to is from the hand of W. G. Lambert.

	Plates
British Museum	
K 1453 *Counsels of a Pessimist*	30
1743+10858 *Theodicy* May go with K 3452+Sm 147	22
1835+8198+8200+9116 *Ox and Horse*	48
2024+2951+2983 *Bilingual Proverbs*	58, 59
2518+DT 358 *Ludlul* II	4
2765 Part of a prayer? See p. 288.	19
2951 See K 2024+	
2983 See K 2024+	
3182+3187+3312+5121+5459+6823+8232+9356+9699+10587+13430+13794+Sm 311 +Sm 1398 [K 9356 does not make a physical join, but certainly goes with the other pieces] *Šamaš Hymn*	33, 34
3187 See K 3182+	
3291 Commentary on *Ludlul*	15–17
3312 See K 3182+	
3323+Rm 941 *Ludlul* II May go with K 8396	6
3364 *Counsels of Wisdom*	28
3452+Sm 147 *Theodicy* May go with K 1743	20, 25
3456+DT 43 *Ox and Horse*	47
3474+8233+Sm 372 *Šamaš Hymn*	35, 36
3641 *Fable of Fox*	53
3650 *Šamaš Hymn*	35, 36
3972 *Ludlul* II	5
4160+13184 *Bilingual Proverbs*	60
4207 *Bilingual Proverbs*	61
4327+4605+4749 *Bilingual Proverbs* May go with K 15227 and 80–7–19, 130	60
4347+16161 *Bilingual Proverbs*	61–63
4539 Of uncertain content. See p. 260.	65
4605 See K 4327+	
4749 See K 4327+	
5121 See K 3182+	
5459 See K 3182+	
5688 *Bilingual Proverbs*	60
5797 *Popular Sayings*	55
5932 *Theodicy*	22
6435 *Fable of Fox*	53
6823 See K 3182+	
6935 *Ludlul* II	7
7638 *Bilingual Proverbs*	59
7654 *Bilingual Proverbs* May go with K 7674+	60
7674+11166+13568 *Bilingual Proverbs* May go with K 7654	64

		Plates
K 7897	*Counsels of Wisdom* Probably goes with K 8282	27, 29
8051	Incantation. See p. 322.	33
8197	*Ox and Horse*	48
8198	See K 1835+	
8199	*Ox and Horse*	48
8200	See K 1835+	
8206	*Bilingual Proverbs* May go with 80-7-19, 286 and 80-7-19, 289	58, 59
8216	*Bilingual Proverbs*	63
8231	*Counsels of Wisdom*	28
8232	See K 3182+	
8233	See K 3474+	
8282	*Counsels of Wisdom* Probably goes with K 7897	27, 29
8315	*Bilingual Proverbs*	64
8338	*Bilingual Proverbs*	64
8396	*Ludlul* II May go with K 3323+Rm 941	5
8413	*Fable of Willow*(?)	44
8463	*Theodicy*	19, 23
8491+13929	*Theodicy*	21, 22
8566+13771	*Fable of Willow*(?)	44
8567	*Fable of Fox*	53
8570	*Fable of Fox*	52
8577	*Fable of Fox*	52
8592	*Fable of Riding-donkey*	53
8714	*Fable of Fox*. See p. 346.	54
9050+13457	*Bilingual Proverbs*	64
9116	See K 1835+	
9237	*Ludlul* I	3
9290+9297	*Theodicy*	21, 22
9297	See K 9290+	
9356	See K 3182+	
9699	See K 3182+	
9724	See p. 345.	17
9834	*Ox and Horse*	47
9908	Precepts? See p. 117.	30
9952	Fragment of historical epic? See p. 296.	12
10301	*Theodicy*	19
10503(+ Sm 2139)	*Ludlul* I. See p. 30.	3
10523	*Dialogue of Pessimism*	38
10587	See K 3182+	
10652	*Counsels of Wisdom*	29
10802	Fragment of catalogue, see p. 63, and *JCS* 11. 11. It goes with K 9717 (P. Haupt, *Das babylonische Nimrodepos*, no. 51)	19
10858	See K 1743+	
10866	*Šamaš Hymn*	33
10916+12029	*Ox and Horse*	48
11166	See K 7674+	
11608	*Bilingual Proverbs*	64
12029	See K 10916+	
12042	*Ox and Horse*	47

		Plates
K 13184	See K 4160+	
13247	Popular Sayings	55
13430	See K 3182+	
13457	See K 9050+	
13568	See K 7674+	
13770	*Counsels of Wisdom*? See p. 106.	27
13771	See K 8566+	
13794	See K 3182+	
13830	*Dialogue of Pessimism*	38
13929	See K 8491+	
15227 with 80–7–19, 130	*Bilingual Proverbs* These two almost certainly go together, though there is no physical join. They may also go with K 4327+	65
16161	See K 4347+	
16171	*Bilingual Proverbs*	64
Sm 61	*Bilingual Proverbs*	65
147	See K 3452+	
311	See K 3182+	
372	See K 3474+	
1033	*Šamaš Hymn*	33
1398	See K 3182+	
1745	*Ludlul* II	4
2139	*Ludlul* I [see K 10503]	
DT 1	*Advice to a Prince*	31, 32
43	See K 3456+	
151	*Ludlul* II	6
358	See K 2518+	
Rm 941	See K 3323+	
79–7–8, 245	Bilingual fragment? See p. 230.	58
80–7–19, 130	See K 15227	
283	*Counsels of Wisdom*? See p. 107.	27
286	*Bilingual Proverbs* May go with K 8206 and 80–7–19, 289	59
289	*Bilingual Proverbs* May go with K 8206 and 80–7–19, 286	58
83–1–18, 237	Incantation. See p. 341.	57
472	*Šamaš Hymn*	34, 35
Ki 1902–5–10, 32	*Ox and Horse*	47
BM 32214 = S+ 76–11–17, 1941	*Ludlul* I, II May go with BM 32694	4
32694 = S+ 76–11–17, 2463+2478	*Ludlul* I, II May go with BM 32214	4
33851 = Rm 4. 411	*Counsels of Wisdom*	27, 29
34633 = Sp II. 116	*Theodicy*	19, 25
34773 = Sp II. 265	*Theodicy*	19, 24
35405 = Sp II. 988+1001	*Theodicy*	20
38283 = 80–11–12, 165	*Bilingual Proverbs*	66
38486 = 80–11–12, 370	*Bilingual Proverbs*	66
38539 = 80–11–12, 423	*Bilingual Proverbs*	67
38596 = 80–11–12, 480	*Bilingual Proverbs*	69
40098 = 81–2–1, 63	*Theodicy* May go with BM 40124	21, 23
40124 = 81–2–1, 90	*Theodicy* May go with BM 40098	20
53309 = 82–3–23, 4344+4473	Exercise tablet, see p. 221. Goes with BM 53555	57

Tablet	Description	Plates
BM 53555 = 82–3–23, 4595	Exercise tablet, see p. 221. Goes with BM 53309	57
55470 = 82–7–4, 43	*Fable of Fox*	54
56488 = 82–7–14, 864	Exercise tablet, see p. 280.	71
56607 = 82–7–14, 989	*Bilingual Proverbs*	70
66882+76506 = 82–9–18, 6876+6960+AH 83–1–18, 1876	Commentary on *Theodicy*	26
76506	See BM 66882+	
98631 = Th 1905–4–9, 137	*Šamaš Hymn*	34
98732 = Th 1905–4–9, 238	*Šamaš Hymn*	33
98743 = Th 1905–4–9, 249	*Bilingual Proverbs*	65

MUSEUM OF THE ANCIENT ORIENT, ISTANBUL

Tablet	Description	Plates
Si 15	*Šamaš Hymn*	33, 36
37+881	*Ludlul* II	6, 7
55	*Ludlul* III	13, 14
881	See Si 37+	
Bo 3157	*Babylonian Proverbs*	72
4209+4710	*Babylono-Hittite Proverbs*	72
A ... 1	*Dialogue of Pessimism*	38
A ... 2	*Dialogue of Pessimism*	38

These two pieces, which go together, are unnumbered, so the above distinguishing marks have been used.

UNIVERSITY MUSEUM, PHILADELPHIA

Tablet	Description	Plates
CBS 4507, Rev. 54–58	*Counsels of Wisdom*	29
14235	*Babylonian Proverbs*	70
N–3395	*Bilingual Proverbs*	71
UM 29–15–330	*Bilingual Proverbs*	68

VORDERASIATISCHES MUSEUM, BERLIN

Tablet	Description	Plates
BE unnumbered	*Bilingual Proverbs*, see p. 274 (no copy given)	
VAT 657	*Dialogue of Pessimism*	38
8573 and Photo Assur S 4825		73

An exercise tablet with extracts as follows:

Obv. 1–18: three lines each from tablets XVIII–XXIII of *Ḫarra* (identified by B. Landsberger)

Rev. 3–5: from *Ḫargud*; cf. VAT 10071. 14 and VAT 10756. 11

Rev. 6–7: unidentified bilingual hymn to Šamaš

Rev. 8–9: unidentified extract

Rev. 10–11: MUL.APIN I = *CT* 33. 4 obv. II. 46–47 (identified by A. Sachs)

Tablet	Description	Plates
8807	Popular Sayings	55–57
8830	*Tamarisk and Palm*	43
9303	*Ludlul* IV(?)	18
9442	*Ludlul* IV(?) May go with VAT 10538	18
9933	*Dialogue of Pessimism*	37
9943	Work similar to *Theodicy*	25
9954	*Ludlul* III	12
10071 with 10756	Exercise tablets with extracts:	73

These two exercises, henceforth A and B, can be taken together as they offer consecutive

	Plates
extracts from the same works. The lexical extracts have been identified by B. Landsberger.	
A 1–2, B 1–3 = *Erim.ḫuš* II. 234–40	
A 3–5, B 4–7 = *Erim.ḫuš* III. 12–21	
A 6–8, B 8–10 = *Diri* I. 247–53	
A 9–11 (no continuation on B) = Commentary on *Šumma izbu* 121–3, though the Commentary probably depends on a lexical series from which the extract here is made.	
A 12–14, B 11–13 = *Ḫargud*, see *MSL* V. p. 81	
B 14–17 (nothing antecedent on A) are unknown; more *Ḫargud*?	
A 15–16, B 18–19 = *Maqlû* IV. 134–40	
A 17–18, B 20–21 = *Šamaš Hymn* 138–41	
A 19–20, B 22–23 = *Ludlul* I. 82–85	
A 21–22, B 24–25 = *Enūma Eliš* I. 22–25	
A 23–24, B 26–27 = *Era Epic* I. 73–76	
VAT 10102 *Tamarisk and Palm*	41-42
10148 *Fable of Fox* Copy of E. Ebeling	53
10151 *Instructions of Šuruppak*	30
10154 *Fable of Fox*	52
10174, Obv. 12–17 *Šamaš Hymn*	36
10251 *Bilingual Proverbs*	58, 59
10349 *Fable of Fox*	52
10538 *Ludlul* IV(?) May go with VAT 9442	18
10567 *Theodicy*	23
10601 *Ludlul* II May go with VAT 10657	6
10610 Bilingual *Hymn to Ninurta*	32
10657 *Ludlul* II May go with VAT 10601	6
10756 See VAT 10071	
10810 *Bilingual Proverbs*	67, 68
11100 *Ludlul* I	3
11193 *Fable of Fox*	49
11556 *Fable of Fox*	54
*11556 *Counsels of Wisdom* Copy of E. Ebeling. 11556 is the false number given to *KAR* 329; the correct number has not been ascertained.	29
11565 *Ludlul* I Copy of E. Ebeling	74
12995 *Nisaba and Wheat*?	44
13836 and Photo Assur S 6814 *Fable of Fox*	50, 51

IRAQ MUSEUM, BAGHDAD

	Plates
IM 53946 *Tamarisk and Palm*	39–40
53975 *Tamarisk and Palm*	39–40
Both copies of J. J. A. Van Dijk	

ARCHAEOLOGICAL MUSEUM, ANKARA

	Plates
SU 1951, 10 *Ludlul* I Copy of O. R. Gurney	1, 2
1951, 32 *Ludlul* II Copy of O. R. Gurney	8–11
1951, 173+1952, 100+142 *Nisaba and Wheat* Copy of O. R. Gurney	45, 46
1952, 100+142 See SU 1951, 173+	
1952, 138+169+181 A–D Excerpt from fable? Copy of O. R. Gurney	55
1952, 212+291 with 302 *Ludlul* IV(?)	18
1952, 257 *Nisaba and Wheat* Copy of O. R. Gurney	45

	Plates
LEIDEN, de Liagre Böhl Collection	
Leiden 853 *Proverbs*, see p. 267. Copy of E. Weidner	68
Tablet once owned by H. Rassam, present location unknown	
Rassam *Fable of Fox?* Copy of T. G. Pinches	49

ADDENDA

K 9810 *Ludlul* I. See p. 343.	74
Sm 1420+1729 *Fable?* See p. 212.	43
BM 54821 = 82–5–25, 1150 *Ludlul* III. See p. 344.	74
65461 = 82–9–18, 5448+AH 83–1–18, 2116 *Šamaš Hymn*. See p. 346.	75
VAT 10357 *Counsels of Wisdom* **d**. See p. 345.	75
10522 *Ludlul* I *LKA* 24, no copy given. See p. 343.	
10569 *Ludlul* II. See p. 344.	74
11179 *Ludlul* III. See p. 344.	74
17157 *Counsels of Wisdom* g. See p. 345.	75

CUNEIFORM TEXTS

SU 1951, 10 **(m)**

Obv.

SU 1951, 10 (m)

Rev.

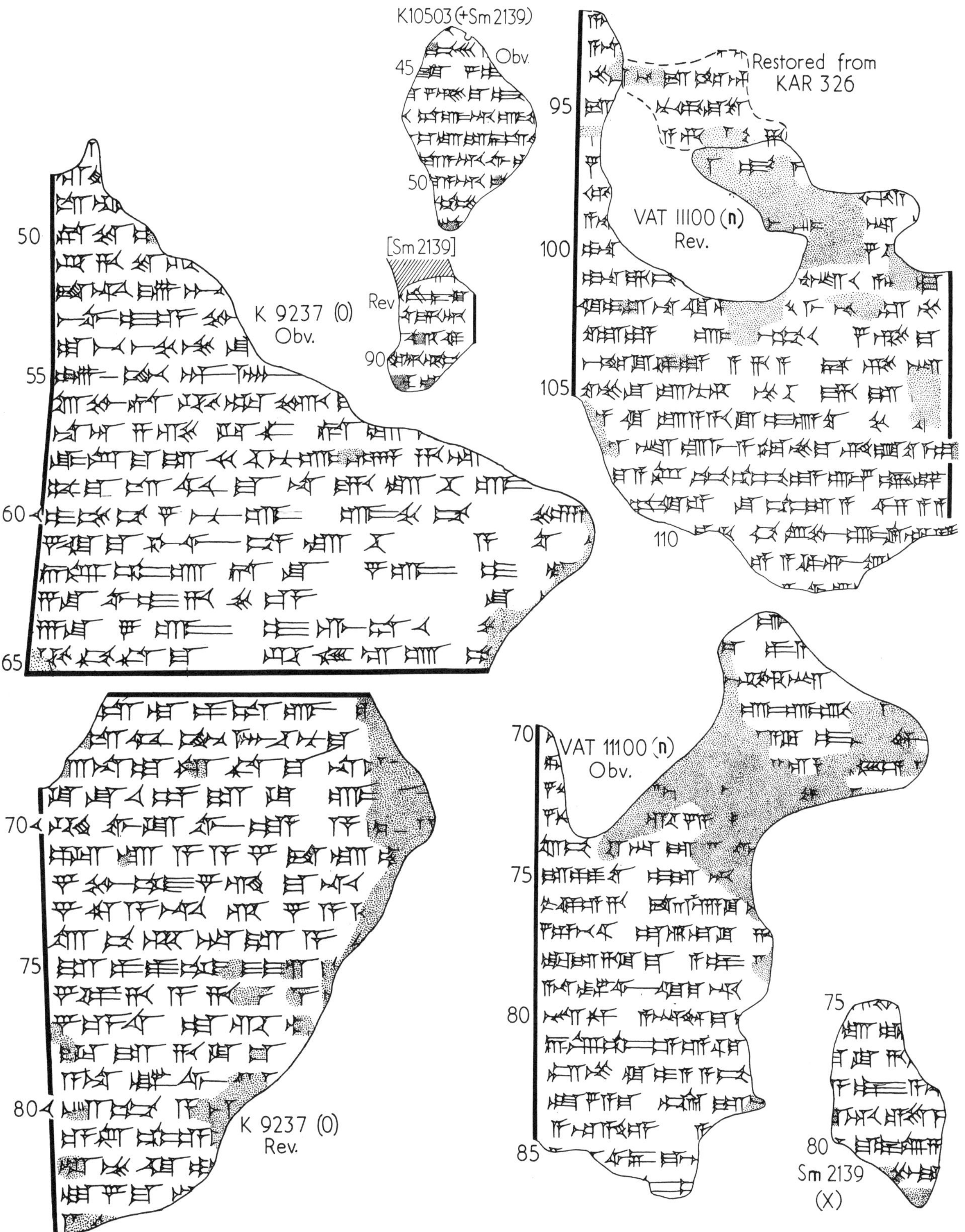
K10503 (+Sm 2139)
Obv.
[Sm 2139]
Rev
Restored from KAR 326
VAT 11100 (n)
Rev.
K 9237 (0)
Obv.
VAT 11100 (n)
Obv.
K 9237 (0)
Rev.
Sm 2139
(X)

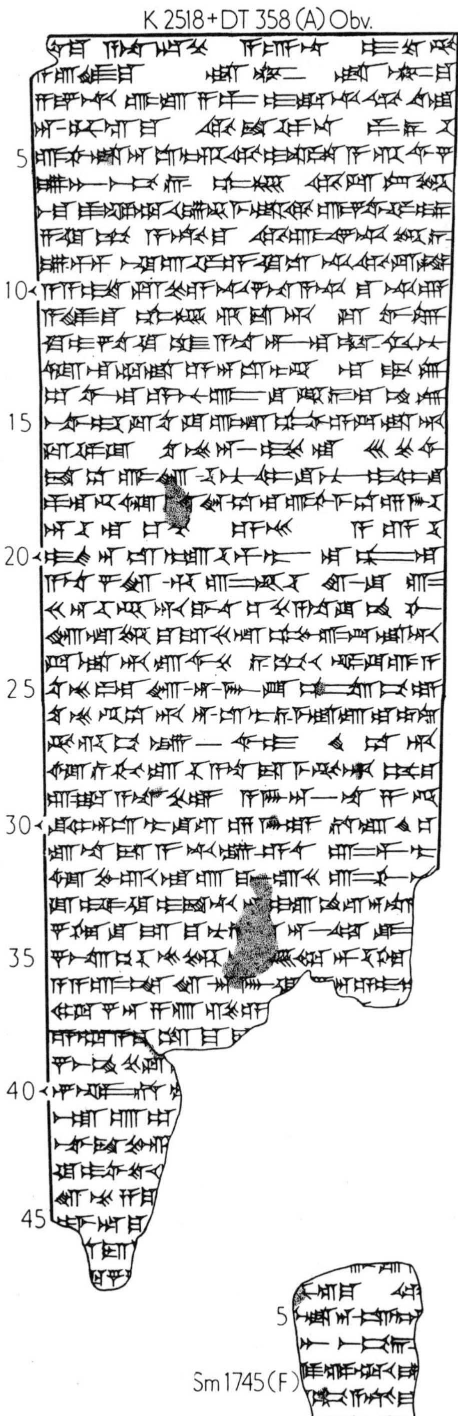
K 2518+DT 358 (A) Obv.
Sm 1745 (F)

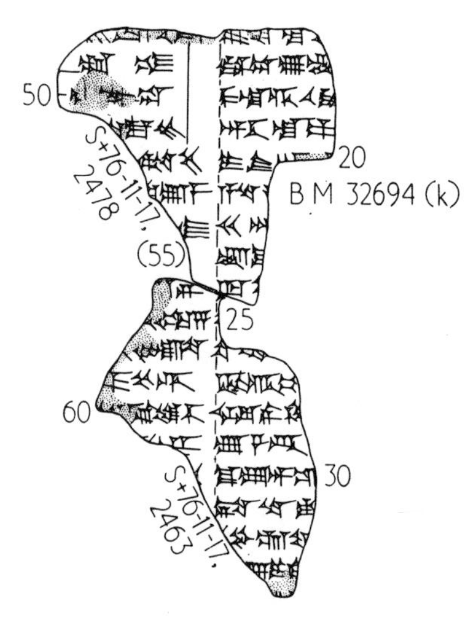
B M 32694 (k)
S+76-11-17, 2478
(55)
S+76-11-17, 2463

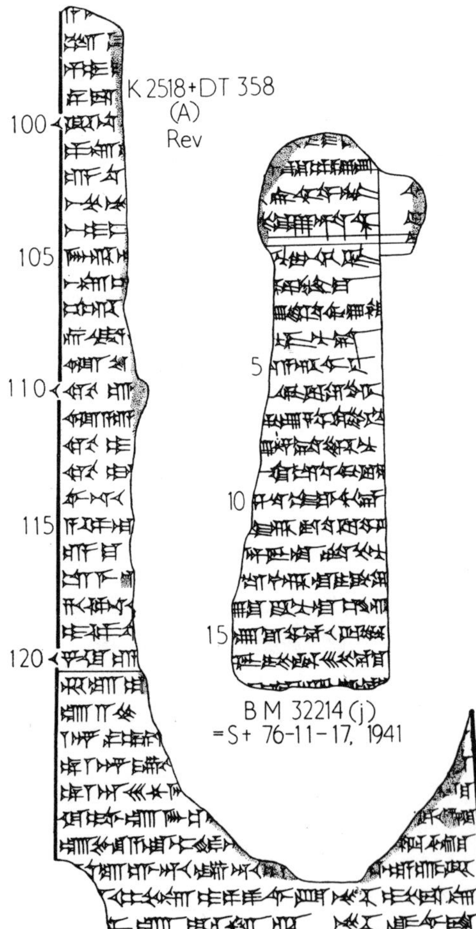
K 2518+DT 358
(A)
Rev
B M 32214 (j)
=S+ 76-11-17, 1941

K 3972 (B)
Obv

K 3972 (B)
Rev.

K 8396 (c)
Obv.

K 8396 (c)
Rev.

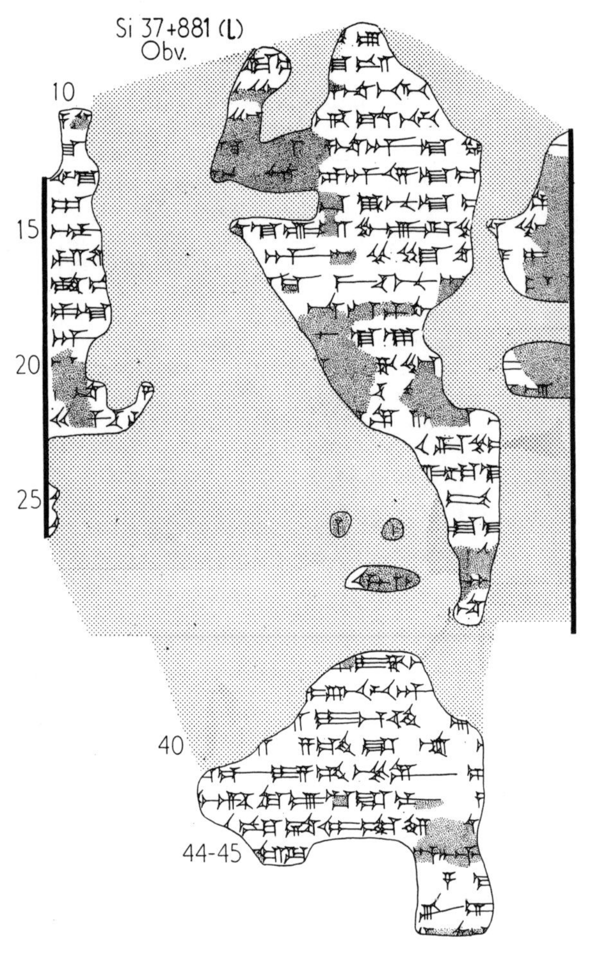
Si 37+881 (L)
Obv.
10
15
20
25
40
44-45

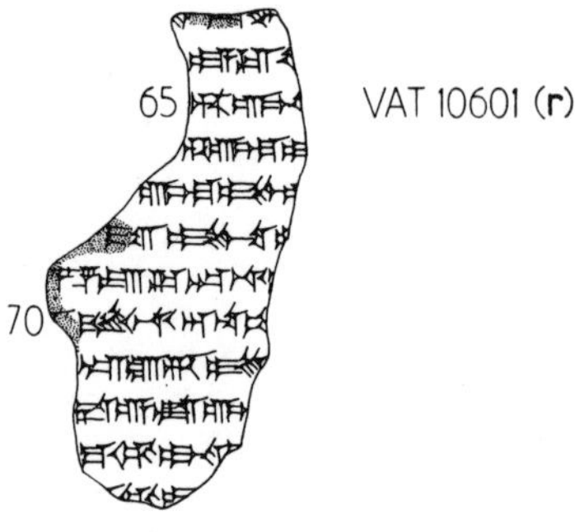
VAT 10601 (r)
65
70

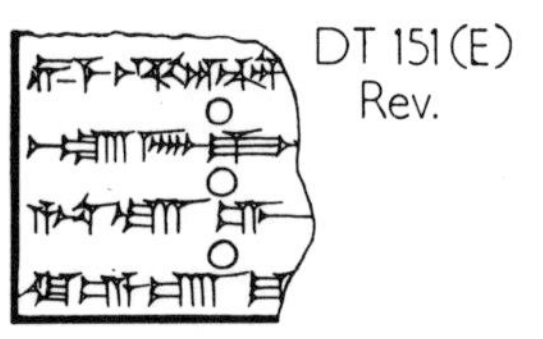
DT 151 (E)
Rev.

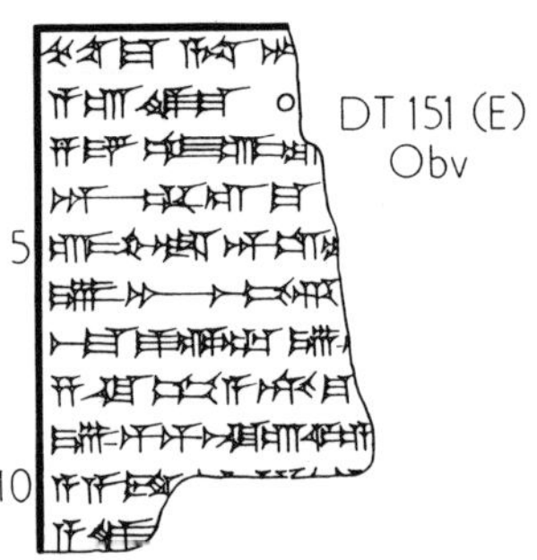
DT 151 (E)
Obv
5
10

K 3323+Rm 941 (D)
105
K 3323 Rev.
110
115
Rm 941
120

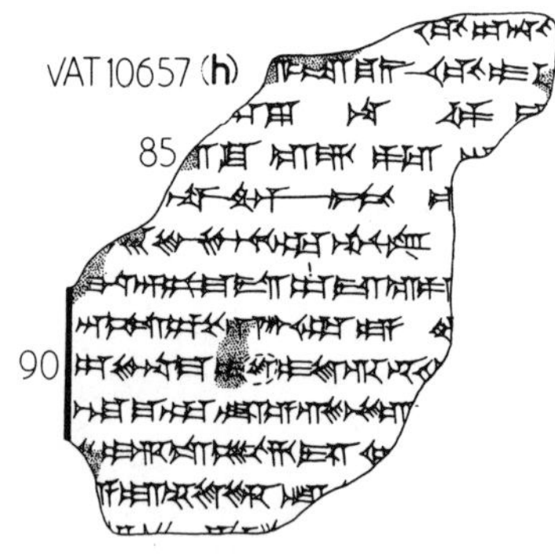
VAT 10657 (h)
85
90

20
K 3323+Rm 941
Obv.

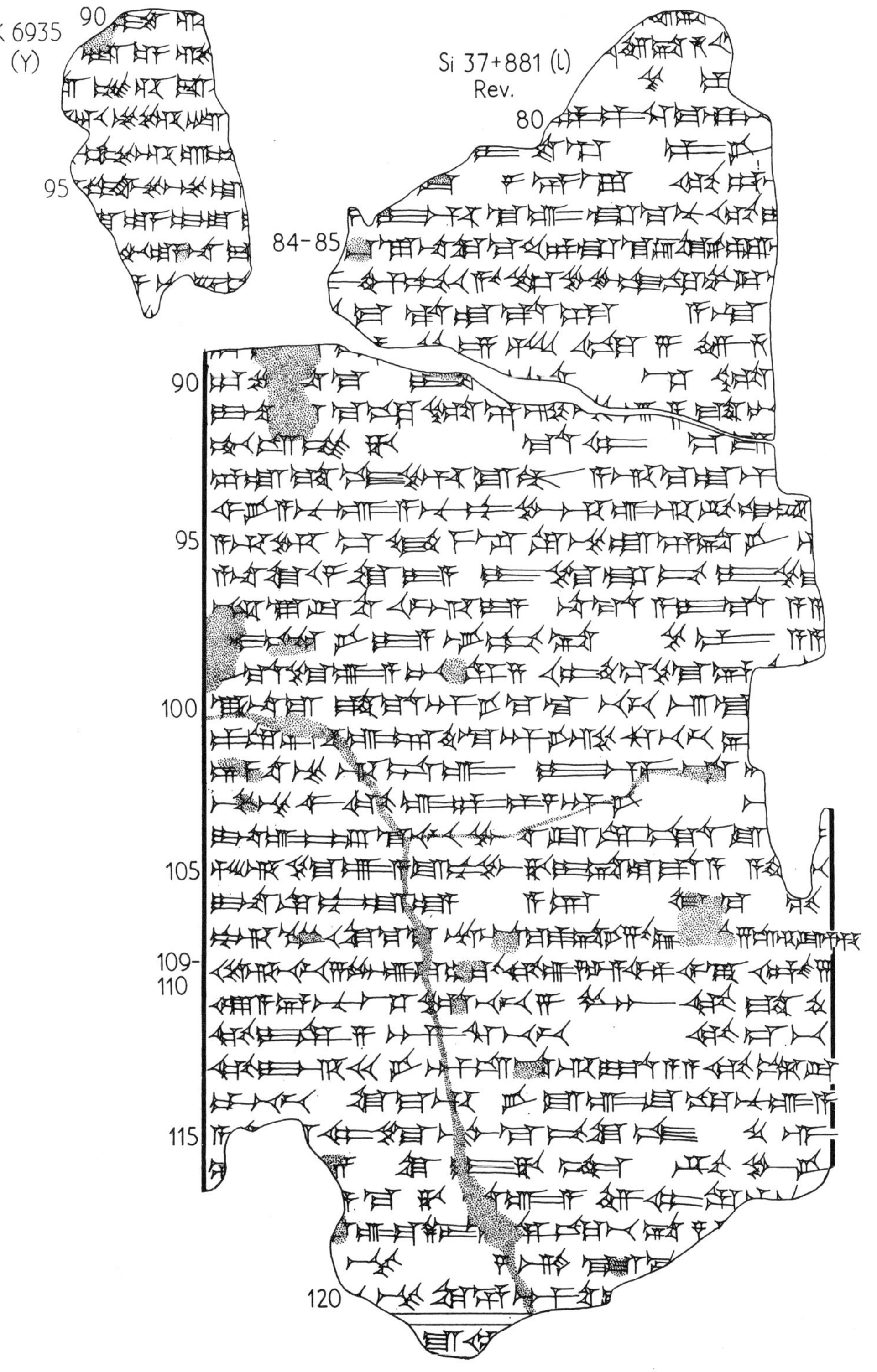
K 6935
(Y)
Si 37+881 (l)
Rev.

SU 1951, 32 (i)

Obverse

SU 1951, 32 (i)

Obv. cont.

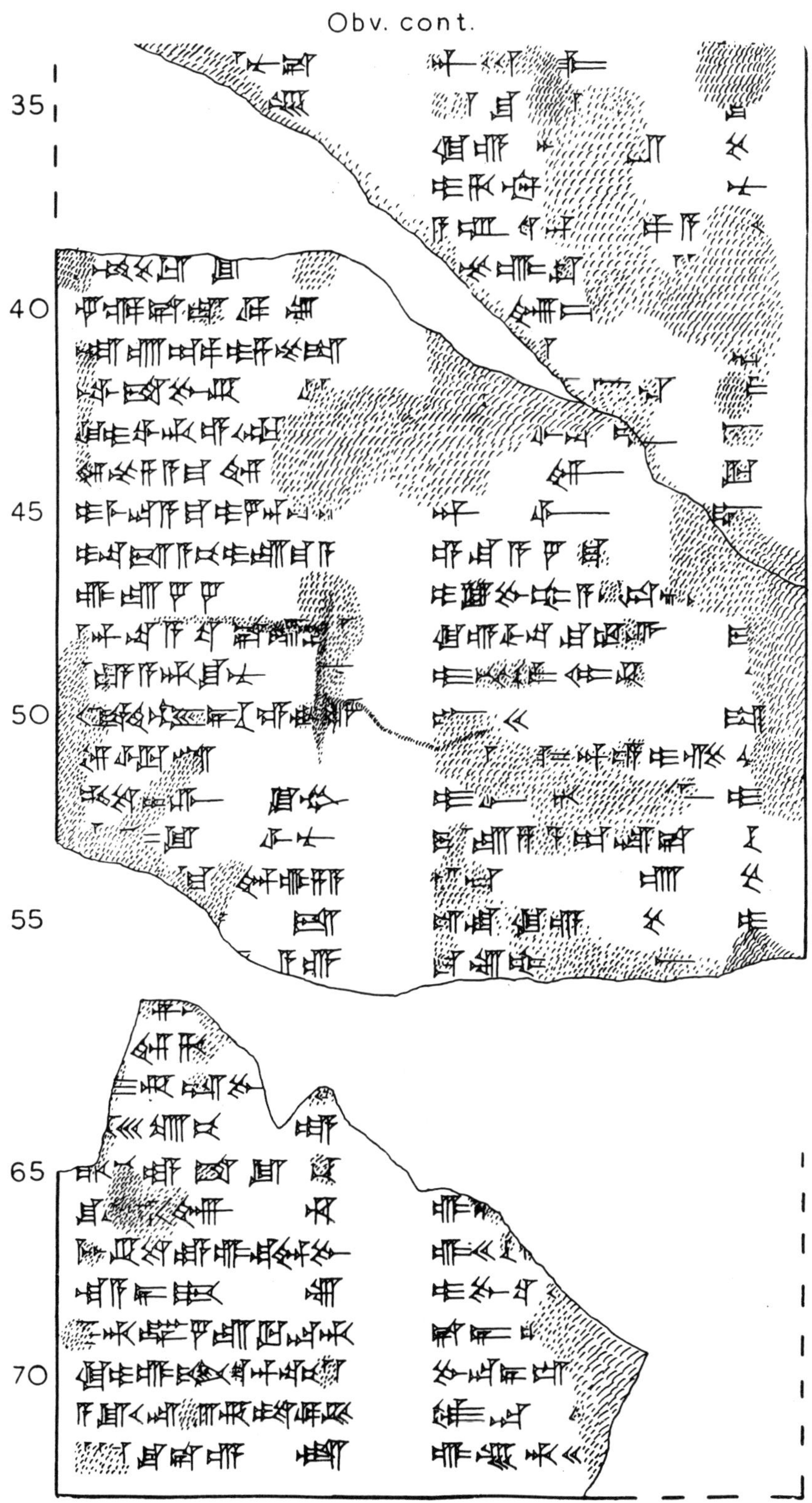

SU 1951, 32 (i)

Reverse

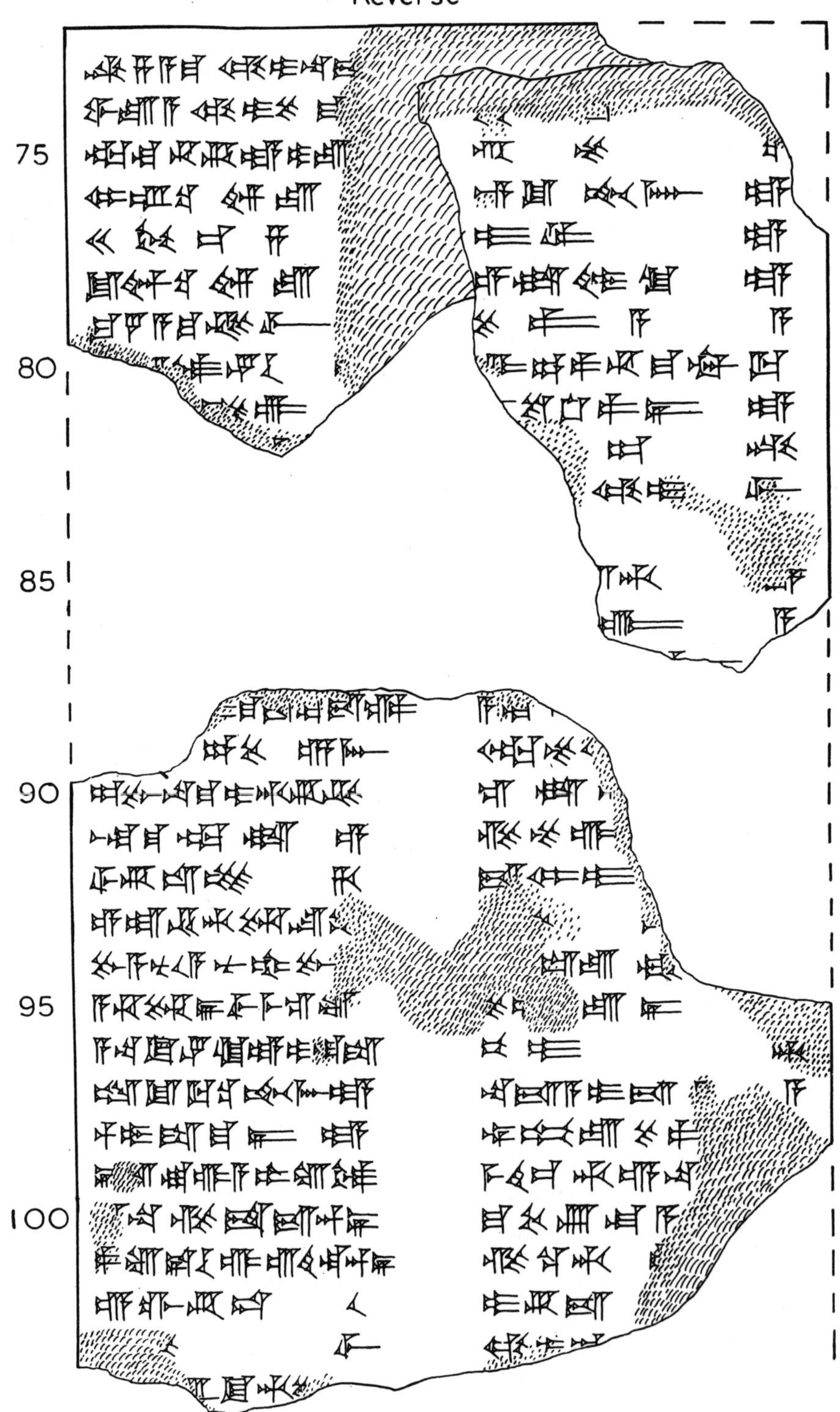

SU 1951, 32 (i)

Rev. cont.

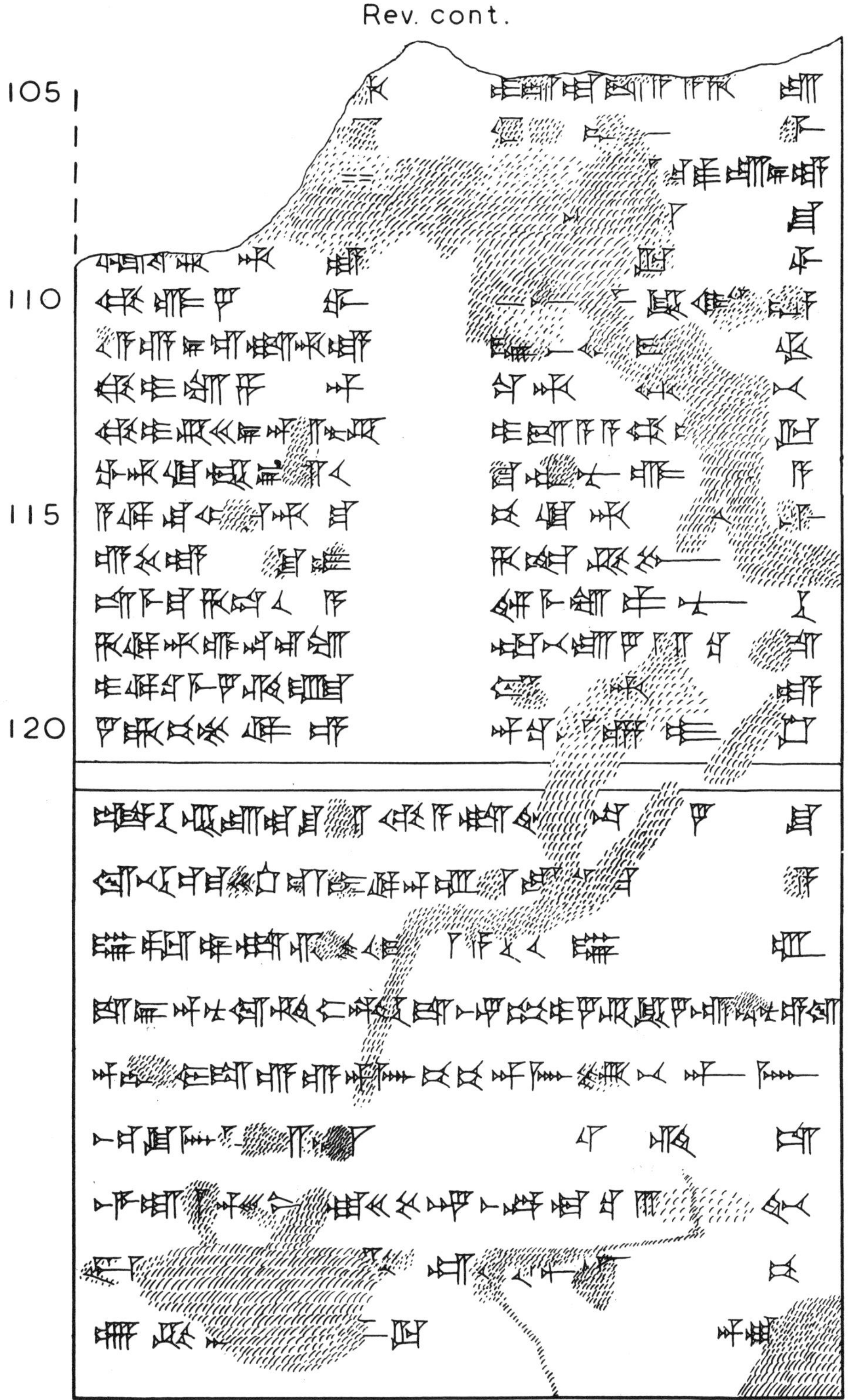

VAT 9954 (p)
Obv.
VAT 9954 (p)
Rev.
K 9952
Obv.
Rev.

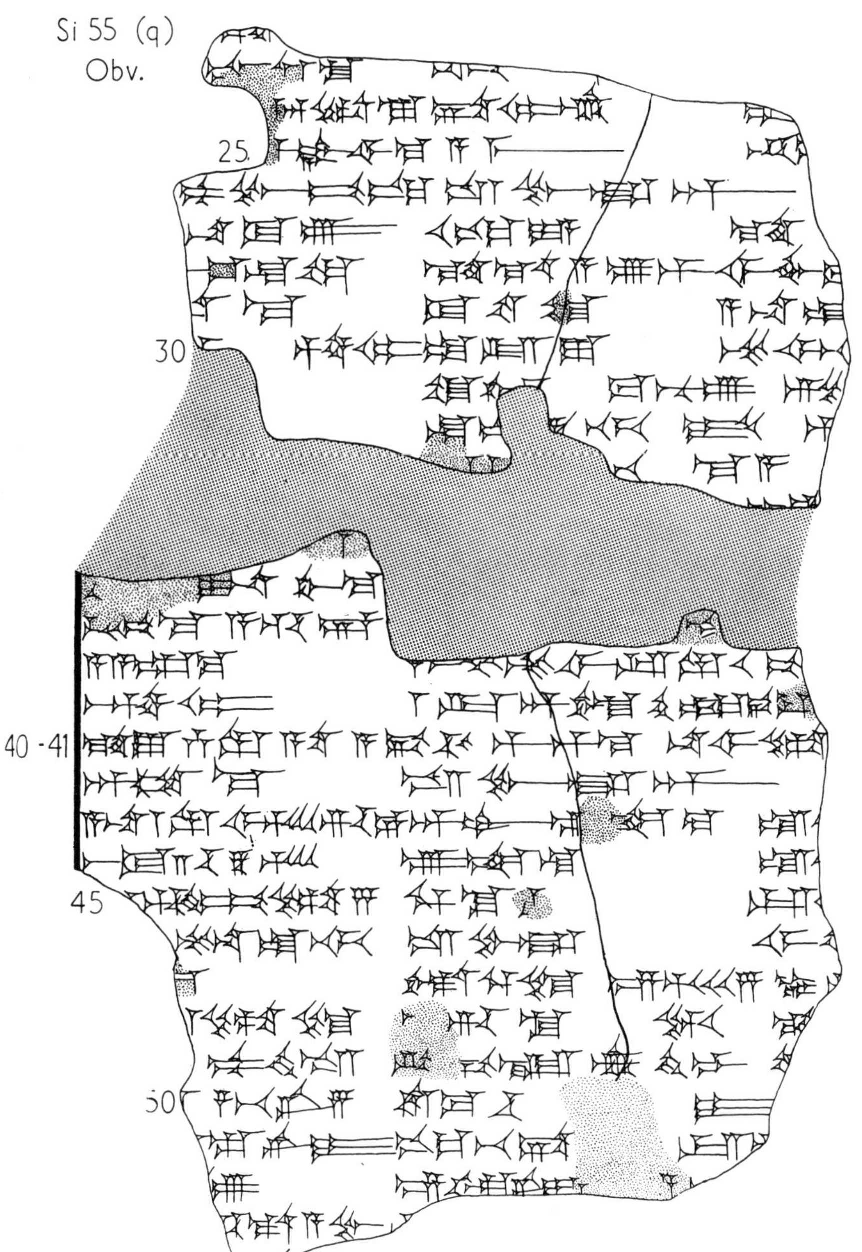
Si 55 (q)
Obv.

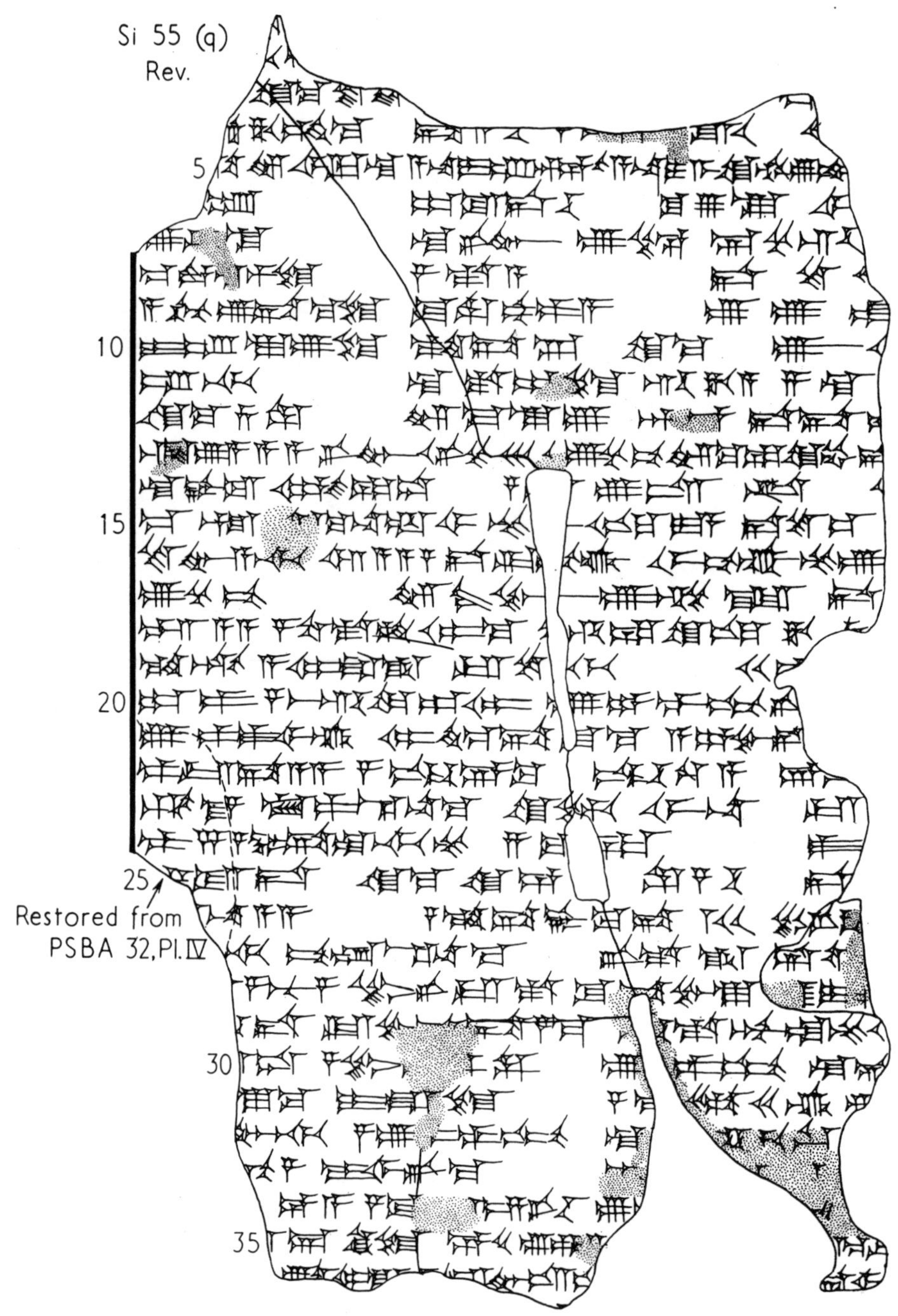
Si 55 (q)
Rev.
5
10
15
20
25
Restored from
PSBA 32, Pl. IV
30
35

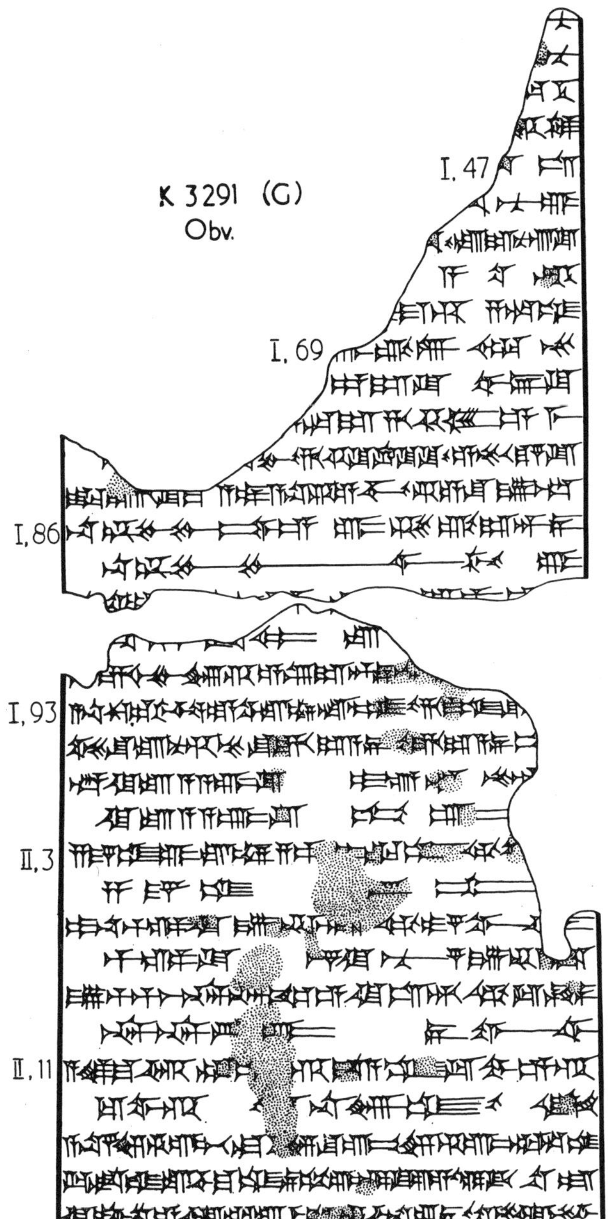
K 3291 (G)
Obv.
I, 47
I, 69
I, 86
I, 93
II, 3
II, 11

K 3291 (cont.)

II,44

II,69

II,90

II,98

III,1

III,60

a

K 3291 (G)
Rev.

K9724

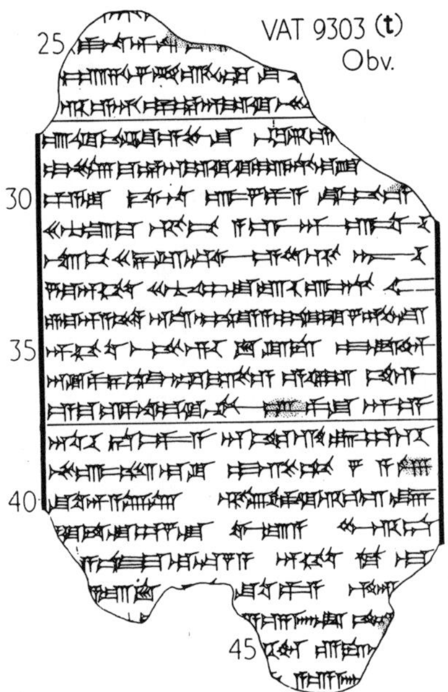
VAT 9303 (t)
Obv.

VAT 9303 (t)
Rev.

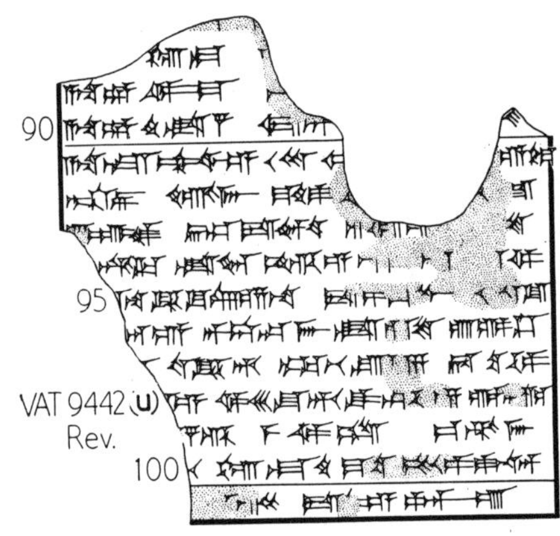
VAT 9442 (u)
Rev.

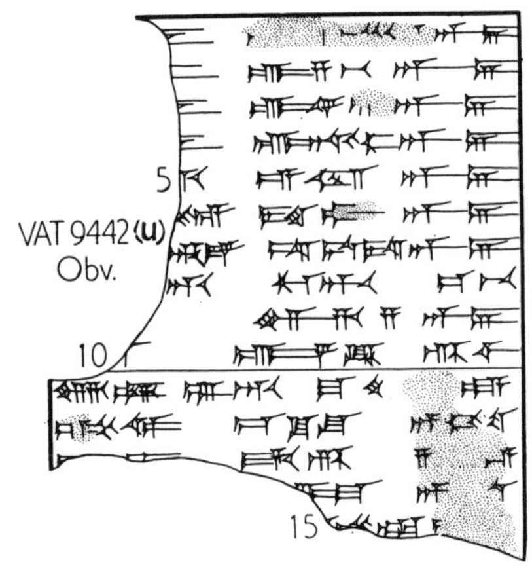
VAT 9442 (u)
Obv.

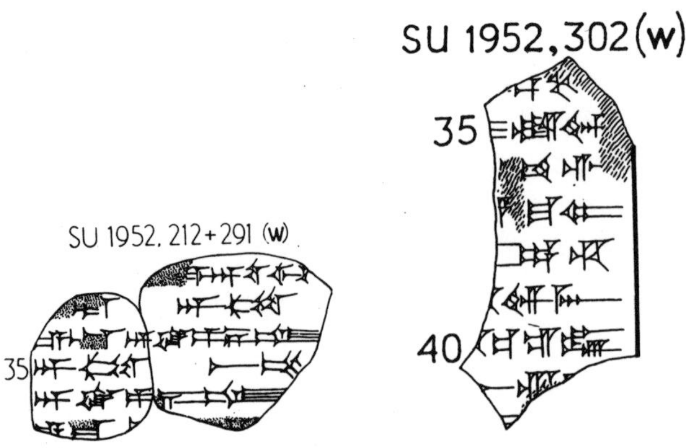
SU 1952, 212+291 (w)
SU 1952,302 (w)

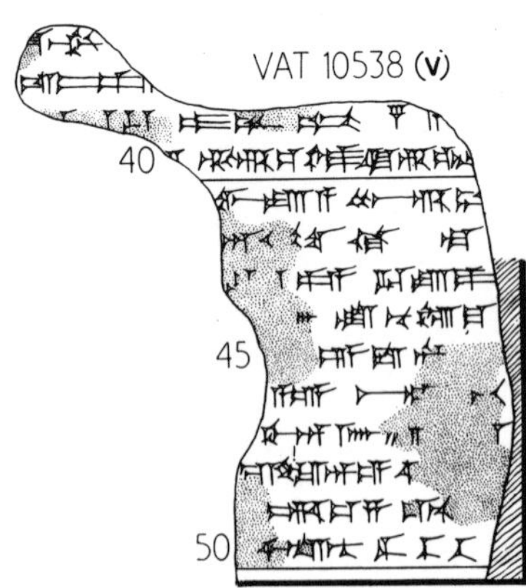
VAT 10538 (v)

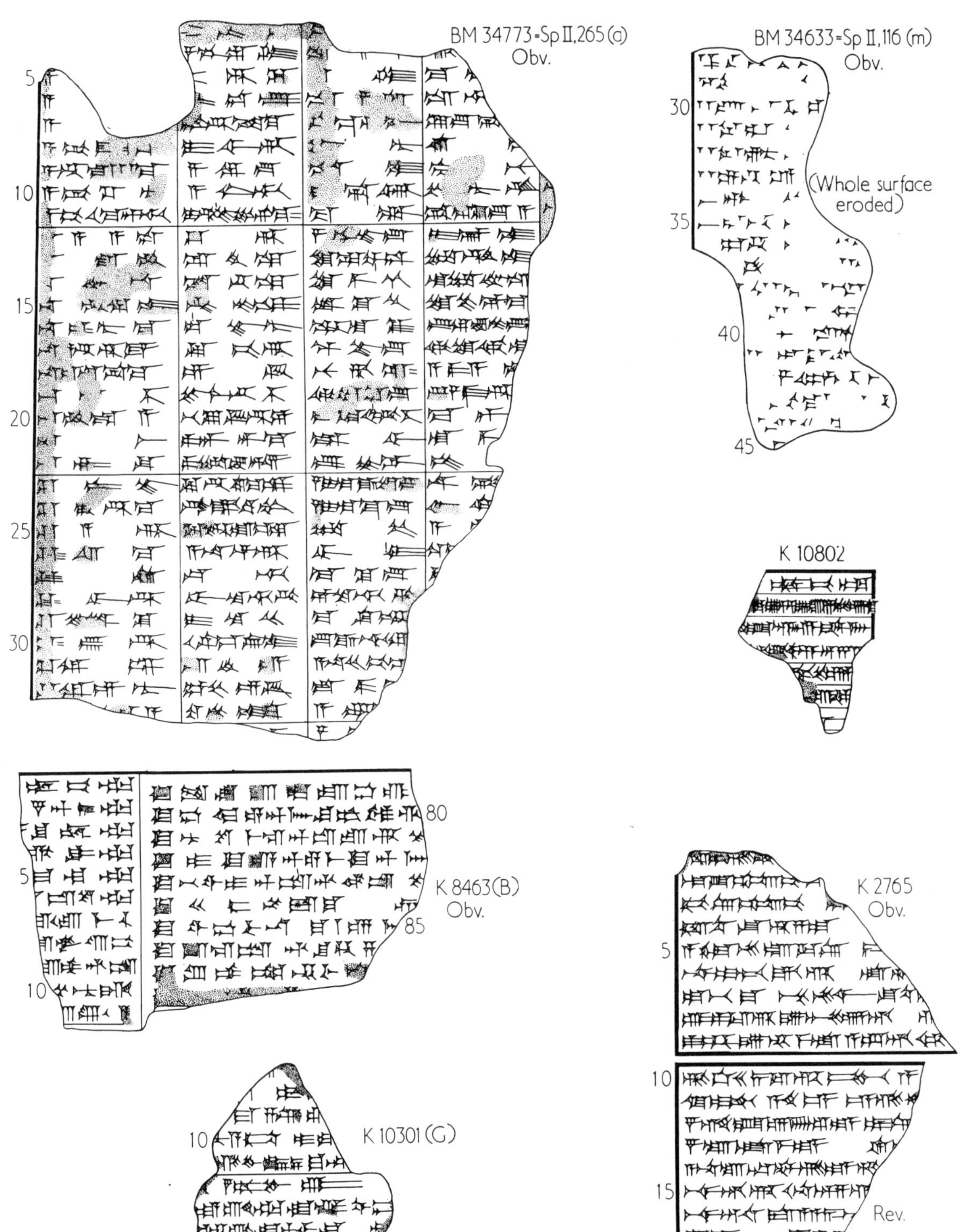
BM 34773=Sp II,265 (a)
Obv.
BM 34633=Sp II,116 (m)
Obv.
(Whole surface eroded)
K 10802
K 8463 (B)
Obv.
K 2765
Obv.
Rev.
K 10301 (G)

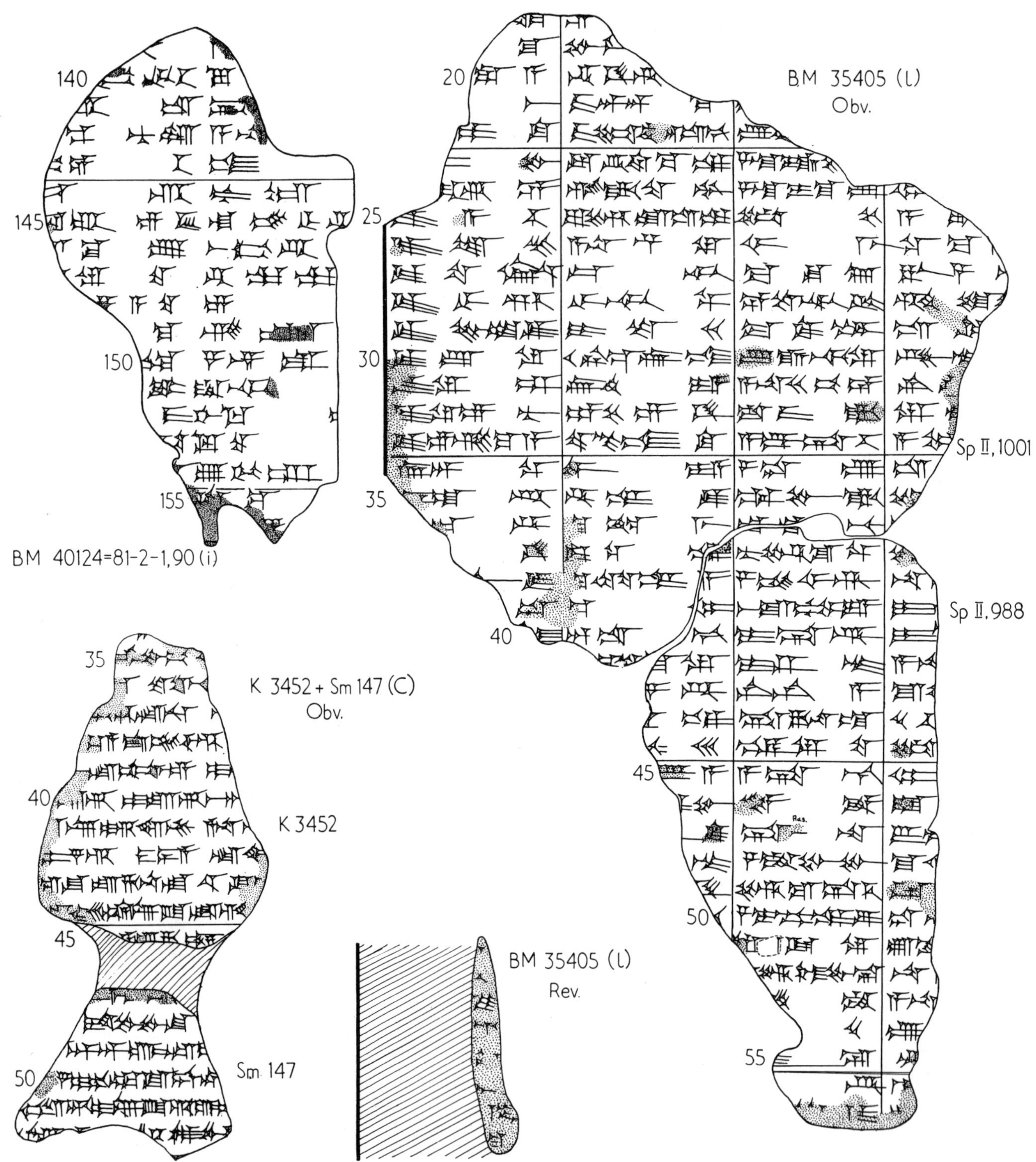
140
145
150
155
BM 40124=81-2-1,90 (i)
20
25
30
35
40
BM 35405 (l)
Obv.
Sp II,1001
Sp II,988
45
50
55
Ras.
35
K 3452 + Sm 147 (C)
Obv.
40
K 3452
45
50
Sm 147
BM 35405 (l)
Rev.

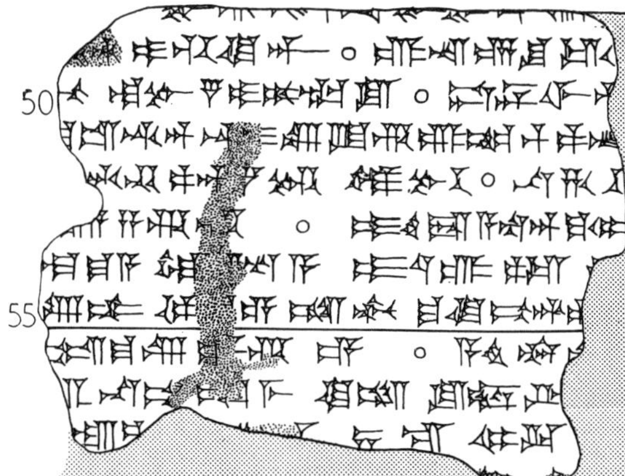

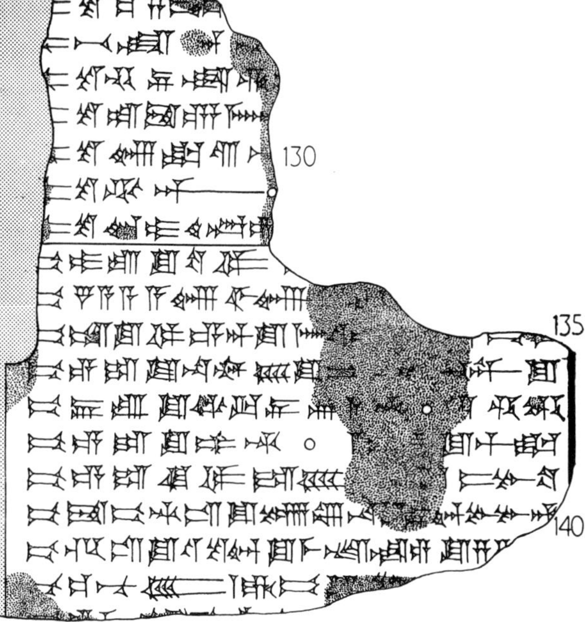

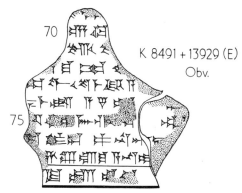

K 9290+9297 (D)

Obv.

K 8491 + 13929 (E)

Obv.

BM 40098 = 81-2-1, 63 (j)

Obv.

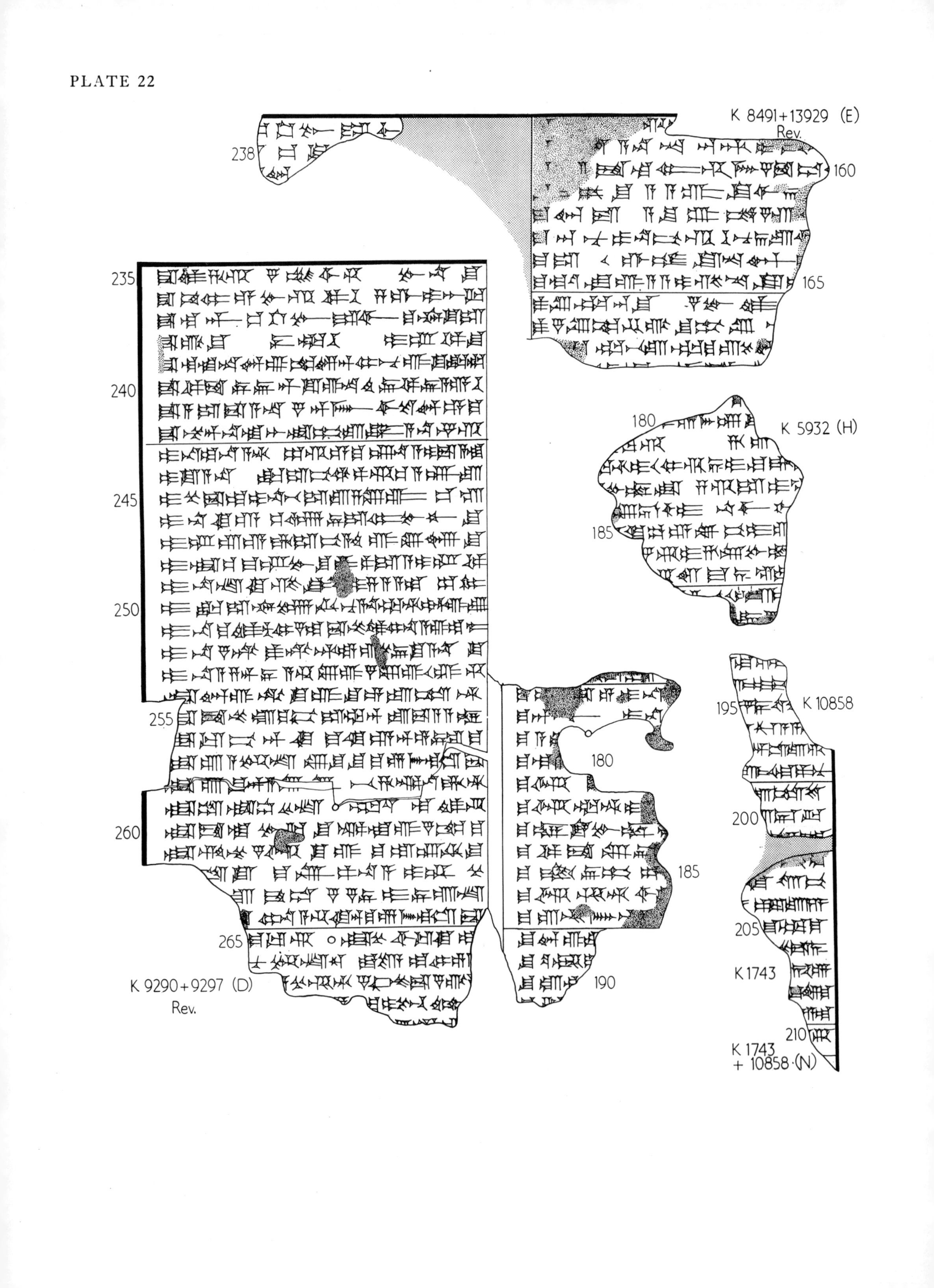

K 8491+13929 (E) Rev.

K 5932 (H)

K 10858

K 1743

K 1743 + 10858 (N)

K 9290+9297 (D) Rev.

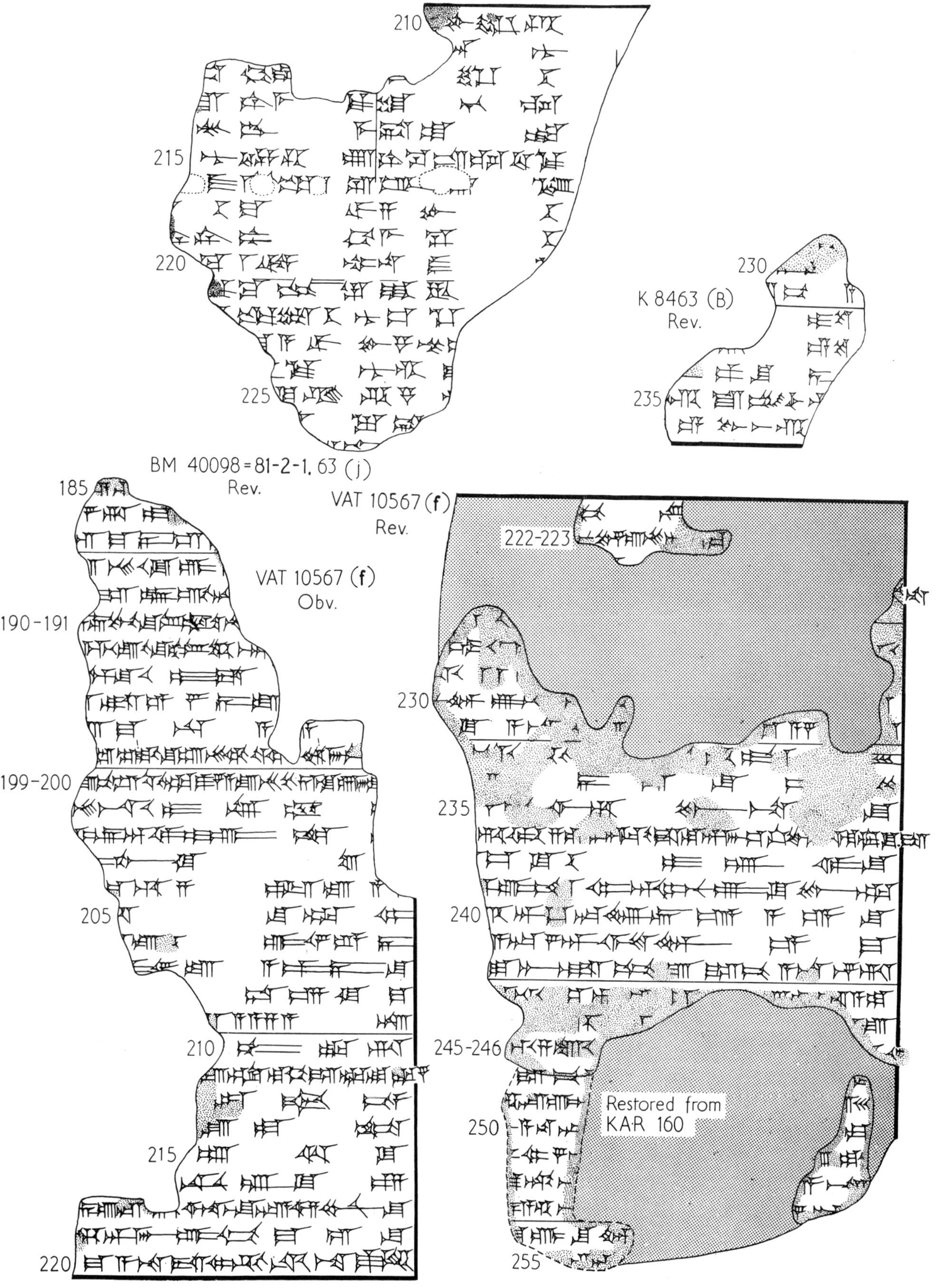

210
215
220
225
BM 40098 = 81-2-1, 63 (j)
Rev.
230
K 8463 (B)
Rev.
235
185
190-191
199-200
205
210
215
220
VAT 10567 (f)
Obv.
VAT 10567 (f)
Rev.
222-223
230
235
240
245-246
250
255
Restored from
KAR 160

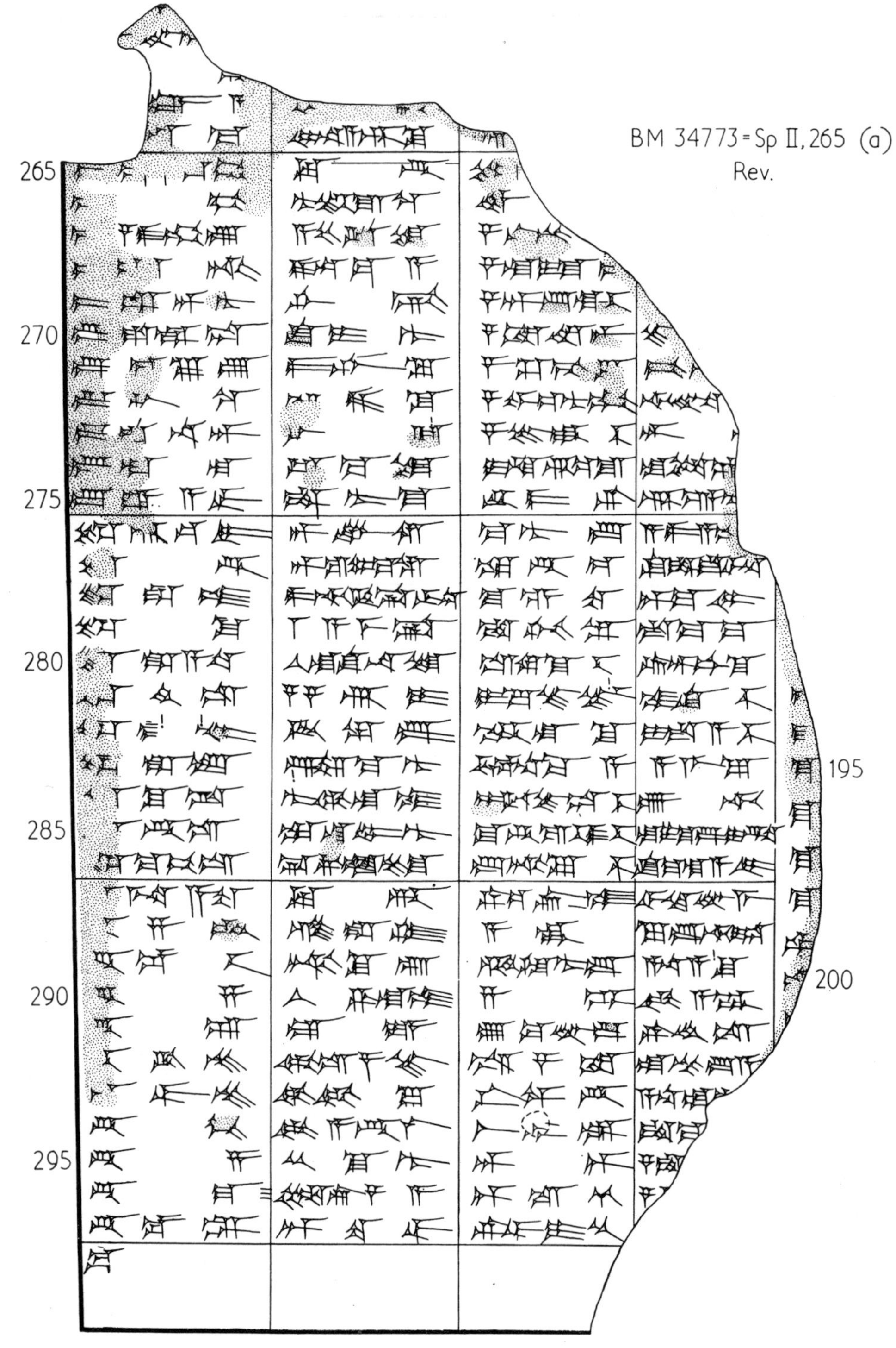
BM 34773 = Sp II, 265 (a)
Rev.

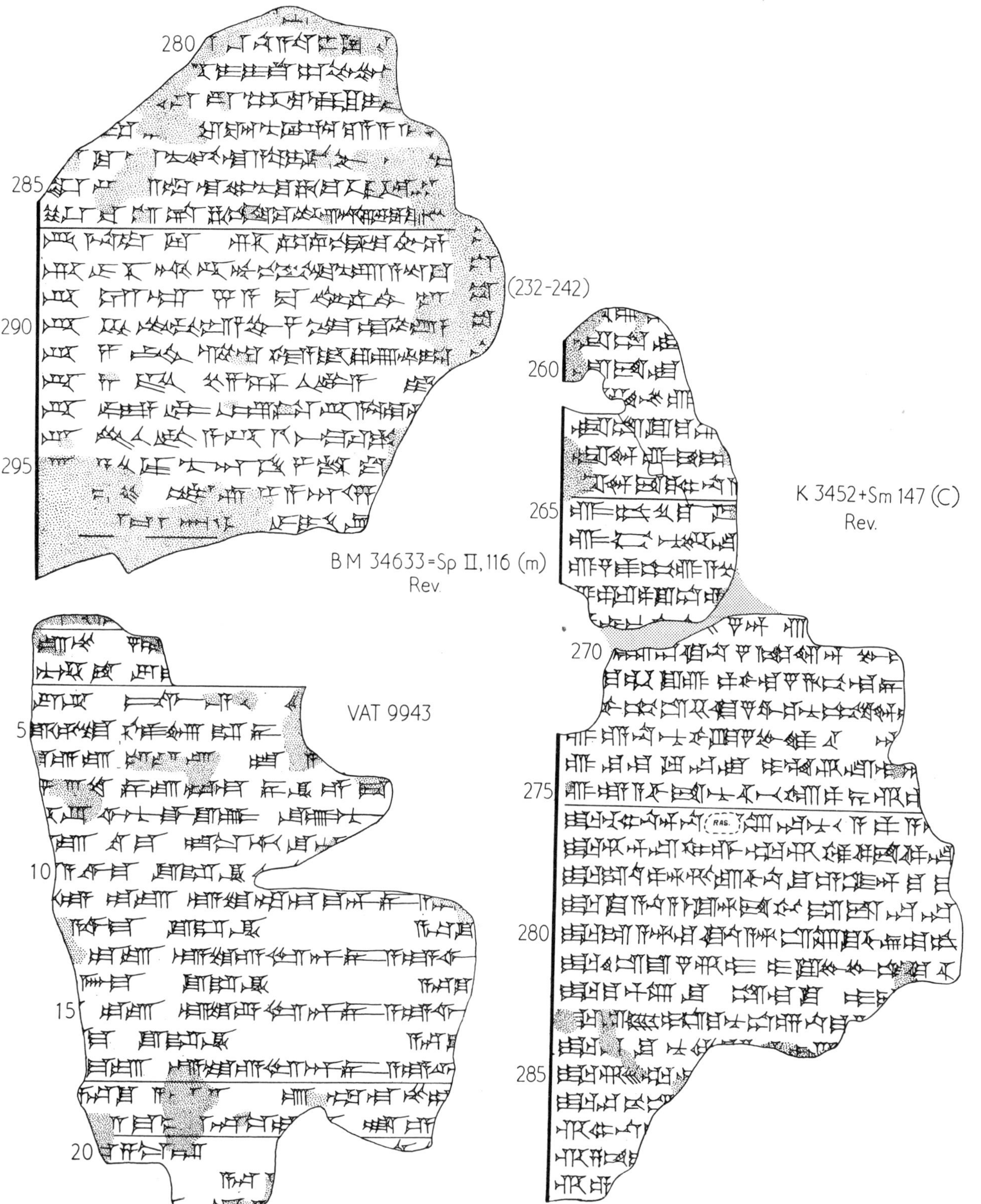

280
285
290
295
(232-242)
B M 34633=Sp II, 116 (m)
Rev.
260
265
270
275
280
285
K 3452+Sm 147 (C)
Rev.
VAT 9943
5
10
15
20

196
206
217
224
244
260
284
BM 66882+76506
Rev.
Upper edge
10
29
41
48
61
79
82-9-18, 6876
BM 66882
82-9-18, 6960
BM 66882+76506
Obv.
BM 76506= AH 83-1-18, 1876

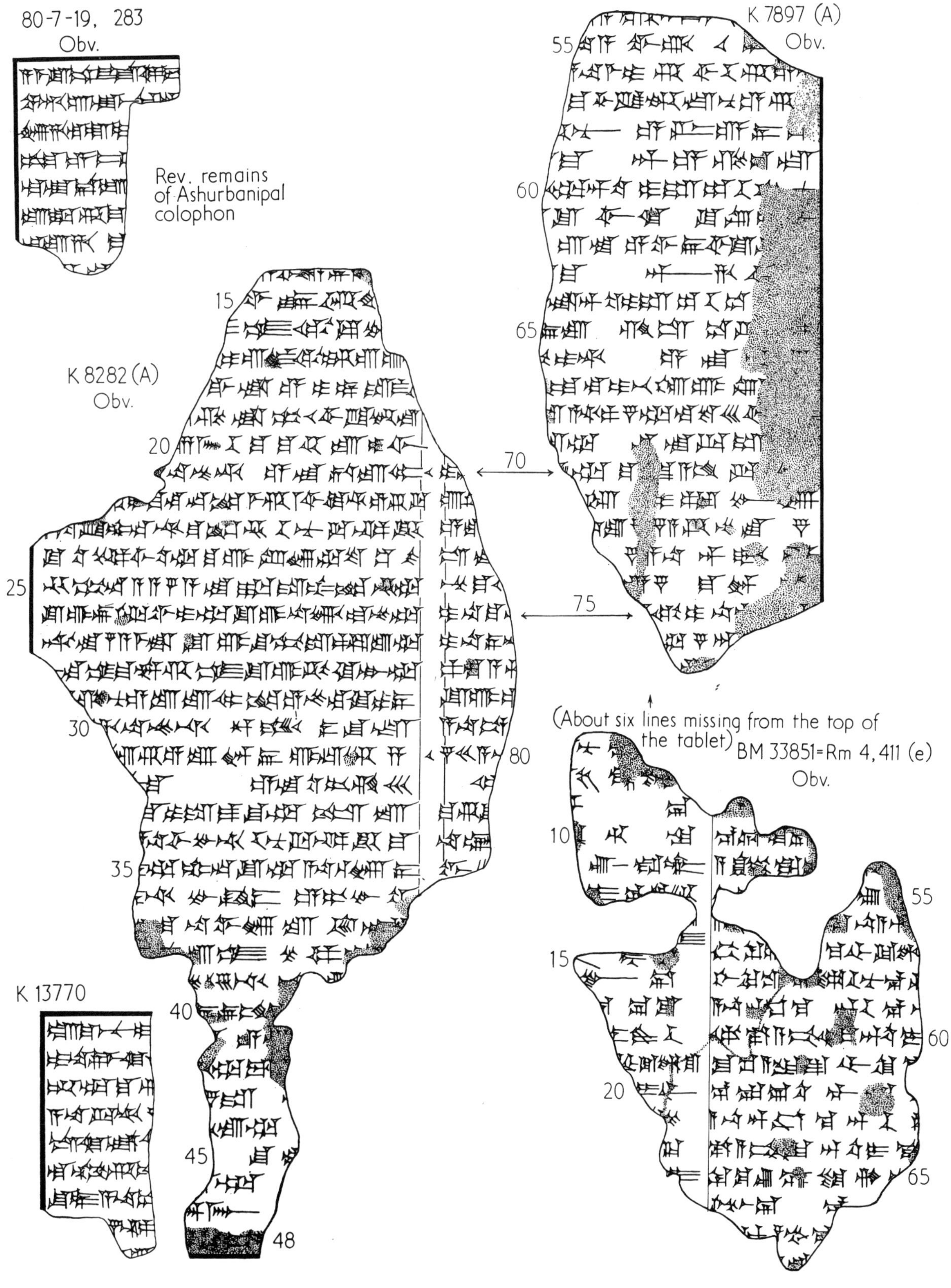
80-7-19, 283
Obv.
Rev. remains of Ashurbanipal colophon
K 7897 (A)
Obv.
K 8282 (A)
Obv.
70
75
80
(About six lines missing from the top of the tablet)
BM 33851=Rm 4, 411 (e)
Obv.
K 13770
48

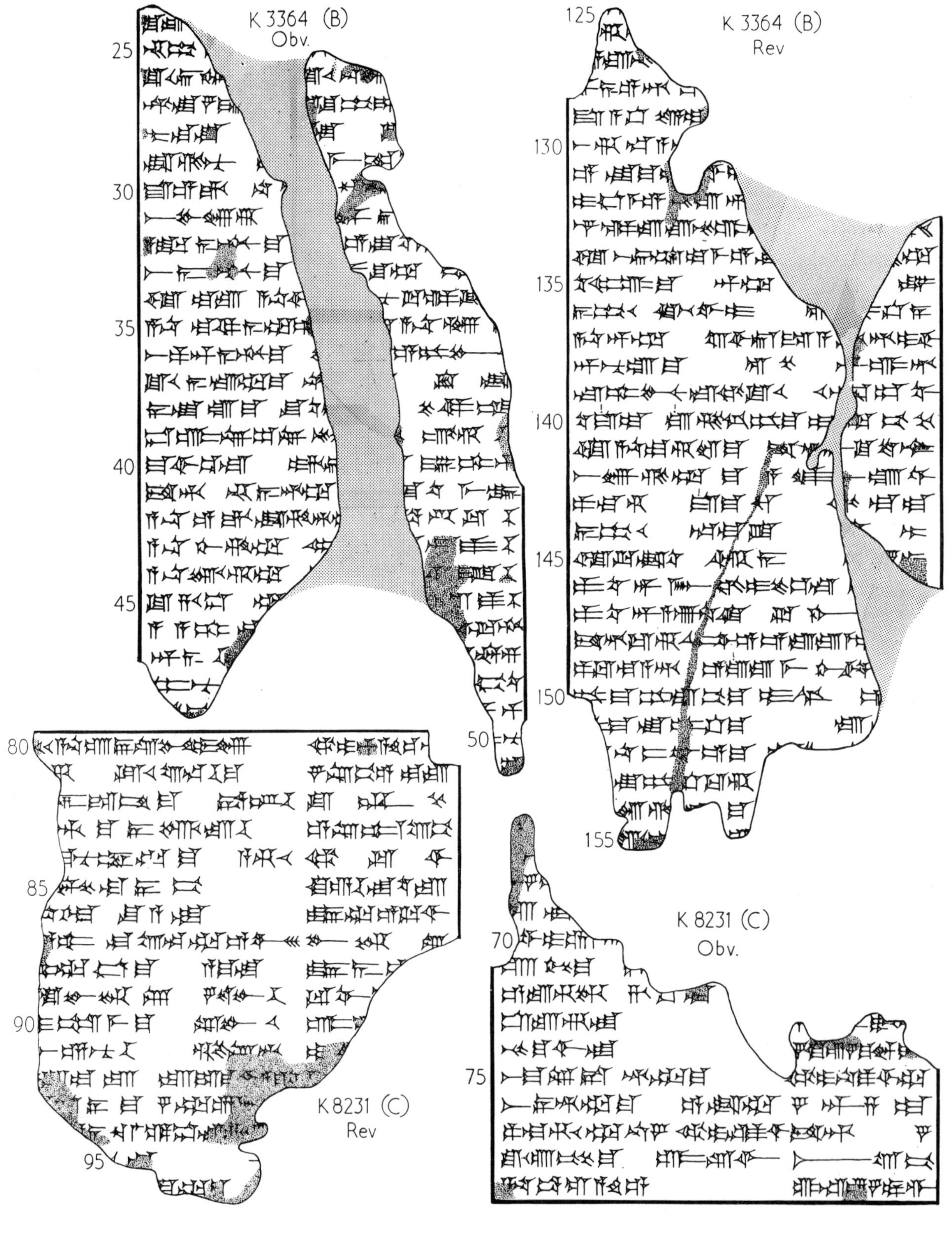
K 3364 (B)
Obv.
K 3364 (B)
Rev
K 8231 (C)
Rev
K 8231 (C)
Obv.

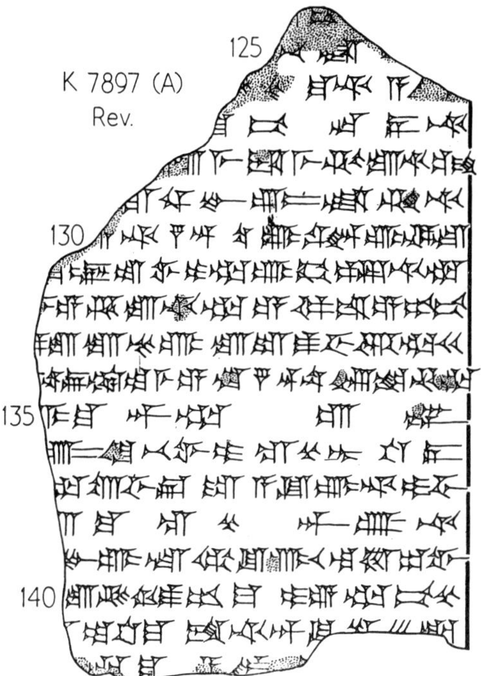
K 7897 (A)
Rev.
125
130
135
140

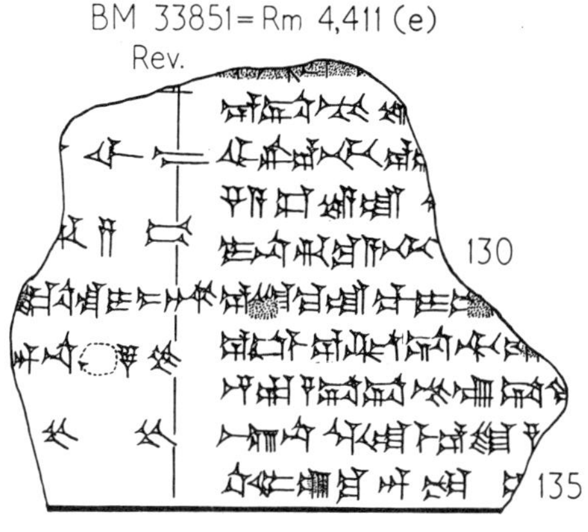
BM 33851=Rm 4,411 (e)
Rev.
130
135

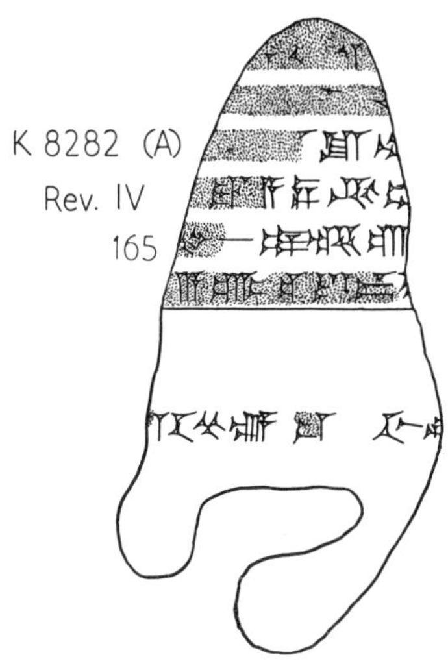
K 8282 (A)
Rev. IV
165

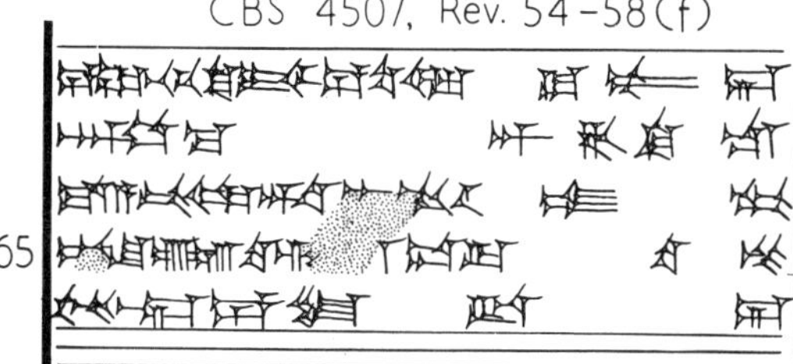
CBS 4507, Rev. 54-58 (f)
65

KAR 329 (d)
15
15
20
20

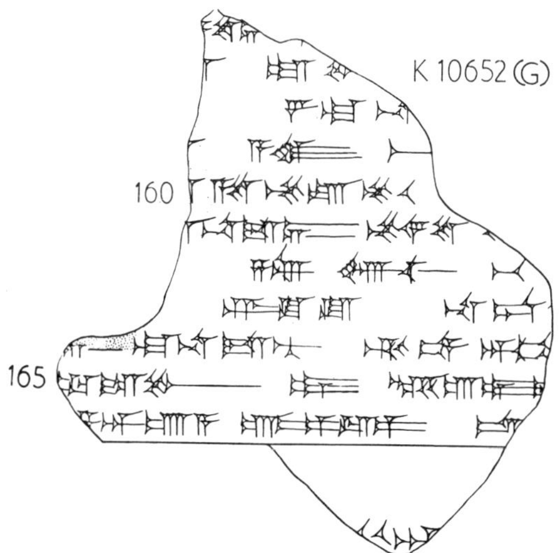
K 10652 (G)
160
165

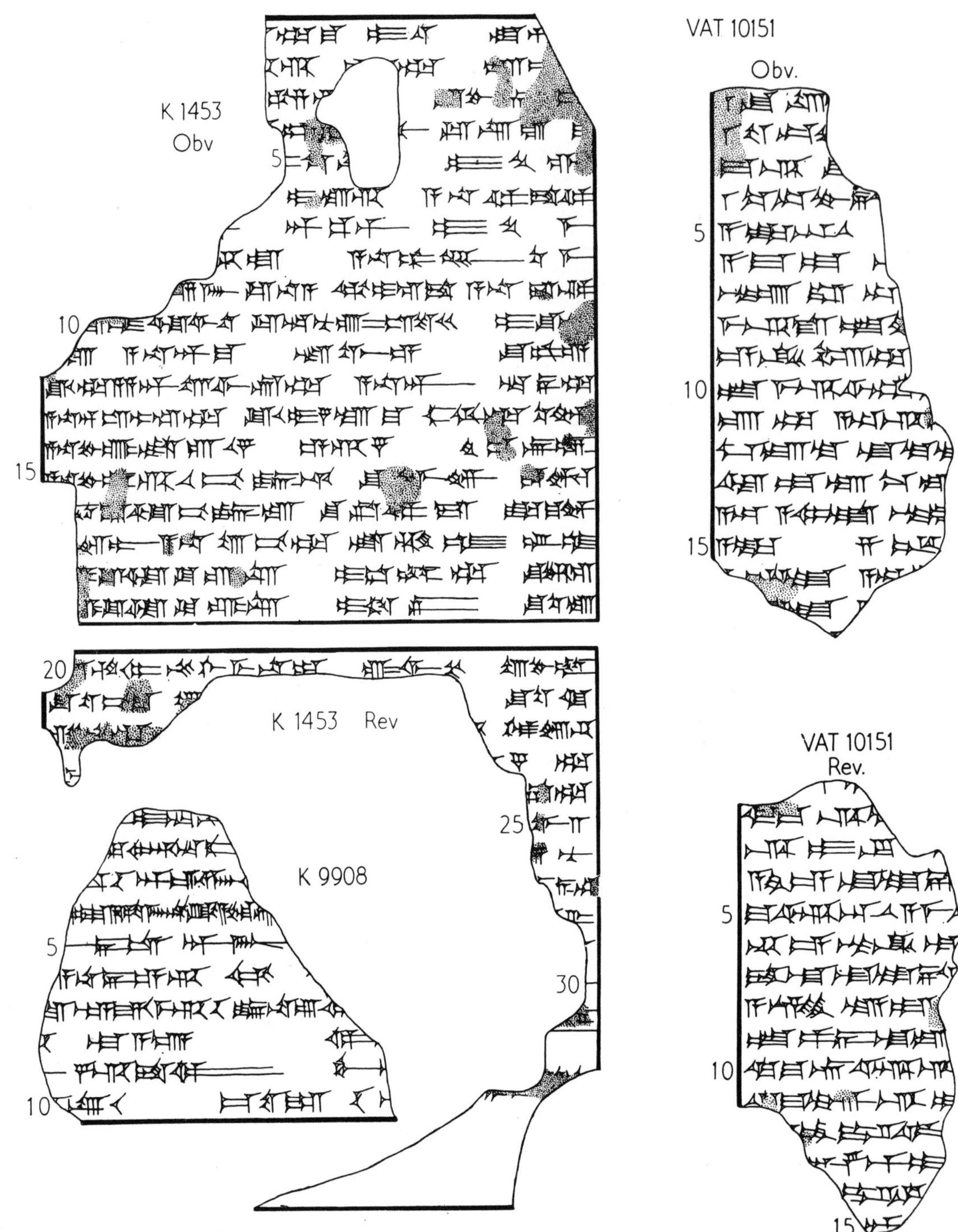
K 1453
Obv
VAT 10151
Obv.
K 1453 Rev
K 9908
VAT 10151
Rev.

DT 1 Obv.

DT 1 Rev.

Ashurbanipal Colophon

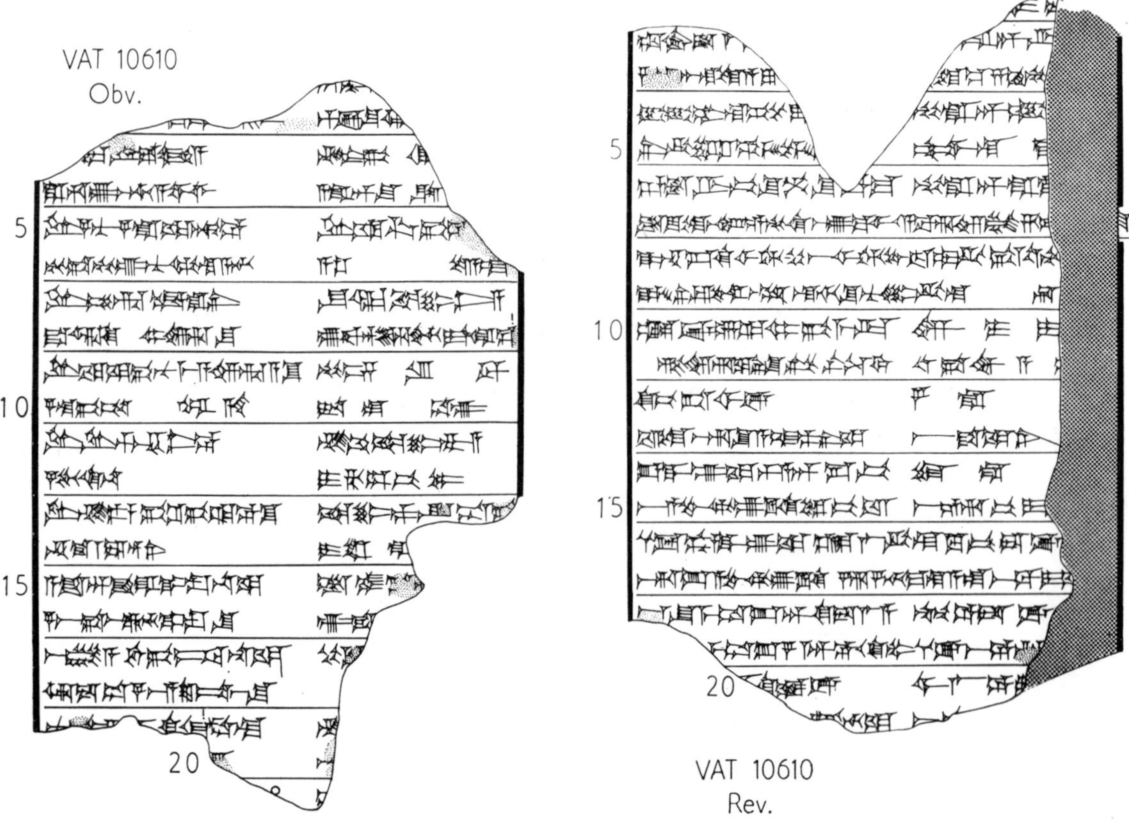

BM 98732 (F)
=Th 1905-4-9, 238

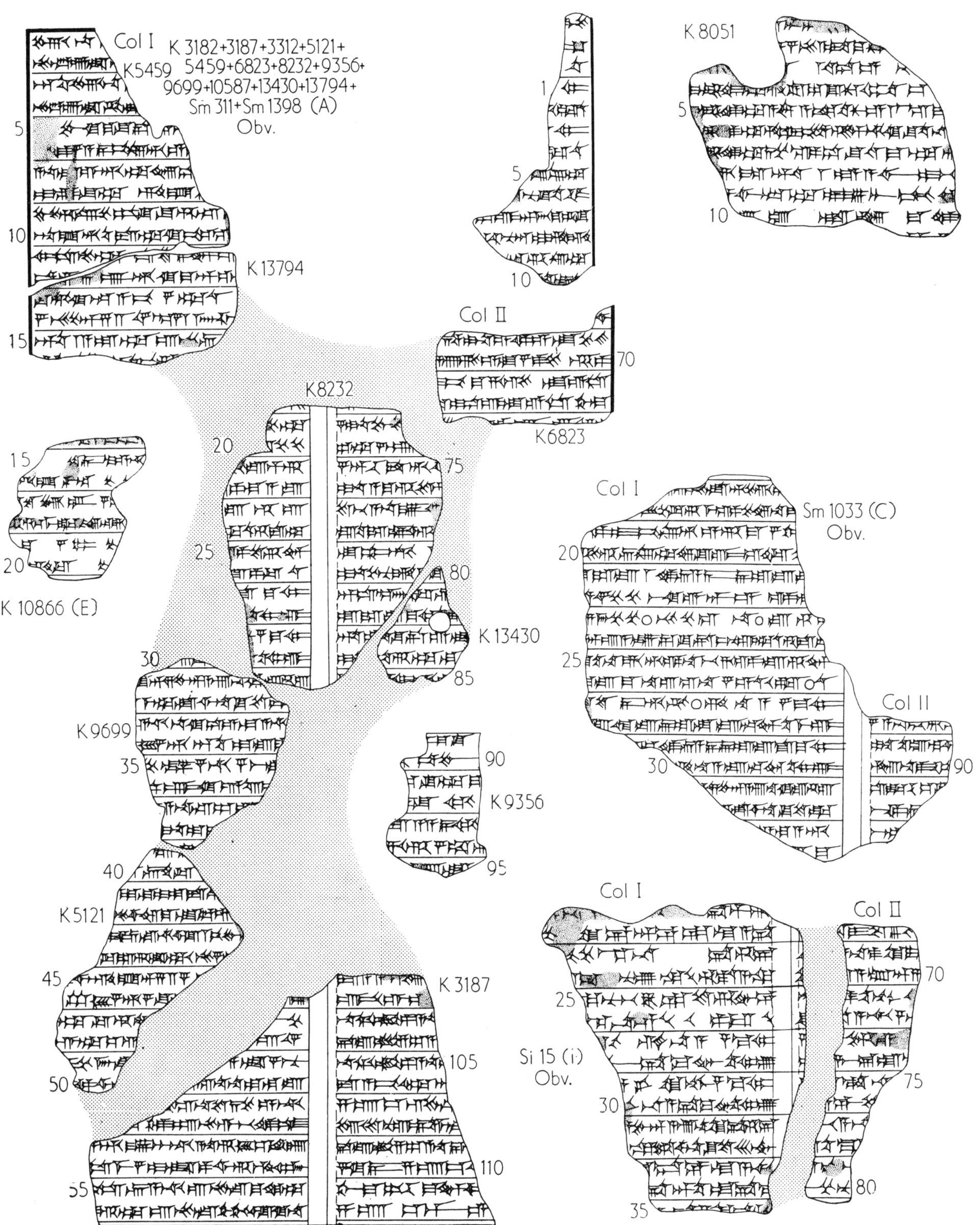

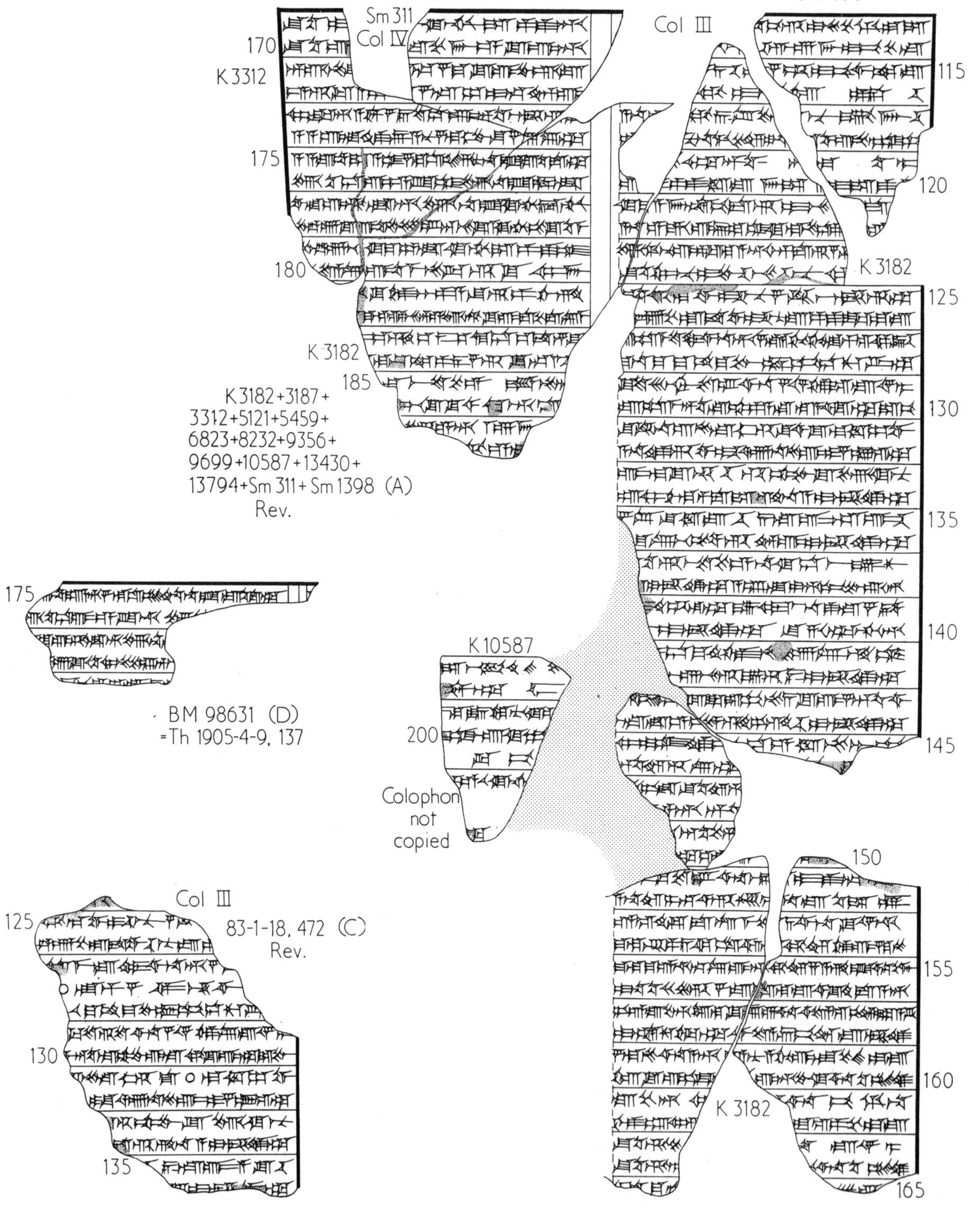
Sm 311
Col IV
Col III
Sm 1398
K 3312
K 3182
K 3182
K 3182+3187+
3312+5121+5459+
6823+8232+9356+
9699+10587+13430+
13794+Sm 311+Sm 1398 (A)
Rev.
BM 98631 (D)
=Th 1905-4-9, 137
K 10587
Colophon
not
copied
Col III
83-1-18, 472 (C)
Rev.
K 3182

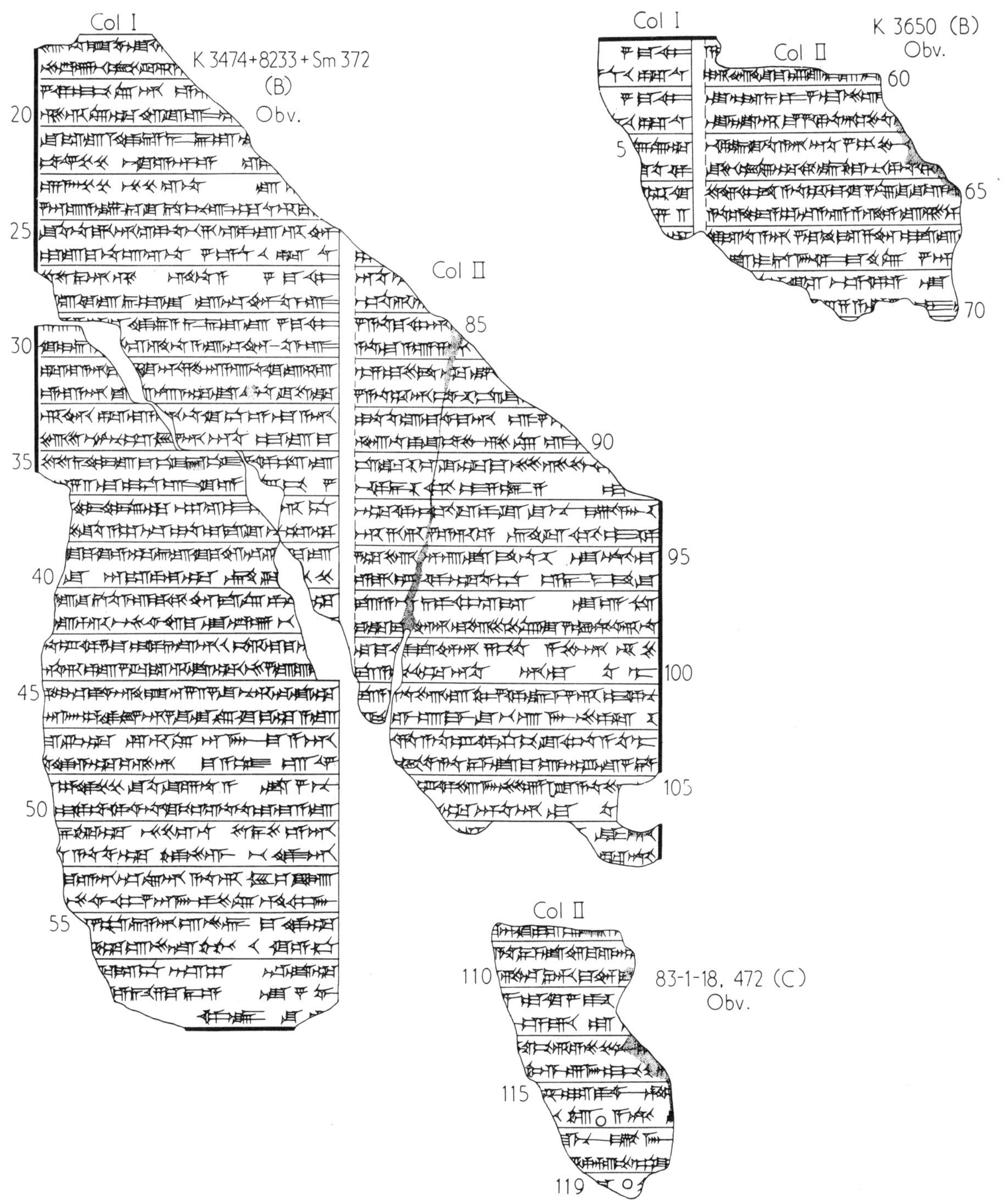
Col I
K 3474+8233+Sm 372
(B)
Obv.
Col II
Col I
Col II
K 3650 (B)
Obv.
Col II
83-1-18, 472 (C)
Obv.

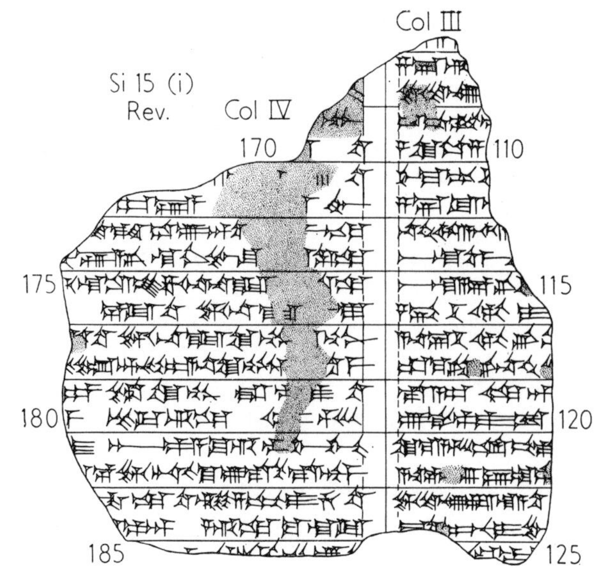
Col III
Si 15 (i)
Rev.
Col IV
170
110
175
115
180
120
185
125

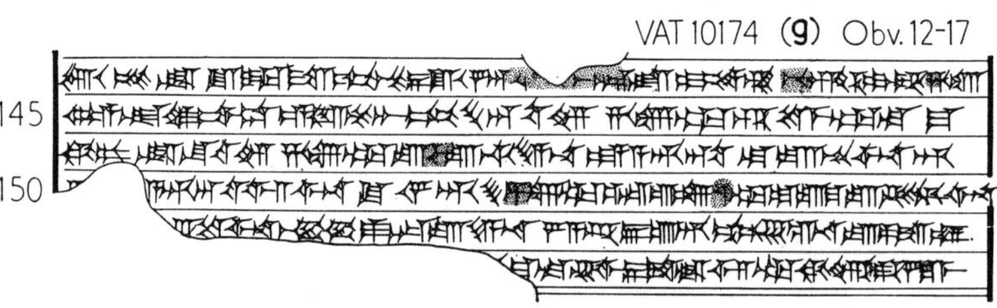
VAT 10174 (g) Obv. 12-17
145
150

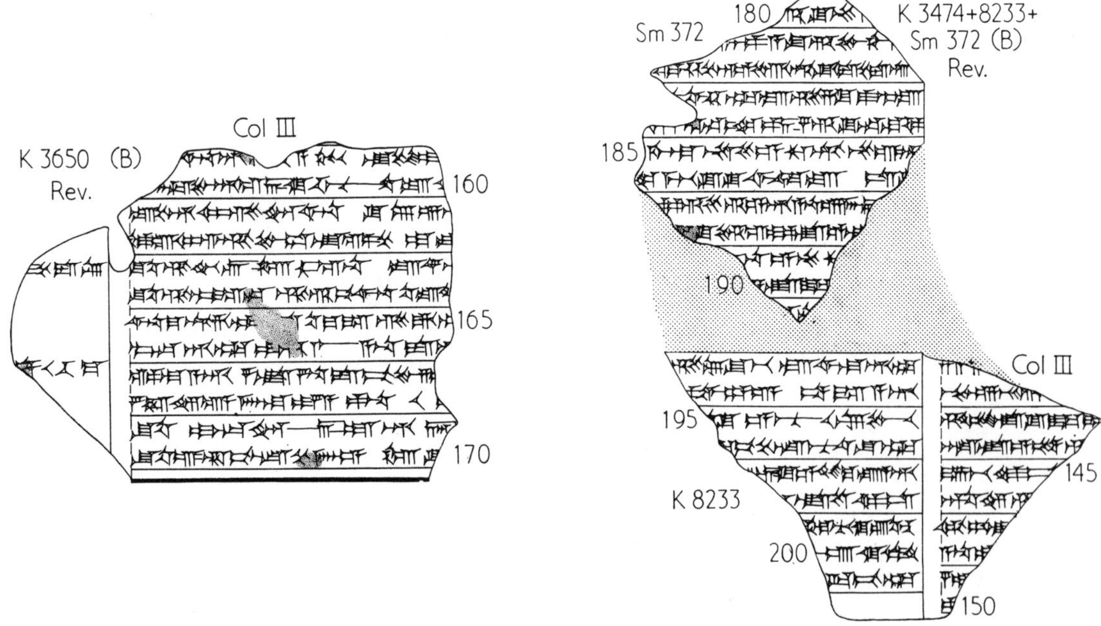
Col III
K 3650 (B)
Rev.
160
165
170
Col IV
180
K 3474+8233+
Sm 372 (B)
Rev.
Sm 372
185
190
Col III
195
145
K 8233
200
150

VAT 9933 (a)
Obv.

VAT 9933 (a)
Rev.

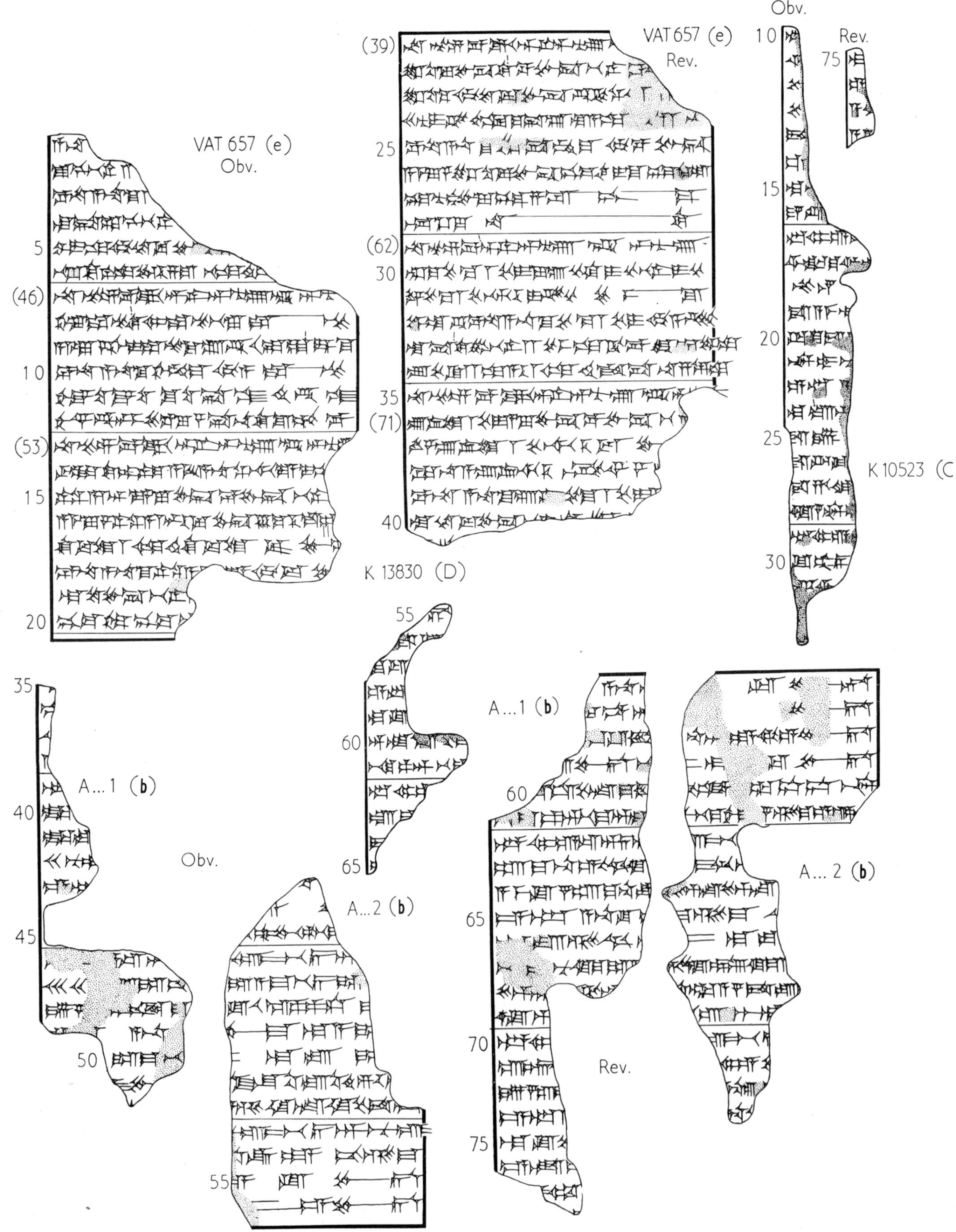
VAT 657 (e)
Obv.
VAT 657 (e)
Rev.
Obv.
Rev.
K 10523 (C)
K 13830 (D)
A...1 (b)
Obv.
A...2 (b)
A...1 (b)
A... 2 (b)
Rev.

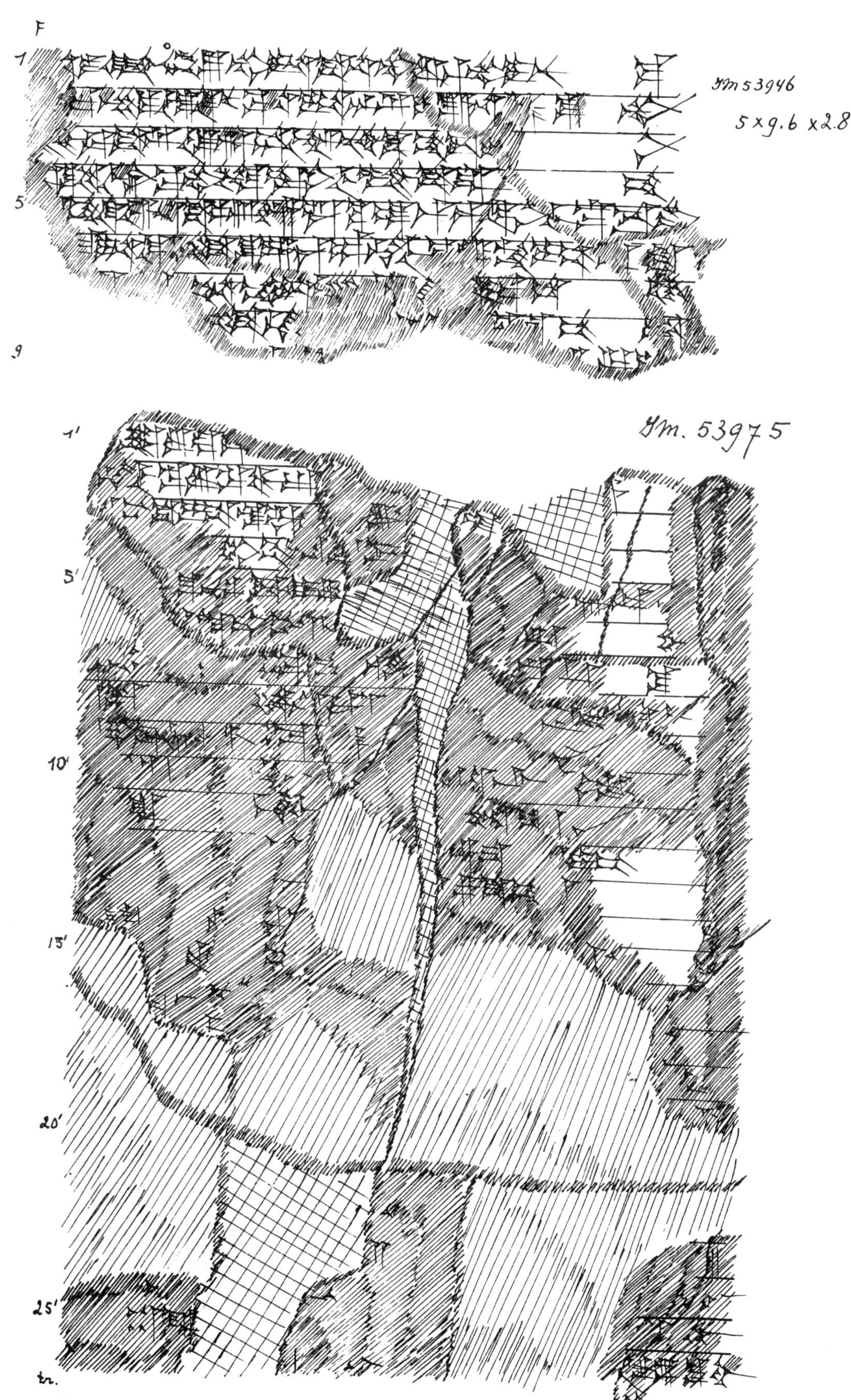

La correspondance des ll. coupées n'est pas certaine

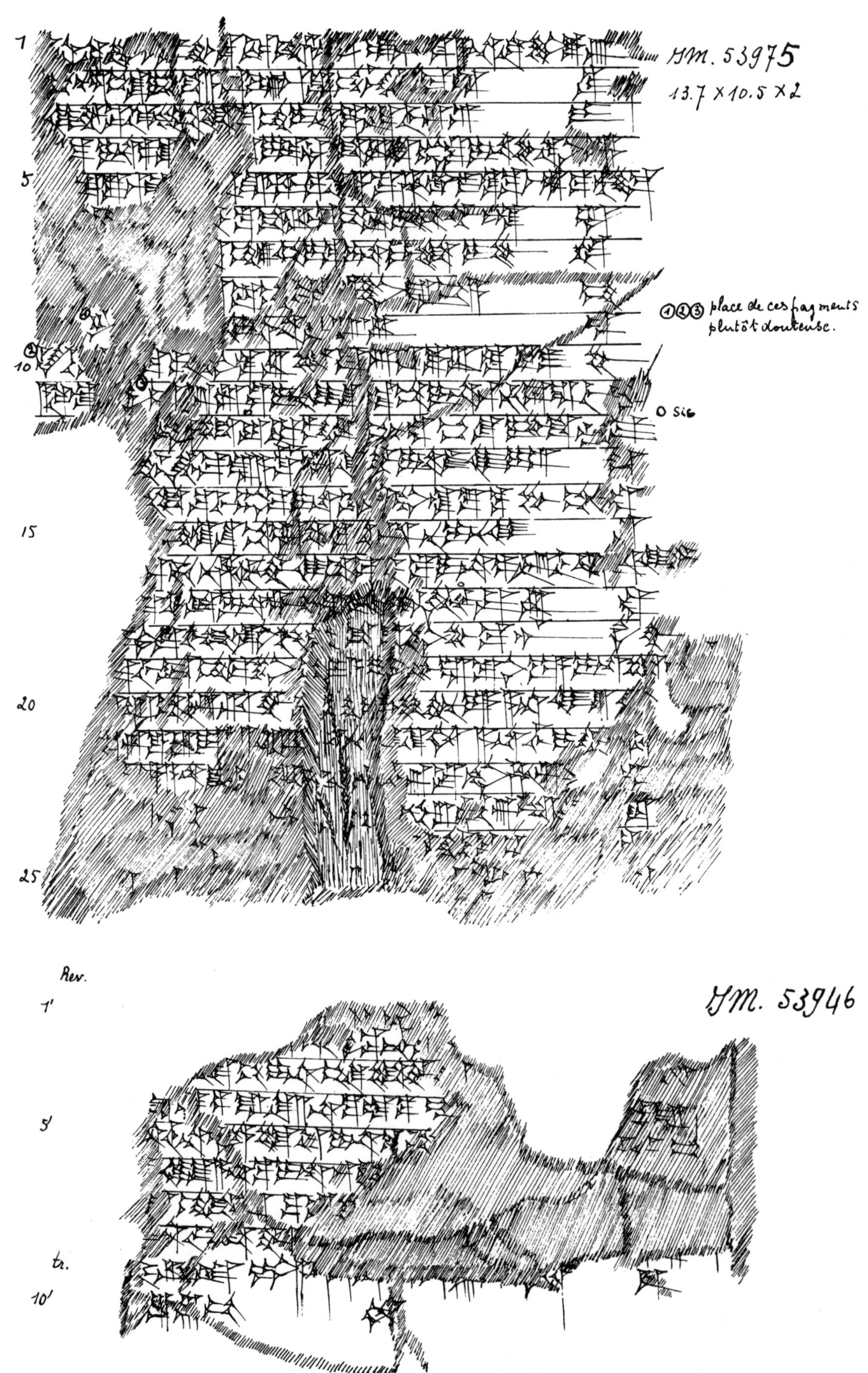
YM. 53975
13.7 × 10.5 × 2
①②③ place de ces fragments plutôt douteuse.
O sic
Rev.
tr.
YM. 53946

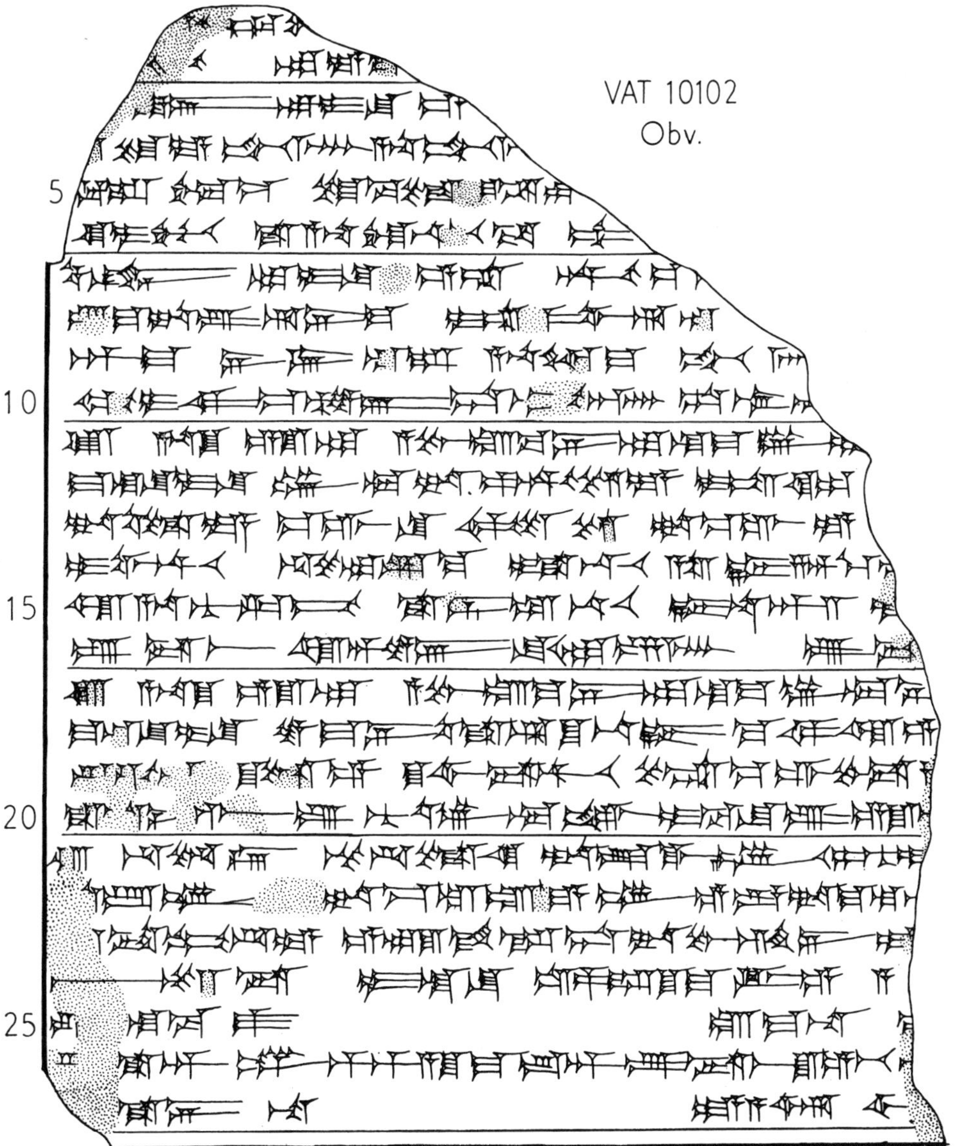
VAT 10102
Obv.

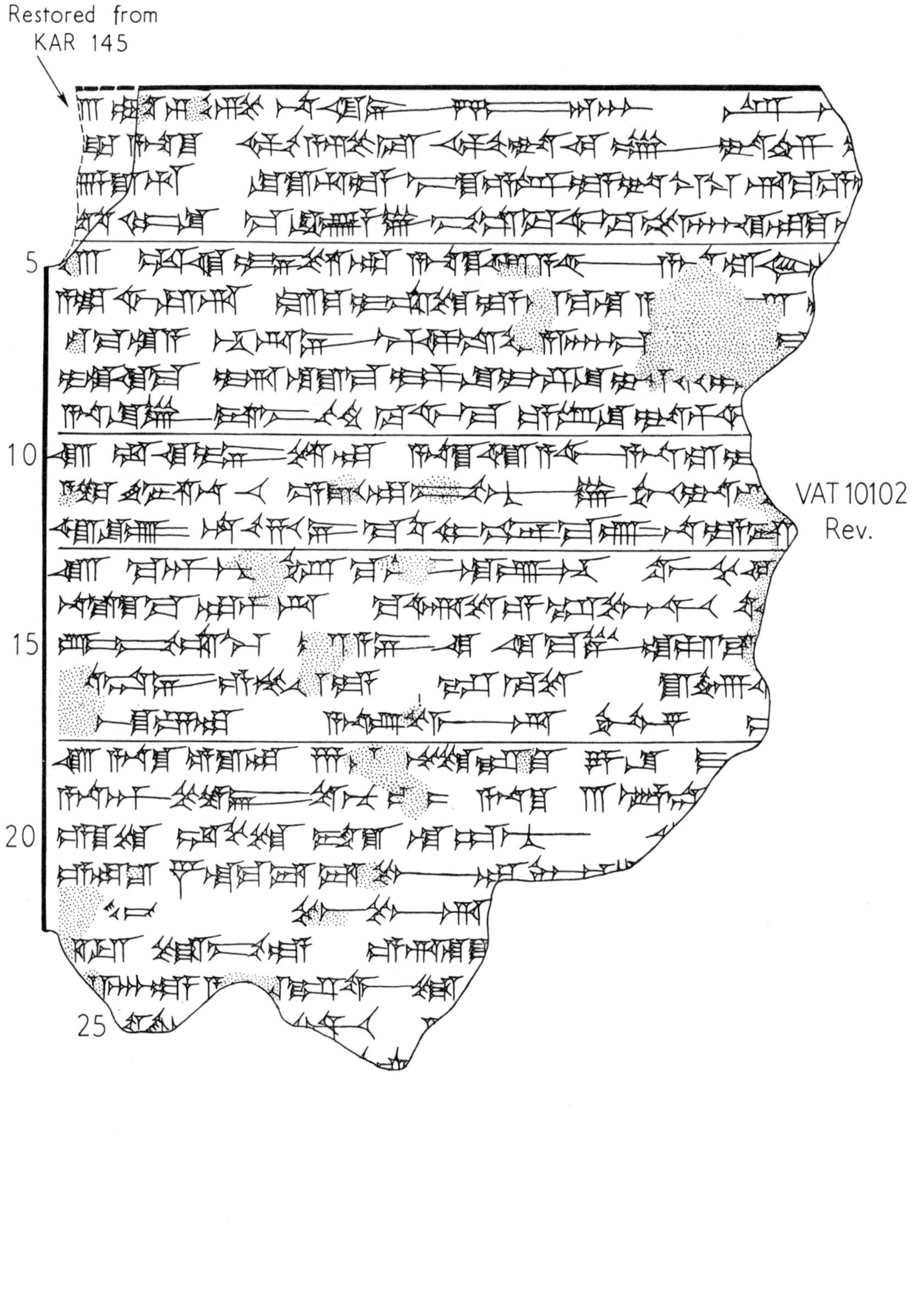

Restored from KAR 145

VAT 10102 Rev.

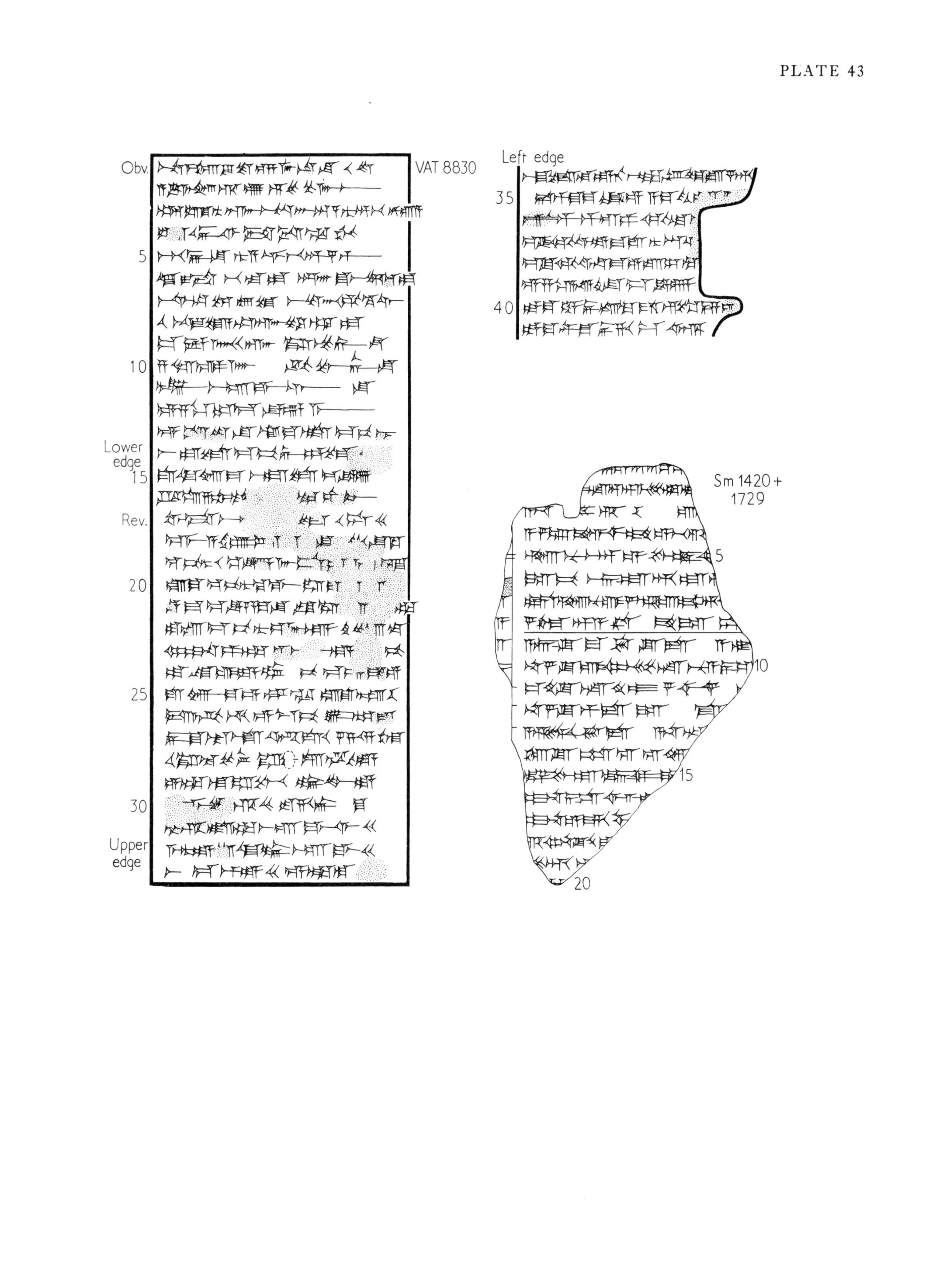

VAT 8830

Obv.

Lower edge

Rev.

Upper edge

Left edge

Sm 1420 + 1729

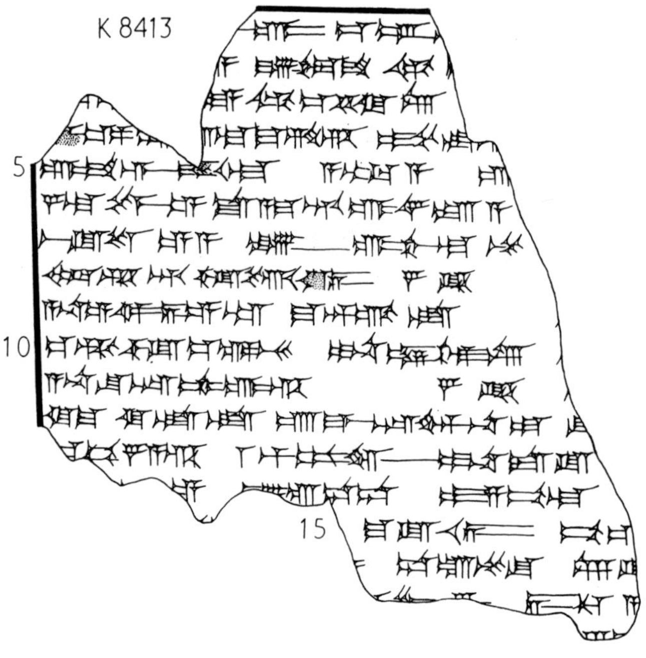
K 8413

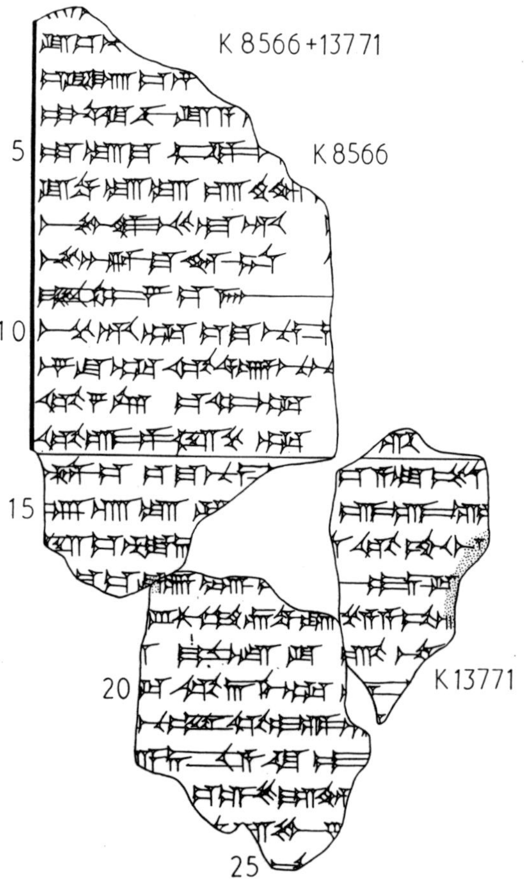
K 8566+13771
K 8566
K 13771

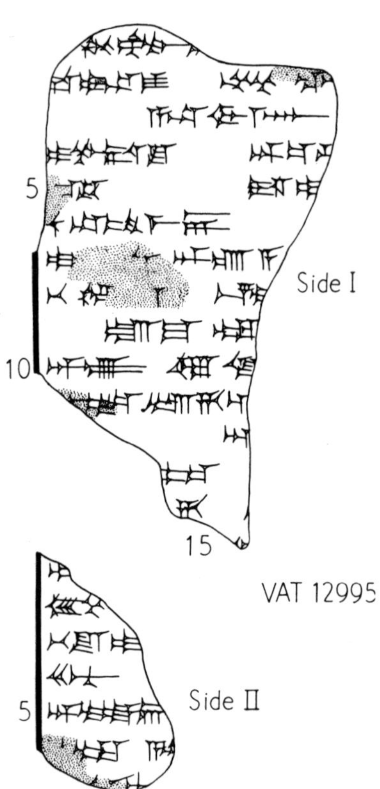
Side I
VAT 12995
Side II

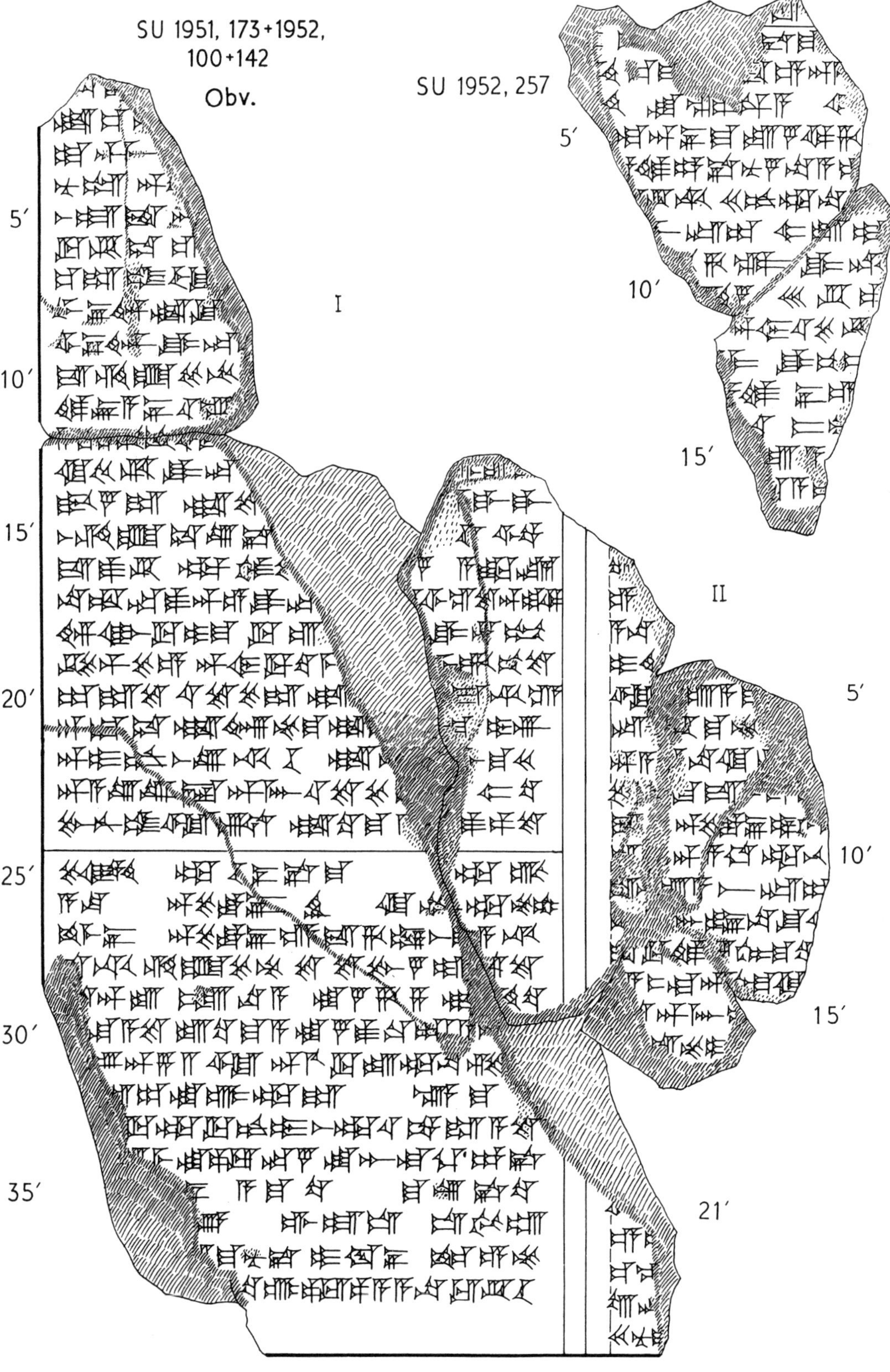
SU 1951, 173+1952,
100+142
Obv.
SU 1952, 257
I
II

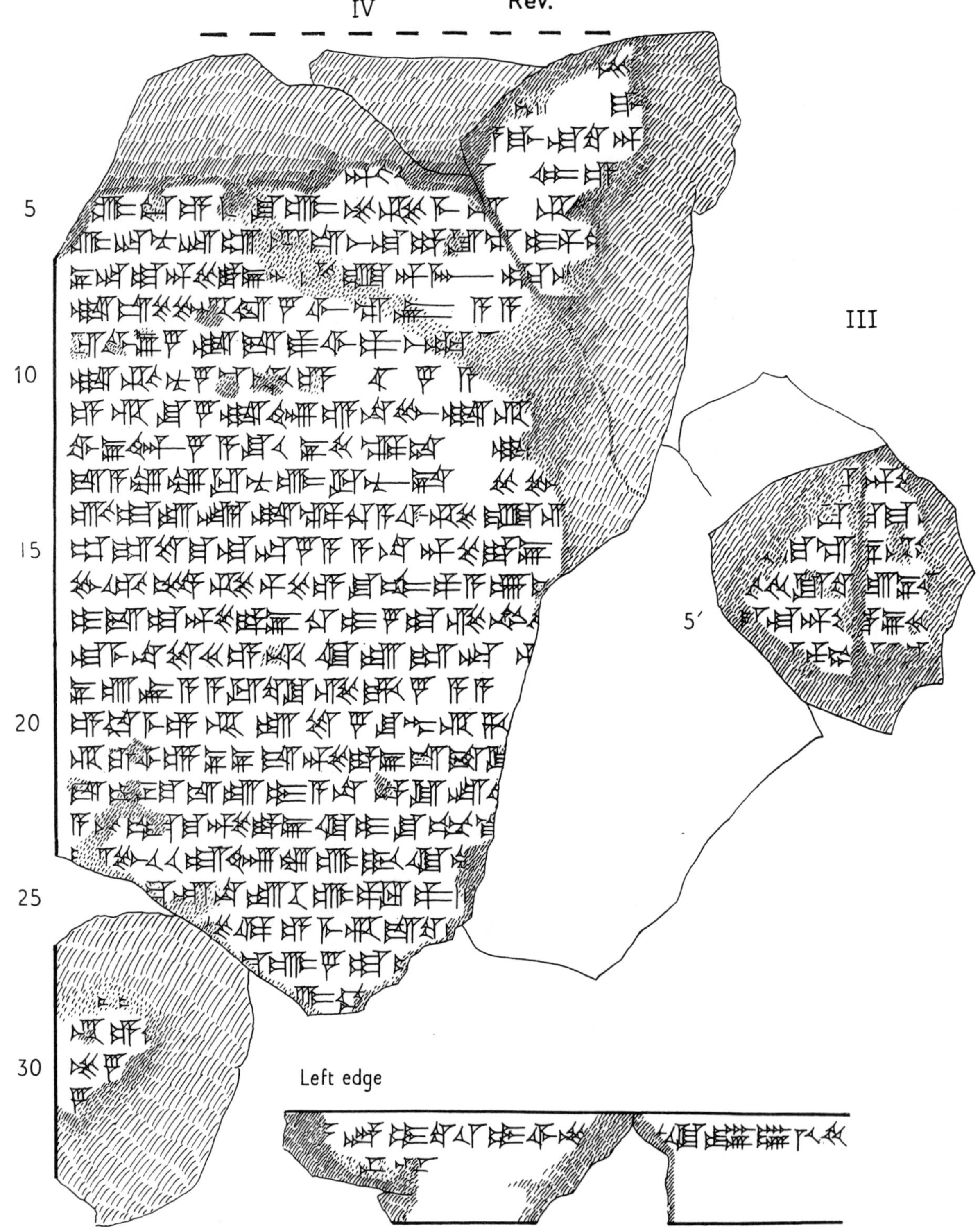
SU 1951, 173+1952,
100+142
Rev.
IV
III
5
10
15
20
25
30
5′
Left edge

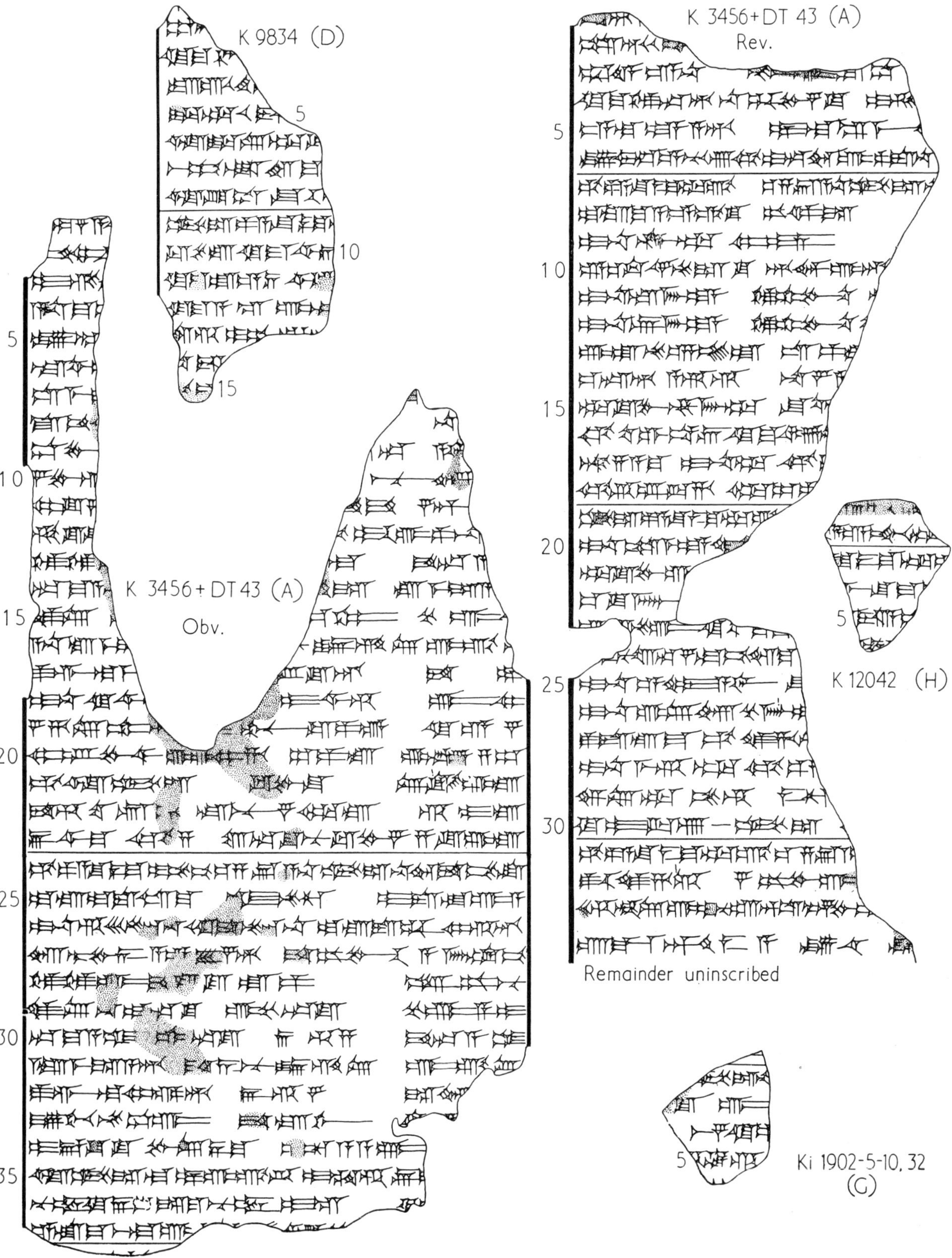
K 9834 (D)
K 3456+DT 43 (A)
Rev.
K 3456+DT 43 (A)
Obv.
K 12042 (H)
Remainder uninscribed
Ki 1902-5-10, 32
(G)

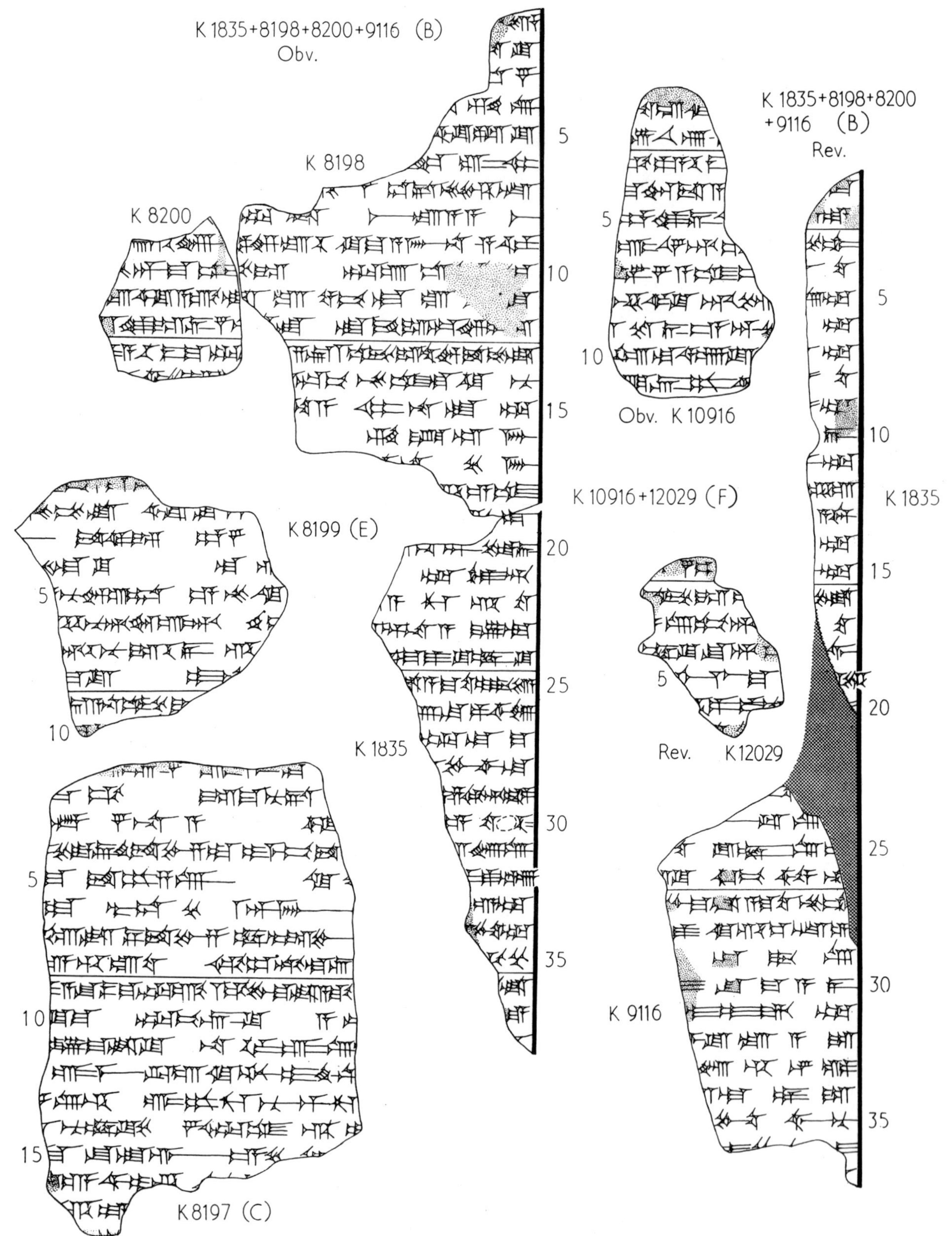
K 1835+8198+8200+9116 (B)
Obv.
K 8198
K 8200
K 8199 (E)
K 1835
K 8197 (C)
Obv. K 10916
K 10916+12029 (F)
Rev. K 12029
K 1835+8198+8200
+9116 (B)
Rev.
K 1835
K 9116

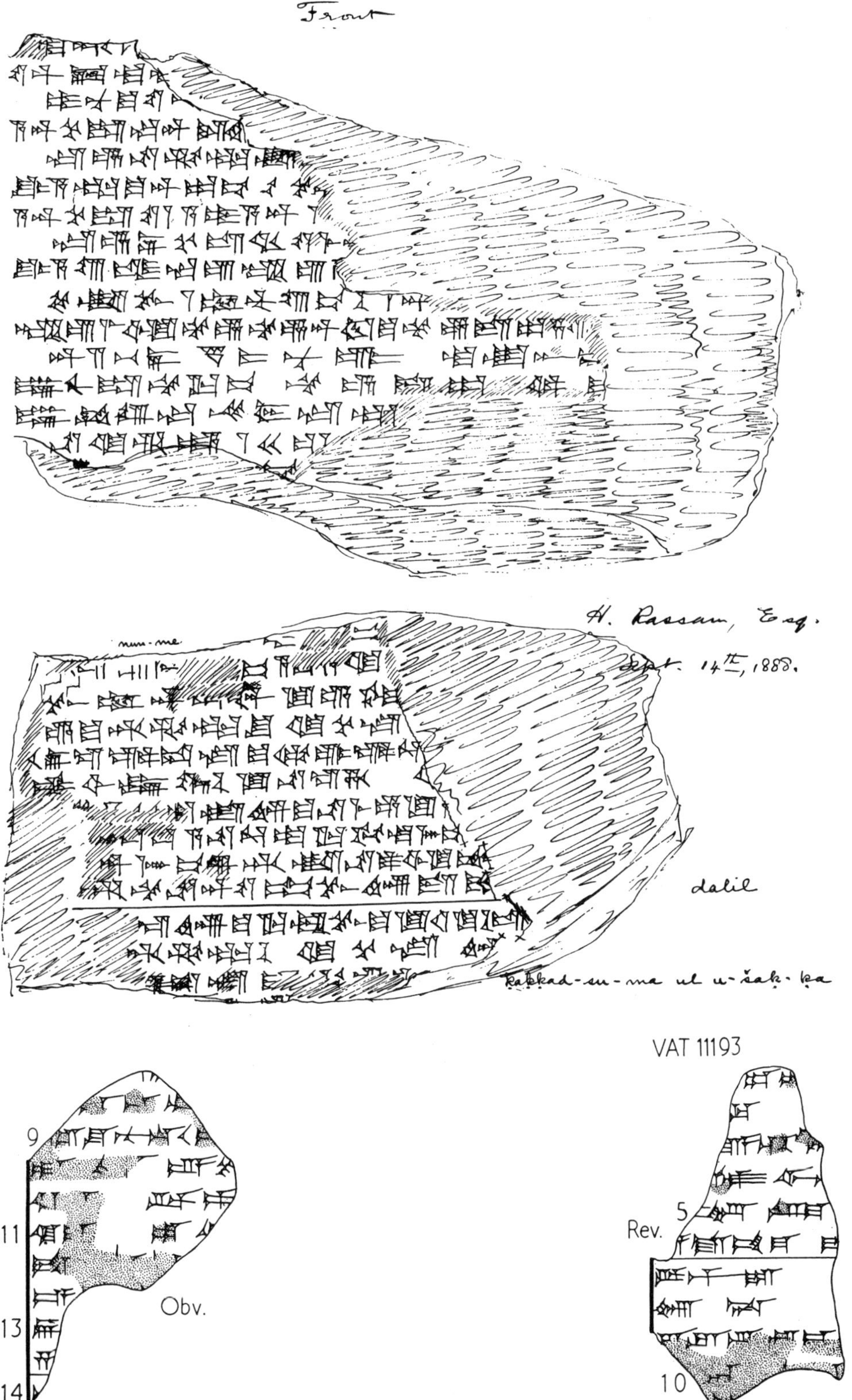
H. Rassam, Esq
Front
num-me
H. Rassam, Esq.
Sept. 14th, 1888.
dalil
kakkad-su-ma ul u-šak-ka
VAT 11193
9
11
13
14
Obv.
5
Rev.
10

VAT 13836 and Photo Assur S 6814 (b)

Obv.

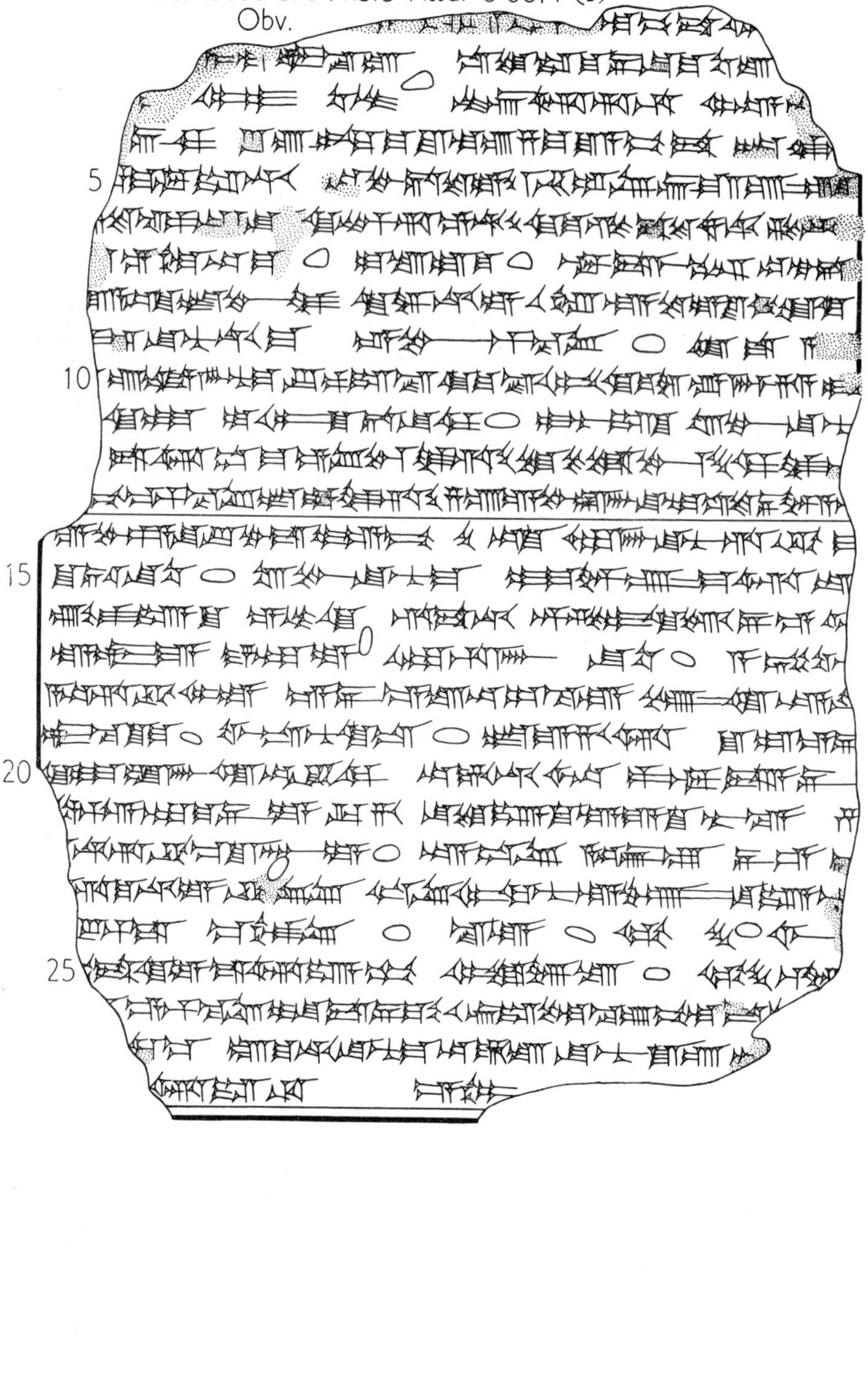

VAT 13836 and
Photo Assur S 6814
(b)
Rev.

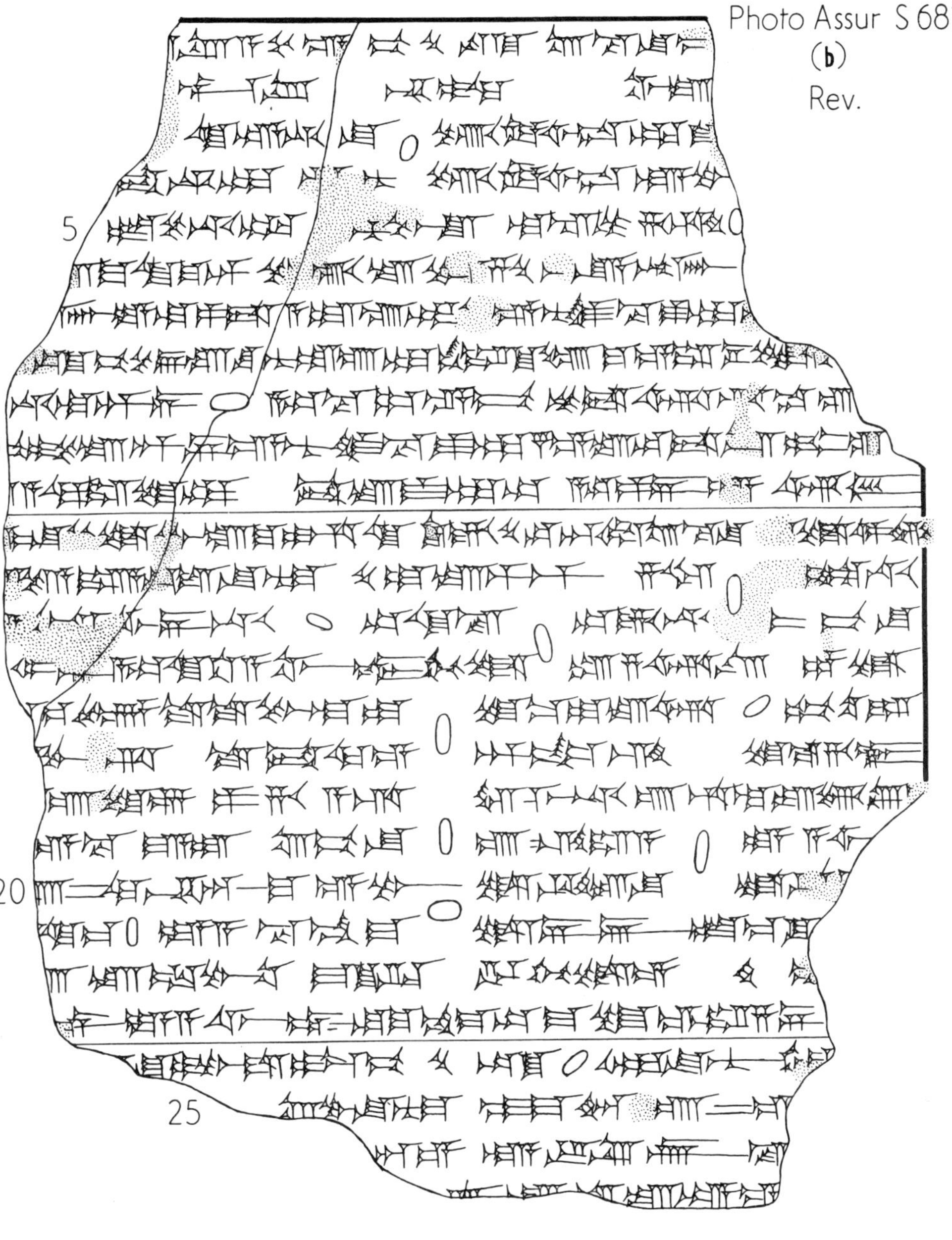

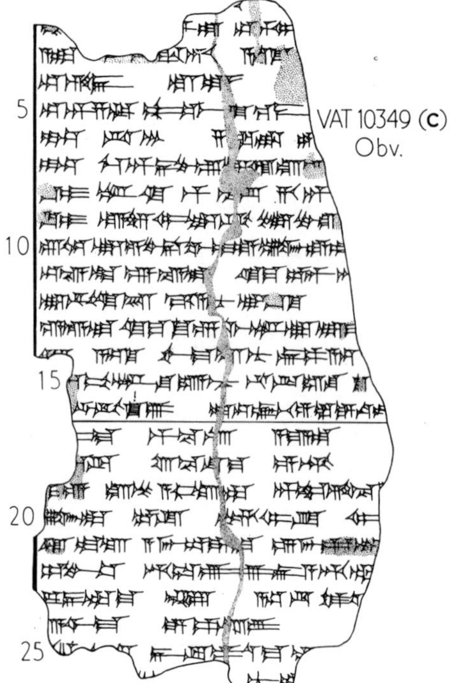

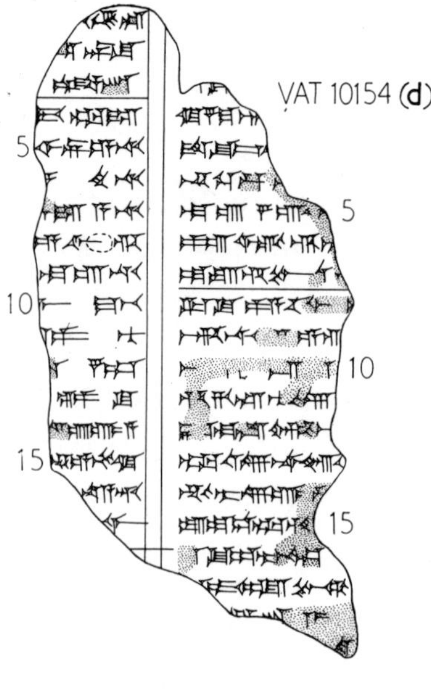

K 8577 (I)

VAT 10349 (c)
Rev.

K 8570 (G)

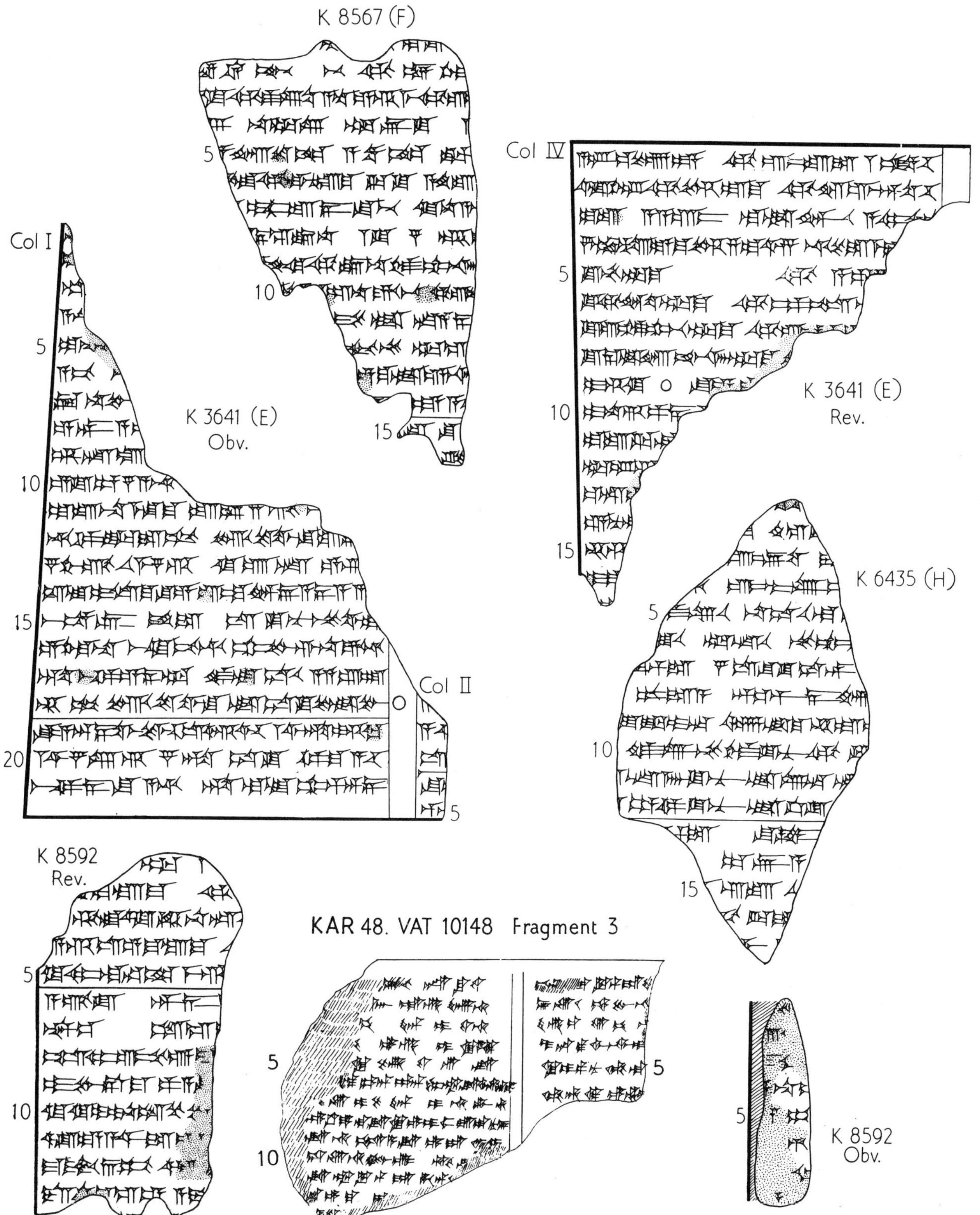
K 8567 (F)
Col I
K 3641 (E)
Obv.
Col II
Col IV
K 3641 (E)
Rev.
K 6435 (H)
K 8592
Rev.
KAR 48. VAT 10148 Fragment 3
K 8592
Obv.

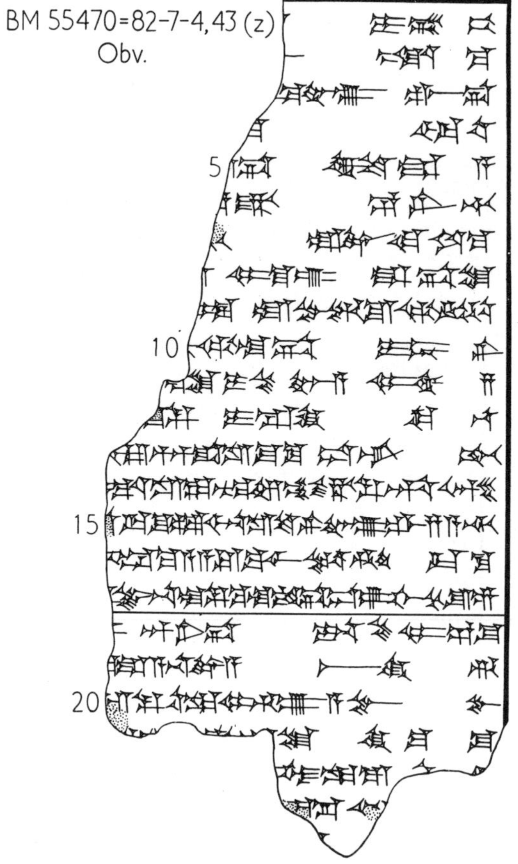
BM 55470=82-7-4,43 (z)
Obv.

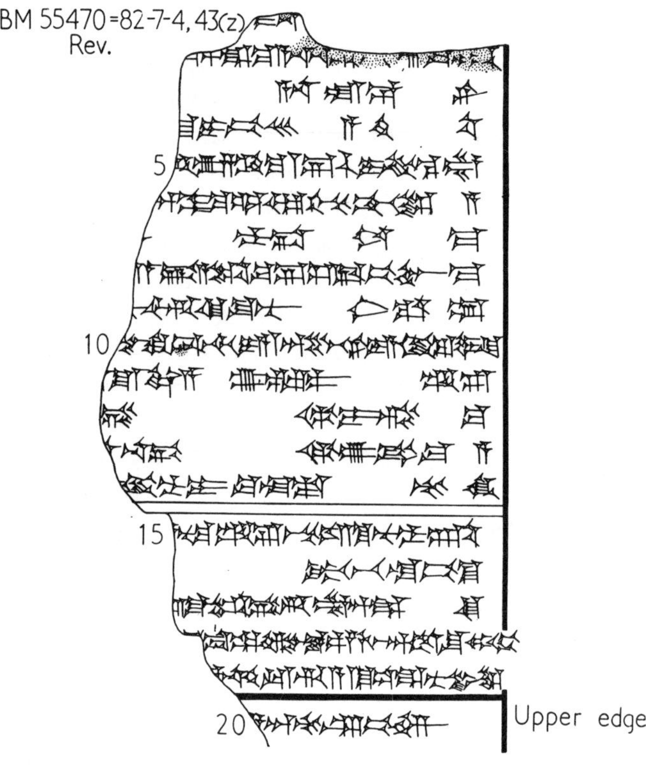
BM 55470=82-7-4,43(z)
Rev.
Upper edge

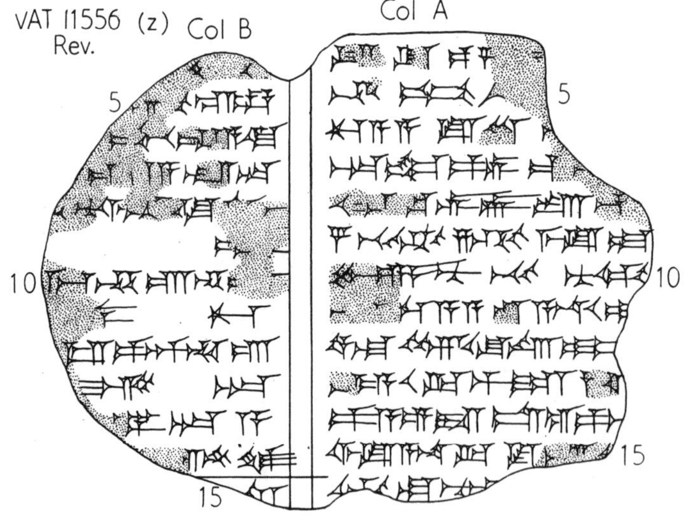
VAT 11556 (z)
Rev.
Col B
Col A

K 8714 (Z)

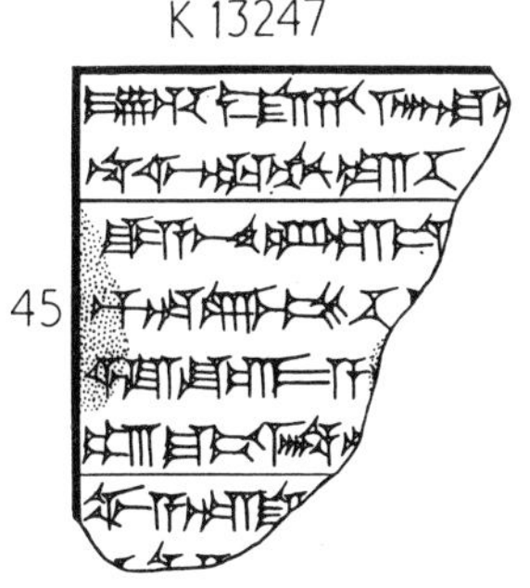

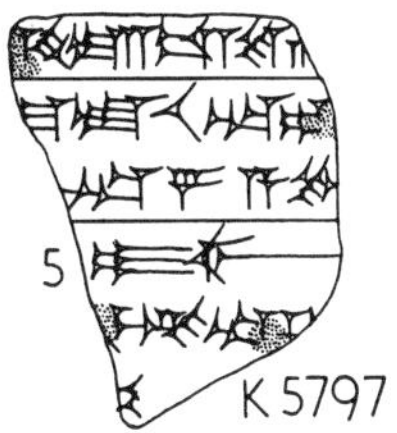

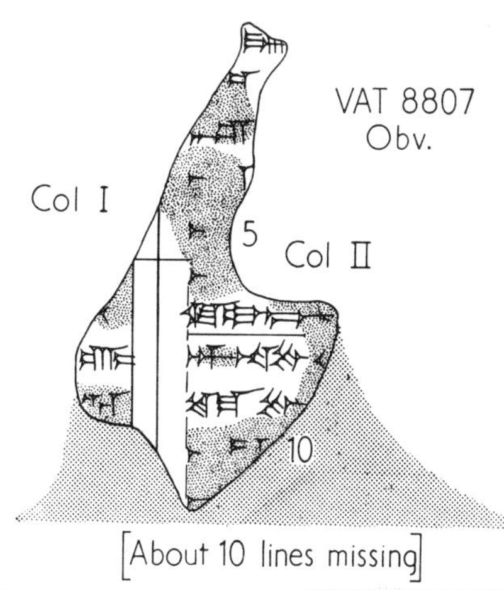

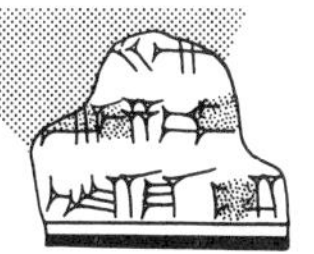

SU 1952, 138+169+181 A–D

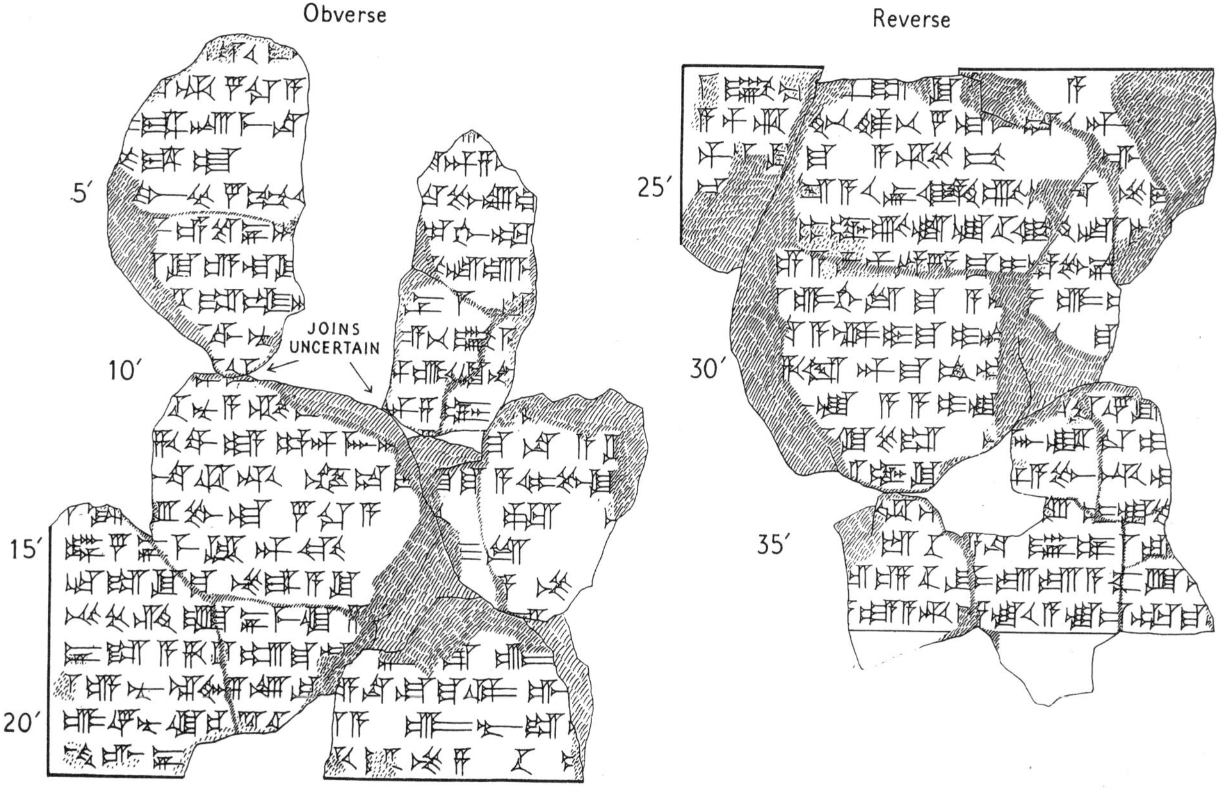

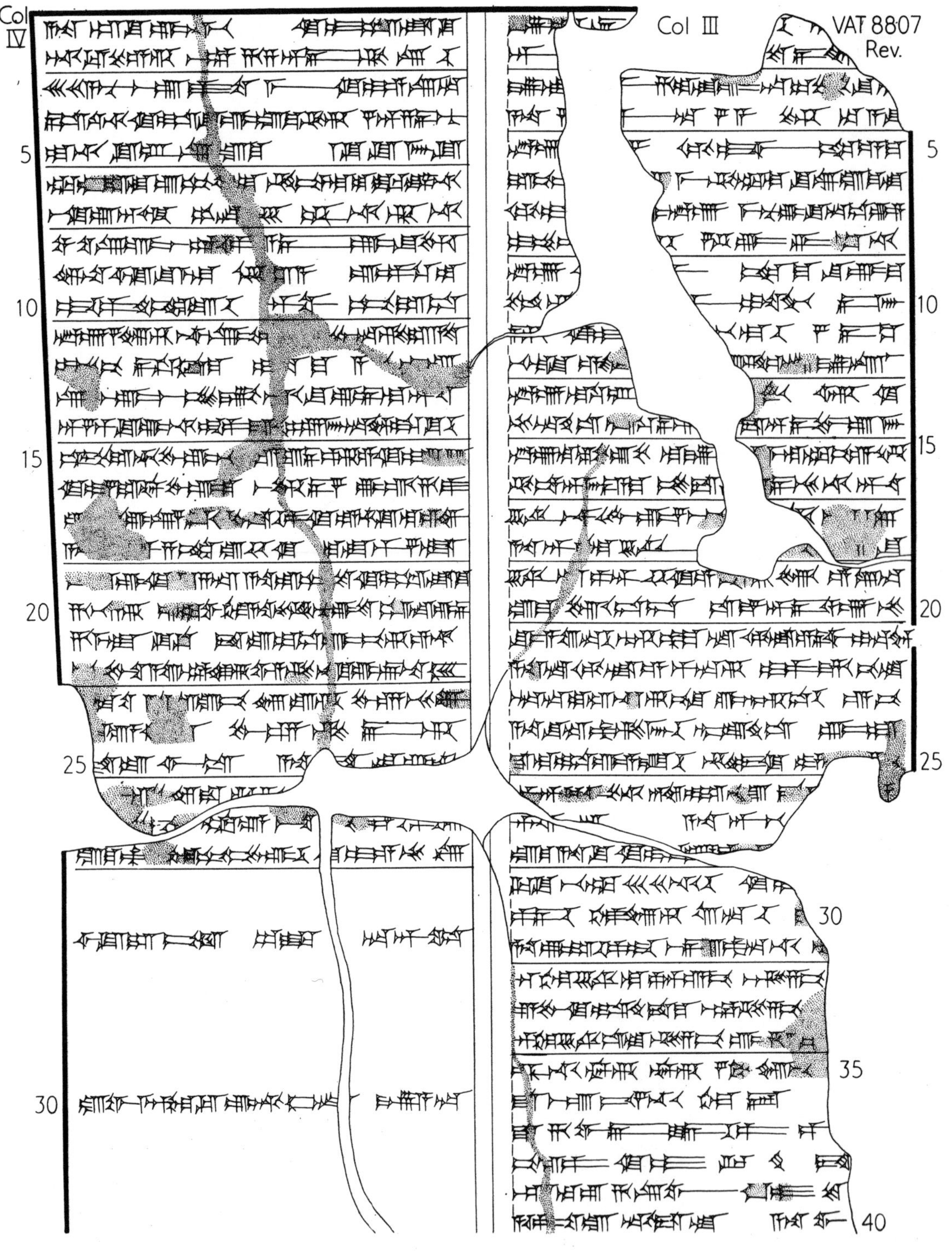
Col IV
Col III
VAT 8807
Rev.

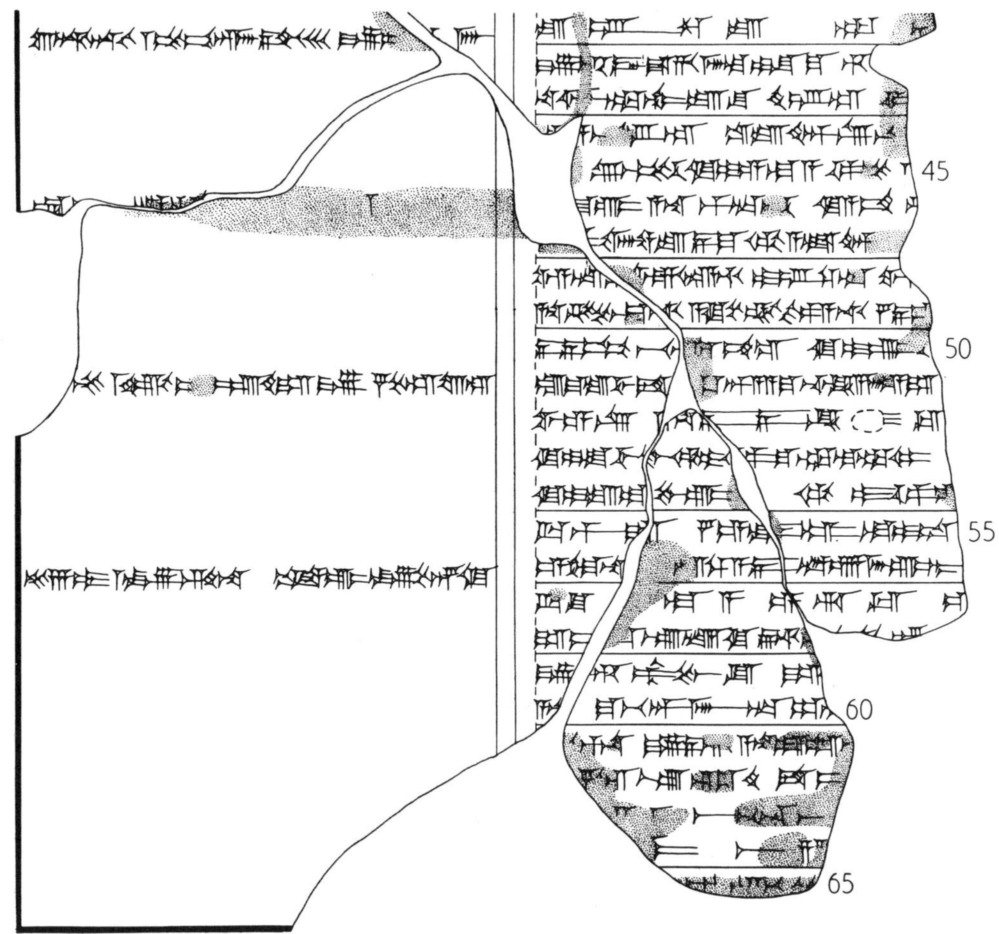
45
50
55
60
65

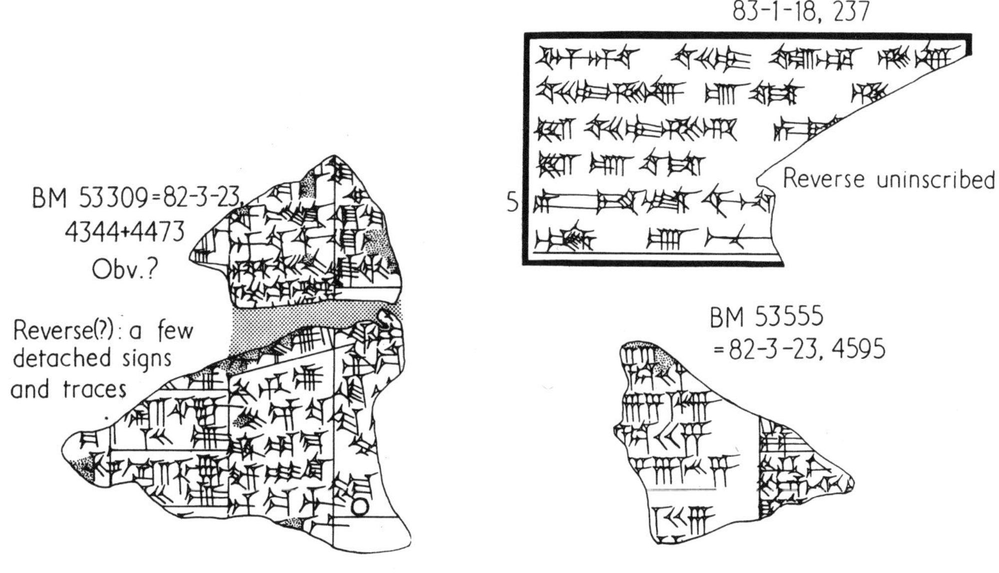
83-1-18, 237
5
Reverse uninscribed
BM 53309=82-3-23,
4344+4473
Obv.?
Reverse(?): a few
detached signs
and traces
BM 53555
=82-3-23, 4595

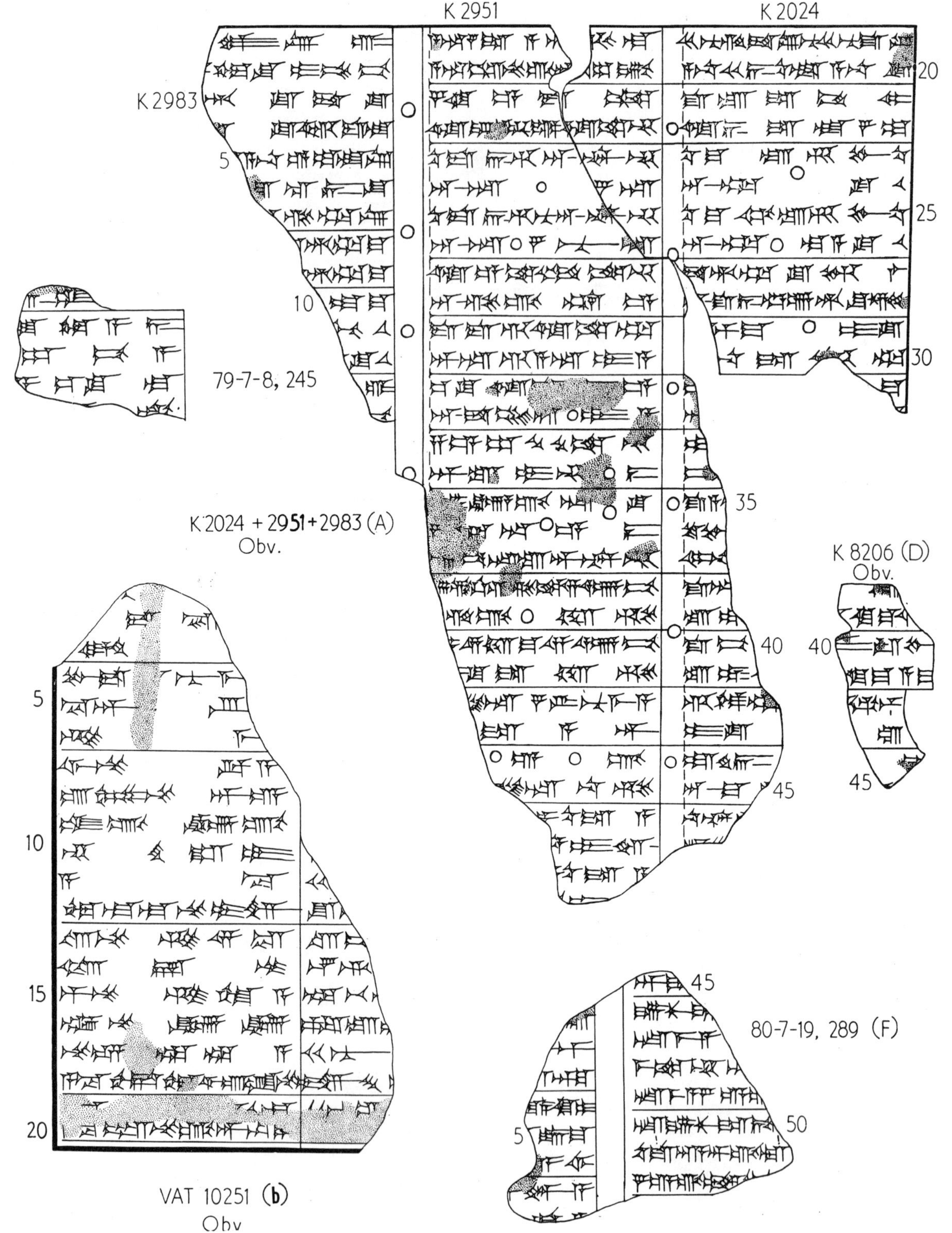
K 2951
K 2024
K 2983
79-7-8, 245
K 2024 + 2951 + 2983 (A)
Obv.
K 8206 (D)
Obv.
VAT 10251 (b)
Obv.
80-7-19, 289 (F)

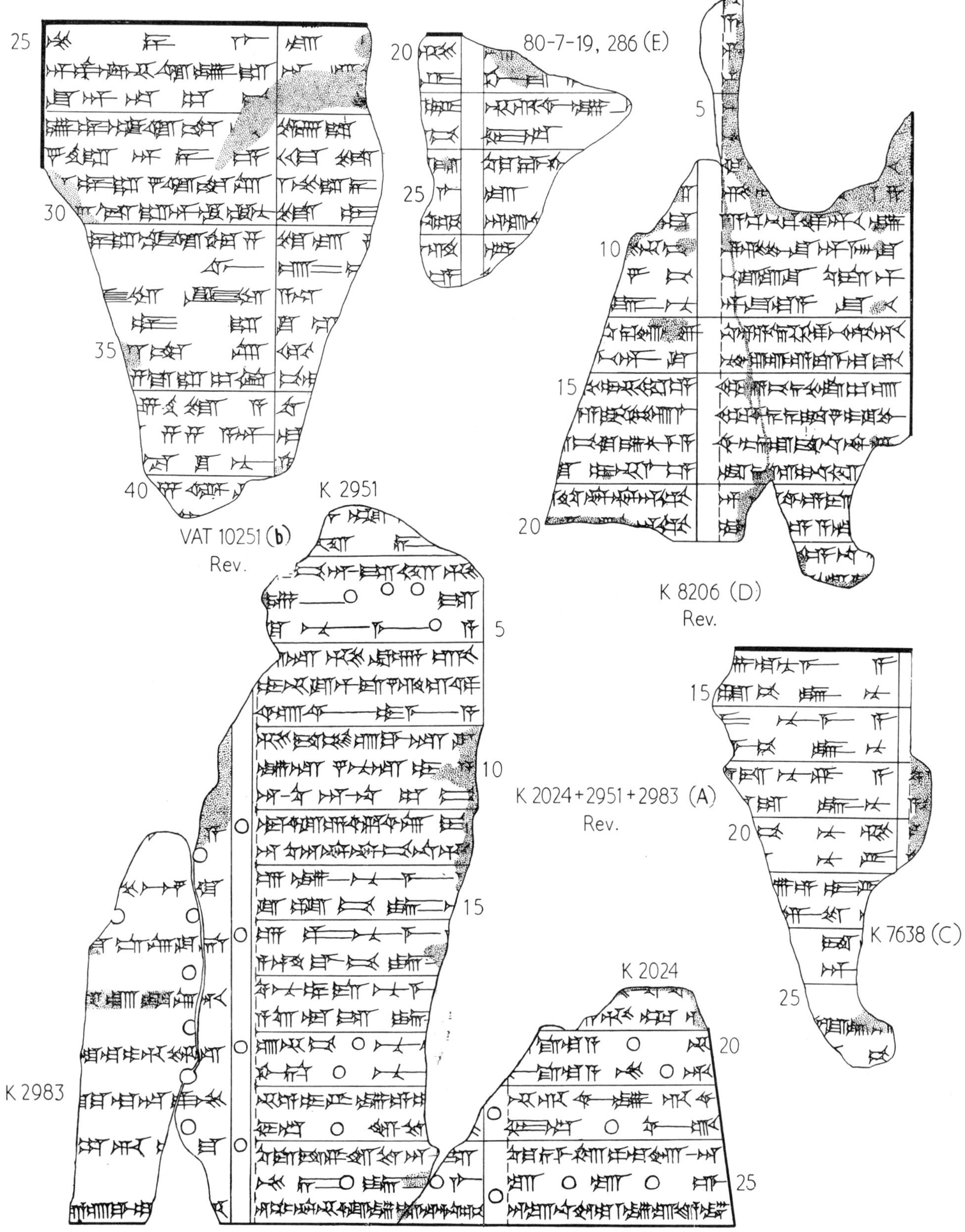
VAT 10251 (b)
Rev.
80-7-19, 286 (E)
K 8206 (D)
Rev.
K 2951
K 2024+2951+2983 (A)
Rev.
K 2983
K 2024
K 7638 (C)

K 7654
K 5688
Col II
K 4327+4605
+4749
Obv.
Col III
Col I
K 4327+4605
+4749
Rev.
Col IV
Col VI
K 4160+13184

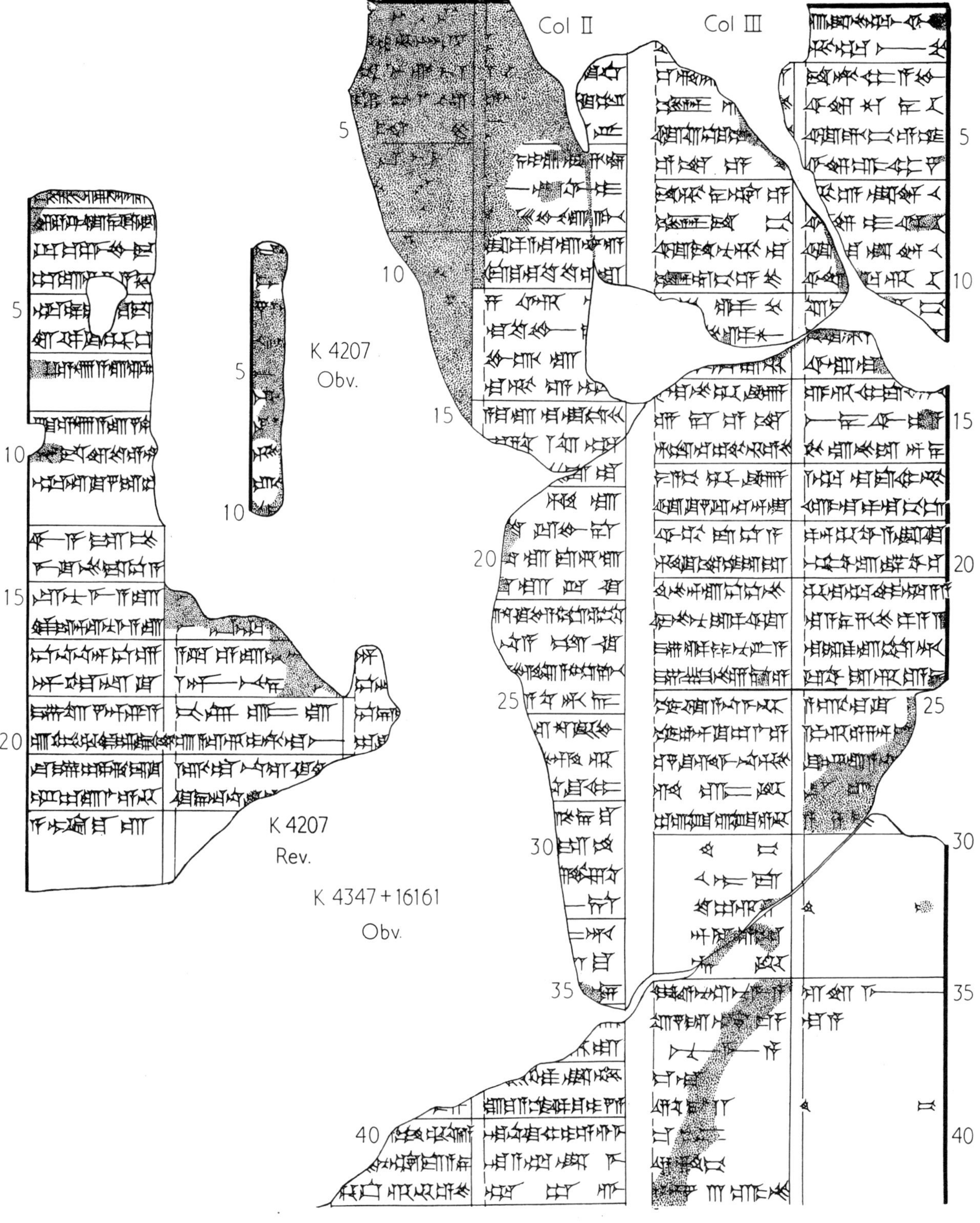
Col II
Col III
K 4207
Obv.
K 4207
Rev.
K 4347 + 16161
Obv.

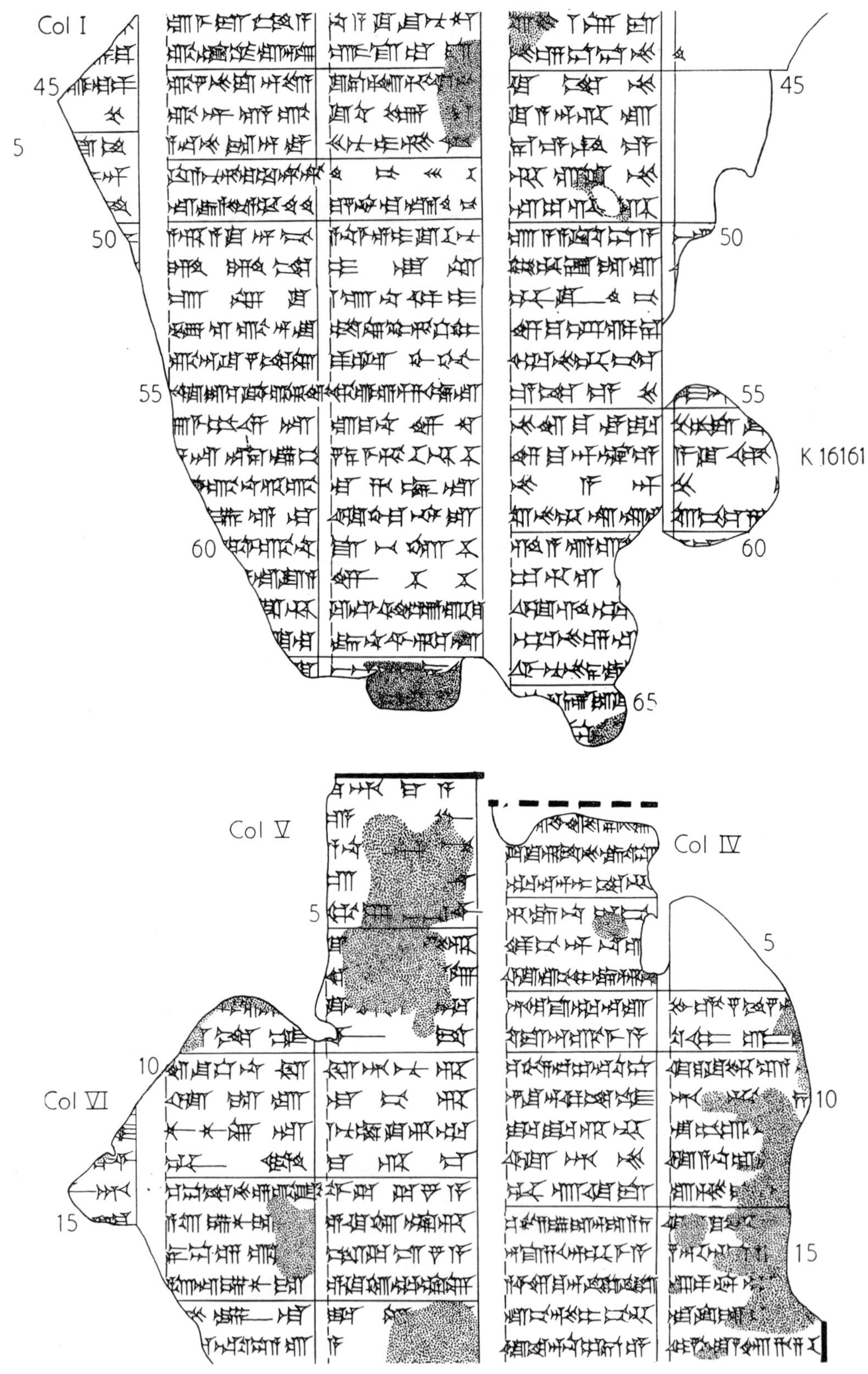
Col I
K 16161
Col V
Col IV
Col VI

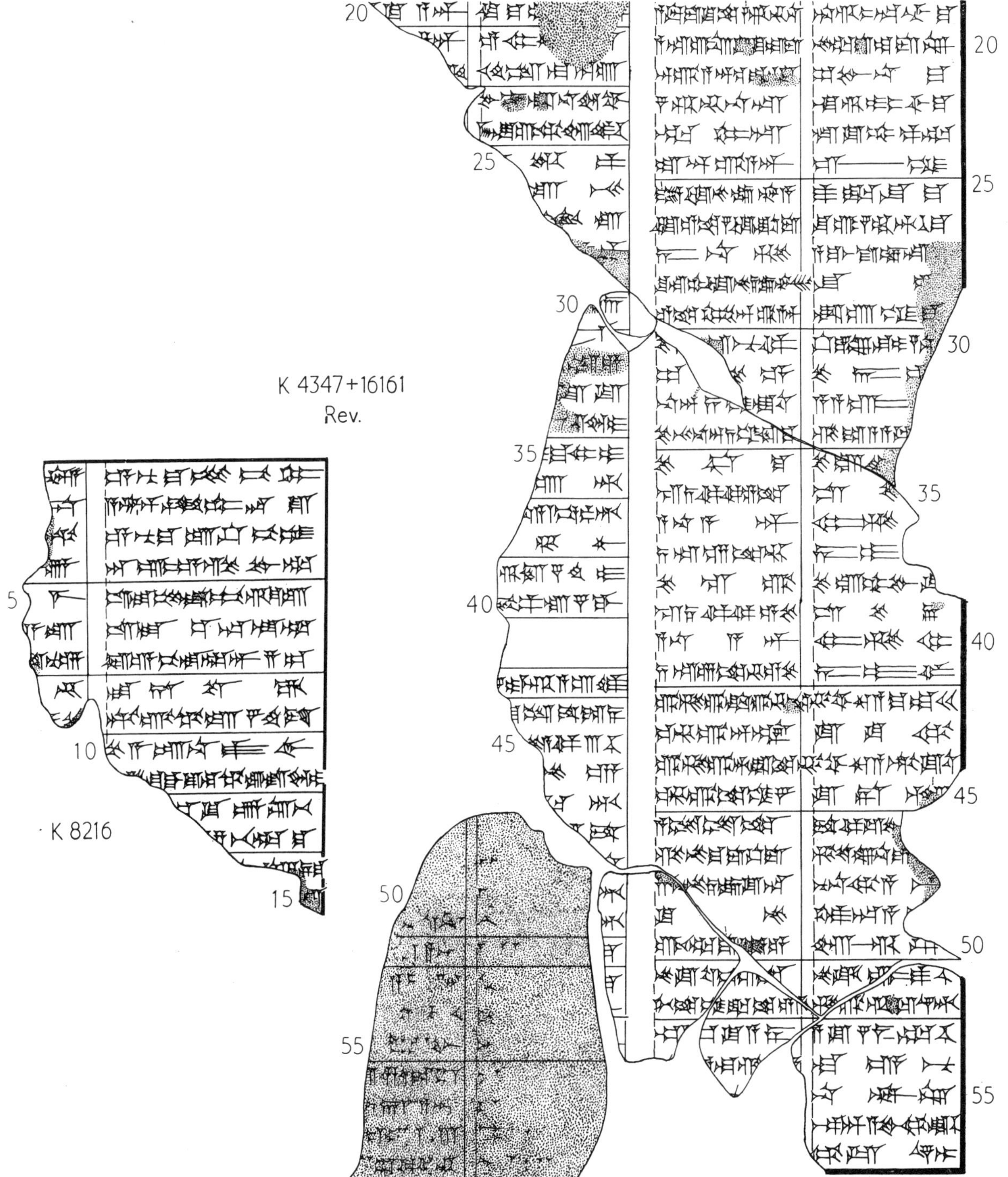
K 4347+16161
Rev.
K 8216

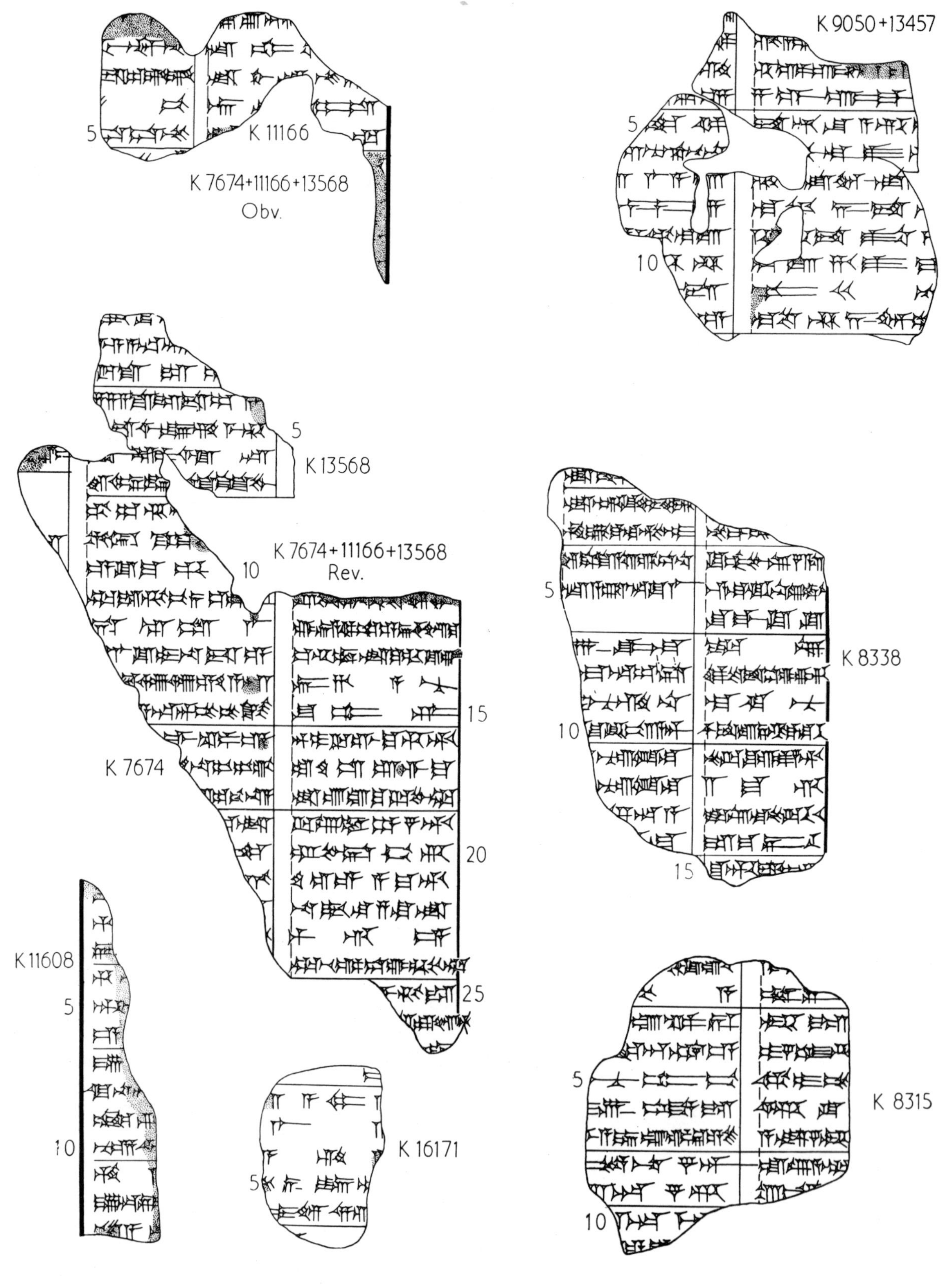
K 11166
K 7674+11166+13568
Obv.
K 9050+13457
K 13568
K 7674+11166+13568
Rev.
K 7674
K 8338
K 11608
K 16171
K 8315

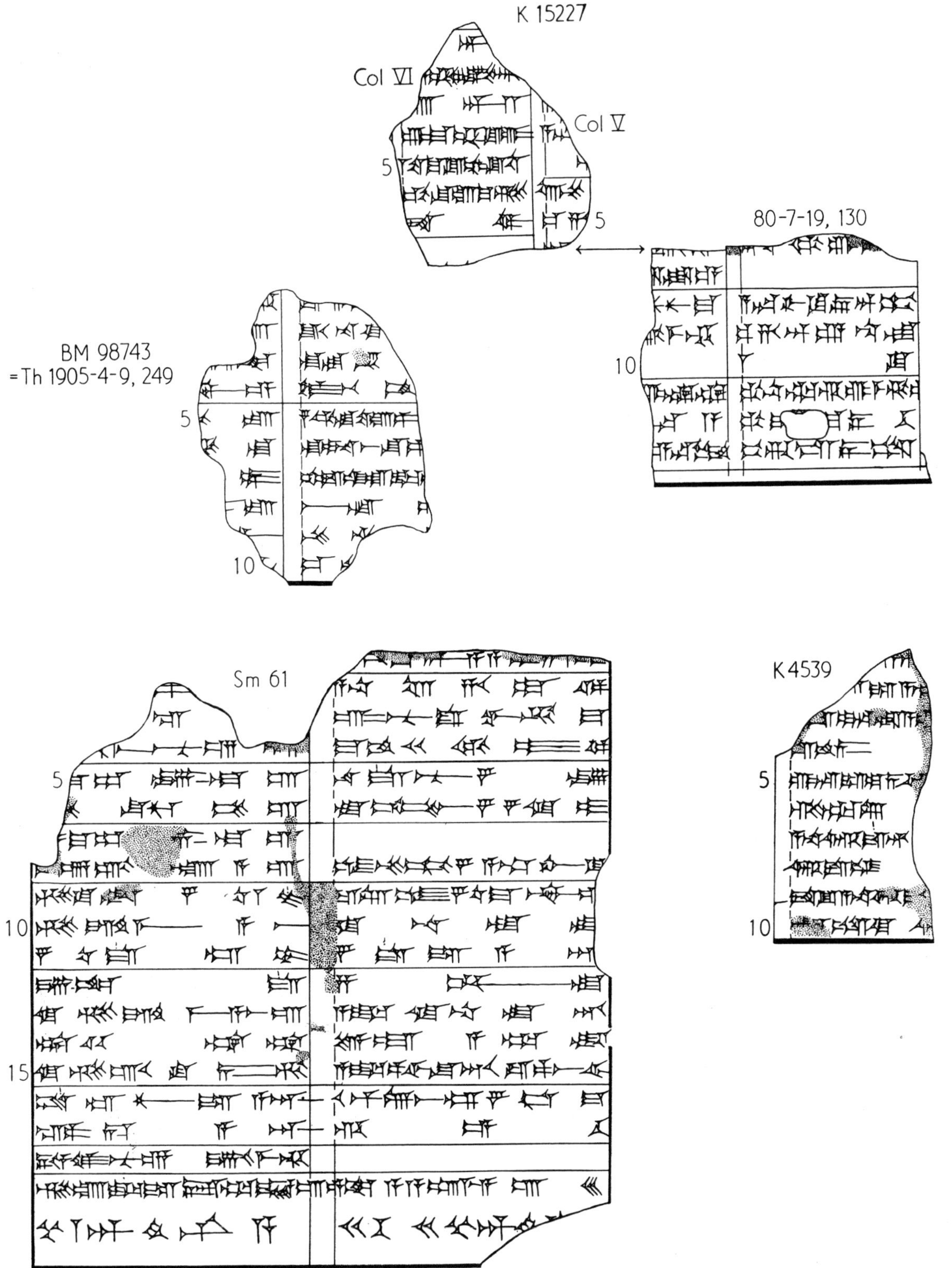
K 15227
Col VI
Col V
5
5
80-7-19, 130
10
BM 98743
=Th 1905-4-9, 249
5
10
Sm 61
5
10
15
K 4539
5
10

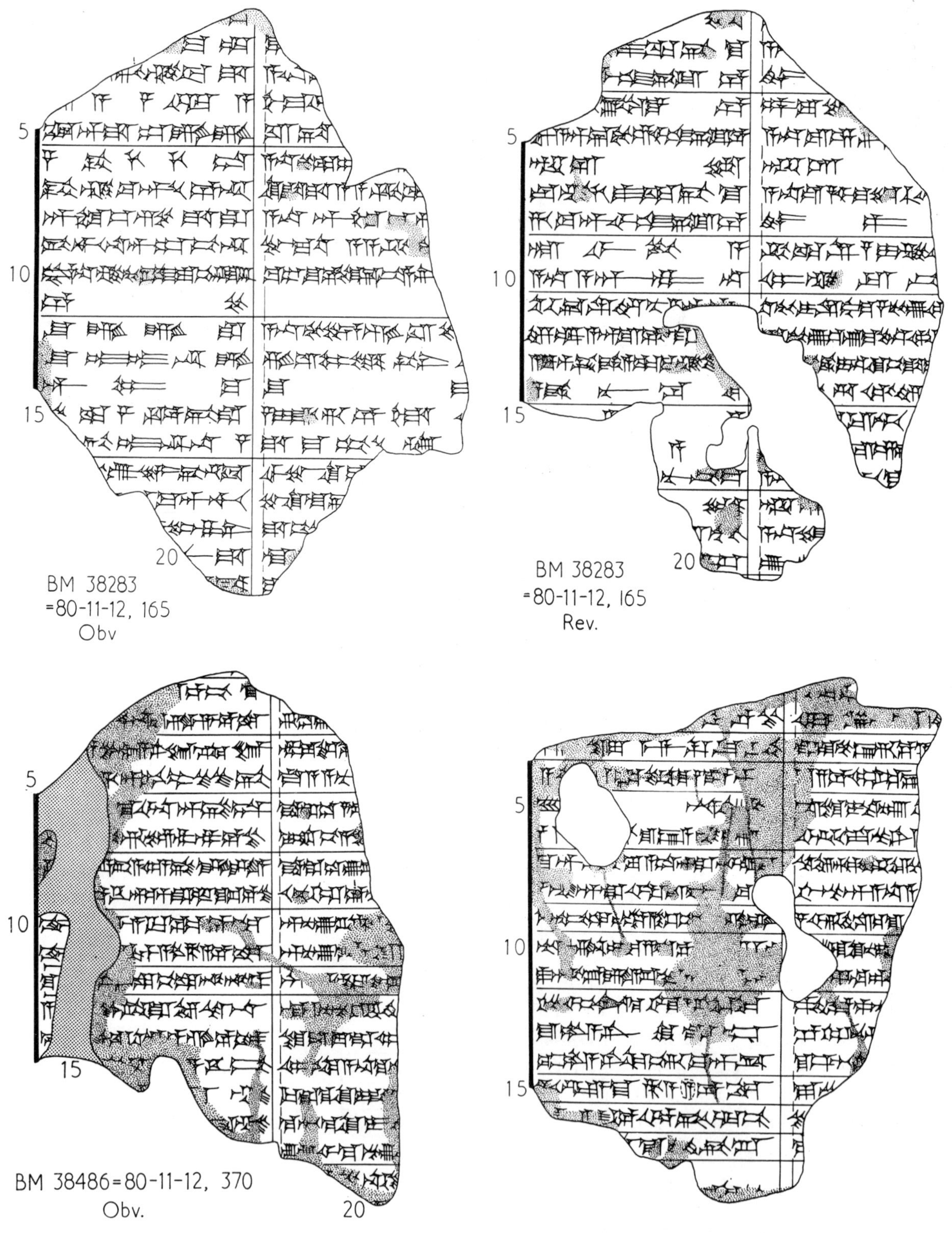

BM 38283 =80-11-12, 165 Obv

BM 38283 =80-11-12, 165 Rev.

BM 38486=80-11-12, 370 Obv.

BM 38486=80-11-12, 370 Rev

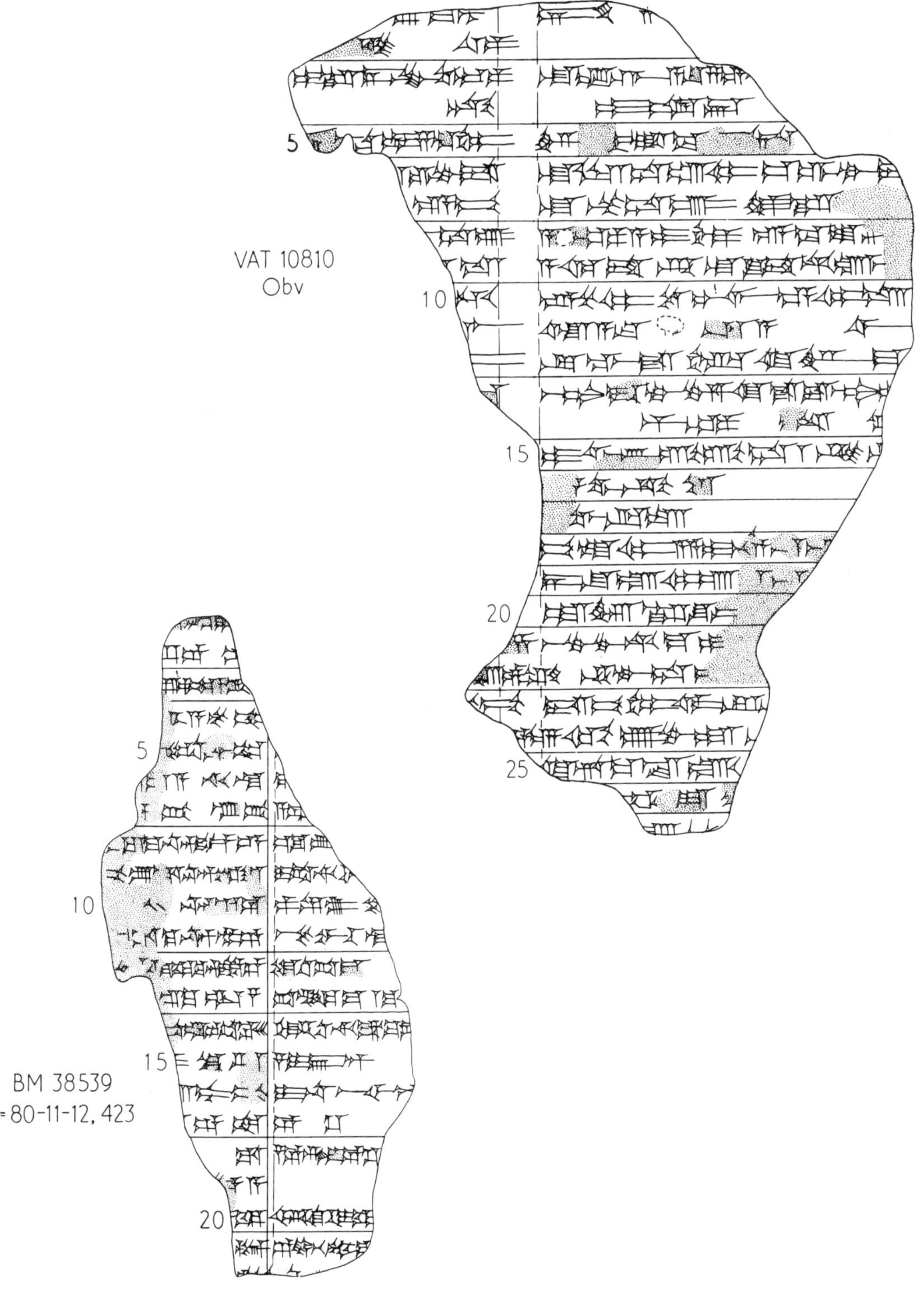
VAT 10810
Obv
BM 38539
=80-11-12, 423

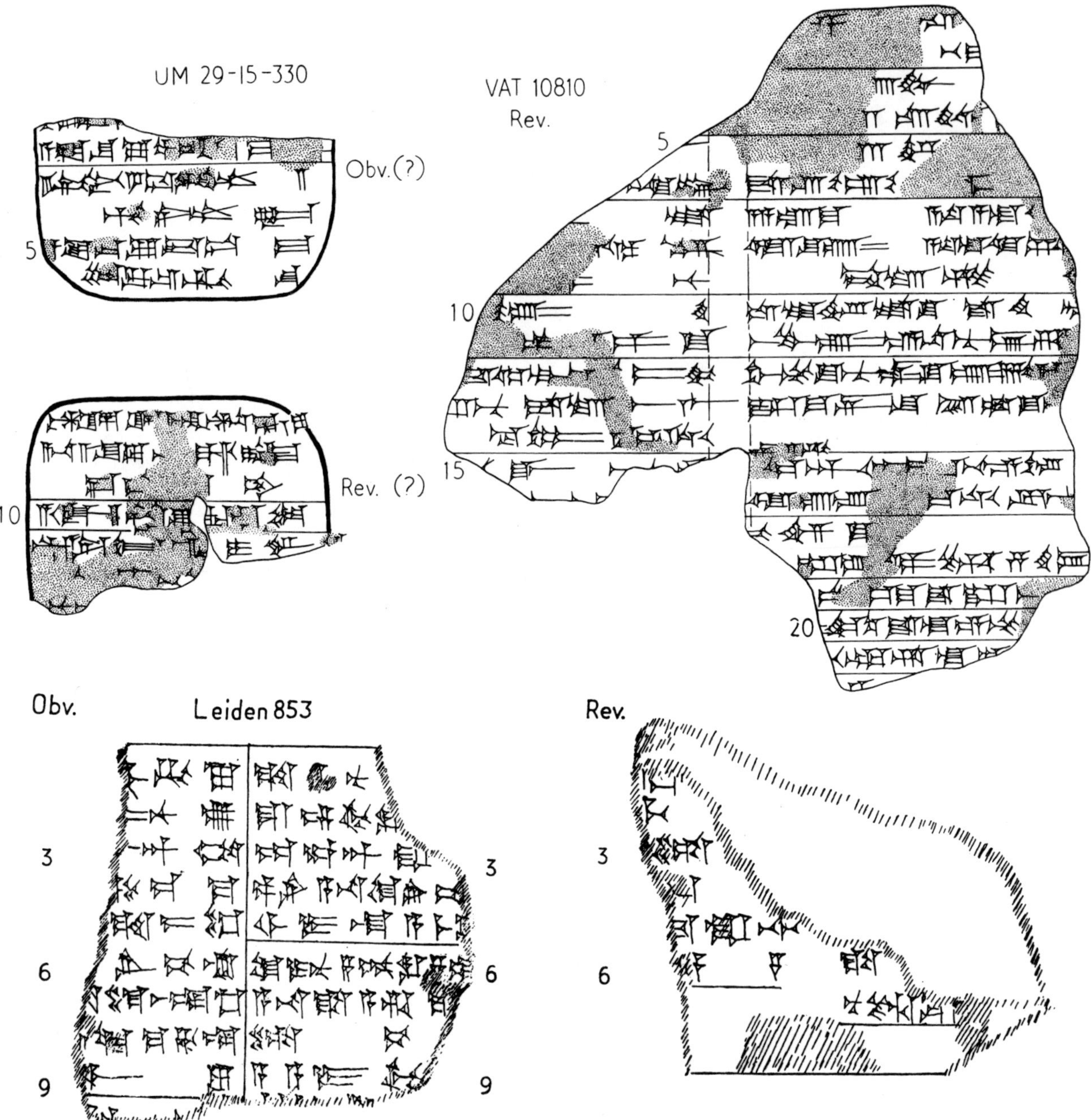

Kindly found and collated in Leiden by Kraus and Frankena, who report: Obv. II. 1 reads clearly *da-pa-nu*. The signs are as Weidner copied them, but DA, not ID, becomes clear by comparison with ID, obv. I. 5. PA is damaged but sufficiently clear.

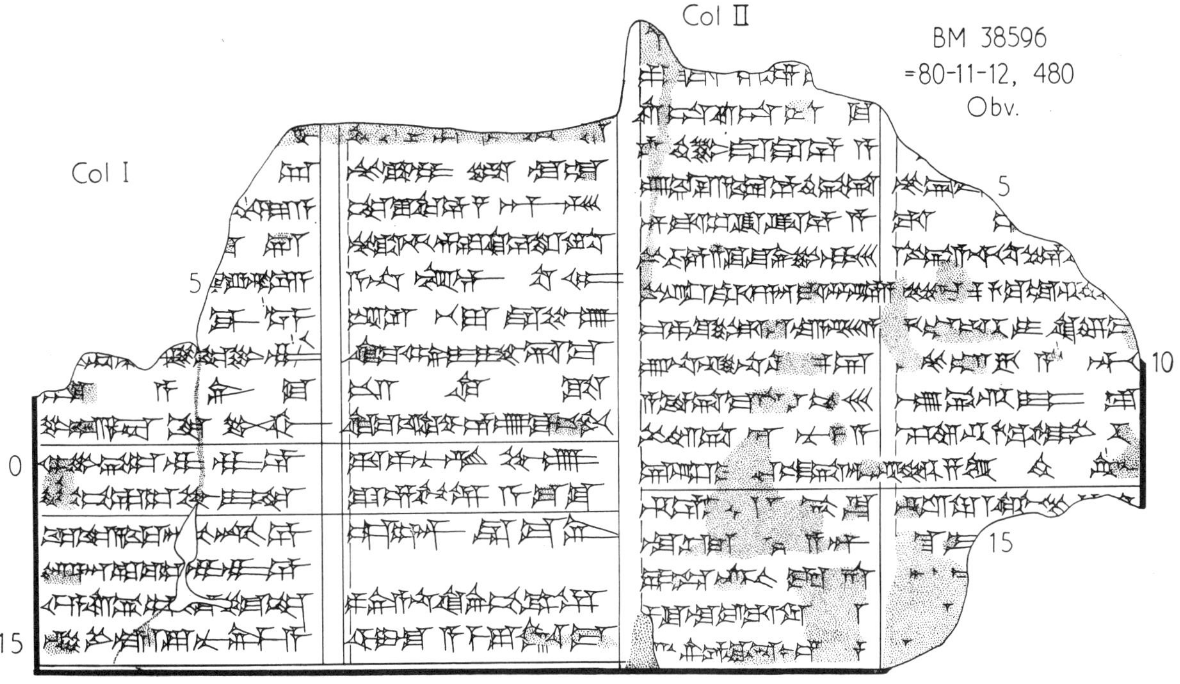
Col I
Col II
BM 38596
=80-11-12, 480
Obv.

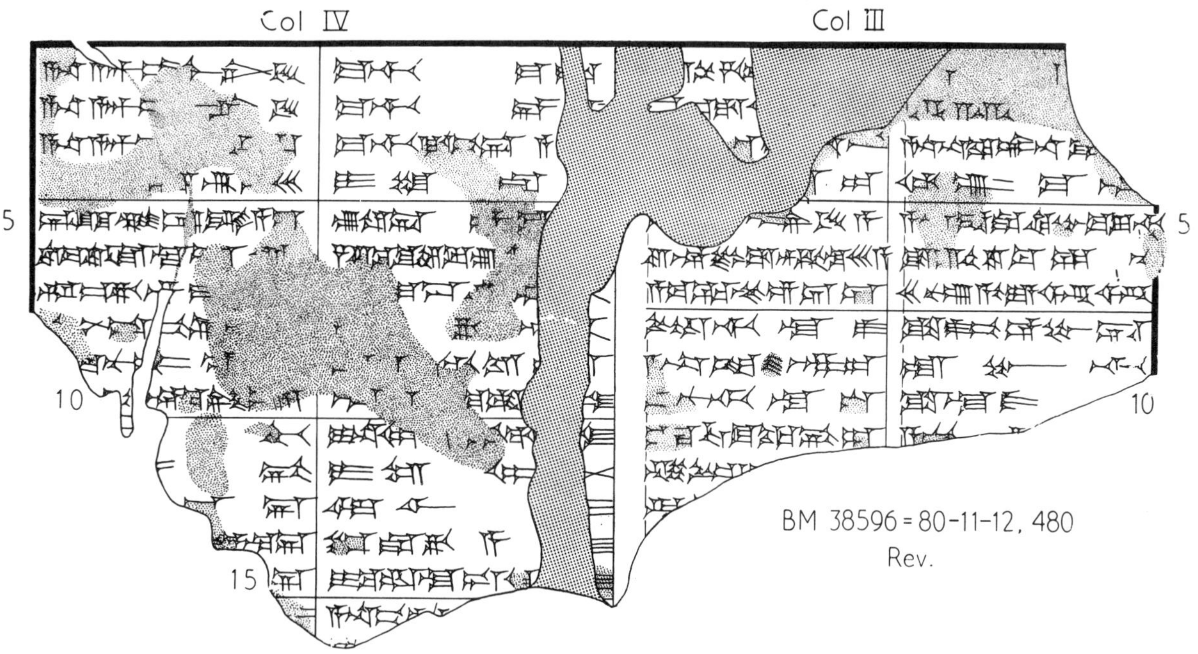
Col IV
Col III
BM 38596=80-11-12, 480
Rev.

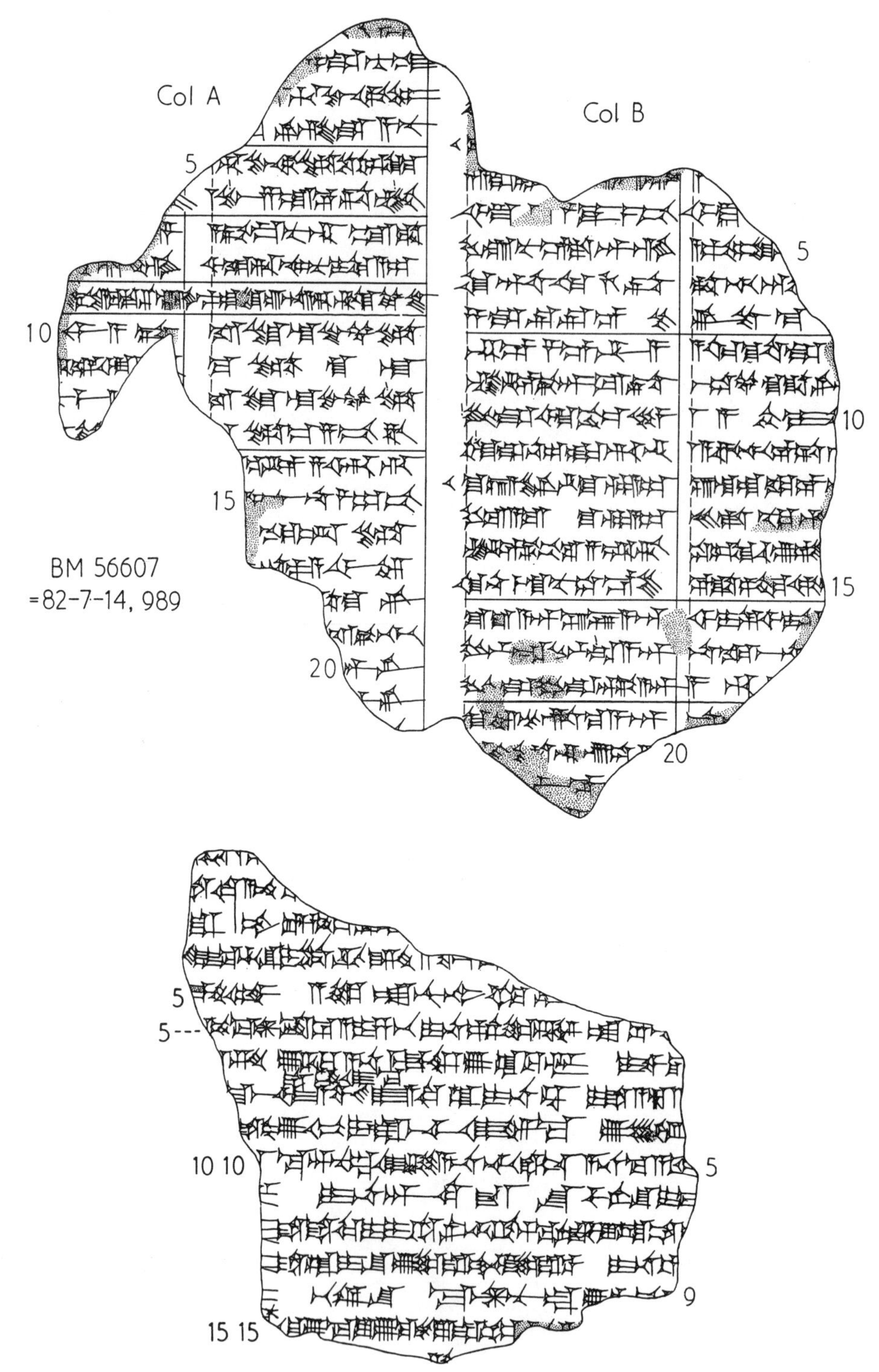

CBS 14235

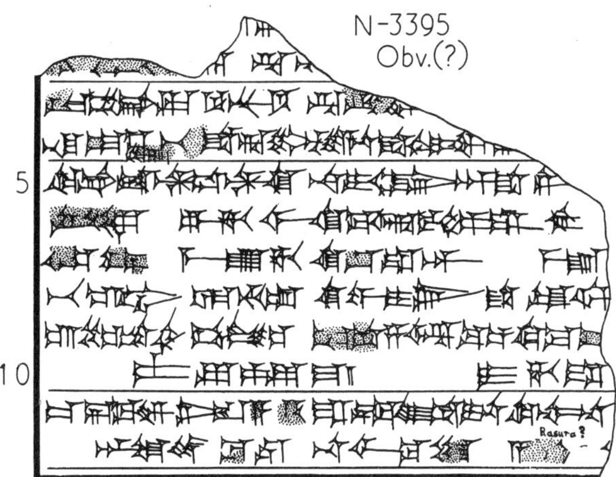

Rev. IV
1-3
4-7
8-10
11-16 and 17-22 (Composite text)

BM 56488
=82-7-14, 864

° This sign is apparently an overrun from the next column.

N-3395
Rev.(?)

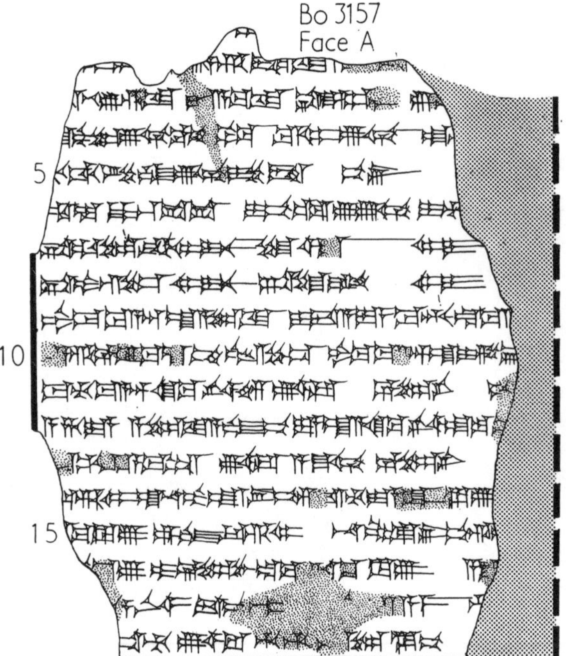
Bo 3157
Face A

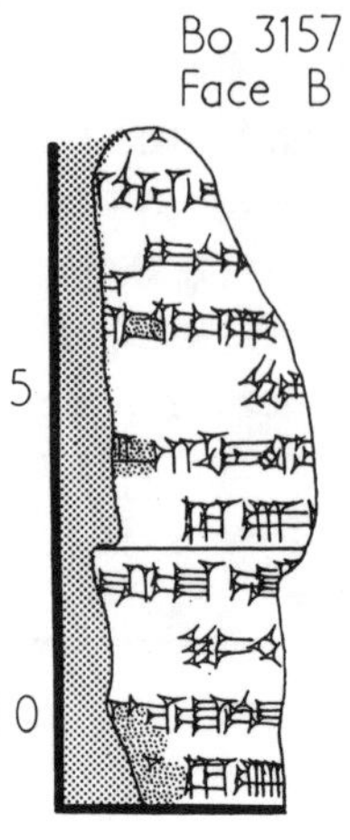
Bo 3157
Face B

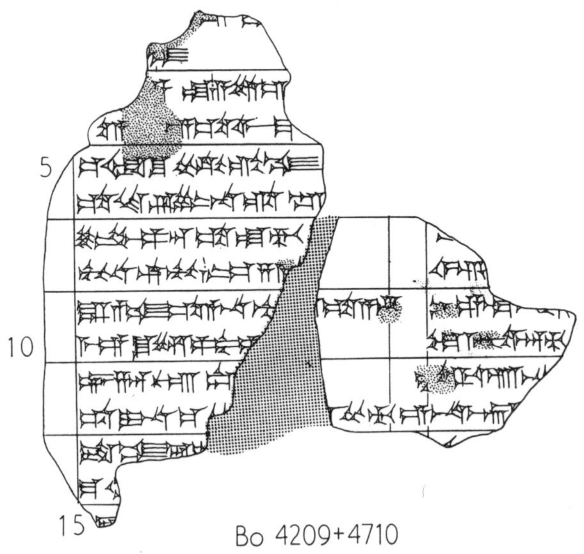
Bo 4209+4710

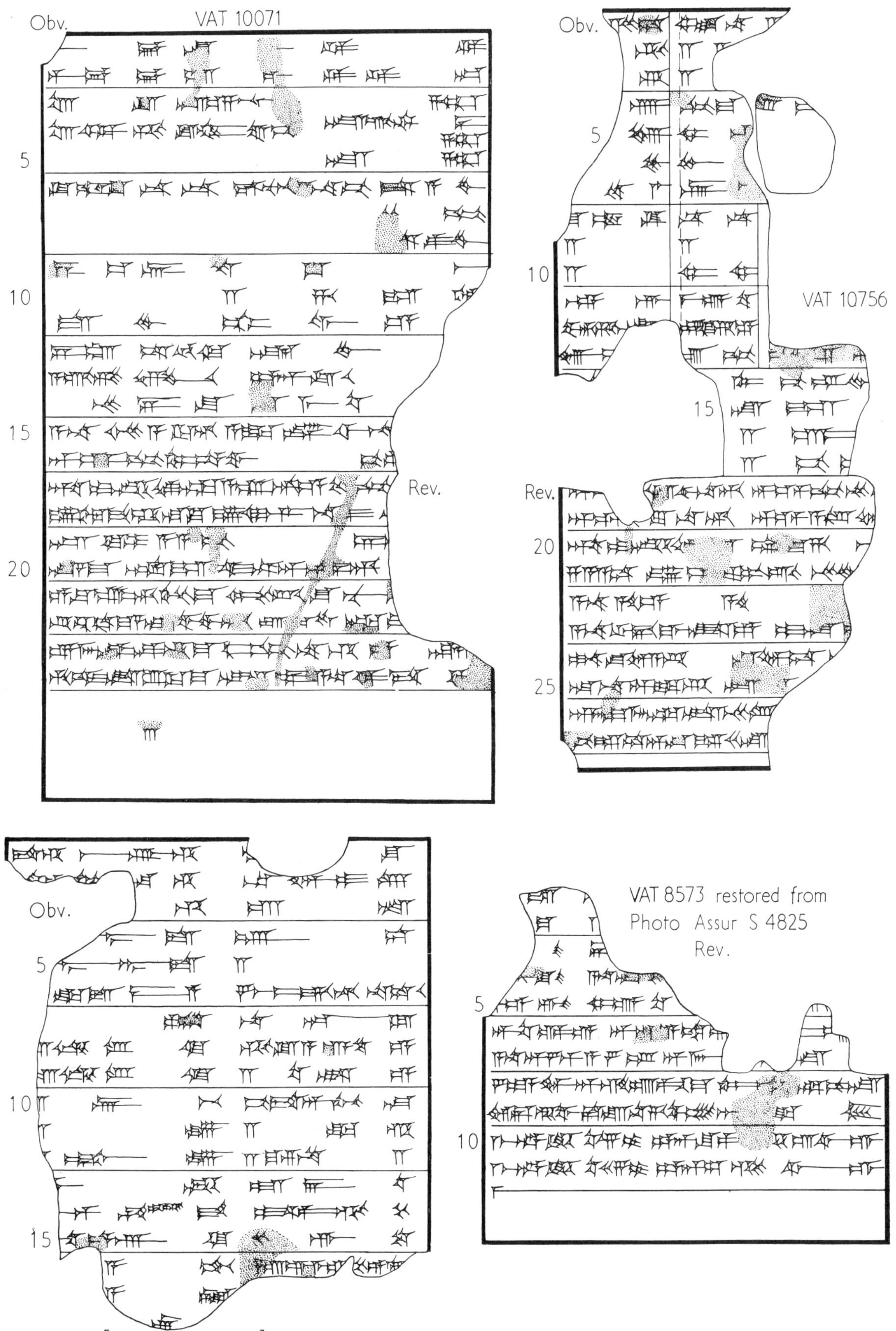
Obv.
VAT 10071
Rev.
Obv.
VAT 10756
Rev.
Obv.
[very little missing]
VAT 8573 restored from
Photo Assur S 4825
Rev.

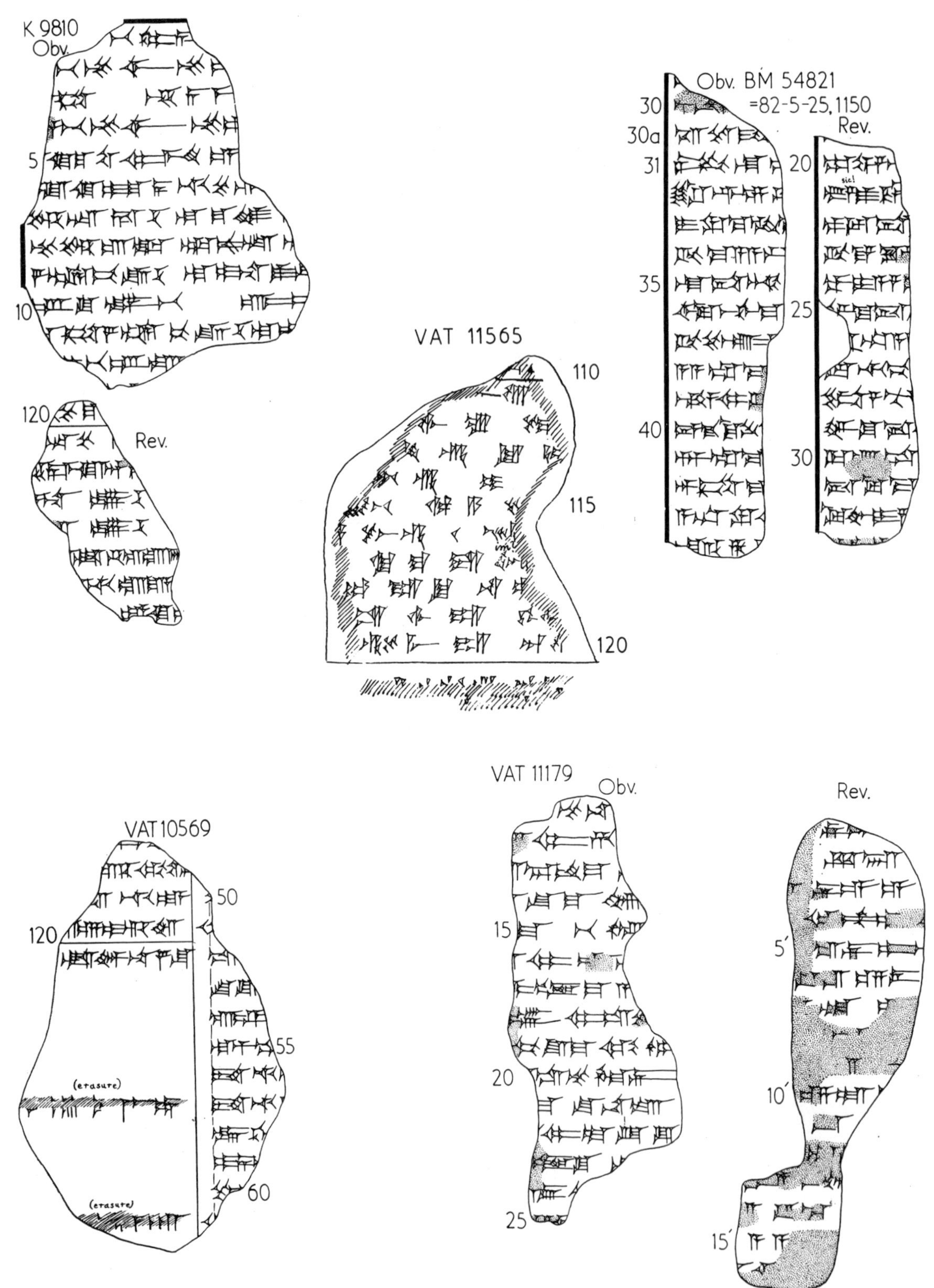
K 9810
Obv.
5
10
120
Rev.
VAT 11565
110
115
120
Obv. BM 54821
=82-5-25, 1150
Rev.
30
30a
31
35
40
20
sic!
25
30
VAT 10569
50
120
55
(erasure)
(erasure)
60
VAT 11179
Obv.
Rev.
15
20
25
5'
10'
15'

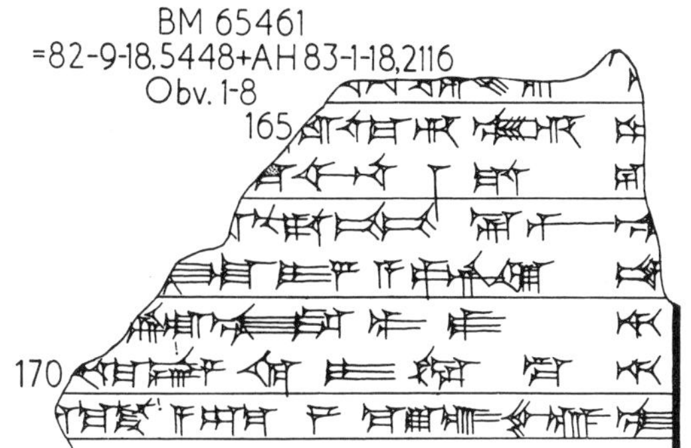
BM 65461
=82-9-18,5448+AH 83-1-18,2116
Obv. 1-8
165
170

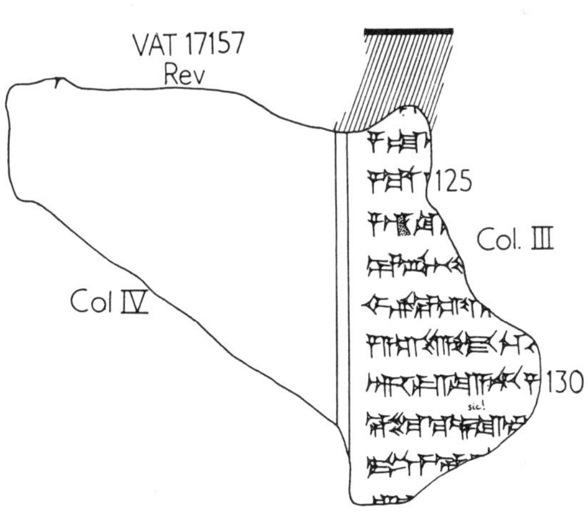
VAT 17157
Rev
125
Col. III
Col IV
130
sic!

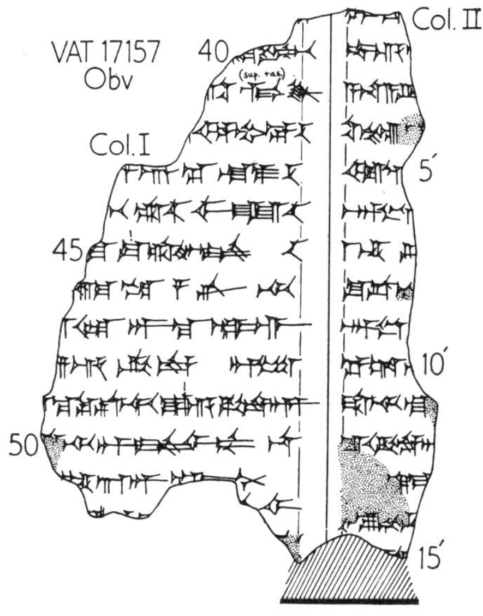
VAT 17157
Obv
40
Col. II
(sup. ras.)
Col. I
5′
45
10′
50
15′

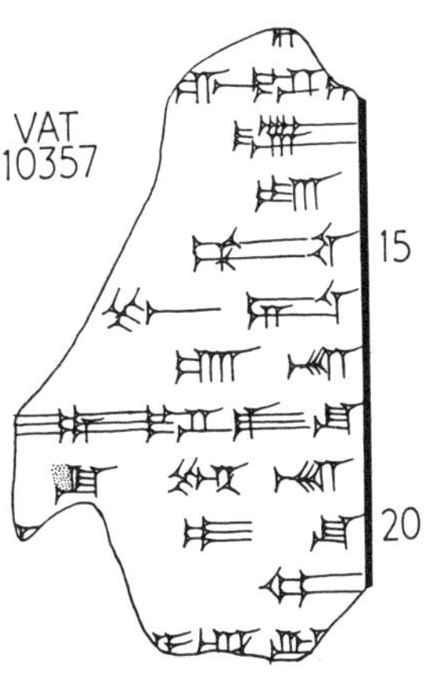
VAT
10357
15
20